THE ROUTLEDGE COMPANION TO JAZZ AND GENDER

The Routledge Companion to Jazz and Gender identifies, defines, and interrogates the construct of gender in all forms of jazz, jazz culture, and education, shaping and transforming the conversation in response to changing cultural and societal norms across the globe. Such interrogation requires consideration of gender from multiple viewpoints, from scholars and artists at various points in their careers. This edited collection of 38 essays gathers the diverse perspectives of contributors from four continents, exploring the nuanced (and at times controversial) construct of gender as it relates to jazz music, in the past and present, in four parts:

- Historical Perspectives
- Identity and Culture
- Society and Education
- Policy and Advocacy

Acknowledging the art form's troubled relationship with gender, contributors seek to define the construct to include all possible definitions—not only female and male—without binary limitations, contextualizing gender and jazz in both place and time. As gender identity becomes an increasingly important consideration in both education and scholarship, *The Routledge Companion to Jazz and Gender* provides a broad and inclusive resource of research for the academic community, addressing an urgent need to reconcile the construct of gender in jazz in all its forms.

James Reddan is Associate Professor and Director of Choral Activities and Music Education at Western Oregon University, USA.

Monika Herzig is Senior Lecturer in the Paul H. O'Neill School of Public and Environmental Affairs at Indiana University, USA.

Michael Kahr is Chair of Jazz at the Gustav Mahler Private University of Music in Klagenfurt and Senior Lecturer at the Institute for Jazz at the University of Music and Performing Arts in Graz, Austria.

Routledge Music Companions offer thorough, high-quality surveys and assessments of major topics in the study of music. All entries in each companion are specially commissioned and written by leading scholars in the field. Clear, accessible, and cutting-edge, these companions are the ideal resource for advanced undergraduates, postgraduate students, and researchers alike.

The Routledge Companion to Jazz Studies
Edited by Nicholas Gebhardt, Nichole Rustin-Paschal, and Tony Whyton

The Routledge Companion to Popular Music Analysis: Expanding Approaches
Edited by Ciro Scotto, Kenneth Smith, and John Brackett

The Routledge Companion to the Study of Local Musicking
Edited by Suzel A. Reily and Katherine Brucher

The Routledge Companion to Music Cognition
Edited by Richard Ashley and Renee Timmers

The Routledge Companion to Screen Music and Sound
Edited by Miguel Mera, Ronald Sadoff, and Ben Winters

The Routledge Companion to Embodied Music Interaction
Edited by Micheline Lesaffre, Pieter-Jan Maes, and Marc Leman

The Routledge Companion to Music, Technology, and Education
Edited by Andrew King, Evangelos Himonides, and S. Alex Ruthmann

The Routledge Companion to Sounding Art
Edited by Marcel Cobussen, Vincent Meelberg, and Barry Truax

The Routledge Companion to Music and Visual Culture
Edited by Tim Shephard and Anne Leonard

The Routledge Companion to Music and Modern Literature
Edited by Rachael Durkin, Peter Dayan, Axel Englund, Katharina Clausius

The Routledge Companion to Jazz and Gender
Edited by James Reddan, Monika Herzig, and Michael Kahr

THE ROUTLEDGE COMPANION TO JAZZ AND GENDER

*Edited by James Reddan, Monika Herzig,
and Michael Kahr*

Routledge
Taylor & Francis Group

NEW YORK AND LONDON

First published 2023
by Routledge
605 Third Avenue, New York, NY 10158

and by Routledge
4 Park Square, Milton Park, Abingdon, Oxon, OX14 4RN

Routledge is an imprint of the Taylor & Francis Group, an informa business

Library of Congress Cataloging-in-Publication Data
A catalog record has been requested for this book

ISBN: 978-0-367-53414-1 (hbk)
ISBN: 978-0-367-63032-4 (pbk)
ISBN: 978-1-003-08187-6 (ebk)

DOI: 10.4324/9781003081876

Typeset in Bembo
by Newgen Publishing UK

This volume is dedicated to the memory of **Dr. Patrice Dawn Madura Ward-Steinmann (1952–2020)**. Dr. Ward-Steinmann was Professor of Music Education at Indiana University. She was also an accomplished pianist and vocalist and one of the leading researchers in choral music pedagogy and vocal jazz improvisation. Her book *Becoming a Choral Music Teacher: A Field Experience Workbook* (Routledge, 2018) is one of the field's essential textbooks. For the second edition, she added a special chapter on gender issues and LGBT awareness. She was in the process of synthesizing her 20 years of research on the identification of predictors of vocal improvisation skills into a model for teaching and learning vocal jazz improvisation for this volume at the time of her untimely death. She shared the following findings with us, the synthesis of numerous quantitative correlational studies and the synopsis of her model:

Effective vocal improvisation is motivated by significant others and a supportive environment; develops through immersion in the study of the musical style through extensive and specific practice strategies, listening experiences, private lessons, and ensemble participation; and manifests in strong musicianship, stylistic command, originality, and interactional synchrony. Gender does not appear to significantly limit or enhance one's ability to vocally improvise.

Unfortunately, her contribution was never completed and, on June 4, 2020, we lost our mentor and friend and one of the most dedicated and accomplished music teachers and researchers. I had the privilege of being her colleague and friend here at Indiana University and witnessed the deep impact she had on the students and on the field. Most importantly, she documented for us that gender and improvisational ability are not corelated and that the issues that inhibit equal participation, as discussed in this volume, are social and cultural constructs and subject to change. In her memory, may the knowledge presented in this book serve as a call to action towards inclusive participation in the creative process of jazz.

In loving memory
Monika Herzig

And Co-Editors
James Reddan, Michael Kahr

CONTENTS

FIGURES AND TABLES

Figures

Tables

PREFACE

The idea of this book was developed at the 2019 Documenting Jazz Conference in Dublin, Ireland. After many research presentations and meetings, it was clear that more research and resources about gender and jazz were needed in the scholarly literature. However, the intent of this collection of scholarship is not to merely fill a gap. The intent is to identify, define, and interrogate the construct of gender in all forms of jazz, jazz culture, jazz history, intersectionality of gender and race, and education in order to shape and transform the discourse on this important topic as it relates to changing cultural and societal norms across the globe. With the rise of the #MeToo movement, attention to gender inequalities in the workplace, culture, on stage, and much more, there is an urgent need to address gender and the construct of gender in jazz in all forms.

In the current world climate, the topic of gender is complex and fraught with controversy depending on who you talk to, individual perceptions and definition of gender, and value systems. Most of the discussions and advocacy efforts at this point focus on Classical music traditions with a strong emphasis on women in jazz and men versus women within such discourse. The definition of gender has changed and evolved in relation to societal norms, politics, social justice research, stereotypes, historical significance, and education. Furthermore, pre-colonial societies, specifically Native American and Hindu cultures, traditionally practiced a more gender fluid concept, rather than the artificial binary construct adapted later by Western cultures. To this end, we have sought to approach the topic of gender in jazz using a broad and global definition. This is to say that within this text, gender is not defined simply as male and female (i.e., biological sex). With over fifty terms currently used related to gender and gender identity, the term *Gender* (emphasis added) is meant broadly to include all possible definitions, including male, female, transgender, gender non-conforming, non-binary, cis-gender, and any other definition currently used in the vernacular. As gender identity becomes an increasingly important consideration in both education and scholarship, our approach to this volume was to provide a broad and inclusive resource of research for the academic community. However, we must also consider that to deviate from Gender outside of its typical binary definition can be difficult and is also important to consider in the larger conversation because gender itself is a controversial construct.

While reading the many contributions contained in this volume, it will be important to note how the term *Gender* and gendered terms are being used and applied. In many cases, contributing authors have noted how they are using gendered terminology within the context of their article, while others have noted their own positioning within the larger discourse.

Jazz as an art form has a troubled relationship with gender. In order to understand the issues and work towards solutions in education and practice, we decided to include a breadth of perspectives from discussions of Gender in jazz education (K–college), music, improvisation, art, policy, advocacy, history, identity, sexuality, race, and more. Scholars focused on issues of gender identity, male and female gendering within the jazz world, jazz appreciation, pedagogy, and theory in addition to many other important areas and offer discussions and possible solutions. It is our hope that this edited volume will be an essential resource for students and scholars alike for classes in research methodologies, jazz history, musicology, ethnomusicology, gender studies, jazz pedagogy, and psychology and other areas of inquiry.

As we considered the topic of Gender in jazz, we contemplated what issues needed to be addressed and what would be the best way to understand the topic as broadly possible. The authors represent a diverse group in terms of geographics, backgrounds, approaches, race, and gender and provide us with a wide range of perspectives. While every attempt was made to invite authors as diverse as possible, the final selection is also influenced by individual availability, time constraints, interest, and experiences. Essays in the current volume were proposed by contributors based on invitation from the editors because of their current knowledge and differing points of view about Gender and jazz. Moreover, we have tried to be careful to honor the ground-breaking research published by many scholars in this field. In that spirit, this text offers many new ideas built upon the contributions of scholars in the field prior to this text as a next step to continued discourse and change. More importantly, we hope that the essays presented herein will serve as a stepping stone for change where needed, for new advocacy, and revised pedagogy towards a more diverse approach to the creation, teaching, and presentation of the art form jazz.

Finally, all viewpoints presented throughout the volume are solely by the chapter authors and their interviewees and may not reflect the views and opinions of the editors. We would like to express our gratitude to Routledge and Taylor & Francis for believing in this project and its importance. We would also like to thank all those authors who have contributed their time, expertise, and wisdom to this important edition.

James Reddan, Monika Herzig, and Michael Kahr

ACKNOWLEDGEMENTS

Completing this volume has been no small undertaking. There are many people the editors would like to thank and acknowledge who have helped to make this volume possible.

First, we would like to extend our deepest thanks and gratitude to Natali Rimoun Jouzi and Elaine Lee, graduate assistants supported by the Indiana University O'Neill School of Public and Environmental Affairs for all their help with communications, organizing, and tracking all the contributions throughout their process. Their help was crucial in bringing this volume to fruition over the past two years.

Second, we must extend our thanks to Constance Ditzel and Routledge/Taylor & Francis for her belief in the success and importance of this volume. Her help and encouragement have truly been inspiring.

Third, we thank the many contributors, reviewers, and scholars who have supported the development of this work and its importance to our field and profession.

Furthermore …

James Reddan would like to thank his colleagues in Music, Creative Arts Division, and College of Liberal Arts and Sciences at Western Oregon University for their support and encouragement to produce this work. Thank you to Jason Stieber and Fern Reddan for all your love, encouragement, help, and support during this process.

Monika Herzig would like to express her gratitude for the support of the Indiana University Arts Administration program and her family, Peter Kienle, Zackary and Jasmin Herzig.

Michael Kahr would like to thank the institutional and personal support at Jam Music Lab University and extends his gratitude to Rainer Kahr, Maryam Sadr-Salek, and Kimiya Lilien Kahr.

PART 1

Historical Perspectives

1

"THE FRIVOLOUS, SCANTILY CLAD 'JAZZING FLAPPER,' IRRESPONSIBLE AND UNDISCIPLINED"

Jazz as a Feminine Domain

Bruce Johnson

Introduction

Relative to overall jazz practice and discourse, the role of women has been neglected. David Ake, writing as recently as 2019, noted the "pervasive sexism that continues to surround neotraditional aesthetics and practices," and that there has never been a female member of the Lincoln Center Jazz Orchestra, describing it as a "locker-room mentality" (Ake, 2019, p. 82). This gendering has led to some significant occlusions in jazz historiography: Patrick Burke refers for example to the argument that Asian-American musicians have been excluded from the US-centric jazz *mythos* through a form of "feminization," lacking "the masculine creative force supposedly essential to jazz" (Burke, 2019, p. 192). In the twenty-first century there has been a growing body of literature on women in jazz (Burke, 2019, p. 189), including such studies as Williams (2007), which critiqued the jazz/masculinity nexus. Much of this literature is reviewed in Rustin and Tucker (2008, pp. 10–19), who also include significant essays pertinent to this one in their collection (see for example Taylor, Hairston, Baade, McMullen). With increasing numbers of exceptions (see for example Arvidsson, 2014), largely driven by a growing interest in the global jazz diaspora, the bulk of the literature on women in jazz has been primarily focused on African American women, and is also framed by a postwar "high art" aesthetic, which is itself overwhelmingly a masculinist construction already saddled with gender politics, the result of which is rather like trying to argue the case for "jazz-as-art" by deploying a discourse written for a Eurocentric high art tradition in which jazz starts out at an insuperable disadvantage (see Johnson, 2011).

My focus here is on gender politics that underpin a global and therefore transracial phenomenon—the "Modern Woman"—and in relation to an interwar conception of jazz as a highly corporeal form of popular culture rather than intellectualized form of "high art". And I also wish to enlarge the idea of "actant," beyond that of a musician. That is, someone who plays a significant role in a social practice or formation. The "jazz world" is not brought into existence solely by musicians, a model derived from the "great artist" *mythos*. It is also created by a range of actants that include the communities of promoters, the media, pundits and commentators, and what we now think of as audiences.

DOI: 10.4324/9781003081876-2

And, I argue, this was far more significantly the case during the period I am discussing—the 1920s—when jazz was not only a music for dancing, but was regarded as much as a dance as an instrumental performance. Today we understand jazz to be a genre of musical performance, produced by (mainly male) musicians in a dedicated performance space, what is in effect a stage. But this was not how jazz was understood in the early decades of its history. Apart from on-stage vaudeville performance in its very earliest diasporic formations, jazz was produced by dance bands but also by the bodies of the dancers, just as, say, a tango is "produced" by those who dance it (see further Johnson, 2000, pp. 64–66; Johnson, 2020, pp. 146–148). To dance to jazz was to "perform" jazz.

Today's idea of a dedicated "jazz venue" or jazz club is very much a development from the late 1930s, and to a great extent this itself has been masculinised by another shift. The range of venues in which jazz might be performed in the 1920s was much broader than is now implied by the term "jazz venue." If I tell you that I am playing a prestigious jazz gig tonight, the image that comes to mind is of a musical event entirely devoted to jazz, a music performed by a group of performers identified as jazz musicians, located on a dedicated performance space, for an audience that is close to static. Few such scenarios existed during the 1920s, partly because, as a music for dancing—an audience in motion—jazz would be just one "hot" component of a modern dance or cabaret band's repertoire. In addition, the range of venues in which such a band would perform was far broader than is the case for a "jazz group" today. Vaudeville, for example, was particularly associated with the earliest jazz, and was also not so rigidly masculinised. To attempt to imaginatively inhabit the 1920s conception of jazz is to discover that, in gender terms, and especially outside the United States, it was primarily women who were the conduit through which the music was seen as entering the local cultural landscape. Jazz was racialized (emanating from black US musicians) but also feminized.

Yet the perception of jazz as a perennial site of masculinity persists, and even the introduction to a very insightful collection of essays on gender in jazz asserts categorically that, "From its birth, … jazz history and criticism has [sic] been couched in the language of nation, race, and masculinity" (Rustin and Tucker, 2008, p. 16). The masculinization of jazz has become axiomatic: "jazz has remained, since its earliest days, an overwhelmingly male domain" (Ake, 2002, p. 64). This chapter is based on a challenge to that assumption, arguing that during the interwar period, and particularly the 1920s, jazz was feminized, the domain of the independent-minded "New Woman" or "Modern Girl."[1] The terms describe the emergence of a newly independent young female eager to occupy a place in the public sphere, who threatened received notions of the proper place of women in society. It was a phenomenon not only of a leisured class fashion *du jour*, but which traversed the class spectrum, reflecting also changes in the situation of the working and serving class of women that had been gaining momentum since the late nineteenth century (see Schwartz, 2019).

This chapter takes as a case study a scandal in Australia in 1928, where the Musicians' Union of Australia (MUA) had long resisted the importation of foreign musicians on the grounds they were depriving local musicians of employment. This posture was hardened by racism in the case of a visiting US African American revue, "The Colored Idea". In collaboration with various state agencies and the yellow press, the MUA succeeded in securing the deportation of the Revue's band, not, however on grounds of protectionism, nor even primarily of race politics, though the latter were harnessed. The lever for the deportation was a public "moral panic" exploitation of the widely perceived association between African American jazz and the modern girl, of women as the conduit through which jazz entered and threatened the local culture. In the 1920s, jazz was a feminine domain.

On 21 January 1928, the African American revue The Colored Idea opened the Sydney season of their Australian tour. The revue's band, Sonny Clay's Plantation Orchestra, was a jazz group whose members included alumni and future members of US bands led by such luminaries as Jelly Roll Morton, Kid Ory, Louis Armstrong and Duke Ellington. The reviews of the first performance in the Tivoli theatre set a pattern in which the band was the star of the Revue: "Sonny Clay's Idea burst like a ray of colored sunshine on the patrons of the Tivoli yesterday afternoon. The band is all your dreams of jazz come true" (Egan, 2020, p. 171). To the reviewer in the lifestyle journal *Everyones*, the band demonstrated that "jazz as played by a European and jazz as played by a real Negro are entirely different. It is all in the Syncopation" (Sutcliffe, 1997, p. 8). The revue was such a success that it was booked for a return season after their commitments in Melbourne, where they enjoyed the same level of acclamation: A review of their opening night on 20 February in the city's main daily newspaper, *The Age*, enthused over "the unrestrained, exotic quality to be expected of the originators of jazz" (Sutcliffe, 1997, p. 10).

Thus far, the band had performed as part of an imported stage revue under contract on an international touring circuit. But their popularity led to a widely publicised invitation to perform in their own right for the Australia Cup midnight dance in late March at the city's premier dance palais, The Green Mill, a highly sought-after gig that would normally have gone to a local band. Five days before the dance it was reported in the press that representatives of the MUA had met with the prime minister in Canberra to seek an embargo on foreign musicians taking work from locals; "Discussion turned strongly on visiting American players" (Sutcliffe, 1997, p. 10). Then, as reported in both the Melbourne and Sydney press, a few days before the scheduled dance, police, with a reporter in tow, and following lengthy surveillance through a window from across the road, raided an apartment in East Melbourne where, the press reported, "a number of young girls were associated with Negroes" (Sutcliffe, 1997, p. 11). The "Negroes" were members of Sonny Clay's band, and the Melbourne newspaper *Truth*, whose reporter had accompanied the police, slathered over the discovery of "empty glasses, half dressed girls, an atmosphere poisonous with cigarette smoke and the fumes of liquor," and general "abandoned behaviour" (Johnson, 2010, p. 10). The only charges that could be devised against the young women was for vagrancy, a charge often used to prosecute prostitutes, none of which in any case succeeded. The musicians had broken no laws, but all their performances were cancelled, and they were ordered to leave the country on pain of formal deportation back to the United States. The Federal Cabinet determined that "No more Negro entertainers are to be admitted into Australia" (Sutcliffe, 1997, p. 11).

This story has been told before by historians in various degrees of detail, (see, for example, in chronological order Sales, 1974; Bisset, 1979/1987, pp. 43–45; Sutcliffe, 1997, pp. 3–13; Hall, 1997, 1998; Johnson, 2010; Cassells, 2013; O'Connell, 2016, 2021; Egan, 2020, pp. 24–42). But the narrative has been refracted primarily through the prisms of race, xenophobia and employment protectionism: A culture, exemplified in the MUA, opposing the importation of foreign, and especially non-white, non-British musicians who would steal employment from the locals as well as introduce forms of cultural contamination. As Cassells (2013) has pointed out, these accounts occlude the flashpoint of the whole event: The women without whom the crucial scandal would never have eventuated, whose rendezvous with the US jazz musicians provided the decisive leverage in securing the band's deportation. When Cassells gave the women's identities as individuals, for the first time we rediscovered their socio-economic profile, and also gain a sense of how far they became the local public scapegoats for the whole affair through media hyperbole. Cassell expounds this is in such impressive detail it would be superfluous to replicate her arguments here. But I want to extrapolate a further point; she makes much of the threat of miscegenation but makes little of the genre of music that brought the black men and white women together—jazz.

The Colored Idea scandal is a case study in the central role of women in the understanding of jazz in the early interwar period, when the music was undergoing its first and crucial stages of globalisation. I have set out this case in broad terms (Johnson, 2020, pp. 139–152), and I want to re-examine The Colored Idea episode through that prism of gender politics, arguing that it was this that finally provided the decisive leverage to deport the last African American jazz band to officially perform in Australia for decades to come. And this could only have happened because jazz at that time was closely aligned with the young modern girl.

My interest here is in the ease with which the media were able to situate the women at the centre of the scandal as the "frivolous, scantily clad 'jazzing flapper', irresponsible and undisciplined." That characterisation was from an article called "A Million Women Too Many" in the 5 February 1920 issue of the UK paper, the *Daily Mail*, in which the overabundance of unmarried British women is blamed for male unemployment and emigration, and the decline of the family, and warned of the threat to morality of the "modern independent girl" pursuing pleasure for pleasure's sake (Melman, 1998, pp. 18, 19). Melman's study was of the UK, but continuing research into the Modern Girl of the 1920s confirms that this was a global perception, spanning East and West (see Weinbaum, 2008). Such studies also incidentally confirm that the anthem of the Modern Girl was jazz. It is extremely puzzling that, as quotations above regarding the perennial masculinization of jazz indicate, this "incidental" insight has not been transferred to any significant degree to jazz scholarship. To develop this argument, we need to explore two contesting forces: The framing culture, of which the MUA was a microcosm, and the image of the Modern Girl in Australia in the late 1920s.

The Musicians' Union of Australia

The Musicians' Union of Australia (MUA) was established in 1916, growing out of various organisations that had emerged from the late nineteenth century that sought to unionise the profession; by the year of the visit of The Colored Idea, it was at the peak of its lobbying power, with 5,000 members (Arthur, 2003, p. 348). It had by this time become "highly protectionist, ... and pursuing a policy of total exclusion of foreign musicians" (Dreyfus, 2013, p. 17). This posture was a microcosm of the larger political context, as reflected in the White Australia Policy (WAP), based on the Immigration Restriction Act of 1901, the same year as the act of Federation that brought the single nation of Australia into existence. The spirit of the Act was articulated in a speech given by former Prime Minister Billy Hughes at the National Party conference in March 1928 in which, apart from implicitly expressing regret that the "niggers" had not been lynched, he "reaffirmed" the policy in no uncertain terms: "We believe in a White Australia ... and a British White Australia at that" (Dreyfus, 2013, p. 84). Unsurprisingly, African American musicians were among those targeted by this racist xenophobia, aggravated by the Australian Commonwealth Band's recent local union ban on performance in the United States during its otherwise very successful international tour (Hall, 1998, p. 179). Nationalist Party Senator J.F. Guthrie alluded to this in a letter he wrote in response to the visiting Kentucky Jubilee Singers in 1929, in which he inveighed against

> nigger bands and nigger singers. The Commonwealth Band, which performed with marked success in Europe, was insulted in America, and not allowed to perform there. I saw a band of fat niggers arrive at Spencer Street [station, in Melbourne] last week. I asked who they were and who had imported them. They replied—"We are the Kentucky Singers, under engagement in Australia to the theatre people." Ye gods and little fishes! Foreign films, foreign 'talkies' teaching our children to mutilate in every way the English language, canned foreign music, imported nigger singers.
>
> *(Egan, 2020, p. 181)*

The MUA formally adopted the WAP at its annual conference in 1925, and it was not removed from the federal rule book until 1961 (Dreyfus, 2013, p. 119). It was an attitude that "was no different from that of any other Australian Union of the time" (Dreyfus, 2009, p. 7) and a reflection of a general xenophobia and racism that went back to the nineteenth century (Egan, 2020, pp. 23, 25). Its deployment against African American jazz musicians had precedent: In 1923 Tom Carlyon sought permission from the Department of Home and Territories to book a black US jazz band into the ballroom of the Esplanade Hotel in Melbourne's beach-side suburb of St. Kilda. The refusal became a precedent for subsequent applications (O'Connell, 2016, p. 244).

The ostensible mission of the MUA in relation to imported players was the protection of employment for Australian musicians, gaining increased urgency from the late 1920s as the emergence of the 'talkies' reduced employment of musicians, rising to 4/5ths of MUA membership by the late 1930s (Arthur, 2003, pp. 348–349). The union argued that imported US dance bands were taking employment from local musicians who were quite capable of providing dance music of the same quality (Dreyfus, 2013, pp. 80, 82, 83). Initially, jazz bands were accepted because they would boost demand for the music and therefore increase employment for Australian jazz orchestras, but as unemployment became more severe at the end of the 1920s, they too were regarded as a threat. In 1928 the MUA lobbied the government for controls over the importation of musicians and in 1929 introduced a ban on union membership for non-British musicians (Arthur, 2003, pp. 348–349).

This policy placed the MUA at odds with entrepreneurs who wanted to import bands under contract through touring circuits, to present various styles of music of a quality that they insisted could not be found locally (Dreyfus, 2013, p. 64). From February 1929 the union introduced rules that in effect excluded foreign musicians, also drawing a distinction between those who entered the country under a contract, and those who entered individually as free-lance musicians. The former obviously brought the union into tension with entrepreneurs, and these disputes were conducted publicly, while the latter cases were handled within the union. The whole process was muddy, the distinction porous (see Dreyfus, 2013, pp. 63-4), but fundamental was the protectionist policy of the MUA, fuelled also by racism, as opposed to the interests of entrepreneurs who wished to serve the public taste for international styles presented at the highest standard.

Industrial disputes were settled through an arbitration system in which representatives of the sector involved were able to participate. In the entertainment and leisure environment of the 1920s, the MUA was a very strong lobbying force, with direct access to the highest level of government. In cases affecting the employment conditions of musicians, the general secretary of the MUA together with another union representative, such as the national president, would play an active role. Regarding imported musicians, "a small cohort of union officials was able to usurp the authority of the system in order to counter the real or imagined threat" (Dreyfus, 2013, p. 64, see also 69). During the period under discussion here, the Federal president of the MUA was Frank Kitson, who was also the secretary of the New South Wales branch. He had been a powerful influence in the union since 1916, and became central in the formation, advocacy, and enforcement of policy as the union's delegate in the arbitration process regarding foreign musicians, which he vehemently and litigiously opposed throughout his tenure in those offices from 1924 to his death in 1951 (Dreyfus, 2013, pp. 57–58).

At the same time, Kitson was an experienced and canny political player, skills which served him and the MUA very effectively during The Colored Idea episode. Within the union movement, the arrival of this revue, with its African American jazz band, was a double affront. It represented not just a potential threat to employment for Australian musicians, even though it was a stage band for revue with a contained touring schedule. It was also an offense against the racism institutionalised in the WAP, to which the union was explicitly committed. It was the former consideration that was argued most vigorously, though of course the latter was a (sometimes) covert factor. But the MUA under Kitson also understood the importance of public opinion: "Characteristically, MUA rhetoric attached itself to popular causes as a means of strengthening its appeal" (Dreyfus, 2013, p. 66). As we shall see further below, throughout the 1920s there was a feverish appetite for the latest in US dance bands, and above all, jazz.

Kitson well understood the importance of marshalling public opinion. In opposing an application for union membership by two Italian musicians in mid-1928, Kitson appealed to a general interwar suspicion of Italian immigration, using the press to publicize his arguments that these non-English speaking foreigners would not be competent as orchestral players in Australia (Dreyfus, 2013, p. 77). In this he was assisted by the cultivation of an alliance with Ezra Norton, owner of the Melbourne newspaper *Truth* ("The People's Paper"), also opposed to the importation of foreign musicians (Dreyfus, 2013, p. 109). It was an alliance that would prove invaluable in the union's fight with the Sonny Clay band from The Colored Idea. Kitson used the same tactic against Italian musicians imported to open the new Regent Theatre, and when theatrical company J.C. Williamson Ltd. imported twelve Italians for their Grand Opera season, while the original agreement with the union had been for only five. The union "was able to link its feelings of resentment to general public concerns about Italian migration" (Dreyfus, 2013, p. 83). Similarly, his relentless campaign against the Jewish refugee Weintraub Syncopators from 1937 exploited a deep vein of anti-Semitism among the Australian public (Dreyfus, 2013). These cases exemplified how the MUA could, in engaging with the public through the press, deploy arguments which had popular appeal, but which in fact masked the more basic and general objection by the MU to foreign imported musicians.

But The Colored Idea and its jazz band presented a very different problem as far as public opinion was concerned. As entrepreneurs recognised, there was a strong public demand for imported bands that could present the latest in American dance music. In 1924 the Harry Yerkes US band was imported to play a season at the Wattle Path dance palais in Melbourne. The MUA appealed against this to the Industrial Registrar, on the grounds that the contract should have gone to local musicians. The appeal failed, the Registrar declaring that Australians could not "get that rhythm that is essential in the dancing halls nowadays." The employer backed up this judgement by reference to public taste:

> We boosted an Australian Band when the Americans were here but the public wanted an American band. We tried very hard to keep the Australian orchestra but public opinion was against it. As a matter of fact our own men were unable to get the same rhythm as the Americans.
>
> *(Dreyfus, 2009, p. 10)*

The feeling that the US musicians were able to produce the rhythmic feel appropriate for the latest in modern dance was frequently expressed in the interwar period. In her memoir of growing up in the 1920s, Kathleen Mangan recalled the excitement caused by the visit of the US fleet in Melbourne in July 1925. As the daughter of the celebrated Australian painter Frederick McCubbin, she was in a position to receive an invitation to a dance on the USS *Pennsylvania*:

> When our party arrived, a little late, … the band was playing and the ball was in full swing. They had two bands that night, each composed mainly of brass instruments with excellent saxophonists that set your feet a 'tingle the moment you walked on board.
>
> *(Mangan, 1984, p. 196)*

As far as the general public was concerned, the *dernier cri* of US dance music trumped union concerns, and protectionism in entertainment counted for little. Australia had a long history of enthusiastic, if sometimes patronising, reception of coloured US troupes (see for example Egan, 2020, pp. 32, 66). The appeal of The Colored Idea was much enhanced by the fact that it incorporated a band with credentials in the latest of the new genres in popular music—jazz. As noted above, the revue, and in particular its band, was a hit with the public. The reviews were breathlessly enthusiastic, and that these were not simply press hyperbole tends to be confirmed by an interview I conducted on February 13, 2012 with a highly lucid 104 year old Grace (Gay) Stell (b. January 11, 1908), in a nursing home in the Victorian rural town of Euroa. She had attended a performance of the revue in Melbourne, and although she could recall little detail about the show, her most vivid memory was of the public excitement it caused.

The engagement of the band to play the ball at the Green Mill was outside its stage contract, and the union could have had a case for imposing an embargo, on the basis of the 1925 precedent cited above, but public enthusiasm for the band had already led one reviewer in Sydney to declare that "if Sonny is allowed to depart without affording us a chance to strut our stuff to his syncopation, every cabaret and dance hall management deserves bankruptsy [sic]" (Sutcliffe, 1997, p. 9). In light of the failure of its opposition to the Yerkes band a few years earlier, the MUA understood that to impose a ban on the dance performance would certainly have been a public relations disaster for them. It was necessary to exploit a different set of concerns, to activate a deeper, pre-existing moral panic in which racism and gender politics converged: The infiltration of the exotic primitive jazz through the agency of the sexually undisciplined modern girl.

To an extent the stage had been set in the previous year. In August 1927 the vocal group, The Coloured Emperors of Harmony, arrived in Australia for a season. Unfortunately the 'harmony' was disrupted when, eagerly headlined in the press, one female member of the troupe stabbed her husband in a jealous rage (Egan, 2020, p. 161), providing all the elements that would surface later with The Colored Idea: Black Americans and their music, sex, lack of restraint. It so happened that Dick Saunders, the victim of the highly publicized stabbing only months prior to the arrival of The Coloured Idea, was now the revue's MC (Egan, 2020, p. 175).

The MUA's opposition to foreign imports was able to be refracted through several other sites of public anxiety which obligingly converged: The odium that attached to jazz, to blackness, and deep moral panic about the New Woman. When it came to harnessing broad popular opinion, it was not the threat to the employment of local musicians that was deployed, but the politics of race and gender, of miscegenation, of sexual dynamics, in this case, the intimate complicity that was recognised between young women and jazz.

The Modern Girl and Jazz

The liberated profile of the Modern Girl and her synergy with urban modernity has been amply documented at an international level (see especially Weinbaum et al., 2008; on South East Asia, see also Keppy, 2019). That nexus has a distinctive inflection in the case of Eurocentric settler Australia, where conquering the rural "bush" to lay the foundations of primary industries was the emblem of muscular masculine production. By contrast, the city was a place of heedless consumption, emasculating, decadent, a space where leisure was given over to modern American fripperies like "jazz parties." This divide became a pervasive trope in the prolific early Australian silent film industry (on the gender politics of this divide see further Johnson, 2000, pp. 69–78; Moore, 2012, pp. 103–106). The Australian experience of World War I sharpened this contrast between a virile pre-industrial rural tradition and decadent modernity. For the men who served in the conflict, the experience of modern technology was of death and maiming. Australia's proportion of casualties was 16 per cent higher than Britain's and, during the interwar years, the continuing disability of 77,000 veterans of the First Australian Imperial Force (AIF) and the death of three veterans per day from wounds was a continuing reminder of the impact of military modernity (on casualty rates see Robson, 1982, pp. 202–203; Dreyfus, 2013, pp. 231–232). Norman Lindsay, a major cultural influence of the era, wrote of "Man":

> But we only have to turn to his actions in mass; his collective impulse expressed in his commercial greeds; his activity in manufacturing implements of destruction, his last war, and the war he is now preparing for, … to realize that this animal, for all his rituals in religion, his conventions in sociology, his prattle of humanitarianism, and all the surface effects of civilization in city streets and civil life, is just as savage and dangerous as he was a million years ago.
>
> *(Lindsay, 1960, p. 89)*

For such men and for the physically and mentally wounded veterans, modernity was a sickness. There was a gender dynamic underpinning these circumstances, exemplified neatly in the establishment of London's Endell Street Military Hospital. Its 500 beds were given over to wounded war veterans, but it was entirely staffed by women (see a full study, including of its suffragette background, Moore, 2020).

For women, the war opened up public spaces for employment and leisure which continued to expand postwar (Matthews, 2005, pp. 71, 83–84, 86–88). During the 1920s Australia had not only recovered from the financial depression of 1896, but was enjoying a very high level of prosperity (Matthews, 2005, pp. 20–21, 25), and this was of particular benefit in expanding leisure opportunities for women. In the early 1920s the Sydney Tivoli vaudeville and variety theatre inaugurated after-noon matinees specifically catering to women: Children were admitted at half price and "Ladies of discernment will find in its cheerful surroundings an entertainment economic, and in excellent taste" (Van Straten, 2003, p. 74).

For young women, modernity was liberating. Major Australian poet Kenneth Slessor wrote a series of poems between 1928 and 1933, collected in 1983 as *Backless Betty from Bondi* (all page numbers refer to this collection). Among the profiles of the Modern Girl which he celebrates are cinema usherettes ("Firefly" p. 6), typists/secretaries ("Underwood Ann" p. 10), nurses ("Nightingale" 1930, p. 14); she wears revealing lingerie ("Pantette" p. 31) and bathing costumes ("Backless Betty from Bondi"—"HER EYES ARE FULL OF WIRELESS" p. 32), she travels ("Streamer's End" p. 17). She skis better ("Skis and Shes" 11), out-hikes ("She Keeps on Walking" p. 12), and outsurfs ("She Shoots to Conquer" p. 13) her male counterpart, a common scenario of the 1920s as in the song 'Flappers in the Sky', in which young women pilot an aircraft leaving behind "mere man" (see fur-ther Johnson, 2020, pp. 140–141).

Modern technology gave women a consumer's leisure paradise in the postwar era: Movies, gramophones, radio, and a growing abundance of labour-saving domestic commodities, all on dis-play in the proliferating women's life-style magazines, department stores and what we would now call multiplex entertainment venues (see further for example Mackay, 1994; Matthews, 2005, pp. 57–58). New hotels

> rivalled the department stores in providing lunches and teas for ladies who stopped and chatted. They offered their palm courts for modern women to enjoy a cocktail and a cigarette and a spin on the dance floor, and their ballrooms entertained both public and private dances and balls. By the mid 1920s, these hotels had become renowned not alone for their grandeur, but for their dance bands and jazz rooms.
>
> *(Matthews, 2005, p. 53)*

Cinema provided relatively inexpensive entertainment that, with its creches, particularly catered for women—70 per cent of Australian cinema attendees in 1927 were female (Johnson, 2000, p. 62). But film narratives also presented models for new ways of being a woman (Matthews, 2005, pp. 81–82; Moore, 2012, p. 126) and advertisements for American films spoke of "brilliant men, beautiful jazz babies, champagne baths and midnight revels" (Brisbane, 1991, p. 181). Cinema also offered employment opportunities, in film production and in the picture palaces as usherettes, in box offices and kiosks and as musicians—the majority of cinema pianists improvising from pastiches for the silent movies were women (Whiteoak, 1999, pp. 14, 66).

Along with cinema, the massive global spread of social dancing became a site of "the emer-ging social and moral economy" and in fact the two complemented each other as movies brought "images of the dancing stars, their frocks, their steps and demeanour" (Matthews, 2005, p. 85). In the 1926 Australian film *Greenhide*, the young protagonist Margery is identified both for her diegetic party guests and for the movie audience by presenting the spectacle of herself improvising a solo dance to the accompaniment of a jazz band (see Johnson, 2000, pp. 69–76). Notorious Sydney bohemian Anna Brennan (daughter of the equally notorious poet/academic Christopher) was celebrated for tap dancing on table tops (Moore, 2012, pp. 129–130). That is, dancing, and especially alone with extravagant extroversion, became a form of self-production, a visible demonstration of agency. Self-presentation as spectacle was an important way of proclaiming the identity of the Modern Girl (see Conor, 2008, pp. 227–228) and the jazzing—that is, dancing—flapper was very much a spectacle of the decade, as in the hit song from the 1920s, "Wait Till You See My Baby Do the Charleston."

And, as in this case, the latest in modern dance was "the jazz." The association of the liberated young woman, the 'flapper', with jazz and jazz dancing was pervasive in social practice, in cinema, in lifestyle journals (on cinema see Johnson, 2000, pp. 59–76, on life-style journals see Mackay, 1994; Moore, 2012, pp. 121, 134). Its brassy sounds were integral to the rising volume of urban modernity, as in the sonic collage of Jean Curlewis's prose poem "The City": "Jazz. Traffic. Noise. Trams … Sirens. Steel Hammers clanging" (Matthews, 2005, p. 46). The young modern girl was "the incarnation of the Jazz Age" (Matthews, 2005, p. 65). In 1925 the newspaper *Truth*, which would lead the charge in publicizing The Colored Idea scandal of 1928, published a poem called 'Recipe for a Flapper', which included the lines,

> Take a handful of girl of about seventeen …// Soak in the foetid atmosphere of a City until all Modesty and // Rationality disappears. // Cover the face with a thick, double or triple layer of // Cosmetic, and stain two fingers of the right hand brown …// Fill with the notion that Jazz is the noblest work of God and // garnish with a trifle of slinky dress and considerable legs. Over // all sprinkle the dust of Complete Conceit.
>
> *(Matthews, 2005, p. 66)*

Those "considerable legs," dancing, confirmed the corporeality of jazz as it was understood during the 1920s, a very different music from the cerebral exercise it became after World War II as exemplified in bands like the Modern Jazz Quartet. The visiting Peruvian contralto singer Margarite d'Alvarez had declared to the press in 1922, "I am crazy about jazz, and I think that it possesses a certain rhythmic essence which creates movements of the body that nothing else can equal" (Brisbane, 1991, p. 180). Jazz dancing gave the body new ways to advertise itself, to be, in public. And that "way of being" inevitably overlapped with sexuality. The famous Sydney bohemian Dulcie Deamer declared that women "jazzed" (that is, again, dancing, as in "waltzed" or "tangoed"), as a form of "sexual adventure, and to allow our repressed polyandrous instinct to get a breath of fresh air" (Johnson, 2000, pp. 66–67). The US term "jazz belle" was originally slang for prostitute (Dreyfus, 1999, p. 43). And women not only "jazzed" as dancers, but as performers, and as such were equally likely to be tainted with the sexual aura surrounding jazz. Among the "new pool" of women's bands in 1920s Australia, Dreyfus documents the band Lynette and her Six Redheads, who included jazz and comedy in their repertoire. Encountering hostility from male bands, with their risqué outfits, bright red wigs and sexy presentation, they were regarded as morally dubious: "Hussies! They must come from Sydney" (Dreyfus, 1999, p. 59). That they debuted in Sydney just months after the Coloured Idea scandal could not have diminished the image of moral dubiety (Dreyfus, 1999, pp. 60–61). Jazz, sex, and the liberated modern women formed a semiotic unity.

My purpose now is to draw the foregoing together to document the way in which this perceived association was deployed to make a moral case that provides leverage in public opinion. The women at the center of the scandal were constructed as examples of the Modern Girl who threatened public decency by acting as the channel through which the contaminations of modernity and modern dance music—jazz—entered Australian culture.

The five young women involved were a seamstress, a live-in nanny, two domestic servants, a typist—"ordinary working-class women"—their ages ranging from seventeen to twenty-three, (Cassells, 2013, p. 9). But these mundane and humanizing details were swamped in the press reports by a strident emphasis on their scandalous association with the African American musicians. The *Truth* led its report with the headlines: "WHITE GIRLS WITH NEGRO LOVERS: Raid Discloses Wild Scene of Abandon; Flappers, Wine, Cocaine and Revels" (Johnson, 2010, p. 5). Egan has gathered a pungent national sample, in which headlines include "SORDID STORY NEGRO NIGHT PARTY WITH WHITE GIRLS, MELBOURNE" (*Sydney Sun*); "NEGROES AND GIRLS. RAID ON A FLAT. Disgraceful Conduct Alleged" (*West Australian*); "LUSTFUL ORGY. NEGROES AND WHITE WOMEN. DISGUSTING CONDUCT IN MELBOURNE FLAT" (*Courier*) (Egan, 2020, p. 174). The police fed details to the public through their briefings to the press, including the information that different groups of women were entertained by the musicians every night, and that the "girls were naked" (O'Connell, 2016, p. 249). One of the arresting police officers, Constable Leslie Saker, giving evidence before the magistrate, was reported as claiming that from his surveillance post across the road he witnessed "wild dancing" and the musicians "pulling around" the girls, though he also admitted that his vision was much restricted by a tree outside the window. He declared that in the flat he found cigarettes, wine and hinted at cocaine. The suspicion that he was indulging in prurient embellishment is fortified by his response to the magistrate's enquiry as to why no charges of offensive behavior had been laid: That he didn't have sufficient evidence (Cassells, 2013, pp. 11–12).

Public indignation was massive, in a way that a union ban could never have achieved. An angry crowd of between 700 and 800, mostly men, assembled outside the court when the women came before the magistrate (Cassells, 2013, p. 11; O'Connell, 2016, p. 249; Sales's source (1974, p. 77) gives a figure of "no less than a thousand men … inquisitive to learn what sort of female would associate with men of another race"). The powerful Returned Soldiers and Sailors Imperial League passed a motion that the WAP should be strengthened to prevent white women from "consorting with negroes" (Cassells, 2013, p. 16), and in Federal Parliament, the MP for Bass in Tasmania demanded to know if any action was planned over the episode; the Minister for Health informed him that "the negroes will sail from Australia on Saturday next," and that in future applications for admission by foreign performers would be more carefully scrutinized (Egan, 2020, p. 174).

As the various police statements in the media and in court suggest, however, the narrative fed to and devoured by the public was in many ways a strategic fiction, playing on anxieties about the Modern Girl, her tastes and lifestyle. Cassell's study in particular suggests that the scandal was driven by a characterization of the women as the conduit of all that was threatening to a conservative order. While it was clear that there were regular parties involving the jazz musicians and what would now be called local groupies, the embellishments by the press and the media were all calculated to inflame moral panic over the modern girl—indeed it appears that the musicians remained largely anonymous, a collective homogeneous Other; one of the young women was reported as declaring "These boys are American, and they are interesting" (Sales, 1974, p. 78). The press reported the presence of a sixth girl named as Irene McCollough who boldly escaped out a window. Cassells' detailed research suggests that no such woman existed (Cassells, 2013, p. 5), but the story certainly heightened the image of the defiant and independent spirit of these young women. *Truth* also published what it claimed were extracts from a diary belonging to one of the women, but which was most probably a fiction. The extracts confirmed all too strongly that this woman, and by association the others involved, were promiscuous and sexually deviant. The diary obligingly included a list of around thirty lovers, referred to abortions, hidden pregnancies, an illegitimate child adopted out, and, most scandalizing of all recorded her wish to "renounce her race" for love of an African American (Cassells, 2013, p. 15). Thus, it was not the MUA's protectionist concern for its members, but miscegenation, the contamination of the white race and white culture, that lay at the heart of the public furor. The vehicle of this contamination was the "jazzing flapper" and its musical mediation was jazz. Jazz, that is, was in the 1920s not a site of heroic male artistic *agon* as it came to be in the post-World War II era, but of subversive female emancipation.

This raises the question of how and why the gendering of jazz was so fully reversed in the post-World War II era that its gender politics of the 1920s seems to have been all but forgotten in jazz studies. The full elaboration of that argument must be for another time, but it would center on several cultural shifts over that period. The Colored Idea was a single, contained scandal. But the fear of cultural contamination mediated by women became pervasive during World War II, when the US garrison included a large proportion of black servicemen (Cassells, 2013, p. 6). This wartime anxiety was followed by a broader attempt to drive women back to domesticity from the enlarged public space which two world wars and the interval between them had made available. This deep conservatism of the postwar decades colluded with a significant shift in the status of jazz. What, in the 1920s, had been a form of popular culture rooted in the corporeality of dance (very much a female domain), was becoming in the 1950s, an art form, created and engaged with through masculinist intellectual labor (for an invaluable case study in this shift see Schlicht, 2008).

In summary, there were many forces at work behind the deportation of the Clay orchestra. They included the hostility of the MUA to foreign musicians, aggravated by the Commonwealth Band embargo, the union's formal commitment to the WAP, the separate contractual arrangements at The Green Mill entered into by the band, all underpinned by a broader xenophobic and racist streak in Australian culture. But, apart from harnessing racism, none of these was presented as such in mobilizing public support for the deportation: It became a matter of gender politics, of the "contamination" of Australian society by black jazz musicians through the medium of the independent-minded young woman and her music. It was not men who opened the door to this new American music. It was the "jazzing flapper."

Note

1 The distinction is discussed with fine nuance in Weinbaum (2008, pp. 9–10), who nonetheless concludes that the two categories are "intertwined", and that both "found political inspiration in popular female performance and spectacle" (Weinbaum, 2008, p. 10).

References

Ake, D. (2002). *Jazz Cultures*. University of California Press.

Ake, D. (2019). After Wynton: Narrating Jazz in the Postneotraditional Era. In N. Gebhardt, N. Rustin-Paschal and T. Whyton (Eds.), *The Routledge Companion to Jazz Studies* (pp. 77–86). Routledge.

Arthur, B. (2003). Industrial Relations. In J. Whiteoak and A. Scott-Maxwell (Eds.), *Currency Companion to Music and Dance in Australia* (pp. 348–349). Currency House/Currency Press.

Arvidsson, A. (Ed.). (2014). *Jazz, Gender, Authenticity: Proceedings of the 10thNordic Jazz Research Conference, Stockholm August 30–31 2012*. Publikationer från jazzavdelningen, Svenskt visarkiv, nr 25.

Baade, C. (2008). "The Battle of the Saxes": Gender, dance bands and British nationalism in the Second World War. In N. T. Rustin and S.Tucker (Eds.), *Big Ears: Listening for Gender in Jazz Studies* (pp. 90–128). Duke University Press.

Bisset, A. (1987). *Black Roots White Flowers: A History of Jazz in Australia*. ABC Enterprises (Updated from the original 1979 edition).

Brisbane, K. (Ed.). (1991). *Entertaining Australia: An Illustrated History*. Currency Press.

Burke, P. (2019). Race in the New Jazz Studies. In N. Gebhardt, N. Rustin-Paschal and T. Whyton (Eds), *The Routledge Companion to Jazz Studies* (pp. 185–195). Routledge.

Cassells, K. (2013). Sex, Scandal and Speculation: White Women, Race and Sexual Desire in the Colored Idea Scandal,1928. *Lilith: A Feminist History Journal*, No. 19 (pp. 4–17).

Conor, L (2008). "Blackfella Missus Too Much Proud": Techniques of Appearing, Femininity, and Race in Australian Modernity. In A. E. Weinbaum, L. M. Thomas, P. Ramamurthy, U. G. Poiger, M. Y. Dong, T. E. Barlow (Eds.). *The Modern Girl Around the World: Consumption, Modernity, and Globalization* (pp. 220–239). Duke University Press.

Dreyfus, Kay (1999). *Sweethearts of Rhythm: The Story of Australia's All-girl bands and Orchestras to the End of the Second World War*. Sydney: Currency Press.

Dreyfus, K. (2009). The Foreigner, the Musicians' Union, and the State in 1920s Australia: A Nexus of Conflict. *Music & Politics* 3(1), Winter (pp. 1–16).

Dreyfus, K. (2013). *Silences and Secrets: The Australian Experience of the Weintraubs Syncopators*. Monash University Publishing.

Egan, B. (2020). *African American Entertainers in Australia and New Zealand: A History, 1788–1941*. McFarland.

Hairston, M. (2008). Gender, Jazz and the Popular Front. In N. T. Rustin and S. Tucker (Eds.), *Big Ears: Listening for Gender in Jazz Studies* (pp. 64–89). Duke University Press.

Hall, R. (1997). White Australia's Darkest Days. *The Sydney Morning Herald Good Weekend,* 15 March (pp. 17–22).

Hall, R. (1998). Black Arms on White Shoulders: Billy Hughes and the Scum of America. In R. Hall, *Black Armband Days: Truth from the Dark Side of Australia's Past* (pp. 171–185). Vintage.

Johnson, B. (2000). *The Inaudible Music: Jazz, Gender and Australian Modernity.* Currency Press.

Johnson, B. (2010). Deportation Blues: Black Jazz and White Australia in the 1920s. *IASPM Journal: Journal of the International Association for the Study of Popular Music,* 1 (1). Online at www.iaspmjournal.net/index.php/IASPM_Journal/article/viewFile/297/502.

Johnson, B. (2011). Hear Me Talkin' To Ya: Problems of Jazz Discourse. In Tony Whyton (Ed.), *Jazz* (pp. 21–32). Ashgate. Originally published 1993. *Popular Music,* 12(1), January (pp. 1–12).

Johnson, B. (2020). *Jazz Diaspora: Music and Globalisation.* Routledge.

Keppy, P. (2019). *Tales of Southeast Asia's Jazz Age: Filipinos, Indonesians and Popular Culture, 1920–1936.* NUS Press.

Lindsay, J. (1960). *The Roaring Twenties: Literary Life in Sydney New South Wales in the Years 1921–1926.* The Bodley Head.

Mackay, M. (1994). Almost dancing: Thea Proctor and the modern woman. In M. Dever (Ed.), *Wallflowers and Witches: Women and Culture in Australia 1910–1945* (pp. 26–37). University of Queensland Press.

Mangan, K. (1984). *Daisy Chains, War, then Jazz.* Hutchinson of Australia.

Matthews, J. J. (2005). *Dance Hall and Picture Palace: Sydney's Romance with Modernity.* Currency Press.

McMullen, T. (2008). Identity for Sale: Glenn Miller, Wynton Marsalis, and cultural replay in music. In N. T. Rustin and S. Tucker (eds), *Big Ears: Listening for Gender in Jazz Studies* (pp. 129–154). Duke University Press.

Melman, B. (1988). *Women and the Popular Imagination in the Twenties: Flappers and Nymphs.* St Martin's Press.

Moore, T. (2012). *Dancing with Empty Pockets: Australia's Bohemians Since 1860.* Murdoch Books.

Moore, W. (2020). *Endell Street: The Women Who Ran Britain's Trailblazing Military Hospital.* Atlantic.

O'Connell, D. M. (2016). Contesting White Australia: Black Jazz Musicians in a White Man's Country. *Australian Historical Studies,* 47(2) (pp. 241–258).

O'Connell, D. (2021). *Harlem Nights: The Secret History of Australia's Jazz Age.* Melbourne University Press.

Robson, L. L. (1982). *The First A.I.F.: A Study of its Recruitment 1914–1918.* Melbourne University Press.

Rustin, N. T. and S. Tucker. (2008). Introduction. In N. T. Rustin and S. Tucker (Eds.), *Big Ears: Listening for Gender in Jazz Studies* (pp. 1–28). Duke University Press.

Sales, P. M. (1974). White Australia, Black Americans: A Melbourne Incident, 1928. *The Australian Quarterly,* 46(4) (pp. 74–81).

Schlicht, U. (2008). "Better a Jazz Album than Lipstick" (Lieber Jazzplatte als Lippenstift): The 1956 Jazz Podium Series Reveals Images of Jazz and Gender in Postwar Germany. In: N. T. Rustin and S. Tucker (Eds.) *Big Ears: Listening for Gender in Jazz Studies* (pp. 291–319). Duke University Press.

Schwartz, L. (2019). *Feminism and the Servant Problem: Class and Domestic Labour in the Women's Suffrage Movement.* Cambridge University Press.

Slessor, K. (1983). *Backless Betty from Bondi.* (Ed. Julian Croft). Angus and Robertson, first published 1928–1933.

Sutcliffe, M. (1997). Sonny Clay and The Coloured Idea. *Australian Record and Music Review,* 35, October (pp. 3–13).

Taylor, J. (2008). With Lovie and Lil: Rediscovering two Chicago pianists of the 1920s. In Nicole T. Rustin and Sherrie Tucker (Eds.), *Big Ears: Listening for Gender in Jazz Studies* (pp. 48–63). Duke University Press.

Van Straten, F. (2003). *Tivoli.* Thomas C. Lothian Pty.

Weinbaum, A. E., L. M. Thomas, P. Ramamurthy, U. G. Poiger, M. Y. Dong, T. E. Barlow. The Modern Girl as Heuristic Device (2008). In A. E. Weinbaum, L. M. Thomas, P. Ramamurthy, U. G. Poiger, M. Y. Dong, T. E. Barlow (Eds.), *The Modern Girl Around the World: Consumption, Modernity, and Globalization* (1–24). Duke University Press.

Whiteoak, J. (1999). *Playing Ad Lib: Improvisatory Music in Australia 1836-1970.* Currency Press.

Williams, L. (2007). Black Women, Jazz and Feminism. In E. M Hayes and L. F. Williams (Eds.), *Black Women and Music* (pp. 119–133). University of Illinois Press.

2

"I'VE GOT THE HAITIAN BLUES"

Mamie Desdunes and the Gendered Inflections of the Common Wind

Benjamin Barson

A Note from the Author: Throughout this chapter I use the term *gender* to refer to both gender and sex whilst acknowledging that strictly speaking, sex is designated by biological differences, and gender is socially constructed. As this chapter also addresses prostitution, I have, following activists who work on the issue, prioritized the term "sex workers" when referring to people who sell erotic services, including sex.

At this point, I want to clarify that I am an able-bodied cisgender and heterosexual male from the United States. This has allowed me to pursue my professional ambitions from a position of privilege, unhindered by the structural disadvantages experienced by women, Black, Indigenous, or People of Color (BIPOC) individuals, or others from social or economically disadvantageous milieus. Therefore, I cannot claim to write this chapter from a position of experience. To partly alleviate this lack, I have aimed to use sources by female or non-binary authors, primarily.

Introduction

Mamie's Blues … [is a] bird who migrates or emigrates or immigrates or transmigrates, roadblock jumper, smuggler,

a song which

is inevitable, is rain and bread and salt, something completely beyond national ritual, sacred traditions, language and folklore: a cloud without frontiers, a spy of air and water, an archetypal form, something from before, from below.

It is a piece that delivers listeners "back to a betrayed origin," a musical ethos that demonstrates that "perhaps there have been other paths and that the only one they took was maybe not the only one or the best one" (Cortazar 1987, p. 195–198). So wrote the Argentine exile in Paris, Julio Cortázar, in his landmark work 1963 choose-your-own path novel (what he called an "Anti-Novel") *Hopscotch*.

Like Cortázar, I also consider "Mamie's Blues" to be something of a "betrayed origin" in how we narrate and tell the story of jazz. This is a piece that contemporary musicologists now consider to be the first twelve-bar jazz blues (Hobson 2011), an opinion shared by Buddy Bolden's trombonist,

DOI: 10.4324/9781003081876-3

Willie Cornish, who claimed that this was a song any musician "had to know" in early twentieth-century New Orleans (Cornish in Hobson 2011, p. 3–27). Over multiple interviews, Jelly Roll Morton remembered that it was "among the first blues that I've ever heard" (Russell 1999, 223), and that "Although I had heard them [the blues] previously, I guess it was Mamie [who] first really sold me on the blues" (Lomax 1950, p. 20–21). Then a teenager working as a roustabout on the docks, Morton went to extreme lengths to study with its composer, Mamie Desdunes. "Of course, to get in on it, to try to learn it, I made myself the … the can rusher," a person responsible for bringing heavy barrels of beer from breweries to the brothels, where pianists like Mamie Desdunes played (Morton 1938). The thought of a young Morton, age eleven, carrying heavy barrels of beer to the most upscale brothels in the United States through a highly policed red-light district would be almost comical if it did not also reveal the twisted deprivation in which Black artistry was forced to toil.

Apparently, Morton was not the only prospective student who opted for the can-rushing route to gain proximity to Desdunes. The African American trumpet player Bunk Johnson, who became associated with the New Orleans revival in the 1950s, also recalled playing and studying with Mamie Desdunes. Johnson told Alan Lomax in a recorded interview in March 1949, that he

> knew Mamie Desdoumes [Lomax's spelling] real well. Played many a concert with her singing those same blues. She was pretty good looking—quite fair and with a nice head of hair. She was a hustling woman. A blues-singing poor girl. Used to play pretty passable piano around them dance halls on Perdido Street.
>
> *(Lomax 1950, p. 21)*

Jazz historian Peter Hanley, based on census data, has suggested that Bunk Johnson and Mamie Desdunes were next-door neighbors, and that "There seems little doubt that Bunk and Jelly Roll knew each other well in their early youth and probably competed with each other for the job of Mamie Desdunes' 'can rusher'" (Hanley 2002). Morton and Johnson maintained a friendship throughout their lives, and they both claimed to have "invented" jazz. Perhaps their early training with Mamie Desdunes gave them the confidence to make such an assertion. For all of Morton's eagerness to lay claim to creating a variety of widely shared songs and conventions, he is extremely deliberate in crediting Mamie Desdunes for "Mamie's Blues" on every possible occasion. As he explained in a letter to his label representative,

> Mamie Desdume [*sic*] wrote Mamie's Blues in the late 90s. I don't like to take credit for something that don't belong to me. I guess she's dead by now, and there would probably be no royalty to pay, but she did write it.
>
> *(Russell 1999, p. 223)*

Given the gendered turn in jazz studies, it is surprising that Mamie Desdunes has not had a more visible showing in recent literature. Desdunes herself is a fascinating figure. Born out of wed-lock to Rodolphe Desdunes and Clementine Walker in 1881, Mamie was connected to a lineage of Haitian-descended activists who maintained close connections to the Black republic throughout the nineteenth century. Her uncle, Pierre-Aristide Desdunes, visited Haiti as part of a delegation of free Blacks to discuss possible emigration in 1847. Instead, the Civil War broke out, and he served as one of the first Black soldiers in the Union Army in the *Corps d'Afrique*. He was also an influential poet whose work is often included in anthologies of Afro-Franco literature from nineteenth-century New Orleans (Bell 2011 and 2014). Mamie's father, Rodolphe Desdunes, was a Reconstruction-era activist and author. He organized for land reform and public rights, corresponded with a young W.E.B. du Bois on political strategy and tactics, and published *Nos Hommes et Notre Histoire*, a land-mark account of New Orleans Creoles of Color from a radical and activist perspective (Desdunes 2001). Mamie's brother, the multi-instrumentalist and brass bandleader Daniel Desdunes, participated in a direct-action sit-in during February of 1892. Arrested, Daniel later won his case, setting the stage for Homer Plessy to challenge the constitutionality of segregation four years later in a similar freedom ride, with less sanguine results (Scott 2007; Otto 2011; Vernhettes and Hanley 2014).

Like her family members, Mamie fused arts and political critique, while creating a new form of music that sounded aspects of her Haitian ancestry. But unlike her family members, she did so from the point of view of a woman working in the quasi-dystopian sexual economy known as "the District," or more commonly today as Storyville. Recent literature has complicated the depiction of Storyville as a "good time," highlighting the intersection of the New South variant of capitalism, sex tourism, violent white supremacy, and the disciplining of Black women's bodies (Landau 2013; Adams 2012). "Mamie's Blues" is a remarkable work because it provides testimony and critiques these conditions.

Writing about Mamie Desdunes is difficult because, outside of her death certificate and a few census records, we lack any "hard" archival evidence to prove many claims made about her. In 1893, she made a rare appearance in print media when the New Orleans *Picayune* reported that a "colored girl named Mamie Desdunes" lost two fingers after being run over by a train. (Morton and others corroborate that Mamie had only three fingers on her right hand) (New Orleans *Picayune* 1893). She died in 1908 of tuberculosis at the age of 31, a disease that disproportionately claimed Black and female victims, manifesting New Orleans's health disparities. She died about a decade too soon to have any of her performances recorded. She left no sheet music, and her name does not appear in ads for Storyville's bordellos. Yet it is precisely this archival gap that makes her presence in assorted interviews so suggestive. The reason we know Mamie Desdunes's name was because she profoundly influenced a coterie of early jazz musicians who attest to both (a) her influence as a mentor and (b) the importance of her innovative signature composition, "Mamie's Blues." The song's unashamed celebration of Black women's sexuality was a refrain for a generation of Storyville's blues people. Indeed, it suggests that blues women responded to this dystopian playground through a new expressive culture called the blues.

In this chapter, I argue that the social vision proposed by "Mamie's Blues" contributed to a Black "counterpublic" that resisted the dehumanizing conditions of Storyville while celebrating Black women's right to desire. As Farah Jasmine Griffin wrote in her discussion of Zora Neal Hurston, Black women artists "raise a level of consciousness about the manner in which black women have come to know and feel about their bodies," and thus "provide a path out of this prison" (Griffin 1996, 534). Mamie Desdunes's signature work celebrated the erotic from a woman's perspective, providing an impetus for self-determination through pleasure. That she did so from the point of view of the "prison," in this case, Storyville, suggests that the body was a site of contestation, and her conception of the blues spoke directly to this.

The second half of the piece explores the resonance of Mamie Desdunes's Haitian identity in the work. I suggest that a particularly Haitian form of cultural production can be heard both in her commentary on sexuality and its attendant power relations, as well as in her use of *habanera*-based polyrhythm in the song's bass line (as played by Jelly Roll Morton). By centering how sex workers and musicians of color understood themselves and the values they carved out, I argue that Mamie's Blues offers another genealogy of jazz, one which is antipatriarchal, communal, and Atlantic in scope. It is this betrayed origin to which I now turn.

Locating Mamie Desdunes in Storyville

Storyville was contested terrain, and Black women and men attempted to shape the terms and conditions of employment. Blues was a song form that emanated both from within and without the working-class of a sex tourism economy, and from its inception it had a highly gendered slant. Jazz historian Lara Pelligrinelli has pointed to Jelly Roll Morton's recollection that "chippies" or prostitutes, stood outside cribs and brothels, "singing the blues" to suggest that the blues emerged as a women's vocal tradition, specifically among those directly involved in the sex industry (Pelligrinelli 2008). Pianist Manuel Manetta similarly claimed that it was "Women who sang mostly blues," and this included "Mary Thacker, Alma Hughes and Ann Cook." Manuel Manetta mentioned "Mary Jack the Bear" and "Mamie Desdume" [sic], specifically singling out the latter as "a madam [female pimp] who had a house on Villere Street" (Manetta 1957). Sex workers populated the class of blues women innovators, foregrounding the dual employment of Memphis Minnie and Bessie Smith, both of whom were not only legendary blues singers but also part-time sex workers (Garon and Garon 2014). These occupations were not ancillary to their artistic output. Their cultural work confronted and narrated the logic of this sexual marketplace. This was a class of artistic innovators who held the contradictory and impossible condition of the "commodity who screams" (Moten 2003, p. 12), humanizing supposedly subhuman subjects.

Mamie Desdunes's only recorded composition, among the most diffused and earliest songs of its type, compels a critical reading. The song's first stanzas suggest an interrelationship between feminized poverty and patriarchal family structures. As an alternative, Desdunes suggests liberation can come through erotic pleasure:

> I stood on the corner, my feet was dripping wet
> I stood on the corner, my feet was dripping wet
> I asked every man I met
>
> Can't give me a dollar, give me a lousy dime
> Can't give me a dollar, give me a lousy dime
> Just to feed that hungry man of mine
>
> I got a husband and I got a kid man too
> I got a husband and I got a kid man too
> My husband can't do what my kid man can do
>
> I like the way he cook my cabbage for me
> I like the way he cook my cabbage for me
> Look like he set my natural soul free.
> *(Morton 1938)*

Several points stick out about these lyrics that locate them within what Angela Davis identifies as a "blues legacy, [a] black-working class legacy" of Black blues feminism (Davis 1983, p. 25). Mamie Desdunes's narrative personifies a feminized poverty exacerbated by intersecting social forces. Yet there is also agency and self-determination in these words. Black women were often primary breadwinners in households, and many were heads of household. In multiple censuses, Mamie Desdunes was herself registered as the head of her household, even when she was married (Vernhettes and Hanley 2014). Desdunes's independence was reflected in her lyrics: while her song's protagonist entertained a formal marriage, she does not shy from sexual pleasure ("cooked my cabbage") outside of the relationship; in fact, it is only with her "kid man" that she feels that her "natural soul" is set free. Mamie Desdunes thus precedes by decades the convention of women blues singers using double entendre to express sexuality and to narrate gendered power struggles within the household and the marketplace. For instance, Ma Rainey, who spent a significant amount of time working in New Orleans with some of Mamie Desdunes's collaborators, uses this lyrical technique in several of her songs, including her self-exposition as bisexual in "Prove It On Me Blues" (1928). The dual emphasis on poverty and sexual liberation has a long history in blues lyrics, what Richard Wright identified as the blues' "lusty, lyrical realism charged with taut sensibility" (Wright 1963, ix). In addition to Rainey's work, sexual poetics can be heard in Bessie Smith's (1926) "Young Woman's Blues," Ida Cox's (1939) "One Hour

Mama," and Ethel Water's (1925) "No Man's Mamma Now." Each of these songs openly discusses sexuality within (and in opposition to) patriarchal power structures; they also postdate "Mamie's Blues" by nearly three decades (Carby 1998).

Sung during the height of New Orleans' progressive movement which emphasized social order and patriarchal power structures, it is quite striking that Mamie vocally embraces sex outside of marriage. Based on the limited archival evidence available on Desdunes, this reflected her own life experience. In 1898, Mamie Desdunes moved in with warehouse worker George Duque, and they married in 1900. It seems they almost immediately broke up, because within a year, they were living separately, and Mamie was living alone in the same home, using her maiden name in the 1901 Soard's directory of New Orleans. By the end of her life, Mamie and George had apparently smoothed things over; the 1910 city directory showed George as a resident of the house and Mamie's death certificate reads "Mamie Dugue." While there is no evidence that Mamie or George's sexual activity was driving these break ups, it is clear that they did not share a traditional nuclear family or household. Mamie was herself born out of wedlock, and other illegitimate children of her father, Rodolphe, and her mother, Clementine Walker, lived with Mamie, including her younger sister Edna and her younger brothers John and Louis. Complex and fluid understandings of marriage and extended family households necessitated a different vision of community outside of the heteropatriarchal nuclear family, and Desdunes's lyrics emphasize openness to life's many opportunities for emotional and sexual connection (Edwards 2016; Snook 2018; Vernhettes and Hanley 2014).

"Mamie's Blues" contains a second stanza which expands the song's social criticism, relocating sexuality from the domestic sphere and women's pleasure by highlighting the violent and unequal power relations that undergirded the Gulf Coast's sexual economy. Jelly Roll Morton sings this stanza in his 1939 recording, and it is also present in Bunk Johnson's 1944 recording of the song (Morton 1939; Bunk Johnson and The Yerba Buena Jazz Band 1944). In these other lyrics, Desdunes narrates the disappearance of a loved one through a sex trafficking network that linked New Orleans to the Texas gulf region, with the refrain "Number 219 took my baby away," referring to a train that connected New Orleans with Texas oil boom towns. As the third line, Desdunes explains that "the 217 may bring her back someday." Charles Edward Smith recalled Morton explaining that the 2:19 was the train that "took the gals out on the T&P [Texas and Pacific Railroad] to the sporting houses on the Texas side of the circuit … [and] the 217 on the S.P. [Southern Pacific] through San Antonio and Houston brought them back to New Orleans" (Wald 2016).

With this foregrounding of the 2:19 train, the other stanzas completely change meaning. Poverty's locus is now in the unequal power relations within the prostitution industry and the economy at large. Not only does Desdunes connect feminized poverty to a repressive sexual economy, she lifts up the erased voices of vulnerable migrants. There are only scattered historical records of these trafficked migrant sex workers, destined for these boom towns. Historians of prostitution have documented that towns such Beaumont and Gladys City at the turn of the twentieth century were home to many migrant sex workers (Humphrey 1995). These itinerant workers were especially vulnerable to exploitation, often with few social connections in the towns where they arrived (Balderach 2005).

"Mamie's Blues" shines a light on this social reality, and its story was familiar enough that it struck a chord with Storyville's Black counterpublic. Desdunes foregrounds the social history of a class of invisible migrants whose pain lay at the intersection of commercialized sex, displacement, and modernity. These same forces animated the lifeways of those who made Storyville their new home, where thousands of Black migrants escaped white violence and repression in the sugar parishes to constitute the first wave of the Great Migration whose primary vectors were not South to North but rural to urban (Hahn 2003). The women of Storyville embodied the proletariat of a new sexual economy, but they were also the first audiences and innovators of the music that became known as the blues. Desdunes developed a vernacular critique of capitalism and women's captivity as it was emerging in its modern form. She both archived and aestheticized these iterant workers' struggles.

"Mamie's Blues" showcases the dark side of "progress," and the use of the train is one meta-phor that speaks to this objective. Trains and railroads are a long-standing signifier in blues songs. What was celebrated as industrial development by progressive reformers was experienced as a new entanglement of capital, enclosure, and economic displacement by others. Desdunes paints the 2:19 train in a negative light, as both symptom and cause of alienation, a comment on modernity, cap-italism, and violence against women (see Carby 2008). In Desdunes's rendering, the train is not a force of social or geographic mobility. She understands this industrial vehicle to reflect how the plantation evolved, how its political economy continued to lay claim to the Black woman's body with modern machinery . Desdunes's spotlighting of these subaltern workers speaks to a genre of "decolonial poetics produced by [afro]diasporic communities," poetics which, in the words of Katherine McKittrick (2013), "depict city death not as a biological end and biological fact but as a pathway to honoring human life" (p. 14). Desdunes's narration of these disappeared women thus honors them. Her tale of dispossession and its emotional costs denormalizes "the fungibility of the captive body" (Hartman 1997, p. x), and the blues places this invisible economy on the aural stage for all to hear, and for those who bear witness to say: "enough."

A final and speculative reading of "Mamie's Blues" is heard when we think through the song within her Catholic upbringing. Mamie's training as a pianist was a convention amongst the middle class, French-speaking Afro-Catholic women, and suggests a certain degree of immersion in the culture. According to Jelly Roll Morton, Mamie Desdunes was close friends with French-speaking Eulalie Echo (also known as Laura Hunter), a Vodou practitioner who was also Morton's godmother (Daniels 2003). Vodou, Catholicism, and other spiritual systems powerfully intersected in both Haiti and Louisiana, where a substantial number of Afro-French Creoles traced descent, including Desdunes and Echo (Dagget 2016; Johnson 2016). It is thus quite improbable that Mamie somehow existed outside of Catholic mores, and therefore striking that Genesis 2:17 through 2:19 are passages that correlate with the creation of women as instruments of male pleasure.

> But of the tree of the knowledge of good and evil, thou shalt not eat of it: for in the day that thou eatest thereof thou shalt surely die. The LORD God also said, "It is not good for the man to be alone. I will make for him a suitable helper." And out of the ground the LORD God formed every beast of the field, and every fowl of the air; and brought them unto Adam to see what he would call them: and whatsoever Adam called every living crea-ture, that was the name thereof.
>
> *(Genesis 2:17-2:19)*

"2:19 took my baby away" may refer to both this verse of scripture and a historic train line that trafficked prostitutes, laying siege to the patri-centric rendering of human creation and pro-posing an alternative narrative rooted in the reality of women's exploitation as well as pathways to pleasure outside of Christian decorum. While there is no recorded testimony from contem-porary listeners of the piece to support this interpretation, blues and Christianity intersected liberally in early twentieth-century New Orleans, perhaps most directly within in the widely cited evidence that trumpet player Buddy Bolden attended Baptist services in the same halls that he performed in on Saturday night, partially as an attempt to translate Black liturgical aes-thetics into popular music (Marquis 2005). Such a reading is even more plausible when one considers the litany of early-twentieth century blues repertoire which employed biblical motifs and appropriated religious channels of expression (Levine 1977). Angela Davis considers the blues to have been condemned by Black church leaders in the first decades of the twentieth century specifically because it "drew upon and incorporated sacred consciousness and thereby posed a serious threat to religious attitudes" (Davis 1998, p. 8). Whether or not "Mamie's Blues" directly referenced (or critiqued) scripture, it certainly channeled a sacred sense of sexuality and mourned the loss of those disappeared by demonic forces.

"Mamie's Blues" had a dual imperative: to reclaim sexuality and desire from plantation social relations while theorizing the political meanings of Black woman's conscription into a new sexual economy. This is broadly in tune with the observations put forward by scholars of Black women's history, who have suggested that the erotic and sexuality were markers of post-emancipation cultural transformation. "[What] is most striking is the way the blues registered sexuality as a tangible expression of freedom.... Sexuality thus was one of the most tangible domains in which emancipation was acted upon and through which its meanings were expressed" writes Angela Davis (1998, p. 8, 23–24). Similarly, Saidiya Hartman argues that for Black women Philadelphians who migrated from the South, "an everyday act of fucking" should be thought of as "the center of this revolution in a minor key" as both blues lyric and its hybrid tonality became poignant repositories of this new structure of feeling based on sexual emancipation (Hartman 2019, p. 117–118).

New Orleans's jazz musicians were certainly aware of these contestations between sex, autonomy, and the power of capital and the state. Danny Barker was one of many who commented on the power relations of the sex industry. Describing an incident in the year 1919, he wrote that

> The police in New Orleans were making it tough for the madames and their girls to make a dollar (that is, a peaceful one), so they spread the news and called a meeting of all the big shots in the District, the pimps, madames, whores, gamblers, hustlers, bartenders and all the owners of joints.

Musicians also attended. Held at Peter Lala's, "the District's number one cabaret," on a Sunday evening, the event included speeches and performances by Joe Oliver's band. Barker suggests that organizers of this event strategically used specific songs and styles produced by Joe Oliver to arouse the sentiments of their audience:

> [Madame] Ready Money told Joe Oliver to play the blues real sad, which he did. Then, when the crowd returned to their seats, she had the drummer Ratty Jean Vigne, roll his snares and she pleaded sadly with tears in her big blue eyes for attention. You could hear a pin drop as she informed the gathering of the many humiliating abuses she had constantly received from the brutal police of New Orleans which they all knew so well. She then told them of her plan to organize them. She proposed that each person present come up to the table where she stood, sign their name and pledge twenty dollars as an active member, which most of them did. She had Joe Oliver play the spiritual Down by the Riverside so the crowd could march up to her and rally to the cause.... She blew kisses to the crowd and yelled, "We'll show them goddamned police!" Everybody screamed, yelled and clapped their hands and they balled till the next morning to the music of Joe Oliver.
>
> *(Barker 1998, p. 67-68)*

Much like "Mamie's Blues," Oliver's simultaneously aestheticized a profound pain and celebrated a liberated future. The coordination between Oliver and Madame Ready Money is presented by Barker as a piece of theater, suggesting more than a passing familiarity among sex workers with blues and jazz songs, sounds, and their emotional impacts. This event was so successful that the following week, another iteration was put together, this time under the helm of a benevolent society organized by and for sex workers. An advertisement saved by Barker reveals its level of detail:

"Black Sis," "Rotten Rosie," and "Lily the Crip," were sex workers ("sporting girls") with leadership positions in this organization. In their very presence on this pamphlet, they announce their intentions as political subjects and resist intimidation and stigmatization. They demand recognition as workers, women, and human beings. Women's blues reflected and contributed to this process, creating a movement that was not anti-male but rather anti-sexist, what bell hooks might have called a "feminism for everybody" (hooks 2000). Joe Oliver's presence at both events is significant because

The First Grand Ball and Soirée to be given at the Economy Hall May 2, 1919, by the
HELPING HAND BENEVOLENT AID AND PROTECTIVE ASSOCIATION

Organized on April 7, 1919, for the aid and protection of sick, needy, helpless, disabled, aged and persecuted Sporting girls and Madames who are confined to hospitals, pest houses, houses of correction, criminal institutions, jails and penitentiaries.

Officers

Black Sis: President
Rotten Rosie: Vice President
Mollie Hatcher: Secretary
Mary Meathouse: Recording Secretary
Warmbody Stell: Financial Secretary
Barrel of Fun: Sgt. at Arms

Ready Money: Treasurer
Ida Jackson: Ex Officio
Lily the Crip: Delegate
One-Arm Edna: Sick C'ttee
Bird Leg Nora: Trustee
Bob Rowe: Director

Reverend Sunshine Money: Pastor

MUSIC FURNISHED BY JOE OLIVER'S BAND
Admission 50c. Pay at the Door

Figure 2.1 Advertisement for the Helping Hand Benevolent Aid and Protective Association Ball. Source: Public Domain, also printed in Barker (1998).

it suggests that musicians worked alongside sex workers in ways that were not merely exploitative or ancillary. This was the environment that "Mamie's Blues" contributed to and was shaped by. Just as Desdunes evinced a concern for the unnamed women shuttled away to Beaumont, Texas, to work far from home in conditions they could not control, so too did the "Helping Hand Benevolent Association" and its Vice President, "Rotten Rosie" express a commitment to furnish "aid and protection" for the "sick, needy, helpless, persecuted, disabled, aged and persecuted sporting girls and Madames," who could be "confined" to hospitals as well as penitentiaries. The focus on disability and the implicit critique of hospitals, prisons, and mental institutions (where Buddy Bolden was then languishing) as sites of disciplinary power anticipates Foucault's observation that "as medicine, psychology, education, public assistance, 'social work' assume an ever greater share of the powers of supervision and assessment, the penal apparatus will be able, in turn, to become medicalized, psychologized, educationalized" (Foucault 1977, p. 306). These activists' language also is a "pre-echo" of twenty-first century movements that fight for the rights of sex workers and people with disabilities.

While Danny Barker's legitimacy as a truth-teller has been called into question by several historians, (Wald 2020) his recounting of these Joe Oliver concerts on behalf of sex workers—imagined or not—serve as windows into the nature of the ideological and political battles that roiled New Orleans's sex industry and its workers' relationships with the state, police forces, and white civil society during the first decades of the twentieth century. Historians of Storyville have documented how Black sex workers fought against police brutality and racist zoning laws in both organized movements and spontaneous acts of defiance (Landau 2013, Adams 2012, Long 2005) and Barker's stories certainly illuminate the issues and the players in the contest over spaces, dignity, and self-determination and complicate the stereotypical image of New Orleans jazz musicians as single-minded pleasure-seekers.

Mamie Desdunes's work portends to the power of women's radical cultural tradition to sustain a Black counterpublic sphere within a highly regimented capitalist economy whose prime commodity, marketed to white consumers, was interracial sex (Landau 2013). In 1900, Black women made up 38 percent of this workforce, and were often the lowest paid, sometimes making as little as fifteen cents a transaction (Foster 1990). Major financial interests bankrolled Storyville and displaced low-income families in New Orleans, while white supremacist politicians organized violent militias to wreak havoc on the Black rural agrarian organizing in Louisiana's sugar parishes (Landau 2013; Gould 1984; Scott 2005). The supply of Black labor in New Orleans' sex industry was thus directly correlated to the formation of post-Civil War racial capitalism. Trombonist Kid Ory marveled at how the shift system of prostitutes functioned as "clockwork" (Ory in Landau 2013, p. 369) and one madam described the almost industrial regularity and emotional toll of the work: "It was a life regular as sunrise: regular joy, misery, hope, lack of hope, and ideas of suicide. A shrug-off of the present, a numb idea of the future, too. We all lied to each other about the future, and to ourselves as well" (Kimball 1970, 86).

Out of such limited social possibilities, New Orleans sex workers produced a vibrant counterpublic that honored and acknowledged Black women's pain as the basis for building an intersectional, interethnic movement for social justice and counter-plantation values (Casimir 2020). Mamie Desdunes was an innovative composer who helped construct this common sense by creating one of the most popular, and perhaps the first, twelve-bar blues. It is essential to understand the blues as a counterculture, one that contested these social forces that laid claim to Black bodies as commodities. And the fascinating paradox is that such songs were sung during the point of transaction, as piano players often played alongside prostitutes or took regular gigs in brothels. Desdunes lived in both worlds and thus was able to critique as one who had experienced its alienation.

Informing Mamie Desdunes's artistry and political voice is her identity as a Haitian-descended woman. In the following section, I explore Desdunes's connection to the Black Atlantic and the Haitian diaspora more specifically, which over the nineteenth century reproduced a rich and important tradition of speaking truth to gendered power.

The Latin Tinge and the Haitian Diaspora

In her 1923 composition "Haitian Blues," New Orleans vocalist Lizzie Miles relays her abuse at the hands of an unfaithful husband:

> Daddy's been cheating
> he's been mistreating
> gave me a beating for some abuse
> Now I've learned my lesson
> and I'm confessin'
> I wish that I had never been born
> I'm leaving town
> 'cause I've got the Haitian Blues
> Boo hoo hoo hoo[1]

Miles seems to imply that there was something particularly "Haitian" about being the victim of infidelity and abuse, and localized this particularity in New Orleans. While there is no evidence the two worked together, Mamie Desdunes and Lizzie Miles were both Creoles of Color who claimed Haitian ancestry, as was Jelly Roll Morton (who claimed that Lizzie Miles was his "favorite vocalist") (Tucker 2004, p. 324). In fact, "Mamie's Blues" reinterpreted Haitian musical devices in its base line and core rhythms, notably those now called *habanera* and *tresillo* rhythms. I hear these Atlantic bass lines as gestures rich with abolitionist signification. While Desdunes's lyrics commented on women's sexualities within and against the sex industry at large, she simultaneously overlayed a rhythmic cadence that was specifically and semiotically evocative of Creole of Color identification with the Haitian diaspora in New Orleans.[2]

When we zoom out in time and place, we can observe that these works by Mamie Desdunes and Lizzie Miles were not aberrations, for across the nineteenth century Caribbean, Haitian diasporic traditions created a way of talking about, and talking back, to gendered and sexual power structures. In this section, I argue for a particularly Haitian hermeneutics which critiqued slavery and coerced sex during the 19th century, and how this historic tradition provides both an Afro-Caribbean and a gendered genealogy for the development of jazz-blues. This is what I believe is hidden within Jelly Roll Morton's statement that "Mamie could really play those blues": how it differed from ragtime in that it overlayed African American and Afro-Caribbean traditions, which both in turn affected the development of jazz.

Mamie Desdunes was born out of wedlock to an African American mother, Clementine Walker, and a prominent Haitian descended activist father, Rodolphe Desdunes, and the latter grounded himself in New Orleans' Creole of Color community. To suggest that Mamie's identity was "Creole of Color" would be reductive, as she was likely alienated from her father while she worked in an industry that contemporaries of her father publicly detested (Cheung 1997), and the fact that she sang exclusively in English also differentiated her from Creole of Color singers (Vézina 2015), but her training as a pianist suggests that she was raised and educated within Creole of Color familial and gendered conventions (Tucker 2004). These mixed-race, French-speaking African-descended peoples were largely free during antebellum Louisiana history and a group with a strong sense of historical identity and social cohesion. They have been the subject of an enormous amount of commentary, and recent historiography is fairly split on their class and social role, with some commentators pointing to their complicity with slavery and their racist statements against non-mixed race African Americans (Wegmann 2105; Ake 2002), while others highlight their revolutionary republicanism, their service to the Union Army, their pivotal role during Reconstruction, and their ongoing connections to Haiti (Bell 1997; Scott 2007; Woods 2017). We do not have sufficient space in this chapter to address this tension. For our purposes, I believe identification with the Haitian republic and its anti-racist, anti-slavery project was a marker of an egalitarian political sensibility within the Creole of Color community, albeit one that not all Creoles of Color shared (Brickhouse 2007).

There is extensive evidence of Haitian-derived rhythms in "Mamie's Blues," such as the *habanera* and *tresillo*." Several scholars have noted that *tresillo*, *habanera*, and *cinquillo* rhythms are all based on a similar set of rhythms which are rooted in different interpretations of a "4 against 3" hemiola. They are characteristic of several genres of Afro-Cuban and French Afro-Caribbean music (Floyd 1999). They are quite prominent in Jelly Roll Morton's performances of the piece and became a major part of his piano style for the rest of his career.

My contention is that these rhythmic conventions became organically linked to a brand of Black Atlantic politics and antipatriarchal storytelling with roots in the Haitian Revolution. Refugees from Saint-Domingue, as colonial Haiti was named, more than doubled the population of New Orleans from 1791 to 1811 and tripled its free community of color (Dessens 2008; Fiehrer 1991; LaChance 1988). The musicologist Christopher Washburne has pointed out, "The musical influence of the Saint-Domingue refugees was vast," noting that in addition both cultural practices, institutions, and creolized rhythmic traditions such as the *tresillo* arrived with the Haitian immigrants (Washburne 2020, p. 54). Sara Johnson argues that these "musics were built upon the migratory labor of black artists and their publics" and that it is therefore "not surprising that the cinquillo resurfaced in communities where Saint-Domingue migrants resettled. Cuba provides a case in point" (Johnson 2012, p. 144). Accompanying these musical forms were

Figure 2.2 Measures 8–15 of "Mamie's Blues," as played by Jelly Roll Morton. The left hand of the piano alternates between a Habanera and a Tresillo rhythm. The arrows outline where a three quaver lengths, or eighth notes, accents are placed above the Habanera/Tresillo bass line.

Source: Transcription done by author from Morton 1938.

not only specific rhythms but also "barbed observations about racial and sexual hierarchies" in different slave societies. These "observations" travelled with the enslaved migrants and their music, to Jamaica, Puerto Rico, Cuba, and Louisiana.

The adjectives "Spanish" and "French" have contributed to erasing Haiti/Saint-Domingue's contribution to New Orleans musical culture. For instance, Baby Dodds recalled that

> In the downtown district where the Creoles lived, they played blues with a Spanish accent.... They lived in the French part of town and we lived uptown, in the Garden district. Our ideas for the blues were different from theirs. They had the French and Spanish style, blended together.
>
> *(Russell 1999, p. 23)*

Jelly Roll Morton himself perhaps mostly widely popularized the concept and the phrase called the "Spanish tinge." In an interview with Alan Lomax, he explained, "Of course you got to have these little tinges of Spanish in it … in order to play real good jazz.... I'll give you an idea what this, the idea of Spanish there is in the blues" (Morton 1938). One of his collaborators, Walter "Foots" Thomas, recalled Morton's orientation as well: "I always felt his melodies came from New Orleans but that his rhythms came from the Latin countries" (Garrett 2008). Contemporary musicologist Charles Garrett (2008, p. 60) hears in Morton's performances of these influences a "sonic metaphor for cultural difference and conflict."

Black commentators who published in this era, however, heard in the *habanera* rhythm a cultural lineage that connected the music of Louisiana specifically to Haiti. Maud Cuney Hare, an accomplished Black pianist and daughter of the famed Texan Reconstruction activist Norris Wright Cuney, published a 1921 compilation titled *Six Creole Folk Songs*, which are full of *habanera* bass lines much like those present in "Mamie's Blues" (Hales 2002). She writes in the book's introduction that these songs were

> Mainly African in rhythm, [and] the music was brought to South American countries and to the West Indies, thence to Louisiana.... Distinct from the mountain song of Kentucky, the Negro Spiritual or the tribal melody of the Indian, the Creoles have added a new note in their gift to the folk-song of America.
>
> *(Hare 1921, p. 3)*

Hare highlights the "West Indies," namely Haiti, as an important waystation for the Afro-Atlantic genealogy. As she works through the sardonic and sarcastic nature of the pieces, Hare explains that "songs of mockery, pointed at times with cruel satire, were common among the Creole songs of Louisiana and the Antilles [Haiti]" (p. 18). Hare also notes that these songs treated themes of gender and sexuality. She writes that the song "Caroline" "sheds light into the tragedy as well as the romance of the young Creole slaves. Marriage, that state of blissful respectability [was] denied to the multitude either by law or social conditions" (p. 18). Hare makes the case that the violence of Southern slave laws was necessary to understand the gender politics of this piece.

Compiled and published in the first two decades of the twentieth century, Hare's anthology reflects how African American musicians of the era understood the *habanera* rhythm and the social-commentary it informed: (a) as a Haitian ("West Indies") derivation, and (b) included in songs of a satirical nature in which gender and plantation sexual relations were held up for critique, contemplation, and ridicule.

Hare was not wrong. Saint-Domingue Black women produced a well-documented body of oral work by nineteenth-century standards. The deeply systemic practice of interracial sex was disavowed in the colonial public sphere, but its nuances were nonetheless communicated in song and poetry that illuminated the contours of this world for both white and Black publics (Burnard and Garrigus 2016). Creole song and poetry produced a space in which enslaved and free women of color could comment on matters that addressed the intersections of race, desire, and power, often critiquing the violent, contradictory sexual relations of the colony or celebrating their own sexual powers. For instance, one late eighteenth century poem depicted an enslaved woman, "Lisette," chastising her lover for escaping to town to have sex with a mistress. She claimed of her foe:

> Her butt is no more than a packet of bones. (*Bonda li c'est paquet zos*)
> She has not a tooth in her mouth, (*Li pas teni dents dans bouche*)
> Her tits are like the sugar cane trash we feed the pigs. (*Tété li c'est blan cochon*)

In contrast, Lisette claims a litany of positive attributes: she claims that she sings like a bird ("Mon chanté tant com zozo"), that her breasts are upright ("Teté moins bougé debout"), and that she is sexually active ("mon gagné canal / D'yo pas lé manqué li," which literally translates to "I have a canal / And no shortage of water for it") (Saint-Méry, quoted in Jenson 2011, 297). Deborah Jenson calls this the "Earliest [recorded] example of female-narrated dissing in the New World African diaspora" (Jenson 2011, 297).

Such dissing and erotic agency travelled with Saint-Domingue refugees and enslaved migrants who fled the Haitian Revolution and Napoleon's reign of terror. For instance, a similar song appeared in Jamaica, another destination for Haitian emigration and where a performance style known as "French Set girls" emerged, marked by women in using handkerchiefs and a heel drumming technique closely tied to Haiti (Abrahams and Szwed 1983, p. 238; Johnson 2012). As in Louisiana, "French" in this instance came to stand in for Haitian where Black peoples were concerned. In Santiago de Cuba, Emilio Bacardí, a Cuban historian whose maternal relatives were planter emigres from Saint-Domingue, recorded a song he overheard during an Afro-Cuban performance:

> Those white men from France, oh shout it! (Blan lá yó qui sotíi en Frans, oh, jelé!)
> They use their (white) wives as a pillow (Yó prán madam yó servi sorellé)
> For caressing black women (Pú yó caresé negués).
>
> *(Fernandez 2000, p. 85)*

This song was derived from a *Tumba Francesa*, meaning "French dance." Like "Spanish tinge," "French" in this case was a misnomer since the *Tumba Francesa* was a set of dances and a song form reproduced by enslaved Haitian communities in Santiago de Cuba, which had the largest concentration of Saint-Domingue refugees outside of Louisiana. Its revolutionary content was derived from its ability to directly insult both the desirability of masters' wives and their fetishizing of their Black female "property" (Johnson 2012, p. 136). In *Tumba Francesa*, the *cinquillo* was heavily present, and musicologist Ned Sublette has suggested that one of its component dances named "frenté" is based on one of Saint-Domingue origin which also appears in Puerto Rican *bomba plena* (Sublette 2004, p. 138; and Cadogan, 2008).

New Orleans was another recipient of *cinquillo* rhythm and its travelling companion, biting sexual commentary, narrated from the point of view of violated women and men of color. Haitian-derived dance forms and song lyrics were observed not only in Congo Square but also on the levees surrounding the city (Dunham 1983, p. 72; Joyaux 1904; Dewulf 2018; Kubik 2017; Mitchell 2018). Camille Thierry, a free man of color, published in 1874 the Creole song "Lament of an Aged Mulatta" from New Orleans. It rings of the style of the Creole poetry heard in Saint-Domingue:

> Listen! When I was in Saint-Domingue,
> Negresses were just like jewels;
> The whites there were ninnies,
> They were always after us.
> In a household,
> Never any fighting,
> The love of a white meant adoration!
> They weren't stingy,
> They were very rich,
> A good *bounda* [ass] was worth a plantation!
> Times have changed, we are sleeping on straw,
> We, whom the planters celebrated…
> Before long a lower-class white
> Will be calling us riff raff!
> *(Thierry 1874, 298–299).*

The reappearance of the political power of *bounda* is, in this case, a marker of descent. Its relative power to the old days—when it was worth a plantation—had disappeared. Other French Louisiana songs of that describe rape and unwanted sexual contact on the part of white men against Black and Creole of Color women have been documented by Tony Russell (1970) and Maud Cuney-Hare (1921).

"Mamie's Blues" should be read as a late-nineteenth century echo of a Haitian and circum-Caribbean women's critique, whereby sexual violence, the Black body, and the erotic were brought out in a Black counterpublic enunciated with musical culture. Storyville's somewhat audacious performance of dissent and critique through blues, performed both for a concert-going public and during the moments of transactional sex, thus has a lot in common with these Afro-Caribbean public arts. An eighteenth and nineteenth Atlantic sexual economy had a built-in critique within its corresponding performance traditions, a practice of symbolic negation in spaces where Black women artists had a circumscribed but still tangible role to signal dissent, ridicule, and reject the terms of engagement. This oral technology of resistance had circulated through the Black Atlantic for the better part of a century, a product of revolution, enslavement, and modernity, and it continued to play an important role in the age of Storyville. The *habanera* rhythm could communicate this history from below in the hands of an expert artist and truth-teller.

Conclusion

In culturally composite countries and, for example, in the case of the Creole cultures of the Americas, advances are accomplished by means of traces.

Edouard Glissant (2006), *Une nouvelle region du monde.*

Storyville was "shut down" by government ordinance in 1917, but the contested nature of the erotic and the sex industry did not suddenly cease to be an important topic for blues women singers. Yet the stirrings of early jazz and their interaction with this sex economy became less pronounced as their classic blues counterparts. Admittedly, the lines were not so firmly drawn, and the recording industry was only beginning to set boundaries between genres which would mark clean divisions between the two. But, in a strange twist, jazz's acceptance as an art form amongst mainstream American society also reproduced bourgeoise and patriarchal ideologies that separated the (male) artist from social and cultural concerns in producing "his" art. When exceptional women instrumentalists "made" it, they were often marketed in ways damaging to their careers and their contributions became posthumously distorted or marginalized (Chilton 2010, p. 201).

Mamie Desdunes not only challenges a male-centric reading of early jazz but also deals directly with the question of Black women's bodies, their desire as well as their containment, as foundational to the music. The embrace of her song by Jelly Roll Morton, Bunk Johnson, and countless others suggests that this variant of social commentary was widely disseminated. It points to how the new music was a space in which Black women (and men) "could discuss, plan, and organize this new world ... the cries of a new society being born" (Woods 1998, 39) As I have shown, these cries were built on a foundation of centuries of Black Atlantic resistance through art, in which the weapons of the weak became the soundtrack of the future.

Mamie Desdunes offers us a lesson in jazz that does not center stars, careers, or egos, but rather social movements and intangible lessons from the narrow cracks offered by glimpses in census archives, death certificates, and a polyrhythmic bass line. Her song demonstrates women's agency and cultural influence within a social context that many modern-day commentators have written off as factories of patriarchal pleasure. It suggests that Black womanist and feminist stirrings were important forces that stirred the creation of new art forms, foundational to the blues form itself. By working through the painful and contradictory negotiation with the erotic through centuries of slavery and capitalist commodification, artists like Desdunes catalyzed new art forms.

In the contemporary moment, it is overdue that jazz educators and historians focus on the relationship of sexuality, women, gendered and racial exploitation, and resistance as central to the art form. In a field still skewed by patriarchal ideologies, women continue to be erased and their struggles and cultural work are considered as separate from the work of iconic artists. But repeatedly, figures like Mamie Desdunes, Mary Lou Williams, Melba Liston, and dozens of others prove this is ideological in nature rather than historical. In that light, we should also take more seriously how male musicians dealt with sexuality in their jazz practice, such as Charles Mingus's self-conscious engagement with the "oversexed" Black male (Rustin-Paschal 2017). Black artists critiqued have followed in Desdunes's footsteps and critiqued their sexualization and fetishization, not only in Storyville, but also against the spectacles of minstrelsy and American popular culture writ large.

Finally, "Mamie's Blues" demonstrates that collaborations between Afro-Caribbean and African American culture were happening in jazz much earlier than what is often assumed. This is why I agree with Cortázar that "Mamie' Blues" is "a cloud without frontiers, a spy of air and water, an archetypal form, something from before, from below." We would do well to continue to study it and hear what it can tell us about gender, women's agency, and the history of Black Atlantic resistance over the past four centuries.

Notes

1 I would like to thank Michael Heller for his help with lyric transcription.
2 For a discussion of piano training as an important part of Creole of Color femininity in New Orleans, see Sherrie Tucker, "A Feminist Perspective on New Orleans Jazzwomen" (New Orleans: New Orleans Jazz National Historical Park, 2004), 41.

Discography

Miles, Lizzie (1923). *Haitian Blues / Your Time Now*. The New Emerson.

Morton, J. R. (1938). *Buddy Bertrand's Blues / Mamie's Blues*. The Complete Congress Recordings. (www.youtube.com/watch?v=I_r5DoSK05E).

Morton, J. R. (1939). *Mamie's Blues*. Commodore Records. (www.youtube.com/watch?v=-rbCAAr-NXc).

Bunk Johnson and The Yerba Buena Jazz Band. (1944). *2:19 Blues*. Ace in the Hole. (www.youtube.com/watch?v=3719cuHZl7g).

References

Abrahams, Roger D., and John F. Szwed, Eds. (1983). *After Africa: Extracts from British Travel Accounts and Journals of the Seventeenth, Eighteenth, and Nineteenth Centuries Concerning the Slaves, Their Manners, and Customs in the British West Indies*. Yale University Press.

Adams, J. (2012). *Wounds of Returning: Race, Memory, and Property on the Postslavery Plantation*. The University of North Carolina Press.

Ake, D. (2002). *Jazz Cultures*. University of California Press.

Balderach, A. S. (2005). *A Different Kind of Reservation: Waco's Red-Light District Revisited, 1880–1920* (M.A. Thesis). Baylor University.

Barker, D. (1998). *Buddy Bolden and the Last Days of Storyville* (A. Shipton, Ed.). Continuum.

Bell, C. C. (1997). *Revolution, Romanticism, and the Afro-Creole Protest Tradition in Louisiana, 1718–1868*. Louisiana State University Press.

Bell, C. C. (2011). "Rappelez-vous concitoyens": The Poetry of Pierre-Aristide Desdunes, Civil War Soldier, Romantic Literary Artist, and Civil Rights Activist. In P.-A. Desdunes, *Rappelez-vous concitoyens: La poésie de Pierre Aristide Desdunes* (pp. 1–19). Les Éditions Tintamarre, Centenary College of Louisiana.

Brickhouse, Anna. (2007). "'L'Ouragan de Flammes' ('The Hurricane of Flames'): New Orleans and Transamerican Catastrophe, 1866/2005." *American Quarterly* 59 (4): 1097–1127.

Burnard, Trevor, and John Garrigus. (2016). *The Plantation Machine: Atlantic Capitalism in French Saint-Domingue and British Jamaica*. University of Pennsylvania Press.

Carby, H. (1998). It Jus Be's Dat Way Sometime: The Sexual Politics of Women's Blues. In R. O'Meally (Ed.), *The Jazz Cadence of American Culture* (pp. 470–483). Columbia University Press.

Casimir, Jean. (2020). "On the Origins of the Counterplantation System." *The Haiti Reader: History, Culture, Politics*, edited by Laurent Dubois et al., Duke University Press.

Cheung, Floyd D. (1997) "Les Cenelles and Quadroon Balls: 'Hidden Transcripts' of Resistance and Domination in New Orleans, 1803–1845." *The Southern Literary Journal* 29 (2): 5–16.

Chilton, Karen. (2010). *Hazel Scott: The Pioneering Journey of a Jazz Pianist, from Café Society to Hollywood to HUAC*. University of Michigan Press.

Cortazar, J. (1987). *Hopscotch* (G. Rabassa, Trans.; 1st Pantheon pbk. edition). Pantheon.

Daniels, Douglas Henry. (2003). Vodun and Jazz: "Jelly Roll" Morton and Lester 'Pres' Young—Substance and Shadow. *Journal of Haitian Studies*, 9 (1): 110–123.

Davis, A. (1983). *Women, Race and Class*. Vintage.

Davis, A. Y. (1998). *Blues Legacies and Black Feminism: Gertrude "Ma" Rainey, Bessie Smith, and Billie Holiday*. Pantheon Books.

Desdunes, R. L. (2001). *Our People and our History: Fifty Creole Portraits*. Louisiana State University Press. (Originally published in 1911).

Dessens, Nathalie. (2008.) "St Domingue Refugees in New Orleans: Identity and Cultural Influences." In *Echoes of the Haitian Revolution, 1804-2004*, edited by Martin Munro and Elizabeth Walcott-Hackshaw, 87–115. University of West Indies Press.

Dewulf, Jeroen. (2018). "From the Calendas to the Calenda: On the Afro-Iberian Substratum in Black Performance Culture in the Americas." *The Journal of American Folklore* 131 (519): 3–29.

Dunham, Katharine. (1983). *Dances of Haiti*. UCLA Center for Afro-American Studies.

Edwards, B. (2016). *Mary Celina Mamie Desdunes Dugue*. RagPiano.Com. http://ragpiano.com/comps/desdunes.shtml.

Fernandez, Pablo Armando. (2000). *Otro Golpe De Dados*. Carieva Editorial.

Fiehrer, Thomas. (1991). "From Quadrille to Stomp: The Creole Origins of Jazz." *Popular Music* 10 (1): 21–38.

Floyd, Samuel A. (1999). "Black Music in the Circum-Caribbean." *American Music* 17 (1): 1–38.

Foster, C. L. (1990). Tarnished Angels: Prostitution in Storyville, New Orleans, 1900-1910. *Louisiana History: The Journal of the Louisiana Historical Association*, *31*(4), 387–397.

Foucault, M. (1977). *Discipline and Punish: The Birth of the Prison*. Knopf Doubleday Publishing Group.

Garon, P., and Garon, B. (2014). *Woman with Guitar: Memphis Minnie's Blues*. City Lights Books.

Garrett, Charles Hiroshi. (2008). *Struggling to Define a Nation: American Music and the Twentieth Century*. University of California Press.

Glissant, É. (2006). *Une nouvelle région du monde*. Gallimard.

Gould, J. (1984). The Strike of 1887: Louisiana Sugar War. *Southern Exposure, 12*, 45–55.

Griffin, F. J. (1996). Textual Healing: Claiming Black Women's Bodies, the Erotic and Resistance in Contemporary Novels of Slavery. *Callaloo, 19*(2), 519–536.

Hahn, S. (2003). *A Nation Under Our Feet: Black Political Struggles in the Rural South, from Slavery to the Great Migration*. Harvard University Press.

Hanley, P. (2002). *Mamie Desdunes*. Doctor Jazz. www.doctorjazz.co.uk/portnewor.html.

Hales, Douglas. (2002.) *A Southern Family in White and Black: The Cuneys of Texas*. Texas A&M University Press.

Hare, M. C. (1921). *Six Creole Folk-Songs with Original Creole and Translated English Text—Sheet Music for Voice and Piano*. C. Fischer.

Hartman, Saidiya. (2019.) *Wayward Lives, Beautiful Experiments: Intimate Histories of Social Upheaval*. W. W. Norton & Company.

Hartman, Saidiya V. (1997.) *Scenes of Subjection: Terror, Slavery, and Self-Making in Nineteenth-Century America*. Oxford University Press.

Hobson, V. (2011). New Orleans Jazz and the Blues. *Jazz Perspectives, 5*(1), 3–27.

hooks, bell. (2000). *Feminism Is for Everybody: Passionate Politics*. London: Pluto Press.

Humphrey, D. (1995). Prostitution in Texas: From the 1830s to the 1960s. *East Texas Historical Journal, 33*(1): 27–43.

Jenson, Deborah. (2011). *Beyond the Slave Narrative: Politics, Sex, and Manuscripts in the Haitian Revolution*. Liverpool University Press.

Johnson, Rashauna. (2016). *Slavery's Metropolis: Unfree Labor in New Orleans during the Age of Revolutions*. Cambridge University Press.

Joyaux, George J., ed. 1904. "Forest's Voyage Aux Étas-Unis de l'Amérique En 1831." *Louisiana Historical Quarterly XXXIX*: 465.

Kubik, Gerhard. (2017). *Jazz Transatlantic: Jazz Derivatives and Developments in Twentieth-Century Africa*. University Press of Mississippi.

Kimball, N. (1970). *Nell Kimball: Her Life as an American Madame*. MacMillan.

Lachance, Paul F. (1988.) "The 1809 Immigration of Saint-Domingue Refugees to New Orleans: Reception, Integration and Impact." *Louisiana History: The Journal of the Louisiana Historical Association* 29 (2): 109–41.

Landau, E. E. (2013). *Spectacular Wickedness: Sex, Race, and Memory in Storyville, New Orleans*. LSU Press.

Levine, L. W. (1977). *Black Culture and Black Consciousness: Afro-American American Folk Thought from Slavery to Freedom*. Oxford University Press.

Lomax, A. (1950). *Mister Jelly Roll: The Fortunes of Jelly Roll Morton, New Orleans Creole and "Inventor of Jazz."* Duell, Sloan and Pearce.

Long, Alecia P. (2005). *The Great Southern Babylon: Sex, Race and Respectability in New Orleans, 1865–1920*. Louisiana State University Press.

McKittrick, K. (2013). Plantation Futures. *Small Axe, 17*(3), 1–15.

Mitchell, Reagan Patrick. (2018). "Gottschalk's Engagement with the Ungovernable: Louis Moreau Gottschalk and the Bamboula Rhythm." *Educational Studies: Echoes, Reverberations, Silences, and Noise: Sonic Possibilities in Education* 54 (4): 415–428.

Moten, F. (2003). *In The Break: The Aesthetics of the Black Radical Tradition*. University of Minnesota Press.

New Orleans Picayune. (1893). July 21.

Otto, J. J. (2011). Dan Desdunes: New Orleans Civil Rights Activist and "The Father of Negro Musicians of Omaha." *Nebraska History, 92*, 106–117.

Pelligrinelli, L. (2008). Separated at "Birth": Singing and the History of Jazz. In N. T. Rustin and S. Tucker (Eds.), *Big Ears: Listening for Gender in Jazz Studies* (pp. 31–47). Duke University Press.

Russell, T. (1970). *Blacks, Whites, and Blues*. Stein.

Russell, W. (1999). *"Oh, Mister Jelly": A Jelly Roll Morton Scrapbook*. JazzMedia ApS.

Rustin-Paschal, Nichole. 2017. *The Kind of Man I Am: Jazzmasculinity and the World of Charles Mingus Jr.* Wesleyan, CT: Wesleyan University Presss.

Scott, R. J. (2005). *Degrees of Freedom: Louisiana and Cuba after Slavery*. The Belknap Press of Harvard University Press.

Scott, R. J. (2007). The Atlantic World and the Road to Plessy v. Ferguson. *Journal of American History, 94*(3), 726–733.

Snook, Claire. (2018). "Mamie Desdunes." November 4, 2018. https://clairesnook.co.uk/2018/11/04/mamie-desdunes/.

Tucker, Sherrie. (2004). "A Feminist Perspective on New Orleans Jazzwomen." New Orleans: New Orleans Jazz National Historical Park.

Vernhettes, D., and Hanley, P. (2014). The Desdunes Family. *The Jazz Archivist, XXVII*, 25–45.

Vézina, C. (2015). Jazz à la Creole. *The Jazz Archivist, XXXVIII*, 38–45.

Wald, E. (2016, June 15). *Mamie's Blues (219 Blues)*. Old Friends: A Songobiography. www.elijahwald.com/songblog/mamies-blues/.

Washburne, Christopher. 2020. *Latin Jazz: The Other Jazz*. Oxford University Press.

Wegmann, A. N. (2015). The vitriolic blood of a Negro: The development of racial identity and Creole elitism in New Spain and Spanish Louisiana, 1763–1803. *Journal of Transatlantic Studies, 13*(2), 204–225.

Woods, Clyde Adrian. (2017). *Development Drowned and Reborn: The Blues and Bourbon Restorations in Post-Katrina New Orleans*. Athens: University of Georgia Press.

Wright, R. (1963). Foreword. In P. Oliver, *Blues Fell This Morning: The Meaning of the Blues* (pp. vii–xii). Jazz Book Club.

3

LIL HARDIN ARMSTRONG AND HELEN JOYNER

The Forgotten Patrons of Jazz

Jeremy Brown

Statement on Gender Identification: In this chapter, I will be referencing the various musicians, authors and other persons named as female/she/her/hers, male/he/him/his. I identify as he/him.

Author Note

Some material in this chapter appears in a Festschrift for Michael Budds (in press), the former editor of the College Music Society "Sourcebooks in American Music Series" and founder of the Budds Center for American Music Studies at the University of Missouri, Columbia, where he was a Professor of Music. This material is interpolated throughout the chapter in no specific order. Portions of this chapter were also presented in a lecture at the 2020 College Music Society National Conference in a paper entitled "Jazz Patronage: The Creation of Opportunity in Jazz Music."

Although it might be their lifeblood in a metaphorical sense, the argument can be made that though music is created by and for musicians, sharing music and connecting to audiences is just as crucial as the creation process in securing cultural value. For this reason, those who support individual artists or musical enterprises must be recognized for their essential role in its history. Patrons have historically occupied a critical position in forming cultural value; in jazz, this crucial function has been filled by lovers and spouses, family members, and colleagues.

The classic model of the patron, an individual of position and wealth eager to encourage composition and performance to enhance his or her social status and bring pleasure, can also be found in the jazz world, although not on as grand a scale. Writers, record producers, concert promoters, and critics can also be considered patrons who celebrate the accomplishments and sustain listeners' and readers' interest in jazz artists' careers. Of these, perhaps most interesting is the contribution of businessmen to the dynamic tradition of jazz patronage. Owners of clubs and the decision-makers for record labels must be acknowledged for their positive impact on the careers of jazz musicians since the days of Storyville. Although they undoubtedly acted out of self-interest, the opportunities they provided and the payments they made for professional services were not all that different from the relationship of Haydn to Lord Esterhazy, of Tchaikovsky to Nadezhda von Meck, or of Stravinsky to Diaghilev.

Of the various types of patrons, jazz artists' wives are overall the most underrecognized. Should they have shown talent as instrumentalists, their accomplishments were often diminished as well. Louis Armstrong, for example, married to Lil Hardin, was painfully harsh (through the lens of the twenty-first century) in his assessment of his former wife, saying: "Read music—yes. As an improviser—Hmmm—terrible"

DOI: 10.4324/9781003081876-4

(Teachout, 2009, p. 75). Yet Lil Hardin was known for a powerful and driving way of playing the piano, a unique style adopted by other prominent musicians. Writer Chadwick Hansen says of white blues pianist Art Hodes (1904–1993): "One can hear something of Lil Hardin in the way he drives with his left hand" (as cited in Martin, 2020, p. 12). Yet, women instrumentalists in jazz were consistently marginalized unless they were glamourous singers. There was, in jazz, an instrument stigma. The working conditions for jazz musicians in the early twentieth century were not considered an environment for women. As historian Gerald Horne summarizes, "there are terrible destructive forces—racism, organized criminality, brutal labour exploitation, battery, debauchery, gambling, from which grew an intensely beautiful art form, today denoted as "jazz" (Horne, 2019, p. 29).

As noted, wives as patrons often figure prominently in jazz artists' success (although they are typically passed over in biographical studies). At the same time, they worked in the background, in a kind of hidden economy. Critic Lauren Du Graf (2017), reviewing the film *I Called Him Morgan*, hits the bull's eye when she writes about Helen Morgan (1926–1996)[1]:

> By centering on Helen, the film has a feminist streak, a badly needed course corrective for a musical genre whose histories overwhelmingly stem from the perspective of men worshipping at the altar of other men. Like Nellie Monk, Lorraine Gillespie, Gladys Hampton, and Maxine Gordon, Helen Morgan labored in an invisible economy of jazz wives who worked behind the scenes to ensure their husbands' success and survival.
>
> *(par. 4)*

Men worshiping at the altar of other men in jazz music was so entrenched and so widely accepted that male (and perhaps female musicians) were not fully aware of how pervasive it was.

Two African American women, in particular, deserve closer study. Lil Hardin Armstrong (1898–1971), a pioneering female jazz pianist of many talents and the second wife of Louis Armstrong (1901–1971), arguably contributed more to American music than any other woman before or after her arrival on the scene (Dickerson, 2002, p. 217). More controversial was Helen Morgan, "who met Lee Morgan on a cold night in New York and killed him on a cold night in New York" (L.R. Thomas, personal communication, October 22, 2020). Nonetheless, she guided Morgan back from the brink of death due to addiction, allowing him and, perhaps more importantly, encouraging him to perform and record numerous additional albums.

Lil Hardin Armstrong

Growing up in Memphis, Lil became familiar with the local musical culture, despite the best efforts of her mother, Dempsey, to discourage her interest in blues and jazz music (Dickerson, 2002, p. 29). Mother and daughter moved to Chicago in 1917 in part because Memphis was

> fragmented by violence, corrupt politics, strained race relations, drug addiction, teen pregnancies, an anti-educational mindset and a stagnant economy. What Dempsey feared most was that Lil's strength—her passion for music—would lead her to Beale street and a life of prostitution.
>
> *(p. 22)*

Lil Hardin attended Fisk University and earned degrees from the Chicago College of Music and the New York College of Music (p. 155).[2] She became not only a champion of her soon-to-be husband, Louis, but an artist of significant accomplishment in her own right. Lil composed the music for some of the best of Armstrong's early recordings, including "King of the Zulus" and "Struttin with Some Barbecue," and co-composed works such as "Hotter than That," "Tears," and "New Orleans Stomp."

Despite her career as a pianist, composer, singer, bandleader, clothes designer, and arguably a co-founder of the American jazz tradition with Louis Armstrong, she remains among the most under-recognized women in music. In part, this is undoubtedly due to her being a jazz instrumentalist in the 1920s. Furthermore, her accomplishments would have been minimized and at the very least considered a novelty by the male instrumentalist-musicians who were accustomed to the culture of men-only on the stage.

The rough and tumble nature of the clubs was a difficult place for a woman performer. King Joe Oliver, who hired Lil to play in the Creole Jazz Band "kept a gun in his cornet case and threatened to use it on musicians whose conduct displeased him" (Teachout, 2009, p. 58). Even Lil gives credit to a man for her ability to as a musician. In 1956, when speaking of her style to play "just as hard as I could just like Jelly Roll did," she credited Jelly Roll Morton, who played for her in a Chicago music store where she worked as a sheet music demonstrator (L.H. Armstrong, 2007, p. 109). In the 1920s, there were few if any female role models for a young woman musician to emulate.

The historical void that characterizes Lil Hardin's legacy was further diffused by the words of her second husband, Louis Armstrong. In his 1954 autobiography, *Satchmo*, Armstrong recounts his first set with the King Oliver's Creole Jazz Band at the Royal Gardens in Chicago soon after arriving on the train from New Orleans in 1923. He describes with admiration and affection, in turn, each member of the band—Baby Dodds, Johnny Dodds, Bill Johnson, Honore Dutrey. When he comes to Lil Hardin, his description has a different tone:

> For a woman, Lil Hardin was wonderful, and she certainly surprised me that night with her four beats to a bar. It was startling to find a woman who had been valedictorian in her class at Fisk University fall in line and play such good jazz. She had gotten her training from Joe Oliver, Freddy Keppard, Sugar Johnny, Lawrence Dewey, Tany Johnson, and many other of the great pioneers from New Orleans. If she had not run into those top-notchers, she would have probably married some prominent politician or maybe played the classics for a living. Later I found out that Lil was doubling after hours at the Idleweise Gardens. I wondered how she was ever able to get any sleep. I knew these New Orleans cats could take it all right, but it was a tough pull for a woman.
>
> *(pp. 237–239)*

Although Louis recognizes that Lil is accomplished in her own right as a performer and a woman with a successful career, one could surmise that he might have been a bit jealous. He is outspoken in his admiration and praise of fellow male musicians but gives Lil little credit for her talent and ambition. Perhaps she had not shown enough allegiance to the young Armstrong (not as much as the other male members of the Creole Jazz Band); she remembers how she "thought he was a bumpkin. . . . I just didn't like him. I was very disgusted" (as cited in Dickerson, 2002, p. 83). Also recalling that her musician friends called him "Little Louis," she writes,

> 'Little Louis, why do they call him Little Louis as fat as he is?' [laughs] Oh boy, mmm, well, I was disappointed all around because I didn't like the way he was dressed, [laughs] I didn't like his hairdo. [laughs] He had bangs. That was the style in New Orleans, he told me later, to wear bangs. And they were sticking right straight out, and I said, 'Whoa, Little Louis.'
>
> *(L.H. Armstrong, 2007, p. 111)*

At the same time, Lil is self-effacing and matter-of-fact, claiming that "from a musical standpoint, jazz didn't mean anything too much to me. Maybe it was because I was as young as I was, and I was interested in the money" (p. 111). It would be understandable for a young African American woman in the 1920s to be concerned about self-preservation and accruing wealth more than creating a new art form.[3] Recruited into the New Orleans Creole Jazz Band by Joe Oliver, Lil nonetheless became a part of the nexus of American jazz in Chicago. The Creole Jazz Band had many admirers and fans, including white musicians who listened to the band play at the De Luxe Café, Dreamland, and the Royal Gardens Café, later renamed the Lincoln Gardens Café. These included Bix Beiderbecke, Hoagy Carmichael (who sat in with the band on piano), and members of Paul Whiteman's band (p. 111). Lil knew this only because Louis and Joe Oliver told her who was listening. She said, "You see, the boys [the white musicians] never talked to me, anyway. They used to talk to Louis and King Oliver and Johnny [Dodds], but they would never say anything to me. Never, never a word said" (p. 112).

There is another perspective to consider as well. When writing about the Chicago power couple of jazz, Louis Armstrong and his wife Lil Hardin Armstrong in the early 1920s, James Dickerson (2002) makes a good point about the origins of jazz:

> At that point in their lives, neither Louis nor Lil saw themselves as the creators of a new type of music. They played music because it paid better than anything else they could do, and most of the time, it was fun and exciting. Neither of them listened to or collected records. The creation of jazz was not an intellectual process for the couple; it was simply a byproduct of the lives they lived.
>
> *(pp. 112–113)*

Blithely unaware of her legacy, or any sense of a feminist outlook in the 1920s, Lil said,

> Most of the musicians didn't know it was going to be important either. We were just playing because sometimes you'd have a date, you wouldn't even bother to write the songs you were going to play until you got to the studio.
>
> *(L.H. Armstrong, 2007, p. 118)*

The twenty-year-old self-proclaimed "Hot Miss Lil" was suddenly a musical sensation (Dickerson, 2002, p. 57). The young Lil and even younger Louis soon began a romantic relationship on the bandstand in the Creole Jazz Band. Their 1924 marriage became the genesis in 1925 of "Louis Armstrong's Hot Five." It is likely that without Lil's compositions, encouragement, and leadership as a bandleader, this group would have never formed and created their iconic recordings.

Although the legacy of Lil Hardin as a piano player is not equal to that of Jelly Roll Morton (1890–1941), her accomplishments when taken as a whole (support of Louis, compositions, recordings, performances, and arrangements) are remarkable. Hot Miss Lil was a savvy, knowledgeable, and ambitious young woman performing in an arena almost entirely composed of men. While women such as blues singer Alberta Hunter (1895–1984) were relatively common, women instrumentalists were rare. Not only that, Lil was by all accounts a hit with audiences, "a sensation among night-club patrons unaccustomed to seeing a gender-mixed band" (Dickerson, 2002, p. 57). An attractive woman, Lil was undoubtedly a skilled piano player as well, earning a position as a featured performer with King Oliver's Creole Jazz Band, considered among the best jazz bands of the day.

Alberta Hunter said of her,

> All you had to do—we knew nothing about arrangements, keys, nothing—all you had to do was sing something like 'Make Me Love You,' and she would be one gone. She could play anything in this world and could play awhile. She was marvelous.
>
> *(as cited in Taylor, 1987, p. 35).*

Lil is likely deserving of much more admiration as an artist, but her advocacy of Louis Armstrong may have overshadowed her accomplishments.

Lil Hardin also had her fair share of critics. In *Pops*, author Terry Teachout (2009) is blunt and even discriminatory when he assesses her contribution to music:

> Lil Hardin Armstrong, as she later preferred to call herself, is one of jazz's most underappreciated figures. It was her own fault, for she never succeeded in turning herself into anything more than a fair jazz pianist, and the solos that she played on the recording she made with Armstrong between 1923 and 1927 range in quality from passable to embarrassing.
>
> *(p. 73)*

Perhaps Teachout was forgetting that this was a new music, still being worked out and rapidly evolving. Furthermore, she was a composer, not only a pianist. The keyboard was often an ensemble instrument—not necessarily a solo instrument—in the early 1920s. Furthermore, Lil's hard-driving style, played in the center one-third of the keyboard, was a powerful rhythmic force for the Creole Jazz Band (Dickerson, 2002, pp. 70–71).

Record producer John Hammond also piled on, likening her to a cartoon character, "a ragtime pianist who always reminds me of Minnie Mouse's playing in the early Disney movies" (as cited in Teachout, 2009, p. 74). Such a remark says more of Hammond's distance and lack of knowledge of the Chicago music scene of the 1920s than it does of Lil Hardin.

In addition to her physical appeal, it is likely that Lil's no-nonsense working style, powerful piano playing, and dedication to "hot music" were attractive to not only her boss at the time, King Oliver, but later Louis Armstrong. Chris Clifton (1938), a trumpeter and friend of Louis and Lucille Armstrong (1914–1983) recalls that "Lil was an excellent and strict leader." Visiting her at her Chicago home in the 1950s, Clifton was invited to sit in with Lil Hardin and her band at the Red Arrow, a suburban Chicago roadhouse. When she called a number he didn't know, "she told me, not mean, but a matter of factly, 'Next time you come to work, know that number'" (Clifton, n.d.).

When Louis joined King Oliver's band in Chicago, playing second to Oliver's lead, Lil helped him negotiate life in the North and pushed him professionally. She believed in Satchmo's talents more than he did (Horne, 2019, p. 59) and probably motivated him to take classical music lessons from "a German teacher" (Teachout, 2009, p. 75). Lil was, in fact, the catalyst for his decision to accept Fletcher Henderson's invitation to come to New York, a move that sealed Louis's national reputation. According to Teachout, Lil's

> contribution to the history of jazz arose not from the quality of her playing, but the nature of her relationship with Louis Armstrong. Not only did she pull him out of Papa Joe's [Oliver's] nest, but she played as important a part in his musical maturation as had Fate Marable.
>
> *(pp. 74–75)[4]*

This is a fine example of the venerable adage: "Behind every great man is a great woman." When Lil noticed that Louis was being taken advantage of by Fletcher Henderson, playing third trumpet with limited solos, she encouraged him to return to Chicago. Though he did not want to, Lil was adamant. "I had to choose between my wife and Fletcher's band," Louis said. "I chose to be with my wife" (Dickerson, 2002, p. 121). When he returned to Chicago, Lil had once again set him up for success. Forming a band named Lil's Dreamland Syncopators, she convinced the Dreamland manager to post a marquee that read: "LOUIS ARMSTRONG—THE WORLD'S GREATEST TRUMPET PLAYER" (p. 120). Not only that, Lil had arranged for Louis to play lead trumpet and make seventy-five dollars a week. "He [Louis] was astonished. He didn't know of another musician who made that kind of money" (pp. 121-122).

Among her most remarkable achievements in modern music and arguably the most unattributed was her involvement in the "Louis Armstrong Hot Five." A 1925 publicity photo shows the "Hot Five" with Armstrong, holding his trumpet sitting at the piano, and Johnny St. Cyr (banjo), Johnny Dodds (alto saxophone and clarinet), Kid Ory (trombone), and Lil Hardin all leaning on the piano gazing at him. John Hammond described Lil's character as follows:

> One of the most lovable people that [*sic*] ever existed in music was Lil Hardin Armstrong, Louis's wife and protector during those early rough days in Chicago. Lil was saintly and kind and no match for the vultures who surrounded Louis in the most creative days of his career.
>
> *(As cited in Dickerson, 2002, p. 217)*

Archival materials in the Louis Armstrong House Museum clearly show a rich and varied artistic connection between the couple that lasted for many years. An undated letter from Louis to Lil in the museum archives shows an open and frank relationship. The chatty and ribald letter, demonstrating the singular personality of the former, appears to have been written around a loan payment to Lil from Louis and demonstrates the unique relationship between the two artists years after they broke up. The letter details the repayment of $163.85, with an additional $36.15 to be sent the following week (L. Armstrong, n.d.). In today's currency, this is well over $2,000!

As noted previously, Armstrong and Hardin, as members of King Oliver's Creole Jazz Band, were among the first to be playing the novel brand of music. Its newly minted description ("jazz") associated with the innovative and incomparable Louis Armstrong, his patron/wife Lil Hardin, the gangster-controlled club scene sustained by the Volstead Act, represented a perfect storm (Porter, 2018).

Helen Joyner

The most controversial of the women known as jazz patrons will probably always be Helen Moore (1926–1996), who saved the life and career of trumpet prodigy Lee Morgan (b. 1938) only to take his life in 1972. The backgrounds and lives of Lil Hardin Armstrong and Helen Joyner were dramatically different. Lil Hardin was an accomplished musician, composer, recording artist, and bandleader, among other talents. Helen Joyner, a non-musician, had no clearly defined career. The narrative of their lives disclosed a crucial common bond, a relatively brief but potent time as the spouses of two of the most famous trumpeters of the twentieth century, Louis Armstrong and Lee Morgan. They supported, encouraged, inspired, and created opportunities for their husbands, arguably more than either of the trumpeters would have had on their own. Both wives were ambitious, tenacious, and destined to move ahead in their lives despite the colossal obstacles of being women, African American, and living through the Jim Crow epoch in America. Though separated by 28 years in age, they could be called feminists, as they lived their lives independently, without reliance on men. Helen Joyner came from impoverished, rural roots in the Jim Crow South. According to her death certificate, she was born in 1924 on a farm in Shallotte, North Carolina, to Ruth Joyner. Helen was also known by the last name of Morgan, More or Moore, with the family name of Joyner: "In 1968 she unofficially adopted Morgan's and was known as Helen Morgan until she died in 1996" (McMillan, 2011, pp. 228–229). Her father is unknown (p. 170). Her mother moved to Wilmington, North Carolina, when she was in her twenties, leaving Helen to be raised by her grandmother "back out in the country" (Thomas, 2006, p. 3). At the ages of thirteen and fourteen, respectively, Helen gave birth to two sons, saying "I had my first child when I was thirteen. See, I was very disillusioned. And then another baby behind that. You see, I didn't learn anything" (p. 6).

An ambivalent mother, Helen left the farm in Shalotte. She moved about forty miles away to Wilmington, a bustling port city during the war years of the early 1940s, leaving her two boys with grandparents. Wilmington was a boomtown crowded with sailors and soldiers who filled the segregated clubs and dance halls.

While in Wilmington, Helen met and married a prosperous local bootlegger, Roy Crawford, an older man in his late thirties, when she was seventeen. Two years later, he drowned at a local beach, leaving Helen a young widow (Thomas, 2014, p. 20–21). Perhaps as a foreshadowing of Joyner's resilience, courage, and sense of self, she told her son Al Harrison a different version of events regarding the death of her husband. Her son recounted that "she killed him because her husband beat her a great deal" (p. 21). Thomas writes, "She got tired of him beating on her, so, one day she stabbed him in the back" (p. 21). But in the interview transcript with Larry Thomas, she simply says, "at the age of 19, he got drowned" (p. 11). Assuming this story is accurate, and not just hyperbole, it did not stop Helen from moving to New York City to live with her deceased husband's family for a time shortly after he died.

Other than her time with Lee Morgan, Helen Joyner's life has been "surrounded by mystery" (McMillan, 2011, p. 170). Arriving in New York in 1945, she started going to clubs and meeting people:

> And then I began to meet other people and started going uptown to the clubs. The first club was the Blue Rhythm up on 145th street 'n Sugar Hill. Little three-piece band—the drummer, singer, and organ player, Della. I can't think of her last name. Let's see Etta Jones. I began to meet all these people. You know I could always fit in. Because I was a talker. And I must say so myself, I was not bad looking, and I used to fit in very nicely with them. And I would be invited to the after-hours joints. But after the clubs would close, that's when you really heard the music. The jam sessions, you know. They would come uptown and really play.
>
> *(Thomas, 2014, p. 39)*

She told Thomas,

> Now it's funny, I met most of the jazz musicians through people who weren't in the jazz world but was in the dope world. Now, see me—I was hip square. That's what they called me. Yeah. You see, I didn't use no heroin.
>
> *(p. 39)*

Her apartment on 53rd street between Eighth and Ninth Avenues, "not too far from Birdland," was known by locals as Helen's Place. It became an after-hours hangout for down-and-out jazz musicians and "a location where they could get a good hot meal. . . . It was a refuge and a safe haven from the hardships of a jazz musician's life" (p. 41).

Moore and Morgan were introduced to each other in 1967 at a New York party (at her apartment) by trombonist Benny Powell (McMillan, 2011, p. 171).[5] What may be an error in McMillan's book is clarified in her interview with Thomas: "I met Lee Morgan through Benny Green, the trombone player I was messing around with at that time" (Thomas, 2006, p. 41). Her first impression of Morgan was a maternal one:

> And I looked at him, and for some kind of reason, my heart just went out to him. I said to myself, 'this little boy,' you know. He didn't have a coat—I said, 'child, it's zero degrees out there and all you have on is a jacket. Where is your coat? And he told me he didn't have a coat 'cause it was in the pawnshop. I told him, 'Well, come on. I am going to go get your coat.' 'You're going to get my coat?' and I said, 'Yeah, and I'm not going to give you the money because you might spend it on drugs. We are going to go and get it.'
>
> *(McMillan, 2011, p. 171)*

Soon, it appeared that a romance had blossomed. Helen became determined to rescue Morgan, nurse him back to health, and restore his career (p. 270). Writer Larry Reni Thomas, who in 1990 had recorded an oral history interview with Helen, which was the nexus of the critically acclaimed film *I Called Him Morgan*, claimed: "she felt sorry for him, then realized he was a way out of poverty, a dream come true!" He went on to say, "she was shocked she could help him out of poverty" (L.R. Thomas, personal communication, October 22, 2020). Helen recovered his trumpet, which he had pawned, and when he was clean, she took over the business aspect of his work and guided him back to performance, saying, "I took over control of Morgan's life" (as cited in Thomas, 2014, p. 87). She "clothed him, fed him, housed him. . . . She found work for him when no one else wanted to hire him and made sure he showed up to his gigs. She even carried his trumpet for him" (Du Graf, 2017, par. 3). Although they never married, she became his common-law wife and took his name. Film critic Peter Rainer (2017) characterized her as a "muse, mother, wife, and manager" (p. 4). The story of their relationship has been addressed in the monograph *The Lady Who Shot Lee Morgan* (2014) and in the documentary film *I Called Him Morgan* (2016).

Lee Morgan recorded as many as twenty-five albums, notably as a sideman on Coltrane's "Blue Train" (1957) and Art Blakey's Jazz Messengers on the Blue Note label. There is every reason to believe that Morgan's life would have ended in 1967 without Joyner's interest and assistance during his rehabilitation. The fact that he returned to the bandstand and recorded numerous albums after her intervention in his life must not be forgotten. The rebirth of Morgan, his return to performing, thanks to Helen, is in some ways similar to what Lil Hardin created for Louis forty-four years earlier when Fletcher Henderson sent a telegram to Armstrong inviting him to play with his New York orchestra.

While the exact date in 1967 when Lee and Helen met and began a relationship is not known, "by the late summer, Morgan began making changes in his career and personal life that showed a concerted effort to establish himself as a bandleader" (McMillan, 2011, p. 167). There is every reason to believe that this rather abrupt change in his demeanor was due to the influence of Helen Joyner. To outward appearances, Morgan was a busy and fully engaged artist, performing on several records after he departed from the Art Blakey Jazz Messengers in 1965, which suggests a vibrant and healthy personal and professional life. His recordings for Blue Note records from 1965 to 1967 included "'The Rumproller,' 'Search for the New Land,' 'The Gigolo,' 'Cornbread,' and 'Delightfulee'" (p. 166). He also "appeared on [more] recent recordings with Art Blakey, Hank Mobley, Freddie Hubbard, and Joe Henderson" (p. 167). "The truth, of course," McMillan continues, "is that Morgan's appearances on recordings since his departure from the Jazz Messengers, while certainly impressive for a horn player, amounted to just a few dozen days of work over a span of two years" (p. 167). His health issues were likely the cause of his infrequent appearances as a performer, however, and "took a toll on his critical reputation, and his name failed to appear in any category of the Down Beat Critics poll of 1967" (p. 167).

One can surmise that the intervention of Helen Joyner in 1967 may have arisen between two recordings for Blue Note he made that year. *Sonic Boom*, a quintet album recorded on two Sundays in April, was composed of Morgan, David "Fathead" Newman, Cedar Walton, Ron Carter, and Billy Higgins (p. 162). Accounts of the recording session suggest Morgan was in poor playing condition, perhaps due to his drug addiction:

> Morgan was underprepared at the April 14 session, but the state of his embouchure could have also been a reason for the session's brevity. From the opening phrase of his solo on *Sonic Boom*, Morgan's tone is vague, and air occasionally escapes from his mouth without engaging the lips. In addition to his inconsistent tone production, Morgan's phrases are short and choppy, especially at the beginning of his solo. Compared to the ease with which he typically played long lines, complete with rhythmic nuances and punctuations, the sound suggests his chops were not capable of sustaining long phrases without tiring.
>
> *(p. 162)*

After the *Sonic Boom* recording session, Morgan "spent nearly three months without working or recording" (p. 163). In this period leading into the summer, Helen's interventions and maternal influences became apparent. Morgan went into the studio and recorded new material for Blue Note that became *The Procrastinator*, released posthumously in 1976. The session included Morgan, Wayne Shorter, Bobby Hutcherson, Herbie Hancock, Ron Carter, and Billy Higgins (p. 163). According to McMillan, "there is an irony in the title *The Procrastinator*, an apt descriptor of Morgan, because the record's eclectic mix of challenging, original compositions and strong ensemble performances comprise one of Morgan's tightest, best-rehearsed record dates" (p. 163). This is further proof of the "Helen effect" and her impact on Morgan's legacy. The recovering trumpeter was aware of her influence in his life and composed a tribute to her, "Helen's Ritual," for the 1968 *Caramba!* album, a medium tempo blues.[6] Morgan's solo on the tune is the second one, after the searching solo of saxophonist Bennie Maupin. Morgan is exuberant, even frenetic at times. The tune ends with a cadential sequence, perhaps a series of thank you's.

Morgan went on to record eight Blue Note recordings from 1967 until his death in 1972. As his music career opened up, he became more renowned as an outspoken activist and was candid about racial inequality and black rights in America. It is unclear just how much Helen had to do with his passion for the fight against racial intolerance, but she likely supported him in this new avenue of expression as much as she did in his music. After Morgan became involved with the Angela Davis campaign, Helen suggested that he "might find a way to help Shirley Chisholm, who was then seeking the Democratic Party's Presidential nomination" (Perchard, 2006, p. 234).

Unfortunately, the relationship between Helen and Lee became increasingly fraught. It is essential to recognize, however, that Helen remained a steadfast companion and supporter to Lee Morgan, and it was Morgan who became abusive and unkind to Helen. In the liner notes to *The Sixth Sense*, a Blue Note record session made some months after *The Procrastinator* in 1967, is a heartfelt tribute to Helen, written by a friend of Morgan, broadcaster Ed Williams:

> Morgan's second wife, Helen, is giving him the respect, encouragement, and support a man needs from his woman. Although her manner is quiet, her love for Morgan is anything but. . . . If Lee is getting more out of music now, chances are it's because he's getting more out of living.
>
> *(p. 182)*

While Helen, "an 'old timer' fourteen years the trumpeter's senior" (p. 233), continued to spend as much time as she could with the much younger Lee, he became increasingly involved with other women. "[Helen] was aware of his activities, and the trumpeter made no effort to hide his relationships from her" (p. 234). Saxophonist Billy Harper believed that "he [Lee] was trying to get away from all the negativity in his life . . . implying that Helen was a part of that negative past" (McMillan, 2011, p. 198). Likely the problems in their relationship stemmed from several reasons. One was Morgan's increasing involvement in political action, including the struggle for racial equality and musicians' struggle for respect. Though supportive to a degree, Helen was likely less engaged with such idealistic pursuits and more concerned with managing Morgan's music career. Another aspect was the resentment resulting from fundamental differences in their temperaments. Kenny Sheffield, a young trumpeter and protege of Morgan, recounts that "Lee was wild; he was a prankster. When Helen walked in, all that playfulness disappeared. She kept Lee in check" (p. 199). It may have been that Morgan's perspective on music and his political action had changed him so dramatically that whatever support Helen had been able to offer him was no longer needed or valid and was resented.

The biographies of Lee Morgan recount many instances of the abuse the young trumpeter heaped on Helen. According to an old friend, he'd come home at night, she's looking out the window watching him make out at the door with a chick, and when she confronted him: You don't know what you're talking about. He'd really do things right in front of her face and then put her down.

(Perchard, 2006, p. 235)

Donna Cox, daughter of Lee Morgan's sister, Ernestine, remembered Helen not so much as Morgan's companion as a mother figure in his life (McMillan, 2011, p. 199). He rewarded her devotion and generosity with humiliating infidelities and anger:

People were saying, she got even more demanding, you're not going to see that guy, and I don't like him, so stay away from her. I don't like you hanging with those people, you're out too late, all of this stuff. They were [like] having rocky, out-in-public arguments. He dumped a bottle of champagne over her head one day, you know, the whole thing, and threw the bottle off, and Bitch, get the fuck out of here, leave me the hell alone, so on and so forth.

(S.B. Harps as cited in Perchard, 2006, p. 232)

Their relationship ended in tragedy. Morgan and his band began an engagement the week of February 15–20 at the New York club, Slugs'. Ironically, it was a gig that Helen had arranged for Morgan. Helen told Larry Thomas, "I remember I called up the man [manager at Slugs'] and got him a week there. And the man said, 'Do you promise?' And I said, 'Yeah, promise, he'll be there'" (Thomas, 2006, p. 49). On the evening of February 18, 1972, Helen came to Slugs' during a horrendous snowstorm, and after a violent argument that saw Morgan hit Helen, she shot him with a handgun. Lee Morgan died soon after the shot was fired.

Challenging as it may be to consider Helen Joyner a patron, one should consider the notion that she was a victim as well. Having given up her life to Lee Morgan in the service of his music, she was unappreciated, humiliated, and abused in return. Without the secure upbringing, education, and resilience of Lil Hardin, Joyner acted out in a crime of passion, morally ambiguous at best. The words at the eulogy for Morgan, as remembered by Helen, are a poignant reminder of what the couple achieved together:

Regardless of what happened, we cannot leave Helen out of this because Morgan was dead to us before she came on the scene. And she brought him back to us, five, six, seven, eight years, you know. She brought him back alive, you know.

(Thomas, 2006, p. 63)

In the end, the differences between Helen Joyner and Lil Hardin Armstrong are vast. Lil was a musician, composer, and bandleader, a cultured and well-educated woman who hailed from a solid family background. Her relationship with Louis Armstrong, though relatively short, was a potent one. She can be credited with untethering his talents, allowing him an international career and a lasting legacy as an iconic American jazz musician.

Helen Joyner came out of what could be described as dystopian roots, giving birth to two children by age fourteen. Still a teenager and after the death of her husband, Joyner, a non-musician with perhaps a high school education, moved to New York in the 1940s. There is little known about her in the ensuing years. Her achievements and career, unlike those of Lil Hardin, are largely unknown. Yet, there were many similarities between them. Like Lil, her relationship with Lee Morgan, though brief, was a powerful one. She brought him back from a premature death due to drug addiction, allowing him to make new recordings and perform with renewed vigor. The legacy of those recordings, *Sonic Boom*, *The Procrastinator*, and *Caramba!*, as well as his compositions from this period, are a part of American jazz history. His contributions with the Jazzmobile Workshop, an outreach program that included concerts, school workshops, and free lessons for children in New York, are important (McMillan, 2011, p. 200). His political beliefs, advocacy for musicians and black rights work, though less widely known, likely inspired others to take up the crucial work to achieve racial equality and a more just society. None of this would have happened without Helen's intervention, encouragement, and support.

Lil Hardin Armstrong and Helen Joyner were two of the most dissimilar women one can imagine. Yet, their legacy as patrons is undeniable and central to the success of their respective husbands.

Notes

1 Helen's maiden name was Joyner. The origins of the last name of More or Moore is not known.
2 Lil took courses in music at Fisk University but never completed a degree. She earned a degree from the Chicago College of Music in 1928 and a post-graduate degree from the New York College of Music in about 1929.
3 Lil claims that she was making more than $100 a week with King Oliver. That works out to about $1340 a week in current US dollars!
4 Fate Marable was the leader of a band that performed on a riverboat that plied the Mississippi from New Orleans to St. Louis and beyond. Armstrong played with Marable from 1918 to 1921, until his departure to Chicago.
5 There are two prominent African American trombonists of this era, Benny Powell (1930–2010) and Benny Green (1923–1977). Helen Joyner mentions Benny Green in the transcript of her interview with Larry Thomas.
6 "Helen's Ritual" opens with a brief quotation of what could be the Benny Golson tune "Killer Joe." While this may be a coincidence, it could also be an inside joke or reference.

References

Armstrong, L. (n.d.). [Letter to Lil Armstrong]. Satchmo Collection (2002.152.1). Louis Armstrong House Museum, New York. Retrieved from https://collections.louisarmstronghouse.org/asset-detail/1094578.

Armstrong, L. H. (2007). Satchmo and me. *American Music*, 25(1), 106–118.

Clifton, C. [n.d.]. Memories from Chris Clifton. [Letter]. Satchmo Collection (2002.152.1). Louis Armstrong House Museum, New York. Retrieved from https://collections.louisarmstronghouse.org/asset-detail/1097629.

Collin, K. (Producer and Director). (2016). *I Called Him Morgan* [Motion picture]. Sweden: Kasper Collin Produktion with Sveriges Television.

Dickerson, J.L. (2002). *Just for a Thrill: Lil Hardin Armstrong, First Lady of Jazz*. New York: Cooper Square.

Du Graf, L. (2017, Mar. 22). From the shadows. [Review of the film *I Called Him Morgan*, produced and directed by K. Collin]. *Reverse Shot*. Retrieved from www.reverseshot.org/reviews/entry/2313/called_morgan.

Hieb. K. B. (2017). [Review of the book *Gender and Identity in Jazz*, edited by Wolfram Knauer]. *Notes* 74(2), 263–265. doi:10.1353/not.2017.0115.

Horne, G. (2019). *Jazz and Justice: Racism and the Political Economy of the Music*. New York: Monthly Review Press.

Martin, R. (2020). *Outside and Inside: Race and Identity in White Jazz Autobiography*. Jackson, MS: University of Mississippi Press.

McMillan, J. S. (2011). *Delightfulee: The Life and Music of Lee Morgan*. Ann Arbor: University of Michigan Press.

Perchard, T. (2006). *Lee Morgan, His Life, Music and Culture*. Oakville, CT: Equinox.

Porter, L. (2018, Feb. 26). Where did 'jazz,' the word, come from? Follow a trail of clues, in deep dive with Lewis Porter. Retrieved from www.wbgo.org/post/where-did-jazz-word-come-follow-trail-clues-deep-dive-lewis-porter#stream/0.

Rainer, P. (2017, Mar. 31). 'I Called Him Morgan' embraces the ambiguousness of the story. [Review of the film *I Called Him Morgan*, produced and directed by K. Collin]. *The Christian Science Monitor*. Retrieved from www.csmonitor.com/The-Culture/Movies/2017/0331/I-Called-Him-Morgan-embraces-ambiguousness-of-story.

Taylor, F. (1987). *Alberta Hunter: A Celebration in Blues*. New York: McGraw-Hill.

Teachout, T. (2009). *Pops: A Life of Louis Armstrong*. Boston: Houghton Mifflin Harcourt.

Thomas, L. R. (2006). *Helen Morgan Interview*. Wilmington, NC: Larry Thomas.

Thomas, L. R. (2014). *The Lady who Shot Lee Morgan*. Drewryville, VA: UBUS Communications System.

4

QUEER AESTHETICS AND THE PERFORMING SUBJECT IN JAZZ IN THE 1920S

Magdalena Fürnkranz

Personal Statement: I'm using the term female for women, lesbians, and trans people who identify as women. The term does not describe any sexual orientation, but gender identities and thus makes the social component of gender visible. I'm using the term queer as an umbrella term for sexual and gender minorities who are neither heterosexual nor cisgender. Queer describes a broad spectrum of non-normative sexual and gender identities and politics. It is a privilege to not have to worry about which pronoun someone is going to use for me based on how they perceive my gender. This chapter is dedicated to persons who are discriminated patriarchally on the basis of their gender identity. In this way, I hope to contribute to increasing the visibility and influence of female★ and queer musicians, as well as intersectional approaches to popular music, and to provide support to emerging scholars from diverse and underrepresented populations.

Introduction

Historically, queer musicians have been marginalized as artists in jazz and popular music. Considered to be novelty acts in a world of hegemonic masculinity and valued more for exoticized performances, as Sherrie Tucker noted in *When Did Jazz Go Straight? A Queer Question for Jazz Studies*, even before jazz came out as the "official soundtrack of heterosexual love and romance" (Tucker, 2008, p. 1) its queer musicians had to work hard to be accepted for their ability. In the period known as the Jazz Age, erotic heterosexual desire lost the stigma of perversion and takes center stage as the new straight norm. Well known female performers of the Harlem Renaissance among them Bessie Smith "The Empress of the Blues," Ma Rainey "The Mother of the Blues," Alberta Hunter, Jackie "Mom" Mabley, Gladys Bentley, Josephine Baker, and Ethel Waters cultivated a lesbian or at least a bisexual image. Dancing as an expression of music associated with African American individuals promoted a queer setting for its protagonists. Dancers like Leon James and Al Minns were rumored to have been queer performers during the period of the Harlem Renaissance.

One of the female protagonists in Harlem's nightlife, who was historicized as a queer performer, was Ma Rainey. In 1925, Ma Rainey was arrested for taking part in an orgy involving the women in her chorus, furthermore the singer was reported to have been several times in trouble with the police for her lesbian behavior. Gladys Bentley challenged heteronormative constructions of sexuality in the 1920s. Dressed in a white tuxedo, she was famous for obscene lyrics about her female lovers and flirted on stage with women in the audience. A performer, who made her journey from the United

DOI: 10.4324/9781003081876-5

States to Europe, was Josephine Baker. While many historians and biographers have denied that Baker was queer, her sexuality was a central part of her life (Garber, 2013, p. 122). As Lester Strong stated, "it's the fact that nearly everything she did expressed desires and needs that deviated significantly from the prescribed social norms of the Jazz Age" (Strong, 2006).

In order to get an overview of queer aesthetics and the performing subject in jazz in the 1920s, I focus on selected musicians based on artist's biographies and their public image. My perspective poses questions of how queer identities are constructed, represented, and negotiated in jazz in the 1920s to understand what role the legacy of these selected musicians plays in jazz history, in popular culture, and in LGBTQ+ music. Paying particular attention to body politics, I discuss Josephine Baker's appearance in the revue *Black on White* in Vienna in 1928; a performance that was described as a threat to Viennese culture.

Historical Precedents

Looking back in the narrative of a queer history of Black popular music through seeking examples of sexual fluidity in performance, we find one particular *persona*. Jim Crow, also referred to as Jump Jim Crow or sometimes John Crow, was a song and dance performed in blackface by white minstrel performer Thomas Dartmouth "Daddy" Rice from 1828. Its origin was described by several sources as Rice meeting an elderly Black stableman with a crooked leg and deformed shoulder (Lhamon, 2003, p.vii; Oakley, 1997, p. 22; An Old Actor's Memories, 1881), while the actor was touring through river towns. The man sang about Jim Crow and punctuated each stanza with a little jump (Lhamon, 2003, p.vii; Oakley, 1997, p. 22; An Old Actor's Memories, 1881). The unproven encounter happened in Louisville, Kentucky. The two actors Rice and Edmon S. Conner were engaged at the city's theater, which overlooked a stable at the back. They saw an elderly slave working and at the same time performing a song and a dance in the stable yard. "Rice watched him closely, and realized that here was a character unknown to the stage. He wrote several verses, changed the air somewhat, quickened it a good deal, made up exactly like Daddy and sang it to a Louisville audience. They were wild with delight" (Edmon S. Conner, cited in An Old Actor's Memories, 1881).

According to Conner, the stable was owned by a white man named Crow, whose name the elderly slave adopted. In the 19th century, the song "Jim Crow" became a great hit and Rice performed as "Daddy Jim Crow" all over the country. The first song sheet edition appeared in the early 1830s, published by E. Riley (Lott, 2013, p. 23). As a key initial step in a tradition of popular music in the United States, "Jump Jim Crow" was based on the imitation of Black people. A couple of decades in the late nineteenth and early twentieth centuries, the mockery genre exploded in popularity with the rise of the minstrel show.

Thomas D. Rice used the body of an African American slave as a projection surface for white, heterosexual disguises of blackness, which he combined with music. The black body was sexualized and entangled in a supposedly amusing game of power and dominance. Rice as a half-naked slave applying black face and wrapped in rags performing a crippled dance gave the starting point for the sexualization of black bodies in the entertainment business.

Regarding the "birth of jazz," the white hegemonic storyline of jazz history is commonly front-loaded into the origin stories of the birthplace of the genre in the brothels of New Orleans. However, historians of New Orleans jazz have negated this assertion; unlike early sex workers in the late 1890s, jazz performers were not restricted to the red-light district of New Orleans that was called Storyville. In fact, jazz was played at dances sponsored by Catholic churches, social clubs, lawn parties, fish fries, and other settings. Even though historians have tried to disapprove this assertion, it is still difficult to find a common jazz narrative that does not locate the birth of jazz in the brothels of Storyville (Tucker, 2008, p. 5).

Jazz and Heteronormativity in the Jazz Age

In the 1920s, Jazz in New York was played and enjoyed by many people from different ethnical backgrounds, classes, and sexual identities. In the narrative of the so-called Jazz Age, the trope of hyper-sexuality was alleged to the image of Black musicians. Fantasies of Black culture became a haven for white modernists, rejecting the hegemonic straight lines, while simultaneously benefiting from their lineage. As Sherrie Tucker (2008) stated "jazz in the 'Jazz Age' aided in making heteronormativity sexy" (p. 6). Thanks to Tucker's work, we have an approach to rethink the historical tangles of sexuality, race, and gender in jazz studies.

By starting to reconsider queer aesthetics in the Jazz Age, I will focus on Harlem's nightlife in the 1920s and 1930s. The so-called Harlem Renaissance is a term used to describe the artistic, cultural, and social activities that happened between the end of World War I and the mid-1930s. Harlem was a cultural mecca, represented by Black writers, artists, musicians, and scholars, individuals who were in search for a place to freely express their creative talents. During this time, the American civil rights activist, Pan-Africanist, author, and editor William Edward Burghardt "W. E. B." Du Bois encouraged artists to leave the South. This artistic and political renaissance involved a new revolutionary spirit and a resulting demand for civil and political rights (Garber, 1989, p. 319). In this spirit a queer subculture in Harlem was born that was still partially repressed. When sexuality was represented within art, such repression became even more apparent.

Queer-oriented events usually took place in the heart of Harlem at parties and costume balls held at buffet flats and speakeasies (Peppers, 2013). A speakeasy, also known as "blind pig" or "blind tiger," was an illegal establishment that sold alcoholic beverages. These establishments became popular in the United States during the Prohibition era that lasted between 1920–1933 and longer in some states. The sale, manufacture, and bootlegging of alcoholic beverages was banned throughout the United States during that time. These establishments largely disappeared after Prohibition was ended in 1933. The queer-oriented parties tended to be private and were known under the term "rent parties," which were "the best place for Harlem lesbians and gay men to socialize, providing safety and privacy" (Garber, 1989, p. 320). Costume balls as "spectacles in color [where] both men and women could dress as they pleased and dance with whom they wished" (Langston Hughes, cited in Garber, 1989, p. 323) were more popular because of their legality and their easier accessibility to a larger public. In retrospect, it could be said that speakeasies and costume balls acted as safe spaces for queer individuals, where they could express themselves freely from social restrictions.

Well known male★ and female★ performers of the Harlem Renaissance cultivated a homosexual or at least a bisexual image. Al Minns, for example, was an energetic dancer with a wild leg style. He was in the famous Whitey's Lindy Hoppers' top group, known as The Harlem Congaroos, and also appeared in the popular soundie *Hot Chocolate* (Berne, 1941). As the youngest dancer in this group, he was particularly fit and flexible. His dancing partner, Leon James, was one of the main Swing dancers with the Whitey's Lindy Hoppers, he also danced with the Shorty Snowden Trio and won several dance competitions.

The duo, also known as "The Jazz Dancers," initially conceived as a novelty act, tried to keep the Lindy Hop dance alive. Two men expressively dancing together in the 1930s, also appearing on US television programs in the 1950s and 1960s such as *DuPont's Show of the Week* (see *Al Minns and Leon James on DuPont Show of the Week* (1961 TV series)), conveyed an exoticized image.

Ma Rainey—Queering the Mother of the Blues

One of the female, allegedly queer, protagonists in Harlem's nightlife was Ma Rainey. The singer was reported to have been several times in trouble with the police for her lesbian behavior (Davis, 1999, p. 40). Rainey was one of the earliest American professional popular music singers (Southern, 1997) and also one of the first generation of blues singers to record, therefore she is sometimes referred to as the "Mother of the Blues." She was born as Gertrude Malissa Nix Pridgett in September 1882 (Eagle and LeBlanc, 2013, p. 87) or on April 26, 1886 (Oliver, 2001). The starting point for the myth that surrounded her public persona is the date of her birth, Rainey claimed that she was born on April 26, 1886 in Columbus, Georgia (Lieb, 1983, p. 2). Her date of birth can be questioned, however, as the

1900 census indicates she may have been born in September 1882 in Alabama. Bob Eagle and Eric LeBlanc suggested that her exact birthplace was in Russell County (Eagle and LeBlanc, 2013, p. 87).

She started her career as a young teenager and became known as Ma Rainey after her marriage to Will Rainey in 1904. The couple traveled with the popular Rabbit Foot Minstrels billed as "Ma and Pa Rainey, Assassinators of the Blues" (Palmer, 1984). The Rabbit Foot Minstrels were wintering in New Orleans, where Ma Rainey met numerous popular musicians, among them Joe "King" Oliver, Louis Armstrong, and Sidney Bechet. During that time the popularity of blues music increased, consequently Ma Rainey became popular (Lieb, 1983, p. 5). Sandra Lieb stated that sometime between 1912 and 1916, Rainey must have met the young blues singer Bessie Smith. Smith's sister-in-law, Maud Smith, later developed the story that Rainey kidnapped Smith and forced her to join the Rabbit's Foot Minstrels, where she taught her to sing the blues (Lieb, 1983, p. 15). Concerning her role as vocal coach for Smith, Rainey has been deliberately sexualized by contemporaries for her uncommon role as a female mentor.

An increasing demand for recordings by Black musicians started in the late 1910s. In 1923, Ma Rainey signed a recording contract with Paramount Records, the same year her first recording was made. She was not the first Black woman to be recorded; the vaudeville singer Mamie Smith started recording in 1920 (Lieb, 1983, p. 29). From 1923 to 1928, Rainey made over 100 recordings, including well-known tunes among them: "Bo-Weevil Blues" (1923), "Moonshine Blues" (1923), "See See Rider Blues" (1924), "Black Bottom" (1927), and "Soon This Morning" (1927). By calling her the "Mother of the Blues," the "Songbird of the South," the "Gold-Neck Woman of the Blues," and the "Paramount Wildcat," Paramount marketed her extensively (Lieb, 1983, p. 25). Linda Dahl described her exoticized performances as follows, "[by] wearing beaded headbands, waving giant ostrich fans and blowing kisses, she would emerge on stage from a huge box made to look like a phonograph" (Dahl, 1984, p. 119). She was popular for her style of singing, highlighting her vocal and phrasing abilities (Lieb, 1983, p. 24). This assumption cannot be confirmed due to the fact that her voice was never adequately captured on records (Giaimo, 2016).

Rainey recorded exclusively for Paramount, a company that was known for its below-average recording techniques and poor shellac quality. The myth of "Ma Rainey, the queer blues singer" is one of the motives that shaped her image in today's popular culture. By taking a closer look at her queer image, Rainey's themes and lyrics seem as innovative as her methods. The topics of her songs were infidelity, abandonment, and heartbreak, which was not uncommon for a blues singer, but her songs' protagonists were more interested in self-justice than to hang their heads and cry. As Angela Davis pointed out, Rainey's songs were full of women who "explicitly celebrate their right to conduct themselves as expansively and even as undesirably as men" (Davis, 2011, p. 481) by drinking, carousing, even baiting law enforcement.

Robert Philipson stated in his 2011 documentary *T'Ain't Nobody's Bizness: Queer Blues Divas of the 1920s* that Ma Rainey was one of a number of Jazz Age artists who might be described as queer by modern audiences. Although her sexuality wasn't public knowledge, her sexual interests were used to create an extraordinary image. "The blues was the area where alternative sexuality was most visible," claimed Philipson in his documentary. Sam Chatmon, a guitarist for Ma Rainey's tent show in Jackson (Mississippi), believed that Rainey and Bessie Smith were lovers (Lieb, 1983, p. 18). Others have not only tended to romantically link her to Smith, but to have introduced Bessie Smith to lesbian relationships in the early years of their collaboration. "Carousing and sexual adventure were not uncommon. In this light, it has often been suggested that Ma Rainey's influence over the young Bessie Smith was more than professional" (McGaskomay, 2015). Chris Albertson detailed in a biography of Smith that Ma Rainey "and a group of young ladies had been drinking and were making so much noise that a neighbor summoned the police, [who arrived] just as the impromptu party got intimate" (Albertson, 2003). He stated that everyone but Rainey fled through the back door. She was arrested for "running an indecent party" but bailed out the next morning by Smith (Albertson, 2003).

It has been speculated that this incident might have inspired "Prove It On Me Blues," a 1928 song. Meagan Day described the song in her 2016 article as "a response to rumors about Rainey's lesbianism, which circulated after she was arrested in 1925 for participating in an orgy with multiple women" (Day, 2016). "Prove It On Me Blues" was recorded with Her Tub Jug Washboard Band and released in June 1928, with the songwriting being attributed to Rainey. "Went out last night with a crowd of my friends," Rainey sang over a strutting beat. "They must've been women, 'cause I don't like no men. It's true I wear a collar and tie, makes the wind blow all the while." Rainey referred to her outfit, including a collar and tie, clothing that is usually attributed to men. Regarding the fact that she "doesn't like men," she wore men's clothes and therefore replaced the male dominance in the group. "Went out last night, had a great big fight. Everything seemed to go on wrong. I looked up, to my surprise. The gal I was with was gone." The big fight underlined her dominant position. She specified this position by stating that the girl she was with is gone. "Where she went, I don't know. I mean to follow everywhere she goes; Folks say I'm crooked. I didn't know where she took it. I want the whole world to know." A longer lasting relationship can be assumed because Rainey sings, "I mean to follow everywhere she goes." With the line, "I want the whole world to know," Rainey clearly alluded to her public image and at the same time mystified herself with the following line, "They say I do it, ain't nobody caught me. Sure got to prove it on me," that is repeated several times. The song concludes with, "Wear my clothes just like a fan. Talk to the gals just like any old man," a trope that was picked up for Paramount's ad for the song that featured a drawing of Rainey in a three-piece suit and a fedora. She seems to chat up some ladies, while being watched by a policeman from across the street underlined by the words, "What's all this? Scandal? Don't fail to get this record from your dealer!"

Philipson (2011) stated that the song was "basically an explicitly lesbian anthem of celebration" and later adds, "You didn't see that anywhere else." Angela Davis mentioned the overtly lesbian lyrics of Ma Rainey's "Prove It On Me Blues" and Paramount's ad for the song in the essay, "I Used To Be Your Sweet Mama: Ideology, Sexuality and Domesticity in the Blues of Gertrude 'Ma' Rainey and Bessie Smith" as follows, "Ma Rainey's sexual involvement with women was no secret among her colleagues or her audiences; and, in fact, the advertisement for this release consisted of a drawing of the blueswoman sporting a man's hat, jacket and tie and obviously attempting to seduce two women on a street corner" (Davis, 1995, p. 259). She also claimed that the promotion of a song with such explicit advertisements of homosexual behavior by female popular singers in the 1920s, influenced not only later historical developments but simultaneously "suggests that the influence of homophobia within the black community was not so powerful as to enshroud lifestyles that challenged the stereo-typical notions of women's realities" (Davis, 1995, p. 260). J. Halberstam (1997) claimed that this advertisement provided "evidence of not only overt lesbian identifications but also a lively culture of cross-dressing" (p. 113). Davis (1999) described "Prove It On Me Blues" as "a cultural precursor to the lesbian cultural movement of the 1970s, which began to crystallize around the performance and recording of lesbian-affirming songs" (p. 40). Davis assumption is clearly underlined by Paramount's promotion of the song by using a queer trope. Although Ma Rainey was never associated with cross-dressing, her lyrics and the image that Paramount created for her clearly influenced the queering of the Mother of the Blues in popular culture.

Gladys Bentley—A Cross-Dressing Performer in a White, Heteronormative Culture

Another performer of the Jazz Age time was Gladys Bentley who, according to Linda Dahl (1984) was "a popular Harlem entertainer and male impersonator" (p. 111). Born as Gladys Alberta Bentley on August 12, 1907 in Philadelphia (Eagle and LeBlanc, 2013, p. 333), she was famous for being an alto singer and piano player, typically wearing a signature tuxedo and top hat. J. Halberstam (1997) described her as "regularly cross-dressed in a tuxedo and she sang songs about 'bulldaggers'" (p. 113).

By analyzing Gladys Bentley's performance persona, it quickly becomes visible that her queer image was constituted primarily through her clothing and style of performance.

Bentley started her career at the age of 16, when she moved from Philadelphia to New York City. She began establishing herself as a pianist, filling in for pianists at night clubs and playing the rent party circuit. Bentley appeared the first time in New York's historical record in the year 1928 ("Gladys Bentley A New Blues Star on Okeh Electric Race Records," cited in Church, 2018, p. 7). A friend told Bentley that a night club in Harlem called the Mad House needed a pianist right away. The audience responded enthusiastically to Bentley's performance, hence the manager hired Bentley on the spot (Church, 2018, p. 7). Soon after, she started working at the Harry Hansberry's Clam House on 133rd Street, one of the city's most notorious gay speakeasies, which was looking for a male pianist. The narrow, smoky speakeasy featured Gladys Bentley, a 250-pound, masculine, Black lesbian, who performed all night long in a white tuxedo and top hat. Bentley, a talented pianist with a growling voice, was celebrated for inventing obscene lyrics to popular contemporary melodies. Langston Hughes (cited in Garber, 1989) called her "an amazing exhibition of musical energy" (p. 322). Due to her success, Bentley started performing in men's attire, wearing "white full dress shirts, stiff collars, small bow ties, oxfords, short Eton jackets, and hair cut straight back" (Bentley, 1952, p. 94). By this time, she had become so popular that she was featured regularly in prominent Black newspapers. From 1928 to 1930, her name became synonymous with the Clam House (Church, 2018, p.7). The entertainer was famous for her scandalous improvised lyrics to popular songs, encouraging her audiences to join in on the lewd choruses. The writer Wilbur Young (1939) stated that "Bentley specialized not in singing the blues but rather in ad libbing the lyrics of popular songs." At that time she began performing at the Ubangi Club on Park Avenue, where she was accompanied by a pianist and backed up by a chorus line of drag queens (Boyd, 2001, p.18). While hundreds of clubs became targets of police investigations and were subsequently shut down, the Ubangi Club was allowed to continue operation for a number of years.

According to Wilbur Young (1939), Bentley "toned her songs down somewhat so they were now called risqué" and the chorus line of drag queens was replaced with female dancers known as the Ubangettes. The local community censored the Ubangi Club for serving white guests, consequently Bentley had lost the support of many Harlemites because she focused on the patronage of wealthy whites (Church, 2018, p. 32).

In retrospect, Bentley was the only performer to publicly exploit her lesbian identity. At the height of her career, she openly flaunted her lesbianism, even reportedly marrying her white lesbian lover in a much-publicized ceremony in Atlantic City in 1928 (Jones, 2012, p. 7; Serlin, 2004, Brathwaite, 2013). The image that the singer conveyed, paired with her popularity as a visible, confident, cross-dressing, queer, Black performer in a white, heteronormative culture already produced "Gladys Bentely"; a key figure in the stories and myths of Harlem Renaissance writers, novels, and entertainment columns of the era. The myth that established Bentley's image started in her childhood. "The beginning of my story, shocking but true, goes back to my childhood days," Bentley (1952) stated and added, "My mother was very bitterly against having a girl. She had prayed and made all preparations for a boy until having a son became an obsession with her" (p. 95). Bentley claimed that her mother had refused nursing her and concluded with, "It seems that I was born different. At least I always thought that. In later years I learned that 'different' people are made not born" (p. 95). She remembered being teased by her schoolmates for wearing her brothers' clothes to school at the age of nine or ten. Bentley's self-expression, clearly received as masculine during her childhood, collided with her sociopolitical background. Her family, acquaintances, and schoolmates were aware of her challenge to heteronormative culture, class, and gender perceptions. According to the singer in a 1952 article, the unique aspect of her image was "the way I dressed" (Bentley, 1952, p. 94). Photographs of Bentley show her wearing lipstick with darkened and shaped eyebrows in white or black tie and tails. Her public performances were limited to nightclubs or speakeasies in

Harlem. Some audience members believed Bentley was a man or a male transvestite while others thought she was a lesbian (Jones, 2012, p. 6; Harrison 1990), who growled and scatted like a trumpet on the 1928 recording of "How Much Can I Stand?" (Dahl, 1984, p. 98).

Artists, who were active in the entertainment field, were well aware of the success of Bentley's cross-dressing performances. In fact, cross dressing was not only fashionable, it created an image actresses and singers, such as Marlene Dietrich, Judy Garland, or Josephine Baker conveyed all over the Atlantic. In retrospect, these entertainers were seen as chic cross-dressing women, who performed occasionally in drag underlining their performance personae on stage and not extending this habit into their personal lives. The perception of Bentley's beauty, race, skin tone, short hair, cross dressing, being overweight, continuing flirtations with women, and voice limited her access to a larger audience (Jones, 2012, p. 7). She was not the mainstream public's idea of a woman entertainer. Though her personal life was discussed as much as her performances, her songs took part in the cultivation of a queer image.

By taking a closer look at Bentley's lyrics, I will focus on the song "Worried Blues," recorded for Okeh in New York City in 1928. The song is considered her most popular, as it can be found on many blues compilations. The topic of the song corresponds to the repertoire of female blues singers, Bentley's lyrics deal in general with being mistreated and abused by men. In "Worried Blues," she embodies an empowered and independent woman. The song starts out with "what makes you men folks treat us women like you do," later she adds, "I don't want no man that I got to give my money to," and, "I give my man everything from a diamond ring or dough." The song's character, which positions itself clearly as female, is capable of caring for herself. It underwent a metamorphosis of empowerment and warns the men folks at the song's end, "the next thing I'm gonna give him six feet in the cold, cold ground."

While Bentley was harassed for wearing men's clothes in the 1920s and 1930s, she would recant her homosexuality during the ultra-conservative McCarthy Era. Bentley's strategy included wearing dresses, marrying, undergoing a hormone therapy, and claiming to have been cured. In her 1952 autobiographical essay, announcing "I Am a Woman Again" in its title, Bentley publicly showed her private life and yielded to oppression of class and sexual identities. "At some point during the late 1940s and early 1950s she subjects herself to expensive estrogen treatments" (Jones, 2012, p. 11). According to Bentley, her physician had revealed to her that "your sex organs are infantile" and hadn't "progressed passed the age of a fourteen-year-old child" (Bentley, 1952, p.95). The entertainer described the treatment as social behavior-changing, as it allowed her to take on a new gendered role as a heterosexual, middle-aged, middle-class housewife (Bentley, 1952, p. 95). Photographs of Bentley preparing dinner, making a bed, writing her autobiography, and selecting jewelry illustrate the article. These photographs work as a proof of Bentley's "domestication," which was made possible by a successful hormone therapy.

In retrospect, Gladys Bentley was overtly cross dressing; her lyrics and the image she created influenced her life narrative. Although her queer way of life was deconstructed during the McCarthy Era, her popularity in Harlem's nightlife, as well as her reputation and image appear in discussions of literary artists from the Jazz Age period and in the discourses of popular culture focusing on queer subjects in its history.

Josephine Baker—A "Threat" to the Viennese Culture

Josephine Baker started her career in the United States in the musical *Shuffle Along* by Eubie Blake and Noble Sissle as a "comedy chorus girl." This character was usually a girl at the end of the series of dancers. She made the audience laugh by awkward movements and was the star of the show's finale. These qualities laid the foundation for Baker's further career: grotesque, parodic traits combined with a special dancing talent. In 1925, Baker made her journey from the United States to Paris. After appearing in the show *La Revue négre* in Paris with her famous banana belt, she became a star practically overnight. Her performances were characterized by a mixture of art forms. Dance was the central element; the artist's signature dance was the Charleston, combined with exotic movements it contrasted the classical dance tradition of Europe. Although Baker started her career as a dancer, she began singing and acting as well. Through documentations of her vocal interpretations on recordings and in movies, her self-created image is accessible to popular culture. Concerning Baker's sexual identity, her son Jean-Claude Baker the author of *Josephine: The Hungry Heart* (2001) has opened up the discussion by calling his mother a "lover of women" in her biography, never attempting to deny her affairs with women throughout her life. In retrospect, Josephine Baker led one queer life, she might or might not have been bisexual, nevertheless her sexuality on and off stage constructed a certain image. Her self-expression consisted of desires and needs that deviated from the social norms of the 1920s and 1930s.

The origin of Baker's exoticized image is the "danse de sauvage," the "Dance of the Savages," first performed by her in *La Revue négre*. Her performance in the famous banana belt on the stage of the Folies Bergère was the decisive moment for her popularity, drawing a picture she was bound to in popular culture. The costumes, made of plush bananas, and Baker's nakedness were the significant details of her image. The rhythmic, isolated movements of her seemingly boneless body, paired with grotesque poses, served the stereotypical sexualized fantasy of the erotic beauty derived from an exotic place called the jungle. Baker's "banana dance" reveals two essential characteristics of her performance: her costume and her dancing. Her naked skin worked as a surface of the sexualized racial differences for the European audience, combined with a multitude of possible perspectives of interpretation concerning her costume. The border between desire and identification seemed blurred. The viewer was not safe from the strange other, but drawn into a scenario by himself pulling the strings (Cheng, 2011, p. 47). Baker's movements were based on dance steps and elements that emerged from the context of an African American heritage. In the environment of minstrel and vaudeville shows, moderate forms of Ballroom dances had been popularized. The characteristics of the African dance are movements that can also be found in Baker's dance style. The Charleston and its most distinctive features, the trembling body, the changing X and O legs, as well as the inside and outside rotating feet, were associated with Baker. Of particular note in her performance was the combination of dance elements with parodic gestures, including the twisting of the eyes, the "monkey walk," imitating the nod of a chicken as well as stretching out the haunches as the conclusion of her dancing; elements borrowed from the minstrel tradition. Baker's extreme embodiment of the "primitive" can thus be understood as a masquerade. Michael Borshuk noticed to that effect, "Baker's parodic dances exposed the error of the converse assumption in the schema: that blacks were inherently inferior primitives" (Borshuk, 2001, p. 50). By challenging the audience's uncertainty about the meaning of her dance, Baker played with colonial symbols and the desire of the viewers. In the environment of the music hall, she found a place of colonial fantasies, where she was allowed to play out the ambivalence of her performance.

La Revue négre ran from October until the end of November at the Théâtre des Champs- Elysées and completed its run in a smaller theatre at the end of December in 1925. Following the show's success in Paris, Josephine Baker played a few performances in Brussels and Berlin in 1926 (Horak, 2013, p. 516). Baker's first trip to Berlin signified a change of track for her career supported by the theatre director, intendant, and theatrical producer Max Reinhardt, who first saw the artist performing in New York in 1925. Reinhardt wanted Baker to stay in Berlin by offering to train her as a "proper actress" in the tradition of the German-language theater of the early twentieth century. Baker decided to stay with the Folies Bergère and returned to Paris. As she recalled in her autobiographical account, the reason why she left Berlin was primarily because parts of the music for her new variety show were to be composed by Irving Berlin (Baker et al., 1995 p. 49).

By this time the new Parisian star, Josephine Baker and her reputation as exotic performer had reached Vienna. Moriz Scheyer was reporting from Paris; he described Josephine Baker as "a ruler, an empress" (Moritz Scheyer 1927, cited in Horak, 2013, p. 517). Roman Horak asserted that with the aforementioned description, "Scheyer cannot resist relating this image to that of another Empress Josephine, namely Napoleon's wife" (Horak, 2013, p. 517). When it was announced that Baker would appear in Vienna, taking over a part in a vaudeville show in 1928, her possible presence in Vienna was discussed in various newspapers and magazines. Conservative groups had lobbied the Vienna City Council; two days after Baker's arrival, the council withdrew permission for Baker to perform in the Ronacher Theater, into which her manager had booked her. This happened because of a small technicality, some formal concession that the theater manager had failed to obtain (Wood, 2010). The Ronacher had only one license as a variety theater, which is why the manager booked the Johann Strauss Theater, which had a concession for revue and operetta. The show *Black on White* was premiered in the Johann Strauss Theater on March 1, 1928 and played for three weeks to packed houses. On March 28, at two o'clock in the afternoon, the journalist Georg Braun hit the window of a cinema's display case in the Lower Austrian town of Stein, took out three photos of Josephine Baker, and ripped them apart in rage. Although the culprit was reported by the cinema owner, he was acquitted by the regional district court of a charge of property damage. The judge recognized in his malefaction an act of "moral self-defense" (Lamprecht, 2009, p. 150). However, the Baker affair had long since run its course; the criminal act of the journalist is only the late end of a campaign against Josephine Baker.

Newspaper articles constructed an image of Baker that was based on stereotypes of racism and sexism and on the assumption that she was seriously attacking the values of traditional European culture, threatening the Viennese culture (Horak, 2013, p. 525). A heated debate for or against Josephine Baker, similar to classical political debates, took place, and simultaneously Baker was featured in forms of a new, modern entertainment press that was present in Vienna at that time. Reports on the arrival of Baker in Vienna, on her various pets, her likes and dislikes were offered to the reader (Horak, 2013, p. 520). A feature called "Josephine Baker-Bulletin" in the *Wiener Allgemeine Zeitung* informed about her sleepless nights and documented her ten suitcases of clothes, which contained, amongst other things, 137 outfits, 196 pairs of shoes, and 64 kilos of powder (*Josephine Baker-Bulletin*, 1928). In Austria, a country with no music hall tradition, most of the population wasn't aware of the kinds of shows in which Baker appeared. Nevertheless, Vienna had been plastered with posters of a nude Baker wearing nothing but pearls and an ostrich feather. All the significant newspapers reported on the revue, so consequently they can be used to give an impression of the show. The revue consisted of a total of 42 scenes or pictures; Baker performed in only five of them (Horak, 2013, p. 520). The impressions were diverse; not only of the show, but also of Josephine Baker's performance. Emil Kläger, reviewer of the *Neue Freie Presse*, was impressed by Baker, "Such a surprise: this woman is negro kraal and the latest in Parisian fashion at one and the same time" (Kläger, 1928). Ernst Fischer from the *Arbeiterwille* described her as "beautiful negro [who] was too natural, too uncomplicated, too unerotic for the Viennese" (Fischer, 1928). The Austrian media did not mention Baker's sexuality; the othering took place on the levels of origin, skin color, and an artificial attributed naturalness. Josephine Baker, as exoticized construct, triggered the fascination with her ambiguity in the midst of a dialectical field of tension between white and Black. Depending on the viewer's perspective, Baker appeared as barbaric original, as uncivilized, as an incarnation of secret wishes, as erotic-mysterious, and simultaneously grotesque.

Conclusion

By analyzing queer lines in specific jazz contexts, focusing on Ma Rainey, Gladys Bentley, and Josephine Baker, who were historicized as queer performers in the Jazz Age, this chapter concludes that the aforementioned female artists worked as cultural precursor to the queer movement of the 1970s and to queer musicianship in a society structured by heteronormativity, patriarchy, white supremacy, and neoliberalism. In the reception, analysis, and historicization of Baker, Rainey, and Bentley straightening and queering happened over and over. "Genders can be neither true nor false, neither real nor apparent, neither original nor derived. As credible bearers of those attributes, however, genders can also be rendered thoroughly and radically *incredible*" (Butler, 1990, p. 180, original emphasis). Black, negro, too natural, undesirable, bulldagger, too unerotic, entertainer, ruler, empress lover, cross-dressing, self-assured, domesticated, blues singing, piano playing; these categorization and classification constituted a specific image of these three female artists, who contributed to their reception in jazz history and at the same time informed more radical possibilities for subsequent generations and current queer musicianship.

References

Albertson, C. (2003). *Bessie*. Yale University Press (Kindle Edition).

"An Old Actor's Memories: What Mr Edmon S. Conner Recalls About his Career." (1881, June 5). *New York Times*. Retrieved from Padgett, K. *Blackface! Minstrel Shows*. http://black-face.com/jim-crow.htm. Original Source: https://timesmachine.nytimes.com/timesmachine/1881/06/05/98559069.pdf.

Baker, J. and Boillon, J. (1995). *Josephine*. Marlowe.

Baker, J.-C. (2001). *Josephine Baker: The Hungry Heart*. Cooper Square Press.

Bentley, G. (1952, August). I Am a Woman Again. *Ebony*, 7(10), 92–98.

Borshuk, M. (2001). An Intelligence of the Body: Disruptive Parody Through Dance in the Early Performances of Josephine Baker. In D. Fischer-Hornung and A. D. Goeller (Eds.), *Embodying Liberation. The Black Body in American Dance* (pp. 41–58). Lit Verlag.

Boyd, N. A. (2001). Same-Sex Sexuality in Western Women's History. *Frontiers: A Journal of Women's Studies*, 22(3), 13–21.

Brathwaite, L. F. (2013, Mar. 11). Gay Jazz Club During Harlem Renaissance Gets One Last Hit—A Wrecking Ball. *Queerty*. www.queerty.com/ubangi-club-gay-harlem-renaissance-20130311.

Butler, J. (1990). *Gender Trouble: Feminism and the Subversion of Identity*. Routledge.

Cheng, A. A. (2011). *Second Skin. Josephine Baker and the Modern Surface*. Oxford University Press.

Church, M. M. (2018*). If This Be Sin: Gladys Bentley and the Performance of Identity*. [Doctoral Dissertation, University of South Carolina]. Scholar Commons. https://scholarcommons.sc.edu/etd/4706.

Dahl, L. (1984). *Stormy Weather: The Music and Lives of a Century of Jazz Women*. Pantheon.

Davis, A. (1995). I Used to Be Your Sweet Mama: Ideology, Sexuality, and Domesticity in the Blues of Gertrude 'Ma' Rainey and Bessie Smith. In E. Grosz and E. Probyn (Eds.), *Sexy Bodies: The Strange Carnalities of Feminism* (pp. 231–265). Routledge.

Davis, A. (1999). *Blues Legacies and Black Feminism: Gertrude 'Ma' Rainey, Bessie Smith, and Billie Holiday*. Vintage.

Davis, A. (2011). Ideology, Sexuality and Domesticity. In S. C. Tracy (Ed.), *Write Me a Few of Your Lines: A Blues Reader* (pp. 470–502). University of Massachusetts Press.

Day, M. (2016, July 1). Bulldykers and Lady Lovers: The Rumors About Lesbian Blues Singers Were All True. *Timeline*. https://timeline.com/lesbian-blues-harlem-secret-f3da10ec2334.

Eagle, B. and LeBlanc, E. S. (2013). *Blues: A Regional Experience*. Praeger.

Fischer, E. (1928, March 8). Die schwarze Schmach in Wein [sic!]. *Arbeiterwille*.

Garber, E. (1989). A Spectacle in Color: The Lesbian and Gay Subculture of Jazz Age Harlem. In M. Duberman, M. Vicinus, and G. Chauncey (Eds.), *Hidden From History: Reclaiming the Gay and Lesbian Past* (pp. 318–331). NAL.

Garber, M. (2013). Bisexuality and the Eroticism of Everyday Life. Routledge.

Giaimo, C. (2016, April 27). The Queer Black Woman Who Reinvented the Blues. *Atlas Obscura*. www.atlasobscura.com/articles/the-queer-black-woman-who-reinvented-the-blues.

"Gladys Bentley A New Blues Star on Okeh Electric Race Records." (1928, September 26). *New York Amsterdam News*.

Halberstam, J. (1997). Mackdaddy, Superfly, Rapper: Gender, Race, and Masculinity in the Drag King. *Queer Transexions of Race, Nation, and Gender*, 52/53, 104–131. www.jstor.org/stable/466736.

Harrison, D. D. (1990). *Black Pearls: Blues Queens of the 1920s*. Rutgers University Press.

Horak, R. (2013). 'We Have Become Niggers!': Josephine Baker as a Threat to Viennese Culture. *Culture Unbound*, 5, 515–530.

Jones, R. V. (2012). How Does a Bulldagger Get Out of the Footnote? Or Gladys Bentley's Blues. *ninepatch: A Creative Journal for Women and Gender Studies*, 1(31), 1–17.

"Josephine Baker-Bulletin." (1928, February 5). *Wiener Allgemeine Zeitung*.

Kläger, E. (1928, Mar. 2). Die Baker tanzt. *Neue Freie Presse*.

Lamprecht, W. (2009). *Jazzkritik in Österreich. Chronik, Dokumente, Stellungnahmen*. Löcker.

Lhamon, W. T. (2003). *Jump Jim Crow Lost Plays, Lyrics, and Street Prose of the First Atlantic Popular Culture.* Harvard University Press.

Lieb, S. (1983). *Mother of the Blues: A Study of Ma Rainey.* University of Massachusetts Press.

Lott, E. (2013). *Love and Theft: Blackface Minstrelsy and the American Working Class.* Oxford University Press.

McGaskomay, J. (2015, May 14). The Mother and the Empress: Ma Rainey and Bessie Smith. *Biography.* www. biography.com/news/bessie-smith-ma-rainey-biography.

Oakley, G. (1997). *Devil's Music.* Da Capo Press.

Oliver, P. (2001). Rainey, Ma (née Pridgett, Gertrude). *Grove Dictionary of Music and Musicians.* Oxford University Press.

Palmer, R. (1984, Oct. 28). The Real Ma Rainey Had a Certain Way with the Blues. *The New York Times.* www.nytimes.com/1984/10/28/theater/the-real-ma-rainey-had-a-certain-way-with-the-blues.html.

Peppers, M. (2013, July 11). The Lesbian Blues Singers of 1920s Harlem: How Speakeasies and Underground Jazz Bars Became a Home-From-Home for New York's 'Sexual Deviants'. *Daily Mail.* www.dailymail.co.uk/femail/article-2360792/The-lesbian-blues-singers-1920s-Harlem-How-speakeasies-underground-jazz-bars-home-home-New-Yorks-sexual-deviants.html.

Scheyer, M. (1927, January 5). Josephine. *Neues Wiener Tagblatt.*

Serlin, D. (2004). *Replaceable You: Engineering the Body in Postwar America.* University of Chicago Press.

Southern, E (1997). *The Music of Black Americans: A History*, W. W. Norton & Company.

Strong, L. Q. (2006). Josephine Baker's Hungry Heart. *The Gay & Lesbian Review.* https://glreview.org/article/article-959/.

Tucker, S. (2008). When Did Jazz Go Straight? A Queer Question for Jazz Studies. *Critical Studies in Improvisation/ Études critiques en improvisation,* 4(2), 1–16. www.criticalimprov.com/index.php/csieci/article/view/850/1410

Wood, E. (2010). *The Josephine Baker Story.* Omnibus Press (E-Book).

Young, W. (1939). Gladys Bentley. *Biographical Sketches: Negroes of New York.* Schomburg Center, New York Public Library: WPA Writers Program.

Videography

Berne, J. (Director). (1941). *Soundie: Hot Chocolate ("Cottontail")* [Film]. R.C.M. Productions.

Al Minns and Leon James on DuPont Show of the week [TV series]. (1961). www.youtube.com/watch?v=KJsBa2u9aMQ.

Philipson, R. (Director). (2011). *T'Ain't Nobody's Bizness: Queer Blues Divas of the 1920s* [Film]. Shoga Films.

5

BLACK AGAINST THE STAVE

Black Modern Girls in British Interwar Jazz

Jessica Chow

Clarifying Statement: Although this research focuses specifically on the cisgender women in the Blackbirds cast, it is worth noting that the Modern Girl body of research includes different genders across the spectrum with additional areas that remains to be researched. One of the many traits of the Modern Girl was her androgynous style and sexual liberation (briefly explored later in this chapter). Further selected readings related to different gender identities and sexualities in the context of global Modern Girls includes *Fashioning Sapphism* (Doan, 2000), *Becoming Modern* (Chadwick and Latimer, 2003), *Becoming Modern Women* (Suzuki, 2010), and *Making Modern Love* (Sigel, 2012).

The "Apotheosis of Jazz": Blackbirds of 1926

Along with the global popularity of jazz increasing in the interwar period, so too was the notion that women were gaining increasing financial independence to participate in consumerism and leisurely pursuits. These circumstances allowed women to engage in modernity and consumerism, creating a model of women termed 'The Modern Girl.' The Modern Girl's vitality and jazz-loving style was a contrast to the bleak devastation of World War I. With identifying features of short, bobbed hair and a slim athletic body, she was seen in all forms of media; from fashion advertisements commodifying her, to real performers who embodied her likeness. According to The Modern Girl Around the World (Weinbaum et al., 2008) research group based at the University of Washington and their Tokyo-based sister research group, the Modern Girl can be identified as "including bobbed hair, painted lips, provocative clothing, elongated body, and open, easy smile" (p. 2). Furthermore, the research group argued that these visual traits, although with variations between different portrayals, were universal in many different countries around the world, including the United States, China, Germany, and Britain (Weinbaum et al., 2008).

Despite these identifiable visual attributes of the Modern Girl, The Modern Girl Around the World Group believed she was not just an aesthetic phenomenon; she represented ideas of modernity, women's rights, and changing gender roles for all women. Her figure was commodified by consumerism, controlled and challenged by governmental ideas and by societies, as well as representing a change in gender roles globally. Her critics argued that these women were symbols of immorality and detrimental to the image of the nation. So broad was her influence and appeal that the research

DOI: 10.4324/9781003081876-6

group proposed several key themes that characterized her, three of which will be explored in more detail. In brief, these are:

- The Modern: This theme questioned the factors that contributed to the Modern Girl's modernity and its defining features.
- The Girl: This theme questioned the classification of the term 'the girl' in media and its different iterations of her image around the world.
- Visual Economics: Looking from a visual perspective, this theme explores the idea of Modern Girls becoming increasingly visible in public roles, and their appearance being commodified.

In contrast to the highly female-centered scope of The Modern Girl study, the academic discourse surrounding jazz is often orientated to male music figures and a limited canon of selected masterpieces. In *Jazz Among The Discourses*, Krin Gabbard (1995) wrote that while he remains hopeful that future jazz studies will incorporate research from musicology, sociology, critical theory, and other disciplines, jazz history has been mostly written by non-academic jazz critics. Gabbard continued that this resulted in the romanticization of favored male jazz artists. Catherine Tackley (née Parsonage) (1999) furthered Gabbard's opinion that the canonization of jazz music "led to a typified, linear history of the genre that has essentially served to strengthen and perpetuate the notion of jazz as 'America's classical music'" (p. ix). Gabbard's ideas were inspired by poet David Meltzer in his book *Writing Jazz* (1999) – an anthology of historical writings on jazz by African American musicians, critics, writers, and poets (Gabbard, 1995; Meltzer, 1999). In Writing Jazz, Meltzer suggested the notion that the idea and terming of 'jazz' was invented by White people in an attempt to colonize and control the genre (Meltzer, 1999). Nathaniel Mackey (1995) furthered this by theorizing that changing the word 'jazz' from noun to verb meant "the erasure of Black inventiveness by white appropriation" (p. 77). He proposed that that the noun was a "white commodification" that "obscures or 'disappears' the 'verb' it rips off, Black agency, Black authority, Black invention" (p. 77). As Mackey, Tackley, and Meltzer believed, jazz history was largely authored from a White-dominated perspective that selected key figures and events that fit into this ideal canon of jazz timeline, overlooking many performers and performances that did not fit into this idealized history. Therefore, here I look further from this canon by exploring how the Black Modern Girls studied were indeed influential with both jazz enthusiasts as well as the general British public. It is because of this that I build on gradually growing attention towards the contribution of Black female performers to British interwar jazz by combining the highly female-oriented studies of the Modern Girl research. There are limitations in resources and material artifacts as many early jazz recordings are either destroyed, missing, contain inaccurate information or otherwise non-existent. In this chapter I will not analyze the jazz music itself; rather, I will use the subject genre and the role of Modern Black Women involved as a means by which to contextualize the social, cultural, and political significance they had.

A key definition that needs to be considered for this chapter is the term, 'girls'. *The Modern Girl Around The World* (2008) research group raised concerns on addressing modern women as 'girls' as it signifies immaturity (pp. 8–10). In addition, the group notes the term 'girl' (as well as 'boy') is associated with derogatory meanings as it was a racial insult in the Jim Crow era United States. These terms often implied 'backwardness' and were used to marginalize Black Americans. Despite this, the group raised the point that the term 'girl' was popular in England from the 1880s onwards, representing "working-class and middle-class unmarried women who occupied an ephemeral free space between childhood and adulthood" (2008). In addition, the term 'girl' is often used in jazz discourses (such as 'chorus girls') to relate to youth and vitality.[1] Therefore, I will be using the term 'girl' to describe the Black Modern Women discussed in this chapter.

For this chapter, the *Blackbirds* jazz revue produced by British theater manager Charles Cochran, which ran at the London Pavillion from 1926 to 1927, will be used as a case study to examine the wider context of Black women in British interwar jazz culture. This chapter is divided into four sections. First, there is a brief exploration of the setting of the revue and its perceived modernity and an 'authentic' depiction of Black culture for British audiences. The second section will address the metaphorical masks used as different identities to veil and control oneself during performances. Third, I discuss the varying perception of Black and Modern Girl's visible bodies, situated within Foucault's body's power dynamic and the gaze of the audience. Further examinations of how Black female performers' skin complexion and bodies became a subject of discussion within the press leads to the final section, where I look at the overview of the Black Modern Girl's agency.

Setting the Stage

On 11 September 1926, the revue *Blackbirds* written by White New York-based Russian émigré Lew Leslie and produced by White British producer Charles B. Cochran opened at the London Pavillion at Piccadilly Circus after showings at *Les Ambassadeurs,* the glamourous theater in Paris. The principal star of the show, Florence Mills, was a Black American woman who had previously performed at the same theater in Cochran's (1923) *Doverstreet to Dixie. Doverstreet to Dixie* was divided into two parts; the first part presented performances from an all-White ensemble, and the second part consisted of an all-Black cast (Egan, 2004). This arrangement was apparently due to British actors' appeal to the British Home Office for protection, forcing Cochran to split his show to encompass a British cast in the first half of the revue ("C.B Cochran Scrapbooks 36", n.d.). In 1927, a similar issue recurred with the Blackbirds revue when an application was made to the Ministry of Labour for a "renewal of the permits without which no foreign artist is allowed to work in this country" ("C.B Cochran Scrapbooks 36", n.d.). A resulting 'Alien Restriction Act' established that 50 percent of an orchestra should be composed of British subjects (*Daily Chronicle*, 1927, May 11). This act may have been adopted because British performers were possibly resentful of the foreigners taking their job opportunities due to the popularity of African American style, which shows the anxieties of maintaining British identity.

The Blackbirds of 1926 was one of the first all-Black jazz performance revues seen in London. The initial start of Blackbirds was delayed due to difficulties with transporting costumes to London as Edmond Sayag, the manager of *Les Ambassadeurs* had claimed a contractual right for Blackbirds to continue in Paris for an additional ten weeks. Additionally, there was animosity within the orchestral band with White musicians refusing to perform alongside Black musicians. This was resolved with a "No work-full pay" agreement with White musicians to prevent a labor action from the union (Egan, 2004). Despite these setbacks, Cochran's Blackbirds' revue successfully opened with the Plantation Orchestra in September 1926, netting almost a thousand pounds in the opening night's two shows (Egan, 2004). For many of the White British audiences, Blackbirds was representative of the 'jazz craze'. The *Manchester Guardian* described Blackbirds as "Jazz in Its Most Strident Form", whereas *The Sackbut* praised that Blackbirds was the "apotheosis of jazz" (*Manchester Guardian*, 1926; *The Sackbut* 1926).

In addition to representing jazz, Blackbirds appeared to be an exclusive and possibly first glimpse into the expectation of Black culture for the White audience – an experience that they possibly perceived as foreign, exciting, and exotic. In an article published in *The Sackbut* in October 1926, Horace Shipp enthusiastically wrote of his experience watching the Blackbirds revue. Shipp said the lyrics in songs by Black performers contained "double meanings, symbolizing the most exotic and up-to-date vices" and that he was puzzled with the ambiguity of several phrases such as " 'love', 'heart', 'girl', 'mammy', 'home', 'rose', and 'chillun'"(1926). As well as the 'authentic' dialogue in the revue, there was praise for the 'realism' of the Blackbirds sets. An article in the *Dancing Times* titled Notes on Decor described in detail that although the settings were considered 'simple' in comparison to the opulence in Cochran's other shows, they were highly praised for their authenticity (Fussel, 1926). This is in part perhaps due to details such as the wheel paddle in "A Levee inn on the Mississippi" as well as the huts in "Jungle nights in Dixie land", which were reminiscent of Indigo Jones sets. Brian Ward (2014) wrote in *Music, Musical Theater, And The Imagined South In Interwar Britain* that interwar Black musical theater performances such as Blackbirds were often set in two types of popular settings (pp. 39–72). On one hand, performances that were set in Harlem during the Harlem Resistance represented a bustling setting of a fast-paced urban and modern life (Ward, 2014). In contrast, shows such as Blackbirds were set in 'Down South' or 'Dixieland' – a nostalgic countryside fantasy location that Ward described as "pastoral, organic place of tradition, stability, and clearly delineated racial, gender, and class hierarchies – a land of timeless certainties and a safe haven from the disorienting flux of modern, increasingly urban life" (Ward, 2014, p. 46). For the audience, the differentiation between the two types and the one that Blackbirds were designed into was clear. After the 1936 remake of Blackbirds, in an article for *Theatre World*, E. Mawby Green warned audiences not to "confuse the Southern Negro with the hot-cha Harlem type" (Ward, 2014, p. 64).

In Jean Baudrillard's *Simulacra and Simulation*, Baudrillard theorized the idea of a simulated space (or imitated reality) that uses symbols and imagery to represent realism within another space (Baudrillard, 1983). Baudrillard (1983) gives an example of television, writing that the audience are active participants in constructing the simulated reality by projecting their self ideals and identity back to the television. Therefore, using Ward's theory that performances like Blackbirds are fictitious realities that the audience projected their own anxieties of modernity upon, Blackbirds could be considered a simulated world or microcosm using stereotypical signs and symbols that the White audience perceived were part of Black culture. As Ward noted, this anti-modern depiction of traditional culture within jazz was comforting Britain in a period of uncertain rapid industrial and social transformation. In an article in *The Outlook* (1927) the author stated that although the performers in Blackbirds "did not exactly furnish an entertainment suitable for a vicarage lawn in a garden suburb" they made the audience feel that "just the other side of the threshold we ourselves are still feral" (*The Outlook*, 1927, May 7). Shows such as Blackbirds represented a microcosmic glimpse into Black culture for the White audiences, giving them a sense of racial superiority in the interwar period that demanded the stability of the national identity.

In May 1927, Blackbirds was moved out of the London Pavillion to accommodate Cochran's new show (*Daily Chronicle*, 1927, May 11). The Blackbirds cast then toured around major cities in Britain, but the strenuous schedule as well as five years' worth of continuous performances took a toll on Mills's health, and she had to be flown back to New York in an attempt to recover (Egan, 2004). Unfortunately, Mills's health never recovered and she died of tuberculosis two months after her arrival in New York, aged just thirty-one (Egan, 2004). The media's eulogies for Mills and the thousands that flocked the streets in Harlem to attend her funeral highlighted her impact on society and her legacy. Her musical talent, which earned her a great salary, as well as her religious beliefs, love for her mother, charitable deeds, and her public campaigning for racial equality were all subjects of the media's attention. Mills's romanticized life story as the daughter of two ex-slaves and her rise to stardom from a young age, was an inspirational story that caused her death to be lamented in the media ("C.B Cochran scrapbooks 36", n.d.). Mills paved the way for future Black jazz musicians in the industry.

Performing Masks and Playing Roles

In Erving Goffman's *The Presentation of Self in Everyday Life* (1956) and his following writings such as *Frame Analysis* (1974), he explores the theory that it is innate in society to adopt different identity performances in daily interactions, depending on location and situation (Goffman, 1956; 1974).

Goffman uses the drama metaphor of a 'mask' that can veil oneself in face-to-face interactions, and that different masks are used in different situations and to different audiences (Goffman, 1956; 1974). Another dramaturgical theory that is useful in this chapter study of Blackbirds is that of American philosopher and gender academic Judith Butler, who wrote an article titled "Performative Acts and Gender Constitution: An Essay in Phenomenology and Feminist Theory" in the *American Theatre Journal* (Butler, 1988). In this article and in Butler's following academic writings, such as *Gender Trouble* (1990), she proposed the idea that gender is a construct of expected roles within society. These dramaturgy theories, if studied through the previously explored Baudrillian lens, signify that the roles the Blackbirds cast performed were a reflection of the audience's own self as well as British interwar society.

These dramaturgical ideas of Goffman and Butler relate to the academic discourses that Modern Girls also participated in performing different roles or masks. In the chapter titled "Racial Masquerade: Consumption and Contestation of American Modernity" from *The Modern Girl Around the World*, Alys Weinbaum (2008) presents the idea that masks and masquerade were associated with the Modern Girl due to its popularity and representation in various different media during the interwar period (pp. 120–121). Weinbaum (2008) says further that because masks are inherently associated with "dress-up, sartorial display, and cosmetic use", a consumer culture was made possible as the masks represented a form of "racialized femininity" (p. 120). As Weinbaum (2008) argues, by being able to control the wearing of these masks, one is able to achieve the status of being 'modern'. Furthermore, the ability of purchasing and wearing these racial masks or "racial masquerade", allows one to show their "otherness" and distance themselves to the character that the mask is presenting, and those that were unable to participate in this activity were "pre-modern" or "primitive" (p. 121). Therefore, as Weinbaum suggests, "blackfacing" and minstrel performances were types of racial masks that were capable of being controlled and a symbol of modernity.

This analogy of wearing masks to represent a new character is interesting in the context of the Blackbirds revue as, although there is no evidence that the women themselves participated in blackfacing for this production, there were a couple of acts where a racial mask was donned. For example, in a scene titled "Chop Suey for One", a Black performer (John Rucker) used blackface by darkening his skin with cork, and another Black performer (Sydney Perrin) wore stereotypical Asian clothing to play a racially charged and "yellow-faced" character called "Ah Sing" (*London Pavilion*, 1927). Although not as extreme as "blackfacing" or "yellow-facing", another form of dressing of a different race that the cast of Blackbirds participated in was through their Asian and Native American inspired costumes, wearing headpieces such as a feather headdress or turban. Alys Weinbaum (2008) explained the notion of non-White performers playing a racial char-acter in this manner: "In distancing themselves from Blackness such performers gained entry into whiteness" (p. 124). Thus, by participating in this racial masquerade that was normally engaged in by White performers, these Black performers were almost able to shake off and control their racial differences.

Including the stereotypical role-playing of other races that the Blackbirds cast performed, there were audience expectations of the cast to intensify their Black identities. When Lew Leslie reintroduced the 1934 edition of Blackbirds to London's Coliseum Theatre, he was quoted saying, "The great thing I try to impress upon all these young people is not to 'go white,' So many of them, when they come over here, try to forget their origin and talk like Europeans, act like Europeans, think like Europeans. I tell them No! Be yourselves" (Ward, 2014, p. 62). This view was likely from a business standpoint, rather than empathy for the Black performers' autonomy, as according to Brian Ward (2014), Leslie "appreciated that it was the perceived racial authenticity of his performers that was 'responsible for the Blackbirds' remarkable vogue 'among white audiences'" (p. 62). The Blackbirds cast therefore performed stereotypical roles expected of them such as a "mammy" figure or an "exotic" beauty like that of Black American-born performer Josephine Baker during the start of her career, as this was easier to market (Wood, 2000).

The highly contested "mammy figure" that dates back to the 1830s, was a fictional character of an enslaved Black woman who was often depicted as helping with domestic housework such as cooking and looking after White children (McElya, 2009). Although this figure was a fictitious character, nonetheless, she symbolized an idea of the "[American] national past and political future that blurs the line between myth and memory, guilt and justice, stereotype and individuality, commodity and humanity" (McElya, 2009, pp. 3–4). In Blackbirds this mammy figure, characterized by her voluptuous figure and bandana-wearing style, played a dominant role in the set design with a large cardboard illustration serving as the backdrop for the opening scene. In addition to the visual representation, several of the songs referenced the mammy figure played by Black African American performer Edith Wilson, including "Mammie's Birthday" and "Mammie's Day in Dixieland" (*London Pavilion*, 1927). A newspaper review of Blackbirds wrote that it was 'natural' for Black performers to sing these sentimental songs about their mothers, but when "ordinary" performers (presumably White) do so, it sounded "cheap and foolish" (*Star*, 1926). These additions to the revue shows the attempt to add perceived Black culture which conformed to the mostly White audience's expectations of the Black female figure.

The existence of the mammy figure in the Blackbirds review additionally raised ideas about motherhood and domestic roles. For example, an author named 'The Gallery Girl' praised the mammy portrayal in the *Star* newspaper, but criticized the lack of real Black children to complete the "perfect picture" (*Star*, 1926, August 20). The same critic wrote in another review a few months later criticizing the lack of male figures in the revue, calling for "Better Balanced Homes!" (*Star*, 1927, January 15). In the article titled *No Bouquets For Father – Why?*, The Gallery Girl wrote that " 'Mammie' gets a very good, good show, while father is not even allowed to put in an appearance in the wedding scene. Father, not mother, it must be remembered, usually holds the purse" (*Star*, 1927, January 15). The mammy figure became a powerful image of motherhood and domesticity – a role which would not otherwise have been considered innate in Black women's nature during this period (McElya, 2009). Therefore, despite women's growing financial independence with an increasing number of jobs available for the interwar Modern Girl, the mammy model contrastingly was expected to be a domestic and mother figure – limiting potential job prospects for Black women.

This conflict between women's roles as a domestic motherly figure and modern women seeking opportunities outside traditional household roles was a prominent debate during the interwar period. In the discourses surrounding the Japanese equivalent of the Modern Girl, the Moga, academics such as Sharon Minichiello wrote about these contesting models of women. One of these models represented 'free' and seemingly Western ideas of the "threat of cultural and sexual liberation" (Minichiello, 2001, p. 19). In contrast, the other female model represents an old-fashioned "Good Wife/Wise Mother" a traditional and domestic figure that was often promoted by the Japanese government as an antidote to the supposed sexual deviance of the Modern Girl (Minichiello, 2001). It could be argued that the Black mammy figure represented in Blackbirds is similar to this Japanese "Good Wife/Wise Mother", as she is similarly old-fashioned, domestic and unthreatening to existing moral principles. Any divergence from this stereotypical mammy role expected of Black women was seen as immoral attempts to be Western or acting 'too White,' echoing criticisms that met the Japanese Modern Girl.

Carol Tulloch (2016) offered a different perspective on the mammy figure in *The Birth of Cool*. Tulloch (2016) considered that the characteristic apron donned by stereotypical mammy figures (including the Blackbirds's version) was symbolic of "freedom in the constrained frame of colonialism" (p. 38). The apron as well the headwrap or bandana (seen in the Blackbirds depiction) were visual signifiers of social status and occupation, recognizable in the West as they were seen regularly in advertisements and later in Hollywood films such as 1939's *Gone With the Wind* (Tulloch, 2016, pp. 31–49). Tulloch (2016) further proposes that these garments were translated through different mediums, and symbolized the "women's ability and right to work, and their movement from one place to another" (p. 49). She believed that they were components in the ability to transform and style the body in the pursuit of both political and/or personal freedom (Tulloch, 2016). Considering Tulloch's analogy, the mammy figure was comparable to the Modern Girl figure as she too was a female character depicted in media through visual material culture signifiers symbolizing women's freedom of movement and work through a traditional lens. I argue that Black female performers who traveled from the United States to Britain simultaneously represented modernity, as well as captured the public's imagination of far-away 'exotic' worlds, which epitomizes the inherent contradiction faced by women in this period between; a growing freedom of movement and ability to work, and archetypal cultural stigma forcing this expression through traditional perceptions.

This far-away and exotic fantasy was intensified in the "Jungle Nights in Dixieland" scene where Mills and other female performers were dressed in grass skirts and bralet sets. The commercial photographs that were taken from this scene and printed in the newspapers show Mills brandishing a staff-like stick with a snarling face, perpetuating the 'savage' stereotype. In another photograph we see Mills sitting cross-legged on the floor of a grass hut with the chorus girls hunched over, hands on their wide-spread legs (Figure 5.1). It could be argued that although the women were racially

Oct. 13, 1926 — *The Sketch* — 87

Coloured Artists' Revue at the London "Pav."

" JUNGLE NIGHTS IN DIXIELAND " : MISS FLORENCE MILLS AND THE PLANTATION GIRLS.

Figure 5.1 Reprinted from "Coloured Artists' Revue at the London 'Pav.'", The Sketch, 1926, October 13, p. 87.

Source: Courtesy of Victoria and Albert Museum, London.

objectified, the fetishism of these women gave Black women empowerment to be sexually implicit. Angela Davis (1998) wrote that music of this period, such as the blues, allowed women and men to autonomously express sexual love that was previously rarely expressed during slavery (p. 4) – for example, in the song 'Don't Advertise Your Man' sung by Edith Wilson in the second edition of the 1926 Blackbirds revue. This was possibly a rendition of a song by the same name recorded in 1924 by African American Clara Smith (Martin Gibbs, 2012, p. 200). Smith's version gives advice to women "to be wise" and that it is "alright to have a little bird in the bush, but it ain't like the one that you've got in your hand", which I believe shows growing acceptance of women's agency and independence in relationships (Smith, 1924).

Another gender identity that was challenged in Blackbirds was Florence Mills's cross-dressing portrayal of a Black boy, "Sammy", in the opening act (Modern, 1927, March 14). Sammy may have been purposely chosen as it relates to the derogatory name to refer to Black people of the period – "Sambo" from the childrens' story book depicting a Black boy in *The Story of Little Black Sambo* (Bannerman, 1899). Cross-dressing and androgynous stylings such as this were traits of the Modern Girl model. According to Liz Conor, adopting "mannish fashion" allowed the Modern Girl to be able to challenge and divert away from sexual responsibilities of motherhood (Conor, 2004). Conor continues that by parodying masculinity, this in turn intensified the Modern Girl's sexual mobility and agency by being able to control the illusion of their gender spectacle (Conor, 2004). As American political scientist Michael Rogin wrote, by cross-dressing one is able to comparably expose the rigid boundaries and categories of identity that "Whites should be Whites" and "Blacks should be Blacks" (Rogin, 2007, p. 32). With Mills cross-dressing as a Black male, she challenged the ideas of how a Black woman should appear and act.

Performing Black Bodies

In Jayna Brown's book *Babylon Girls: Black Women Performers and the Shaping of the Modern*, Brown studied interwar Black female bodies' value and symbolisms when "in motion". Brown likened the chorus girls' bodies to industrial capitalism due to their disciplined movements, which include "principles of uniformity, precision of routine, and efficiency of movement" (Brown, 2009, p. 164). Brown argues that they embody the industrial development of this period, writing, "In the age of electricity and machines, the human body in its various motor capacities became the form through which the modern was designed" (Brown, 2009). Further to this, the chorus girls' uniformity through their matching dance movements, appearance, and costumes was comparable to factory mass production where repetition and 'sameness' are created. Similar to Brown, Jill Green used Foucault's ideas of 'docile bodies' from *Discipline and Punishment* to analyze how dancers' bodies are reflective of power, control, and surveillance in society (Green, 2002, pp. 99–126). Here, the definition of the "docile body" is a "body that is manipulated, shaped, trained, which obeys, responds, becomes skillful and increases its forces" (Foucault, 1975/1979, p. 136). Furthermore, Foucault believed that "a body is docile that may be subjected, used, transformed and improved" (Foucault, 1975/1979, p. 136). Therefore, Green theorized that the dancers' bodies can be classified as 'docile' as they "require a system of codification and methods that are, like Foucault's socialized bodies, under meticulous control and surveillance" (Green, 2002, p. 111). Like Brown's analogy, performing bodies are subjected to authoritative social power that is controlled through discipline. These ideas of performing bodies when applied to Black women under the White gaze raises many interesting discussions surrounding surveillance and power of the period. Like the previously mentioned ideas that Blackbirds' set design became a reflection upon self for the audience to either empathize with or contrast against the performers, similar comparisons were made with the skin colors of the women themselves.

The cast members were often accused of not acting and appearing like the racist stereotypes expected of them. For example, the *Daily Herald* accused the Blackbird performers of cheapening their Black culture by attempting to conform to American beauty standards. It wrote that,

> for the Blackbirds are deracialised, with a touch of colour snobbery. Their chorus girls have a white standard of beauty to which they approximate as closely as paint and powder will allow. Their comedians even go to the length of disguising themselves under the ludicrous make-up of a 'Christie Minstrel nigger' with ebony face and enormous thick red lips
>
> *(Daily Herald, 1926)*

An article in the *Empire News* described Florence Mills as a "white negress" and wrote that the audience were fascinated with the cast's ability to appear White due to their blonde bobbed, curl-less wigs and lighter complexion (1926). This article was possibly written in attempted good faith due to the author possibly noticing the similarity between White people and the Blackbirds cast, writing that "sooner or later, however, the barrier must be broken down. While you watch the chorus of the Pavilion show pointing their toes and frisking their frocks, you begin to wonder how long it will be before their race awakens" (*Empire News*, 1926). Therefore, Blackbirds possibly gave audiences a sense of familiarity by offering a glimpse into Black culture and, although it was enmeshed with racist implications, was an early step in paving the way to racial equality.

Despite Blackbirds being the initial steps for racial familiarity of the performers in this revue, there were still anti-miscegenation opinions and fears of immorality from critics. This was particularly apparent in an act showing a Black couple (Edith Wilson and Johnny Hudgins) in bed together. This scene was initially heavily criticized by reviewers when Wilson was mistaken for a White woman due to critics being "deceived by the lady's complexion cream" (*Sphere*, 1926). This illustrates that there was still discrimination against depicting a mixed-raced couple. Despite Black culture being seen as immoral by critics, an article in the *Sphere* (1926) wrote that because of the "naiveté of the Blackbirds' mannerism" there was no offence to this suggestive scene in bed and avoided negative criticism that they would have received if they were a White couple instead (p. 20). Another article wrote that the bed scene was so "childishly proud" and "unsophisticated" that the journalist found no objection to the scene (*Sunday Express*, 1926, September 12). This may suggest that White audiences dismissed and belittled Black couples' sexual implications as merely innocent behaviour or "child-like fooling around", unable to have adult sexual impulses and not taken seriously as equivalent adults.

During the interwar period, female bodies became visible and "touchable", with fashion designed to reveal more flesh and, in particular, slender limbs (Steele, 1985). The media often openly discussed women's bodies in a manner that differed from previous generations (Steele, 1985). This was reflected in the coverage of the Blackbirds revue, which focused on commenting on the skin tone and the body shapes of these black women (notably more greatly than they focused on the men). Women were often portrayed by food-associated adjectives to describe shades such as "coffee", "cream", and "feasts of colour". A brief article in the *Sunday Pictorial* titled 'All Shades' wrote that some of the chorus girls are "coffee-coloured, with lots and lots of milk, not to mention a lump or two of sugar" (*Sunday Pictorial*, 1926, June 19). In addition to commenting on the Blackbird cast's skin color, the media often scrutinized Florence Mills's body figure. Mills's "slender frame" and thin "bird-like legs'" were often the subject of the British media's attention (Egan, 2004, p. 174). According to her husband, Kid Thompson, this attention to Mills's legs caused her to be body-conscious and she used pads to attempt to build up her legs to appear bigger (Egan, 2004). However, this was either not very successful or she soon abandoned the attempt (Egan, 2004). Jane Nicholas (2015) described this

GIRL SINGERS' WINTER BATHING.

SPRING is in the board, if not in the air, when "The Blackbirds," a singing trio at the London Pavilion, go bathing on the Kenwood estate, London.

Figure 5.2 Reprinted from "A Blackbird Pie", *The Illustrated Sporting and Dramatic News*, 1927, March 3.
Source: Courtesy of Victoria and Albert Museum, London.

transformation of the body as a means of "disciplining the body in order to develop a certain status of modern femininity" (p. 39). The interwar period was overwhelmed with modern feminine ideals on how to care for, perform, and create a desirable body (Nicholas, 2015, p. 39).

These opinions on Mills's slender frame were reflected in how she was illustrated in the media. Illustrations such as Figure 5.2, from *The Illustrated and Dramatic Sporting News* depicted Mills's figure as elongated and an almost androgenous body shape. The androgenous and slender body were key characteristics of the Modern Girl and of 1920s fashion (Steele, 1985). The 1920s was associated with youthfulness, which may have been affected by post-war disillusionment with the older generation that let the youth die in the war (Steele, 1985). According to Valerie Steele (1985), the 1920s female's fashion minimized the breasts (which were associated with older and mature women) and accentuated '"long", "straight", "shapely" legs, which were associated with youth"' (p. 239). These slenderized depictions of Mills that followed the 1920s ideals were a contrast to the voluptuous curved figure of the 'mammy' archetype.

Off-stage the Blackbirds cast additionally showed off their bodies as they posed for photos for different newspapers wearing their swimming costumes at bathing parties (Figure 5.3). As Minichiello (2001) wrote, "Along with short hair, another characteristic of the Modern Girl was her healthy physique and athleticism" (p. 20). This period saw an increase of women in public participating in sports. These activities allowed women the freedom to socialize with each other and with the other sex – publicly show off their figures, as well as tone and shape the body to conform to the new athletic body ideal (Skillen, 2013, p. 131). Therefore, activeness and youthful vitality, as well as a display of the healthy body as in Figure 5.3, showing a photograph of the Blackbirds cast, promoted an idealized modern lifestyle to other aspiring Modern Girls. Silverberg (2001) addressed this idea of the commodification of young women's bodies and the display of long legs in particular as a key definition of the Modern Girl. This photo with the cast purposely posing their legs in the air on show was likely using their athletic bodies for promotion of the Blackbirds revue.

A BLACKBIRD PIE.

Figure 5.3 Reprinted from "Girl Singers' Winter Bathing", *Liverpool Courier*, 1926, November 26.
Source: Courtesy of Victoria and Albert Museum, London.

Florence Mills as a Role Model

Due to the success and popularity of the Blackbirds, the cast reached celebrity-like status. Florence Mills was conscious of her power as a performer in the public view, saying, "I like my work on the stage, because it is the quickest way of showing white people that we are really very like them" (Mills, 1926, September 14). During her residence in Britain, Mills often used her renown to express her opinion on racial equality, writing several articles in newspapers and periodicals. For example, in 1927 Mills published an article shortly after the end of the Blackbirds review and before her departure back to the United States. In a piece titled "A Famous Blackbirds' Farewell: When Will Christian Britain Abandon Racial Prejudice?" Mills wrote that despite the mass popularity of Blackbirds that spread across the country in different forms (including on the gramophone) and outside London, her heart ached as Black people still faced racial inequality (Mills, 1927, November 3, p. 4). Mills (1927) wrote of the irony of media praise for the Blackbirds revue alongside articles on the banning of Black people in dance halls and restaurants (p. 4).

Due to Mills publicly campaigning for racial equality, many Black women saw her as a role model. A fan who described herself as 'Madame Davis' enthusiastically wrote to Mills from her home in Holborn:

> Last night I saw your 'show' and never was there a heart prouder than mine, being one of yourselves: I think you are wonderful – yes wonderful indeed I write this to tell you (as a colour woman like yourself) I do thank your whole company for being able to show the white people, who think we are nobody – because we are 'colour' that we can stand side by side and beat them at their own game. Well done, daughter of the Motherland.
>
> *(Gillett, 2010, p. 484; Bressey and Romain, 2018)*

Although "Madame Davis" praised her performance, it was Mills's role as a racial ambassador that was the main source of Davis's admiration (Bressey and Romain, 2018, p. 388). Furthermore, as Caroline Bressey and Gemma Romain (2018) wrote, it was Mills's embodiment of a modern Black woman that was "working, successful, political and candid" that was the cause for such high praise from Davis (p. 390). Thus, for Black women, Mills was an iconic figure who not only gave a voice to racial discrimination, but was a pioneer in promoting the image of the Black Modern Girl.

Mills was additionally a muse for White audiences, particularly due to the high profile attendees to Blackbirds. According to Bill Egan (2004), author of Florence Mills's biography, this enthusiasm for the Blackbirds revue resulted in Black people being increasingly accepted and entertained in respectable social circles (p. 174). It was regularly reported by the media that the then Prince of Wales (later King Edward VIII) attended performances numerous times with his fellow high-society associates. It is estimated that the prince enjoyed the revue so much that he visited between eleven to sixteen times – or more (Egan, 2004, p. 175). Egan further noted that the royals were "the apex for England's class-conscious society, and the large aristocracy and upper-middle class were always keen to follow their lead in matters of fashion in taste" (Egan, 2004, p. 176). Additionally, Blackbirds was a great inspiration for associates of the Bright Young People/Bright Young Things (BYP/BYT); a new generation of wealthy young male and female aristocrats and socialites mostly based in London and Oxford. Many of these associates included key literary and artistic figures such as photographer Barbara Ker-Seymer, artist Edward Burra, and artist Cecil Beaton amongst many others (Egan, 2004, p. 177; Romain, 2017, p. 90; Burra, n.d.). These members of the Bright Young People were so inspired, they reportedly held Blackbirds-themed fancy dress parties. According to Egan (2004), on one occasion guests had to impersonate a living personality, and several turned up as versions of Florence Mills (p. 177). From this anecdote we can glean that perhaps the Blackbirds performers were perceived more as muses and inspiration for the upper echelons of British society than would otherwise have publicly been expected.

In addition to her impact on jazz, art, and literature, Mills was often considered a fashion icon both on and off stage. On stage, the media covered in detail the costumes that were worn by both the audience members and performers in the revue with one reviewer writing that the costumes were "curiously fascinating" due to the "contrast of dusky skin and shimmering white ostrich feathers over chiffon" (Roberts, 1926, January 21). Another article speculated whether dark colored store mannequins in the fashionable London's West End were the result of Florence Mills and the Blackbirds's influence (*Daily News*, 1927, February 10). Likewise, after Mills's death in November 1927, media nationwide advertised stockings with a shade called "Florence Mills" dedicated to the late singer, from several stocking producers such as Eve's Stockings, Robinson and Cleaver's, and D.M. Brown (*Liverpool Echo*, 1928, January 18; Robinson and Cleaver's, 1929, June 24; D. M.

Brown, 1932, April 4). These examples demonstrate that Black women were often restricted to racialized beauty standards due to their skin color, however, they had influential agency as fashion icons for commodity culture.

Despite their broad influence in different echelons of society, including fashion and design, the Blackbirds cast were still separated as racially different. Jeffrey Green (1987) wrote that it was likely that these Black performers who mingled with high-society "perceived the elements of snobbery, sexual curiosity, sympathy for the underdog, and respect for artistic and professional talent in that society" (pp. 431–434). Consequently, the performers were often still seen as a novel commodity or as outsiders to these social circles. In the introduction of *The Modern Girl Around the World*, the research group wrote that commodities such as fashion and beauty products

> traffic in ideas about gender, race, and modernity; trade flows enabled them to materially connect different parts of the world. As marketed and exchanged goods with monetary values, their spread and sale was driven by the capitalist logic of supply, demand, and profitability.
>
> *(Weinbaum, 2008, p. 19)*

Thus, their celebrity-like status made these Black female performers vessels of the British public's market demands for appropriating Black culture.

External to the revue, Mills and the cast members dedicated themselves to social causes such as touring hospitals and charities. Newspapers reported that Mills anonymously gave gifts to hospitals and shelters two or three times a week, garnering her the nickname "Florence 'Nightingale' Mills" by the *Sunday Chronicle* (*Sunday Chronicle*, 1927, March 13). In addition to this, Mills set aside a "substantial" part of her salary for charity (*Sunday Chronicle*, 1927, March 13). These philanthropic deeds were accidentally discovered as she had been borrowing Lew Leslie's car (*Sunday Chronicle*, 1927, March 13). This suggests that Mills was ardent to help social causes without relying on her celebrity status. Publicly, Mills and other members of the cast supported several causes, including Bethnal Green's Hospital for Children as well as performing for over a thousand disabled veterans (*Star*, 1926; *Daily Telegraph*, 1926; *Daily Sketch*, 1926). The widely reported charitable public deeds were likely good publicity for the revue, with Cochran being aware and organizing the actions.

Conclusion

There is a strong correlation between the global spread of jazz and the Modern Girl image. As British music conductor Henry Coward declared in 1926, "You can trace jazz in the modern girl, even in the way she walks" (1926, October 1, p. 5). Indeed, jazz became an outlet for how the Modern Girl image was consumed and jazz performers became the forefront of its visual image distribution globally.

This chapter has aimed to examine how the Black female jazz performers in Blackbirds related to the Modern Girl model and how they navigated these multiple racial and gendered roles in British society. In order to make a comparison, the themes outlined in this chapter's introduction from *The Modern Girls Around the World* will be re-examined in the context of the Blackbirds cast in Britain. To recapitulate, these are "The Modern", "The Girl" and "Visual Economics".

Although there is no found evidence that these women identified themselves as 'Modern Girls' and there are limitations on examining their own agency in the performance as most of their actions were directed by Cochran, these Black women fought racial challenges against a heavily male-dominated industry. There is a lack of existing research on the comparisons between the Black women in British jazz and the Modern Girl model, likely due to their under-representation in historical archival material.

Note

1 Interwar British media such as *Punch* magazine made associations between chorus girls and the representation of Modern Girls (see *Punch*, 1920, February 11). In Charles Cochran's article "Choosing a Chorus Girl" for *The London Magazine*, Cochran explains his selection process (Cochran, 1923). Cochran describes the multi-talented English chorus girl of 1923 as "of bright, alert expression; often with bobbed hair; of slim ankles and slender build" and a contrast to the chorus girls from twenty years or so prior (Cochran, 1923, p. 20).

References

Baudrillard, J. (1983). *Simulations*. New York: Semiotext (e).

Bressey, C., and Romain, G. (2018). Staging race: Florence Mills, celebrity, identity and performance in 1920s Britain. *Women's History Review, 28*(3), 380–395. doi: 10.1080/09612025.2018.1493119.

Bannerman, H. (1899). *The Story of Little Black Sambo* (1st ed.). London: Grant Richards.

Brown, J. (2009). *Babylon Girls: Black Women Performers and the Shaping of the Modern* (1st ed.). Durham: Duke University Press.

Burra, E. (n.d.). *Papers of Edward Burra: 1901–70S*. [Collection of personal papers and sketches] (TGA 771). Tate Archive, London.

Butler, J. (1988). Performative Acts and Gender Constitution: An Essay in Phenomenology and Feminist Theory. *Theatre Journal, 40*(4), 519–531. doi: 10.2307/3207893.

Butler, J. (1990). *Gender Trouble* (1st ed.). London: Routledge.

C.B Cochran Scrapbooks 36. [Collection of scrapbooks] (GB 71 THM/97/36). V&A Theatre and Performance Department, London.

Chadwick, W., and Latimer, T. (2003). *Becoming Modern: The Modern Woman Revisited: Paris Between the Wars* (1st ed.). New Brunswick, NJ: Rutgers University Press.

Cochran, C. (1923). "Choosing a Chorus Girl". *The London Magazine*.

Conor, L. (2004). *The Spectacular Modern Woman* (1st ed., pp. 248–249). Bloomington: Indiana University Press.

Coward, H. (1926, October 1). Jazz in the Modern Girl. *Sheffield Daily Telegraph*. Retrieved from www. britishnewspaperarchive.co.uk. p. 5.

Daily Chronicle. (1927, May 11). "Bombshell for "Blackbirds"—White Orchestra Must Play at Revue: Whitehall Order. *Daily Chronicle*.

Daily Herald. (1926, September 13). All Coloured Artists – "Blackbirds"—An Exhilarating Revue for London. *Daily Herald*.

Daily News. (1927, February 10). Thinking Black. *Daily News*.

Daily Sketch. (1926, November 23). *Daily Sketch*.

Daily Telegraph. (1926, November 18). Not Forgotten Association. *Daily Telegraph*.

Davis, A. (1998). *Blues Legacy and Black Feminism* (1st ed.). New York: Pantheon Books.

D. M. Brown. (1932, April 4). D. M. Brown's Sale of Stockings. *Dundee Courier*.

Doan, L. (2000). *Fashioning Sapphism: The Origins of a Modern English Lesbian Culture* (1st ed.). New York: Columbia University Press.

Egan, B. (2004). *Florence Mills: Harlem Jazz Queen* (1st ed.). Lanham: MD: Scarecrow Press.

Empire News. (1926). Unknown Title. *Empire News*.

Foucault, M. (1979). *Discipline and Punish: The Birth of the Prison* (A. Sheridan, Trans.). New York: Vintage. (Original work published 1975).

Fussel, G. E. (1926). Notes on Decor: "Blackbirds". *Dancing Times*.

Gabbard, K. (1995). *Representing Jazz*. Durham: Duke University Press.

Gillett, R. (2010). Jazz and the Evolution of Black American Cosmopolitanism in Interwar Paris. *Journal Of World History, 21*(3), 484. doi: 10.1353/jwh.2010.0000.

Goffman, E. (1956). *The Presentation of Self in Everyday Life* (1st ed.). New York: Doubleday.

Goffman, E. (1974). *Frame Analysis* (1st ed.). Boston: Northeastern University Press.

Green, J. (1987). High Society and Black Entertainers in the 1920s and 1930s. *New Community, 8*(3), 431–434.

Green, J. (2002). Foucault and the Training of Docile Bodies in Dance Education. *Arts And Learning Research Journal, 19*(1), 99–126.

Liverpool Echo. (1928, January 18). *Liverpool Echo. Negro Touch in Fashions*.

London Pavilion. (1927). *Blackbirds of 1927 Programme* (2nd ed.). London: London Pavilion.

Mackey, N. (1995). Other: From Noun to Verb. In *Jazz among the Discourses* (1st ed.). Durham: Duke University Press.

McElya, M. (2009). *Clinging to Mammy* (1st ed.). Cambridge: Harvard University Press.

Meltzer, D. (1999). *Writing Jazz* (1st ed.). San Francisco: Mercury House.

Mills, F. (1926, September 14). Florence Mills on Prejudice. *Daily News*.

Mills, F. (1927, November 3). A Famous Blackbirds' Farewell: When Will Christian Britain Abandon Racial Prejudice? *Nottingham Journal*. p. 4.

Manchester Guardian. (1926, September). "Black Birds" - Jazz in Its Most Strident Form *Manchester Guardian*.

Martin Gibbs, C. (2012). *Black Recording Artists, 1877–1926* (1st ed.). Jefferson: McFarland.

Minichiello, S. (2001). *Taishō Chic: Japanese Modernity, Nostalgia, and Deco* (1st ed.). Seattle: University of Washington Press.

Modern. (1927, March 14). *Four and Twenty Blackbirds*. Modern.

Outlook, The (1927, May 7).

Nicholas, J. (2015). *The Modern Girl: Feminine Modernities, the Body, and Commodities in the 1920s*. Toronto: University of Toronto Press.

Parsonage, C. (1999). *Jazz among the Discourses*. Durham: Duke University Press.

Punch. (1920, February 11). *"Old-fashioned aunt: 'Good heavens, child! You're not going out like that? You look like a chorus-girl'"* [Cartoon].

Roberts, F. (1926, January 21). Fashions from Stage and Stalls. *Illustrated Sporting and Dramatic News*.

Robinson and Cleaver's. (1929, June 24). *Robison and Cleaver's Summer Sale Begins Today*. Belfast News-Letter.

Rogin, M. (2007). *Blackface, White Noise: Jewish Immigrants in The Hollywood Melting Pot* (1st ed.). Berkeley: University of California Press.

Romain, G. (2017). *Race, Sexuality and Identity in Britain and Jamaica* (1st ed.). London: Bloomsbury Publishing.

Shipp, H. (1926). *Upon Not Being So Black as We Are Painted. The Sackbut*, 79–80.

Sigel, L. (2012). *Making Modern Love: Sexual Narratives and Identities in Interwar Britain (Sexuality Studies Series)* (1st ed.). Philadelphia: Temple University Press.

Skillen, F. (2013). *Women, Identity, and Sports Participation in Interwar Britain. In Consuming Modernity: Gendered Behaviour and Consumerism before the Baby Boom* (1st ed., p. 131). Toronto: UBC Press.

Smith, C. (1924). Don't Advertise Your Man. Retrieved 8 February 2020, from https://archive.org/details/Clara_Smith-Dont_Advertise_Your_Man

Sphere. (1926, September 25). The Lighter Side of Life. p. 20.

Star. (1926, August 20). A Gallery Girl Writes. *Star*.

Star. (1926, November 22). Blackbirds for Ex-Soldiers. *Star*.

Star. (1927, January 15). No Bouquets for Father—Why? *Star*.

Steele, V. (1985). *Fashion and Erotism: Ideals of Feminine Beauty from the Victorian Era to the Jazz Age* (1st ed.). New York: Oxford University Press.

Sunday Chronicle. (1927, March 13). Mystery Woman's Pilgrimage—Florence "Nightingale" Mills. *Sunday Chronicle*.

Sunday Express. (1926, September 12). *Negro Artists in a Revue: Challenge to White Dancers – A Bedroom Scene*.

Sunday Pictorial. (1926, June 19). All Shades. *Sunday Pictorial*.

Suzuki, M. *(2009). Becoming Modern Women: Love and Female Identity in Prewar Japanese Literature and Culture* (1st ed.). Stanford: Stanford University Press.

Tulloch, C. (2016). *The Birth of Cool: Style Narratives of the African Diaspora* (1st ed.). London: Bloomsbury.

Ward, B. (2014). Music, Musical Theater, and the Imagined South in Interwar Britain. *The Journal of Southern History, 80*(1), 62.

Weinbaum, A. and Modern Girl Around the World Research Group. (2008). *The Modern Girl Around the World*. Durham: Duke University Press.

Wood, E. (2000). *The Josephine Baker Story*. Sanctuary.

6

TRUMPET MEN

Performances of Masculinity in Jazz

Aaron J. Johnson

Gender Terms in the Chapter: Despite reservations, I have used the terms male and men, and female and women rather freely and interchangeably. An exception is that that when discussing school-aged pre-adults, I have used girl and boy. A concern has been when discussing the subset of the population who do not identify as male, I have sometimes felt forced to use non-male, with the reservation that this normalizes maleness. There may be an occasion where I used "female and non-binary" in place of non-male. I consider myself as cis-gendered African American male.

> *The very essence of leadership is that you have to have vision. You can't blow an uncertain trumpet.—Theodore Hesburgh*
>
> *Trumpet players see each other, and it's like we're getting ready to square off or get into a fight or something.—Wynton Marsalis*
>
> *When two trumpet players first meet, they shake hands and at the same time say, "Hi! I'm better than you!"—Traditional trumpet joke*
>
> *Well, my sister played trumpet. Can you imagine having a sister blowing the trumpet around the house?—Freddie Hubbard*

Within jazz's culture and among a spectrum of instruments gendered as male, the trumpet stands out. It screams for attention, it engages in a puckish and signifying side commentary, it exerts a soft-spoken, cryptic but unquestioned authority via muted and crinkly whispers, and seldom assumes a supporting role. The trumpet demands the spotlight even if it has to steal it. In a remarkably masculinist culture, the trumpet is often regarded as a supremely masculine instrument. This chapter considers modes of jazz masculinity involving the trumpet, the trumpet's iconic stature in jazz, and its persistence as an instrument that is highly gendered as male. The musical styles of two major trumpet innovators are considered with respect to their own performances of jazz masculinity, and these two styles are related to enduring African male archetypes. Within the range of cis-gendered American males, a range of masculine performance styles can be found among the jazzmasculinity of two leading jazz trumpet players of the post-bop era: Freddie Hubbard and Lester Bowie provide two points along a wide range of styles.[1] Associated primarily with straight-ahead jazz, Hubbard was highly regarded and sought after by avant-garde players as well. Despite early roots in R&B, Bowie

DOI: 10.4324/9781003081876-7

was almost completely associated with the avant-garde. As artists on different poles of the jazz axis in the 1960s and 1970s and beyond, Hubbard and Bowie offer the opportunity to examine expressions of masculinity and to trace those conceptions within the African American aesthetic space.

Jazz studies present unique opportunities to examine the social interactions of race, class, and gender in a context atypical of American life in general. Within the world of jazz, at least, black musicians were not only respected, but assumed to be *authentic*—the real thing where jazz was concerned—and innovative. One is tempted to add *authoritative*, but black authority was constantly undermined by the interpretative, explanative mediation of white interpreters. On the job at least, Black male jazz musicians have been unusually able to express their masculinity largely free of the emasculating restrictions of Jim Crow America.

Racial control in the United States has been thorough, complex, and multifaceted, an uncountable set of mechanisms required to fully implement American anti-black racism. In show business, practices concerning black intellect and the performances of gender faced unique challenges, when African American performers held the stage before passive white audiences. For example, the American vaudeville tradition held that blacks could only appear before white audiences as comedy teams. A solo black comedian implied a black person who had the audacity to address whites directly, and that a black woman or man had the standing to command the attention of whites with her or his own wits. The staging of the black comedy team allowed for the charade that the white audience was merely overhearing entertaining black banter. In 1944, the pioneering comedian Timmie Rodgers (1914–2006) broke ground "when he did the unimaginable: put on a tuxedo and walked onstage in front of a white audience. By himself" (Watson, 2008). Jazz, of course, has played a role in erasing these boundaries. Well before 1944 Black jazz musicians like Duke Ellington had white fans and admirers in clubs, on stage, and on radio (Johnson, 2013).

When Rogers "refused to shuffle out in the blackface that was prevalent among black entertainers of the time or to speak the broken English many accepted as standard 'darky talk'" he was perhaps following the lead of jazz musicians such as Nat Cole, Fats Waller, and Earl Hines, who had already appeared solo before white audiences and earned their respect (Watson, 2008).

The Trumpet and Jazz Masculinity

Trumpet playing has been associated with leadership. The great volume and high range of the trumpet called attention to the instrument, and trumpet players seem aware of its power. Dizzy Gillespie is thought to have said the trumpet is the leader because it's the loudest. Harry "Sweets" Edison said "a trumpet is the loudest instrument that you can play. And the hardest. When they used to bring kings and royalty in, they had those big, long trumpets, you know. That got attention, man. That got attention" (Barnhart, 2005, p. 90).

Krin Gabbard (1992) has decoded the Hollywood film practice of a binary of phallic and post-phallic jazz trumpet playing and film imagery. "Hot" phallic players display hysterical intensity, range, and speed while "cool" post-phallic players display the qualities of the introvert or ironist. Trumpet players have constituted a durable jazz subject from *Young Man with a Horn* (1950) to *Miles Ahead* (2015) with the inability of either "hot" or "cool" players to perform analogized to male potency.

Despite a number of fine female trumpet players – including Ingrid Jensen, Rebecca Coupe Franks, Tanya Darby, Liesl Whittaker, Dolly Jones, Laurie Frink, and Ernestine "Tiny" Davis – the instrument and the occupation are considered stereotypically male. A modest social media row over a blogpost ranking of the top-fifty jazz trumpet players was concern that the obscure but underrated Louis Smith (26th) placed ahead of Clark Terry (28th), not the fact that the ranking did not include a single woman.[2]

Kathleen McKeage (2004) studied gender and participation in high school and college instrumental jazz ensembles, concisely observing that "jazz is a musical style that has historically not been open to women instrumentalists" (p. 344). Her data showed declining female participation in jazz with each successive increase in educational level, possibly because as young women inch towards professionalism, they are increasingly confronted with jazzmasculine behavior. In the preface of her history of jazzwomen, Linda Dahl (1989) wrote,

> clearly, the qualities needed to get ahead in the jazz world were held to be 'masculine' prerogatives: aggressive self-confidence on the bandstand, displaying one's 'chops' or sheer blowing power; a single-minded attention to career moves, including frequent absences from home and family.
>
> *(p. x)*

In other words, an embrace of jazzmasculinity.

Ingrid Monson (1995), a trumpet player herself, identified many white musicians as idealizing the image of the stereotypically dangerous black male, concluding that "the symbolic intersection of masculinity, music, and race perhaps explains the persistence of jazz as a fraternity of male musicians" (p. 405). It follows then that observers of jazz, regardless of race, would see the practice of jazz musicianship as a masculine activity.

"Masculine" and "Feminine" Instruments and Jazz as Competition

A study of the gender stereotyping of instruments ranked respondents' characterizations of eight commonly played instruments and created a spectrum from most masculine to most feminine—drums, trombone, trumpet, saxophone, cello, clarinet, violin, and flute. Given the supporting role of the drummer and the marginal role of the trombone as post-swing era band leaders, this leaves the trumpet regally at the ultraviolet end of the masculinity-as-leadership spectrum (Abeles and Porter, 1978; Abeles, 2009).

Although men play all the commonly used Western musical instruments, it is interesting to consider the dual nature of gender stereotyping of instruments. From the author's personal experience in school band and orchestra programs, the very instruments girls are encouraged to play—flute, clarinet, violin—are the instruments that boys, usually as a result of peer pressure, do not want to play. These instruments in turn are considered "sissy" instruments—many a boy violinist or flautist has had to defend himself on the way home from school or lessons. Contrary to the expected correlation between tessitura and gender association, the trumpet sits atop the brass "family" with predominantly male players.

In addition to its loudness, the trumpet, like other brass instruments, is often associated with the physical strength required in the players facial (embouchure) and core (diaphragm) muscles (Frederiksen, 1996). Brass instruments exploit the harmonic or overtone series to produce different notes, and the easiest and most comfortable notes to play are those that correspond to the lowest several partials. The higher notes on any brass instrument require an increasingly strong or firm embouchure (to correctly select among the increasingly narrow upper partials), the rapid movement of air, and other skills, among them being the ability of the player to manage a great deal of tension in the facial muscles of the embouchure while achieving a very relaxed attitude concerning all other musculature. Thus, in the culture of trumpet playing, the ability to play higher than others, along with other technical proficiencies (speed, clean articulation, flexibility in range) can be paramount in displays of trumpet prowess.[3]

As an undergraduate it occurred to me that the stylistically challenged young trumpet players of my university big band had adopted the Olympic motto "*Citius, Altius, Fortius*" as their guiding musical aesthetic. Gillespie could indeed play faster, higher, and louder than any of his peers, and while simultaneously creating the hippest, slickest, tastiest, and coolest music of anyone. Gillespie could get away with playing the clown prince, a less-threatening role that helped his commercial success but drew both the love and ire of Miles Davis. In the masculine world of Olympic trumpet playing, Davis recognized Gillespie as the gold medalist. Gillespie's enviable prowess as a trumpeter allowed Davis to tolerate his "clowning" onstage behavior (Davis and Troupe, pp. 83 and 163).

Stereotypically masculine behavior involves displays of physical prowess, the projection of confidence, swagger, and other demonstrations of fitness. However, the African American imperative of "coolness" favors the performance of difficult acts with the appearance of nonchalance and grace. For Robert Farris Thompson (1983), coolness lies at the center of Yoruba culture. "Coolness is the correct way you represent yourself to a human being" (p. 13). And "constant smiling is not a Yoruba characteristic. Sealed lips, frequent in Yoruba statuary are a sign of seriousness" (p. 13). These traits can be found in the bearing and posture of the modern black jazz musician, particularly those shaking free of the minstrel past. Davis was embracing coolness while critiquing Gillespie's clownishness. Bebop players, beginning in World War Two and continuing in the postwar atmosphere, were agents of their own desire for dignity and change. They worked good hours, they were skilled, they were respected (at least by fans), they dressed well, they used their intelligence, and sometimes they made a decent living. Thompson (1983) reminds us that coolness was part of the process and

> a part of character. To the degree we live generously and discreetly, exhibiting grace under pressure, our appearance and our acts gradually assume virtual royal power. As we become noble, fully realizing the spark of creative goodness God endowed us with ... we find the confidence to cope with all kinds of situations. This is *àshe*.
>
> *(p. 15)*

This is naturally only one of a number of competing behavioral modes. Musicians still displayed petty jealousies, nursed grudges, felt overlooked, overworked, and under-appreciated, drank to excess, and took drugs. But many jazz musicians did demand and expect respect and did carry themselves with coolness. Being cool, looking cool, and showing physical prowess was not enough to enforce the masculinity of the jazz world, however. Male behavior that intentionally or unintentionally discourages the participation of women in jazz is also an important factor.

#MeToo

The #MeToo movement that grew exponentially in 2017 has exposed additional connections between male behavior, the participation of women, and the masculinist spaces of jazz. In sharing their adverse experiences, women and LGBTQ+ musicians have described a range of hostile behaviors and sexual misconduct that range from rude and snide remarks to physical battery. These behaviors can negatively affect all aspects of musicians' careers, including institution-based education, informal training, hiring, rehearsing, touring, and performing, and eventually may drive women from the field. Prior to the 1970s most musicians, even those with college-level music training, acquired their jazz training in informal networks of apprenticeships and mentorships (Berliner, 1994; Monson, 1996). While a spirit of sharing and fraternity generally existed between apprentice and senior musicians, the informality of those associations encouraged cliques and reinforced the power of "old boys' networks," conditions bound to work against the excluded and overlooked women jazz musicians.

Whereas the hiring and training processes in classical music have implemented a degree of transparency consistent with the institutionalized nature of its largest entities—conservatories, symphony orchestras, and opera companies are all subject to conduct codes, bylaws, and even HR departments—the corresponding lack of such institutional structures in jazz has allowed these informal processes to go unchecked. (Although the #MeToo movement has brought significant scandals to light in classical music as well!) In each of the (sometimes concurrent) phases of a musician's career—training, hiring, rehearsing, performing, and touring—respect for the individual is a prerequisite. Respect for women jazz musicians can be undermined by

- *Quid pro quo* sexual harassment. When sexual favors, or even agreeing to dates, are a term of employment or required to "get the gig."[4]
- Hostile work harassment. Unwelcome sexual behavior such as repeated rude comments, constant "passes," even bullying can create a hostile work environment on stage, in rehearsals, on the tour bus, while traveling, or even on social media.[5]
- Physical danger.[6]
- Chummy hiring decisions. Networks of friends often exclude women, sometimes intentionally, sometimes unconsciously.
- Lack of respect for ability. Some men refuse to take women seriously as musicians or assume they are only getting gigs based on their gender or attractiveness.
- Overemphasis on physical appearance. Men (and women) can be conflicted about the relationship between appearance and performing skill with regards to women, though often, but not always, male appearance is a secondary concern.
- Abuse of power. In jazz there are seldom figures as powerful as studio heads or opera directors, but abuse of power can take place in almost any asymmetric relationship. One area of consistent problems in jazz is between teachers and students, especially at the university or conservatory level, where in addition to being subject to unwanted sexual behavior, female students face harassment, lack of support, and even active discouragement by male instructors.[7]

In short, women musicians face serious obstacles in getting hired and, perhaps to a lesser extent, in carrying out their performing duties. Though these conditions are not new, the trend towards college-level training holds new promise for improving conditions for women jazz musicians. Based on my professional experiences in the New York jazz scene over the years, an emerging generation of young male jazz musicians has had significant exposure to female peers in their own education and appear less resistant to female co-workers.

Women jazz musicians have been activated by recent events. They have been speaking out, writing essays and opinion pieces, and having conversations about these issues (Vandever, 2018; Thurman, 2017; Berliner, 2017). Organizations, such as Women in Jazz, have mobilized with the intent to (1) dismantle barriers and inequities; (2) create opportunities for members to perform, work, learn, and participate in jazz; and (3) provide an established voice to represent women and non-binary people in jazz.[8] A very recent development is the code of conduct—addressing workplace harassment, diversity in programming and curating, and promoting processes for resolving workplace issues—developed by the fourteen-member We Have Voice Collective.[9]

Two Trumpet Men

As the post-bop mainstream consensus in jazz began to wane in the mid-to-late 1960s, the avant garde was finding itself in full flower, although in a significantly smaller garden of commerce. By the 1970s, Miles Davis was in seclusion, Lee Morgan had been killed, Dizzy Gillespie was a (relatively) static icon artistically speaking, and Wynton Marsalis had not yet emerged as the icon of the future. Of the many outstanding jazz trumpet players of the time, let us consider Freddie Hubbard and Lester Bowie as fine examples to discuss the state of jazz trumpet masculinity in the post-civil rights era.

Ready for Freddie

Freddie Hubbard had been a "bad" cat on the trumpet since the early 1960s, and his iconic status continues to the present day, undiminished by his passing in 2008. Hubbard's musicianship and trumpet mastery made him the player of choice on an astonishing variety of projects. Although primarily a straight-ahead (and very hard) bebop player, Hubbard recorded on *Free Jazz* (1961) with Ornette Coleman and on *Ascension* (1960) with John Coltrane. In the 1970s, Hubbard recorded a series of LPs slickly produced by Creed Taylor, whose commercial successes helped usher in the smooth jazz genre, though Hubbard never fully abandoned straight-ahead jazz.

Hubbard came from the vibrant Indianapolis jazz environment that produced J. J. Johnson, Slide Hampton, and the Montgomery brothers, Monk, Buddy, and Wes. Hubbard outgrew Indianapolis—the black jazz player lifestyle, including the entitlement to keep company with white women, ran counter to Indiana's parochial values (Yanow and Hubbard, 1979). Hubbard enjoyed rapid success in New York, recording with John Coltrane at age twenty and entering into a great friendly rivalry with fellow trumpeter Lee Morgan, who had recorded *Blue Train* with Coltrane a year earlier at age nineteen—a rivalry later captured musically on the LPs *Night of the Cookers Vols. 1 and 2* (April, 1965).[10] Hubbard has been a towering influence for young brass players through his own recordings as well as those led by Art Blakey, Curtis Fuller, Herbie Hancock, Eric Dolphy, and Wayne Shorter.

The "manly" aspects of Hubbard's trumpet playing are in plain view in a number of statements he has given over the years.[11] On what attracted him to the trumpet as a kid: "I just liked the way it sounded, it was the loudest instrument and intense" (Yanow, p. 44). On his family's influences: "Well, my sister played trumpet. Can you imagine having a sister blowing the trumpet around the house?" (p. 44). Actually it sounds like he couldn't. On how hard he played when he came to New York: "Dizzy used to tell me that I am playing too hard. He used to say to not give everything. Miles used to tell me that too" (p. 44). Hubbard should have heeded Davis's advice for, during his last decade, he suffered from a chronic injury to his embouchure, an injury he has admitted came from playing too hard when he should have tried to heal a far more minor problem.[12]

Hubbard worked both sides of the jazz street, from the most orthodox associations in the straight-ahead community, such as Art Blakey and the Jazz Messengers, to free jazz playing with Ornette Coleman, Eric Dolphy, and Archie Shepp, and with the free-jazz-with-skills crowd exemplified by musicians such as Andrew Hill and Joe Chambers. In all his recordings, Hubbard played with fire, notable virtuosity, and with a great deal of forcefulness. It is clear from his own statements that he has a competitive and virile approach to trumpet playing. He spoke admiringly of his contemporary and rival Morgan:

> I never saw any man do the stuff he did, do what he did and play. He used to scare me to death … he'd blow me out. I was playing slicker than hip lines but he would blare me out. He had a bigger sound somehow.
>
> *(Yanow, p. 45)*

Hubbard played the "role" of Miles Davis in the V.S.O.P. quintet Herbie Hancock organized in the late 1970s. The quintet reunited Hancock, Shorter, Tony Williams, and Ron Carter of Davis's remarkable 1960s group. He told of his mixed feelings about the experience of standing in for one of jazz music's greatest icons – "Those guys acted like they expected Miles Davis to be there, but it was me instead. My shit was stronger than theirs. I let them know that I was Freddie Hubbard not Miles" (Yanow, p. 48). If that statement didn't indicate that Hubbard could experience male anxiety, his remark that Dizzy Gillespie's "style is so unique that it makes me sound like a gargling baby playing beside him" certainly did. The young Booker Little had provided some competition back in Indianapolis: "Booker Little would run me off, because they played fast. They tried to see how fast they could play" (Mandel, 1978, p. 17). Hubbard, however, knew no bounds to his sense of competitiveness, even jokingly remarking, "I play the trumpet because I figure, 'if Gabriel can do it, I can do it'" (Yanow, p. 48).

A remarkable example of Hubbard's bravura approach to the trumpet can be found on the 1963 Art Blakey and the Jazz Messengers recording of "Skylark."[13] The track is Hubbard's feature and adheres to the compressed format typical of studio ballad recordings where the abbreviated improvised chorus is split between piano and trumpet. Hubbard's reentry at the bridge is a staggeringly abrupt and rapid sixteenth note ascent to his high G over high C, a note he holds at fortissimo for five full beats before launching into an astonishing run of approximately 92 notes played over the next 12 beats on a single breath. It is just the kind of majestically impressive passage that Hubbard was noted for.

Hubbard's approach to the trumpet has reflected a very conventional approach to masculinity, featuring Gabbard's phallic trumpet playing. Hubbard's playing is powerful, aggressive, loud, brash, swift, and agile; his style demonstrates a tremendous affinity for "running the changes." Hubbard operated very much in the mode of jazzmasculinity that David Ake (1998) has posited as challenged by Ornette Coleman's possible re-masculation of jazz and its reward systems. Hubbard's performative jazzmasculinity is indicative of the resiliency of conventional indices of masculinity.

The 5th Power

Lester Bowie was born in 1941, three years later than both Lee Morgan and Freddie Hubbard. Perhaps the career paths of outsiders Bowie and fellow trumpeter Don Cherry are so different from those of insiders Hubbard and Morgan because they came to New York at much later stages in their respective developments—Bowie arriving from Chicago and Cherry from Los Angeles. Bowie was born in Frederick, Maryland, and raised in St. Louis. It was there that he experienced performing a wide range of Black music and was a co-founder of the Black Artists' Group (BAG). Before arriving in Chicago and becoming immersed in the experimental jazz scene there, Bowie gained R&B experience touring with Jerry Butler, Jackie Wilson, and Joe Tex (Wilmer, 1971). It was in Chicago that Bowie linked up with the AACM, joining saxophonist Roscoe Mitchell in a band that evolved into the Art Ensemble of Chicago, one of the first AACM bands to become known outside of Chicago.

The Art Ensemble was one of free jazz's most venerable bands with origins in the late 1960s and a continuing, if reduced, presence today. The classic lineup lasted until the mid-1990s and featured Bowie and Mitchell, along with bassist Malachi Favors Maghostut, saxophonist Joseph Jarman, and percussionist Famoudou Don Moye. The Art Ensemble was known for costumed performances, including face paint, and their employment of diverse instruments, including conch shells, banjos, extremely large (bass- contrabass), and small (sopranino) saxophones, and many small percussion instruments.[14]

Though the Art Ensemble was a cooperative, Bowie's impact on its eclecticism was evidenced by their two 1970 LP collaborations with Bowie's then wife, Fontella Bass ("Rescue Me"), *The Art Ensemble of Chicago with Fontella Bass* and *Les Stances A Sophie*. Both projects include elements of bebop, free jazz, collective improvisation, and R&B grooves. Bowie remained with the Art Ensemble until his death in 1999 from cancer, but also led or participated in several other noteworthy ensembles. The cooperative band, The Leaders, composed of pianist Kirk Lightsey, bassist Cecil McBee, saxophonists Chico Freeman and Arthur Blythe, and Famoudou Don Moye on drums was a completely different concept from the Art Ensemble (even though Bowie still wore his trademark white lab coat) with the players occupying more conventional roles on their instruments. In this sextet setting, it is quite clear how Bowie's trumpet practices differ from Hubbard's. Bowie's voice is quiet and diffuse, featuring more low register playing and displaying his penchant for vocal effects, such as half-valve notes, growls, and smears.[15] Perhaps Bowie is best known for Brass Fantasy, his avant-pop band that supported his featured trumpet with a backing ensemble of drums, three trumpets, two trombones, French horn, and the anchoring presence of Bob Stewart on tuba. In Brass Fantasy, Bowie the postmodern ironist is on full display—the 1986 LP *Avant Pop* featured songs made popular by Whitney Houston ("Saving All My Love"), Willie Nelson/Patsy Cline ("Crazy"), Fats Domino ("Blueberry Hill"), and The Dells ("Oh, What a Night").[16]

In contrast to Hubbard's swagger—Saint Louis Cardinals pitcher Dizzy Dean famously said about swagger, "It aint braggin' if you can do it"—Bowie described his trumpet facility more modestly.

> I really don't have fantastic chops, actually I'm one of the weakest trumpet players around, but I have learned a lot from being weak. Because my chops aren't inherently strong, anything I play that the sound is strong is because of something I have had to learn.
>
> *(Wilmer, 1971, p. 13)*

Bowie evolved in a simultaneously forward- and backward-looking style that influenced others and broadened the hard-bop trumpet vocabulary considerably. Robert Palmer (1978) said of Bowie, "Though he can be a singing evocative melodist when he chooses, Bowie also commands an unprecedented vocabulary of half-valved groans, roars, squeal and other, essentially vocal sounds" (p. D30). If the scientific and methodical Hubbard bears all the marks of the modernist, Bowie's trumpet art was post-modern. Valerie Wilmer (1971) describes his palette: "Bowie's tonal spectrum embraces the story of jazz. The wide vibrato that echoes New Orleans will follow hard on the spattering, snarling note-cluster. Squeezed half-valves"—one of the few effects embraced by Hubbard as well—"nudge at carefully constructed lines. The phutt-phutt of a motorcycle mocks the pretentiousness of other musicians. There is hokum aplenty, humor, anger, sorrow. But above all, irony" (p. 13). In his scientist's or doctor's white lab coat Bowie performed a winking postmodern response to the elaborate non-Western costumes and face paint worn by his Art Ensemble colleagues.

Flash of the Spirit

Both Freddie Hubbard and Lester Bowie impacted jazz at the highest levels. Hubbard was named a NEA Jazz Master in 2006.[17] In addition to Bowie's important roles in BAG and the AACM, the Art Ensemble of Chicago and Brass Fantasy expanded the audience for avant garde jazz and were templates for future ensembles with non-standard instrumentation. Bowie was elected to the DownBeat Hall of Fame a year after his death in 2001. In connecting their masculinity models to the Yoruba *orishas* Shango and Eshu-Elegba, I hope to demonstrate than African American modes of masculinity are not derived simply from emulation of American white culture, but also include African origins.

The humorous and playful nature of Lester Bowie brings to mind the African trickster figure Eshu-Elegba, while the bold, forward, and volcanic style of Freddie Hubbard recalls Shango. Though the Yoruba orisha has a deceptive nature that can produce truly negative consequences, Bowie's presentation resembles Elegba in many respects. Bowie's signifying nature, mimicking, at times mocking, at times commenting, echoes Elegba's methods. In Elegba's service, trickery is not merely about deceit, but more importantly about power.

> *Eshu*, like Hermes, has the power to bind and release. With charms he produces sleep, breaks locks, and becomes invisible. He is described as being able to transform himself into a bird, become like the winds, or appear as other persons. He confuses [our] recognition by throwing dust, blinking his eyes, and clapping his hands. He causes people to lose their way in the forest by pointing his staff, or, with the sacrificial items they have offered, enables them to avoid pitfalls. His is the "secret action," and, as Brown (1969: 19) notes, "'secret action' means magic." *Eshu* the trickster is *Eshu* the magician, the one who possesses the *oogun* which has the power to transform.
>
> *(Pemberton, 1975, p. 26)*

This passage fits Bowie and his music on many levels. His music is varied, "Great Black Music—Ancient to Future," and is well represented by his own coinage "avant-pop." By costumes and through humorous and sarcastic gestures, he misdirects his audience and distracts them from where they think they are headed, and from the seriousness of his music's content. Eshu is a troublemaker, and *agent provocateur*. Bowie, according to musicians who worked with him, loved to signify—in the old-fashioned Black southern vernacular sense—to stir up conflict within his band, just for the entertainment value. In an obituary article, jazz critic Gary Giddins called Bowie "the most bourgeois of underminers, the wiliest jazz provocateur of his generation" (Giddins, 1999).

Elegba is also the orisha of the crossroads, often alluded to in blues culture, as in the mythology of Robert Johnson. Bowie's music is at the metaphorical crossroads of jazz traditions, R&B, the avant garde, funk, and gospel. Pemberton points out the masculine symbolism associated with Elegba. Returning to the discourse of the phallic, observers have noted the sexual symbolism of the upswept hairstyle, associating "long hair with libidinous energy, with power and aggression, with unrestrained sexuality, and with uninhibited instinct." Interestingly, Lester Bowie tended to wear his hair in an upswept style once known as a fade. Eshu is sometimes portrayed blowing a flute or whistle, which again some observers have linked to the sexual orality of thumb-sucking or pipe smoking. Again, interestingly, Bowie had a thing for cigars, which became something of a trademark. Giddins (1999) commented on the cigar as a clue to his mode: removed he was straightforward, but "in his mouth you half expected to hear the heh-heh-hehs that occasionally marked his records."

If Bowie is Eshu-Elegba then Hubbard is Shango, the "thunder king." The power of Shango streaks down in meteorites and thunderstones. Robert Farris Thompson (1983) notes Shango's dual embodiments, that of "warrior and lover" have been

> stylized into the particularities of a piece of seventeenth-century sculpture—the fertilizing thrust of the thunderstone into the earth indicated by an image carved in wood, pointing to his penis with one hand while indicating the source of that energy by pointing to the sky with the other hand.
>
> *(p. 92)*

Pemberton (1977) reports that in the *oriki* Sango is portrayed as unpredictable, capricious, self-serving, as one who "rides fire like a horse," who "takes by force," who

> does as he pleases, who is the death that drips 'to, to, to.' He is also the giver of children, the one who imparts his beauty to the woman with whom he sleeps. He is a source of medicine. He wrinkles his nose at liars, reverses the fortunes of the rich, strikes the one who is stupid. Lightning, the leopard, and the gorilla image his power, energy, and potency.
>
> *(p. 20)*

One cannot help but note that many of the above characteristics describe the jazzmasculine image of a line of powerful rain-making trumpet virtuosi stretching from Louis Armstrong, Roy Eldridge, and Dizzy Gillespie through Freddie Hubbard, Roy Hargrove, and Freddie Hendrix. Considering the widely romanticized notions of bandstand battles and cutting contests, warrior and lover fits Hubbard well.

Conclusion

Jazz is one of the few areas in American culture that African American men have felt safe to project masculinity, and humanity, as they see fit.[18] Whites have been dazzled by the excellence, inspiration, and ingenuity of Black jazz musicians since the music emerged early in the twentieth century, and the leading figures of jazz have been recognized as the intellectual and innovative leaders that they are. In creating their jazz lives, African American trumpet men (and drummers and pianists and saxophonists) have been performed jazzmasculinity according to modes that, like the music itself, combine elements from Africa, America, and Europe and, significantly, are not patterned exclusively after white norms.

As it has provided a unique space in American culture in which Black masculinity is much less restricted by historical racial restraints, it is also recognized that jazz, as with so many other sectors of American life, has done little to accommodate the concerns and prerogatives of women desiring full participation. As such, jazz provides a valuable means to explore modes of performance of Black masculinity, particularly in a field of endeavor where the innovative and leading figures—those whom both novice and experienced practitioners look to emulate—are African American men. Such explorations are both overdue and timely. Overdue, as masculinity has for too long gone unchallenged and uncritiqued, too long accepted as related to biology. In celebrating the all too rare unfettering of Black masculinity in jazz, there is a risk of ignoring its negative impacts. Such explorations are also timely. The #MeToo movement brought new focus of the oppressive weight of unchecked jazzmasculinity on women and non-binary jazz people.

Jazz is hardly responsible for the longstanding gendering of musical instruments in Western culture, but jazz does little to counter those trends. By various mechanisms, these gender associations with instruments begin with grade-school students. At that early age, participation in instrumental music is more balanced, but female participation in jazz ensembles declines with age. Those women who persevere despite the systemic obstacles are still facing the unfavorable conditions that discourage all looking to have music careers. However, there is some promise due to the increasing role of institutional jazz training in bringing young women and men together as student musicians.

I have tried to show how the trumpet in jazz was and is still a locus of Black masculinity, but also that masculinity can be expressed on the trumpet in ways other than the more expected strutting and posturing, and that there is also a trickster tradition of misdirection and irony present in the African American tradition as alternative sources of power. Both the trickster and the earth-mover are found in West African cultures, and these modes of masculinity are frequently in conflict but also in harmonic coexistence. It is wise to realize that within the Black community, any observed performance of masculinity lies within a spectrum of possibilities, rather than stand as the singular representation as it may be seen in the non-Black community. This issue has direct and important consequences in the present; a unifying concern in the Black Lives Matter cases is the degree to which unarmed African American males are perceived as dangerous and life-threatening, even twelve-year-old, Tamir Rice.

For jazz, at least, there is some hope. There is no reason why the freedom to express one's masculinity cannot coexist with the full and welcome participation of women in jazz. The persistent calls to raise consciousness on gender in jazz has increased opportunities for women, and there is the hope that more recent generations of male musicians trained alongside women are more respectful of women's abilities and rights.

Let the trumpet sound.

Notes

1 "Jazzmasculinity" is concept introduced by Nicole Rustin-Paschal (2017) that relates to the demonstration of behaviors by musicians of all genders meeting or exceeding the homosocial norms associated with excellence and virtuosity of jazz practices. Female musicians, Rustin-Paschal asserts, perform jazzmasculinity by "embracing the aggression, competition, arrogance, discipline, and creativity of men—and at times, doing it better than men."

2 Charles Waring, "The 50 Best Jazz Trumpeters of All Time" *Udiscovermusic.com*

3 Quoted in Gillespie's autobiography *To Be or Not to Bop*, trumpeter Duke Garrett admitted to such competitive behavior; "Dizzy's playing—it was different, and it was accuracy of chord structure. Before, we trumpets had just been screaming and trying to see who could play the loudest and who could get the highest." (Gillespie, 1979, p. 239).

4 In the overwhelmingly male jazz environment of the past with limited opportunities for women instrumentalists,, female singers bore the brunt of *quid pro quo* harassment. "If you want to be a Rae-lette, you gotta 'let Ray,'" was a story well-known among musicians. As the alpha male, many bandleaders have felt entitled to *droit du seigneur.*

5 Trombonist Kalia Vandever, who wrote an impactful blog post in 2018 about her experiences at Julliard, described a high school experience of being the only young woman amidst twenty-five young men in at a jazz camp. After the camp she learned from a friend she had made there that "the first night of the week, all of the guys had congregated and made bets on who I would hook up with. To their disappointment, I 'hooked up' with no one."

6 Pianist and composer Mary Lou Williams was raped traveling to Chicago to join a band. (Kernodle, 2014).

7 Saxophonist Camille Thurman wrote that after the arrival of a new and unprotective high school teacher at a prestigious arts high school the experience left her totally disillusioned.

> By that time, we were all graduating and had endured two years of being completely disrespected. I went to school wanting to learn and instead left crushed, depressed, angry and traumatized. By then, I wanted nothing to do with music. I had actually quit playing. My self esteem, spirit and confidence were gone and I really believed that I couldn't play.
>
> *(Thurman, 2017)*

8 http://wearewijo.org/

9 The We Have Voice Collective is Fay Victor, Ganavya Doraiswamy, Imani Uzuri, Jen Shyu, Kavita Shah, Linda May Han Oh, María Grand, Nicole Mitchell, Okkyung Lee, Rajna Swaminathan, Sara Serpa, Tamar Sella, Terri Lyne Carrington and Tia Fuller. The code of conduct can be seen at their website, wehavevoice.org.

10 Lee Morgan enjoyed a career very much parallel to that of Hubbard, perhaps initially more successful considering Morgan's hit recording "The Sidewinder." However, Morgan, unlike Hubbard, was not really associated with the avant-garde; even as a side-musician his recordings were straight ahead. Morgan was shot and killed in 1972 in an incident that involved his romantic entanglements.

11 Quotes from Freddie Hubbard website http://home.ica.net/~blooms/hubbardhome.html accessed 12/3/2007.

12 Private conversation with trumpeter David Weiss. Weiss had been working with Hubbard for several years, trying to help re-establish Hubbard's playing career.

13 Art Blakey and the Jazz Messengers, *Caravan*, Riverside LP 9438 (1963)

14 For photos see the Art Ensemble of Chicago Website. To see vintage versions of the website use the "wayback machine" at http://web.archive.org

15 *The Leaders,* directed by Frank Cassenti, New York: Rhapsody Films, ca1990. VHS tape.

16 Lester Bowie Brass Fantasy, *Avant Pop,* Polygram Records, 1990, LP.

17 Despite the gendered title, the first female Jazz Master was named in the fifth year (1987) of the award and a consistent effort to be mindful of gender exclusion has resulted in, aside for some droughts, the induction of a female for every six new awardees, the latest being the 2021 selection of Terri Lynn Carrington

18 And certainly, performing masculinity as they see fit has had demonstrated negative consequences for those not male.

References

Abeles, H. (2009). Are Musical Instrument Gender Associations Changing? *Journal of Research in Music Education*, *57*(2), 127–139.

Abeles, H. F., and Porter, S. Y. (1978). The Sex-Stereotyping of Musical Instruments. *Journal of Research in Music Education*, *26*(2), 65–75.

Ake, D. (1998). Re-Masculating Jazz: Ornette Coleman, "Lonely Woman," and the New York Jazz Scene in the Late 1950s. *American Music*, *16*(1), 25–44.

Barnhart, S. (2005). *The World of Jazz Trumpet: A Comprehensive History and Practical Philosophy*. Milwaukee: Hal Leonard.

Berliner, P. (1994). *Thinking in Jazz: The Infinite Art of Improvisation*. Chicago: University of Chicago Press.

Berliner, S. (2017). An Open Letter to Ethan Iverson (and the Rest of the Jazz Patriarchy). www.sashaberlinermusic.com/political-and-socialcommentary-1/2017/9/21/an-open-letter-to-ethan-iverson-and-the-rest-of-jazzpatriarchy.

Brown, N. O. 1969. *Hermes the Thief*. New York: Vintage Books.

Burke, P. L. (2008). *Come in and Hear the Truth: Jazz and Race on 52nd Street*. Chicago: University of Chicago Press.

Cohen, H. G. (2010). *Duke Ellington's America*. Chicago: University of Chicago Press.

Dahl, L. (1989). *Stormy Weather: The Music and Lives of a Century of Jazzwomen*. New York: Limelight Editions.

Davis, M., and Troupe, Q. (1989). *Miles, the Autobiography*. New York: Simon and Schuster.

Frederiksen, B. (1996). *Arnold Jacobs: Song and Wind*. Gurnee, IL: WindSong Press.

Gabbard, K. (1992). Signifyin(g) the Phallus: "Mo' Better Blues" and Representations of the Jazz Trumpet. *Cinema Journal, 32*(1), 43–62.

Giddins, G. (1999, December 14). Lester Bowie 1941–1999. *Village Voice.*

Gillespie, D. (1979). *To be, or not … to BOP: Memoirs.* Garden City, NY: Doubleday.

Hallam, S., Rogers, L., and Creech, A. (2008). Gender differences in musical instrument choice. *International Journal of Music Education, 26*(1), 7–19.

Johnson, A. J. (2013). A Date with the Duke: Ellington on Radio. *The Musical Quarterly, 96*(3/4), 369–405.

Kernodle, T. L. (2004). *Soul on Soul: The Life and Music of Mary Lou Williams.* Boston: Northeastern University Press.

McKeage, K. M. (2004). Gender and Participation in High School and College Instrumental Jazz Ensembles. *Journal of Research in Music Education, 52*(4), 343–356.

Mandel, H. (June 15, 1978). Freddie Hubbard: New Direction, Fresh Perspective. *DownBeat, 45(12),* 17–19, 50–51.

Monson, I. T. (1995). The Problem with White Hipness: Race, Gender, and Cultural Conceptions in Jazz Historical Discourse. *Journal of the American Musicological Society, 48*(3), 396–422.

Monson, I. T. (1996). *Saying Something: Jazz Improvisation and Interaction.* Chicago: University of Chicago Press.

Monson, I. T. (1999). Monk Meets SNCC. *Black Music Research Journal, 19*(2), 187–200.

Palmer, R. (1978, December 3). The Lyrical Trumpet of Lester Bowie. *New York Times.*

Pemberton, J. (1975). Eshu-Elegba: The Yoruba Trickster God. *African Arts, 9*(1), 20–92.

Pemberton, J. (1977). A Cluster of Sacred Symbols: Orişa Worship among the Igbomina Yoruba of Ila-Qrangun. *History of Religions, 17*(1), 1–28.

Ramsey, G. P. (2013). *The Amazing Bud Powell: Black Genius, Jazz History, and the Challenge of Bebop.* Berkeley: University of California Press.

Rustin-Paschal, N. (2017). *The Kind of Man I am: Jazzmasculinity and the World of Charles Mingus Jr.* Middletown, CT: Wesleyan University Press.

Thompson, R. F. (1983). *Flash of the Spirit: African and Afro-American Art and Philosophy.* New York: Random House.

Thurman, C. (March 2017). #METOO: A story of resistance and resilience in the music industry. *Allegro, 121(3).*

Vandever, K. (2018). Token Girl. *medium.com.*

Watson, D. M. (February 3, 2008). Timmie Rogers: Revolutionary for a new black comedy. *The Virginian-Pilot.*

Wilmer, V. (April 29,1971). Lester Bowie: Extending the Tradition. *Down Beat, 38(9),* 13, 30.

Wilson, A. (1985). *Ma Rainey's Black Bottom: A Play in Two Acts.* New York: New American Library.

Yanow, S., and Hubbard, F. (June 1979). Record Review Interview: Freddie Hubbard. *Record Review Magazine.*

7

HARD BOP COOL POSE

Bebop, the Blues, and Masculinity in the Music of Lee Morgan

Keith Karns

This chapter deals with masculinity and male gendered modes of expression. Masculinity is not a biological inevitability; rather it is reinforced through experience and relationship. In reference to historical figures, I adopt the gender pronouns most commonly used in the historical record. In reference to other sources, I have used gender-neutral pronouns. My goal as a jazz musician, educator, and scholar is to help contribute to a community where people of all gender identities and all races can express themselves through this music.

This chapter looks at the intersection of race and gender in jazz. More specifically, it focuses on how masculinity is expressed sonically in hard bop. Hard bop was the style of jazz popular in the mid-1950s through the mid-1960s in black communities in New York, Philadelphia, Pittsburgh, Detroit, and Chicago (Mathieson, 2013). Hard bop represents something of a common practice period in modern jazz education. This is in large part due to the influence of hard boppers such as Art Blakey, Horace Silver, John Coltrane, Miles Davis, Sonny Rollins, Dexter Gordon, Cannonball Adderley, Clifford Brown, Max Roach, and others.[1] Understanding the intersection of race and gender in hard bop will give us a better understanding of the relationship between these elements in modern music.

The terms *jazz*, *bebop*, and *hard bop* are generally accepted for this music in jazz scholarship, yet they are anything but precise. It can be challenging to draw distinctions between bebop, hard bop, and *post-bop* performance. For example, the version of "Confirmation" recorded by Art Blakey and Horace Silver on the live album *A Night at Birdland* (Blakey, 1954) aligns closely with bebop, despite the fact that Blakey, Silver, and the rest of the band are all musicians closely associated with hard bop. In addition, the distinction between bebop and hard bop was one that the musicians of the time did not make. It was more common for musicians to refer to bebop or hard bop as *modern music*, or *playing modern* (Monson, 1995, p. 406). This is reflected in scholarship that does not draw a distinction between these two styles and simply refers to both bebop and hard bop with the term bebop or *bop* (Owens, 1995; Ake, 2002). Additionally, many contemporary jazz artists such as Nicholas Payton (2011) have rejected all conventional terminology for jazz. They link the established terms to efforts by white record executives and promoters to profit from black American music. Still, the terms jazz, bebop, and hard bop are generally accepted in jazz scholarship and jazz education and, so even though they are problematic, in the interest of clarity I will use them for the course of this discussion.

DOI: 10.4324/9781003081876-8

Hard bop can be considered both a continuation of bebop as well as a broadening of musical palette in the bebop style. Hard bop preserved the musical language and performance practice of bebop, but also embraced a variety of additional musical sounds and styles. These styles included *traditional blues, black gospel music, R&B, world music, Tin Pan Alley*, and *twentieth-century classical music* (Monson, 2007, p. 71).

Blue Note Records—the label most closely associated with hard bop—marketed the music through its "hip" aesthetic. *Hipness* in the post-war era aligned with a worldview that valued "individuality, nonconformity, spontaneity, authenticity, and direct, unmediated self-expression" (White, 2011, p. vii). Hipness was one of the ways these primarily black jazz musicians separated themselves from other musicians as well as from mainstream society (Monson, 1995). In the classic work *Blues People*, Amiri Baraka (1963) described the black jazz musicians of the mid-twentieth century as part of an avant garde counter culture that challenged entrenched modes of white power. While typically celebrated in men, the values of hipness were generally discouraged in women. This is often cited as one of the barriers for women entering and continuing in jazz (Wehr, 2016).

Jazz and Gender

In recent years the social barriers women and non gender-conforming people have faced in jazz spaces have begun to receive more critical attention. For example, Erin Wehr's (2016) work on tokenism and stereotype threat detailed the ways in which women have struggled to find identity in masculine spaces. Sarah Provost (2017) detailed how women such as Lil Hardin and Mary Lou Williams adapted to and subverted male-dominated spaces and masculine modes of expression. Nicole Rustin (2005) continued this line of thought in her discussion of female genius in jazz and its relationship to masculinity. It is generally agreed upon that conventional jazz spaces are inherently masculine, but we have not yet fully explored exactly how masculine expression functions musically. This has important implications, not only for how we understand jazz and gender, but also the intersection of race and gender in jazz.

Gender is learned and reinforced through experiences and relationships that remind individuals of socially accepted gender roles (Pelzer, 2016, p. 18). Masculinity, then, can be described as the means by which the male-gendered identity attempts to confront or resolve problems, disputes, or other insecurities through seeking approval and validation (Fournier and Smith, 2006, p. 147). Fournier and Smith argue that this process is never-ending. The competitive nature of temporary success spurs individuals to strive for loftier, more challenging goals, fostering a never-ending cycle in which participants must prove their manhood. In jazz, this means not only that performance practice tends to reinforce conventional masculine gender roles, but also that this is a constant state in which masculine identity must be reified through dress, speech, behavior, and jazz performance.

At first glance this might seem to imply a purely dysfunctional mode of masculinity in jazz. While masculine spaces in jazz have certainly been problematic in terms of providing a safe space for people of all gender identities to express themselves, this mode of expression can also be seen as a means with which black jazz musicians not only confronted the very real insecurities faced by many black men, but also challenged mainstream—that is to say, white—views of black masculinity.

Herman Gray (1995) wrote that this music and the musicians who made it "enacted a black masculine that not only challenged whiteness but exiled it to the cultural margins of blackness—that is, in their hands, blackness was a powerful symbol of the masculine" (p. 401). Majors and Billson's (1992) seminal work *Cool Pose: The Dilemmas of Black Manhood in America*, can be used to draw a connection between the hip imagery we associate with hard bop musicians and black masculinity. They argued that the cool image adopted by black men represents an alternative to conventional modes of masculinity available to black men. This *cool pose* presents a facade of poise, power, control, and invulnerability. It is a survival mechanism that black men use to navigate a world in which they face alienation, limited access to power, and limited access to conventional resources. Like Fournier and Smith, Majors and Billson described cool pose as a façade of masculinity that must be constantly proved. "If [cool pose fails, masculinity fails" (p. 28). A key component of this discussion is how black masculinity challenges entrenched norms of white hegemony: "Self representations of black masculinity in the United States are historically constructed by and against dominant (and dominating) discourses of masculinity and race" (Gray, 1995, p. 401).

Bell hooks (2004) continued this mode of inquiry, arguing that the cool facade adopted specifically by black male musicians could be used as a blueprint by other black men to transcend poverty and alienation in urban life (p. 23). Niyi Afolabi (2007) developed this further, arguing that the regenerative aspect of cool pose and black masculinity can be viewed not only a means of proving one's masculinity, but also subverting entrenched systems of racial oppression (p. 460).

Like conversations regarding hipness, cool pose has mostly been discussed in terms of visual and popular culture representations of blackness such as dress and speech. However, many, such as Majors and Billson (1992), hooks (2004), and others linked cool pose specifically to musicians and their music. One study, by Regina Bradley (2012), expands the view of cool pose to consider how it is manifested sonically in the music itself.

Bradley has done this by introducing the concept of *Hip Hop Sonic Cool Pose*. Hip Hop Sonic Cool Pose examined the musical and nonmusical elements of *hip hop* and contextualizes them in terms of black masculinity. Some of the musical elements identified by Bradley include instrumentation, sampling, auto-tune, and vocal timbre. The non-musical elements identified are primarily vocalizations such as the laugh of rapper Tupac Shakur or the grunts of Rick Ross.

Bradley used Hip Hop Sonic Cool Pose to describe the varying and often conflicting performances of cool and black masculinity in hip hop. For example, in the comparison of rappers Rick Ross and Drake, Bradley argues that Ross's brand portrayed a "forceful and hard hitting" interpretation of black masculinity (p. 60). This can be heard in Ross's non-musical vocalizations as well as in the instrumentation. Drake, by contrast is positioned on the opposite end of the spectrum from Ross, portraying vulnerability in a way that is not often present in commercial rap. This too Bradley argues, can be heard in Drake's vocalizations and the instrumentation of his music. According to Bradley, differing interpretations of masculinity can be heard in the music through the combination of various musical elements.

I am interested in identifying sonic cool pose in the context of jazz, specifically in hard bop. Current scholarship has yet to fully address how race and masculinity can be heard sonically in jazz. For example, in Monson's (1995) analysis of hipness, much of the discussion centers on the accoutrements of hipness—zoot suits, horn rimmed glasses, posture, the idiosyncratic speech patterns of beboppers—but does not identify how hipness can be heard in the music. David Ake (2002) identified mainstream jazz in the 1950s—hard bop—as a vehicle for what he refers to as conventional modes of black masculine expression. Ake's argument focuses on how Ornette Colman's music challenged this conventional masculinity, but does not devote much time to exploring conventional masculinity in hard bop.

Lee Morgan is something of an avatar of the hard bop style, often referred to as the "quintessential hard bopper" (Rosenthal, 1992, p. 4; Monson, 2007, p. 76). Morgan's style is often identified through his use of the blues, but Morgan is also a significant figure in jazz because he is one of the chief links in the chain of trumpet players stretching from Louis Armstrong through Roy Eldridge, Dizzy Gillespie, and Clifford Brown. This legacy is ongoing, continued today by players like Terrell Stafford, Nicholas Payton, Terence Blanchard, and Wynton Marsalis. Morgan's approach to this music is therefore representative of common performance practices adopted by many hard bop musicians. This is what Benjamin Givan (2014) referred to as musical dialect (p. 211). Using Morgan as a model, I will examine two musical elements of hard bop: (1) bebop, and (2) the blues. How these two musical elements are applied has a direct impact on how cool pose is constructed and how masculinity is projected. This chapter will close with a discussion on cool pose in contemporary performances of hard bop and suggestions for future research.

Bebop and the Blues

Thomas Owens (1995) described bebop as "the lingua franca of jazz" (p. 4). Bebop was pioneered in the 1940s by black musicians such as Charlie Parker and Dizzy Gillespie. While there have certainly been many advances in the realm of jazz expression since the bebop era, Owens is correct in asserting that bebop remains a potent force in jazz.

Bebop is characterized by improvisation on the chords—or *changes*—of a tune. Melodic content in bebop outlines the changes in a way that embraces chromaticism and dissonance. The harmonic content of this music largely follows the rules of functional harmony based in the Western European tradition. Bebop is generally associated with fast tempos. This produced aesthetic values that prized instrumental technique, and harmonic and melodic complexity.

Today bebop is commonplace but, in the 1940s, it emerged in semisecret jam sessions. Only those initiates who paid their dues at sessions such as the famous ones at Minton's Playhouse were able to play or even understand this music (Ake, 2002). The result was a musical culture that rejected the status quo. It was at once avant garde and subversive and challenged the commodification and commercialization of swing. Bebop reified the roots of jazz by bringing it outside the mainstream, and realigning it with its folk roots as a secret, subversive style of black American music (Baraka, 1963, p. 181).

In the mid-twentieth century, jam sessions were one of the main places where musicians learned and practiced the art of bebop playing. Here, young and experienced players alike could engage in what is often described as a pugilistic display of musical ability. At stake was honor, glory, admiration, prospects for a better gig, and possibly the "amorous favors" of a member of the audience (Ake, 2002, p. 67). Accounts of the famous jam session at Minton's Playhouse paint a picture akin to trial-by-combat in which players are weighed and measured by their ability to navigate key changes, odd chord substitutions, and blazing fast tempos (Gillespie and Frasier, 1979, p. 144).

What can account for the value beboppers placed on virtuosity? Certainly, this established a musical aesthetic that was at once new and distinct from swing. However, as we consider the competitive nature of bebop and the ever present need to prove oneself, we must also conclude that this indicates a decidedly masculine set of musical values. If masculinity is something that must constantly be proved, in the context of bebop, soloists must constantly demonstrate their musical prowess lest they be deemed unworthy. In a situation where every solo must be the "hippest" solo of the night, beboppers necessarily adopted the aesthetics of power and invulnerability that they projected through their music.

The expression of power in bebop is more than the establishment of a hard-hitting personal brand. For black jazz musicians, the expression of power was a means by which they could address the insecurities faced by black men in America, challenge conventional interpretations of black manhood, and challenge white hegemony (Gray, 1995; hooks, 2004; Afolabi, 2007). If we consider bebop to be the expression of Western European—that is to say white—harmony through music pioneered and performed by black men, bebop subverts an artifact of white culture—tonal harmony—and repurposes it as an instrument of black cultural expression. From this perspective, instances of bebop—particularly in the hard bop style that are wedded to traditional blues and other statements of black music—project an image of black power and dominance over white modes of harmonic expression.

The blues has been an integral part of jazz since its very first iterations in New Orleans at the dawn of the twentieth century. While by no means absent in the playing of beboppers such as Charlie Parker, Dizzy Gillespie, and others, traditional blues styles had fallen out of favor with many bebop musicians in the 1940s (Deveaux, 1997, p. 343). This had changed by the mid-1950s when the affirmation of more traditional forms of the blues and black folk music by musicians such as Horace Silver and Art Blakey became a hallmark of the hard bop style (Monson, 2007, p. 71).

One reason for this was the shifting political debates surrounding race in the black community during the 1950s and 1960s. The fight against Jim Crow laws led to a reification of traditional black music among black artists and audiences. This included spirituals, black gospel music, the blues, and R&B. When hard bop musicians brought traditional blues back into their music, it was both an affirmation of blackness, and black masculinity, and provided a wider range for emotional expression in jazz.

Despite important contributions by female blues artists such as Bessie Smith, Ma Rainey, Sister Rosetta Tharpe, and others, authenticity in blues performance was typically derived from heterosexual black masculinity (Adelt, 2010, p. 1; Monson, 2007, p. 78). Yet the blues remained a complicated space where traditional modes of masculinity could be challenged (hooks, 2004). It offered a platform for black men to express their feelings in a way that may not have been socially acceptable in other formats. This provided space for the many—and in some cases contradictory—performances of black masculinity in black American music.

The blues is manifested in hard bop in several different ways. The first is in compositional approach. This includes tunes that follow the 12-bar blues form as well as tunes that share similarities, such as Morgan's "The Sidewinder" (Morgan, 1963). Harmony was another way in which traditional blues was affirmed in hard bop. The resurgence of the traditional V^7-IV^7 turnaround in m. 9 of the blues rather than the bebop variant ii^7-V^7 is perhaps the most obvious example of this—as is evidenced in tunes like "Tom Cat" (Morgan, 1964). Musical phrases—both in compositions and in improvised material—relied much more heavily on blues melody than had been done in strict bebop settings. For example, in Morgan's solo on "Confirmation" (Smith, 1979), Morgan adheres to a generally bebop-oriented approach—however three times in his solo he ends a long bop passage with the minor blues scale (see Figure 7.1). Here, the blues functions as a vehicle to raise the energy level of the solo. This functions not only by providing musical contrast to the bebop convention of extending diatonic scale material with chromatic passing notes, but also by moving the line into the upper register of the trumpet. This can be heard at the end of the A section in the second chorus. The combination of bebop with traditional blues and other forms of black music offered greater opportunities for musical contrast, even on tunes that adhere to a bebop-oriented sensibility as can be heard in Morgan's solo on "Confirmation."

Figure 7.1 depicts the three instances in which Lee Morgan played the blues in his solo on the tune "Confirmation," which is based on a 32-bar AABA form (Smith, 1979). All three instances of the blues come at the end of an A section and function as a means of resolving a phrase back to tonic in F major. For instance, Morgan's solo lines in the second A sections of the first and second chorus are derived from the F minor blues scale. A vertical harmonic analysis would identify a species of harmonic alteration, that is, a $D^{7\#5\#11\#9}$ chord anticipated on the A minor chord, but this is not

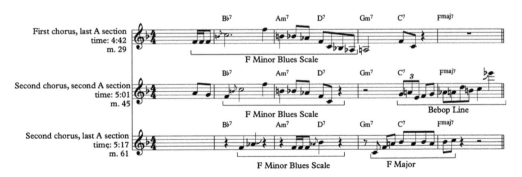

Figure 7.1 Blues phrasing on Lee Morgan's solo on "Confirmation." This figure depicts all three instances of the blues heard in Morgan's solo.

fully descriptive of how this material functions in relation to the tune, which is important to our understanding of Morgan's application of the blues tradition in jazz. While Bb (#5), Ab (#11), and E# (#9) all represent alterations of the D^7 chord (the E# is pragmatically notated as the enharmonic equivalent F), this analysis negates the essence of the line—particularly the E# interfering with its fundamental meaning as the tonic. These pitches are not just outlining a particular chord, they imply the blues in relation to the key.

The strength of the blues does not come from its harmonic stability, but from the connection to the blues and black folk music. Black music was coded as "manly and virile" (Monson, 2007, p. 78). Therefore, statements of the blues connect jazz performance to a celebrated image of black masculinity.

Badness and Hard Bop Sonic Cool Pose

Cool pose is a way in which individuals can demonstrate and prove their masculinity. The dress, posture, and speech patterns are all accoutrements of cool but, for jazz musicians, authenticity is also related to the music. An important element of masculinity in jazz then becomes the ability to project cool pose sonically. This is what separates the "hip" from the "squares." In Morgan's music, bebop and the blues intersect in a way that not only help to establish Morgan's version of cool pose, but also affirms an image of "badness" (Rosenthal 1992, p. 118).

Badness embodies a similar masculine aesthetic space as hipness, but also represents a more dangerous image. According to Rosenthal (1992), badness implied a sense of imminent violence or danger. Indeed, while Rosenthal indicated certain musical traits can be heard as markers of badness— rhythmic phrasing, blues-inflected passages, and an overall funky approach to the music—he describes "malice" as the key component of badness (p. 118).

Monson (1995) further defined badness by linking it to statements of virility, sex, and commercialism. "'Unabashed badness' and sexual transgression have sold incredibly well.... male jazz musicians have not infrequently enjoyed their reputations for virility and have constructed accounts of themselves that play into the market for this image and its transgressive aspects" (p. 419). Sonically, the musical expression of badness lies in statements of virtuosity and a reification of blackness through the blues in a way that projects an image of power.

Morgan's solo on "Moanin'" is perhaps his most famous expression of power through the blues (Timmons, 1958). Here, the application of the blues is unlike that heard in "Confirmation." We hear longer iterations of the blues, and bebop is more balanced in relation to blues passages. Indeed, bebop is limited almost entirely to the bridge of both choruses. Perhaps the most famous aspect of this solo is Morgan's intro (see Figure 7.2). Morgan opens with a high D above the staff, descending in an arpeggio to outline an Fm^6 chord. Morgan develops this motif twice more before ultimately resolving with descending F minor blues scale.

These phrases are idiomatic to Morgan's music. Even on tunes that might call for more subdued melodies, it is common to hear the application of bebop and blues to invoke power, virtuosity, and badness. Take for example, Morgan's solo on "Along Came Betty" (Golson, 1958). This tune could be a vehicle for a more understated improvisational approach, yet Morgan projects badness in much the same way he did on "Moanin" and "Confirmation." Figure 7.3 shows the bridge to Morgan's solo on "Along Came Betty." Morgan begins with a double-time blues line similar to the material he played on his second A section of "Moanin." He does not develop this for long before quickly moving to double-time bebop for the remainder of the bridge.

Badness can be heard in a different way on "Caribbean Fire Dance" (Henderson, 1966).[2] This solo is distinct from Morgan's work on "Confirmation," "Moanin," and "Along Came Betty" because it shows how Morgan approached modality.

Miles Davis and John Coltrane were among the early pioneers of modal jazz in the early 1950s (Kernfeld, 2003). By the time of this recording in 1966, modality had largely been adopted by most

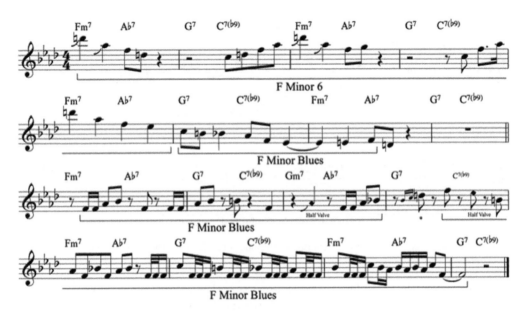

Figure 7.2 The Opening to Morgan's solo on "Moanin.'" Time 0:59, m. 1-16.

Figure 7.3 The bridge to Morgan's solo on "Along Came Betty." Time 1:48, m. 17-24.

hard boppers. Indeed, bebop and the blues are not used anywhere nearly as prominently; instead the A half whole diminished scale and the Eb lydian mode are the primary vehicles heard on the A sections, and the C whole tone scale is the primary scale heard on the bridge.

David Rosenthal (1992) contended that connection to the blues is a key musical component of badness, but he also cited Morgan's solo on "Caribbean Fire Dance" as a prime example of badness, despite the fact that the blues does not play a large role in Morgan's solo, nor in the tune at all. What then can account for the badness of this solo?

The most obvious explanation for this is the register that much of Morgan's solo appears in. Like the opening of Morgan's solo on "Moanin'," this type of playing is a display of both musical strength and technique. Upper register playing has been described as an idiomatic part of Morgan's trumpet style, often tied to bravado and masculinity (Gabbard, 1992; Monson, 2007). Register is certainly a contributing factor to the badness of "Caribbean Fire Dance," but there are other musical elements at play as well.

For example, the groove and rhythms of the piece are loosely based on music from Cuba, Puerto Rico, other parts of the Caribbean, and ultimately West Africa. The interaction between Morgan

Figure 7.4 Morgan's second A on his first chorus of "Caribbean Fire Dance." Time 2:23, m. 9-16.

and drummer Joe Chambers during Morgan's solo as well as the interaction between the horn section and drums in the shout chorus (time 5:35) is particularly significant in this respect.

Modality also plays an important role. Modal jazz often occupies musical space similar to bebop—eighth note lines that outline a particular scale or mode. But if bebop is the application of black melodic language to Western European harmony, modal jazz represents the application of melodic material that was developed primarily by black musicians to harmonic procedures pioneered primarily by black musicians.

Morgan projects a cool pose that is rooted in statements of power, blackness, and badness. This hard-hitting image of near-invincible masculinity was central to Morgan's personal brand and was effective for many hard boppers. For example, among trumpet players of the time, similar versions of sonic cool pose can be heard in the music of Woody Shaw, Freddie Hubbard, and Blue Mitchell. While all distinct artists, all use bebop and the blues—and in some cases elements of post bop and free jazz—to project similar interpretations of masculinity. This is hardly surprising if we consider the similar musical dialect shared between these artists.[3]

This version of cool pose was not the only one employed by hard boppers. Indeed, when we examine the application of bebop and the blues in some of Morgan's contemporaries, we find that these musical elements project a very different version of cool. For example, Horace Silver's iconic solo on "Doodlin'" (Silver, 1954), does not align with the idea of badness in the same way as Morgan.

In Silver's first chorus (see Figure 7.5), rather than contrast the subdued groove oriented blues passages with displays of power through physical and technical pyrotechnics, the pianist stays in the groove and develops blues motifs in a decidedly understated way. This material is very simple, yet it maintains the essence of the blues. Indeed, only the bebop material in m. 8–9, where Silver briefly "runs changes," present any notes not derived from the major or minor blues scale. The bebop material functions less as a tool to communicate power, and more of a brief contrast and means of connecting ideas. This is a much less pyrotechnic approach, and it focuses attention to the blues and groove. If the cool pose we hear in Morgan's solos present an image of power and invulnerability, here the use of the blues projects an image of cool, and subtle—and perhaps sensual—sophistication.

Like hip hop sonic cool pose, sonic cool pose in hard bop can account for the different and at times conflicting expressions of masculinity heard in the music. If we view Morgan's application of cool pose as normative, the expression heard in Silver's music challenges established modes of masculinity in jazz performance. How musical elements converge in performance has a direct impact on how various images of cool are expressed. Sonic cool pose in hard bop reifies the visual and cultural image of "cool" constructed by musicians. In the case of Morgan, the visual image of badness is

Figure 7.5 Horace Silver's first chorus on "Doodlin."

projected through statements bebop and the blues in order to express an unmitigated sense of power. Morgan acknowledged this himself, although perhaps in a somewhat understated way: "Jazz is an extroverted music. I am an extrovert" (Rosenthal, 1992, p. 118). In the context of the individual, this could be seen as a strategy to establish a kind of personal hegemony inside a band or local jazz community. Indeed, Rosenthal (1992) described Morgan's performance on "Caribbean Fire Dance" as making the band—hard bop royalty all—"look like a bunch of sissies" (p. 118). However, I do not believe that this offers a complete picture of the role masculinity plays in this music. In the context of black artistry, the power projected in Morgan's solos can also be heard as a way of confronting the various injustices many black men face. From this perspective the cool pose projected by Morgan through his music was a powerful tool to confront a hard world.

Is Jazz Still Cool?

This discussion has focused on only two elements of hard bop performance, and yet it is obvious that within these confines there are many—and often conflicting—ways in which masculinity is expressed sonically. We have yet to consider how the harmonic developments in the 1950s and 1960s impacted cool pose and masculine expression. Indeed, a long list of musical elements should be examined through this lens.

Hard boppers in the 1950s and 1960s proved their strength, power, prowess—their masculinity—through virtuosic displays of bebop and the blues. Is that still the case today? Is jazz performance still a performance of masculinity? This has important implications for jazz scholarship, jazz performance, and jazz education. Do modern performances of bebop and hard bop represent modern ideas about race and gender, or are modern interpretations of bebop and hard bop performances of a historical, sanitized black masculinity? Perhaps the most important component of this music is how it confronted entrenched modes of power. This is a critical aspect of this music, but do modern performances still accomplish that goal?

Jazz trumpeter Nicholas Payton (2011) addressed the issue of coolness in the aptly titled poem, "On Why Jazz Isn't Cool Anymore." Payton argued that by labeling and marketing jazz, institutions have put boundaries on the music. "The very fact that so many people are holding on to this idea of what jazz is supposed to be makes it not cool" (Payton, 2011). Payton also rejected the label of "jazz" and instead identifies with the term *New Orleans music*. "I play postmodern New Orleans Music. ... My ancestors didn't play jazz, they played traditional, modern, and avant garde New Orleans Music" (Payton, 2011). This reclaims jazz and repositions it in relation to Payton's hometown, the birthplace of jazz, and the black culture of the city. For a New Orleans native this probably does make jazz cool, but is repositioning jazz in this way sufficient to make it cool for the general population? If jazz is not cool, how do contemporary performances of jazz align with masculinity? Is this an example of what Monson (2007) described as a white fascination with "yesterday's blues" (p. 78)? What are the ways that the jazz musicians today construct and express their image? How does that align with the established conceptions of gender, and how is that represented sonically?

In the mid-twentieth century, performance of hard bop was largely an expression of black masculinity made by black men as a means of subverting established notions of black manhood and challenging white hegemony. Jazz is now performed by an international, multiethnic, multi-gendered community. Ted Gioa's (1997) Introduction to *The History of Jazz* described an "Africanization of American Music" in which black music has gradually come to influence much if not all of American Music (p. 3). How have modes of expression changed as jazz styles cross lines of race and gender? Further research on how modes of masculine expression are being repurposed is needed. Coming to grips with how masculinity has been expressed in jazz will go far in helping us construct a more equitable space for jazz performance, scholarship, and education. More research is needed to identify how cool pose and masculinity function in contemporary jazz communities.

Notes

1 Both Miles Davis and John Coltrane recorded in what can be considered a hard bop style in the 1950s, but by the end of the decade both were moving on to different modes of musical expression outside the confines of hard bop.
2 "Caribbean Fire Dance" (Henderson, 1966) is an example of how style blurs in bop. While it contains many of the same stylistic elements of hard bop, the modal harmony and Joe Henderson's "in and out" improvisational approach also align this tune with "post bop."
3 Benjamin Givan (2014) describes dialect in jazz as a set of musical ideas, performance practices and gestures shared between a group of musicians. In the case of Morgan, Shaw Hubbard, Mitchell, they were all contemporaries, and had formative experiences as young people working for some of the same band leaders such as Art Blakey and Horace Silver. It should not be a surprise that these artists share a musical dialect.

References

Adelt, U. (2010). *Blues Music in the Sixties: A Story in Black and White*. Rutgers University Press.
Afolabi, N. (2007) Cool Pose: Masculinity as Regenerative Impulse in Nathan McCall's "Makes Me Wanna Holler." *CLA Journal*, 50(4), 458–472.
Ake, D. (2002). *Jazz Cultures*. University of California Press.
Baraka, A. (1963). *Blues People: Negro Music in White America*. Harper Collins.
Blakey, A. (1954) Confirmation [Recorded by Art Blakey]. On *A Night at Birdland* [CD]. New York: Blue Note Records.
Bradley, R. (2012). Contextualizing Hip Hop Sonic Cool Pose in Late Twentieth—and Twenty-first—century Rap Music. *Current Musicology*, 93, 55–70.
DeVeaux, S. (1997). *The Birth of Bebop A Social and Musical History*. University of California Press.
Fournier, V., and Smith, W. (2006). Scripting Masculinity. *Ephemera*, 6(2), 141–162.
Gabbard, K. (1992). Signifyin(g) the Phallus: Mo' Better Blues and Representations of the Jazz Trumpet. *Cinema Journal*, 32(1), 43–26.
Gioa, T. (1997) *The History of Jazz*. Oxford University Press.
Gillespie, J. B., and Fraser, A. (1979). *To Be or Not to Bop*. Doubleday.

Givan, B. (2014). Gunther Schuler and the Challenge of Sonny Rollins. *Journal of the American Musicological Society*, 67(1), 167–237.

Golson, B. (1958). "Along Came Betty" [Recorded by Art Blakey and the Jazz Messengers]. On *Moanin'* [CD]. New York: Blue Note Records.

Gray, H. (1995). Black Masculinity and Visual Culture. *Callaloo*, 18(2), 401–405.

hooks, b. (2004). *We Real Cool: Black Men and Masculinity*. Routledge.

Henderson, J. (1966). "Caribbean Fire Dance" [Recorded by Joe Henderson]. On *Mode for Joe* [CD]. New York: Blue Note Records.

Kernfeld, B. (2003) Modal Jazz. Grove Music Online. https://doi.org/10.1093/gmo/9781561592630.article. J305400.

Mathieson, K. (2013). Hard Bop. *Grove Music Online*. https://doi.org/10.1093/gmo/9781561592630.article. A2249696

Majors, R., and Billson, J. (1992). *Cool Pose: The Dilemmas of Black Manhood in America*. Lexington Books.

Monson, I. (1995). The Problem with White Hipness: Race, Gender, and Cultural Conceptions in Jazz Historical Discourse. *Journal of the American Musicological Society*, 48(3), 396–422.

Monson, I. (2007). *Freedom Sounds: Civil Rights Call Out to Jazz and Africa*. Oxford University Press.

Morgan, L. (1963). The Sidewinder [Recorded by Lee Morgan]. On *The Sidewinder* [CD]. New York: Blue Note Records.

Morgan, L. (1964). "Tom Cat." [Recorded by Lee Morgan]. On *Tom Cat*. New York: Blue Note Records.

Owens, T. (1995). Bebop *the Music and its Players*. Oxford University Press.

Payton, N. (2011, November 27). On Why Jazz Isn't Cool Anymore. Nicholas Payton, https://nicholaspayton.wordpress.com/2011/11/27/on-why-jazz-isnt-cool-anymore/.

Pelzer, D. (2016). Creating a New Narrative: Reframing Black Masculinity for College Men. *The Journal of Negro Education*, 85(1), 16–27.

Provost, S.C. (2017). Bringing Something New: Female Jazz Instrumentalists' Use of Imitation and Masculinity. *Jazz Perspectives*, 10(2–3), 141–157. https://doi.org/10.1080/17494060.2018.1443966

Rosenthal, D. (1992). *Hard Bop: Jazz and black music 1955–1965*. Oxford University Press.

Rustin, N. (2005) "Mary Lou Williams Plays Like a Man!" Gender, Genius, and Difference in Black Music Discourse. *South Atlantic Quarterly*, 104 (3), 445–462. https://doi.org/10.1215/00382876-104-3-445.

Silver, H. (1954). "Doodlin'" [Recorded by Horace Silver and Art Blakey]. On *Horace Silver and the Jazz Messengers*. New York: Blue Note Records.

Smith, J. (1979). "Confirmation" [Recorded by Jimmy Smith]. On *Confirmation* [LP]. New York: Blue Note Records.

Timmons, B. (1958). "Moanin'" [Recorded by Art Blakey and the Jazz Messengers]. On *Moanin'* [CD]. New York: Blue Note Records.

Wehr, E. (2016). Understanding the Experiences of Women in Jazz: A Suggested Model. *International Journal of Music Education*, 34(4), 472–487. https://doi.org/10.1177/0255761415619392

White, A. (2011). "No Room for Squares:" the hip and modern image of Blue Note Records, 1954–1967 [Doctoral dissertation, Indiana University]. IU Campus Repository. https://iucat.iu.edu/iun/11066841

8

TOWARD A FEMINIST UNDERSTANDING OF JAZZ CURATORSHIP

Kara Attrep

Her singular musical voice encompasses the past, present, and future of jazz (Bill Charlap, on Marian McPartland).

(Hentoff 2011, p. 52)

What does it mean to curate jazz? The *Online Etymology Dictionary* defines a curator as "a guardian; one who has care or superintendence of something." This broad definition of curation provides a jumping off point in order to explore the gendered aspects of curation. This chapter relies on the biography, autobiography, and interviews of four female musicians, radio hosts, and jazz institution directors who have contributed to and significantly shaped the history of jazz: Marian McPartland, Nancy Wilson, LaDonna Smith, and Terri Lyne Carrington. While they have not yet been explicitly framed as major curators of jazz, this chapter explores what it means to intentionally look at how women have shaped and supervised the history of jazz.

There are several institutions, museums, and archives that house the history of jazz. However, Jazz at Lincoln Center (JALC) and the ensemble associated with the institution, the Lincoln Center Jazz Orchestra (LCJO), are the most public-facing jazz organization and ensemble in the United States, setting the focus and tone, and guiding the historical narrative of jazz performed throughout the nation since the late twentieth century. Proving their importance to shaping the narrative of jazz, in the history section of the JALC's website, jazz.org, they explain their mission: "Representing the totality of jazz music, Jazz at Lincoln Center's mission is carried out through four elements— educational, curatorial, archival, and ceremonial—capturing in unparalleled scope, the full spectrum of the jazz experience." Therefore, it is arguably the public institution most associated with the curatorial history of jazz in America. Their importance to the shaping of the historical narrative of jazz is not only foregrounded in their own positioning of their mission but also through the countless scholarly and journalistic articles that have been devoted to JALC and its director, Wynton Marsalis. While the curatorial vision of the JALC is led by Marsalis, the curation of jazz, when explored from a feminist perspective, provides a different understanding of the guardianship of a genre that has such a layered, complicated past.

Curation is usually considered to be the purview of museum exhibition. However, considering the history of jazz through the lens of curation provides insight into the way the history of jazz has been shaped. What does it mean to "guard" the knowledge of a genre? In the case of jazz, its guardians have predominantly been understood to be white men such as James Lincoln Collier, Scott DeVeaux,

DOI: 10.4324/9781003081876-9

Leonard Feather, Ted Gioia, Nat Hentoff, Frank Tirro, and many more, and the institutions these curators have been associated with were either the academy or journalism. Starting in 1987, the curation of jazz history began to shift to Jazz at Lincoln Center. Arguably, the largest institution in the world to support jazz, JALC, under the helm of Marsalis—curator, musician, composer, and bandleader—has grown to represent what jazz is in the United States. The history of Jazz at Lincoln Center is lengthy and has been recounted more fully in other studies. However, understanding the framing of jazz history through JALC is essential. In jazz scholar Eric Porter's (2002) book, *What is this Thing Called Jazz: African American Musicians as Artists, Critics, and Activists,* he provides a thorough examination of the importance of the work being done at Jazz at Lincoln Center and by its leader Wynton Marsalis. Porter also provides a nuanced critique of the institution's mission and its leader. In particular, Porter explains the historical connection of a patriarchal understanding of jazz, especially around the lineage of Louis Armstrong, that has been the basis of the programming and education efforts at JALC. Porter (2002) explains:

> In keeping with his earlier comments about Armstrong, Marsalis describes a patriarchal continuum of jazz artistry and wisdom. Although he expresses a deep respect for women as individuals and performers, he emphasizes the role of men as the carriers of the jazz tradition.
>
> *(p. 311)*

In an article chronicling JALC's expansion in the early 2000s, Timothy Murphy (2004) explains the curatorial focus of Marsalis, JALC, and the Ken Burns documentary *Jazz* that aired in 2001:

> Burns' documentary seems to imply that jazz is no longer a living art form but rather a collection of historically fixed artifacts, museum relics that can best be appropriated through the kind of curatorial logic that Artistic Director Wynton Marsalis's work at Lincoln Center (and on recordings) represents.
>
> *(p. 130)*

The static history of jazz presented and curated by Burns and Marsalis represents a dominant history that has been replicated over the last three decades.

While the curation of visual art through a feminist lens has been critically addressed by several publications and exhibitions, the feminist curation of jazz has been less deliberative. There are jazz festivals devoted to women musicians such as the Mary Lou Williams Women in Jazz Festival at the Kennedy Center, but the critical evaluation of what a feminist curation of jazz looks like has been less forthcoming. Amelia Jones, professor of Art and Design, explains that, "curating *constructs* certain kinds of historical narratives, or in some cases intervenes in existing narratives" (p. 5). Jones further argues that

> while scholarly histories and theories of feminist art and culture are crucial to the feminist projects of expanding histories as well as interrogating the structures through which art is made and historicized, *curatorial practice* is one of the most important sites for the constitution of both historical narratives about feminist art (the histories of feminist art) and feminist theories of curating and writing histories (the feminist histories and theories of art).
>
> *(p. 5)*

While addressing museum curation, Jones's focus on constructing and intervening in narratives of visual art histories through *curatorial practice* can be applied and used to address feminist curation of jazz. I will return to a discussion of how contemporary feminist jazz curation by artists such as Terri Lyne Carrington has specifically addressed JALC, but I will first analyze the work of several important precursors—Marian McPartland, Nancy Wilson, and LaDonna Smith—who used radio and print media to embody a feminist curatorial practice.

Marian McPartland's *Piano Jazz*

Marian McPartland was born in 1918 in England. A pianist from a young age, McPartland studied at the Guildhall School of Music and Drama but left to take a gig as a vaudeville musician. She met trumpeter Jimmy McPartland after World War II, and they married, eventually moving to the United States in 1946. She played with Jimmy frequently but also soon established her own career, notably having a long-standing gig at the Hickory House in New York City. McPartland played with many prominent jazz musicians, and her output of solo albums and work with her various ensembles was impressive. My focus, however, is on her commitment to jazz education, history, and foregrounding the many musicians who formed the past, present, and future of jazz. McPartland's curatorial practice of jazz can be found particularly in her radio series *Piano Jazz*.

Before McPartland recorded her first *Piano Jazz* show in 1978, she secured a grant through the Nixon Administration to do a series of jazz workshops in schools in the DC area. She was committed to jazz education and saw the current popular music of the day eclipsing jazz. As a white Englishwoman, her education efforts were not always met with resounding enthusiasm in the predominantly African American schools in DC. She was criticized by local musicians and music educators who wondered why a white woman was teaching African American music history to African American kids. On the one hand, she seemed to be somewhat unaware of her white, European privilege, and at times held a morally superior attitude about her work in educating youth, especially African American youth, about "their" music. On the other hand, she listened to the community and invited local musicians to join her at the workshops as well as finding

> new routes to the kids' hearts. In one class, she demonstrated how Kool & the Gang's "Jungle Boogie" was a reworking of rhythmic figures Louis Armstrong had pioneered a half century earlier and sparked their interest with the infectious, booming bass line of Herbie Hancock's Headhunters hit "Chameleon."
>
> *(de Barros, 2012, pp. 265–266)*

> She continued her educational work throughout the 1970s, "doing free concerts at youth guidance centers and, eventually, at New York's infamous prisons on Rikers Island and at Attica."
>
> *(de Barros, 2012, p. 268)*

At the same time, McPartland's career was flourishing and, according to Paul de Barros, her biographer, she "saw a rise in income between 1973 and 1978" (p. 265). Additionally, her profile as a musician rose, which de Barros claims was "buoyed," not only "by the jazz education movement," but also by "feminism" (p. 265). In examining McPartland's radio show, *Piano Jazz*, I explore the ways in which McPartland's career, her focus on and approach to jazz education, and her performances were discussed, shaped, and understood in relation to gender. I want to turn to the first *Piano Jazz* shows to highlight how McPartland's role as a curator of jazz was informed and impacted by feminism.

From her experiences leading educational workshops and her active performing schedule, McPartland found herself in a position to be suggested as the host of a radio show. Her friend and composer Alec Wilder was the host of a radio show called *American Popular Song with Alec Wilder and Friends*, but his health was failing, so the network began to look for a replacement. Wilder recommended McPartland (de Barros, 2012, p. 295). Her show centered around interviews with jazz pianists; the first shows with the first producer focused exclusively on piano—even those musicians who were not primarily piano players, such as Dizzy Gillespie, were also expected to play a bit of piano. In 1978, McPartland recorded her first *Piano Jazz* interview. As recounted in her biography,

> [the] interview took place at the Baldwin showroom on October 8, 1978. Her guest was Mary Lou Williams, whom she chose quite consciously, meaning to honor her longtime idol and the most important woman in jazz. McPartland immediately regretted it. Haughty and arrogant, Williams came in with a conspicuous chip on her shoulder and sulked through most of the show. At one point, according to Marian's friend Diana Schwartz, who was at the taping, Williams turned to Dick Phipps [the show's producer] and said outright, 'I should be doing this show.' Which was no doubt precisely how she felt.
>
> *(de Barros, 2012, p. 297)*

While this exchange, at first, appears tense, a closer examination of the show reveals an important exchange between these two trailblazers of jazz piano and history.

In Tammy Kernodle's (2020 [2004]) seminal biography of Mary Lou Williams, she explains Williams's ability to excel in teaching, despite an initial reluctance. She also describes the barriers that were put into place that kept Williams from being a radio show host—barriers that were not typically encountered by white female musicians. Kernodle explains how important her Duke University position was within the context of Williams's career:

> Here was Mary, a black woman who had not graduated high school and never taken a college course, teaching as a college professor.... After years of struggle—fighting against the racism that said she was inferior because of her color, against sexism that said her place was not on stage or on record but in the kitchen..., against the professional jealousy that had robbed her of her proper place in jazz history and had stunted her professional advancement—Mary had entered a period of happiness, stability, and security.
>
> *(p. 266)*

Kernodle explains the intersectional discrimination that occurred throughout Williams' life. Taking these subtle and blatant discriminatory acts into consideration helps to reframe our understanding of this first *Piano Jazz* recording. Williams would have been a highly skilled host, albeit very different than McPartland, and this is evidenced in Williams's successful tenure as a college professor. Institutionalized racism and sexism kept Williams from even being given the chance of hosting such a show.

In the above description of the radio show, it sounds as if it was extremely intense from the outset. However, listening to the show 40 years after it was aired, the tension seems less prevalent. It could be that at the time, Williams's reputation as being contrary and suffering no fools overshadowed the first *Piano Jazz* show. Additionally, McPartland deliberately chose Williams as her first guest as a way to honor her idol, a person McPartland considered to be "the most important woman in jazz" (de Barros, 2012, p. 297). McPartland does, at times, talk over Williams and vice versa, and this comes not only from a spirit of competition between two accomplished jazz musicians but also from McPartland's lack of experience doing a radio show. She had done a bit of radio work, but this was her first time hosting. Later shows demonstrate that McPartland understood when to leave space for the guest to talk and perform. She is clearly excited and nervous during this first recording session. Listening to this interview in a contemporary context, however, demonstrates that while there are some slightly tense moments there is also an abundance of material that highlights the important historical and educational aspects of the show. For instance, the section of the interview after Williams plays her tune "Watch Your Morning Star," highlights the rapport between the pianists. The two musicians have a wonderful conversation about playing in different keys that is both educational and focuses on specific aspects of Williams's career and work. McPartland says, "I love that thing ["Watch

Your Morning Star"] so much but I never do it in that key." Williams then says, "D flat." McPartland says, "Don't you think different keys set up different vibrations?" Williams agrees, "[They] set up different moods, right…. You play differently if it was in another key, you think differently" (1979). This exchange highlights the focus on music performance that was at the heart of McPartland's show.

Another section from the Williams show highlights a component of *Piano Jazz* that seemed to be a recurring feature of the show, that of gender. Williams subtly brings up the issue of gender in her experiences as a professional jazz musician as she recounts her time in Benny Goodman's big band. The moment goes by quickly but other instances similar to this one arose in subsequent episodes.

While McPartland's first recorded *Piano Jazz* show was with Mary Lou Williams, the first show aired was with Dr. Billy Taylor. As a veteran radio show host, educator, mentor, musician, and composer, Taylor seemed the more appropriate choice for the first *Piano Jazz*. The show is casual and easygoing as Taylor and McPartland recall their past gigs and experiences while also having an extended discussion about comping and the lack of improvisation studies in contemporary music education. Taylor's interview on *Piano Jazz* launched an over-thirty-year run that helped further raise McPartland's stature and made her an international spokesperson of jazz. In McPartland's biography, the author, De Basso, explains,

> When asked in an interview if [Taylor] considered it an injustice that a white Englishwoman had become the national spokesperson for American jazz, Taylor said simply, 'That is the society we live in…. She's worked very hard and she earned the respect that she got.'
>
> *(p. 299)*

While Taylor's statement seems to partially confirm a level of injustice in McPartland's stature, it also emphasizes that McPartland is not a charlatan or merely in her role due to privileged status as a white Englishwoman. Like many of her guests, Taylor himself respected McPartland for paying her dues.

While gender rarely became an explicit focus for the *Piano Jazz* shows, it seems to have been an implicit subject that McPartland's guests would spontaneously address. An exchange between Taylor and McPartland illustrates the subtle way discussions of gender arose. Taylor catches himself talking exclusively of male piano players who would visit a small bar, the Hollywood Bar, that had only an upright piano, switching quickly to discussing a female performer, Dorothy Donegan:

> Tatum used to go there, all the piano players used to go there, nothing but piano players…. Everybody would go there and play. Guys would just sit there for hours listening to one another play. It wasn't a competitive thing…. You would just go in and listen to another guy play and if you felt like playing, you'd play. A woman would come in and play. I remember Dottie Donegan came in one time…. Most of the guys there had only heard her do her act. So, they had heard her in the Roxy. But they had never heard her really play.
>
> *(McPartland, April 1, 1979)*

McPartland then says, "she can really play." To which Taylor replies, "She can *play*." Then McPartland adds a stereotypical gendered comment she herself experienced multiple times throughout her career: "I bet no one said she plays good for a chick." Taylor laughs and says, "Believe it!" (McPartland, April 1, 1979). While outside of the scope of this chapter, it is imperative to note the important contributions made by Dr. Billy Taylor in all aspects of jazz. His particular focus on mentorship, education, and performance are integral to understanding jazz history. For an excellent examination of his importance to jazz, see Tracy McMullen's (2021) chapter in *Artistic Research in Jazz: Positions, Theories, Methods.*

Whether the person being interviewed was a man or woman, discussions of gender arose organically. (In the sample cross-section of the twenty shows I listened to out of the over seven hundred, McPartland rarely asked musicians directly about issues related to gender. An example from her show with pianist Dorothy Donegan illustrates this. McPartland had just asked Donegan about her influences and Donegan begins to recall the beginning of her career. She quickly recounts how she was perceived as a player: "They said I used to play like a man. So, I always said I used to play like a heavy man" (McPartland, 1983). McPartland then recounts her own experiences with these types of gendered comments with similar humor.

In McPartland's (1987) book of essays titled *All in Good Time*, she recounts in the chapter titled, "You've Come a Long Way, Baby" that she would receive similar types of "compliments" that addressed her gender:

> I was so busy trying to play as well as I could that I didn't think about [the "compliments"] too much. But finally I asked someone who said, 'You play just like a man' what he meant. He stammered a bit and said, 'Oh, well, you know, I've never heard a *woman* play so *strong*.' Once a man stood at the bar watching me intently and when the set was finished he came over and said with a smile, 'You know, you *can't* be a respectable woman the way you play piano.' For some reason or other, this struck me as a great compliment.
>
> *(p. 8)*

While gender discussions were certainly a part of the show, it was McPartland's focus on the technical aspects of playing jazz that provides a rich archive of jazz performance and theory. Take for instance an example with Dorothy Donegan about her use of Dorian mode in Donegan's rendition of "I Can't Get Started." After finishing "I Can't Get Started," McPartland asks Donegan to demonstrate "some strange chords" she had heard in the tune. Donegan explains that they were "from the Dorian mode." McPartland asks, "can you do that again or was that something that just fell in there by accident?" Donegan replies with a laugh, "No, that was not by accident, it was designed" (McPartland, 1983). Then Donegan proceeds, at McPartland's behest, to play the phrase again. Each show featured sections such as these, moments that focused on creating music and then analyzing the music right after it was performed. This in-the-moment analysis contrasts with how McPartland would humorously deflect sexist commentary as recounted above. The show enabled her to, in some ways, bypass the commentary by taking control not only of the music but also of the commentary *around* the music, thus curating the narrative of jazz.

A key example of this type of musical revelation includes a moment during the Mary Lou Williams interview. McPartland and Williams are talking about rhythm and bass lines and in particular Williams plays a piece she wrote that she says is "a little rock thing." She goes on to explain that "the kids … have been carried away so much into this rock thing and they kinda lost the feeling of jazz." She then explains that the piece "has a rock rhythm" but she has "put the blues back on top of it." McPartland then asks, "can you get them to have that … on two and four rather than … [how] they . . . always clap on one? It's so square." William then agrees, "That is terrible. If you are playing jazz it will just ruin you. But this [piece has its rhythmic emphasis] on 4/4." Williams then speaks and claps "one, two, three, four" (McPartland 1979). She then plays the tune "Rosa Mae" and sings the lyrics she wrote for the piece. This exchange demonstrates Williams's focus on music education, her philosophy of jazz education, and the wide-ranging styles she composed and performed. The discussion about jazz theory also shows how these women shaped the discourse of jazz at the time. Rather than focusing explicitly on gender dynamics, the show seems to offer listeners a clear example of masterful musicians who happen to also be women, indicating a subtle but powerful corrective for a typically male-dominated and masculinist history. And the fact that the host, a competent female musician, can illicit such illuminating musical material further demonstrates an underlying feminist dimension of McPartland's curation of jazz history. For example, one of the most oft-cited exchanges on *Piano Jazz* comes from McPartland's program with Bill Evans, also in the first season of the show. Evans, known for his quiet and reserved manner, opens up about his playing (McPartland, May 27, 1979). This interview, especially a moment where Evans demonstrates the displacement of phrases, has been cited and analyzed in several academic articles and dissertations, further highlighting the show's importance to jazz scholars.

One other aspect *Piano Jazz* highlighted was the range of jazz history and approaches to the music that were not apparent on the stage or in classrooms. Two shows that feature these moments are with Alice Coltrane in 1981 and Cecil Taylor in 1994. Alice Coltrane's *Piano Jazz* appearance features the soft-spoken Coltrane playing several of her own tunes as well as John Coltrane pieces. An exchange that exemplifies a focus on the extra-musical aspects of jazz performance is discussed during the show. In particular, Coltrane and McPartland discuss the practice of meditation (McPartland, 1981). Additionally, McPartland's interview with Cecil Taylor addresses the musical, historical, and spiritual aspects of his music and poetry. Perhaps one of the most substantive interviews of Cecil Taylor ever recorded, McPartland discusses with Taylor his poetry and its connection to nature. At the end of the exchange about his poetry, Taylor explains, "[poetry] helps us to survive the negation [of nature]." McPartland's connection with Taylor on an extramusical level provides insight into his music. The two then go on to play an entirely improvised duet with McPartland admitting, "Listening to you brings out something in me that's not always there." Taylor responds simply, "It's there" (McPartland, Feb. 16, 1994). These exchanges provide an exclusive look into jazz as it is being created and enacted.

For jazz students, fans, and musicians alike, McPartland's approach provides a rare "behind the scenes" glimpse into the creation of jazz. Musicians on *Piano Jazz*, through very little encouragement or questioning, reveal how they do what they do. McPartland's archive of these conversations represents a significant contribution to jazz history and performance and highlights the importance of curatorial practice necessary for enacting a feminist curation of jazz. In particular, McPartland's curation is feminist because, as demonstrated through the examples above, she centered her approach on telling the story of jazz through *listening* versus trying to impose her ideas and theories onto her guests. In Nichole T. Rustin and Sherrie Tucker's (2008) edited volume *Big Ears: Listening for Gender in Jazz Studies*, Rustin and Tucker explain why listening for gender in jazz is integral to understanding jazz history: "Listening for gender in jazz studies shifts the contours of jazz history: the boundaries and definitions of what counts as jazz sounds and *practices* (my emphasis)" (p. 19). McPartland shifts the contours of jazz history by practicing a feminist way of listening and thereby expanding the boundaries of jazz history. She was also comfortable with discussions of gender without needing to foreground them. Additionally, her attention to her guests' individual styles and her ability to easily engage with them through "their" musical language (she was able to interview figures as eclectic as Mary Lou Williams and Cecil Taylor) exemplifies her enacting a feminist curatorial practice.

Nancy Wilson's *Jazz Profiles*

Song stylist Nancy Wilson was featured on *Piano Jazz* in 1994. Similar to the other shows I have focused on here, Wilson addresses, somewhat subtly, issues of gender and the music business during part of her hour with McPartland. Wilson explains,

> I've always respected this business…. Just look at the history, especially females. An awful lot of women, wonderful women, performers, singers, great voices, marvelous, delightful people whose lives were a living hell…. There is something in the business that will do that to you because all these women are not weak. These are wonderful women. What is there that creates this chaos in their lives? So, I put family and home first. I put my happiness before the music.
>
> *(McPartland, 1994)*

Nancy Wilson was born in 1937 in Chillicothe, Ohio. She began her career quite young, having a TV show by the time she was 15. Referring to herself as a song stylist, her career spanned over fifty years, and she performed with musicians ranging from Cannonball Adderly to Hank Jones to Chick

Corea. She also released over 70 albums throughout her long career. She was asked to host a new jazz series for NPR in 1995, and she jumped at the chance. The show, *Jazz Profiles*, aired on NPR from 1996–2005. Former producer for NPR Tim Owens said of the show,

> [c]ollectively, *Jazz Profiles* remains the most comprehensive history of jazz ever recorded. Nearly 200 one-hour shows focused on a single, living jazz artist were created. The series also chronicled the lives of those no longer living—some of jazz's greatest innovators, like Louis Armstrong, Duke Ellington, Charlie Parker and Charles Mingus. Some shows explored topics such as women in jazz, or hallowed places like the Village Vanguard.
>
> *(2018)*

Unfortunately, the overall significance of Nancy Wilson's life and her work with *Jazz Profiles* has not been well documented. However, I would like to highlight several episodes that demonstrate the curatorial importance of the show to jazz history. *Jazz Profiles* differs conceptually from *Piano Jazz* in various ways. While there are interviews, the series focuses on a more documentary style of telling the stories of the people and places of jazz, rather than featuring live performances by the interviewees (as is the case in *Piano Jazz*). This is a different type of curation, one that collects and shapes the stories of jazz in a more cohesive narrative. To illustrate the historical significance of the shows, I turn to the *Jazz Profiles* show that focused on the Village Vanguard. Featuring performers who played in the club as well as interviews with club owners Max and Lorraine Gordon, the show paints a picture of an integral venue and space for jazz that continues to be essential to jazz performance today. The episode focuses on Lorraine Gordon's running of the club after her husband Max Gordon's death. Lorraine Gordon discusses her role as the proprietor of a major jazz club. While not explicitly feminist in the way the Vanguard is featured, the focus on Lorraine Gordon and her integral role in this important space for jazz implies a subtle focus on gender and jazz. In particular, the show highlights a woman shaping and curating a venerated space for jazz, thus showing the importance of the work of women in jazz beyond performance.

Two other shows highlight the importance of the profiles on particular musicians and the rich intersectional history they represent. One show that highlights these intersections is the show profiling singer Abbey Lincoln. As with all *Jazz Profiles* episodes, the show interweaves interviews with the musician being profiled along with their collaborators, as well as music from the performer, providing an intimate documentary-style portrait of jazz. The varied, high quality documentaries represent an important record of the history of jazz shared via prominent media to the general public. One example of this intimacy can be heard in Lincoln's recounting of her childhood home:

> In the winters, I guess it was really cold because this house, on 11.5 acres, there weren't any other buildings around to protect us from the wind and the snow. I don't remember being cold. I remember a chance to sit at the piano that he [her father] had for us too. Mama said there was at one time there were two pianos. There was this upright piano in the living room and I'd go in there and pick out melodies all by myself when I was like 4 and 5 and 6. And I didn't know when I was a little girl that I would have a career and I would learn to be all these things but I have. But it started there, in the house my father built in the country.
>
> *(2002)*

Wilson goes on to explain that, in 1992, Lincoln wrote two songs, one commemorating her father and one her mother. This analysis brings together the personal history of Lincoln's childhood with her career as a singer and composer. The depth of the stories told on *Jazz Profiles* highlight an alternative history to the great-man narrative so often presented in jazz histories.

A similar intimacy can be found in the *Jazz Profiles* episode that featured the career of trombonist and arranger, Melba Liston. In highlighting her early career, the profile of Liston emphasizes the connections and mentoring she had from older musicians, including bandleader Gerald Wilson. In recounting her early career, Liston first discusses her time as a performer. Liston graduated from high school in 1942 and joined the Lincoln Theater band in Los Angeles that same year, and the bandleader, Bardu Ali, quickly discovered Liston's skills at arranging. The bandleader had her write for the theater's stars, including Louis Armstrong. Armstrong was impressed by Liston and encouraged her to take her first solo. However, Liston did not really view herself as a performer. She explained, "I didn't want to solo. I didn't even desire to. No, I was not the solo type. But [I was] 'the girl in the band' so you got to solo" (2008).

However, she would go on to join Gerald Wilson's band, and he praised her for her playing ability; she also fostered Liston's arranging and composing, becoming his assistant. The show highlights her importance as a jazz arranger, through the voices of musicians she worked with, including Gerald Wilson, Randy Weston, and many others. The show also features many recorded examples of her arrangements, allowing listeners to experience them aurally, in addition to providing in-depth musical examination of her arranging. Drummer Charli Persip analyzed Liston's arranging in the *Jazz Profiles* episode:

> "[Hers was] the hardest music I ever played…. [Her music] is different because she's got kind of another harmonic sense. Some of the harmonies are very close. There's a lot of dissonances but the dissonances, as you know, they work. You may use certain notes as passing tones that may be dissonances but then when they pass to the next chord then it blossoms into something very beautiful.
>
> *(2008)*

The intimacy and time afforded to these moments are what make *Jazz Profiles* invaluable to the feminist narrative of jazz. These examples demonstrate that profiling Abbey Lincoln and Melba Liston's careers was an act of feminist reclamation, a critical examination of the music and lives of musicians that rarely occurred in jazz histories and happened even less in the mass media for a general audience. This further highlights the importance of curatorial practice, in this case in a deep dive into a musician's professional life, as a way of enriching the history of jazz. As with the presence of McPartland's voice in *Piano Jazz*, the fact that each episode of *Jazz Profiles* was structured around the narrative presented by an accomplished female jazz artist like Nancy Wilson further emphasizes the role women play as not only performers but also as curatorial guardians of the music.

LaDonna Smith's *the improvisor*

Another important curator, in this case primarily of avant-garde jazz and improvisation, is LaDonna Smith, improvisor, violinist, violist, educator, concert producer, and co-founder and publisher of the journal, *the improvisor* (the international journal of free improvisation), Smith is a native of Birmingham, Alabama, and grew up learning, performing, and fostering improvised music in the southeastern United States. Smith's work has grown to focus on creating a space and a discourse for improvised music globally.

While the shows of McPartland and Wilson highlight the curatorial importance of radio, Smith's publication and founding of the journal *the improvisor* spotlights another form of curatorship that is often overlooked: print media. Started in 1980, *the improvisor*, while no longer published, continues to be available through its archive, which is partially housed online. This archive is rich in the history and sound of the world of improvised music. During the 1980s and 1990s, before the age of the Internet, the focus of a publication on improvised music was invaluable to performers, festival promoters, and scholars alike.

> The publication exists for the purpose of sharing experiences in the world of sound, writings about sound, movement and music, performance events of interest, and to build a network of people and a web of information, in which to further develop and support the act of unabashed creativity and play.
>
> *(http://the-improvisor.org/sitemap.html)*

I argue here for viewing Smith's work as both a curator and an archivist. In particular, the journal was not solely a historical or textual documentary source but also a way for performing musicians to learn about and learn from one another and to connect.

The improvisor is a curatorial space by and for musicians. Articles from its over thirty years in publication range from announcements of workshops to scholarly articles on improvisation in education, improvisation as prayer, and so forth; record reviews; and reflections on live performances. Several of Smith's articles, as well as pieces by other contributors to the journal, address a central goal of the publication, which was to create a "resource for musicians and composers of free improvisation, to share music, ideas" and more (http://the-improvisor.org/sitemap.html). Highly diverse in form and content, the publication, in some ways, mirrors the improvised music scene, wide-ranging, open, and shifting in focus—although it is notable that McPartland and Wilson also both engaged in this open-minded approach, interviewing and featuring musicians from the avant-garde on their more mainstream-focused programs. This open-mindedness, one could argue, is another component of the feminist curatorial practice. Each of the women curators actively sought out more marginalized musicians and genres, utilizing their curatorial lens to bring attention to these musicians and their music.

Representative articles in *the improvisor* illustrate the dedication to improvised music that has been at the core of Smith's career. For instance, in an article Smith wrote for the journal titled, "Improvisation in Childhood: Music Training and Techniques for Creative Music Making," Smith draws from her "fifteen years as teacher and Director of a Suzuki Violin Program" along with her pioneering work as a free improvisor in the United States (n.d.). Smith suggests that,

> Musical creativity should be the first and foremost priority in the teaching of music. In every music lesson, there should be a time for improvisation, for invention, and a time for technical training, and development of the tools, which would include improvisational skills based on free and theoretical styles.
>
> *(n.d)*

Smith advocates for putting into practice an improvisation-centered music education. In many ways, the journal was a space that fostered a community of musicians and practitioners of improvised music. In describing and reviewing the 2000 Guelph Jazz Festival Symposium, Smith explained,

> [t]he colloquium, to my mind, as a unique and powerful presence in the Guelph Jazz Festival week, sets off an internal community inquiry into the making of music, and the social ramifications of it. It brings us to the artists, up close, and creates an opportunity for people and artists to co-mingle, communicate, and learn from each other.
>
> *(2000)*

This sense of community is one that permeates the focus of the articles in *the improvisor* and demonstrates an enactment of curation that centers community and improvisation. Community building is an important component of feminist curation as well as improvisational practices. Improvisation, community, and feminism align in Smith's work and exemplify the intersectional aspects of jazz that Daniel Fischlin and Ajay Heble (2004) discuss in *The Other Side of Nowhere:*

Jazz, Improvisation, and Communities in Dialogue. Fischlin and Heble explain that improvising musicians, such as Smith, "demonstrate … that innovated forms of musical expression can contribute to a formulation of new models for civic life by being sources of empowerment, education, and community building" (p. 25). In her pedagogical work, her writing, and performance, Smith advances a feminist curatorial practice connected with the deep history of community that has long been a part of jazz.

Terri Lyne Carrington's *Institute of Jazz and Gender Justice*

With the establishment of the *Institute of Jazz and Gender Justice* at Berklee College of Music in January of 2019, drummer, bandleader, college professor, and composer Terri Lyne Carrington brought to the fore a component of the jazz narrative that, while present throughout jazz history (as evidenced in the discussions of the musicians above), had not been deliberately institutionalized or even officially acknowledged. Starting with the question, "What would jazz without patriarchy sound like?" Carrington is deliberately enacting a feminist curatorial practice of jazz by directly confronting the role gender has played in understanding and enacting jazz.

This is an approach decidedly different to the curation of jazz than has been the focus of institutions such as Jazz at Lincoln Center. In fact, while shaping the narrative of the history of jazz, Marsalis has included the works of women jazz composers, notably Mary Lou Williams, but has not sought to incorporate women instrumentalists into the Lincoln Center Jazz Orchestra (LCJO) until recently. In fact, in its thirty-year history, the LCJO has only had one female band member tour with them full time, Camille Thurman. In 1995, only a few years after the LCJO was founded, Marsalis was confronted with the question of mentoring and fostering female instrumentalists. In a debate with James Lincoln Collier, it was reported that Marsalis, in defending his hiring practices, recounted how diverse the members of his band were. Marsalis then explained that

> his goal [was] to advance the jazz genre by encouraging young men to continue in jazz. When asked what was being done to help young women learn the genre, Marsalis rolled his eyes and said that he didn't have time for such political correctness. The unspoken answer was nothing.
>
> *(Kavanaugh as cited in Wehr, p. 482)*

As late as 2018, the LCJO's hiring practices around gender equity were still being called into question. Calls for the LCJO to conduct blind auditions, as many symphonic orchestras and classical music ensembles do, have gone unheeded. While LCJO's decisions are disappointing to many women, gender non-binary, gender non-conforming, and transgender people who have been performing, composing, teaching, producing jazz, the *Institute for Jazz and Gender Justice* provides a space for redressing the jazz gender gap.

During the inaugural ceremonies for the institute, keynote speaker and professor of African American literature at Columbia, Farah Jasmine Griffin, explained, "the work of achieving gender justice is not 'women's work" (Lorge, 2019, p. 25). In other words, the focus of the institute is on *gender* equity, not solely on women's equity. However, it is important to note that Carrington, as a woman, took on this renarrativization of jazz by enacting these changes. Carrington also spoke to some common misconceptions about gender justice and how the institute will enact it:

> No, the institute won't be about all-female ensembles and segregating musicians into washroom categories. But it will be about musicians all along the gender spectrum—female, male, non-conforming and non-binary—working together to create music that rises above social constructs based on seeming biological differences. In large part, this work will be

corrective, Carrington said, and a challenge to the basic underpinnings of patriarchy, the system by which women and non-normative individuals are disenfranchised.

(Lorge, 2019, p. 26)

This important corrective is being enacted through a deliberate curatorial practice that Carrington and ethnomusicologist Aja Burrell Wood, managing director of the institute, are programming. While the COVID-19 pandemic undoubtedly curtailed the programming and performances that would have occurred through the institute, virtual events throughout 2020 and early 2021 have focused on discussions on Black Feminism, Jazz and Gender, and virtual performances as well as developing a new book of standards and curating a Jazz and Gender Justice playlist on Spotify. These wide-ranging discussions and varied performances are building a curated narrative on jazz and gender and racial justice. The intersectional work that the Berklee *Institute of Jazz and Gender Justice* provides highlights an important move in the curation of a new jazz narrative. It is also important to note that Carrington took her curatorial practice of jazz to an established institution where jazz teaching and learning are known globally. The fact that the institute is housed and backed by a university helps to establish it as a counter to the narrative that has grown out of standard jazz histories and JALC, through not only performance, but also scholarship, programming, education, and so forth. With the institute, Carrington brings the history of jazz and its curation into focus, allowing for a more inclusive and representative history of jazz than has been enacted before now. Building on the more historiographical work of feminist curators such as McParland, Wilson, and Smith, Carrington and her colleagues offer a more explicitly feminist curatorial framework from which to hear and create jazz.

Conclusion

Marian McPartland and Nancy Wilson's radio shows provide an alternative approach to the framing of jazz history and performance. The year 1987 saw the establishment of Jazz at Lincoln Center with Wynton Marsalis as its curator, and the first concert, titled "Ladies First: A Tribute to the Great Women of Jazz," featured Marian McPartland, along with bassist Steve LaSpina and drummer Joey Baron, playing the music of Mary Lou Williams (de Barros, 2012, p. 331). While it may seem that JALC's positioning of a "Ladies First" concert emphasized a feminist perspective, this was more likely a case of tokenization. As Lara Pelligrinelli (2008) argues (in the context of women singers versus male instrumentalists in jazz), this type of revering women as important "founding mothers" who can then be let go in favor of their more significant male progeny is an unfortunate repetitive feature of jazz history. (p. 32)

As discussed above, JALC now represents the largest organization to champion jazz and, as ethnomusicologist Kimberly Hannon Teal explains,

> The legitimacy that JALC has brought, not just to the contemporary music that is performed there, but also to the venue's particular interpretation of jazz history, continues to be a source of concern because it is difficult for any single organization to act as the primary curator of a diverse tradition.
>
> *(p. 401)*

However, *Piano Jazz* started in 1978, *the improvisor* began its publication in 1980, and *Jazz Profiles* started in 1995. While each of these publications and shows had divergent foci, their contributions to jazz history is no less important than the narrative that is presented, perpetuated, and curated by JALC and the previous histories of jazz published in earlier decades. While McPartland was not solely in charge of booking, producing, or staging performances through *Piano Jazz*, her show was heard around the United States and established an important component of the jazz history narrative. That narrative was one that was absent in the curation of the JALC and previous histories in particular because of Marsalis' lack of employing women or staging women's music (with the exception of Williams). So, at the heart of this is a lack of women's voices, women's curatorial voices or even the acknowledgement that women could shape the narrative of jazz.

Why have women's voices been diminished within the shaping of jazz history? There are a multitude of reasons: sexism, racism, the focus on instrumentalists versus vocalists, and so forth. Women's voices were, in a sense, drowned out by the loud narrative, established by predominantly white, male historians and journalists of jazz in the 1950s through the 1990s, and that was further perpetuated at JALC. However, it is the *curatorial practice* of feminist perspectives that allows for a more complex narrative of jazz to emerge and, by examining the work of McPartland, Wilson, Smith, and Carrington, we can expand the history of jazz to focus not only on the past of jazz but also to reexamine, shape, and expand the present and future of jazz as well.

References

De Barros, P. (2012). *Shall We Play That One Together: The Life and Art of Jazz Piano Legend Marian McPartland*. St. Martin's Press.

Fischlin, D. and A. Heble (Eds.). (2004). *The Other Side of Nowhere: Jazz, Improvisation, and Communities in Dialogue*. Wesleyan University Press.

Hentoff, N. (2011). *At the Jazz Band Ball: Sixty Years on the Jazz Scene*. University of California Press.

Jones, A. (2016). "Feminist Subjects versus Feminist Effects: The Curating of Feminist Art (or is it the Feminist Curating of Art?)" Issue 29. Oncurating.org.

Kernodle, T. (2020 [2004]). *Soul on Soul: The Life and Music of Mary Lou Williams*. University of Illinois Press.

Lorge, S. (2019, February). "Transform the Culture." *Downbeat*, 24–29.

McMullen, T. (2021). "The Lessons of Jazz: What We Teach When We Teach Jazz in College." In M. Kahr (Ed.), *Artistic Research in Jazz: Positions, Theories, Methods*. Routledge.

McPartland, M. (1987). *All in Good Time*. Oxford University Press.

McPartland, M. (Host). (1979, April 1). Billy Taylor. [Radio program]. *Piano Jazz*. NPR.

————. (Host). (1979). Mary Lou Williams. [Radio program]. *Piano Jazz*. NPR.

————. (Host). (1979, May 27). Bill Evans. [Radio program]. *Piano Jazz*. NPR.

————. (Host). (1981, Dec. 4). Alice Coltrane. [Radio program]. *Piano Jazz*. NPR.

————. (Host). (1983). Dorothy Donegan. [Radio program]. *Piano Jazz*. NPR.

————. (Host). (1994, Jan. 15). Nancy Wilson. [Radio program]. *Piano Jazz*. NPR.

————. (Host). (1994, Feb. 26). Cecil Taylor. [Radio program]. *Piano Jazz*. NPR.

Murphy, T. (2004). "Improvisation as Idiomatic, Ethic, and Harmolodic." *Genre*, 37(1), 129–150. https://doi.org/10.1215/00166928-37-1-129.

Owen, T. (2018). Remembering Nancy Wilson: The Best of 'Jazz Profiles.' Retrieved from www.npr.org/2018/12/15/676919863/remembering-nancy-wilson-the-best-of-jazz-profiles.

Pellegrinelli, L. (2008). Separated at "Birth": Singing and the History of Jazz. In N. T. Rustin and S. Tucker (Eds.), *Big Ears: Listening for Gender in Jazz Studies*. (pp. 31–47). Duke University Press.

Porter. E. (2002). *What is this Thing Called Jazz?: African American Musicians as Artists, Critics, and Activists*. Berkeley, CA: University of California Press.

Rustin, N. T. and S. Tucker (Eds.). (2008). *Big Ears: Listening for Gender in Jazz Studies*. Duke University Press.

Smith, L. (n.d.). Improvisation in Childhood Music Training and Techniques for Creative Music Making. Retrieved from http://the-improvisor.org/web%20ARTICLES/Improvisation%20&%20Education.html.

————. (2000). Guelph International Jazz Festival and Colloquium: A Report on the Colloquium. Retrieved from http://the-improvisor.org/web%20ARTICLES/Guelph%20Jazz%20Fest%202000.html.

Teal, K. (2014). "Posthumously Live: Canon Formation at Jazz at Lincoln Center through the Case of Mary Lou Williams." *American Music*, 32(4), 400–422. https://doi.org/10.5406/americanmusic.32.4.0400.

Wehr, E. (2016). "Understanding the Experiences of Women in Jazz: A Suggested Model." *International Journal of Music Education*, 34(4), 472–487.

Wilson, N. (Host). (2001). The Village Vanguard: A Hallowed Basement. *Jazz Profiles*. NPR.

————. (Host). (2002). Abbey Lincoln: The Power of Voice. *Jazz Profiles*. NPR.

————. (Host). (2008). Melba Liston: The Bones of an Arranger. *Jazz Profiles*. NPR.

9

THE GIRL IN THE OTHER ROOM

Generating New Open Knowledge for the Women of Jazz

M. Cristina Pattuelli and Karen Li-Lun Hwang

Introduction

As with most histories, the history of jazz is one dominated by men. Angela Davis, in a panel discussion on jazz and gender, pointed out that while the jazz community has always been one to anticipate and be on the forefront of social change, it has been slow to recognize and reluctant to act on issues of gender inequality. Davis urged jazz musicians and scholars alike to "figure out ways to guarantee that jazz is not left behind while the rest of the world moves forward" (Winter Jazzfest, 2018). The gender gap has become a staple of discourse within the jazz community through panel discussions, documentaries, and exhibitions. A significant body of jazz literature has also been devoted to discussing gender inequality from different perspectives and historical contexts. Noted women in jazz study pioneers include Handy (1981, 1998), Dahl (1989), and Tucker (1999, 2000, 2004, 2008), as well as scholars such as McKeage (2004), Wehr (2016), and Van Vleet (2021).

While issues surrounding jazz and gender seem obvious, at least anecdotally, providing empirical evidence enables us to identify the issue's origin, recognize its context and understand its persistence. As jazz journalist and scholar Lara Pellegrinelli (2017) suggests, hard data and factual evidence, such as the tally of women bandleaders at US jazz festivals, or the percentage of women faculty in jazz academic departments, provide an unbiased way to evaluate gender parity. Such data uncover hidden assumptions and expose discriminatory norms and practices.

Since 2011, the Linked Jazz project[1] has been mining information from jazz historical sources and facilitating its analysis using a new generation of digital tools. Knowing that the practice of jazz was embedded in a rich cohesive social network, the initial aim of Linked Jazz was to show the dense web of professional and personal relationships that tie jazz musicians together. Discovering and analyzing connections between people, places, events, and concepts are essential to understanding the history and evolution of a community. The jazz community, characterized by a high level of interaction and connectivity, is no exception. However, identifying and navigating the web of relationships among jazz musicians requires extensive archival research.

For decades, digital technologies have been applied to cultural content, including jazz archives and special collections, to improve visibility and expand access to the material. Semantic technologies, however, and their most recent implementation—linked open data—afford much more than access. They represent information in the form of structured data. These data have meaning attached that humans, but more importantly, digital systems, can understand and process. In other words,

DOI: 10.4324/9781003081876-10

linked data technologies make information semantically transparent and computationally tractable to enable new forms of sense-making. Linked open data principles are based on a powerful knowledge paradigm that sees connections as producers of meaning. Without delving too far into the technical details of the development process, machine-readable data is constructed and linked into networked structures. The process is conducted under principles of openness, as linked open data are by definition public and intended to be freely available on the web. Not only are they to be discovered, queried and explored through visualizations, they are also intended to be shared and reused through new configurations and different systems. The network model and flexible framework of these technologies enable us to represent the jazz community as an extensible knowledge graph.

A Relational Cartography of the Jazz Community

Social scientists have long held "the notion that individuals are embedded in thick webs of social relations and interactions" (Borgatti, Mehra, Brass, and Labianca, 2009, p. 892). While invaluable for building critical scholarship, uncovering these relationships, especially in historical contexts, can be a daunting task. Even if the Web has made digital content more accessible, the task of gathering all the possible sources of information needed to support comprehensive analysis still requires a labor-intensive process of sifting through individual collections and digging into discrete documents disseminated through repositories located across the United States and around the world.

Through an automated method of data extraction, we mined a sample of over fifty jazz oral history transcripts. To compile a diverse sample of documents we relied on the rich collections of digitized and transcribed oral histories held by a number of different institutions including Hamilton College, Rutgers University, The Smithsonian, University of Michigan, and University of California, Los Angeles. A baseline of connections among musicians was created under the assumption that if someone mentions another person it is safe to assume a level of knowledge or familiarity with the person referenced. The relation "knows of" was the first connector that linked the jazz musicians in a machine-readable networked structure. Automated methods can only go so far in understanding the semantics carried in textual narratives, so we relied on human interpretation through crowdsourcing to identify connections with more expressive properties of membership, collaboration and personal closeness. With this new layer of semantics, the Linked Jazz Oral History Network grew into a knowledge base comprised of nearly 2000 musicians and jazz affiliates.

Through a tiered development process that was experimental at the time (for details see Pattuelli, Miller, Lange, Fitzell, and Li-Madeo, 2013), text was "alchemically" dissolved and converted into knowledge graphs. While most efforts in the use of semantic technologies were, and mostly still are, concerned with converting existing descriptions of documents into linked data, we focused instead on mining and encoding actual content. We performed text analysis and extracted person entity names from digitized text to generate original knowledge in the form of machine-readable statements, all connected as a semantic chain—a knowledge graph—representing musicians' social relationships.

These linked data-driven graphs are sets of interconnected data that can be queried for direct answers. A more enticing and intuitive way to harness graphs, however, is through visualization. A dedicated visualization tool makes it possible to interact with the network through various configurations—from a global view of the map of relations to radial views centered on individuals and their circles. Figure 9.1 shows, on the left, the network representing connections across the entire corpus of jazz interviews. The larger the image of the musician, the greater the number of connections. On the right is displayed the ego-network of Hazel Scott showing the graph of people who mentioned her.

Each node represents a musician. It is also the starting point for navigating paths of connections that have not been predetermined which, in turn, leads to unanticipated lines of exploration and discovery. Social network analysis studies of jazz musicians based on a mathematically based approach

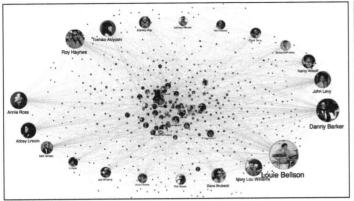 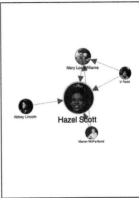

Figure 9.1 Mention-based network rendering: Global view (left) and radial view of Hazel Scott (right).

have been conducted in the past with a focus on contemporary musicians (Heckathorn and Jeffri, 2001, 2003) and discographies (Schubert, 2012). Developed as a demonstrative prototype, our effort showed the potential that a qualitative approach to social network analysis has on the study of facets of influence, reputation, and authority.

Both as a theoretical framework and a methodological approach, this networked structure enables us to see the world not as distinct entities, but as a web of relations. It is a powerful paradigm that responds to the complexity of the world, or, in this case, the intricacies of a community of musicians, by asserting the notion that all entities, including people, are best understood as nodes in a web. The jazz community that emerged from the knowledge graph appeared, on the surface, to reflect mainstream narratives of unproblematic engagement, collaborations and participation. However, indicators of an anomaly started to surface as more oral histories of women jazz musicians were processed. It became apparent that the number of women musicians increased dramatically, revealing that many more women jazz musicians existed but were not accounted for in our dataset. This raised a number of questions and led to the assumption that women in jazz simply mentioned other women in the context of their lives and careers more often than men did. A necessary technical step in the development process is the validation of proper names, which is performed by mapping names against authoritative name directories. When a name is not found in the lists, it needs to be minted and associated to a public unique identifier. Just by quantifying the newly created names (8% of the women mentioned in the entire text corpus), we began to see clear evidence of the ways in which women jazz musicians were excluded from the historical record (Pattuelli, Hwang, and Miller, 2016).

Lack of data, as Onuoha (2018) observed, is often associated with issues concerning the most vulnerable individuals in a given context, suggesting a vacancy of something that should instead be there. As D'Ignazio and Klein (2020) argued, "the phenomenon of missing data is a regular and expected outcome in all societies characterized by unequal power relations" due to systematic disregard and neglect for data about powerless people (p. 38). The omission of data can be extremely revealing and a compelling clue for further investigation. The name discrepancies observed during data collection set off our next phase of research, redirecting us to more closely examine the gender data gap we had detected.

As Wahl and Ellingson (2018) pointed out, "the jazz art world operates on informal but powerful networks of male musicians" who hold the keys to the jazz scene and are the arbiters of the canon (p. 459). Women musicians are often burdened or impeded by stereotypical assumptions underlying their professional competence, especially when compared to male musicians. In other words, the table they are not invited to sit at is set up by meritocratic parameters that all but seal their exclusion. The gender imbalance we noticed coming from the content of oral histories suggested that women musicians were not part of the memory when the memory was constructed by men. These factors framed our research agenda moving forward.

Gendering the Network

To start gathering hard evidence of the gender disparity observed during data collection, we needed to quantify the distribution of jazz artists in the dataset. Counting women might seem like a low-hanging fruit approach, but it provides a critical base measurement of the phenomenon. "Quantification is representation," in the words of data journalist Jonathan Stray (2016), who stated that "Counting is limited, but there are many things that are best known by counting" ("Quantification is Representation" section). We did not have a way to accurately quantify the presence of women in the network until the attribute "gender" was associated to each musician in our dataset. Assigning gender data—a fundamental marker of identity—can be a problematic and often a controversial undertaking. As Björck and Bergman (2018) recently noted, women jazz musicians still describe the "women" label as something that causes discomfort due to the fact that being a woman is often viewed as a mark of inferiority. It could have a negative influence on the way their professional value is perceived, further perpetuating their marginality. Gender neutrality in jazz music, however, also works against women, as "jazz music [is] inherently coded as masculine" and, without a qualifier, would be interpreted as male-created music by default (Björck and Bergson, 2018, p. 50).

Coding personal attributes like gender, and eventually others, was an essential first step in making these aspects computationally tractable. It also facilitated data analysis and visibility. In the Linked Jazz Oral History Network, ensuring women musicians were represented enabled us to advance from basic research questions answered with simple frequency and distribution data, to more complex considerations about the nature of women's participation and contributions. Quantitative evidence that women jazz musicians were part of the jazz scene was key to uncovering this lesser-represented, often-invisible segment of the community.

From a data engineering perspective, the task of assigning gender was not straightforward. Automated approaches to gender identification based on machine-learning techniques were not a viable option, as they were still experimental and prone to error (Cheng, Chandramouli, and Subbalakshmi, 2011). We resorted to harvesting gender from name directories, including the Library of Congress Name Authority File[2] and MusicBrainz,[3] the most extensive and authoritative data hubs at the time (Hwang, 2015). Another limitation was the binary format of "male/man" or "female/woman" with the only option of "unknown" to address missing or uncertain data. It is encouraging to see the expansion in the range of gender descriptors that have emerged since we started working on gender data back in 2014, offering options that extend beyond binary to account for gender fluidity and nonconformity. We should point out that we have yet to encounter a case in our work where a non-binary term is required. It is also worth noting that jazz has been slow compared to other music genres in challenging gender and sex stereotypes. Instead it has actively worked to preserve hetero-normative connotations that align with its hegemonic masculine and inherently heterosexual image (Annfelt, 2003; Davis, 2002; Tucker, 2008).

Visualizing Gender Asymmetries

Once gender was assigned to all the person entities in the Linked Jazz Oral History Network, we shifted from a generalized representation of the jazz community as a social network to a highly focused one that allowed us to examine the dataset through a gendered lens. A dedicated gender view was added to the existing network graph, providing visual evidence at a glance of the unequal ratio between genders for macro analysis.[4] The distribution of men and women was computed through simple tabulation. Of a total of 52 interviews, 41 were with men and 11 with women while people

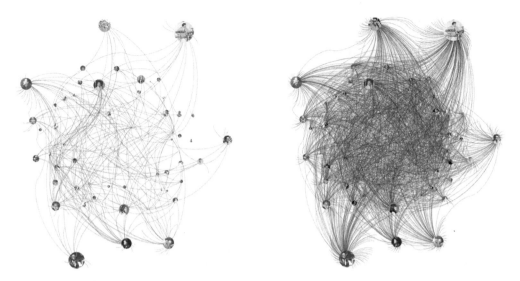

Figure 9.2 Network graph filtered by gender: Women on the left and men on the right.

mentioned included 221 women and 1,695 men. Due to the relatively small sample of oral histories and the limitations of working with prototypes in the initial phase of data collection, we can only consider these numbers as indicative, albeit revealing. More specific configurations display gendered data by distribution of mentions (Figure 9.2).

In the view on the left of the figure, each line connects a woman to the person who mentioned that woman. Similarly, the view on the right displays men mentioned in interviews with connections to the individuals who mentioned them. A comparison of the graphs in terms of line densities clearly illustrates that significantly more men had been mentioned across the corpus of interviews than women. Data were also computed and visualized to show the most-mentioned women. In this instance, key markers were the points of intersection representing people who had been mentioned in more than one interview. The density of the intersections was a strong indicator of the frequency of mentions across interviews denoting acknowledgements from multiple sources. In the graph representing mentioned women, three points were identified as the densest junctions of links corresponding to Sarah Vaughan, Billie Holiday, and Ella Fitzgerald—three celebrated vocalists. They were mentioned by 20, 19, and 17 people respectively. The next most mentioned women were Dinah Washington, Carmen McRae, and Lena Horne, followed by Mary Lou Williams, finally the first instrumentalist, mentioned by 7 people.

Even in a relatively small interview sample like ours, the data indicate a prevalence of high-profile women vocalists, confirming the well-known issue of gender stereotyping that historically confines women to roles of vocalists and pianists (Annfelt, 2003). But women have been playing, as well as singing, from the beginning of the jazz era (Placksin, 1982). Their many contributions as instrumentalists, bandleaders, arrangers, and composers, educators or organizers, however, have seldomly made it into the official chronicles of jazz history. Mainstream narratives have celebrated the male instrumental soloist with his share of individual geniality and energetic self-confidence as the quintessential expression of jazz masculinity. This level of acceptance—membership to the pantheon of jazz—is bestowed upon women instrumentalists only on the condition of their exceptionality (O'Connell and Tucker, 2014). Validation through exceptionality and celebration of uniqueness has resulted in a process of tokenization of women instrumentalists, setting them apart from the professional community and neutralizing broader recognition of women as musicians.

Tallying musicians was the first technical step needed to create a baseline for further inquiry. It was also a direct way to make overlooked and under-recognized women jazz musicians immediately visible and more easily discoverable. Nonetheless, we do not subscribe to the idea that adding missing data back into the existing knowledge base somehow corrects and completes an otherwise male-dominated musical space. As Tucker (2004) pointed out in her study on New Orleans jazz women, adding "lost women" to jazz history would not reshape the general view of jazz as a masculine genre of music (p. 7).

Uncovering women not yet mentioned in earlier interviews and integrating them in the Linked Jazz knowledge graph enabled new and different types of data analysis. As an important feature of the Linked Jazz platform, each relation represented in the dataset is linked to its source, that is, the original excerpt it was derived from. The passages are gendered by default as they are directly associated with their speaker. We can now compute those mentions and discover that, on average across interviews, women mention men at a 10 percent higher rate than women are mentioned by men—28 percent versus 18 percent.[5] Interestingly, not a single woman was recorded by us as mentioned by Sam Rivers in his short interview conducted by Darryl Duncan (Rivers, 1988) or by David Murray when interviewed by Monk Rowe (Murray, 2003). On the other hand, 31 percent—the highest in our selection of interviews—was the share of women derived from Melba Liston's interview with Steve Isoardi (Liston, 1992). The majority of women interviewees cited other women at a rate of 20 percent or more, whereas the majority of men cited women at a rate lower than 10 percent.

The implications of using the property "gender" as a frame for analysis extends beyond quantifying and visualizing the data to include the possibility, for instance, to perform qualitative content analysis. The system allows a researcher to select excerpts with mentions around different focal points. For example, all the passages can be filtered by any musician in our dataset. Figure 9.3 illustrates this case by displaying a sample of quotes from six different oral histories referring to Mary Lou Williams.

Narrators and their gender are listed respectively in the two columns on the left. The broader historical context is always within reach as the original document, linked to each quote, can be easily consulted. This capability provides a new mode of access to primary sources making it possible to navigate their original content from a socio-relational perspective. It also generates a unique research

speakerLabel	genderLabel	blockText
Billy Eckstine	men	Mary Lou is a beautiful person. She's from my hometown, Pittsburgh. Mary Lou I love very much. She's a very accomplished musician.
Annie Ross	women	Yeah, exactly. She was a great cook. She was very funny. One night she said to me, "I'm going to take you to hear Sidney Bechet." At that time in Paris, there was a huge gap between dixieland and modern jazz. I said, "I don't want to hear Sidney Bechet. He's, like, of the old school." She said, "Don't say things like that unless you really know. I want to take you to hear him." We went, and I was amazed. He was something else. He used to collect emeralds, loose emeralds. Carried them in a little black pouch. I remember he gave Mary Lou Williams two or three - could have been four. From then on I was a - I loved Sidney Bechet, because I listened, and I heard. Mary Lou Williams's laugh, that was something that I can still hear. She was a wonderful lady, so talented. In the time she came up, how difficult could that have been?
Vi Redd	women	Oh it's been a pleasure. I think well, you know there are not too many of us around that were active in the 50's and 60's and 70's, and in sound mind and body. And I consider it a blessing that I'm still here to talk about things that have happened in the past and were very significant in terms of jazz history, and in terms of the roles of women in that. Oh we didn't mention Mary Lou Williams
Marian McPartland	women	Well we always said this, like when they had the Kansas City Women's Festival, that was a long time ago, I think you were probably a real young boy then -- I can't remember how long ago, gee maybe it's fifteen or twenty years -- and this was the, like the biggest jazz festival ever. Mary Lou Williams played it and I played it and Toshiko Akiyoshi had her big band, and I mean it was a large event. And they carried that on for three or four years and then ran out of money...
Jane Jarvis	women	The big problem in music, is you had to either go to the education formula, or cast your wits against the world in jazz. Because there was no forum, mind you, eighty years ago. Not eighty years ago, well, in 1929 is when all this took place. In 1929, there was no place for a woman to play jazz. Now I was friends with Mary Lou Williams, because she and Andy Kirk were at the Corbalabum, which was right on my way to Bush Conservatory, and I used to sit and listen to the rehearsals. Big bands used to rehearse, you know, in the afternoons. And that's where I met her.
Buddy Tate	men	More relaxed but still swing. It was more swinging. And they was just having fits and jumping and having fits, and they would be swinging, and those guys would be taking those fine solos and things behind them. And it just swept the whole thing away. It was Chic Webb, well Chic played everything, it had to be up here, you know? It'd be up there, they'd have the midwest thing. Then come Jay McShann after, but they all had a different thing, had a different thing. Andy Kirk had more of a sweet band, people like Pha Terrell, and Mary Lou Williams. They were swinging, but it was softer than Count Basie and people like that. They were good bands in Kansas City then. Musicians came out from New York who were supposed to be the big names, and they'd get a lesson when they'd come to Kansas City. They'd come from New York to Kansas City to get a lesson.

Figure 9.3 Sample of passages where Mary Lou Williams is mentioned.

space where different types of qualitative analysis can be conducted, like sentiment or discourse analysis, to examine gender power dynamics through life-story telling.

New Kinds of Biographies

Adding properties is at the core of data modeling, a key activity in any data-driven project. The original Linked Jazz dataset focused on social relationships representing professional and personal ties among musicians. The inclusion of gender data opened up the possibility of interrogating jazz history through a gendered lens. We would need to model and encode more identity data to convey the multiple facets of musicians' lives, including their social and cultural context, to better understand the full extent of women's contributions to jazz as well as the power dynamics at play in the work environment.

The process of creating an ontology to represent our domain of interest requires full awareness of the possibility to encode into the technical infrastructure the researchers' latent biases and assumptions regarding sexism, racism, or other forms of discrimination. Our modeling work, however, is not carried out in a vacuum or in isolation. Instead, the choice of descriptors to be assigned to musicians is informed by jazz studies literature, the current public discourse on jazz and, whenever possible, input from the archives and jazz communities. This interplay of information sources helps achieve greater diversity and inclusion in the way people's identities are represented in data and makes it possible to formulate more complex queries about their lives and work. For example, Wahl and Ellingson (2018) explained that there have been three key aspects impacting the career of women jazz musicians, especially during the Swing Era: having found a mentor, having married a jazz musician, or coming from a family of musicians. To be able to represent those elements, a number of properties were added to the Linked Jazz ontology to express mentorship and familial relations.

Digital technologies are evolving at a rapid pace, and remarkable progress has been made in the creation of new platforms and tools capable of fully implementing the core principles of openness and shareability that linked data are designed upon. One of the most impactful developments is Wikidata,[6] an expansive multilingual knowledge base that has rapidly become the main source of public-domain data. The information populating Wikidata—structured as linked data—is harvested from Wikipedia as well as contributed by anyone with a Wikidata account in a crowdsourced fashion.

Linked Jazz is a frequent user of the Wikidata knowledge base, both as a consumer and as a contributor of data. We have also been early adopters of Wikibase, the software that powers Wikidata, using a locally installed instance.[7] The two platforms share the same features, including an intuitive user interface that creates a "semantic" record for each of our individual musicians, bands, and performances. Each record consists of an online page that includes relevant information about an entity in the form of linked data. New information can be added effortlessly by any of the researchers involved in the project. One of the marks of quality of the data we enter is their traceability. Because they link back to their original source, they are easily verifiable.

The musician data configurations created represent a new kind of biography that, due to their underlying data structure, becomes an open-ended encyclopedia of networked life narratives. Unlike entries in traditional dictionaries of jazz, these profiles grow incrementally, extending their currency as new bits of content are added. As we expand our dataset with additional data derived from various sources, an interlinked web of previously disparate information emerges. The more-detailed data can be examined in context and speak to both professional and personal, even familial, experiences. An example is offered by Marjorie Pettiford,[8] whose record includes information from bibliographic sources about her membership in two all-women bands—International Sweethearts of Rhythm and Dixie Rhythm Girls—as well as links to her siblings, Leontine and Oscar, inherited from the existing Linked Jazz dataset. Web-shared and seamlessly grounded in their historical sources, these biographical data become, almost naturally, prosopographies to study groups of people from different perspectives and contexts.

By continuing to add new names of women and their data-driven biographies, we lay a path that not only exposes absences and disparities, but also offers the possibility to effortlessly discover and delve into their histories. The new platforms expand in unprecedented ways the range of questions we can pose. Queries that we had only previously envisioned can now be formulated and submitted via a query service.[9] This question-answering system returns an answer in response to a user's question. In other words, rather than the usual list of ranked documents typically retrieved from common discovery systems such as commercial search engines, users obtain direct answers in the form of short texts. We are able, for example, to quantify the ratio of men versus women instrumentalists and women vocalists versus instrumentalists, and can break down the data by gender and type of instrument. Or, if we focus on oral history passages, we can discover which woman instrumentalist was most discussed and how.

Any property of a person entity can be used to query the data, and any property or combination of properties can serve as a lens through which we can explore the many dimensions of an individual musician. As discussed earlier, the attribute of gender was the prerequisite to "seeing" women in the graph. With the inclusion of more identity-defining properties, new possibilities become available to represent the complexity of the women's experience. For example, intersectional analysis is possible thanks to attributes like race, sexuality, class, or nationality/regionality. More sophisticated contextualization enables us to historically situate categories of personal identity in time and space, recognizing their contingency and shifting meaning as social constructs. For example, gender values could be qualified diachronically with a start and end date to account for gender fluidity over time.

The International Sweethearts of Rhythm Case

To begin leveraging our project's technical makeover and explore the affordances that the new data infrastructure offered, we focused on all-women bands of the Swing Era, starting with one of the most successful groups of the time, the International Sweethearts of Rhythm (ISR). During the 1940s, women bands proliferated in the United States, filling the void left by men sent to fight in War World II. For a brief period, the jazz scene was dominated by an array of talented women musicians, including many remarkable instrumentalists who, as Handy (1998) points out, mostly vanished once the war ended.

The ISR was formed in 1937 to raise funds through touring for the Piney Woods Country Life School in Mississippi, a boarding school originally founded by Laurence C. Jones in 1909. The school's mission was to provide an education and teach a trade to African-American youth. The band was composed of members of diverse races and ethnic origins, including Black, Hispanic, Asian, White, and Native American, prompting the use of "International" in the band's name (Handy, 1998). Later, after the band was no longer affiliated with the school, it became the first integrated women's band, and it enjoyed enormous success touring both domestically and overseas until it disbanded in 1949. While a handful of the original members continued to play throughout the next decade or so, ISR as it was originally constituted, came to an end.

Our work with ISR followed a circuitous path. It began with an interview with Zena Latto,[10] a little-known saxophonist from the Bronx who, toward the end of her life, was on a mission to document her life in jazz by putting together her memorabilia. She called the Carnegie Hall archivist in search of a better copy of the flyer for a concert she had played there in 1957 with a group called "Jazz Female" ("Zena's flyer," n.d.). The Carnegie Hall archivist had neither the original, nor any other artifacts documenting this concert, and that is when he shared Zena's story with us. We soon began to weave Zena's story back into the rhizomatic fabric of the Linked Jazz graph. We found two immediate links to the network through her mentor Benny Goodman and Melba Liston, part of the Jazz Female ensemble in that Carnegie Hall concert. Zena played with at least two all-women bands. One was Moderne Moods, an all-women band she formed and led in the 1950s. Not much is known about the band besides Zena's own mention of it and a photograph of a concert announcement. This did not give us enough data to connect the dots. Then she mentioned that she also played with the ISR, which opened up for us a whole new pathway and stream of work.

Zena's is an example of a microhistory that emerges from obscurity, often by accident, albeit a happy one. Carlo Ginzburg, one of the founders of the historical research practice known as "microhistory," has shown the heuristic power of investigating the margins, following the anomalous and the unexpected, focusing on the details, or the traces (Ginzburg, Tedeschi, and Tedeschi, 1993). This framework is, in a broad sense, the inspiration for our efforts to semantically represent individuals and their communities in ways that expose the often-invisible, lost or underrecognized voices, situating them in a meaningful web of relations for encouraging new interpretations.

The ISR provides an interesting and rather unique case study. The historical context during the years in which the band was active (1937–1949) upended the rules, roles, and expectations usually applied to women jazz musicians. The traditional elements that characterize the jazz culture of meritocracy, for example, were suddenly less pressing. In a way, the ISR and most of their sister bands active during the same time period pushed boundaries, defied conventions and had an empowering impact on all women musicians.

Our project started with the creation of the ISR membership roster. Handy's (1998) monograph on ISR served as the main reference source from which information was derived. We were also fortunate to have a remarkable body of literature on jazz women and all-women bands, from Dahl (1989) to Tucker (2000), from which to triangulate and expand the data. As a big band, the roster of ISR included an extensive number of performers who throughout the years reached various degrees of recognition. With the information collected we created records for each of the musicians in our platforms. The relatively limited size of ISR made it feasible to add this extra step of data entry. Out of 72 ISR members identified to date, only 11 had a record in Wikidata, which did not always list the band affiliation, as was the case of Tiny Davis and Carline Ray. Sixty-one records had to be created from scratch directly by us or through other activities we organized, like Wiki edit-a-thons. Despite entering all the information available to us, not all of the musicians had a full record. For example, in some instances, the instruments played were not found. As noted earlier, one of the strengths of open systems like Wikidata or a local Wikibase is the capacity to expand as new knowledge is added. Wikidata is also a public crowdsourcing system and, in our context, has the potential to become a formidable tool for tracing the history of ISR and related bands through the public engagement of volunteers, including researchers and archivists. Every morsel of historical data disseminated through Wikidata is exposed to search engines like Google that can exploit the semantics in their definitions and information tables. We noticed, for example, that data we entered to Vi Burnside's Wikidata page—"Music Group: Harlem Playgirls"—appeared in Google's knowledge panel shortly after our data was added (Figure 9.4).

Our local platform, on the other hand, provides a distinct and curated research environment where biographical profiles and other entities of interest are enhanced with more specific and unique information to support deeper historical inquiry. To this end, we are expanding the range of data sources to include information useful in locating musicians, charting their performances, and mapping their collaborations. This information is often buried in documents like performance announcements, record liner notes, flyers, newspaper clippings, and obituaries. These types of documents are typically the only source of information available to generate the historical record and document voices otherwise undetectable through traditional archival descriptive standards and discovery systems whose limitations are a well-known problem in archival studies. As Woods (1994) noted about pre-Victorian women writers, those who were out of the canon were also absent from archival finding aids or were so inadequately described that they needed to be rediscovered by each new generation of scholars. Through these new methods and tools, we can help address issues of "archival silences" in the field of jazz.

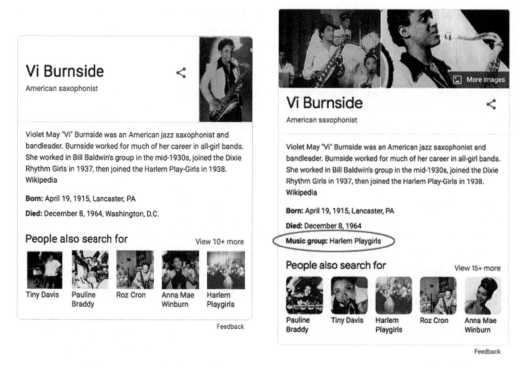

Figure 9.4 Comparison of Google's knowledge panels for Vi Burnside.

By harvesting more ephemeral documents, we expect to not only semantically expand existing records, but to also identify new individuals, bands, and events. We are broadening the spectrum of roles and occupations women played in bands beyond that of performer, to include educator, composer, arranger, founder, and organizer. Capturing spatio-temporal contexts is also a priority for the project. By situating performances and people's life events geographically and chronologically, we hope to be able to map out their individual and collective trajectories and destinations. For example, the underlying question of what women did after leaving the band is always looming. In postwar times, with men back on stage and music tastes changing, the trajectory of ISR and of many big bands, took different turns. Having temporal data in place will allow us to diachronically track their professional and personal paths and analyze patterns of behavior.

Currently, an ISR musician record includes membership properties (*member of*), professional-related properties (*instrument, role, occupation*), personal properties (*related to, educated at*) and identity properties under the category *demographica*. The latter is where gender data are listed and where other descriptors like race, ethnicity, or nationality will be entered. Assigning personal attributes to a historical individual is a form of identity construction that requires great care to mitigate possible assumptions and biases. Following best curatorial practices, we make every effort to represent only values explicitly stated in a referenceable source (see Figure 9.5).

The process of expanding semantic records is made up of iterations, at times prompted by serendipitous findings. We expect this work to progress incrementally, knowing that benefits can be harvested at any time as every additional bit of data makes it possible to draw new connections. An almost organic expansion came from locating neighboring bands whose members had also engaged with ISR. Through cross-referencing and triangulating data from secondary sources, including

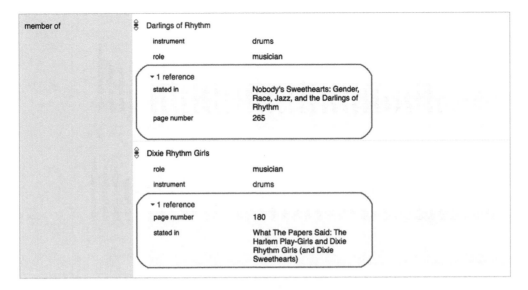

Figure 9.5 Portion of a Wikibase record for Henrietta Fontaine showing reference information for band membership.

Tucker (1999, 2000), Placksin (1982) and Rye (n.d.), in addition to the leading texts by Handy (1981, 1998), we started to record musician participation in multiple bands.

Connecting dispersed pieces of information into openly available records can be particularly helpful for uncovering artistic activities that leave very few material traces. For example, all-women bands have a meager discographic presence. Even ISR, by far the most successful band of that era, only recorded one album. As we continue to gather information about bands, band membership, and (soon) performances, we expect to be able to chart all-women bands as data that are useful for researchers. The data collected to date include a web of fifteen bands connected through their shared members. Figure 9.6 shows musicians from ISR (left column) for whom we were able to locate additional band membership information (opposite column). The snowball effect triggered the discovery of new band members and yielded the list of women musicians in the three far-right columns. The vast majority of these musicians did not have records on Wikidata and required us to create new ones.

This work shares the same ethos that has driven Linked Jazz since the beginning, which is to pioneer ways to graph out segments of the jazz community traditionally at the margins of historically dominant narratives.

Notes

1 The Linked Jazz Project website is available at https://linkedjazz.org.
2 https://id.loc.gov/authorities/names.html.
3 https://musicbrainz.org/.
4 Gendered view of the network is available at https://linkedjazz.org/network/?mode=gender.
5 All mentions of a musician in a single interview are counted as one.
6 www.wikidata.org/.
7 http://base.semlab.io/wiki/Main_Page.
8 http://base.semlab.io/wiki/Item:Q20592.
9 The project's SPARQL query service is available at https://query.semlab.io/.
10 Wikipedia page available at https://en.wikipedia.org/wiki/Zena_Latto.

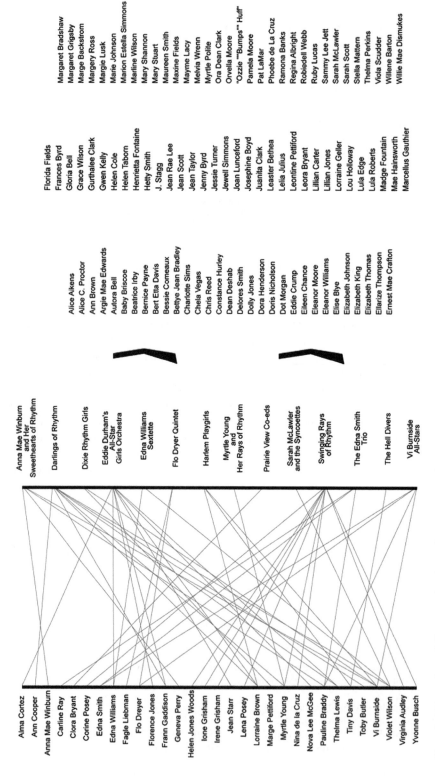

Figure 9.6 Expansion of all-women band members stemming from ISR.

References

Annfelt, T. (2003). Jazz as masculine space. Retrieved from http://kjonnsforskning.no/en/2003/07/jazz-mascul ine-space.

Björck, C., and Bergman, Å. (2018). Making women in jazz visible: Negotiating discourses of unity and diversity in Sweden and the US. *IASPM Journal*, *8*(1), 42–58.

Borgatti, S. P., Mehra, A., Brass, D. J., and Labianca, G. (2009). Network analysis in the social sciences. *Science*, *323*(5916), 892–895.

Cheng, N., Chandramouli, R., and Subbalakshmi, K.P. (2011). Author gender identification from text. *Digital Investigation*, *8*(1), 78–88.

Dahl, L. (1989). *Stormy Weather: The Music and Lives of a Century of Jazz Women*. New York: Limelight Editions.

Davis, F. (2002, September). In the macho world of jazz, don't ask, don't tell. *New York Times*, p. 19.

D'Ignazio, C. and Klein, L. F. (2020). *Data Feminism*. Cambridge, MA: The MIT Press.

Ginzburg, C., Tedeschi, J., and Tedeschi, A.C. (1993). Microhistory: Two or three things that I know about it. *Critical Inquiry*, *20*(1), 10–35.

Handy, A. D. (1981). *Black Women in American Bands and Orchestras*. Metuchen, NJ: The Scarecrow Press.

Handy, A. D. (1998). *The International Sweethearts of Rhythm: The ladies' jazz band from Piney Woods Country Life School*. Lanham, MD: Scarecrow Press.

Heckathorn, D. D., and Jeffri, J. (2001). Finding the beat: Using respondent-driven sampling to study jazz musicians. *Poetics*, *28*(4), 307–329.

Heckathorn, D. D. and Jeffri, J. (2003). Social networks of jazz musicians. In *Changing the Beat: A Study of the Worklife of Jazz Musicians, Volume III: Respondent-driven Sampling: Survey Results by the Research Center for Arts and Culture* (Report No. 43). National Endowment for the Arts Research Division. www.arts.gov/sites/default/files/JazzIII.pdf

Hwang, K. (2015) Enriching the linked jazz name list with gender information. Retrieved from https://linkedjazz.org/?p=1007

Liston, M. (1992). An oral history with Melba Liston/Interviewer: Steven L. Isoardi. Central Avenue Sounds Oral History Project, UCLA, Los Angeles.

McKeage, K. M. (2004). Gender and participation in high school and college instrumental jazz ensembles. *Journal of Research in Music Education*, 52(4), 343–356.

Murray, D. (2003). An oral history with David Murray/Interviewer: Mark Rowe. Hamilton College Jazz Archive, Hamilton College, Clinton, NY.

O'Connell, M. H., and Tucker, S. (2014). Not one to toot her own horn (?): Melba Liston's oral histories and classroom presentations. *Black Music Research Journal*, *34*(1), 121–158.

Onuoha, M. (2018). On missing data sets. Retrieved from: https://github.com/MimiOnuoha/missing-datasets.

Pattuelli, M. C., Hwang, K., and Miller, M. (2016). Accidental discovery, intentional inquiry: Leveraging linked data to uncover the women of jazz. *DSH: Digital Scholarship in the Humanities*, 32(4), 918–924. https://doi.org/10.1093/llc/fqw047

Pattuelli, M. C., Miller, M., Lange, L., Fitzell, S., Li-Madeo, C. (2013). Crafting linked open data for cultural heritage: Mapping and curation tools for the Linked Jazz Project. *The Code4Lib Journal*, (21).

Pellegrinelli, L. (2017). Women in jazz: Blues and the objectifying truth. Retrieved from: https://nationalsawdust.org/thelog/2017/12/12/women-in-jazz-blues-and-the-objectifying-truth/.

Placksin, S. (1982). *American Women in Jazz: 1900 to the Present: Their Words, Lives, and Music*. New York: Seaview Books.

Rivers, S. (1988). An oral history with Sam Rivers/Interviewer: Darryl Duncan. The Nathaniel C. Standifer Video Archive of Oral History: Black American Musicians Located in the African American Music Collection, University of Michigan, Ann Arbor.

Rye, H. (n.d.). What the papers said: The Harlem Play-Girls and Dixie Rhythm Girls (and Dixie Sweethearts). In L. Wright (Ed.), *Storyville 1996/7* (pp. 173–187). Chigwell, Essex, England: L. Wright.

Schubert, A. (2012). Jazz discometrics: A network approach. *Journal of Informetrics*, 6(4), 480–484.

Stray, J. (2016). The curious journalist's guide to data. New York: Columbia Journalism School. Retrieved from www.cjr.org/tow_center_reports/the_curious_journalists_guide_to_data.php#quantificatin.

Tucker, S. (1999). The prairie view co-eds: Black college women musicians in class and on the road during World War II. *Black Music Research Journal*, 19(1), 93–126.

Tucker, S. (2000). *Swing Shift: "All-Girl" Bands of the 1940s*. Durham, NC: Duke University Press.

Tucker, S. (2004). *A Feminist Perspective on New Orleans Jazzwomen*. Lawrence, KS: Center for Research University of Kansas.

Tucker, S. (2008). When did jazz go straight?: A queer question for jazz studies. *Critical Studies in Improvisation/Études critiques en improvisation*, 4(2), 1–16.

Van Vleet, K. (2021). Women in Jazz Music: A Hundred Years of Gender Disparity in Jazz Study and Performance (1920–2020). *Jazz Education in Research and Practice*, *2*(1), 211–227. doi.org/10.2979/jazzeducrese.2.1.16.

Wahl, C. and Ellingson, S. (2018). Almost like a real band: Navigating a gendered jazz art world. *Qualitative Sociology*, *41*(3), 445–471.

Wehr, E. L. (2016). Understanding the experiences of women in jazz: A suggested model. *International Journal of Music Education*, *34*(4), 472–487. doi:10.1177/0255761415619392.

Winter Jazzfest. (2018, July 18). *WJF Jazz and Gender Panel Discussion* [Video]. YouTube. www.youtube.com/watch?v=9nd-j3IyNfI.

Woods, S. (1994). Recovering the past, discovering the future: The Brown University Women Writers Project. *South Central Review*, *11*(2), 17–23. https://doi-org.ezproxy.pratt.edu/10.2307/3189986.

Zena's Flyer. (n.d.). Retrieved from www.carnegiehall.org/Blog/2016/09/Zenas-Flyer.

10

THE RISE OF QUEERMISIA IN JAZZ

Medicalization, Legislation, and Its Effects

Chloe Resler

Clarifying Statement: During the time period discussed, gender identity and sexuality were considered inextricable; this means it is functionally impossible to retroactively apply modern labels to queer people of the era. As such, I have opted to use *queermisia* in place of *homophobia* or *transphobia* unless one of those terms is specifically applicable. I have also avoided modern labels whenever possible, attempting to use only the terms that the people specifically featured used for themselves. When discussing the development of terminology during the first two decades of the twentieth century, I have used homosexuality and heterosexuality in order to faithfully represent the discussions of the period, although those concepts do not map perfectly onto how the modern terms work.

The jazz community and the queer community were once inseparable. During the 1920s, the Harlem Renaissance created a neighborhood where artistic excellence thrived alongside personal freedom and sparked larger cultural reverberations that connected the two communities across New York City. Many musicians and entertainers—such as Gladys Bentley—performed exclusively in drag. Large dance halls, including the Savoy, held integrated drag balls. Rent parties (and their racy sibling buffet flats) were frequented by jazz musicians of all identities. By the 1950s, something had changed. Jazz was a heteronormative art form, and musicians suffered from an environment of intense queermisia. Furthermore, as jazz history began to be cataloged and studied in earnest, there was an ideological split emerging in the historical discussion: Entertainment in opposition to art. This was a framework that often excluded queer performers. Entertainment and art have long been considered one and the same in the LGBTQ+ community. While queermisia had exerted its influence upon the jazz community long before the 1950s, the three decades separating the Roaring Twenties and Dizzy Gillespie's infamous statement, "I don't even know a jazz musician who's a homosexual—not a real jazz musician" (Sales, 1984, p. 1), saw a massive and rapid shift in jazz culture.

The question that naturally follows is, "What happened?" Although the cultural repositioning played out during the twentieth century, its roots lay decades earlier. In cities all around the world, the turn of the twentieth century saw the stirrings of queer liberation. This was a period of sexual revolution; some described the feeling of the 1920s as "shaking off the Victorians." Magnus Hirschfield's groundbreaking work on the science of sexuality and gender, urbanization, and a cultural turn towards independence started breaking down the strict Victorian norms surrounding sex and love. Hemlines crept up. Dancing became a saucier social activity thanks to the burgeoning popularity of African American[1] dances, appropriated and presented by white entertainers. The first two decades of the century also saw movement away from the religious and towards the secular, prompting

DOI: 10.4324/9781003081876-11

philosophical and scientific thought. Harlem was no exception to these trends. This majority African American neighborhood was a place of artistic exploration and innovation. Literary works strove to great heights, and there was a push for greater civil rights and liberties for African Americans. Harlem was the final destination of many people who moved north during the Great Migration and empowered many with relatively increased financial freedom. The welcoming into the community of jazz musicians from New Orleans and other places in the South, as well as the increasing volume of records being printed and bought, made Harlem a space where jazz flourished. There was plenty of work to be had for artists and entertainers, taking place in venues that ranged from rent parties to revues to the stage of the Cotton Club.

One major facet of queer life in Harlem, where amateur queer entertainers and drag queens could dance and compete freely, were the drag balls (See, Herring, Love, and Moffat, 2020). These events, often simply called 'balls', were not a new phenomenon. They had begun in the 1880s, started in Washington, DC, by a formerly enslaved person named William Dorsey Swann. At their height, these events attracted thousands of people from all walks of life and were held all over the Eastern seaboard, including in New York City (Russell, 2008). At first glance, there may not seem to be any association between these massive events and the jazz scene; however, taking a look at a 1932 map of nightclubs in Harlem reveals a world intimately connected. The Savoy Ballroom is one of jazz's most iconic clubs, immortalized in Edgar Sampson's "Stompin' at the Savoy" (1933), recorded by both Chick Webb and Benny Goodman. For those most familiar with swing era jazz, the Savoy is known as a venue where some of jazz's biggest mid-century icons worked in their early careers. Ella Fitzgerald, Thelonious Monk, Dizzy Gillespie, Art Blakey, and Charlie Parker all played there as members of popular orchestras. What is less well-known is that the Savoy hosted several drag balls. Eric Garber said this, concerning the balls of the 1920s and early 1930s:

> Only slightly smaller were the ones given irregularly at the dazzling Savoy Ballroom, with its crystal chandeliers and elegant marble staircase. The organizers would obtain a police permit making the ball, and its participants, legal for the evening. The highlight of the evening was the beauty contest, in which the fashionably dressed drags would vie for the title Queen of the Ball.
>
> *(qtd. in Hawkeswood, 1997)*

The drag balls weren't the only queer events in Harlem. Musicians of all orientations were familiar with, and many frequented, buffet flats. Count Basie recorded a tune called "Swingin' at the Daisy Chain" (1937), supposedly named after a popular establishment. Buffet flats were most numerous in Harlem, but could be found in other cities. Bessie Smith —who was bisexual—brought her niece, Ruby Smith, to one in Detroit in the 1920s. Ruby remembered the flat this way:

> They had a faggot there that was so great that people used to come there just to watch him make love to another man. He was that great. He'd give a tongue bath and everything. By the time he got to the front of that guy he was shaking like a leaf. People used to pay good just to go in there and see him do his act. ...That same house had a woman that used to ... take a cigarette, light it, and puff it with her pussy. A real educated pussy.
>
> *(Chauncey, 1994)*

Given the plethora of spaces that catered to queer clientele, it's evident that Jazz Age Harlem was a place that largely encouraged personal freedom for the queer community. Things began to change, however, in the mid-1930s. The Great Depression hit the world hard, and many Americans blamed the economic downturn on the excesses of the previous decade. As the societal pendulum swung back towards conservatism, heteronormativity became an increasingly powerful force in American society. The subsequent queermisia was reinforced by the trifecta of the redefinition of heterosexuality, the medicalization of queerness, and its subsequent connection to Communism.

In sexology, heterosexuality has generally been considered the "standard" orientation. *Psycopathia Sexualis,* a highly influential work by Richard von Krafft-Ebing detailing "deviant sexuality," was published in 1886. The first English edition was released in 1892. There has been some debate as to the nature of the label "heterosexuality" in the late nineteenth century, with some scholars arguing that "heterosexuality" was a term used solely to medicalize those who did not fit into the Victorian expectation of a single lifelong marriage. It has been posited that under this definition, heterosexuality was not a commonly accepted orientation until the twentieth century; however, there is some evidence that suggests otherwise. This text, one of the first to consider and publish case studies on homosexuality, frequently positions homosexuality and heterosexuality in opposition to each other. On page 255, the English translation reads, "The vita sexualis of these [yearnings]... is entirely like that in normal hetero-sexual love; but, since it is the exact opposite of the natural feeling, it becomes a caricature." (von Krafft-Ebing, 1892). Of course, no matter the general feeling of the sexologists, the field and its views on heterosexuality were not necessarily typical in general society until several decades after *Psycopathia Sexualis* was published (Dean, 2011).

Though heterosexuality made the transition to become the societal standard by the first decade of the twentieth century, queerness continued to be generally considered taboo in dominant culture until nearly a century later. This was due, in part, to decades of unethical research and the conflation of queer identities with medical problems. The roots of sexology were in the 1880s and the field had grown exponentially by 1913, when the first academic association working in the subject was founded. Despite its reputation as taking a progressive view of sexuality, most early work in sexology did not allow for an understanding of queerness as anything other than an inversion and/or disorder. Frequently, homosexuality was tied to other disorders (even when the link did not exist), leading to lingering queermisic stereotypes. For example, Havelock Ellis's work *Sexual Inversion* (1897), the first study of homosexual relationships between men, did not account for the difference between consensual queer relationships between adults and pedophilia. This particular stereotype persists in queermisic rhetoric today. The translation of *Psycopathia Sexualis,* the first appearance of the word "homosexual" in English, deals with same-gender love in a chapter titled "Contrary Sexual Instinct, or homo-sexuality." This chapter can be found in the "General Pathology" section of the book. The insidious historical goal of psychology and psychiatry was, in many cases, eugenics: To cure those who could be cured, and to remove from society those who could not. As the academic respectability of the sexology field increased, so too did the attempts to pathologize, medicalize, and ultimately *cure* queerness.

By 1935, the Committee for the Study of Sex Variants was established, made up of scientists who had expertise in human sexuality and deviant behavior (Minton, 1996). The committee itself was unusually liberal for the time, as it worked with the queer community directly in its studies instead of simply retelling the accounts of queer people without their input. However, the approach taken was distinctly anthropological and othering, which disappointed the queer activists with whom they worked. Furthermore, several scientists on the committee believed it beneficial to encourage the people they worked with to "control their impulses" (Minton, 1996). While this was not at all an unusual position for the time, it signifies their ultimate objectives and the lack of respect the committee held for queer people. This committee was only one example of the various groups instituted to study, quantify, and "solve" queerness. Though it operated for only six years, it is representative of the conventional end goal of the medicalization of homosexuality. The fact that this is one of the few committees that deigned to work directly with their subjects is a further indictment of the attitudes of medical communities toward queerness of the late 1930s and early 1940s.

Due to the legacy of eugenics and ableism, those with mental illnesses have for decades been seen as inherently untrustworthy. When queerness and mental illness were equated, both the medical community and the general public began to see queer people as inherently immoral and untrustworthy. This became particularly problematic as the country steadily marched towards conservatism during World War II. During the war, there were efforts to remove queer people from military positions, but due to the need for bodies and the high percentage of service members who were queer, no order was ever carried out. This did not hold after the war had ended. By the time Senator Joseph McCarthy gave his infamous "Enemies from Within" speech, Communism had been inextricably tied to immorality, and capitalism with morality (Loftin, 2007). Therefore, anyone deemed "immoral" was automatically suspect, alongside those who had progressive political ties (Adkins, 2016). Queer people suffered greatly during the Red Scare, facing removal from their positions and persecution as communists if they were outed due to the perceptions that, (a) queer people were more susceptible to blackmail, and (b) queer people were inherently untrustworthy due to their "illness" (Charles, 2017). This has been well-documented. What has perhaps seen less study is the connection many jazz musicians had to progressive groups, especially during the 1930s and 1940s (Casey, 2016). Influential musicians such as Mary Lou Williams, Billie Holliday, Hazel Scott, and Duke Ellington were involved in leftist politics. In the case of Williams, Holliday, and Ellington, their leftism was expressed in their music. Many other jazz musicians were explicitly involved with communist movements in America during the 1930s. By the 1950s, these ties proved dangerous for those in the jazz community. If someone could be proven to be either a communist or queer, they were liable to lose their cabaret card, and thus access to one of the biggest markets in the United States. When touring, African American musicians already faced discrimination in what they were paid, which hotels they were able to stay in, and where they were allowed to play. Losing access to the New York market would have been a devastating financial blow. Therefore, given that queerness was seen as a potential warning sign for Communism, it became in jazz musicians' best interest to distance themselves from queerness as much as possible (Wilson, 2010). For many African American musicians, vocal queermisia may well have been a protective measure.

Whether popular queermisia was begun by legislation or followed by legislation is something of a chicken-and-the-egg problem, but there is no question that further discriminatory legislation was adopted long before the Red Scare. In 1926 and 1927, several plays with queer themes saw successful runs, including Edouard Bourdet's *The Captive* and Mae West's *The Drag*. *The Captive* was focused on a romantic relationship between two women, and though it was wildly popular and met with critical acclaim, the entire cast was arrested, and the show was forced to close. These shows, alongside many others, sparked a debate about the morality of queer themes in entertainment (Hamilton, 1992). In 1927, a New York City measure, the Wales Padlock Law, was passed preventing theaters from putting on shows that featured queer characters. Only three years later, the film industry's Hays Code was established, preventing queer characters from being shown in anything but an overtly negative light. After Prohibition ended in 1933, New York's State Liquor Authority explicitly prevented bars and other establishments from serving gay clientele. Furthermore, they were not allowed to hire queer people, nor were queer people allowed to gather in bars (Chauncey, 2019). These legislative actions were not the only consequence of the burgeoning conservatism of the decade. In 1931, stewardship of the distribution of cabaret cards was passed over to the New York Police Department, a decision that would prove disastrous (Friedman vs. Valentine, 1941). Cabaret cards were the licenses necessary for entertainers and artists to perform in New York City, and once the police dictated who received them, they were often revoked for drug use, being publicly inebriated, and other offenses that fell under the realm of "degeneracy." This policy was used disproportionately against Black performers; in the common narrative of jazz history, the stories of Thelonious Monk and Billie Holliday, and their brushes with losing their cabaret cards are well known. Queer performers, inside and outside the jazz community, were hit hard as well.

Between 1923 and 1966, a policy of entrapment led to the arrests of more than fifty thousand men in New York City. The New York state legislature "specifically criminalized male homosexual cruising as a form of disorderly conduct," known among police forces as "degeneracy" (Chauncey, 2019). During the decades when entrapment was standard policy, plainclothes policemen would frequent bars, subway stations, and other areas where gay men were known to gather. If the officers were propositioned by one of the men in these places, they would immediately arrest them. The consequences for an arrest of this type were dire for any person: job loss, prison time, being outed to their families, and having their name printed in the newspaper were all possibilities. For performers, having such an arrest on their record often meant losing their cabaret card and being prevented from ever having one again.

Aaron Payne

One such case was the situation of Aaron Payne, a queer entertainer and performer who was not necessarily a part of the jazz community. Payne was a young Black gay man who lost an opportunity to launch a performance career when his application for a cabaret card was denied in 1947. The reasoning for the denial was that Aaron had two prior arrests for "degeneracy" (Chauncey, 2019). Aaron Payne later took the moniker Jason Holliday and was the subject of Shirley Clarke's 1967 film *Portrait of Jason*. While Payne was not an established jazz performer, likely partly a result of his inability to gain a cabaret card, the jazz world took notice after the film was released. The attention was not positive.

The consequence of years of both discriminatory legislation targeting the careers of performers and the construction of heteronormative society was a deeply queermisic jazz culture. In a style representative of the majority attitude by the time of its publishing, musicologist Grover Sales published an article in December of 1984 in Gene Lee's *Jazzletter*, entitled "The Strange Case of Charles Ives or, Why Is Jazz Music Not Gay Music?" The opening sentences of this article read as follows:

> In the 1950s, before the ascendancy of rock turned historic jazz clubs into parking lots and topless joints, San Francisco's Black Hawk, Jazz Workshop and Sugar Hill were nightly camping grounds for a Black homosexual prostitute and would-be entertainer immortalized in Shirley Clarke's documentary film *Portrait of Jason*. Born Aaron Paine, this fluttery engaging poseur called himself Jason Holliday but the jazz world called him Jason the Faggot.
>
> (Sales, 1984)

Leaving aside the slurs Sales chooses to employ regularly throughout the article, there is no reason to assume that Payne was, in fact, a "fluttery, engaging poseur." This article is an illustration of the queermisia that existed in jazz during and after the Red Scare. The very premise that Sales begins with in his approach relies upon the assumption that queer artists have not contributed significantly to jazz. The argument thus follows that, as queer artists have not created serious art, queer artists are incapable of creating serious art, and are therefore an oddity in the jazz world. However, as subsequent case studies show, many musicians creating incredible art were queer and dealt with queermisia in a myriad of ways. Furthermore, this approach necessitates a separation between art and entertainment, wherein entertainment is deemed 'lesser'; this allows queermisic musicians, historians, and observers to place any queer artist into the entertainment category, and to dismiss them. It is impossible to know what Payne's contributions to jazz might have been (although he was undoubtedly a gifted performer with a gorgeous voice and a talent for impressions). However, there is some evidence that established performers within the jazz tradition knew him. As Professor George Chauncey noted, Black singers, including Carmen McRae, gave him work.

Sales's perspective on Payne is indicative of the feelings many had towards queer musicians; his attitude was certainly shared amongst many cisgender and heterosexual jazz musicians and historians. Nowhere is this clearer than in the jazz magazines of the period. One example is this excerpt, from a 1937 article introducing Gene Krupa as the new author of the drumming column of *Metronome*:

> I've tried to do a few things: first, the abolishment of temple blocks. And in using temple blocks as a symbol of sissified, emasculated drummings, instigate a movement against

homo-sexual music. Needless to say, I am heart and soul opposed to these personality bands which play cute, sterile music. Cute music is feminine music and its swing the big-hipped, swishy swing of a fag.

(*Metronome, 1937, p. 14*)

Though this particular brand of queermisia had appeared earlier, with frequent comparisons made between "crooners" and "singers" or "pansies to prize fighters" (*Metronome,* 1933, p. 46), the rhetoric held progressively more and more vitriol as the years progressed. By the mid-1950s, queermisia, and the further connection between the ability to play and cisheteromasculinity, had been solidly cemented in the jazz community. In a stunning example, Horace Silver's 1956 interview with Nat Hentoff on page 18 in *Down Beat* included the statement, "I hope jazz doesn't go too far in a lot of directions it has been going. I can't stand the faggot-type jazz—the jazz with no … no guts. There's too much of that on the present scene." Long gone were the days of the Pansy Craze[2] and the mainstream freedom to express oneself through jazz in queer ways. This queermisia in jazz culture had devastating effects upon queer musicians and their careers. Some musicians went so far as to undergo invasive medical treatments to distance themselves from their reputations and claw back their careers. A notable example is Gladys Bentley.

Gladys Bentley

In the 1930s, Bentley was a respected entertainer, playing across Lenox Avenue from the Cotton Club during Cab Calloway's tenure. She was one of the most popular entertainers on the scene, with many magazines raving about her charismatic performances. Her nightclub was called Gladys' Clam House. Pianist Benny Payne, who later worked for Cab Calloway and recorded for Fats Waller, worked as an accompanist in the Clam House for Bentley during the late 1920s and early 1930s (Pease, 1942). Though she occasionally played piano for herself, she cut several records with Eddie Lang and Joe Venuti. Her work with multiple influential players during this period indicates that her musicality was well-respected in the nightclub scene in Harlem. Her popularity extended beyond the jazz community; she was one of the first African American performers to be allowed to perform in predominantly white clubs during the Pansy Craze (Church, 2018). During a stint in Chicago in July of 1938, her performing is mentioned as a highlight of the South Side on page 6 in *Tempo*:

> Except for Jimmie's [Noone] fine music, the exciting feature of this stop was hearing the infectious toe-tapping of Gladys Bentley, the 'name' of the show, who, when togged in a tux, looked absolutely pickwickian. Gladys is too far on the bulky side to hop much; but she doesn't have to. What she can do with one foot, while supporting her tonnage on a cane, is miraculous! Amusing as is her bawdy repertoire, e.g., *The Old Maids* in version 66, *Give It To 'Em,* and *Gladys Isn't Gratis Anymore,* we found the heel-and-toe obligato so hypnotic that we stayed through a second show for more.

Bentley was a name synonymous with entertaining queer performance throughout the 1920s and well into the 1930s (Wilson, 2010), but her career was in decline by 1938; this particular show was a stop on her way to Hollywood after work vanished in New York. Her brief attempts at career revival in Harlem in 1940 were met with police pushback. After the *New York Daily Mirror* mentioned Bentley, they ordered the club to close and asked that Gladys look for fertile grounds in New Jersey or some other state (Monroe, 1940). Unable to find steady performance work by the mid-1940s, she wrote tunes for Tin Pan Alley and placed advertisements in magazines like *The Music Dial*. She found some work at California gay clubs, like San Francisco's Mona 440, where run-ins with the police often ended with less violence (Boyd, 2001). Though she tried her hand at New York's theater scene a few more times, she was met with small audiences and negative reviews. She returned to Los Angeles in 1950 to take care of her elderly mother and came under scrutiny by government officials due to her previous marriage to a woman. Having already lost a huge chunk of her career, staring down the possibility of losing her freedom seems to have been too much to bear for Bentley, who sanitized her act by retreating into social norms she had once flouted (Wilson, 2010). Between 1950 and her death, she performed exclusively in dresses and picked safer repertoire. Despite her declining career, she had made enough in her early days to live comfortably (by her own account; Bentley, 1952), and her contemporaries still asked her to record with them.

One notable example from this period of her life, recorded in 1952, was her work with Dexter Gordon and Wardell Gray. "Jingle Jangle Jump" puts Bentley's vocal power and characteristic vibrato and phrasing on full display. Vocalists today continue to pull from her stylistic vocabulary, whether consciously or through the influence of later singers who learned from listening to Gladys and other blues singers. In perhaps another attempt to purify her public image, she published an autobiographical piece in *Ebony* magazine in August of 1952. "I Am A Woman Again" was a complete rebranding of Bentley's image, featuring photos of her in a dress and flowered headband posing with Billy Erskine and Louis Armstrong, who came to see her perform, doing household chores for her new husband, and selecting jewelry for a night out (Wilson, 2010). After a lengthy introduction confronting the struggles of queer life in twentieth-century America, she wrote,

> Today I am a woman again through the miracle which took place not only in my mind and heart—when I found a man I could love and who could love me—but in my body—when the magic of modern medicine made it possible for me to have treatment which helped change my life completely.
>
> *(Bentley, 1952)*

She goes on to explain that she underwent hormone therapy to attempt to heal herself.

Despite her best efforts, her career never again had the same relevancy she had enjoyed during the progressive Harlem Renaissance. Critics claimed that the article in *Ebony* was a fabrication to try and rescue her career, and though she sang at clubs and was featured on television in 1958, when she passed away in 1960, she was almost forgotten by the jazz world. In jazz magazines, the news of her death was given a single short article in *Down Beat*, where she is remembered solely as a "male impersonator" (*DownBeat*, 1960). There is no question that Bentley's career was cut short by discriminatory legislation and rising queermisia. The medicalization of queerness and the jazz community's commitment to queermisia led her to undergo physical conversion therapy for the small chance of regaining her career. Even now, she is rarely mentioned in jazz histories, despite her massive public popularity, her relevance among her contemporaries, and her influence over vocal stylistic language. If she is mentioned, she is discussed primarily as an entertainer. Her contributions to the musical legacy of the jazz tradition are ignored. While there is no meaningful difference between performers who were artists and performers who were entertainers (every musician is both, to varying degrees), it is unquestionable that historiographers have prioritized performers that they view as artists. Musicians like Bentley, whose performance aesthetic relied upon entertainment and queer self-expression, are often unfairly dismissed from the common narrative out of hand.

Gladys Bentley's case is an excellent example of a musician who came of age during the relatively freer Jazz Age and was forced to navigate the increasing queermisia that grew from the Swing Era to Bebop. However, her story is not the only queer narrative that can be found in jazz history—queer musicians continued to play and write jazz throughout the century. Billy Tipton, for example, was a pianist, saxophonist, bandleader, and talent broker who began his career in the Swing Era. He was also a transgender man. It was an open secret that many singers who were active in the mid twentieth century were queer, including Billie Holiday and Carmen McRae. Perhaps the most notable queer musician of the period is Billy Strayhorn.

Billy Strayhorn

Strayhorn, born in 1915, was a pianist, an arranger, and the composer of dozens of tunes in the Great American Songbook; he worked closely with Duke Ellington for decades. He was also an out gay man. As one of his friends, another Black gay musician, said:

> The most amazing thing of all about Billy Strayhorn to me was that he had the strength to make an extraordinary decision—that is, the decision not to hide the fact that he was homosexual. And he did this in the 1940s, when nobody but nobody did that. We all hid, every one of us, except Billy. He wasn't afraid. We were.
>
> *(Hajdu, 2013, p. 93)*

His decision to be open and honest about his identity stood in direct contrast to Bentley and most queer musicians of the time, who stayed in the closet. Despite this risky commitment, Strayhorn had a lifelong career and left a lasting impression on jazz composition.

The question that might naturally be posed is: How was he able to do that if jazz culture was truly so deeply queermisic? His anonymous friend, quoted above, believed that Ellington protected Strayhorn and gave him the ability to be open in his personal life. He remarked,

> Billy could have pursued a career on his own—he had the talent to become rich and famous—but he'd have had to be less than honest about his sexual orientation. Or he could work behind the scenes for Duke and be open about being gay. It really was truth or consequences, and Billy went with truth.
>
> *(Hajdu, 2013, p. 94)*

Billy Strayhorn met Duke Ellington when he was only 23 years old. At this meeting, he played for Duke, who was so impressed that Strayhorn was immediately given a job with the orchestra. Strayhorn was profoundly influenced by Classical music, and his writing reflected that. By age 17, when he first composed "Lush Life," his compositions were astonishingly mature and already inflected with the darkness that was characteristic of his work. The complex tonal colors and the subject matter he chose to employ were often at odds with the cheerful and frequently laughing Strayhorn of the 1940s that both his friends and first long-term partner, Aaron Bridgers, remember. However, they become less surprising when one considers the intense maltreatment Strayhorn had already endured by this point; his father, James Strayhorn, was abusive (Hajdu, 2013). Furthermore, coming of age as a queer person in the first half of the twentieth century was unfathomably difficult. Even those who were old enough to experience the relatively tolerant 1920s were often alienated from their families, something Strayhorn experienced briefly with his sister Georgia in the mid-1940s (Hajdu, 2013).

Despite the odds, Strayhorn and Bridgers remained very open about their relationship and frequented New York's gay hotspots. They were together until they parted amicably after Bridgers' move to Paris in 1947, and every time Strayhorn visited Paris, he and Bridgers would spend many hours of the visit together. Despite the many healthy friendships he cultivated, there is no question that Strayhorn spent much of his life unhappy, particularly after he and Bridgers split (Barg, 2013). His desire for the publishing of his work was often disrespected. Nat King Cole, for example, recorded "Lush Life" without Strayhorn's permission, an action made exponentially worse because Strayhorn did not originally want to publish that song due to its personal nature (Hajdu, 2013). Duke Ellington also profited by his position over Strayhorn, though not necessarily for the same nefarious reasons he had been taken advantage of in his early career. He often appeared as a co-composer, or the sole composer, on works on which Billy Strayhorn was the lone writer (Hajdu, 2013). Eventually,

Strayhorn felt that he was not only not being recognized for his work, he was not able to compose what he wanted—he was writing Duke Ellington, not Billy Strayhorn. After several attempts to extricate himself in the 1950s, he was   brought   back by Ellington with the promise of complete creative freedom. To Ellington's credit, Strayhorn's name began appearing on bills for projects he was the driving force behind, like *Such Sweet Thunder*, and he was given more artistic license on theatrical projects. Ellington would also make sure to speak highly of Strayhorn during live performances. However, the media often attributed all of Strayhorn's work to Ellington. In these cases, Ellington would never correct them (Hajdu, 2013). To add insult to injury, when Frank Sinatra reached out to Strayhorn to cut a record, Ellington lost his temper and completely forbade the collaboration. As Strayhorn would later tell Honi Cole, "He said, 'Strays, haven't you heard about the prodigal son? He can't go home again.'" (Hajdu, 2013, p. 240).

In fairness, Strayhorn wasn't completely restricted from doing solo work; however, by the late 1950s, he often seemed to feel that it would be pointless to put much in. Ellington allowed Strayhorn to cut several records of his own, but much to his frustration, they were received as Ellingtonia, rather than his own work (Hajdu, 2013). When asked to perform concerts, he began to express fears that people were only coming to see and hear Duke Ellington, not him. In 1959, Strayhorn cut a record with Johnny Hodges. The album was originally meant to be released under Hodges's name, but due to a conflict with recording contracts, the decision was made to release it as Strayhorn's. Oliver Jackson, the drummer on the session, remembered talking to Strayhorn about it.

> "[H]ere there's finally a record with your own name on it, and it's really Rab's! Isn't that something?" And Billy said, "Oh yes, Oliver. I'm sure there'll be an uprising." Man, he didn't think nobody cared … his own name didn't mean nothing to him no more. Like, fuck it—nobody cares. Why should I?
>
> *(Hajdu, 2013, p. 221)*

Strayhorn drank heavily, suffered through an abusive relationship, slept little, and hardly worked. Those around him recalled that when he wasn't around Bridgers, he seemed deeply sad. Honi Coles recounted that he once asked Strayhorn whether he was happy. As he remembered the conversation, Strayhorn just sobbed.

Things got marginally better in the 1960s after Strayhorn was introduced to Martin Luther King, Jr. The Civil Rights movement captivated him, gave him a reason to return to work. He had broken up with his abusive partner. He composed and arranged more frequently, worked on theatrical projects, and went down South to march. He supported vocalist Lena Horne's desire to get involved and helped her prepare to sing "Amazing Grace" during one of the marches. Unfortunately, his health was beginning to fail. He ended up unable to participate in the march, instead sitting in the bleachers and listening to the speakers. After a brief tour in the Middle East, Strayhorn had difficulty climbing up the short stairs to his friends' brownstone in New York City. He was diagnosed with advanced esophageal cancer in 1964. In the winter of that same year, he met his final partner, Bill Grove. A year later, he played a concert for the Duke Ellington Jazz Society. It was a smashing success. Many people who saw it recall his incredible facility on the piano and his sense of humor. Sadly, it wasn't to last. The cancer spread through his body rapidly, and by 1966, he knew he was dying. Marian Logan, a good friend of his, said,

> Strays finally looked like he had the kind of thing he really wanted, but he knew it wouldn't be for long. He knew damn well it would be all over soon and he couldn't get everything out of it that he should have[;] … he said to me over and over toward the end, "Bill's so great. If they had white boys like that in Pittsburgh, Doll Baby, you wouldn't *know* me."
>
> *(Hajdu, 2013, p. 278)*

Billy Strayhorn passed away, with Bill Grove by his side, on May 31, 1967. The last piece he ever wrote was called "Blood Count." It is characterized by a sense of deep sadness and a pedal point bassline that evokes the sound of an intravenous fluid.

Ellington was shattered. He very nearly was unable to attend the funeral. His son Mercer remembered it this way: "It was a big blow to the old man. He couldn't accept any kind of misfortune[;] … he couldn't accept that Strayhorn really wasn't there anymore" (Hajdu, 2013, p. 289). The deep grief and love Ellington felt for Strayhorn proved problematic for Joe Morgen, who handled the publicity of the event. It was known by those around Ellington's organization that Morgen had always hated that Strayhorn was gay, and he felt it important that the emotion Ellington was feeling couldn't be interpreted as anything other than platonic grief. In order to achieve that, he sent a falsified interview to Leonard Feather that characterized Strayhorn as being too gruff and too busy for a wife:

> For an article on Ellington's initiation of the Strayhorn scholarship in the black digest *Jet*, Morgen provided what he said was material from an unpublished exclusive interview in which Strayhorn defended his bachelorhood. "Look, I'm an individualist. The rugged kind. I don't bat an eye when the fellows in the band call me a character. I'm not fit company for man nor beast. The chosen Eve of my life surely has no reason to put up with that cross-section." Morgen sent the "interview" to Leonard Feather, who commented, "It was quite accurate—as a description of Joe Morgen. Ellington, to his credit, grieved terribly for Billy because he loved him. Unfortunately, some people couldn't accept that any better than they accepted Billy when he was alive."
>
> (Hajdu, 2013, pp. 289–290)

This was not the only postmortem coverage that erased Strayhorn's orientation. Some outlets reported that Lena Horne was cradling him in her arms as he passed away—a complete lie, but the myth has persisted. Billy Strayhorn had given up artistic control and fame in order to live his life honestly, but the jazz world was in no way ready for that honesty.

In Strayhorn's case, there was no less internal anguish than what Bentley suffered. Both artists made the decision to live their lives out, and both experienced marginalization in their artistic and professional development as a result. The two cases were not identical; one of the main differences between them lies in their later treatment within the common narrative. Bentley is often seen as purely an entertainer, rather than an influential vocalist, and is readily ignored for that reason. Strayhorn's long association with Ellington means that, historically, he simply cannot be dismissed, so instead, his queerness is downplayed, erased, overwritten, and his music then safely universalized. Discussions of Bentley's music are vanishingly rare, while Strayhorn's music is completely divorced from the queer experience he often wrote about— both forms of queer erasure in jazz historiography. None of this even touches on the queer musicians who did not achieve the fame of Bentley and were brushed aside by historians as being solely entertainers, incapable of creating great art or influencing the jazz idiom. It also doesn't take into account the dozens of queer performers who were never able to come out due to fears of financial and social repercussions. When the word "faggot" was routinely tossed around on the band bus and one was liable to lose one's job or access to the New York market, how could they? In the face of everything, some of jazz's greatest performers, composers, and arrangers were queer. How many more are we missing? How many were never able to reach the great heights that Dizzy Gillespie, Charlie Parker, Sarah Vaughn, Ella Fitzgerald, and Duke Ellington climbed to?

In Grover Sales' article, he plays up the split between the entertainment world of theater and the art world of jazz, but many jazz musicians wrote and played in theatrical productions, from revues to Broadway. He claims that jazz musicians that came of age in all decades never knew any jazz musicians that were queer. However, we know from Mercer Ellington that Duke, one of the most prominent jazz musicians of the twentieth century, had been "exposed to homosexuality his whole life in the music business. He knew plenty of gay men and women, so there was no question about, 'Hey, is this person a freak or something?'" (Hajdu, 2013, p. 93). This is the danger of the legacy of a queermisic culture that was built between the 1920s and the 1950s. The lack of acknowledgment of the existence of queer people in jazz has prevented many from coming out, and still more from pursuing a career at all. When the story is allowed to be dictated by the words, "the incidence of homosexuality in jazz [is] not only below that in other kinds of music and all the other arts, it [is] far below population norms cited in studies such as the Kinsey report" (Sales, 1984, p. 1), it is ahistorical and doesn't do justice to the dozens of queer stories that can be found in jazz.

Heteronormativity and queermisia did not arise out of a vacuum, nor have they been immutable facts for time immemorial. Medicalization, the conflation of queerness with Communism, discriminatory legislation, and public pushback against queer life all contributed to the construction of a deeply queermisic culture. There were heavy consequences for being queer, for those who were out and those who could not be out. In the decades after the mid-twentieth century, it's become commonplace to assume that jazz and queer identity are fundamentally opposed, precisely because of the ways queermisia affected the environment musicians worked in and the ways jazz history was recorded and interpreted. When art and entertainment are separated in the narrative, queer musicians are left behind. When queerness is something left relegated to private life, the analysis of out queer musicians' work lacks a key part of their life experience—an experience that is as inseparable from a person's perspective as any of their other identities. When prejudice stands between the common narrative of jazz and a fuller knowledge of the truth, all those who love jazz suffer the loss of a rich history full of gifted musicians, their work, and the story of their lives. It is imperative that this gap in jazz history is understood and corrected.

Notes

1 When "African American" is used in this chapter, it refers to the specific African American ethnicity, and not Black culture.
2 The Pansy Craze (1930–1933) was a rise in the underground popularity of drag queens and kings. Queer entertainment became, briefly, mainstream.

References

Abernethy, M., Douglas, M., Nelson, D., Pearson, B., Fitzgerald, C., Moore, R., Pontecorvo, A., Vellucci, J., Horowitz, S., Kavadlo, J., and Ribeiro, A. C. (2015). *Edouard Bourdet's Lesbian Play, "The Captive," Was Certainly Captive of its Time*. PopMatters. www.popmatters.com/edouard-bourdets-lesbian-play-the-captive-was-certainly-ca ptive-of-its-time-2495490331.html.

"According to Douglas Stanley" (1933, November). *Metronome, 49*(11), 46.

Adkins, J. (2016). "These People Are Frightened to Death": Congressional Investigations and the Lavender Scare. *Prologue Magazine*. www.archives.gov/publications/prologue/2016/summer/lavender.html.

Association of Motion Picture Producers, Inc. (1930). *The Motion Picture Production Code*. www.asu.edu/courses/fms200s/total-readings/MotionPictureProductionCode.pdf.

Barg, L. (2013). Queer Encounters in the Music of Billy Strayhorn. *Journal of the American Musicological Society, 66*(3), 771–824. doi:10.1525/jams.2013.66.3.771.

Bentley, G. (1952, August). I Am a Woman Again. *Ebony Magazine*. www.queermusicheritage.com/BENTLEY/Ebony/ebony1.jpg.

Boyd, N. (2001). Same-Sex Sexuality in Western Women's History. *Frontiers: A Journal of Women Studies, 22*(3), 13–21. doi:10.2307/3347235.

Campbell, E. S. (1932). *A Night-Club of Harlem* [Illustration]. https://syncopatedtimes.com/the-harlem-renaissa nce-guide-to-historic-jazz-clubs/.

Casey, B. W. (2016). *Before the Blacklist: How the New York Jazz Community Promoted Radical Politics as an Agent of Social Change Leading Up to the McCarthy Era*. University of Colorado.

Charles, D. (2017). Policing Public Morality: Hoover's FBI, Obscenity, and Homosexuality. In Johnson S. and Weitzman S. (Eds.), *The FBI and Religion: Faith and National Security before and after 9/11* (pp. 134–147). Oakland, CA: University of California Press.

Chauncey, G. (1994, June 26). A Gay World, Vibrant and Forgotten. *New York Times.* www.nytimes.com/1994/06/26/opinion/a-gay-world-vibrant-and-forgotten.html.

Chauncey, G. (2019, June 15). The Forgotten History of Gay Entrapment. *The Atlantic.* www.theatlantic.com/ideas/archive/2019/06/before-stonewall-biggest-threat-was-e ntrapment/590536/.

Church, M. M. (2018). *If This Be Sin: Gladys Bentley and the Performance of Identity.* University of South Carolina. https://scholarcommons.sc.edu/cgi/viewcontent.cgi?article=5705&context=etd

Davis, F., Burton, G., Bey, A., Hersch, F., Kohlhase, C., and Sales, G. (2002, April). *Destination Out* [Panel]. Talking Jazz: Live at the Village Vanguard, New York. www.columbia.edu/cu/najp/events/talkingjazz/transcript1.html.

Dean, J.J. (2011), The Cultural Construction of Heterosexual Identities. *Sociology Compass,* 5, 679–687. https://doi.org/10.1111/j.1751-9020.2011.00395.x.

Ellis, H. (1925). Sexual Selection in Man (Vol. 2). F. A. Davis

Garber, E. (1988). *A Spectacle in Color: The Lesbian and Gay Subculture of Jazz Age Harlem.* Virginia.Edu. http://xroads.virginia.edu/~ug97/blues/garber.html.

Gourse, L. (2001). *Carmen McRae: Miss Jazz.* Billboard Books.

Hajdu, D. (2013). *Lush Life: A Biography of Billy Strayhorn.* Farrar, Straus and Giroux.

Hamilton, M. (1992). Mae West Live: "SEX, The Drag, and 1920s Broadway." *TDR (1988-), 36*(4), 82–100. doi:10.2307/1146217.

Hawkeswood, W. G. (1997). *One of the Children: Gay Black Men in Harlem.* University of California Press.

Loftin, Craig M. (2007). Unacceptable Mannerisms: Gender Anxieties, Homosexual Activism, and Swish in the United States, 1945–1965. *Journal of Social History, 40*(3), 577–596.

"Male Impersonator." (1960, March 31). *DownBeat, 27*(7), 36.

Matter of Friedman v. Valentine, 177 Misc. 437 | Casetext Search + Citator. (1941, November 10). CaseText. https://casetext.com/case/matter-of-friedman-v-valentine-1

Minton, H. (1996). Community Empowerment and the Medicalization of Homosexuality: Constructing Sexual Identities in the 1930s. *Journal of the History of Sexuality, 6*(3), 435–458. Retrieved March 31, 2021, from www.jstor.org/stable/4629618.

Monroe, A. (1940, June 15). Swingin' the News. *The Chicago Defender,* 18.

Muller, E. (1938, July). A Nite on the South Side: Week-End of a Private Secretary. *Tempo, 6*(1), 6.

Pease, S. (1942, August). Benny Payne Was Boy Soprano: Son of Preacher, Cab's Pianist Has Some Unique Musical Ideas to Offer. *Down Beat, 9*(15), 19.

Russell, T. (2008). The Color of Discipline: Civil Rights and Black Sexuality. *American Quarterly, 60*(1), 101–128.

Sales, G. (1984). The Strange Case of Charles Ives, or Why Is Jazz Not Gay Music? *Jazzletter,* 1–8.

See, S., Herring, S., Love, H., and Moffat, W. (2020). "Spectacles in Color": The Primitive Drag of Langston Hughes. In Looby C. and North M. (Eds.), *Queer Natures, Queer Mythologies* (pp. 106–133). New York: Fordham University Press. doi:10.2307/j.ctvsf1qwg.8.

Tough, D. (1937). Down With the Sissies! *Metronome, 53*(12), 14.

von Krafft-Ebing, R., and Chaddock, C. G. (1892). *Psycopathia Sexualis* (2nd ed.). F. A. Davis.

Wilson, J. (2010). "In My Well of Loneliness": Gladys Bentley's Bulldykin' Blues. In *Bulldaggers, Pansies, and Chocolate Babies: Performance, Race, and Sexuality in the Harlem Renaissance* (pp. 154–191). Ann Arbor: University of Michigan Press.

11

CONSTRUCTING A DIVERSE AND INCLUSIVE JAZZ TRADITION

A Uchronic Narrative

Michael Kahr

Author's Statement: I am writing from the perspective of a White, middleclass, cisgender, heterosexual male, which has allowed me to partake in jazz education and subsequent professional life as a jazz pianist and educator without experiencing any disadvantages related to gender. However, as I witnessed several incidents of discrimination towards colleagues during my student years—sadly without fully realizing my personal potential as a catalyst for change—this chapter is dedicated to all advocates for diversity and equality in jazz. I also write from the perspective of my current teaching, research, and quality assurance responsibilities in higher education, which represent my genuine interest and obligation to develop feasible strategies for increasing diversity and inclusion in jazz.

Introduction

Jazz has long been associated with masculinity. During the past century, much academic and vernacular literature has portrayed jazz as having an evolutionary lineage of predominantly male musicians who had developed a distinct African American approach in music. As jazz historians have started to unravel the "complicated and variegated cultural phenomena that we cluster under the umbrella jazz" (DeVeaux, 1998, p. 489), previously forgotten or even ignored "issues of historical particularity" (p. 507) have come to the surface. Studies employing a more differentiated perspective towards gender in the history of jazz have entered the discourse during the past two decades, spearheaded by scholars such as Sherrie Tucker (2000), Erin Lynn Wehr-Flowers (2006), Marie Buscatto (2007/2018) and Nichole Rustin-Paschal (2017). Rustin and Tucker's (2008) metaphorical "big ears" have stood out as a call to listen for gender in jazz as a "critical intervention in the field of feminist theory and music studies" (p. 1), hoping to challenge the field of jazz studies to be "more representative and articulate about its consistencies" (p. 3).

The gender inequities revealed by jazz scholars have also started to be actively addressed by prominent educational institutions, with the Berklee College of Music at the forefront. In 2018, the college initiated the Institute for Gender Justice, which was founded with the aim to do "corrective work and modify the way jazz is perceived and presented, so the future of jazz looks different than its past without rendering invisible many of the art form's creative contributors" (Berklee, 2021). This call for action involves the opposition to discrimination experienced in the past and the ignorance

DOI: 10.4324/9781003081876-12

regarding female contributions in jazz history. Moreover, the institute demands growing recognition of gender-related matters in current discourses in jazz. In the field of education this entails the development of jazz history classes with greater sensibility towards gender, race and intersectionality. For instance, Terri Lyne Carrington's promotion of the creative work of female jazz composers as "new jazz standards" has aimed to raise awareness regarding matters of diversity in the choice of repertoire (Berklee, 2021a). On a larger scale, the Institute for Gender Justice has aimed to contribute to the sustainability of future societies:

> We will foster creative practice and scholarship in jazz within an integrated and egalitarian setting. We seek to engage ourselves and others in the pursuit of jazz without patriarchy and, in making a long-lasting cultural shift in jazz and other music communities, recognize the role that jazz can play in the larger struggle for gender and racial justice.
>
> *(Berklee, 2021b)*

The Berklee College of Music has successfully developed a safe space for jazz without patriarchy and some cities of jazz, such as New Orleans, may reinvigorate the temporarily "forgotten" diversity in their own history (Tucker, 2004). But how about other places, where female contributions to the local jazz histories cannot be identified at all?

One of such places is the Austrian city of Graz. The vast majority of Austrian jazz musicians have been male (Fürnkranz, 2019; Bruckner-Haring, 2017). The jazz scene in Graz was exclusively male for more than two decades after World War II (Kahr, 2016). Despite a gradual shift in support of female performers since the mid-1980s, the ratio is still far from equal. The local male domination was historically grounded by generations of successful men as musicians and key players in relevant local institutions regarding the development of jazz and popular music (e.g. education centers, cultural politics, concert venues, journalism and broadcasting corporations).

This chapter aims to outline an alternate history of jazz in the city of Graz, led by female artists instead of men. What would the jazz history look like if women founded and chaired the relevant institutions? How would women have acted as role models and ensured student recruitment? Which key decisions would have been made in a diverse and inclusive jazz scene and upon what grounds? These questions were addressed in a case study involving the development of an alternate local jazz history, based on a thorough analysis of the prevalent male-dominated structures.

From a psychological perspective, such counterfactual reflection may involve degrees of sentiment and "wishful thinking," however, in the sense of "rational imagination" (Byrne, 2005) it becomes a useful strategy to avoid the reoccurrence of mistakes. As aviation pilots learn from imagining alternative strategies after "near-miss" accidents (Starr, 2021), the proposed construction of a counterfactual jazz history aims to serve the purpose of preparing for the future on the grounds of an "improved" version of the past.

Utopia and Uchronia

Alternate historiography is based on the historical concepts of "Utopia" and "Uchronia". Utopia as an imaginary, non-existent place inhabited by an ideal society was first imagined by Sir Thomas More in his novel *De optimo rei publicae statu deque nova insula Utopia* [Of a republic's best state and of the new island Utopia] (1516). More's storyline depicts concrete concepts for improvement in the society of an imagined island, casting the "real" world as a problematic space. Utopian ideas and ideals have been entertained by authors throughout the centuries, for instance in the form of novels, essays, theatre plays, and movie scripts. If the imagined places represent a less pleasant perspective, Utopia turns into Dystopia (Mills, 1868).

Utopian places are spatial as well as temporal sites of meaning (Hawley, 2004). References to the past, present or the future connect Utopia with the concept of "Uchronia." In 1857, French philosopher Charles Bernard Renouvier published the first version of his novel *Uchronie (L'utopie dans l'histoire)* [Uchrony (Utopia in history): Apocryphal sketch of the development of the European civilization not as it was but as it could have been], sketching the development of European civilization "not as it was, but as it might have been" (Renouvier, 1876). The term "Uchronia" is based on the combination of the Greek words οὐ ("not") and χρόνος ("time") and refers to an alternate time, which does not and has not existed, but might exist as an imagined future, present or past. Uchronian narratives have frequently appeared as "alternate" or "counterfactual" histories in literary genres, such as the scientific romance, counterfactual historiography and science fiction (Worth, 2018). In 2017, Ben Carvers's first comprehensive survey and analysis of alternate histories in Britain, France and America between 1815 and 1915 has shown the use of Uchronia "as a means to reflect on how scientific, cultural, and historical discoveries altered the understanding of the past" (Carver, 2017, p. 1). Moreover, Uchronia has been addressed in various scholarly contexts such as design studies and artistic research (Schmid, 2020), jazz studies (Dunkel, 2018), film studies (Schaefer and Rodríguez-Hernández, 2016), urban planning (Firth, Ferrei and Lang, 2016), and oral historical narratives (Portelli, 1988).

Helga Schmid founded the Uchronia platform to foster "critical and imaginative thought on the contemporary time crisis, challenging current perceptions, and offering alternative ways of being in time. Uchronia explores the multifaceted nature of time in an academic and public context" (Schmid, 2018). Schmid's platform, which involves exhibitions, talks, workshops and texts, builds upon the work of sociologist Helga Nowotny (1994/1989), who discussed Uchronia in relation to the "pressure of time" felt by many across various social groups (p. 132). She claimed that "uchronias, like utopias before them, have a central social function to fulfil: they contain proposed solutions to particular unsolved problems in a society" (p. 141), and described "three current uchronias, the economic, the political and the cultural one" (p. 142): the first path leads into the "Cockaigne of full time" (p. 136) referring to the fulfilment of all the wishes the imagination produces (i.e., more time and money); the second path turns to people's work experience, aiming for "autonomy and self-determination, temporal flexibilization in the interest of employees, new forms of distribution of working time and living time" (p. 137); the third path starts "from a change in temporal rhythms," which refers to a new alignment of habit and linearity with spontaneity, and has "a lot in store for women," as they have more ability to shape human routine in a "less regular fashion" than men (pp. 137–138). Nowotny's differentiation of Uchronia was referred to by Schmid (2017) in her research on current changes regarding the perception of time and its dependence on various sociocultural and temporal conditions. In this context, Uchronia appeared as a form of "temporal utopia," referring to an "attempt to escape the rigidity of clock time through the development of new time concepts" (Schmid, 2017, p. 33).

Uchronic Method

Both, the concepts of Uchronia as an alternate narrative of history and the related "temporal utopia" as a problem-solving concept were applied in this study. The imagination and construction of an alternate history of jazz in Graz involved the reconsideration of real historical events and developments, replacing the real, predominant male-dominated history with an alternate narrative based on female-based perspectives, events and actions. Temporal utopia represents the active endeavor to solve the "problem" of a male-dominated past by employing creativity aimed at the support of advocacy for a more diverse future.

The Uchronia diagram in Figure 11.1 (Renouvier, 1876) depicts a cartography of the actual course of history, marked by the horizontal line from *0* to *a*, and possible routes of divergence, marked by oblique lines between actual events (uppercase letters) and imagined events (lowercase letters). Accordingly, the historical lineage may change at any time, leading to alternative realities which may, however, involve some real events.

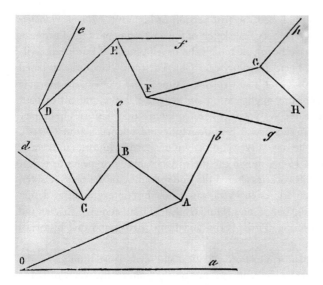

Figure 11.1 Uchronia diagram by Charles Bernard Renouvier in which uppercase letters represent actual events, lowercase letters events that did not happen.

The actual events referred to in the following case study were derived from confirmed knowledge on the male-dominated local jazz history in Graz, which was gathered by a methodical combination of historical research, empirical social research and artistic research as part of the research project "Jazz and the City: Identity of a Capital of Jazz" (Kunstuni Graz, 2021). The project was funded by the Austrian Science Fund FWF and conducted at the University of Music and Performing Arts in Graz from 2011–2013. The historical research stream involved the analysis of a large body of written sources and oral accounts reflecting the history of jazz in the city from 1965 through to 2015 and is published in various articles and a comprehensive monograph (Kahr, 2016, 2017 and 2018). The scrutinized written sources included academic studies and reports, newspaper articles, and manuscripts in private collections. The empirical social research involved qualitative interviews with a selection of participants of the local jazz scene. The artistic research was based on the author's artistic experience as a member of the jazz scene in Graz and resulted in a series of new compositions and historically informed performances of repertoire relevant to the local history (Kahr, 2016a).

The construction of imagined events was based on basic theory of matriarchal societies (Göttner-Abendroth, 2004; Bachofen, 1861). According to Göttner-Abendroth (2004), matriarchal societies were characterized by "perfect mutuality" and "matricilocality" (p. 6), appeared as "consensus societies" (p. 6) and "societies of reciprocities" (p. 7), and involved social criteria resulting in "non-hierarchical, horizontal societies of kinship" (p. 8). Despite the contradictions and ambiguities regarding matriarchy theory in the context of feminism and gender theory (Meier-Seethaler, 2019), matriarchy was merely chosen in this study for its illustrating potential as the exact opposite of the evident patriarchy in jazz. In order to create a vivid example of an alternate history of jazz in Graz, it appeared most fruitful to focus on the most explicit juxtaposition of patriarchy and matriarchy.

Thus, the alternate history outlined below involves imagined perspectives derived from the application of features found in early matriarchal societies onto the real lineage of jazz history in Graz. This also involves ramifications of a wider matriarchic context beyond the jazz scene, including matriarchal structures in society and politics. The alternate history is provided in the right column below, juxtaposed with the verified historic events in the left column. The texts are structured in nine passages that may be read next to each other for comparison. Reciprocal text passages mark incidents of real events as part of the alternate history stream.

Case Study: A Uchronic Narrative of Jazz in Graz

(1)

The early history of jazz in Graz was deeply interrelated with the British occupation after World War II (Kolleritsch, 1995). Since many aficionados had secretly listened to jazz on foreign radio broadcasts during the war, jazz events soon became a symbol of freedom and liberation, and yet, they were critically observed by a conservative elite (Kahr, 2018). Jazz became a lively form of popular entertainment at local bars and dance clubs, however, rather than reducing jazz to entertainment, local cultural politicians sensed its potential as an elitist representation of contemporary art and provided financial support for the development of modern jazz styles as "high art." The local jazz history has been deeply interrelated with the development of the Institute for Jazz at the current University of Music and Performing Arts in Graz, which was founded in 1965 as one of the first academic jazz programs in Europe. The institute has quickly built a reputation as the European center for jazz education and research (Körner, 1969), even though some jazz courses had been organized much earlier. For instance, the jazz program at the Dr. Hoch'sche Konservatorium in Frankfurt am Main was founded in 1928 but shut down by the Nazis in 1933 (Kahr, 2017, p. 47).

(2)

The international reputation of the institute in Graz has played an important role in the formation of a local jazz identity. This involved a high degree of pride and self-esteem, particularly among those affiliated with the foundation of the academic institution (Kahr, 2017, pp. 46-47). All of the founding members and lecturers were male; most of them aged between 25 and 35 with an education in classical music, some had obtained doctoral degrees in musicology or law (Kolleritsch, 1995, pp. 199-208). They participated successfully at national and international jazz competitions and conveyed the image of jazz as a serious art form, worthy as an academic subject alongside the achievements of iconic composers in Classical music.

(3)

Members of the institute participated in a wide range of activities to develop their competences regarding jazz practice, education and research. These involved the organization of concerts with well-known international jazz artists in Graz. Festivals such as Internationale Grazer Jazztage (1965, 1966 and 1974) and Jazz Live (1974–1978), as well as concert series in local venues such as

(1)

The early history of jazz in Graz was deeply interrelated with the social effects of the peacefully united Europe in the early 20th century. The rise of new communication technology and the effects of globalization ensured the early and wide distribution of jazz as a new musical practice. Jazz was consumed through various new media, appreciated as entertainment as well as a form of high art, and was actively practiced by a large part of society alongside repertoires of classical and popular music from all over the world. Jazz musicians of all races, nationalities, religions and gender identities were hired as teachers in schools and private homes to ensure the development of jazz practice as a major contribution to well-being and public health. The community leaders appreciated the artistic activities and provided a sustainable support system for artistic activities. Due to public demand, local musicians founded a specialized jazz program for particularly motivated and talented young musicians at the local music academy in 1965, which later became the current University of Music and Performing Arts in Graz. Since then, the local jazz history has been deeply interrelated with the institute's contributions to the development of jazz practice, education and research.

(2)

The institute in Graz has cooperated with similar institutions across the world, but engagements with local and neighboring communities were of highest priority. The faculty's inclusive activities have played an important role in the formation of a local jazz identity. This involved a high degree of awareness regarding the music's positive impact on the society. The founding members represented the demographical characteristics of the surrounding communities and targeted the fair representation of all age groups and education levels among lecturers. There was little competition: some musicians participated at national and international jazz festivals, while others continued to engage exclusively in local communities.

(3)

Members of the institute participated in a wide range of activities to develop their competences regarding jazz practice, education and research. These involved the organization of concerts with well-known international jazz artists in Graz. Festivals such as Internationale Grazer Jazztage (1965, 1966 and 1974) and Jazz Live (1974–1978), as well as concert series in local venues such as Cave 62, Forum Stadtpark, M 59 and Royal Garden Jazzclub

Cave 62, Forum Stadtpark, M 59 and Royal Garden Jazzclub contributed to a lively exchange between local and foreign artists. The representation of black masculinity raised particular attention among local media and audiences; an outstanding event in this regard was the 1966 appearance of the Max Roach Quintet (Freddie Hubbard, tp; James Spaulding, as; Ronnie Mathews, p; Jymie Merritt, b; and Roach, dr), which resulted in a scandal (Kahr, 2016, pp. 60–62). Alcohol abuse and inappropriate behavior on stage led to the arrest of Hubbard and Spaulding. The incident caused a measure of animosity directed towards the musicians thus detained (who were freed the following day), towards jazz in general, and the organizing members of the jazz institute. Reports appeared in local newspaper articles such as *Kleine Zeitung* on 15 November 1966, with some commentators expressing their disapproval of the supposedly irresponsible use of public money to support such "outrageous" events.

(4)

The jazz institute was first located in the historical Palais Meran close to the city center, which had been built for the Archduke Johann in 1843 and has been owned by the government authorities since World War II. However, after a series of jam sessions in the basement, disputes with members of the classical departments forced the jazz institute's move to a rather run-down temporary location on the city outskirts. After gradual renovation, the building has become the permanent site for jazz education in Graz. As there was no suitable performance space, the institute started a longtime cooperation with a local student dormitory organization to ensure a venue for jazz concerts in a nearby location.

(5)

In 1966, Swedish trombonist, improvisor and composer Eje Eilert Ove Thelin (1938–1990) was appointed as one of the first international professors at the institute (Kahr, 2016, pp. 244–246). Equipped with excellent instrumental skills and a successful international career he soon became the spearhead of a thriving free jazz movement in Graz. Thelin's unorthodox teaching approach stood out in comparison to the rather conservative educational standards at the academy. By teaching at late hours, partly in his home, and by exploring musical concepts outside the stylistic norms of swing and bebop, Thelin built trust among his followers (Piller, 2015), but also attracted distrust among the leading faculty members. The growing tension contributed to a

lively exchange between local and visiting artists. The representation of diversity was taken for granted by concert promoters and audiences.

The media reported about the scope of artistic expression, displaying the musical competence of journalists who often were active musicians themselves. All invited guest performers presented their musical approaches not only on concert stages and in workshops at the jazz institute but participated in a wide range of outreach activities in public places and schools. Frequently, local jazz musicians and their guests were invited by the community leaders to join political discussions and to participate in decision making processes. Occasionally, the community leaders (many of whom had received musical training themselves) performed with local and guest musicians and reflected their artistic encounters in lively discourses thereafter.

(4)

The jazz institute was first located in the historical Palais Meran close to the city center, which had been built by the Archduke Johann in 1843 for educational purposes. After a series of jam sessions in the basement, members of classical departments became interested in cooperative projects, for instance in the form of improvised reinterpretations of historical music by composers such as Clara Schumann, Alma Mahler, Maria Bach, Vera Auer, Jutta Hipp, Nina Simone, Carla Bley and Toshiko Akiyoshi. The building was constantly renovated including barrier-free construction as well as a cafeteria and a large pool for recreation and social interaction between periods of academic study.

(5)

In 1966, Swedish trombonist, improvisor and composer Eje Eilert Ove Thelin (1938–1990) was appointed as one of the first international professors at the institute (Kahr, 2016, 244–246). Equipped with excellent instrumental skills and a successful international career he soon became the spearhead of a thriving free jazz movement in Graz. Thelin's teaching approach matched the long-established standards of student-centered and gender-sensitive learning and teaching at the academy. By teaching at late hours, partly in his home, and by exploring musical concepts outside the stylistic norms of swing and bebop, Thelin built trust among his followers as well as the leading faculty members. Thelin emphasized theculminated in a conflict when one of his students appeared to the performance of Igor Stravinsky's *Ebony Concerto* in a red shirt instead of the black suit and white shirt uniform (Kahr, 2018, p. 444). While the student received a formal warning and was banned from further participation in the orchestra, Thelin's responsibility was critically questioned by the academic leaders. Thelin left Graz after his teaching contract was not renewed in 1972.

(6)

From the 1980s onwards, the institution installed a limited number of professorships dedicated to jazz composition and theory, trumpet, saxophone, trombone, guitar, piano, bass and drums. These positions offered stable salaries and a respected social status. The selection process was highly competitive and required self-esteem and assertiveness of the applicants. Almost all professorships as well as the re-openings upon retirement were filled by men. Singer Sheila Jordan was the first female guest lecturer, conducting a workshop in tandem with Bobby McFerrin in 1985. In 1988, the institute installed a permanent jazz vocal class, led by guest lecturers including Jordan, Lauren Newton, Jay Clayton, Mark Murphy, Andy Bey, Marguerite Juenemann, Michele Hendricks and Tom Lellies. From 2002-2006 Laurie Antonioli filled the first guest professorship for jazz vocals. Since 2006, singer-pianist Dena DeRose has represented the only female full professor at the jazz institute.

(7)

Although the Austrian government—which has exclusively been led by men since its inception in 1918—has ensured free access to higher education since 1972, the number of students admitted to the jazz program was limited. As applicants have continuously outnumbered the available study places, a competitive selection process has led to the rejection of a high number of capable students throughout the years. Some were accepted in a future selection round and some enrolled at other institutions; however, a considerable number of motivated young musicians had to change their education plans. All accepted students, however, have received training of the highest quality and many graduates had successful careers as artists and/or academic leaders (Kahr 2016, pp. 44-45) need to extend the number of female

trombonists and created a special study program, in which he encouraged historical research on women in jazz and invited several female professional brass players to perform as role models for students in and around Graz. Many of his students have established international careers and continued to inspire young female brass players around the world. In 1972, Thelin decided to leave the city of Graz after he was offered a position in his home country.

(6)

Due to the involvement of women across the decision-making processes across all European countries, the legal framework for the academic sector from the early 20th century onwards has been based on mutual trust and bottom-up developments rather than top-down strategies. After a long discussion process involving all members of the institutions, consensus was reached in favor of equality among faculty members and non-hierarchic academic structures. This involved equal status of all lecturers. The faculty at the jazz institute comprised a balanced group of lecturers representing the demographics of the region as well as the diversity of musical approaches in jazz. Lecturers decided freely on their length of tenure and there was no competition for obtaining a particular social status. Public funding ensured the integration of international guest lecturers for shorter or extended periods and the development of new pedagogical approaches beyond the master-pupil type training scheme.

(7)

The Austrian community leaders—comprising a diverse group of people representing the local demographics in Austria—have ensured free access to higher education since 1918. There was no selection process at the jazz institute, which has resulted in a large group of trained jazz musicians. Some students decided to live and work as musicians, while others turned to different careers, integrating the knowledge gained from jazz in other professions and social activities. Some graduates became community leaders, such as drummer Thomas Klestil (1932-2004). He served the Austrian community from 1992-2004 but continued to perform regularly with his ensemble, which at times included his school friend, the well-known pianist Joe Zawinul.

(8)	(8)
As a consequence of the growing research activities at the jazz institute, the International Society for Jazz Research was founded in Graz in 1969 (ISJR, 2021). In the same year, the society started with the organization of international conferences and the publication of the yearbook *Jazzforschung / Jazz Research*, which has been acknowledged as the first periodical in jazz research worldwide (Martin, 1996, p. 11) and the book series *Beiträge zur Jazzforschung / Studies in Jazz Research*, which was complemented by the journal *Jazz Research News* in 2000. In 1971, the Institute for Jazz Research was founded as a separate entity at the current University of Music and Performing Arts in Graz with the aim to establish jazz research as an independent, interdisciplinary branch of musicology (Kolleritsch, 1989, p. 224). Jazz research was defined as an interdisciplinary endeavor encompassing specifically adapted methods methods in systematic, historical and comparative musicology (Kahr, 2021, pp. 208-212). According to the institute's self-definition, one of its most notable research achievements has been "an abundance of in- depth structural analyses of musical genres and individual musicians' styles, based on original transcriptions of audio recordings" (Kunstuni, 2021a). The institute has hosted a large archive of print publications and audiovisual recordings, has contributed to the education of generations of dedicated jazz researchers as well as musicologists with a special focus on jazz and popular music research, and spearheaded the development of jazz research in Central Europe.	As a consequence of the growing research activities at the jazz institute, the International Society for Jazz Research was founded in Graz in 1969. In the same year, the society started with the organization of international conferences, the publication of the yearbook *Jazzforschung / Jazz Research*, which has been acknowledged as the first periodical in jazz research worldwide and the book series *Beiträge zur Jazzforschung / Studies in Jazz Research*, which was complemented by the journal *Jazz Research News* in 2000. In 1971, the Institute for Jazz was extended by a research unit, which later became the International Study Center for Jazz Practice and Research at the current University of Music and Performing Arts in Graz. The center's aim was the interaction and cooperative reflection of scientific knowledge on music and tacit knowledge embodied in the artistic processes. Jazz research was defined as an interdisciplinary endeavor encompassing specifically adapted methods in systematic, historical and comparative musicology as well as arts-based research methods. According to the institute's self-definition, one of its most notable research achievements has been an abundance of in-depth structural analyses of musical genres and individual musicians' styles, based on the practitioners' knowledge as well as original transcriptions of audio recordings. The institute hosts a large archive of print publications and audiovisual recordings, has contributed to educate generations of dedicated jazz artists and researchers, and inspired the development of artistic research as an academic discipline.
(9)	(9)
Over time, the achievements of the jazz institutes, and their function as an international hub for the jazz scene, have influenced local jazz identity. The dominance of men has been mirrored across all sectors of the local jazz scene (Kahr, 2016, pp. 409- 434). Despite the general high appraisal for jazz associated with black masculinity (Kahr, 2016, pp. 201 and 415), the first African American professor was appointed not before 2006 at the institute.	Over time, the achievements of the jazz institutes, and their function as an international hub for the jazz scene, have influenced local jazz identity. The long history of diversity and inclusion among faculty and students regarding gender, race, age, physical conditions and religious beliefs has been mirrored across all sectors of the local jazz scene, which became internationally known as the "Graz model."

Conclusion

This case study presents the radical experiment of remembering the history of jazz in Graz as it has not happened. The construction of an alternate jazz history of gender diversity and equity on the grounds of an otherwise male-dominated narrative was based on Utopian and Uchronian approaches. The projection of an Utopian narrative of the past appeared as a Uchronian path to resolve the social and structural ramifications of the real, long-lasting domination of men in jazz. From this perspective the real history of jazz in Graz may appear as a dystopia, while the Uchronian version projects new socio-cultural conditions. The experience from this experiment may help to visualize and realize long-term goals regarding gender diversity and equity, rather than falling into the trap of reiterating the problems of one's own past.

As recent research has revealed, women still struggle with bias and barriers in approaching leadership positions across industries (AAUW, 2016). As proposed by the United Nation's Sustainable Development Goals (United Nations, 2021), gender equity is a fundamental human right, hence, advocacy and action are required. Rather than relying on the hopeful "not-yet" Utopian schemes derived from feminist visions (Gilarek, 2015), a Uchronic perspective of a diverse jazz history provides a more pragmatic "What if?" Utopia of diversity and inclusion in jazz. As "rational reasoning" in psychological terms participates to "identify causes of outcomes and form intentions for the future" (Byrne, 2013), the vivid imagination of a "better" version of the past may help to identify the specific problems involved with male-dominated jazz histories and encourage developing concrete paths towards the future.

This study has outlined alternate memories of a local jazz history, which could replace the memories of the real past. The construction of these alternate memories has rested on the author's imagination, which was informed by the results of musicological research on real historic events as well as knowledge embodied in the artistic participation as a member of the jazz scene in Graz. The author's creation of an alternate history can thus be understood as a form of artistic research (Kahr, 2021a), establishing altered preconditions for the creation of new art and new artistic encounters based on memories of a diverse and inclusive jazz tradition which has not existed but may have existed and should exist in the future.

References

AAUW (2016). Barriers and bias: The status of women in leadership. www.aauw.org/app/uploads/2020/03/Barriers-and-Bias-nsa.pdf.

Bachofen, J. J. (1861/1992). *Das Mutterrecht: Eine Untersuchung über die Gynaikokratie der alten Welt nach ihrer religiösen und rechtlichen Natur.* English edition (1992). *Myth, Religion and Mother Right.* Princeton University Press.

Berklee Institute of Jazz and Gender Studies. (2021). What Would Jazz Sound Like in a Culture without Patriarchy? https://college.berklee.edu/jazz-gender-justice.

Berklee Institute of Jazz and Gender Studies. (2021a). New Standards. www.jazzandgenderjustice.com/.

Berklee Institute of Jazz and Gender Studies. (2021b). Mission, Values, and Vision. https://college.berklee.edu/jazz-gender-justice/mission-vision-values.

Bruckner-Haring, C. (2017). The development of the Austrian jazz scene and its identity 1960-1980. *European Journal of Musicology, 16*(1), 136–157. https://doi.org/10.5450/ejm.2017.16.5784.

Buscatto, M. (2007/2018). *Femmes du jazz: Musicalités, féminités, marginalisations.* CNRS Editions.

Byrne, R. M. J. (2005). *The Rational Imagination: How People Create Alternatives to Reality.* MIT Press.

Byrne, R. M. J. (2013). Counterfactual reasoning. In D.S. Dunn (Ed.), *Oxford Bibliographies in Psychology.* Oxford University Press. doi:10.1093/obo/9780199828340-0017.

Carver, B. (2017). *Alternate Histories and Nineteenth-century Literature: Untimely Meditations in Britain, France, and America.* Palgrave.

DeVeaux, S. (1998). Constructing the jazz tradition. In R.G. O'Meally (Ed.), *The Jazz Cadence of American Culture* (pp. 484–514). Columbia University Press.

Dunkel, M. (2018). Darcy James Argue's uchronic jazz. In W. Knauer (Ed.), *Jazz@100. Darmstadt Studies in Jazz Research 15* (pp. 129–142). Wolke Verlag.

Firth, R., Ferrei, M. and Lang, A. (2016). Future(s) perfect: Uchronian mapping as a research and visualisation tool in the fringes of the Olympic Park. *Livingmaps Review, 1*(1), 1–15. http://livingmaps.review/journal/index.php/LMR/article/view/21.

Fürnkranz, M. (2019). Zur Situation von Instrumentalistinnen im österreichischen Jazz. In M. Pfleiderer and W.-G. Zaddach (Eds.), *Jazzforschung heute: Themen, Methoden, Perspektiven* (pp. 37–58). Edition EMVAS.

Gilarek, A. (2015). The temporal displacement of utopia and dystopia in feminist speculative fiction. *Explorations: A Journal of Language and Literature, 3,* 34–46.

Göttner-Abendroth, H. (2004). Matriachral society: Definition and theory. In G. Vaughan (Ed.), *The Gift, Il Dono: A Feminist Analysis.* Meltemi editore. http://wunrn.com/wp-content/uploads/013106_matriachial_society.pdf.

Hawley, J. C. (2004). Mapping utopia: Spatial and temporal sites of meaning. In M. A. Bartter (Ed.), *The Utopian Fantastic* (pp. 17–22). Praeger Press.

ISJR. (2021). International Society for Jazz Research. https://jazzresearch.org/.

Kahr, M. (2016). *Jazz & the City: Jazz in Graz von 1965 bis 2015.* Leykam.

Kahr, M. (2016a). *Jazz & the City (and me …).* [CD Recording] Alessa Records ALR 1047.

Kahr, M. (2017). The jazz institutes in Graz: Pioneers in academic jazz and their impact on local identity. *European Journal of Musicology, 16*(1), 45–59. https://doi.org/10.5450/ejm.2017.16.5778.

Kahr, M. (2018). Jazz in Graz von 1965 bis 2015. In F. Bouvier, W. Dornik, O. Hochreiter, N. Reisinger and K. M. Schmidlechner (Eds.), *Historisches Jahrbuch der Stadt Graz 48* (pp. 435–451). Stadt Graz.

Kahr, M. (2021). Jazz in Graz in den frühen 1970er-Jahren: Institutionen, Personen, Entwicklungen. In S. Prucher, S. Herkt, S. Kogler. S. Matiasovits and E. Strouhal (Eds.), *Auf dem Weg zur Kunstuniversität: Das Kunsthochschul-Organisationsgesetz von 1970. Veröffentlichungen zur Geschichte der Universität Mozarteum Salzburg 15,* (pp. 204–220). Hollitzer.

Kahr, M. (Ed.) (2021a). *Artistic Research in Jazz: Positions, Theories, Methods.* Routledge.

Kolleritsch, E. (1989). Ein neuer Zweig der Musikwissenschaft, des praktischen Musikstudiums und der Musikpädagogik: Das Institut für Jazzforschung und die Abteilung für Jazz an der Hochschule für Musik und darstellende Kunst in Graz. *Artis Musicae, 36*(3), 223–227.

Kolleritsch, E. (1995). *Jazz in Graz Von den Anfängen nach dem Zweiten Weltkrieg bis zu seiner akademischen Etablierung: Ein zeitgeschichtlicher Beitrag zur Entwicklung des Jazz in Europa.* Beiträge zur Jazzforschung/Studies in Jazz Research 10. Akademische Druck- und Verlagsanstalt ADEVA.

Körner, F. (1969). Graz: Zentrum der Jazzforschung. *Jazzforschung/Jazz Research, 1,* 8–14.

Kunstuni Graz. (2021). Jazz and the City: Identity of a Capital of Jazz. https://jazzforschung.kug.ac.at/en/research/research-at-the-institute/external-funding/jazz-the-city-identity-of-a-capital-of-jazz/.

Kunstuni Graz. (2021a). Institute for Jazz Research. https://jazzforschung.kug.ac.at/en/institute/institute-for-jazz-research/about-us/.

Meier-Seethaler, C. (2019). Matriarchatstheorie und feministische Geschlechterforschung: Eine Positionsbestimmung. www.theoriekritik.ch/?p=3625.

Mills, J. S. (1868). Public and parliamentary speeches – Part I – November 1850 – November 1868. https://oll.libertyfund.org/title/kinzer-the-collected-works-of-john-stuart-mill-volume-xxviii-public-and-parliamentary-speeches-part-i#preview.

More, T. (1516). *De optimo rei publicae statu deque nova insula Utopia: Libellus vere aureus, nec minus salutaris quam festivus* [Of a republic's best state and of the new island Utopia]. www.gutenberg.org/files/2130/2130-h/2130-h.htm.

Nowotny, H. (1994/1989). *Time: The Modern and Postmodern Experience.* Translated by Neville Plaice. First published in German as *Eigenzeit: Entstehung und Strukturierung eines Zeitgefühls.* Polity Press.

Piller, L. (2015). *Das Wirken des Jazz-Posaunisten Eje Thelin in Graz und sein Einfluss auf die Entwicklung des Free Jazz (1967–1972)* [MMus thesis, University of Music and Performing Arts in Graz].

Portelli, A. (1988). Uchronic dreams: working class memory and possible worlds. *Oral History 16,* 46–56.

Renouvier, C. (1876). *Uchronie (l'Utopie dans l'histoire): Esquisse historique apocryphe du developpement de la civilisation européenne tel qu'il n'a pas été tel qu'il aurait pu être* [Uchrony (Utopia in history): Apocryphal sketch of the development of the European civilization not as it was but as it could have been]. 2nd edition (first edition published in 1857). Bureau de la Critique philosophique XVI. https://gallica.bnf.fr/ark:/12148/bpt6k833574/f1.item.

Rustin-Paschal, N. (2017). *The Kind of Man I am: Jazzmasculinity and the World of Charles Mingus Jr.* Wesleyan.

Rustin, N. T. and Tucker, S. (Eds.) (2008). *Big Ears: Listening for Gender in Jazz Studies.* Duke University Press.

Schaefer, C. and Rodríguez-Hernández, R. (2016), From utopia to uchronia: After-images of revolutionary history in contemporary Mexican film. *Studies in Spanish and Latin American Cinemas, 13*(2), 137–157.

Schmid, H. (2017). *Uchronia: Time at the Intersection of Design, Chronosociology and Chronobiology* (PhD thesis, Royal College of Art).

Schmid, H. (2018). Uchronia. https://uchronia.world/.

Schmid, H. (2020). *Uchronia: Designing Time.* Birkhäuser. https://doi.org/10.1515/9783035618112.

Starr, W. (2021). Counterfactuals. In E. N. Zalta (Ed.), *The Stanford Encyclopedia of Philosophy (Summer 2021 Edition).* https://plato.stanford.edu/archives/sum2021/entries/counterfactuals/.

Tucker, S. (2000). *Swing Shift: "All-girl" Bands of the 1940s.* Duke University Press.

Tucker, S. (2004). A Feminist Perspective on New Orleans Jazz Women. NOJNHP Research Study. University of Kansas. www.nps.gov/jazz/learn/historyculture/upload/New_Orleans_Jazzwomen_RS-2.pdf.

United Nations. (2021). Sustainable development goals: Goal 5. www.un.org/sustainabledevelopment/gender-equality/.

Wehr-Flowers, E. L. (2006). Differences between male and female students' confidence, anxiety, and attitude toward learning jazz improvisation. *Journal of Research in Music Education, 54,* 337–349. https://doi.org/10.1177/002242940605400406.

Worth, A. (2018). Uchronia. *Victorian Literature and Culture, 46*(3–4), 928–930. https://doi.org/10.1017/S1060150318001201.

PART 2

Identity and Culture

12

PLAYING THE PART

A Social-Psychological Perspective on Being a Girl in Jazz

Erin L. Wehr

Author's Statement: I would like to acknowledge the women who have shared their experiences in jazz culture. Their courage and perseverance make it possible to move towards an understanding of learning jazz from the perspective of someone identified as a *girl*. I use the term "girl" to illustrate the childhood experience, and "identified as" to represent the perspective of an individual, regardless of personal preferences of sex and gender, categorized by others as a girl in social contexts. As song titles reflect jazz culture (Monson, 2008), I refer to song titles in headings to connect the explored gender concepts with traditionally accepted elements of the jazz language.

"Girl Talk"

There is an "uncomfortableness" associated with being a girl in jazz that has been navigated by females throughout jazz history (Healy, 2016; Monson, 2008; Oliveros, 2004; Provost, 2017; Rowe, 1995). The introduction of jazz into school music education programs brought both opportunities and challenges for girls as jazz culture, even in educational settings, is primarily masculine (Alexander, 2011). The possible conflict between a girl's vision of her adult life and the jazz culture is understood (Dahl, 2004; Eccles, 1987), however, school music study is not limited to the purpose of developing music careers. Jazz contributes much to education, including history and social awareness (Bierman, 2020), self-expression (McPherson and Hendricks, 2010), skills for understanding current music (Ciorba and Russell, 2014), and finding one's musical voice (Provost, 2017). A review of female participation in jazz education from a social-psychological perspective can provide insight into the girl in jazz experience. Social-psychology also provides theories to guide institutional change for increasing girls' participation in jazz.

Advocating for Girls "I Should Care"

Advocating for including girls in jazz education is essential. Initially, gender and jazz research lacked a foundation for inquiry. Masculinity, competition, and gender-appropriate roles were commonly understood facets of the jazz culture, yet these concepts needed to be documented to justify inquiry into the nature of the gender imbalance in jazz. Women who dared to speak and publish on gender and jazz have allowed others to follow (Tucker, 2001/2002). Also deserving of appreciation are the

DOI: 10.4324/9781003081876-14

men who have asked where the girls are. Collier (1995) shared that some jazz musicians attribute the gender issue in jazz to a victim mentality. Some women, possibly aware of this perspective, have hesitated to discuss gender and risk one's acceptance in the field (Hall and Burke, 2020). A continued justification for teaching jazz to girls is needed to counteract cultural suggestions that girls don't need jazz and jazz doesn't need girls.

"All the Things You Are"

Jazz is a cultural and artistic creation of African-American contribution that developed in the United States, influencing popular and art music around the world (Bierman, 2020). Jazz is as important for girls as for boys to understand American history in a depth not available from traditional history books (Goodrich, 2008), including a combination of musical cultures and traditions initially from Africa, Europe, Cuba, and the Caribbean. Jazz reflects society and includes lessons on diversity, equity, and equality from both written history and through song. Music theory and form in jazz provide foundations for understanding the development of popular music styles. Jazz is both written and improvised, harmonically and rhythmically complex, art music and popular music, and a genre that values personal creativity and expression (Bierman, 2020). Participation in jazz gives girls an opportunity to be creative, expressive, and heard while also challenging creative cultures that silence women (Bassett et al., 2020; Steinberg, 2001).

"Farewell Blues"

School jazz programs help to preserve jazz as a functioning art form. Students participating in jazz programs become jazz consumers (Willard, 2014). Jazz improvisation belongs in music education (Steinberg, 2001), and should include jazz performance, history, theory, and appreciation (Ciorba and Russell, 2014). Women are a significant part of our education system and teaching girls jazz continues jazz education in our schools.

"Nice Work if You Can Get It"

Both boys and girls need musical experiences that allow creativity and expression (Provost, 2017), which are uniquely provided in jazz education. By not experiencing jazz, girls limit their potential in music careers (Delzell, 1994/1995; McKeage, 2004). The US Bureau of Labor Statistics Occupational Handbook (2021) predicts only 1 percent growth in occupations for musicians, suggesting a highly competitive work environment. Truity (2021) and the Bureau of Labor Statistics (2006) suggested that knowing multiple musical styles and instruments is helpful for music careers. Tucker (2001/2002) described music education careers as traditionally acceptable venues for women in jazz, however, women need solid teaching and performing experiences in jazz to prepare them for teaching jazz. Jazz study provides a pathway for understanding and creating music in popular culture while broadening music skills for careers in music (McPherson and Hendricks, 2010). However, as much as girls need jazz, jazz needs girls as part of keeping jazz relevant and preserving jazz contributions to history and society (Willard, 2014).

Gender in Jazz Education "I Got a Right to Sing the Blues"

In 1971 jazz programs were developing in American schools (Worthy, 2013) while Congress enacted the Title IX Education Amendments bringing an expectation of gender equity in schools (AAUW, 2000). However, fifty years later jazz education continues to be reported as male-dominated/patriarchal, competitive, sarcastic, excluding, and as having an environment of sexual misconduct and power relationships (Alexander, 2011; Caudwell, 2012; Collier, 1995; Hall and Burke, 2020;

MacDonald and Wilson, 2006; McKeage, 2004; Olin, 1995; Olin and Aberg, 1995; Oliveros, 2004; Shanley, 2009; Valenti, 2018).

Improvisation ability by gender was compared in early music education research with no significant differences reported (McDaniel, 1974; Hores, 1977; Bash, 1984). Porter (1984a) published two articles in the *Music Educators Journal* recognizing creative contributions and experiences of successful women in jazz. Porter acknowledged that most were pianists, piano and singing were more acceptable female roles, and playing a brass instrument historically had not been considered a proper choice. Porter (1984b) also reported that while men were appreciated throughout the process of developing jazz skills, women were judged more quickly by jazz critics suggesting higher expectations for female acceptance.

Jazz music is not learned alone in a practice room but rather is experienced, practiced, and performed in group settings (Macdonald and Wilson, 2005) where, if a girl is not an accepted member of a group, the process of learning self-expression through improvised music becomes complicated due to social (Macdonald and Wilson, 2006) or social-psychological (Wehr, 2016) factors, particularly when the improvised language is considered inappropriate for a girl (Monson, 1995). The experience of being the only female in a jazz group is frequently reported throughout jazz history (Bassett et al. 2020; McCord, 1985; McKeage, 2004), and when combined with gender stereotypes contributes to social-psychological dynamics that can hinder learning processes. McCord (1985) contributed that if there is a woman in a group, she is often the only one. Male and female jazz experiences differ (Macdonald and Wilson, 2006; Olin and Aberg, 1995; Wehr-Flowers 2006, 2007), and become more complicated when males and females are not equally represented (Wehr, 2016).

The International Association of Schools of Jazz began a jazz education publication in 1994 called *Jazz Changes* (Collier et al., 1994). The first publication referenced females only twice in two pictures, a singer and a keyboardist, both acceptable female roles (Porter, 1984a). The second publication headline read "Women in Jazz: Why Aren't There More Women in Jazz Education?" Both an article and editorial acknowledged the lack of females as a widespread issue in the field of jazz and called for ongoing discussion. Collier stated that few women audition, and even fewer have the needed skills for jazz programs (1995). Interestingly, after the gender discussions in two issues of *Jazz Changes* there was very little continued discourse in the publication on women. Change is slow, and the problem is not limited to American music with similar reports of few women entering jazz programs in Norway (Annfelt, 2003); Australia, (Bassett et al., 2020; Hall and Burke, 2020; Healy, 2016; Valenti, 2018) and the UK (Caudwell, 2012; McAndrew and Widdup, 2021).

Studies at the turn of the century continued to explore the female jazz experience. Madura (1999) reported no gender differences in learning vocal jazz improvisation. Steinberg (2001) identified a jazz gender imbalance and introduced social-psychological issues in jazz by calling attention to the possibility of gender-role stereotyping in student/teacher interactions in rehearsals, contests, and clinics. McKeage's (2004) study followed contributing a list of gender and jazz issues with the last two items particularly related to social-psychological theory: (a) instrument choice limiting jazz access; (b) limited number of available spots; (c) jazz courses not required for degrees; (d) jazz courses not counting towards degrees; (e) girls less comfortable in jazz programs than other ensembles; and (f) girls not able to connect purpose to jazz participation.

May (2003) identified jazz improvisation as a single construct with self-evaluation as the best predictor of jazz improvisation achievement. May theorizes that girls may avoid jazz improvisation due to a lowered confidence level which suggests self-efficacy (Bandura, 1997) as a theoretical understanding of the jazz and gender relationship. Tucker (2003) described women in jazz as being marginalized and often marketed and consumed visually rather than for their music suggesting issues of stereotype (Kanter, 1993; Steele, 1997; Steele and Aronson, 2005). Tucker (2004) analyzed the term jazz community and the meaning for women in jazz suggesting a social-psychological setting

145

(Bandura, 1997). Oliveros (2004) also connected social-psychology theory to the female jazz experience through describing solo-status environments, uncomfortableness in male-dominated groups, and discouraging experiences with male teachers.

Males and females participating in high school and college jazz bands reported having significantly different perceptions towards jazz including females having less confidence and more anxiousness with a less positive attitude towards jazz (Wehr-Flowers, 2006). A follow-up study (Wehr-Flowers, 2007) on gender differences in music education students towards jazz identified gender as a single main factor with follow-up analysis revealing significant gender differences on the following self-efficacy contributing variables (Bandura, 2006b): (a) females being more anxious; (b) females reporting a difficult social climate and lack of peer support; and (c) females having less locus of control, more skepticism, and lowered self-efficacy for learning jazz. Monson (2008) shared an intimate portrait of her navigation of jazz culture reinforcing social-psychological issues for girls in jazz. including: (a) being the only female or one of very few; (b) being placed in token roles such as seductress; (c) feeling like a "walking stereotype"; and (d) feeling that being a woman was somehow disqualifying. These studies and writings collectively demonstrated a move towards understanding gender dynamics in jazz as a social-psychological phenomenon (Bandura, 2001). In particular, the introduction of Bandura's (1997) self-efficacy theory, Kanter's (1993) tokenism theory, and stereotype threat (Steele, 1997; Steele and Aronson, 2005) have been directly and indirectly implied as major contributors to the question of why girls avoid jazz participation.

Instrument Choice "Don't Blame Me"

Much attention has been given to instrument choice in music education research, including the sex-stereotyping of instruments (Abeles, 2009, Abeles and Porter, 1978; Delzell and Leppla, 1992; Griswold and Chroback, 1981; Steinberg, Tarnowski, 1993; Zervoudakes and Tenur, 1994), restricted participation in music due to peer-pressure and sex-typing of instruments (Conway, 2000;), understanding stereotypes (Conway, 2000; Green, 1997; Johnson and Stewart, 2004, 2005; Marshall and Shibazaki, 2011), concern for sex-stereotyping effects on students (Abeles, 2009; Abeles and Porter, 1978; Abeles et al., 2014; Doubleday, 2008; O'Neill and Boultona, 1996), and understanding how we can change the perceptions of instrument stereotyping (Bruce and Kemp, 1993; Eros, 2008; Harrison and O'Neill, 2000). A small group of researchers reported change in instrument choice research, including a lessening of degree of stereotype (Delzell and Leppla, 1992), an increase of females choosing male associated instruments (Zervoudakes and Tenur, 1994), and girls being more likely to choose a male-associated instrument in band settings (Abeles, 2009).

In 1988, Barber attributed a gender inequity in jazz participation to instrument choice. Many have since cited gender-based differences in instrument choice as a primary reason for the lack of females in jazz (Alexander, 2011; Barber, 1988; Delzell, 1994/1995; McKeage, 2004; Tucker, 2001/2002). Though sex-stereotyping of musical instruments appears to offer an explanation to the gender and jazz problem, instrument choice for school music (Green, 1997) and jazz participation (Wehr, 2016) has roots based in culture and gender stereotype. Girls' instrument choices and female jazz participation rates share similar gender issues but do not indicate the same causes or solutions. Though some overlap exists, to attribute the gender problem in jazz to something outside of the jazz culture such as instrument choice is to not have "Big Ears" for listening for gender in jazz (Tucker, 2001/2002).

> I advocate … ear-training that would enable jazz researchers to better listen for gender in … jazz studies. Listening for gender will be helpful … to those of us wanting to understand sexism and the experiences and contributions of women in jazz, but also to anyone wishing to develop more complex frameworks for addressing the histories, sounds, functions, and

meanings of this fascinating and multifaceted music. Without listening for gender ... jazz studies risks overlooking a category of analysis that closely follows race ... as the social category most capable of deconstructing this dominant discourse.

(p. 377)

Just as sex-stereotyping of instruments warrants study, so does the gender imbalance in jazz. Blaming the lack of females in jazz on children's instrument choices should be replaced with research seeking to understand the female jazz experience (Caudwell, 2012; Teichman, 2020). The jazz field is not just *dominated* by men, it is *overwhelmingly* masculine (Provost, 2017). Jazz was identified as the most sex-typed genre with stereotypes "overwhelmingly confined to jazz" (North et al., 2003, p. 139). Valenti (2018) identified from a survey of female jazz-trained instrumentalists that the male-dominated environment, the competitive culture, and a lack of female mentors and role models adversely affected their jazz study.

Steinberg (2001) reported a slight majority of females playing piano in a study of participation at school jazz contests, but females took only 29 percent of the piano solos. Piano as a socially acceptable instrument for girls (Tucker, 2001/2002) should have at least equal participation if the gender issue is related to instrument choice. Instrument choice does not align with jazz and gender research, instead putting the focus of the problem on the child instead of jazz culture. However, stereotyping of musical instruments in combination with social-psychological factors in jazz culture may be a contributing factor.

Researchers reported girls increasingly choosing male-associated instruments for band participation (Abeles, 2009; Zervoudakes and Tenur, 1994) yet gender imbalances in jazz continue. There appeared to be a dramatic attrition rate in jazz for women between high school and college, and as jazz study became more advanced (McKeage, 2004; Shanley, 2009; Zervoudakes and Tanur, 1994) demonstrating that girls participated in jazz then chose to quit. As girls' participation in jazz increases, girls improvising does not increase (McKeage, 2004; Rowe, 1995). Steinberg (2001) reported females soloing less than males at school jazz festivals, even when accounting for the male to female ratios, but only on piano and saxophone, which are considered more gender neutral (Abeles, 2009; Zervoudakes and Tanur, 1994).

Piano and string bass are not typical band instruments yet are necessary in school jazz bands and are often played by band members as secondary instruments. Flute and clarinet are utilized in jazz music, often as secondary instruments, yet teachers were reported as limiting students to one instrument and discouraging their jazz participation (McKeage, 2004; Shanley, 2009). Are teachers encouraging the learning of secondary instruments when serving the teacher and the band instrumentation, but not when initiated by, or serving, the student interested in learning jazz?

Researchers found instrument choice to not be a significant factor in the jazz and gender problem (McAndrew and Widdup, 2021; Wehr-Flowers, 2007). Continuing the instrument choice explanation as a single contributor to the gender and jazz issue can be perceived as avoiding the gender and jazz issue. If the gender imbalance in jazz is attributed to girls' instrument choices, then the jazz field avoids responsibility and justifies a lack of action to include girls in jazz programs. Though the typical high school jazz band has a limited instrumentation—historically flute, clarinet, bass clarinet, French horn, and violin among others—have been used professionally in both small groups and big band settings. Instrument choice can be an excuse to build jazz education around the instrumentation on readily available published charts, however charts are available with expanded instrumentation. Jazz competition can be used as an excuse to not use expanded instrumentation due to adjudication based on authenticity, however one might question the authenticity of jazz programs limiting jazz education to a big band experience with limited instrumentation.

McPherson and Hendricks (2010) in a broad study of students in 6–12 grade found that school music ranked low in comparison to other subjects, and music outside of school ranked high. Their recommendations for improving school music programs include (a) a broader scope of performance options including more personal creative expression; and (b) encouraging opportunities for autonomous, self-directed learning. Small jazz groups of varying instrumentation fit this description and allow for a broad range of instrumental participation.

Social-Psychological Theories "All Alone"

Bandura (1989) described human functioning in social-psychology as resulting from interactions among the person, their behaviors, and how they perceive others to react to their behaviors. This interaction affects future behavior, including what challenges one accepts and the perseverance in pursuing those challenges (Schunk and Pajares, 2005; Stajkovic et al., 2018). Wehr (2016) suggests three social-psychological theories as a lens to understanding the gender experience in jazz: (a) tokenism (Kanter, 1993); (b) stereotype threat (Steele and Aronson, 2005); and (c) self-efficacy theory (Bandura, 1997).

Tokenism "Solitude"

Tokenism (Kanter, 1993), also referred to as solo-status, describes a culture where females are the only female, or one of a very few. Tokenism in Kanter's setting shouldn't be confused with another use of the term tokenism referring to hiring representatives from underserved groups for appearances. Jazz is characterized as a patriarchal society (Dobson, 2010; MacDonald and Wilson, 2006) where solo-status for females is common, particularly as jazz study becomes more advanced (McKeage, 2004). Kanter suggested 15 percent or less of a token group creates potential for stereotype. Even in groups with a greater percentage of females, one can perceive tokenism in the broader field. Kanter (1993) described the difficulty of being in male-dominated environments according to four role traps that women fall into: mother, kid sister/pet, seductress, and iron-maiden. These role perceptions allow a generalization of women by fitting women into stereotypical roles, each relating to a token woman's sexuality. By living up to the expected role as part of "fitting in," a token loses her individuality. Kanter's research is with token women in a corporation, and later applied to the jazz field (Wehr, 2007, 2016). The existence of this sense of isolation and exclusion for female tokens in jazz has been well documented (Healy, 2016; Kavanaugh, 1995; McKeage, 2002; Monson, 2008; Valenti, 2018).

Mother "My Mammy"

The mother role involves taking care of and serving men (Kanter, 1993). Mother-role tokens are rewarded for their service rather than their professional contributions and may include taking on helpful/supportive roles. Reports of the mother role in jazz include men having difficulty seeing women as more than a mother (Provost, 2017) and females being asked to fulfill motherly tasks (Alexander, 2011).

Kid-Sister/Pet "Sister Sadie"

The kid-sister/pet role is characterized by a woman being accepted by the group as a plaything. Women in this role avoid being viewed as competition and are instead included in the group as a novelty valued for providing amusement (Kanter, 1977). Olin (1995) shared her perception of some women in jazz not taking themselves seriously, and Steinberg (2001) documented women band members being referred to as novelties (Steinberg, 2001). Tucker (2001/2002) reported novelty as overshadowing the potential of women to be respected as musicians.

Seductress "The Seductress"

The seductress role characterizes the woman as a sex-object valued for her looks rather than her musicianship. This role leads to jealousy from the group if a woman is closer to one man, or a negative perception if she is viewed as too friendly to all (Kanter, 1993). Kavanaugh (1995) shared that isolation is common unless the girl is dating one of the boys. Healy (2016) described the difficulty in navigating feelings of being looked at sexually. Monson (2008) explained the uncomfortableness of navigating relationships with band members based on who was trying to date her. Monson also described a guest singer filling a gender appropriate role as being treated with chivalry while Monson wasn't given basic courtesy. Caudwell (2012) reported audience assumptions that a woman in jazz must be dating one of the band members.

Iron-Maiden "Hard Hearted Hannah"

The iron-maiden role describes the woman demonstrating confidence and/or blocking sexual interests while avoiding association with other token roles (Kanter, 1993). Healy (2016) described females in jazz as concerned about being perceived as bossy and having to nullify their sexuality to avoid being treated as a trinket. Accepting an iron-maiden role allows a female to coexist as a professional while avoiding being perceived as a seductress, mother, or kid-sister. The result, however, often includes social isolation. Tucker (2001/2002) shared the expectation that women are mothers and housewives, and that women choosing to participate in jazz culture were perceived as sexual spectacles (seductress), novelties (pet), or masculine women (iron-maiden).

Stereotype Threat "They Say I'm Different"

Stereotype threat (Steele, 1997; Steele and Aronson, 2005) is the fear of confirming a negative stereotype. A negative stereotype in jazz includes playing like a girl, or for a girl, also playing like a man. Kanter's (1993) token roles as stereotype are reported by jazz women (Monson, 2008). If a woman plays like a man, she is too aggressive and stereotyped as an iron-maiden. If a woman sounds feminine, she is stereotyped as a pet, mother, or seductress. If a singer, she is likely viewed as seductress and valued for her looks rather than her musicianship. Tucker (2003) described female stereotypes in jazz as "inauthentic" spectacles, hypersexual or asexual, and/or women taking on male roles. Navigating stereotype roles can cause confusion and contribute to the uncomfortableness experienced by women in jazz (Monson, 2008; Rowe, 1995; Shanley, 2009; Tucker, 2001/2002). Jazz as a predominantly male, sex-typed genre (North, Colley, and Hargreaves, 2003) creates an environment where token females may lack confidence and underperform (Tavani and Losh, 2003) due to stereotype threat (Steele, 1997; Steele and Aronson, 2005). Sometimes the only way to avoid confirming a negative stereotype in jazz is avoidance, ultimately contributing to fewer women in jazz (Bandura, 2013). Fewer girls pursuing jazz study continues solo-status and stereotype threat environments.

Teichman (2020) made a case for jazz education as discriminatory through implied pressure to adhere to heteronormative roles. The female jazz experience, with a potential combination of solo-status and negative stereotype, establishes an environment for stereotype threat (Wehr, 2016), which can be more detrimental to women's performance than either condition alone (Inzlicht and Ben-Zeev, 2000; Sekaquaptewa and Thomas, 2003). Stereotype threat can reduce motivation when associated with negative group perceptions, regardless of one's capabilities (Steele, 1997; Steele and Aronson, 2005). Monson shared, "Gender socialization was finally doing its work on me ... having finally got it...that jazz was a quintessentially masculine music, I suddenly felt like a walking stereotype" (Monson, 2008, p. 274).

Self-Efficacy Theory "I Believe"

Ciorba and Russell (2014) suggested success and positive outcomes in jazz are related to student motivation. Social-psychology and self-efficacy theory (Bandura, 1997) provide guidance for helping students develop confidence leading to persistence and motivation. Self-efficacy is a type of confidence that is task-specific that can be increased by designing learning experiences. Bandura's self-efficacy theory includes four facets having potential to build or reduce self-efficacy: (a) mastery experiences; (b) vicarious experiences; (c) social persuasion; and (d) physiological states.

Positive Mastery Experiences "Do It Again"

Mastery experiences are small, multiple successes that build confidence for a specific task (Bandura, 2006a) and have been reported as the strongest contributor for building music performance efficacy (Zelenak, 2014). Instruction on jazz improvisation, specifically aural methods, have been shown to improve self-efficacy for improvising jazz (Watson, 2010).

Negative Mastery Experiences "I Can't Get Started"

Failures undermine self-efficacy, especially if occurring before confidence is established (Bandura, 2006a). Goals that are unreachable, or tasks assigned without skill building, set up students for failure. Asking a student to improvise without first guiding the student in learning jazz vocabulary can reduce self-efficacy for improvisation. Learning environments that induce anxiety or uncomfortableness can hinder the ability to learn and have mastery experiences.

Positive Social Persuasions "I Believe in You"

Social persuasions include voiced and perceived messages from others communicating belief in one's potential to be successful at a task. Positive social support alone has little effect in promoting self-efficacy. Telling a girl that she can improvise without first building skills reduces self-efficacy as she will lose trust in a teacher who says what she doesn't believe is true. When skills are developed and mastery experiences occur, then positive social support can contribute to the mastery experience (Bandura, 2006a).

Negative Social Persuasions "Whisper Not"

Negative social persuasions include voiced and perceived messages from others communicating disbelief in one's ability to be successful at a specific task and can be extremely powerful in lowering self-efficacy and reducing motivation (Bandura, 2006a). Social persuasion as evaluative feedback can raise or lower self-efficacy depending on how it is presented (Bandura, 1997). As self-efficacy increases, negative social persuasions become less effective. Monson (2008, pp. 279–280) shared, "When I finally had self-confidence about … playing, I was no longer upset by these comments."

Positive Vicarious Experiences "Because of You"

Vicarious experiences involve identifying with role models for achieving a specific task. There must be a shared experience, such as gender, race, age, and so forth, for increasing self-efficacy (Bandura, 2006a). Role models were suggested for increasing female participation in jazz (Alexander, 2011; McKeage, 2004). Steinberg (2001) stated that role models are particularly important during adolescence, the time when girls are making choices about jazz participation.

Negative Vicarious Experiences "All by Myself"

Experiencing solitude, without role models in your chosen field, reduces self-efficacy, as does observing role models fail (Bandura, 1997). A lack of role models in jazz has been well documented (Barber, 1999; Shanley, 2009; Valenti, 2018). Fewer women in the jazz field translates into fewer possibilities for connecting girl students with female role models, however, role models and mentors can be useful based on other qualities such as instrument, hometown, or being willing to provide positive guidance (Monson, 2008).

Positive Physiological States "Feeling Good"

Physiological states contribute to self-efficacy through one's interpretation of experiencing physiological activation. Elevated heart rate as part of anticipation and excitement is one example. Heightened arousal if interpreted as manageable can contribute positively to attention and focus for learning. Positive feelings about a learning or performing experience build self-efficacy for attempting future challenges (Bandura, 1997).

Negative Physiological States "Heebie Jeebies"

Heightened physical and affective states in stressful situations can be interpreted as signs of vulnerability or dysfunction. In music performance anxiety, negative self-interpretation of physiological states cycles into anxiety lowering task self-efficacy. Physiological states are especially pertinent to musicians where physiological states can impede a successful performance. Jazz improvisation practiced/rehearsed in group settings can induce performance-type anxiety. Physiological states including stress reactions, tension, anxiety, and altering mood can contribute to lower functioning, affecting one's ability to learn and perform (Bandura, 1997). A heightened sense of anxiety/uncomfortableness has been reported by females in jazz (Alexander, 2011; Healy, 2016; Shanley, 2009; Wehr, 2006, 2007).

Teaching Jazz to Girls: A Self-Efficacy Approach "Watch What Happens"

Utilizing social-psychological theories can help change jazz education environments into positive learning environments for teaching jazz skills. Ultimately, teaching jazz to girls involves increasing their individual beliefs of their ability to successfully learn and perform jazz. Teaching for confidence in jazz includes: (a) reducing tokenism and stereotype threat in jazz learning environments; (b) teaching for small successes in attaining jazz skills; (c) providing mentoring and role models to help manage negative social persuasions; and (d) helping students to understand and manage anxiety in jazz environments.

Teaching Environments "This Could Be the Start of Something Big"

Positive environments for females in jazz include safe spaces without tokenism and stereotype threat (Kanter, 1993; Steele, 1997; Steele and Aronson, 2005). Students are more open to experiment and create if they foresee success. Ideal jazz learning environments would have balance of gender, however, even 15–35 percent of females can reduce tokenism (Kanter, 1993). Finding ways to offer jazz instruction to all students, regardless of instrument (Alexander, 2011) would expose more students to jazz study and possibly reduce competition in the jazz environment. Encouraging girls to find their own sound and creating all-female groups (Steinberg, 2001) or small groups of like-minded students are options for creating safe spaces for building improvisation skills (Wehr, 2016). Other inclusive jazz teaching options include flute jazz ensemble reading vocal jazz arrangements up one octave and combos reading flexible instrumentation charts and/or reading lead sheets.

Create and Celebrate Small Successes "Pick Yourself Up"

Creating small successes in jazz improvisation may be challenging as many school music teachers have not had training in jazz improvisation. Steinberg (2001) suggests all students solo with first providing quality instruction early in music education programs to build skills and confidence. Band programs often focus on music reading and discourage learning music by ear. Jazz is a musical language with its own set of phonics that must be heard and imitated, whether from recordings or teacher demonstration. To develop self-efficacy for speaking the jazz language, one must learn jazz as a language. Develop your jazz skills for modeling the jazz language for students, attend a jazz improvisation camp, or host a jazz improvisation camp for your students. Help students to begin learning the jazz language through providing them accessible solos for transcription.

In the competitive environment of jazz, winning is subjective. Unclear goals and parameters for success lower self-efficacy (Bandura, 2013). A competitive environment complicates the development of self-efficacy in that a good attempt could be viewed as failure if there isn't a win. Setting specific and achievable goals as part of the learning process and celebrating small successes help to create mastery experiences.

Mentors, Role Models, and Negative Messages "Please Be Kind"

Cultivating a class/rehearsal environment where judgments and stereotyping are not acceptable is essential for developing self-efficacy, including pairing positive messages with small successes. Goodrich (2007) found benefits from employing a peer mentoring program in a high school jazz ensemble. Monson (2008) reported having a long line of encouraging directors and teachers guiding her in mastery learning experiences and introducing her to jazz cultural experiences. By the time she had to deal with negative and disrespectful band mates and directors she had enough skills and confidence to carry her in the jazz culture. Students need to avoid and/or be protected from negative environments while they are building their skills and confidence.

Much of the discourse in jazz and gender refers to the need for female role models (Alexander, 2011; Bandura, 2006a; McKeage, 2004; Steinberg, 2001; Valenti, 2018). Providing access to female jazz clinicians, attending contests with female adjudicators, and making connections with female jazz professionals provides role models and builds trust with the director making this effort. Increasing access to female jazz artists can shift the perception of jazz culture for all students.

Acknowledge Physiological States "I Should Care"

Tokenism, stereotype threat, and lack of self-efficacy can increase anxiety in jazz education environments manifesting as fear of derogation, cognitive block, and physical tenseness including elevated heart rate, shakiness, and dry mouth (Wehr, 2007). Helping students understand increased physiological states as part of learning jazz can help students manage rather than fear the increased anxiety responses. Reducing tokenism, controlling for stereotype threat, and creating safe learning spaces can help reduce anxiety by attending to mastery experiences, social persuasions, and vicarious experiences.

"The Best is Yet to Come"

National Public Radio has published the NPR Music Jazz Critics Poll since 2013. Pellegrinelli et al. (2021) shared that from 2017–2019 women accounted for only 11–16 percent of core personnel in ranked projects. However, in 2018 and 2020, 3 of the top 10 new releases were led or co-led by women. In 2019, 5 of the top 10 new releases were led or co-led by women. According to Kanter's (1993) tokenism theory we are approaching numbers that move women in jazz out of tokenism status. Centers for women in jazz are being created at major jazz colleges and universities including the Berklee School of Music Institute of Jazz and Justice (n.d.), and the UNT Jazz and Gender Equity Initiative (n.d.). Jazz at Lincoln Center now lists females on their sub list. Opportunities for including women in jazz exist, particularly in our school jazz programs, if we accept the challenge.

References

Abeles, H., and Porter, S. (1978). The gender-stereotyping of musical instruments. *Journal of Research in Music Education, 26*, 65–75. https://doi.org/ckmqkm.

Abeles, H. (2009). Are musical instrument gender associations changing? *Journal of Research in Music Education, 57*, 127–139. https://doi.org/dr5xd2.

Abeles, H., Hafeli, M., and Sears, C. (2014). Musicians crossing musical instrument gender stereotypes: A study of computer-mediated communication. *Music Education Research, 16*, 346–366. https://doi.org/gh7w.

Alexander, A. (2011). "Where Are the Girls? A Look at the Factors that Limit Female Participation in Instrumental Jazz." Unpublished manuscript, University of Southern California, Los Angeles. www.arielalexander.com/live/video_popup.php/Thesis_females_jazz.pdf?filename=dl_file&gallery=true&id=5&download=1&start_dl=1.

American Association of University Women (AAUW). (2000). *License for Bias: Sex Discrimination, Schools, and Title IX.* Marlow and Company.

Bandura, A. (1997). *Self-efficacy: The Exercise of Control.* Freeman.

Bandura, A. (2001). Social cognitive theory: An agentic perspective. *Annual Review of Psychology, 52*, 1–26. https://doi.org/dqmktz.

Bandura, A. (2006a). Adolescent development from an agentic perspective. In F. Pajares and T. Urdan (Eds.). *Self-efficacy Beliefs of Adolescents,* (pp. 1–43). Information Age Publishing.

Bandura, A. (2006b). Guide for constructing self-efficacy scales. In F. Pajares, and T. Urdan, (Eds.) *Self-efficacy Beliefs of Adolescents,* (pp. 307–337). Information Age Publishing.

Bandura, A. (2013). The role of self-efficacy in goal-based motivation. In E. A. Locke and G. P. Latham (Eds.), *Development in Goal Setting and Task Performance* (pp.147–157). Taylor and Francis.

Barber, D. (1999). A study of jazz band participation by gender in secondary high school instrumental music programs. *Jazz Research Proceedings Yearbook 19*, 92–99.

Bash, L. (1984). "The relationship among musical aptitude, musical achievement, psychosocial maturity, sex, age, preliminary improvisation performance and the acquisition of improvisation performance skill." *Jazz Research Papers, 4*, 6–12.

Berklee School of Music Institute of Jazz and Justice. (n.d.). *Berklee School of Music.* https://college.berklee.edu/jazz-gender-justice.

Bierman, B. (2020). *Listening to Jazz.* Oxford University Press.

Bruce, R., and Kemp, A. (1993). Sex-stereotyping in children's preferences for musical instruments. *British Journal of Music Education, 10*, 213–217. https://doi.org/cz7bjk

Bureau of Labor Statistics, U.S. Department of Labor (2006/2021). *Occupational Outlook Handbook, Musicians and Singers.* www.bls.gov/ooh/entertainment-and-sports/musicians-and-singers.htm.

Ciorba, C., and Russell, B. (2014). A proposed model of jazz theory knowledge acquisition. *Journal of Research in Music Education, 62*(3), 291–301 https://doi.org/gh7z.

Caudwell, J. (2012). Jazzwomen: Music, sound, gender, and sexuality. *Annals of Leisure Research, 15*, 389–403 10.1080/11745398.2012.744275.

Collier, G. (1995, Spring). Women and jazz, jazz and women: New riffs on an old tune. *Jazz Changes, 2*(1), 5.

Collier, G., Gill, J., and Turkenburg, W. (1994, Spring). Editorial. *Jazz Changes, 1*(1), 2.

Conway, C. (2000). Gender and musical instrument choice: A phenomenological investigation. *Bulletin of the Council for Research in Music Education, 146*, 1–16. https://doi.org/gh7z.

Dahl, L. (2004). *Stormy Weather: The Music and Lives of a Century of Jazz Women.* Limelight Editions.

Delzell, J. (1994/1995). Variables affecting the gender-role stereotyping of high school band positions. *Quarterly Journal of Teaching and Learning, 4*(4)/*5*(1), 77–84.

Delzell, J., and Leppla, D. (1992). Gender association of musical instruments and preferences of fourth grade students for selected instruments. *Journal of Research in Music Education, 40*, 93–103. https://doi.org/gh7z.

Doubleday, V. (2008). Sounds of power: An overview of musical instruments and gender. *Ethnomusicology Forum, 17*, 3–39. www.jstor.org/stable/20184604.

Eccles, J. (1987). Gender roles and women's achievement-related decisions, *Psychology of Women Quarterly, 11*, 135–172. https://doi.org/d9hwz3.

Eros, J. (2008). Instrument selection and gender stereotypes: A review of recent literature. *Update: Applications of Research in Music Education, 27*(1), 57–64. https://doi.org/fb2t4q.

Goodrich, A. (2007). Peer mentoring in a high school jazz ensemble. *Journal of Research in Music Education, 55,* 94–114. www.jstor.org/stable/4494336.

Goodrich, A. (2008). Utilizing elements of the historic jazz culture in a high school setting. *Bulletin of the Council for Research in Music Education, 175,* 11–30. www.jstor.org/stable/40319410.

Green, L. (1997). *Music, Gender, Education.* Cambridge: Cambridge University Press.

Griswold, P., and Chroback, D. (1981). Sex-role associations of music instruments and occupations by gender and major. *Journal of Research in Music Education, 29,* 57–62. https://doi.org/cmx3dq.

Hall, C., and Burke, R. (2020). Talkin' all that jazz: Unsilencing gender in music. *Lens.* https://lens.monash.edu/@politics-society/2020/09/15/1381258/talkin-all-that-jazz-unsilencing-gender-in-music.

Harrison, A., and O'Neill, S. (2000). Children's gender-typed preferences for musical instruments: An intervention study. *Psychology of Music, 28,* 81–97. https://doi.org/dpvpbr.

Healy, B. (2016, August 1). Be a good girl or play like a man: Why women aren't getting into jazz. *Biddyhealy.* www.biddyhealey.com/blog/2016/6/18/be-a-good-girl-or-play-like-a-man.

Hores, R. (1977). A comparative study of visual and aural-oriented approaches to jazz improvisation with implications for instruction. (Doctoral dissertation, Indiana University, 1977). *Dissertation Abstracts International, 39*(04), 2121A.

Inzlicht, M., and Ben-Zeev, T. (2000). A threatening intellectual environment: Why females are susceptible to experiencing problem-solving deficits in the presence of males. *Psychological Science, 11,* 365–371. www.jstor.org/stable/40063543

Johnson, C., and Stewart, E. (2004). Effect of sex identification on instrument assignment by band directors. *Journal of Research in Music Education, 52,* 130–140. https://doi.org/bx4xh4.

Johnson, C., and Stewart, E. (2005). Effect of sex and race identification on instrument assignment by music educators. *Journal of Research in Music Education, 53,* 348–357. https://doi.org/bvdw4m.

Kanter, R. (1993). *Men and Women of the Corporation.* Basic Books.

MacDonald, R., and Wilson, G. (2005). Musical identities of professional jazz musicians: A focus group investigation. *Psychology of Music, 33,* 395–417. https://doi.org/dr8b9x

MacDonald, R., and Wilson, G. (2006). Constructions of jazz: How jazz musicians present their collaborative musical practice. *Musicae Scientae 10,* 59–83. https://doi.org/dr8b9x.

Madura, P. (1999). Gender and vocal jazz improvisation skills. *Jazz Research Papers, 19,* 30–34.

Marshall, N., and Shibazaki, K. (2011). Instrument, gender and musical style associations in young children. *Psychology of Music, 40,* 494–507. https://doi.org/d4rv6n.

May, L. (2003). Factors and abilities influencing achievement in instrumental jazz improvisation. *Journal of Research in Music Education, 51,* 245–258. https://doi.org/cmqw6v.

McAndrew, S., and Widdup, P. (2021). The man that got away: Gender inequalities in the consumption and production of jazz. *European Journal of Cultural Studies, 24,* 690–716. https://doi.org/gh72.

McCord, K. (1985). The conceptualization of women in jazz. *Jazz Research Papers, 61,* 128–139.

McDaniel, W. (1974). "Differences in Music Achievement, Musical Experience, and Background between Jazz-improvising Musicians and Non-improvising Musicians at the Freshman and Sophomore College Levels" (Doctoral dissertation). Proquest Dissertations and Theses Database. (UMI No.7513794).

McKeage, K. (2004). Gender and participation in high school and college instrumental jazz ensembles. *Journal of Research in Music Education, 54,* 343–356. https://doi.org/bwrcdv.

McPherson, G. and Hendricks, K. (2010). Students' motivation to study music: The United States of America. *Research Studies in Music Education, 32,* 201–213. https://doi.org/crzvkg.

Monson, I. (1995). The problem with white hipness: Race, gender, and cultural conception in jazz historical discourse. *Journal of the American Musicological Society, 48,* 396–422. https://doi.org/ggttf3..

Monson, I. (2008). Fitting the part. In, N. Rustin and S. Tucker (Eds), *Big Ears: Listening for Gender in Jazz Studies* (pp. 267–287). Duke University Press.

North, A., Colley, A., and Hargreaves, D. (2003). Adolescents' perceptions of the music of male and female composers. *Psychology of Music, 31,* 139–154. https://doi.org/cp738m.

Olin, M. (1995, Spring). Inspiration and support. *Jazz Changes, 2*(1), 7.

Olin, M., and Aberg, L. (1995, Autumn). The purpose of gals'in'jazz. *Jazz Changes, 2*(3), 4.

Oliveros, P. (2004). Harmonic anatomy: Women in improvisation. In D. Fischlin and A. Heble (Eds.), *The Other Side of Nowhere: Jazz, Improvisation, and Communities in Dialogue* (pp. 50–70). Wesleyan University Press.

O'Neill, S., and Boultona, M. (1996). Males' and females' preferences for musical instruments: A function of gender? *Psychology of Music, 24,* 171–183. https://doi.org/fn8rx4.

Pellegrinelli, L., Effinger, S., Elizabeth, J., Grunenberg, K., Horn, R., Sebesky, G., and Weiner, N. (2021, January 12). Equal at last: Women by the numbers. *NPR.ORG.* www.npr.org/2021/01/12/953964352/equal-at-last-women-in-jazz-by-the-numbers.

Porter, L. (1984a). "She wiped all the men out": Jazzwomen part I. *Music Educators Journal, 71*(1), 43–52. www.jstor.org/stable/3396332.

Porter, L. (1984b). Jazzwomen part II: "You can't get up there timidly." *Music Educators Journal, 71*(2), 42–51. https://doi.org/b5fw3f.

Provost, S. (2017). Bringing something new: Female jazz instrumentalists' use of imitation and masculinity. *Jazz Perspectives, 10*(2–3), 141–157. https://doi.org/gh73.

Rowe, E. (1995, Spring). Gender and swing. *Jazz Changes, 2*(1), 5–7.

Sekaquaptewa, D., and Thompson, M. (2003). Solo status, stereotype threat, and performance expectancies: Their effects on women's performance. *Journal of Experimental Psychology, 39*, 68–74. https://doi.org/bz4k5x.

Schunk, D., and Pajares, F. (2005). Competence perceptions and academic functioning. In A. Elliot and C. Dweck (Eds.). *Handbook of Competence and Motivation* (pp. 85–104). The Guilford Press.

Shanley, V. (2009). *Jazz and Gender: Teaching Improvisation to Girls.* (Publication No. 1507). University of Northern Iowa Graduate Research Papers. https://scholarworks.uni.edu/grp/1507.

Steele, C. (1997). A threat in the air: How stereotypes shape intellectual identity and performance. *American Psychologist, 52*, 613–629. https://doi.org/br4sk4.

Steele, C., and Aronson, J. (2005). Stereotypes and the fragility of academic competence, motivation, and self-concept. In A. Elliot and C. Dweck (Eds.), *Handbook of Competence and Motivation* (pp. 436–456). The Guilford Press.

Steinberg, E. (2001). " 'Take a Solo': An Analysis of Gender Participation and Interaction at School Jazz Festivals" (Publication No. 3029732) [Doctoral dissertation, University of the Pacific]. ProQuest Dissertations and Theses Global.

Tarnowski, S. (1993). Gender bias and musical instrument preference. *Update: Applications of Research in Music Education, 12*, 14–21. https://doi.org/btxc77.

Tavani, C., and Losh, S. (2003). Motivation, self-confidence, and expectations as predictors of the academic performances among our high school students. *Child Study Journal, 33*(3), 141–151.

Teichman, E. (2020). Pedagogy of discrimination: instrumental jazz education. *Music Education Research, 22*(2), 201–213. https://doi.org/gh76.

Truity. (2021). Musicians and Singers. *Career Profiles.* www.truity.com/career-profile/musician-or-singer.

Tucker, S. (1999). Telling performances: Jazz history remembered and remade by the women in the band. *Oral History Review (26)*, 67–84. www.jstor.org/stable/3675691.

Tucker, S. (2001/2002). Big ears: Listening for gender in jazz studies. *Current Musicology, (71-73)*, 375–408. https://doi.org/gh77.

Tucker, S. (2003, January 20). Women in jazz. *Grove Music Online.* https://doi.org/gh78.

Tucker, S. (2004). Bordering on community: Improvising women improvising women-in-jazz. In D. Fischlin and A. Heble (Eds.), *The Other Side of Nowhere: Jazz, Improvisation, and Communities in Dialogue* (pp. 244–267). Wesleyan University Press.

UNT Jazz and Gender Equity Initiative (n.d.). *UNT College of Music Jazz Studies.* https://jazz.unt.edu/unt-jazz-and-gender-equity-initiative.

Valenti, T. (2018). *A survey to investigate the participation of female jazz-trained instrumentalists at WAAPA and in Perth's professional music scene.* Edith Cowan University Repository. https://ro.ecu.edu.au/theses_hons/1522.

Watson, K. (2010). The effects of aural versus notated instructional materials on achievement and self-efficacy in jazz improvisation. *Journal of Research in Music Education, 58*, 240–259. https://doi.org/cdk4g4.

Wehr, E. (2016). Understanding the experiences of women in jazz: A suggested model. *International Journal of Music Education, 34*, 472. https://doi.org/gh79.

Wehr-Flowers, E. (2006). Differences between male and female students' confidence, anxiety, and attitude toward learning jazz improvisation. *Journal of Research in Music Education, 54*, 337–349. https://doi.org/d8ggf2.

Wehr-Flowers, E. (2007). *An Exploratory Model of Jazz Self-efficacy and Gender.* (Publication No. 3281418) [Doctoral dissertation, University of Iowa]. ProQuest Dissertations and Theses Global.

Willard, J. (2014, March 26). Jazz audience development: The gender factor. *NewMusicUSA*, https://nmbx.newmusicusa.org/jazz-audience-development-the-gender-factor/.

Worthy, M. (2013). Jazz education. In *The Grove Dictionary of American Music: Vol. 4*, in Charles Hiroshi Garrett (Ed.), (2nd ed., pp. 475–478). Oxford University Press. https://doi.org/gh8b.

Zelenak, M. (2014). Measuring the sources of self-efficacy among secondary school music students. *Journal of Research in Music Education, 62*, 389–404. https://doi.org/10.1177/0022429414555018.

Zervoudakes, J., and Tanur, J. (1994). Gender and musical instruments: Winds of change? *Journal of Research in Music Education, 42*, 58–67. https://doi.org/bnxsrm.

13

GENDER, SEXUALITY, AND JAZZ SAXOPHONE PERFORMANCE

Yoko Suzuki

While recalling his experience of attending a concert given by the International Sweethearts of Rhythm in his youth, legendary tenor saxophonist Jimmy Heath (1926–2020) told me, "Vi Burnside played so strong that she was accused of being a man or a lesbian" (J. Heath, May 4, 2000). This was my first encounter with the close relationship between a musically strong female saxophonist and homosexuality. Inspired by authors such as Linda Dahl (Dahl, 1984), Leslie Gourse (Gourse, 1995), and Sherrie Tucker (Tucker, 2000), I was interested in why there are few female instrumentalists recognized in jazz history. Especially, Tucker's work showed a number of women who performed in all-female swing bands during the 1940s, and I wondered why many of them could not continue performing after World War II. Though performers' sexuality was not a main focus in my research, a number of female saxophonists shared experiences of being (mis)identified as lesbians. In addition, some women mentioned that they often struggled to establish friendship and mentorship with male musicians due to unwanted sexual advances.

This chapter investigates how gender and sexuality intersect in the world of jazz instrumentalists through ethnographic and archival research. My ethnographic fieldwork, which was mostly done from 2008 to 2010 in New York City for my dissertation (Suzuki, 2011), included interviewing jazz veterans Jimmy Heath, Frank Wess, Billy Taylor, Lou Donaldson, Lonnie Smith, and thirty female jazz saxophonists as well as attending concerts by the informants. I begin with discussing two African-American female saxophonists, Vi Burnside (1915–1964) and Willene Barton (ca.1925–2005), who were often associated with homosexuality. By examining the ways newspaper articles reported as well as how fellow musicians described them, I will explore how their excellence in jazz performance was associated with homosexuality. Then I will illustrate the contemporary jazz scene, where the same type of assumptions about strong female players and homosexuality still existed. I use the term female and woman interchangeably to describe female-identified people. Drawing on theorists such as R. W. Connell (1995), Judith Halberstam (1998), Michael Kimmel (1994), and Adrienne Rich (1980), I will elucidate how gender expressions and sexual orientations tend to be conflated in the perception of jazz performance. Further, I argue that gender norms in jazz are strongly associated with heterosexuality and patriarchy. Due to this heteropatriarchy, women, regardless of their sexual orientations, often suffer sexual harassment in jazz. Though being identified as lesbians and experiencing sexual misconduct are seemingly two different issues, they are intertwined and based on heteropatriarchy that has persisted in the jazz world.

DOI: 10.4324/9781003081876-15

Vi Burnside and Willene Burton

Violet Burnside, best known as a featured soloist of the International Sweethearts of Rhythm, was born in Lancaster, PA in 1915. According to her obituary in the *Afro-American*, Burnside studied music at a conservatory in New York City ("Vi Burnside, World's Greatest Female Saxophonist, Dies Here," *Afro-American*, 1964). She played in a few different all female bands before joining the Sweethearts of Rhythm in late 1943. She participated in the group's USO tour in 1945 and stayed in the band until 1948. During these years, Burnside became popular among musicians and predominantly Black jazz fans as a through concerts and reports in the Black press.

Burnside had a successful career as a soloist in one of the most prominent all-girl big bands during the 1940s and as a bandleader at the end of the 1940s and the early 1950s. All of her existing recordings, however, are as a sidewoman (though as a main soloist) of the International Sweethearts of Rhythm, which are scattered on several different albums. The only readily available CD, *Hot Licks: Rare Recordings from One of the Best American All Girl Big Bands of the Swing Era,* was released in 2006, sixty years after her prime time. Other recordings are out of print, but several video clips are available on YouTube (MusicandDancing4Ever, 2014, International Sweethearts of Rhythm. n. d.). Although these recordings are not of particularly high quality, we can hear her robust sound and solid technique especially demonstrated in the up-tempo songs.

Burnside died in 1964 in Washington DC. Although she disappeared from historical Black newspapers around November 1955, the obituary reported that she performed at a jazz festival in D.C. in 1964. While she did not earn the recognition she deserved or was not given enough opportunities to be recorded, she was "known among musicians and fans as a strong swing-style improviser" (Suzuki, 2012). How did audiences and fellow musicians perceive her? Since her active years were the 1940s and the first half of the 1950s, there are few musicians alive who still remember Burnside.

In 2009 I interviewed Jimmy Heath again about his experience with female saxophonists in general. Our conversation moved from contemporary female saxophonists to historical ones, and he talked about Burnside as well. Unlike his neutral statement nine years earlier, Heath clarified that he perceived her as a homosexual woman. He equated Burnside's strong playing with masculinity and her homosexuality, "being who she was." In his mind, Burnside's saxophone performance was not "womanly"; thus, it was "manly." Consequently, a woman who plays "like a man" would be homosexual. His ideas also strongly suggest that a person's sexuality serves as their core identity, determining who they are and what they do.

Frank Wess (1922–2013) mentioned that Burnside was still active in New York perhaps in the 1960s, and he actually played with her. I asked him in what context he played with her and how she sounded. He recalled that they sometimes played together in jam sessions at a place called Colonial Inn in Queens, New York: "She didn't play bebop. She played in an older style … like swing …. She was gay, you know" (F. Wess, personal communication, August 31, 2009). While Wess did not display any homophobic attitudes, I found it interesting that he particularly remembered that Burnside was gay. Perhaps, Burnside being gay stuck out in his memory because Burnside's status as a strong player was associated with her being gay in his mind.

On the other hand, a conversation with Billy Taylor (1921–2010) progressed quite differently:

> There were so many women who were really good musicians I have come in contact with in my lifetime. There are almost as many good female ones as male ones. It's a shame that that part of it is not written about, because it's a part of history, and just it's ignored.
>
> *(B. Taylor, personal communication, August 8, 2009)*

After a respectful conversation about Burnside, I asked, "Some people I interviewed mentioned that she played very strong like a man, and she was gay. Did people talk about it?" He answered:

Yes, that's one of the reasons that perhaps she didn't get as much of attention without mentioning that aspect of her life because ... gay people in show business were accepted in a way that they were not by the general public. That part was hard to live with for anybody, and there was less of it within the show business.

I was struck that Taylor did not mention Burnside's sexual orientation until I asked. "Well, I forgot about it until you asked me" (B. Taylor, personal communication, August 8, 2009).

It is hard to speculate whether the subject did not come to his mind or he deliberately avoided it. However, it is obvious that Taylor has quite different attitudes toward the relationship between jazz saxophone playing and sexuality than those held by Heath and Wess. All three interviewees praised Burnside's playing as strong and brilliant. However, while her homosexuality was important for Heath and Wess to mention when talking about her saxophone performance, it was merely additional information that has nothing to do with her playing in Taylor's story.

Willene Barton was born in Oscilla, Georgia circa 1925, and her family moved to Long Island, New York, when she was ten. Soon she started to study the clarinet and switched to tenor saxophone when she entered junior high school. After graduating from Manhattan High School, she started to study with saxophonist Walter Thomas and guitarist/trombonist/composer Eddie Durham. Through them, she secured an audition for a Sweethearts spin-off band Anna Mae Winburn was organizing in 1952 (Placksin, 1982, p. 228). After playing with several different all-female groups, Barton started to play with organist Dayton Selby, with whom she made her only recording, *The Feminine Sax,* in 1957. In this recording, she demonstrated her technical mastery as well as bluesy and hard-swinging feelings with a gutsy, throaty sound. Barton's performances with her all-female groups at jazz clubs were often featured in Black newspapers that often depicted her as beautiful, sexy, and feminine ("Band Routes," 1959, "What Stars Are Doing Along Stem," 1959).

Although many jazz musicians did not even recognize her name, I found a few people to interview. My conversation with alto saxophonist Lou Donaldson (b. 1926), who has been active in the jazz scene since the early 1950s and is also known for his outspokenness, demonstrates his views on gender, sexuality, and saxophone playing.

> In the 50s, in New York [Barton] was working with Jazz Sisters. Jazz Sisters was a Black group, they used to play at Small's Paradise [in Harlem]. Paula Hampton on drums, Jean something, Bertha Hope on piano, Gloria on bass. ...Everybody in the band was a dyke.
> (L. Donaldson, personal communication, August 10, 2009)

Donaldson's statement clearly contradicted my archival research. Barton's group in the 1950s, which included Gloria Coleman, was called the Four Jewels, but neither Hope nor Hampton was a member. Barton played with these two musicians in the 1970s, and the group was called the Jazz Sisters. In our conversation, Donaldson mixed up some facts, and his story may not be plausible. However, I found the way he remembered and told the story to be revealing. In his mind, Barton was active in the 1950s, playing with the group called the Jazz Sisters, who consisted of gay Black women. He mentioned Barton being gay when I asked her age, not her sexuality. Further, he mentioned that Barton's male musical partner was also gay.

He even said, "They [members of Jazz Sisters] would steal your girlfriend" (L. Donaldson, personal communication, August 10, 2009), suggesting that these women were interested in women. Why did he give me all the information I never asked for? Donaldson clearly associates these talented and successful female jazz instrumentalists with homosexuality. He chose to talk about these musicians' sexuality because he considered it to be important information about them. Apparently, Donaldson thought that these female instrumentalists and a gay male organist were *outside* the perceived heteronormativity.

Subsequently, I interviewed Dr. Lonnie Smith (1942–2021), the organ player who worked with Barton in the 1960s. According to him, Barton hired him in her band when she needed an organist for a show at the Purple Manor. Smith said, "She could play! She was strong" (L. Smith, personal communication, August 12, 2009). With the information from Donaldson in mind, I asked him if he and other musicians talked about Barton and her bandmates' sexual orientation. He was hesitant to answer the question and said, "We knew that [they were gay], but they did that to keep up with the guys" (L. Smith, personal communication, August 12, 2009). Perhaps, he meant that Barton and other female instrumentalists acted like men in order to get along well with other male musicians. Then he suggested that her "manliness" comes from both her strong saxophone playing and her mannerisms. Interestingly, unlike Smith, Donaldson never mentioned how Barton talked or acted. In other words, while Donaldson seemed to associate Barton's homosexuality with her strong playing, Smith uncomfortably disclosed her homosexuality (though he never said the word) suggested by her saxophone performance as well as her demeanor, which helped her to blend into the male dominated jazz scene as "one of the guys."

Both Donaldson and Smith's description of Barton challenges her image depicted in the old newspapers: she was one of "the sexiest saxophonists" in a bare shoulder dress showing her feminine figure in several pictures ("What Stars Are Doing Along Stem," 1959). Further, in the article, "Willene Barton Feels: Female Musicians Can't Create Ideas," Robinson (1964, p. 17) of the *Pittsburgh Courier* wrote about Barton's personal life, including an anecdote about a "boyfriend," which is unrelated to the main subject of this article—how she feels about her fellow female musicians. I shall not speculate on Barton's sexual orientation, but this portrayal clearly constructs Barton as being heterosexual. In other words, Robinson as well as other authors from the historical Black newspapers attempted to confine Barton *within* the norms of heterosexuality.

Though both Vi Burnside and Willene Barton had a successful career, especially in their peak years in the 1940s and 1950s respectively, they are rarely written about in jazz history books. While some musicians remembered these women as musically strong players, their ability was often associated with their homosexuality. More importantly, ideas displayed both in newspapers and musicians' statements are based on the strict heterosexist gender norms, which will be explored later. This connection between jazz instrumental performance and female homosexuality is also prevalent in the contemporary jazz scene.

Female Jazz Saxophonists—Are You Gay?

While conducting interviews with female saxophonists, many of them shared their experience of being identified as lesbians by fellow musicians and the audience. Why are talented female saxophonists assumed to be gay? While the conflation of gender expressions and sexual orientations has been discussed in various fields (Rieger, 2010; Jones, 2016; Clifford, 2020), here, I will explore the association of female instrumentalists with lesbians in the context of jazz saxophone performance. I suggest that this equation consists of three assumptions: (1) Jazz is a "masculine" music genre (Suzuki, 2016); therefore, (2) females who play jazz very well, especially on instruments normally associated with men, should be masculine; (3) masculine females are gay. Although the first statement might sound over-generalized, jazz instrumental performances are filled with stereotypically masculine elements, and masculine approach to the genre has been emphasized and embraced among both musicians and audiences for many years. In the dominant discourse of jazz history, legendary, innovative, notable jazz instrumentalists have been predominantly men. Therefore, jazz music tends to be associated with typical masculinity, manliness, or characteristics of men. This masculinity, or "hegemonic masculinity," is based on heterosexuality and patriarchy. According to Connell (1995, p. 76), however, "with growing recognition of the interplay between gender, race, and class it has become common to recognize multiple masculinities." Further, she suggests that hegemonic masculinity is not a fixed character type but the one that occupies the hegemonic position in a given pattern of gender relations. Though different types and versions of masculinities are present in jazz performances (some of them may be perceived as feminine or effeminate), one type of masculinity that some have tried to preserve and others have sought after is the one associated with romanticized notions of African-American men, namely, Black masculinity. This is why talented female saxophonists often receive the comment (meant to be a compliment), "You sound like an old [heterosexual] Black man," as discussed below.

The second assumption, "females who play jazz very well, especially on instruments normally associated with men, should be masculine," needs to be unpacked. It is perhaps fair to say that women who can play masculine music very well on a masculine instrument are masculine. Yet, how are they masculine? This is related to both their visual appearance and their saxophone sound. Visually, a woman playing the saxophone is not pretty or feminine in conventional ways. The shape of the saxophone can represent a phallic symbol as the trumpet does in a slightly different way (Gabbard, 1995), and a saxophonist has to put the mouthpiece in her mouth. In addition, while playing the saxophone, a performer's cheeks and neck are swollen and veins come out. When improvising, a performer is engaging with a creative process and her face often contorts and her mouth frowns. Some of my interviewees mentioned that they hate to see the pictures or videos of themselves playing because they hardly look pretty. Further, as some of my informants told me, female jazz saxophonists tend not to dress too femininely because they want to be recognized as musicians first, not as women. While they do not try to look like a man, they often choose to wear a pair of pants instead of a skirt/dress and do not wear too much make-up or jewelry, which sharply contrasts with how female jazz singers are expected to dress on stage.

Aurally, their playing is often perceived as masculine. Most interviewees have received comments, such as, "I've never seen a woman playing sax *like that*." This suggests that people have expectations of how a female saxophonist would sound and appear visually. One specific comment Janelle Reichman received from an audience member explains it better: "We saw you come up there, you're this skinny little timid looking woman, and we couldn't believe that the sound came out" (J. Reichman, personal communication, August 17, 2008). This comment clearly shows that Reichman's masculine tenor saxophone sound and her conservative yet feminine look (or just her being a young white woman) did not match in this audience's mind. Grace Kelly (G. Kelly, personal communication, October 26, 2009) shared an episode that she once sent her recording to enter a saxophone competition, which was blindly reviewed. She was selected as one of the finalists and the judges were amazed and said, "Oh my god, we had no idea you're the thirteen-year-old Asian saxophonist. We thought you were a forty-year-old Black man." As these examples demonstrate, a majority of stakeholders in jazz associate musical sound with certain type of body—we have assumptions at least about a performer's sex, race, and age, and expect a certain type of attire depending on musical genres. When we hear a musically strong jazz saxophone performance, we tend to imagine a male performer, which evokes masculinity.

Now, can women be masculine? In his groundbreaking work, *Female Masculinity*, Halberstam (1998) claims that existing scholarship has studied masculinities as being possessed by men. Halberstam suggests that female masculinity has its own cultural history and not simply a derivative of male masculinity and that studying female masculinity helps us to understand male masculinities. In exploring and historicizing diverse forms of female masculinity, he concentrates on a variety of queer female masculinities because he believes that female masculinity becomes problematic and disturbs gender norms when it involves nonnormative sexuality. According to Halberstam, female masculinity becomes threatening and unacceptable when coupled with lesbian desire. In his discussion of the stone butch, a mode of female masculinity, Halberstam writes "Because masculinity has seemed to play an important and even a crucial role in some lesbian self-definition, we have a word for lesbian masculinity: butch" (1998, p. 120). Some butches demonstrate their masculinity in clothing and hairstyle, and "others actually experience themselves as male" (Gayle Rubin, quoted in

Halberstam,1998, p. 120). These descriptions of lesbian masculinity significantly differ from masculinity "performed" by female jazz saxophonists. While they may sometimes wear mannish clothes, they do that for blending into other men on stage, not for wanting to feel like a man (one exception is discussed in Stokes, 2005, p. 31). Masculinity of some butches is visually perceived, and in others' cases, masculinity is linked to their identity. In addition, masculinity here is related to sexual desire for women. Though there are some lesbian jazz saxophonists in this study, my discussion of masculinity does not necessarily involve lesbian desire. In the case of female jazz saxophonists, their masculine performance is produced aurally by musical sound and visually by the body that is sincerely and seriously engaged in music making. To Halberstam, masculine performance of female jazz saxophonists may not be as disturbing as that of butch lesbians in society at large since it does not involve desire for women. Masculinity performed by female jazz saxophonists, however, would threaten and disturb gender norms that have been persistent in the jazz world precisely because it does *not* involve lesbian desire.

The third assumption, "masculine women are gay," derives from an assumed connection between gender and sexuality. As shown in the cases of Vi Burnside and Willene Barton, only masculine men and feminine women exist under the heterosexist gender norms that have been persistent in the jazz world. Therefore, those who are outside the norms are "queer"/homosexual. In addition, this view is also related to men's anxiety that they are not sufficiently masculine. For example, Black heterosexual males may fear that their masculinity is subverted in American society due to their experiences as Black men. Moreover, men in general possess anxiety because of the fragility of hegemonic masculinity. Michael Kimmel quotes sociologist Erving Goffman's statement,

> In America, there is only "one complete, unblushing male": a young, married, white, urban, northern heterosexual, Protestant father of college education, fully employed, of good complexion, weight and height, and a recent record in sports. Every American male tends to look out upon the world from this perspective.... Any male who fails to qualify in any one of these ways is likely to view himself ... as unworthy, incomplete, and inferior,

And Kimmel asserts that this is the definition of "hegemonic" masculinity (Kimmel, 1994, p. 125). R. W. Connell (1995, p. 79) also states,

> Normative definitions of masculinity, as I have noted, face the problem that not many men actually meet the normative standards. This point applies to hegemonic masculinity. The number of men rigorously practicing the hegemonic pattern in its entirety may be quite small.

Therefore, hegemonic masculinity throws many heterosexual men into a state of anxiety. As a result, heterosexual men tend to become insecure about their own masculinity, desire to see the display of male masculinity in other heterosexual men, hate to see the lack of masculinity in gay men, and feel threatened by performed masculinity as demonstrated in the example of female jazz saxophonists. Moreover, since insecure heterosexual men are intimidated by performed masculinity, they try to associate masculine heterosexual women with homosexuality and situate them outside of the matrix where only heterosexual men and women are present. This is one of the reasons why female jazz saxophonists tend to be invisible regardless of their presence in the jazz world.

Sexual Misconduct and a Lesbian Advantage Myth in Jazz

Many female saxophonists I interviewed mentioned difficulties in developing camaraderie with fellow male musicians and finding male mentors, both of which are crucial to be successful in the jazz scene. Alto saxophonist Matana Roberts also writes in her self-published essay titled "Gender Issues in Jazz and Improvised Music Part 1,"

> You really start to notice the differences when a few male musicians who use [sic] to be your mentors recognize your budding womanhood as a chance for them to use their influence to be sexual leeches. It's at this point that you have to develop certain emergency bells in your psyche—watching carefully to make sure you are not vulnerable to those creepy guys out there that really don't have your creative growth in their best interest.

Researchers have discussed that women in male-dominated occupations experience sexual harassment more than women in female-dominated or gender balanced industries (Gruber et al., 2005, Haas et al., 2010, Raj et al., 2020). Jazz is notoriously male-dominated, and many factors, including hiring practice and workplace environments, tend to allow sexual misconduct to happen. Sexual misconduct in general can often be concealed and is not always reported immediately (Schneider, 1991). Especially, jazz was one of the fields where sexual misconduct had not been revealed for many years. One of the reasons for this can be strong respect for older, legendary, and mostly male musicians in the genre. Unlike many other popular music genres in which young talents attract attention, legendary musicians are extremely valued and revered in jazz. Though jazz education has been more and more institutionalized, direct mentorship is still crucial for young aspiring musicians. Hiring practice often relies on word-of-mouth and recommendation by established musicians who tend to recommend their students. Younger musicians are dying to have renowned musicians as their mentors. In mentor–mentee relationships, lessons and rehearsals can take place in private spaces. Further, jazz performances often happen late night at dimly lit places where alcohol is served. In other words, a workplace can be someone's living room, hotel room, bar, and nightclubs in jazz. In this backdrop, female musicians' aspiration for career advancement can be abused by established male musicians.

Inspired by the #MeToo movement, several sexual harassment cases in jazz have been reported mainly in the context of higher education in recent years. The case involving the two saxophonists, Steve Coleman (b. 1956) and Maria Grand (b. 1992), one of the founding members of the We Have Voice collective, stood out especially because of the abusive nature of their relationship and the defamation lawsuits filed by both parties. Coleman, a recipient of a MacArthur fellowship, Guggenheim fellowship, and Doris Duke Performing Arts award, has been instrumental in the New York jazz scene since the 1980s. A Swiss saxophonist, Grand moved to New York City in 2011, two years after she initially met Coleman at his workshop during her visit to New York City. Coleman v. Grand was filed in October 2018, and Grand countersued Coleman immediately. The lawsuit was triggered by the letter Grand wrote and circulated among her close friends in the industry in 2017. Since the letter was included as an exhibit in Coleman's complaint against her, it is publicly available (Coleman v. Grand, 2018). It details their relationship, which started as teacher-student but quickly became a romantic and abusive one. Grand admits that she was "maybe slightly manipulative, to be honest" (Coleman v. Grand, 2018) in the beginning of their relationship. She was aware that she could become Coleman's student due to her attractiveness as a young woman. However, there is no doubt that Grand was extremely vulnerable to Coleman. In February 2021, the United States District Court for the Eastern District of New York issued summary judgment in favor of Grand (Coleman v. Grand, 2018). In the summary, Grand's statement is considered to be "public interest" as part of the growing consciousness regarding the #MeToo movement and demonstrates her intention that is more about raising awareness with sexual misconduct in the music industry than defaming Coleman. Further, the Court identifies Grand's statements as protected opinions, while Coleman had failed to show that Grand "acted with actual malice" (Coleman v. Grand, 2018). This is a significant win, which hopefully encourages people in abusive relationships to speak out.

As mentioned above, while women in the male-dominated occupations are at greater risk to experience unwanted sexual advances from male superiors, several authors discussed a "lesbian advantage" in male-dominated workplaces. For example, one study about female firefighters in the UK finds that lesbians experience lower levels of sexual harassment or unwanted sexual attention in the workplace (Wright, 2008). Is this true in the jazz world?

Kristy Norter and Virginia Mayhew, both identified as lesbians, proved it the opposite way. Norter (personal communication, July 20, 2008) told me her experience when she first moved to New York City: She went to a late-night jam session at a jazz club for networking. After she played, a well-known young male bassist approached her and said, "You sound great. Do you have a card? Do you wanna hang out and have some sessions?" Since she liked the idea of having sessions with him, they exchanged their cards. That night, she emailed the bass player hoping to arrange a jam session. He immediately responded saying, "I thought you're cute. Do you wanna go on a date?" Norter was upset because the male bassist took advantage of her aspiration to make connections and be successful in the New York jazz scene. She said, "If he said, 'I don't really like your playing, but do you wanna go on a date?' That would have been much better." Clearly the male bassist used his power as a man and a successful jazz musician to get what he wanted. Mayhew started to work with a legendary male instrumentalist in the early 1990s (V. Mayhew, personal communication, August 10, 2009). When she got a gig at the old Birdland in the mid-1990s, she hired him. But right before the gig, he told Mayhew that he would not do the gig unless she sleeps with him. Mayhew unwillingly decided to hire somebody else, and the management of the club was extremely unhappy because they wanted her to play with somebody with a big name. This also shows that the legendary musician used his power and status to manipulate Mayhew's ambition for success.

Did Norter and Mayhew's lesbian identities change the way these male musicians interact with them? It is possible that they read these women as heterosexual. It is also possible that they were uncertain of these women's sexual orientation. Another possibility is that they deliberately challenged these women's homosexuality in hope of changing/ "fixing" it. In whichever case, they were put in a vulnerable position as a woman. Cassity (personal communication, July 24, 2008) mentioned that she once pretended to be a lesbian to avoid sexual advances. "You know what happens? They still hit on me." In these cases, women's sexual orientation does not matter to the interaction with heterosexual male musicians who attempt to sexually take advantage of vulnerability of female musicians.

Relationship between Sexuality and Music

Tenor saxophonist Janelle Reichman (personal communication, August 17, 2008) said, "This is what really interests me is that if you take all the female jazz musicians in the world and pull them together, you're gonna have a higher percentage of lesbians than in just the general population." I found it intriguing that some of my female informants assumed the connection between jazz and lesbianism. In fact, in both formal interviews and casual conversations with random musicians, both men and women, I have heard a number of stories and rumors about lesbian musicians in jazz. Some current or former members of the all-female ensemble Diva frequently complained that people asked them how many of the members are gay and if they have been hit on by lesbian members. These speculations are never made regarding all male big bands. More importantly, people hardly assume that male jazz instrumentalists are gay.

Why is the assumption that there are more lesbians in jazz than in general population plausible to some people? In fact, I must admit that I had the impulse to speculate on the relationship between jazz and lesbian women and the scarcity of gay males in jazz. It seemed to be reasonable to think that "masculine" music attracts "masculine" people, including many (but not all) lesbians and heterosexual men. Assumptions such as Reichman's, regarding lesbian population in the jazz community, appeared convincing prior to careful considerations. As this project progressed, however, I have come to realize that the issue is not so simplistic. It is difficult to identify lesbians in the first place. There is a wide variety of non-heterosexual desire, and self-identification as a lesbian is also elastic. One may identify herself as a lesbian in one situation, but not in another. Coming out as a lesbian is another issue. One might come out in one place, but not in another, which also involves safety and comfortableness. In the case of the Diva Jazz Orchestra, its all-female membership as well as leader Sherrie Maricle's alternative sexuality may be creating a safer and more comfortable environment for lesbian instrumentalists to come out. Therefore, it is not logical to expect the same ratio of lesbians to be present in the jazz world. And for the same reasons, it is also difficult to determine the ratio of lesbians in the general population.

Lisa Parrott believes that being gay and being a jazz musician are not related (personal communication, August 12, 2008). "Because I have been a jazz musician a lot longer than I have been gay, and my music hasn't been changed since I became gay." She emphasized, "For me personally, the bigger issue was still more about being female playing music rather than being gay playing music." In the jazz world, according to Parrott, gender matters more than sexuality for women. Parrott's disassociation of her homosexuality from her music is similar to what an out gay jazz pianist Fred Hersch mentioned in his interview with David Hajdu (2010). However, we cannot generalize these two musicians' views to conclude that there is no connection between a person's sexuality and their music. In fact, there might be some people who claim that their music represents or deeply involves with their sexual orientations.

Musicologist Suzanne Cusick (1994, p. 69), in her personal account of her relationship with music, ponders over "whether there might be a lesbian aesthetic, that is, a preference for certain kinds of music that somehow reflected the patterns of lesbian desire or lesbian pleasure." Defining "lesbian" as "not an identity … but rather a way I prefer to behave, to organize my relationship to the world in a power/pleasure/intimacy triad." She suggests, "*this* meaning of 'lesbian' can be detected in my musicality" (Cusick, 1994, p. 73). She finds "love" in music and lesbian relationship with her "love" in both her teaching and performing music. In addition, the ecstatic feelings of both listening to and performing music are often compared to human sexual experiences. Yet, these experiences are rather individual than general, and not specific to homosexuality or heterosexuality. In other words that there is no universal quality of homosexual or heterosexual music. Therefore, the connection between jazz and gay women and heterosexual men is nothing more than speculation based on heterosexist gender norms.

Conclusions

In the case of Burnside, both Jimmy Heath and Frank Wess remembered her as a good musician, but in their stories her strong playing was associated with her perceived homosexuality. Both Heath and Wess are far from chauvinistic or homophobic. Rather, they actually have helped female instrumentalists in developing their careers by hiring them and recommending them to other musicians. What is questionable in the way they talked about Burnside is their strong adherence to a binary construction of sex and gender, one based on heterosexuality. To them, Burnside's strong saxophone playing is a masculine gender signifier that constructs her as homosexual. In addition, Heath presents his idea of "lesbian identity" as the source of homosexual women's strong playing. He named a few other female jazz musicians (both African-American and white women) he identifies as lesbians and mentioned that they also play aggressively. He believes in an essentialized identity possessed by all lesbian women. Though Heath's attitude is rooted in his generation, the underlying idea is problematic because there is no universal identity of lesbians, heterosexuals or any other categories. Moreover, as Adrienne Rich (1980) argues, there is a wide range of women-identified experiences, what she calls "lesbian existence," whether they identify themselves as lesbian or not.

Similarly, Barton is remembered by Lou Donaldson as a strong "dyke" saxophonist. Donaldson's account of Barton and the musicians she performed with excludes these musicians from his idea of normative gender and sexuality. The way Donaldson told the story is radically different from the way Heath and Wess did. While both Heath and Wess never displayed a homophobic attitude and were respectful to Burnside, Donaldson almost made fun of those "strange" musicians he thinks are "dykes." At the same time, however, their fundamental ideas are the same. In their minds, strong playing of these female saxophonists is associated with their homosexuality.

The association between musically strong female saxophonists and lesbianism is persistent in the jazz world, which manifests in different levels since norms of gender and sexuality can function as stereotypes as well. Older male jazz musicians' comments referring to tenor saxophonists Burnside and Barton as a lesbian or "dyke" and the comments contemporary female saxophonists received may be considered as prejudiced or ignorant. Yet, the same idea can be seen in subtler ways, such as in the speculation about the connection between lesbian population and male-dominated fields. Although the latter may seem to be more reasonable and plausible than the former, both are based on the same heterosexist gender norms that are usually taken for granted. Female jazz saxophonists' masculinity is performed by stereotypically "masculine" musical sound, attitudes, and their body as a musician that is absorbed into the creative moment whether the performer is heterosexual or homosexual. Their musical performances strongly evoke images of a male body as where the musical sound originates. In other words, these women perform the saxophone outside gender norms. Under the strict heterosexist matrix, women outside gender norms are automatically associated with homosexuality.

At the same time, because of the same heterosexist matrix, female instrumentalists who are not categorized into lesbians or "dykes" are considered to be sexually available to men. As discussed earlier, many women experience difficulty to develop as professional musicians due to unwanted sexual advances from their male colleagues and mentors. In both mentor-mentee relationships and professional contexts, women often experience sexual harassment as seen in the case of Maria Grand and Steve Coleman. While their case is rather extreme, I am certain that most female jazz instrumentalists have experienced some kind of sexual misconduct by male musicians. Since female musicians are often the only woman on the bandstand, they are subconsciously "bracing," as Esperanza Spalding mentioned (Chinen, p. 196, 2019). Contrary to "lesbian advantages" in other male-dominated fields, even some lesbian instrumentalists experienced sexual harassment.

Sexuality is not a simple binary of heterosexuality and homosexuality. Instead, there are various sexual desires and orientations that are not simply categorized into heterosexuality or homosexuality. While heterosexuality has been taken for granted and considered as "normal," it is a "man-made institution," in which "male power is manifested and maintained" (Rich, p. 637, 1980). In the context of the jazz world, where this "compulsory heterosexuality" has been persistently present, women are either heterosexual who can be the object of men's sexual desire, or "dykes" who do not fit into this man-made institution.

Further, sexual orientations are not stable identities of people. Drawing on Judith Butler's idea of gender performativity, Moya Lloyd (1999, p. 197) states, "['Straight' and 'queer'] do not identify or represent particular groups of subjects. One 'is' never straight or queer, merely in a condition of 'doing' straightness or queerness." As one of my interviewees who I thought was lesbian came out as heterosexual, one can "perform" sexuality. How should female saxophonists "perform" sexuality in order to comfortably navigate and be visible/audible in the jazz world? Women who demonstrate strong musical proficiency tend to be perceived as lesbians and excluded from the heterosexist gender norms. Yet, women who play strong and "perform" heterosexuality are more threatening to men than lesbian musicians. In addition, (hetero)sexual harassment is common to both heterosexual and homosexual women. Therefore, women have to negotiate both heterosexist and sexist discourse of jazz. In order for these women to be heard and seen in jazz, heteropatriarchal gender norms in the jazz world have to change, which, in turn, encourages us to imagine the musical sound that is free from the stereotypical notion of femininity and masculinity.

Of course, gender and sexuality cannot be fully understood without taking other identity categories such as race and ethnicity into consideration. It is not coincidental that the two female saxophonists who were identified as lesbians were Black because femininity has been historically associated with whiteness (Hunter, 2005). The power relationship between Steve Coleman, an African-American man, and Maria Grande, a white European woman, stems not only from their gender and sexuality but also from Coleman's ethnic background that granted him authority in jazz. "Intersectional dynamics are not static, but neither are they untethered from history, context, or social identity" (Crenshaw, p.1426, 2012). It is urgent and crucial for us to recognize various intersecting factors that marginalize female instrumentalists, which will change the dynamics for the next generation.

References

Band routes. (1959, September 19). *Pittsburgh Courier*, A7.

Chinen, N. (2019). *Playing Changes: Jazz for the New Century*. Vintage Books.

Clifford, N. (2020). Re-imagining masculinity: Prince's impact on millennial attitudes regarding gender expression. In Mike Alleyne and Kirsty Fairclough (Eds.), *Prince and Popular Music: Critical Perspectives on an Interdisciplinary Life* (pp. 117–128). Bloomsbury.

Coleman v Grand (2018) https://unicourt.com/case/pc-db1-douglas-coleman-v-grand-871772.

Connell, R. W. (1995). *Masculinities*. University of California Press.

Crenshaw, K. W. (2012). From private violence to mass incarceration: Thinking intersectionally about women, race, and social control. *UCLA Law Review* 59, 1418–1472.

Cusick, S. (2006/1994). On a lesbian relationship with music: A serious effort not to think straight. In P. Brett, E. Wood, and G.C. Thomas (Eds.), *Queering the Pitch: The New Gay and Lesbian Musicology* (pp. 67–84). Routledge.

Dahl, L. (1984). *Stormy Weather: The Music and Lives of a Century of Jazzwomen*. Limelight Editions.

Gabbard, K. (1995). Signifyin(g) the phallus: Mo' better blues and representations of the jazz trumpet. In Krin Gabbard (Ed.), *Representing Jazz* (pp. 104–130). Duke University Press.

Gourse, L. (1995). *Madame Jazz: Contemporary Women Instrumentalists*. Oxford University Press.

Gruber, J. et al. (2005). *In the Company of Men: Male Dominance and Sexual Harassment*. UPNE.

Haas, S. D. et al. (2010). Sexual harassment in the context of double male dominance. *European Journal of Work and Organizational Psychology* 19 (6), 717–734.

Hajdu, D. (2010, January 31). Giant steps—The jazz pianist Fred Hersch. *The New York Times*. www.nytimes.com/2010/01/31/magazine/31Hersch-t.html.

Halberstam, J. (1998). *Female Sexuality*. Duke University Press.

Handy, D. A. (1981). *Black Women in American Bands and Orchestras*. Scarecrow Press.

Hunter, M. (2005). *Race, Gender, and the Politics of Skin Tone*. Routledge.

International Sweethearts of Rhythm (n.d.) *Playlists* [YouTube channel]. YouTube. Retrieved July 19, 2021 from www.youtube.com/channel/UC_UoxsVuXnS7_akQK8v7Nmg.

Jones, A. L. (2016). Are all the choir directors gay?: Black men's sexuality and identity in gospel performance" In Portia K. Maultsby and Mellonee V. Burnim (Eds.), *Issues in African American Music: Power, Gender, Race, Representation* (pp. 272–296). Routledge.

Kimmel, M. S. (1994). Masculinity as homophobia: Fear, shame, and silence in the construction of gender identity. In H. Brod and M. Kaufman (Eds.), *Theorizing Masculinities* (pp. 119–141). Sage Publications.

Lloyd, M. (1999). Performativity, parody, politics. *Theory, culture, and society* 16(2), 195–203.

MusicandDancing4Ever. (2014, September 5). *The International Sweethearts of Rhythm-Best Female Jazz Band* [video]. YouTube. www.youtube.com/watch?v=WczP3PyHt20&t=843s.

Placksin, S. (1982). *American Women in Jazz, 1900 to the Present: Their Words, Lives, and Music*. Wideview Books.

Raj, A. et al. (2020). Gender parity at work and its association with workplace sexual harassment. *Workplace Health and Safety* 68(6), 279–292.

Rieger, G. et al. (2010). Dissecting "gaydar": Accuracy and the role of masculinity-femininity. *Archives of Sexual Behavior 39*, 124–140.

Rich, A. (1980). Compulsory heterosexuality and lesbian existence. *Signs* 5(4), 631–660.

Roberts, M. (n.d.) Gender issues in jazz and improvised music Part 1. In *Fat Ragged*, 4–7.

Robinson, M. (1964, November 21). "Willene Barton feels: Female musicians can't create ideas." *Pittsburgh Courier*.

Schneider, B. E. (1991). Put up and shut up: Workplace sexual assaults. *Gender & Society 5* (4), 533–548.

Stokes, W. R. (2005). *Growing up with Jazz: Twenty-four Musicians Talk about Their Lives and Careers*. Oxford University Press.

Suzuki, Y. (2011). *"You Sound Like an Old Black Man": Performativity of Gender and Race among Female Jazz Saxophonists*. University of Pittsburgh.

Suzuki, Y. (2012). Burnside, Vi(olet May). *Grove Music Online*. Retrieved 19 Jul. 2021, from www.oxfordmusiconline. com/grovemusic/view/10.1093/gmo/9781561592630.001.0001/omo-9781561592630-e-1002227886.

Suzuki, Y. (2016). Gendering musical sound in jazz saxophone performance. In Walfram Knauer (Ed.), *Gender and Identity in Jazz* (pp. 85–96). Jazzinstitut Darmstadt.

Tucker. S. (2000). *Swing Shift: "All-girl" Bands of the 1940s*. Duke University Press.

Vi Burnside, World's greatest female saxophonist, dies here. (1964, December 15). *Afro-American*, 15.

What stars are doing along stem. (1959, May 16) *The Chicago Defender*, 18.

Wright, T. (2008). Lesbian firefighters: Shifting the boundaries between masculinity and femininity. *Journal of Lesbian Studies* 12(1), 103–114.

14

A CLASH OF IDENTITIES

How Aspects of Gender and Identity in Jazz Influence Both the Music and Its Perception

Wolfram Knauer

Magnus Hirschfeld, the German sexologist and first advocate for homosexual and transgender rights, argued in 1910 that gender is an unstable category of humanness, that masculinity and femininity are mostly social constructs, not empirical entities. The male and the female as absolute representations of their sex, Hirschfeld wrote, are "abstractions, invented extremes" (Hirschfeld, 1910, p. 122).[1]

In an essay about "Typisch Deutsch", the typical German element in music, the musicologist Ekkehard Jost found that phrases starting with "typical" usually denote stereotypes and clichés and, thus, as Jost argued, should be treated with socio-psychiatric rather than musicological approaches. After discussing some aspects often associated with Germanness in music, he concluded that most of them would be better described by the term "specific to" than "typical of" (Jost, 2014, p. 29 and 43).

Let's keep both of these caveats in mind when looking at issues of identity in jazz, when asking about what we hear as "typical of" certain musicians, styles, places, gender(s).

Hirschfeld makes us aware of the element of abstraction—and thus unjust simplification—which any reflection about human acts automatically engages in. Jost reminds us of the fact that the focus we as analysts use to describe music will automatically reduce the analyzed object to a cliché, something both larger and smaller than the person or personal style we try to describe.

In this essay I want to look at a number of clichés that we take for granted about music, about jazz, about musical interaction and its representation of humanness, and I want to ask about the degree of abstraction involved in such clichés, about the range of varieties implied by them, about what is considered the norm and what not, about how such ideas of aesthetic, social and human norms come into being and how they influence our enjoyment, our understanding of, and our reflections about music and jazz.

I will begin with a look at stereotypes pinned to musicians by the industry, the mass media, the public, or by themselves. I will then look at specific shaping factors: especially such based in family, religion, race, ethnicity, and geography. While I will stay away from the subject of women in jazz, which is discussed elsewhere in this volume, I will briefly touch upon "camp" in jazz, before rounding up with a final survey of the different influences which shape (a) a musician, (b) a musical style, (c) his or her representation in the media, and (d) the audience's perception.

DOI: 10.4324/9781003081876-16

The Shy, Sensitive, Funny, Sophisticated, Angry Black Man: Concepts of Identity

Before looking at different aspects of what "identity" actually might mean in respect to music, let's look at the term itself. Psychology differentiates between social identity, personality and the self-concept (Turner and Onorato, 1999). Ethics might differentiate between personality, identity and character (Narvaez and Lapsley, 2009). When *we* talk about identity in the arts, though, we usually refer to a mix of all four of these categories, a mix of artistic self-conception, moral image, result of media marketing, and audience projection. Charles Mingus as the angry Black man; Duke Ellington as the suave and sophisticated artist; Bill Evans as the introvert musical philosopher; Dizzy Gillespie as the extrovert raconteur and entertainer; Archie Shepp as the political protester; George E. Lewis as the artist as scholar; Keith Jarrett as the sensitive, at times touchy performer; Robert Glasper as the self-confident voice of a new generation. All such categorizations have been put on the respective artists by the media, but are grounded in some part of who they actually are. Dizzy was funny, and Jarrett is touchy, and Ellington was suave, and Mingus could become angry. Yet, Dizzy also was a very serious man with a clear political position; Jarrett got into most-inspired playing once he felt safe at his piano; Ellington had a clear outline for his musical as well as aesthetic path; and Mingus could be outright funny in the middle of his anger. This is not so much different, of course, of the way we see others, family, friends, colleagues, or strangers: We acknowledge certain aspects of their personality which may become the moment's "identifier" of that person. Some of these aspects probably will be part of what we often call their "identity", others may be marketing strategies, often exaggerating a real strength of the person in question.

How the artist perceives himself or herself, might be something completely different. Musicians often won't think so much about where they are coming from, as they are simply exploiting all the possibilities of influences which have shaped them. When Robert Glasper uses hip-hop elements, when Vijay Iyer hopes for "out-of-body experiences" during improvisation; when Jan Garbarek uses Nordic folk elements in sound, melody and his harmonic approach, they don't follow any of these paths because they "want to express their individuality", but because they have to, because that is the language they have learned to express themselves in. "Play yourself" is the mantra of the jazz world, but playing who you are is not a concept, it is a prerequisite for making art. What other people will make out of what they hear depends on how far their and the artists' experiences might overlap.

While there are many different approaches to the concept of "identity", then, I will use the term as meaning a composite of self-perception and external perception shaped through the interaction in different, sometimes overlapping, circles and/or communities, as well as through a constant validation of these perception(s) through feedback from peer groups, the audience or the media.

Let us look at different scenes, then, in which "identity" is being shaped, at how it may reflect in music, and at what is being perceived by whom.

Gullah and Geechie on Central Park West: How Community Shapes Identity

At the core of our identity are factors which shape us as individuals interacting with our environment. The first kind of interaction we have is with our mother, then our parents, our immediate family, our neighborhood, our village, our town, our childhood friends, kindergarten, school, our teachers, sports teams, our church and/or religious community. All of these environments are the ones we grow up in and which will have a tremendous impact on our cultural, moral and social understanding, and curiosity.

Apart from family, religion seems to have a big impact on musical identity—more so if the religious environment was especially strong during your childhood and your musical coming of age. This holds true for musicians rooted in the gospel call-and-response of the Black church, but it holds true as well for Protestant German churches, which shaped so many who grew up listening to the hymns, singing either in the congregation or the choir, and learned a musical vocabulary which would shape their musical approach. To really have an impact, though, such musical and ritual influences have to be present over a span of time. To go to one opera might enlighten you and make you extremely curious. To be at church every Sunday and in between, knowing the liturgy and all the possible reactions during the service by heart is something completely different.

When it comes to jazz, what is being called "race" has always been and continues to be a decisive set of distinctions. Discourse about "authorship" or "ownership" of jazz, which have been part of jazz history since its inception, are mainly about respecting origin and innovation, about giving credit and making sure that such credit is not just lip service.

Jazz history has different phases of this Black / white dichotomy. The stereotypical mapping of jazz history often identifies "Black" or "white" stylistic directions through major figures which spearhead the respective styles, but also by using musical arguments, with "Black" standing for a freer approach to improvisation, for a more daring rhythmical concept, for harmonic adventures, for risk, for a consciousness of the blues; and "white" on the other hand standing for a stronger impact of composition, for more "setness" in rhythmical or harmonic approaches, for a safer, often more commercial road taken, for a consciousness of art in a very European sense.

As with most stereotypes, some of these attributions may make sense, others are completely misguided. One needs to know the position of whoever speaks to understand the connotations. Defining a certain piece of music as "Black" can mean something completely different if this definition comes from a Black musician, from a white musician, from a Black or white American jazz fan, from a European jazz fan, or from one who is not a jazz aficionado (from wherever). Also, the definition can be influenced by whom these individuals are talking to: to fellow musicians on stage; to competing musicians on the local, national or international scene; to jazz critics; to those who are not jazz critics; to jazz fans; to a general audience, and so on and so forth.

Finally, the definition will always be influenced by the attempted message: Do I include myself in the group I am identifying the music with or do I consciously try to dissociate myself from it? Am I referring to this identifying principle predominantly for musical or for social reasons? The question always is: Where do I see myself by identifying with a specific descriptor; and: How do I want to be seen?

Let's look at how one can juggle different sets of identity for different means.

Wynton Marsalis identifies himself as a musician in the Black tradition of his home town, New Orleans. He makes sure to also identify with a tradition spanning from the Mississippi Delta to New York through (especially) Duke Ellington and some other, usually Black, musicians who make up the canon of his public jazz identity. At the same time Marsalis used his excellent networking skills to build up Jazz at Lincoln Center as a major concert and education venue, as a meeting place and social forum, not *just* for jazz, but always connected to this music.

In a way, Marsalis tried to redefine the hipness of jazz by establishing a more acceptable version of hip than the underground notion of how jazz had been and continues to be associated with among the cognoscenti. He used some of the tools of the world of Western classical music to bring the social acceptance of "jazz" to a different level. Some say that he established a "clean" venue to replace the dive perception of dirty and noisy jazz clubs, a place where jazz can become a marker for cultural and social distinction even if you don't quite know what the music is about—similar, in a way, to a visit to the opera house, which often is not just about the music.

Marsalis juggles different sets of identities to achieve his general aim, to further the social acceptance of jazz. His New Orleans identity gives him street credibility. His success as a classical musician gave him respect in the arts world from early on. His networking skills and public image give him influence. His management identity, the achievement of actually getting JaLC to run successfully, has made him a powerful player in the field of jazz awareness. He is seen as a traditionalist by most, but sees himself also as a modernist, who tries to renew jazz by emphasizing the existing vocabulary as well as aesthetic guidelines for its rhythmic concept, for melodic invention, sound colors, and musical interaction. His musical identity is clearly different from his business identity, and both have an influence but are not synonymous with the identity he wants us to see, that is, his public image.

Marsalis is a good example, because he always tries to be in control both of his musical identity (his aesthetic credo) and his public image (see Broecking, 2011). Official statements, interviews, books about him or in collaboration with him constitute his public persona. Concert performances, record albums, musical collaborations constitute his aesthetic persona. From time to time he changes elements of his public perception by specific moves, which can be seen as artistic and tactical moves at the same time: by his reference to *Black Codes* for instance or by his oratorio *Blood on the Fields*, which at a time when many in the jazz world saw him mainly as a traditionalist, progress-unfriendly representative of a new corporate jazz concept made sure to emphasize his obligation to the Black cause. Geography is at the core of jazz's legacy and has been used to identify whole stylistic developments of the music's history. Musicians from New Orleans over the decades were proud of their hometown and bonded even after they left home to live and work in other bands and cities. The Chicago-based Austin High School Gang is an early case of an educational community turning into local / geographical identity. The memories of Kansas City jam sessions come to mind, New York's 52nd Street and, most importantly the West Coast / East Coast duality in the 1950s—which even were declared as being stylistic identities for musicians grouped into the specific schools (for all the above see, for example, Ostransky, 1978).

Most geographical factors which eventually became part of what might be called a musical identity can be analyzed as being clear group identities based upon what I would call "real" communities: groups of people bound together through place, educational background, church and/or religion, work places (and this also includes venues, festivals, touring circuits). Being from Detroit or Philadelphia meant you grew up in a jazz scene which encouraged intergenerational learning (see Stryker, 2019; Allen, 1997). Being from Chicago or St. Louis may have given you the chance to learn from the AACM's or the Black Artist Group's inter-arts perspectives (see Lewis, 2008; Locker, 2004). Being from Boston may have encouraged musical experiments stirred more easily in an academic environment. Being from San Francisco you grew up with a specific look at life, being from rural Alabama (and being Black or white) would probably be a completely different thing.

How, though, does geographical identity translate into music? The answer is simple if your geographic origin has clear musical traditions, whether they are rooted in folklore, in strong church activities or in other cultural practices. I want to point out one example which impressed me immensely because it brings together a couple of different aspects of geographical identity.

From 2005 I have been involved in an initiative which documents the history of Black music and especially the African-American contributions to jazz in Charleston, South Carolina, as well as the Low Country around that city. Similar to New Orleans, Charleston had been a major slave market. Different from the cotton fields of the South, the rice plantations of the low country of South Carolina and coastal Georgia had heavily relied on the traditional farming expertise of slaves who had been cultivating rice for many generations in West Africa. They had developed techniques of keeping the plants flooded and yet not destroy the harvest by flooding too much. While elsewhere in slave-holding America, in order to prevent slave uprisings, the masters had made sure that their slaves would speak English and not be able to communicate in their original languages, plantation owners in these coastal regions, because of the traditional knowledge of their slaves, did not force them to break up family or original community bonds. Thus, in the Low Country, memories of African traditions survived much more unimpaired than elsewhere, as has been documented in studies on the Gullah language, on farming techniques, on story-telling, food and music (see Chandler, 2018). During one of the conferences I attended in Charleston, the drummer Quentin Baxter talked about his Gullah background, about how the Gullah dialect had become a clearly distinguishable inflection in everyday language in South Carolina, Black or white. But more, Baxter insisted that with music being so close to language the Gullah dialect showed up in musical tone inflections, and in his own concept of rhythm, the Gullah ostinato, as he called it. He spoke lines in Gullah, focusing on the rhythm of speech, and followed that with a series of percussion lines, involving pitch, rhythmical taps, accents, repetition (see https://youtu.be/m7bWI3cp-8w, from 4:30, accessed 24 March 2021).

Baxter's argument was purely musical: "I grew up in a community," he said, "which informed my feeling of pitch, rhythm, timbre, and micro-form. My music is heavily influenced by a translation of such aspects of language." Quentin Baxter plays jazz—he performs regularly with Monty Alexander and René Marie, and was Freddie Cole's drummer—but I am sure it is this approach, his rhythmic expertise, and his clear sense of identity which is favored by some of the artists he has performed with over the years. Baxter is a virtuoso percussionist, who brings energy, intensity, a steady swing to the bandstand. Few may know where it comes from, but he himself knows that part of this musical identity is the church and his Gullah upbringing in South Carolina.

"Do I Sound Straight?" Or: At an Ellingtonian Camp Meeting

The filmmaker David Thorpe released a documentary in 2015, *Do I Sound Gay?*, in which he digs into the stereotype of the gay voice. I read a review about the film by Michael Schulman on the *New Yorker* website (Schulman, 2015) just as I came home from a concert at Darmstadt's state opera house with the Kurt Elling group featuring the German trumpeter Till Brönner. The music had been great, professional artists all of them with perhaps a little too much perfection, for my taste, and a bit too little daring. The two headliners greeted each other on stage with awkward embraces, those hugs that don't get too close, heads not touching, a pat on the shoulder of the other showing who's the boss. It felt, to me at least, like heterosexual showmanship, as if the stars on stage had a testosterone competition they wanted to hide from the audience. Before that I tended to think of a "gay voice" as an oddity in itself: If there is a gay voice, is there anything like a "straight voice"? On that stage, though, I clearly felt just that, a "straight voice": in the behavior of the two artists towards each other, in the cool, humorous announcements by both Elling and Brönner, in the patronizing gestures offering the applause to the respective other. The "gay voice", if anything, is related to the double entendre of African-American speech. Just as Signifyin' has a lot of reasons and is perceived differently from the in-group than from the out-group, *camp* is implying community but also pride about being who you are. So what, it says, you think this is not appropriate? Let's make it an art form.

So, is there a "gay voice" in jazz? The openly gay pianist Fred Hersch performed at the 2014 OutBeat festival in Philadelphia, advertised as America's "first queer jazz festival". Before, though, in a letter to *DownBeat* magazine, Hersch took offense both to the term "queer" and to the notion of playing "gay jazz" (Hersch, 2014). Nobody likes stereotyping, whether it's about a voice or an instrument, about styles, about ethnic or racial roots, about gender, about sexual orientation. Why can't we be judged by "who we are", by "how we write or play", by the result of our work instead of by the perspective people have of us? Why? Because we need those perspectives. As musicians, as critics, as scholars, as listeners. Music allows us to develop and compare our individual perspective, it encourages us to try out and accept other perspectives, and it helps us to acknowledge development in our aesthetic taste.

The campiest example in my book comes from one of the masters of our music, Edward Kennedy "Duke" Ellington. Ellington's announcements were beautiful, using the most elegant words and pronunciations he could master. There is a legendary recording from the early 1960s of Duke Ellington posing as a journalist interviewing Billy Strayhorn. It is revealing in the many levels of identity both of these musicians appropriate and question at the same time. Ellington's love for flowery words has much to do with his love for sound colors. His concert announcements blend in with the way he treats the pieces his orchestra plays. In the interview with Strayhorn, who was openly gay, though, much of this, at least from a gay man's perspective, turns into pure camp, a play with words, giving up all pretense or rather, building up new ones so transparent that it is clear they are for play and love and not for fight and competition. One has to listen to the tone of voices, here, but for lack of a sounding page, here are Ellington's first two questions and Strayhorns answers, which are "very informative", as Ellington acknowledges (Ellington/Strayhorn, 2010, p. 8):

DUKE ELLINGTON: Mr. Billy Strayhorn, how do you do, Sir. I am here, representing Mr. Ralph Gleason—I am sure you know him, he is an editor and publisher of jazz, he is an authority on jazz, and, of course, he is a noted columnist for the *San Francisco Chronicle* and many other papers, a recognized authority, internationally. And I am, as I said before, representing Mr. Gleason, and he sends his regards to you. I personally..., Well, I met you myself in the late 30s in Pittsburgh, you may not recall the occasion or the place, but I did meet you. And I'd like to know, or rather, Mr. Gleason's readers would like to know something about you, a little more about you than they do know. Where were you born?

BILLY STRAYHORN: Well, Sir, I was born in Dayton, Ohio.

DE: Yes ... What year?

BS: What did you say?

DE: In what year?

BS: In what year? Well, all I know is that it was A.D.

DE: A.D.

BS: Yes

DE: Yes. Well, Mr. Strayhorn, that's very informative. Thank you, Sir.

Ellington is a good case in point in other respects as well. He *was* royalty, in jazz and offstage, and as royalty does, he would wear silk and satin, have his hair done, look good whether on stage or off, because whenever he left his room it felt like he was giving an audience to those around him. What *is* his identity? Sign-painter from Washington, DC, stride pianist, composer of songs and revues, bandleader? Mastermind, experimenter, businessman? Entertainer, ladies' man, aesthetic conscience for his generation and generations to come? (see Knauer, 2017, pp. 270–271).

Ellington's strength was his ability to compile the musical talent around him, structure it in a way that it became more than it would ever have been on its own. He had a vision, and his vision was musical just as it was political, aesthetic, and social. "We love you madly", he would shout out to his audiences, anywhere, and what he meant was, "We love you, no matter who you are because our music transcends ethnic differences, because our music is universal." In his band, Ellington was a collector of musical identities. He never had been interested in streamlined musicians for his orchestra. If you were perfect but one could not hear where you came from, you were not for him. The chalumeau register of Barney Bigard's clarinet, the sinewy alto saxophone of Johnny Hodges, the wa-wa sounds coming from Tricky Sam Nanton's trombone, or the cello-like beauty of his section mate Lawrence Brown, the plunger and growl work of Cootie Williams, the fascinating half-valve technique of Rex Stewart, the air-filled tenor sound of Ben Webster, the aggressive laziness in Paul Gonsalves' playing, the theatrical percussion of Sonny Greer—most of these musicians would have had a hard time in any other band, but Ellington was hungry exactly for such musical individuality. The parts in his band book are not titled "1st alto", but "Rabbit" (for Johnny Hodges), not "1st trumpet" but "Cootie" (for Cootie Williams). And when the musicians left the band the pieces might leave the repertoire until somebody came along who had something similar to add or something completely different yet personal.

To round up, let us briefly review other factors which shape identity and look at how they might actually translate into music.

So, Who am I, and Will You ever Know Me?

We already defined ethnicity or "race" as a most important factor in the United States, even more so than elsewhere.

We mentioned geography, West Coast jazz for instance, which grew out of economic necessity and evolving communities more than out of any ethnic traditions. We might talk about national identity being shaped not so much by nationality per se but by the specific cultural and educational systems (the system of a French central state for instance versus the cultural sovereignty of the 16 federal states in Germany).

We might talk about the influence of language on music, looking at sound aspects, melodic flow or rhythmic peculiarities like, just as a small example, the fact that in Czech you usually pronounce the first syllable, which makes upbeat phrases in music feel more unnatural than downbeat phrases.

We mentioned religion, and, of course, music always is close to spirituality, so identity can be shaped by a specific spiritual awakening through music as well. You might have had the epiphany of music talking to you, personally; music may have become an extremely personal companion to you as a listener; you may have had out-of-body experiences seemingly "getting lost" in improvisation, a feeling which can be described in a myriad of ways, scientifically as well as spiritually ("God plays through me").

We can talk about gender attributes and what these social norms mean, both for musicians and listeners (see Rustin and Tucker, 2008). The same applies to the sexual identity of anyone involved, the experience, for instance, that for social reasons more than as a realistic fact, the gay or lesbian subcultures and the jazz scene hardly seem to overlap.

Social status and how you deal with it is another element. You may have an educated background, come from a wealthy family or you may have dropped out of school and gone through a hard childhood. Any of these aspects may leave you either strong or not so strong, depending on how you deal with what you've been dealt with, how you are able to develop pride for your heritage, no matter what it is … or not.

Physicality can become an altering factor in your identity, if your health falters, if you are handicapped or getting up in age. However: Chick Webb's spinal tuberculosis, contracted at the age of 3 and leaving him with a hunched back and walking problems, didn't hinder him from becoming one of the most successful drummers, and seeing the small-sized Michel Petrucciani perform his virtuoso solos despite the glass bone disease he had to live with seemed to be more important for the audience as an "identifying" element of his art than for the pianist, himself, who felt like he was no different from other men in his love for music, women and wine.

Aspects of character certainly will influence your art quite decisively. Whether you're aggressive or rather shy, direct or holding back, an extrovert or an introvert, self-confident or self-conscious might eventually come out in your music, and by that I mean in what you play, how you interact with other musicians and how you present your music to the audience.

As much as your identity is shaped by all the different impacts on you as a person, you will decide how you weigh the circles you move in very individualistically. Apart from interacting in the jazz world, you may be a family person, or your non-musical job may take up most of your time; you may have a circle of friends you spend quality time with, or be a member of a sports club. You may like to travel, be a party animal, or be a reading hermit, a loner.

Identity is who you are, what you have been shaped by, but also who you decide you are, which of the many possibilities of social and cultural interaction you choose to adopt for yourself.

None of the decisions you make will make you a better or worse jazz musician. They will shape who you are, how you approach and solve problems, though, and if jazz is about something, it is about constant and spontaneous problem solving. It is not so much your identity than it is the way how you are able to accept whatever identity, or identities, you have chosen for yourself in this both conscious and subconscious process of your personal development, which will influence how you deal with musical problems.

Which brings us to the big issue: How to change the world. There will always be those who demand immediate recognition of all aspects of gender and identity in society. There are those who see structural discrimination at work because they feel that issues addressed are not inclusive enough or ignore other injustices. On a personal note, I tend toward pragmatism. I have seen changes in the society I live in within the last decades when it comes to the recognition of gender and sexuality that I would not have deemed possible many years ago. Is the situation perfect? Far from it! Is the discourse necessary? Absolutely! I feel encouraged by a young generation making demands for causes, even if I may view them differently. I may feel uneasy by what I often perceive to be a strong moral tone or by the unforgiving stance that some of these demands seem to take. Yet, it's the discourse that counts. I feel encouraged that young musicians, jazz musicians at that, participate in these debates, from #MeToo through Black Lives Matter, Friday for Future, all the way to most recent and very specific demands of some young German musicians asking for intersectionality in the advisory board and jury of the Deutscher Jazzpreis (German Jazz Award) which was first awarded in June 2021 (www.musiciansfor.org). As long as we keep talking, debating, demanding, perspectives will shift. As long as perspectives shift, reality will change.

Beyond Category

I would like to conclude by getting back to the caveats I gave in my introduction. Magnus Hirschfeld made us aware of the element of abstraction—and thus unjust simplification—when it comes to gender issues. Sometimes, though—and Hirschfeld's explanation comes exactly from this point of view—we might just need this abstraction to single out specific musical traits. Ekkehard Jost had argued for the term "specific to" instead of "typical of", trying to back down from the representational perspective of a musician's style standing for something that might be more than the musician's personal experiences. That makes sense, and yet we will want to identify the communities the artist interacts with in order to fully grasp motivations or inspirations for his or her creative work. Recent publications—actually the whole field of what has been called New Jazz Studies—are doing exactly that: looking at the music and the different circles it resonates in, identifying the fields for exploration not as universal explanations but as highly individual perspectives which, however, will allow us a better view of the whole picture.

When some years ago we organized our Darmstadt Jazzforum conference around the subject of "gender and identity in jazz" (Knauer, 2016), I noticed misunderstandings among colleagues, journalists, musicians, fans about that subject. There were those who read "gender" and understood "women". There were those who read "identity" and added either "sexual" or "national" in their mind. There were those who asked, "So are you going to talk about the ditch between American and European jazz?" What I am interested in, though, is to learn how all of these self-ascribed or externally ascribed identity-related influences which end up constituting the personal styles of musicians relate to aesthetic directions the musicians take. I quoted Fred Hersch, who was not happy with the word "queer" or the idea of "gay jazz". There are so many female musicians who argue that their musical approach has nothing to do whatsoever with them being women. At the Darmstadt conference, Sherrie Tucker stated that she wished every time people spoke about "women in jazz" they would really be thinking "diversity in jazz" (Tucker, 2016, p. 257). There are European musicians who will vehemently deny any influence of their nationality on their art. And yet, where you come from is where you go to. Your life and work experiences will shape what you say and how you present yourself to the world. That's the wonderful thing about the human species and art: We all live in the same world, and yet, each of us has his or her own perspective of it. Thus, to get to know the influences that shape someone else's artistic being will not only help us to understand the other, but will make us see our own identity from a different perspective.

Note

1 In the German original: "Derartig absolute Vertreter ihres Geschlechts sind aber konstruierte Extreme, Abstraktionen, in Wirklichkeit sind sie bisher nicht beobachtet worden."

References

Allen, George E. (1997). Contributions of Philadelphia African American Musicians to American Jazz Music from 1945 to 1960. Philadelphia: Temple University [PhD thesis].

Broecking, Christian (2011). *Der Marsalis-Komplex. Studien zur gesellschaftlichen Relevanz des afroamerikanischen Jazz zwischen 1992 und 2007*. Berlin: Broecking Verlag.

Chandler, Karen (2018). Bin Yah (Been Here). Africanisms and Jazz Influence in Gullah Culture. In Wolfram Knauer (ed.), *Jazz @ 100. An Alternative to a Story of Heroes. Darmstädter Beiträge zur Jazzforschung, Bd. 15* (pp. 226–245). Hofheim: Wolke Verlag.

Ellington, Duke, and Strayhorn, Billy (2010). Duke Ellington interviewing Billy Strayhorn. *Duke Ellington Society of Sweden Bulletin*, 18/4 (November 2010), 8–9.

Hersch, Fred (2014). Chords and Discords. Hersch on OutBeat. *DownBeat*, 81/9 (September 2014), 10.

Hirschfeld, Magnus (1910). Die Zwischenstufen-Theorie. Sexual-Probleme. *Zeitschrift für Sexualwissenschaft und Sexualpolitik*, 6, 116–136.

Jost, Ekkehard (2014). Über einige Problem beim wissenschaftlichen Umgang mit dem Begriff des Typischen und über den Versuch, ihn auf sinnvolle Weise durch einen anderen zu ersetzen. In Dietrich Helms and Thomas Phleps (eds.), *Typisch Deutsch. (Eigen-)Sichten auf populäre in diesem unserem Land* (pp. 29–44). Bielefeld: transkript.

Knauer, Wolfram (2016). *Gender and Identity in Jazz. Darmstädter Beiträge zur Jazzforschung, Bd. 14*. Hofheim: Wolke Verlag.

Knauer, Wolfram (2017). *Duke Ellington*, Ditzingen: Reclam.

Lewis, George E. (2008). *A Power Stronger than Itself. The AACM and American Experimental Music*. Chicago: University of Chicago Press.

Locker, Benjamin (2004). *BAG. "Point from Which Creation Begins." The Black Artists' Group in St. Louis*. St. Louis: Missouri Historical Society Press.

Narvaez, Darcia, and Lapsley, Daniel K. (2009). *Personality, Identity, and Character. Explorations in Moral Psychology*. Cambridge: Cambridge University Press.

Ostransky, Leroy (1978). *Jazz City. The Impact of Our Cities on the Development of Jazz*. Englewood Cliffs, NJ: Spectrum/Prentice-Hall.

Rustin, Nichole T., Tucker, Sherrie (2008). *Big Ears. Listening for Gender in Jazz Studies*. Durham, NC: Duke University Press.

Schulman, Michael (2015). Is There a "Gay Voice"? In *The New Yorker*, 10 July 2015. www.newyorker.com/culture/culture-desk/is-there-a-gay-voice (accessed 24 March 2021).

Stryker, Mark (2019). *Jazz from Detroit*. Ann Arbor: University of Michigan Press.

Tucker, Sherrie (2016). A Conundrum is a Woman-in-Jazz. Enduring Improvisations on the Categorical Exclusions of Being Included. In Wolfram Knauer (ed.): *Gender and Identity in Jazz. Darmstädter Beiträge zur Jazzforschung, Bd. 14* (pp. 240–261), Hofheim: Wolke Verlag.

Turner. John C, and Onorato, Rina S. (1999). Social identity, personality, and the self-concept. A self-categorizing perspective. In Tom R. Tyler, Roderick M. Kramer, Oliver P. John (eds.): *The Psychology of the Social Self* (p. 11–46), Mahwah, NJ: Lawrence Erlbaum Associates Publishers.

15

"I'M JUST ONE OF THEM"

Gender in Jazz Competitions

Matthias Heyman

Introduction

Shortly after winning the prestigious Thelonious Monk Institute of Jazz International Competition in 2013, tenor saxophonist Melissa Aldana was asked about becoming the first female instrumentalist to take first place.[1] She responded, saying, "Even though I know that is a big deal, because I'm the first one, I never felt different because I'm a female. I felt I was competing with all those great, young musicians and I'm just one of them" (Ashton, 2013a, para. 4). This comment suggests that, in the context of this competition, Aldana felt the need to downplay her gender and firmly align herself with her fellow finalists and semifinalists, all 12 of whom were male.[2]

Her response may have been a reaction to the strong focus on her gender by the press. Virtually all headlines emphasized her being the first woman instrumentalist (and, to a lesser degree, the first South American) to win this contest. As much attention went to her gender and nationality (Aldana hails from Chile), she may have felt that her artistry was not given proper due, as is evidenced by more recent remarks made in the context of the release of her 2019 album *Visions*: "I don't really like how reviews of the album keep focusing on the word female and Latina rather than the substance of the influence" (Derdeyn, 2019).

Yet, the unicity of her achievement cannot be denied. In the 30 editions that have been held between 1987, the year of the Monk competition's inception, and 2019, the final edition, Aldana remains the only woman to win an instrumental edition of this major, international jazz contest. While gender inequality is an issue in all jazz industry branches, this seems even more so in the competition milieu. Are competitions less hospitable to women than, for example, festivals or educational institutions? If so, what are the reasons for this? What can contest organizers do to address gender equity? This chapter aims to answer the above questions and provide a better understanding of the role gender plays in the context of international jazz competitions.[3]

Focus: Monk Competition and Jazz Hoeilaart

With a history dating back to the 1920s, jazz competitions can be found throughout the world in all forms, from solo to big band, and for all levels, from young child to seasoned professional (Heyman, 2020, p. 442). Due to this prominence, these "tournaments of value" act as a powerful

DOI: 10.4324/9781003081876-17

context for (re)producing or challenging particular cultural meanings, including those relating to gender (Appadurai, 1986, p. 21). Despite their assumed gender neutrality—for example, many competitions employ a blind audition system for their preliminary selection—competitions seem to reinforce the notion of jazz as a hypermasculine milieu. This is suggested by surveying the gender balance in the Monk competition and the Jazz Hoeilaart International Jazz Contest, worldwide two of the oldest ongoing international jazz competitions.[4] Their longevity provides ample data, and their singular scope and focus allow for diverse perspectives to be considered. For example, Jazz Hoeilaart is a band-based contest, whereas the Monk competition is a solo contest designed every year to showcase a prescribed instrument, including vocals. Furthermore, while both music tournaments attract international participants, the latter draws predominantly US-based applicants (ca. 79% in the finals), while for the former, most contestants hail from the wider European region (ca. 88% in the finals).

The Jazz Hoeilaart International Jazz Contest, a competition aimed towards pre-professional bands, was founded in 1979 in Hoeilaart, a rural municipality located east of Brussels, Belgium's capital. Although Albert Michiels, the contest's founder, was no music professional, he quickly managed to develop Jazz Hoeilaart, held annually, from a small local competition to a major international one. By 1987, there were already submissions from 17 countries with bands from the United States and India among the finalists. In 2015, Jazz Hoeilaart was taken over by Muziekmozaïek Folk and Jazz, a professional support center for jazz and folk music. They sought to further professionalize the competition, for example, by moving it to the central city of Leuven and renaming it B-Jazz International Contest.[5] The typical selection procedure consists of a preliminary blind audition of eligible submissions (e.g., average age of maximum 30 for the entire band), upon which six bands are selected to perform a 40-minute live set with no limitation regarding repertoire or style, except the inclusion of a mandatory, pre-selected composition by a Belgian jazz musician. As a result, most bands will play their own music and only rarely the standard repertoire.

The first edition of the Monk competition was held in 1987, one year after its mother organization's foundation, the Thelonious Monk Institute of Jazz, a non-profit music education organization based in Washington, D. C. Among the Institute's founders were established performers such as trumpeter Clark Terry, opera singer Maria Fisher, and drummer T.S. Monk, the notable pianist's son.[6] This solo competition, which is held annually, is one of the Institute's activities, others being poised more towards education (e.g., Jazz in the Classroom) or public outreach (e.g., the International Jazz Day, co-organized with UNESCO). It has a strong connection to the professional jazz community, as is evidenced by its esteemed cast of judges, such as saxophonist Wayne Shorter or singer Dee Dee Bridgewater. The typical selection procedure consists of a preliminary blind audition of eligible submissions (e.g., maximum age of 30), upon which approximately 12 individuals are selected to perform a 15-minute live set. Three contestants are selected for the finals, in which they are required to perform a live set featuring two compositions. While the preselection comprises specific requirements (e.g., the inclusion of a post-1970 composition), there are no limitations regarding repertoire or style in the semifinals and finals. (For some editions, the inclusion of a Monk composition was mandatory.) As all semifinalists and finalists need to perform their sets with the resident rhythm section, most will refrain from performing original compositions that require extensive rehearsing and instead showcase their solo skills on standard repertoire.

These two competitions cannot be straightforwardly compared with each other or with other contests, nor are they representative of all jazz competitions. They do, however, offer a pertinent insight into gender within the jazz competition milieu. With this in mind, let us survey the gender balance among contenders in both competitions. As noted, the sampled data is limited to a female/male binary as data that reveals a broader spectrum of the participants' gender is not available.

Gender Balance in Jazz Competitions: The Data

For Jazz Hoeilaart, all participants in the 40 editions between 1979 and 2019 were surveyed. A total of 322 bands contended in the finals, ranging from soloists (twice) to big bands (four), with quartet being the most common format (123). This results in an estimated 1,336 individuals (of 18 bands, the exact personnel, including their gender, is not known). Of these 1,336 finalists, 38 were female, a mere 2.8 percent. As Annfelt (2003) explained, jazz has a "traditional 'division of labour'" (para. 2) with a "gendered division of roles" (para. 7), resulting in the vast majority of women in jazz being vocalists, followed by what Lorge (2019) calls "gendered instruments" (p. 28) such as the piano, flute or violin.[7] This is reflected in the data: Seventeen of these 38 women were vocalists (44.7%), compared to only five male vocalists. Of the remaining 21 female finalists, seven played the piano and five played the (acoustic or electric) bass, somewhat surprising given this instrument's typically gendered role. Remarkably, 16 of the 38 women (42.1%) participated after 2015, when Jazz Hoeilaart was taken over. This is something I explore in more detail below. Another aspect worth observing is that out of a total of 322 bands, 11 were female-led (3.4%), several of which account for an increase in the participation of women. This is exemplified by the Norwegian all-female quartet Jazz'isters (1995), the Kika Sprangers Large Ensemble (2018), a twelvetet from the Netherlands with six female musicians, the Belgian septet Aishinka (2019), which comprises four female members, or O.N.E. Quintet, a Polish all-female band (selected for the aborted 2020 edition). It is likely no coincidence that many bands led by women comprise a significant number of female musicians. Notwithstanding historical research on all-female bands (e.g., Tucker 2000), this particular observation remains unexplored in literature.

For the Monk competition, all participants in the 30 editions between 1987 and 2019 were surveyed. As noted, the Monk competition annually focuses on a distinct instrument. Still, it does not employ a fixed revolving schedule whereby a particular instrument automatically returns every two or three years (as is the case with several classical music competitions such as the Queen Elisabeth Competition). Which instrument is featured seems to be decided arbitrarily, although it is notable that the more "popular" or "mainstream" instruments such as piano (eight editions), saxophone, and vocals (five editions each) are showcased significantly more. By contrast, hand drum (2000) and trombone (2003) have been featured only once.

As the Monk competition consists of a semifinal and a final round, I analyzed two data sets. Unfortunately, the data set for the semifinals is incomplete as I was unable to find the names of the semifinalists of various editions before the mid-2000s. Therefore, this data is sampled from the last ten editions, starting in 2008 (there was no competition in 2016 and 2017). In these ten editions, 125 individuals participated in the semifinals, 20 of whom were women (16%). Of the ten editions, two were dedicated to vocals. As a result, 17 of the 20 female semifinalists (85%) were vocalists (as opposed to six male vocalists). The three female instrumentalists to be selected for the semifinals were bassist Linda May Han Oh (2009), saxophonist Melissa Aldana (2013), and pianist Liya Grigoryan (2018). For the finals, a complete data set of 30 editions is available: 110 individuals participated in the finals, 19 of which were women (17.2%). One of these 19 women, the singer Charanée Wade was a finalist twice (Fourth Prize in 2004, Second Prize in 2010), a unique occurrence. As noted, of the 30 editions, five were dedicated to vocals. As a result, 16 of the 19 female finalists (84.2%) were vocalists (as opposed to only two male vocalists). The three female instrumentalists to push through to the finals were guitarist Sheryl Bailey (1995), trombonist Karin Harris (2003), and Aldana (2013), none of whom played instruments typically coded as female.

While only a small number of women pushed through to the semifinals of both surveyed competitions, even fewer won first place. In the 40 editions of Jazz Hoeilaart, only two bands comprising women took first place, in both instances after the 2015 re-organization. The Daahoud Salim Quintet (2017) and Aishinka (2019, see Figure 15.1) account for five of the

Figure 15.1 The Belgian septet Aishinka, here shown during a 2021 live-streamed performance, comprises four women, one pianist and three vocalists. In 2019, the band won the "Grand Prix Albert Michiels" at the B-Jazz International Contest. Photograph copyright by Patrick Clerens. Reproduced with permission.

total 38 women finalists, with three of these five being vocalists. For the Monk competition, this number lies slightly higher: In the 30 editions, six women placed first, all save one, Aldana (2013), in dedicated vocal editions.

The above data reveals an outspoken gender imbalance in both competitions' contenders, with the estimated percentage of women finalists being 2.8 percent for Jazz Hoeilaart and 17.2 percent for the Monk competition. This discrepancy may be explained through the difference in contest design, with the Monk competition organizing dedicated vocal editions, which are sure to attract a significantly higher number of female contenders. When removing vocalists from the data, this discrepancy lessens: female instrumentalists account for 1.5 percent of finalists in Jazz Hoeilaart and 2.7 percent of finalists in the Monk competition. These figures confirm that gender disparity is a significant issue within the jazz competition milieu. This becomes even more obvious when placing these numbers in a broader context of data available on gender balance in jazz, particularly with regards to higher education.

For example, between 2012 and 2017, the most recent period for which data are available, an average percentage of 7.1 women graduated from the five US institutions that graduated the most jazz performance students in higher education (Data USA, Diversity section). While data for Belgium are lacking, the neighboring countries provide insight into Western Europe's situation. According to a 2019 study, in France, 25.5 percent of all jazz students at music conservatoires were women, while 18 percent of the educational staff was female (Martin and Offroy, 2019, p. 4). As can be expected, the vast majority of these women were vocalists, 71 percent of the students and over 90 percent of the educators (Martin and Offroy, 2019, pp. 8 and 10). For UK music conservatoires, gender data relating to jazz students are unavailable, but a 2020 survey indicates that the proportion of female jazz staff is 11 percent, the majority being vocal teachers (Raine, 2020, p. 19). For Germany, data on gender in an educational context is absent. Still, generic data indicates that in 2016, 20 percent of professional jazz performers were women, albeit with the proviso that the share of female musicians is more significant among younger generations (Renz, 2016, p. 10). Furthermore, 51 percent of these women were vocalists (Block, 2020, p. 20).

As the data above address distinct aspects, these cannot be compared side-by-side, nor can they be compared with the data sampled from both jazz competitions. Still, they offer a broader framework to understand the data retrieved from the discussed jazz contests. Most apparent is the predominance of vocalists, which applies not only to the competition milieu but also within the educational and professional sector, something that not only can be gleaned from the above data but is also well documented in the literature (e.g., Annfelt, 2003; Pellegrinelli, 2008; Wahl and Ellingson, 2018). Another pertinent observation is that the percentage of women finalists in both competitions under discussion, 2.8 percent for Jazz Hoeilaart and 17.2 percent for the Monk competition, lies significantly lower than the 25.5 percent of female jazz students at French conservatoires or the 20 percent of female professionals in the German jazz community. While no causal conclusions can be drawn from this data, this seems to imply that jazz competitions are even less conducive to the participation of women than higher education or the professional sector.

Gender Inequality in Jazz Competitions: Possible Causes

There may be various reasons why jazz competitions such as the two under scrutiny attract so few submissions by female jazz musicians, with even fewer pushing on to the finals and, ultimately, first place. In many instances, the causes are the same as those in other branches of the jazz industry, such as (mainly tertiary) music education and the live music circuit. For example, G. Robinson (2020) highlighted the "importance of representation when discussing diversity and inequality" (Representation section, para. 1). Virtually all jazz industry branches, including jazz competitions, rely significantly on gatekeepers, individuals or committees of (often self-proclaimed) experts in charge of an evaluation and selection process, for example, educators, booking agents, and critics. As these "gatekeepers are, and have always been, disproportionately male" (para. 4), as C. Robinson (2019) wrote, a hierarchy arises by which a select network, often belonging to what can be considered an "old boys' club," holds sway over a large number of musicians, many of whom are in an economically or socially disadvantageous position: Performers rely in part on concert bookings for their income, prospective students need to pass auditions before being admitted to a music conservatoire, appearing in jazz polls and critics' year-end lists impacts album sales.[8]

In the context of jazz contests, these gatekeepers are the organizers and adjudicators. The latter seem to wield the most impact in the short term as they are immediately involved in selecting, evaluating, and ranking the contenders and, ultimately, consecrating the winner(s). Typically, organizers have no direct influence on the selection process of the candidates, but in the long term, they impact the design, structure, and overall presentation of a competition, for example, through outlining the competition rules, which include the candidates' eligibility. Moreover, as McCormick (2015) asserted, competition organizers "draw from their networks to identify panelists who have the expertise and a reputation for being both fair and congenial" (p. 185). Parallel to gatekeepers in other branches of the jazz industry, contest organizers and adjudicators tend to be predominantly male.

In the 30 editions of the Monk competition, a total of 166 jury members participated in the (semi-)finals, all of whom were (or are) internationally renowned jazz musicians, such as producer and trumpeter Quincy Jones or saxophonist Wayne Shorter.[9] Several of them were invited multiple times, such as pianists Danilo Pérez (four times) or Herbie Hancock (five times). Therefore, a distinction needs to be made between the (relative) number of jury slots and the (absolute) number of individual judges. Out of a total of 166 jury slots, 25 were filled by women (15%). Of these 25 "female slots," 16 were in the five vocal editions. When excluding multiple participation, a total of 122 unique individuals who served as Monk competition jurors, the vast majority of whom were American. Of these 122 individuals, 17 were women (13.9%), five of whom participated as a judge multiple times, such as vocalist Dee Dee Bridgewater (four times). The majority of the 17 female adjudicators were vocalists; seven jury members were instrumentalists: five pianists, one saxophonist, and one drummer. This, again, confirms the systemic division of gendered roles in jazz, the majority of both female contenders and female judges being vocalists.

Jazz Hoeilaart has had an average of seven jury members per edition, resulting in approximately 264 judges over a total of 40 editions. While journalists or concert promotors on occasion acted as adjudicators, the majority were prolific performers, most of whom were (or are) primarily active in the Belgian jazz milieu, such as saxophonist Etienne Verschueren and pianist Nathalie Loriers. Since 1989, virtually every edition had at least one (and often several) adjudicator(s) from outside Belgium, but none came from outside Europe. Many jury members appeared multiple times, on one occasion even up to 18 times. When omitting such multiple participations, a total of 68 individuals served as a Jazz Hoeilaart juror. It was not until 1999, 30 years after Jazz Hoeilaart's creation that the first female judge appeared, and since then, women have acted as adjudicator 20 times out of a total of 264 jury slots (7.5%). In absolute numbers, however, there were seven women among the 68 unique judges (10.2%): three pianists, two vocalists, one bassist, and one concert promoter. As noted above, the number of female contenders increased after the new organization took over, but so did the number of female jury members: after 2015, five individual women filled seven of the 29 available jury slots.

As data from both competitions reveal, very few individual women acted as judge: seven in the 40 editions of Jazz Hoeilaart and 17 in the 30 editions of the Monk competition. This lack of representation in the highly visible and influential position of adjudicator may indeed discourage young women from considering partaking in a competition. "[Y]oung people in the early stages of their careers should see themselves represented within the higher power structures" (Representation section, para. 1), explained G. Robinson (2020), elaborating that "[f]emale representation in leadership positions within any institution is crucial to creating a gender-diverse and supportive environment and is essential in eradicating underlying systematic oppression" (Representation section, para. 1).

But the issue of gender representation is not limited to the level of the jury alone. While G. Robinson (2020) referred to "[f]emale representation in leadership positions" (Representation section, para. 1), a similar principle applies to the field of contenders. As McCormick (2015) argued:

> Music competitions provide an arena for [the] public construction of collective identities to take place. When candidates are seen not as individuals but as representatives of groups (e.g., women, Americans, Asians), the event becomes an arena where the boundaries of the civil sphere are called into question and the possibilities of the incorporation process becomes symbolically engaged.
>
> *(p. 68)*

This may partly explain the media's emphasis on Melissa Aldana's gender: her victory represented a victory for all female instrumentalists. Yet, with so few women participating in both these highly prestigious contests, be it as a candidate or as a juror, the process of incorporation, to paraphrase McCormick (2015), cannot be fully engaged, and Aldana's win remains an anomaly, firmly entrenching the jazz contest as a male-dominated domain.

While the underrepresentation of women impacts gender equality in virtually all jazz industry branches, other factors are more exclusive to jazz competitions. Music contests are built on the (admittedly, utopic) principles of fairness and inclusiveness, with equal treatment of all contenders at its core. Yet, the public perception of a competition and the rhetoric surrounding it often reveals implicit gender bias. As such, the image a contest conjures up may impede the very act of entering a competition. When considering the premodern history of music competitions, it is evident that contests or related events such as the competitive festivals held by southern German Meistersinger guilds were aimed almost exclusively at men (McCormick, 2015, p. 33). The early twentieth century saw the rise of the modern international music competition in the format we still know today (McCormick, 2015, p. 38). Eligibility by gender was rarely restricted—the Anton Rubinstein International Competition, with its founding in 1890 arguably the first modern competition, being a notable exception to that rule (McCormick, 2015, p. 39). Although most modern competitions, be it in classical music or jazz, did not impose any restrictions on gender, they remained androcentric spaces throughout much of the twentieth century. Performers considering submitting their candidacy may not be fully conscious of this history, but they are undoubtedly aware of other cultural competitions, prizes, and awards, many of which are highly visible and inform and shape one's understanding of a contest.

Furthermore, certain similarities exist between cultural competitions and sports competitions. In the latter case, competitions are typically organized along a strict gender binary, with separate leagues, series, and tournaments for men and women to alleviate any possible physical (dis)advantages stemming from one's assigned sex. Yet, sports competitions are primarily male-oriented, and the male athlete is normative: male athletes or teams are more celebrated by the media, receive better sponsorship deals, are better paid, and so forth. As Caudwell (2010) demonstrated, a strong connection between the rhetoric used in sports and jazz exists. Through a number of examples of what she terms the jazz-sport analogy, she maintained that,

> styles of play and bodily practices in jazz and sport are produced by dominant ideas surrounding embodied performance and the citation of gender. The elements of this dominant aesthetic—individual, "natural," competitive and equipped—operate in jazz and sport to produce gendered versions of creativity and "beauty."
>
> *(Caudwell, 2010, p. 246)*

Such analogies extend to combat metaphors with which jazz is rife. Machismo expressions such as "cutting contests," "band battles," and "chasing saxophones" (as exemplified by some of Dexter Gordon's 1947 recordings) live in many jazz musicians' historical imaginations, and larger-than-life (and indeed often fictional) stories such as the infamous but false near-decapitation incident of saxophonist Charlie Parker have become part of popular culture.[10] The use of sport and combat metaphors that confirm typical gender ideologies is characteristic of what McCormick (2015) called a "game frame" (p. 89). She wrote that, "[o]ne of the more popular metaphors in this vein has been the description of competitions as a 'musical Olympics'" (McCormick, 2015, p. 89), the type of analogy used by Ashton (2013b, para. 1) and Friedwald (2017, para. 5) in their description of the Monk competition. Another remarkable example of such a sports metaphor is the description of the jury of the 2019 competition as the "Murderer's Row [sic] of modern jazz guitar masters" (West, 2019, para. 4), a reference to the now-legendary baseball hitters of the 1927 New York Yankees.

This game frame also operates on a subtler level—for example, when music critics discuss "competitors' repertoire choices as if they were game strategies, pointing out the challenges they present for each individual performer and the possible advantages and disadvantages they could bring" (McCormick, 2015, p. 105). Likewise, the focus often lies on a contender's "physical feats" (McCormick, 2015, p. 105), as evidenced from these reviews from the 2019 guitar finals, with Cecil Alexander displaying "finger work [that] was unbelievably quick and lithe" (West, 2019, para. 7), while Evgeny Pobozhiy held "a pyrotechnic display of physical dexterity" (West, 2019, para. 8) and "threw his whole body into the performance, gyrating and gesticulating with the same fury as his fingers flew across the fretboard" (Sinnenberg, 2019, para. 8).

As McCormick (2015) recognized, the use of this game frame, with its sport and combat metaphors, "invite[s] a particularly gendered interpretation of musical performance. When the music competition is portrayed as a physical contest, it reinforces the tendency for virtuoso musical performance to be interpreted as a display of masculinity" (p. 106). As the jazz–sport analogy (Caudwell, 2010) and the cutting mentality (Walker, 2010) already present in jazz discourses coincide with and are amplified by the game frame (McCormick, 2015) inherent to the discourse on music competitions, it is not surprising that jazz competitions can be perceived as a hypermasculine field.

Besides a lack of female representation and the public perception of a competition as androcentric, the "male gaze" is another factor that may contribute towards gender inequality in jazz contests. While Mulvey's male gaze theory (1975) centered on women as sexual objects in a cinematic context, a similar principle can be applied to the context of jazz competitions, although not necessarily within a framework of sexuality. As noted, competitions hinge on an (assumed) notion of impartiality, but all participants—organizers, jurors, competitors, audiences—enter a contest with their particular set of beliefs and values, not only of competitions but also of the music itself. Jazz is often understood as a "universal and transcendent music, an autonomous art with the same romanticized ideals as western art music" (Whyton, 2010, p. 68). But even though "the ideal of autonomous musical meaning [...] should render the social characteristics of the performer irrelevant" (p. 152), McCormick (2015) clarified that "the effects of gender, age and race cannot be avoided, especially in live performances where the audience can gaze on the musical body of the performer" (p. 152). Following Green (1997), she argued that

> the gender of the musical performer is not merely an extramusical association; it enters into the interpretation of musical meaning, becoming intrinsic to the listening experience. Male and female musicians have different relationships to their audiences because the bodily display involved in the performance of music is enmeshed in gender ideologies.
>
> *(McCormick, 2015, p. 152)*

The most prominent audience members—i.e., those with the most agency—of a competition are the jury panelists. As noted, Jazz Hoeilaart and the Monk competition judges predominantly were experienced jazz performers who enjoyed long and prolific careers. For example, saxophonist Jimmy Heath, who began his professional career in the mid-1940s, was invited to judge the Monk competition four times between 1991 and 2013. By this last time, he was 87 years, to date the oldest judge to have participated in the Monk competition. While adjudicators would not consciously discriminate against women contenders, it stands to argue that having being part of an androcentric culture for so long profoundly shapes their understanding of the culture of jazz.

While many take jazz to be a meritocracy—including saxophonist Sonny Rollins, a contemporary of Heath (as cited in Wahl and Ellingson, 2018, p. 446)—Wahl and Ellingson (2018) indicate that this "ideology of meritocracy" is only one of "two contradictory cultures," the other being "a culture of exclusion [that] relies on essentialist gender distinctions, and structures the occupation in ways that either excludes women or only allows them to fulfill feminized roles within jazz" (p. 446). As exemplified by numerous testimonies (e.g., Tucker, 2000; Enstice and Stockhouse, 2004), many (mostly men) in jazz exhibit "[t]aken-for-granted beliefs about how gender impacts individual capabilities and conventions of instrumentation and performance" (Wahl and Ellingson, 2018, p. 447). They may think of women as inferior musicians, "lacking the same abilities as their male peers" (Wahl and Ellingson, 2018, p. 447), indeed a form of the male gaze: everything is considered from a masculine perspective, the male instrumentalist being normative. Furthermore, within this framework, the female singer is often sexualized, conforming to "the stigmatised stereotype of a female vocalist looking pretty at the front" (G. Robinson, 2020), something that disadvantages this type of competitor even further. Again, it is unlikely that female contenders would have been deliberately excluded or ranked lower than their male counterparts— this would be inadmissible under competition rules. But a juror's value system of jazz would be shaped by the male gaze, especially if he had been a long-standing member of the jazz community, pursuing much of his career at a time when women were even more marginalized than they are today. Therefore, an implicit gender bias may impact or cloud one's judgment, leading to fewer women being selected, ranked, and consecrated in jazz competitions.

The causes I discuss above are by no means the only ones that help explain the significantly lower number of female competitors, let alone female finalists and winners. Several other possible causes are left uninvestigated in this chapter, particularly those that operate on the individual level and can therefore not be easily generalized, such as low self-efficacy (Wehr, 2016, p. 480).[11] However, the outlined causes do lay bare some of the more pertinent issues at stake in moving towards a more gender-inclusive notion of jazz competitions.

Towards Gender-equal Jazz Competitions: Potential Solutions

As can be expected, there is no fix-all solution to redress the gender balance in jazz competitions. For example, altering eligibility criteria is a precarious procedure as changes that could impact the assumed impartiality are undesirable. For this reason, introducing a gender quota, for example, would be shunned by many competition organizers, as would any other structural change that could be perceived as disadvantageous to one or more of the actors. For example, for decades, holding blind auditions has been standard practice in classical ensembles and orchestras to help disable the male gaze. But holding "blind competitions" would not allow for the presence of a live audience, as such withholding the organization of a critical revenue stream.[12]

However, a first and crucial step—and something this chapter aims to achieve—is to reflect on one's accountability. For contest organizers, it would be worthwhile considering the effect a more gender-balanced jury panel could have. For critics reporting on competitions, it would be worthwhile scrutinizing one's writing style for any unnecessary and gendering sport or combat metaphors. Jury guidelines could help raise awareness of implicit gender bias in the evaluation process. Again, these are not magical measures that will instantly lead to more gender-inclusive contests but combined and effectuated in an enduring manner, they will help open up further the field of jazz competitions for women.

The B-Jazz International Contest, the re-envisioned Jazz Hoeilaart, offers a tentative case in point. As noted, 16 of the 38 female competitors participated after 2015 (42.1%), when a new organization took over jazz Hoeilaart. Similarly, in the 40 editions, the two only bands comprising women to have won first place participated after 2015. Last, of the seven female judges over the 40 editions, five were invited after 2015. When asked if this was the result of a conscious strategy, Filip Verneert, the contest director, and Pablo Smet, the contest administrator, said this was not the case, or at least not consciously, for example, through "positive discrimination," as Verneert put it (personal communication, January 20, 2021).[13]

However, the organization did change its jury policy to ensure that the panel of judges is more representative of the field of contenders (personal communication, January 20, 2021). Before 2015, Jazz Hoeilaart had a fixed pool of adjudicators. As noted, many judges were invited multiple times, over time resulting in a network of "usual suspects." McCormick called this type the "professional juror" (p. 191), "instrumentalists whose names are not as widely recognized, but who have established careers in performing and teaching" (p. 192). To ensure some degree of continuity and prevent valuable expertise from being lost, the new organization maintained a select number of pre-2015 judges, but several new jurors were invited. Still, it implemented a new policy whereby a jury is only invited after the finalists have been designated (personal communication, January 20, 2021). This allows the organizers to be more flexible and respond to particular needs: if a band featuring (a) vocalist(s) is selected, one or more vocalist-jurors will be invited as these are more skilled in the technicalities of singing and tend to be less biased towards vocalists (personal communication, January 20, 2021).[14] Furthermore, as such adjudicators are usually women, the male gaze is at least partially eased.

Additionally, the most recent editions comprised several significantly younger jury members, another conscious decision by the current organizers (personal communication, January 20, 2021).

For example, of the six jurors in the 2019 edition, two were younger than thirty. By contrast, in the 2019 edition of the Monk competition, the two youngest of the six judges were in their mid-forties. Younger generations, performers or otherwise, generally are more conscious about gender, women's empowerment, and social justice, especially given the prominence of social movements such as the #MeToo movement. Compared to older generations, they are more used to studying and working in gender-inclusive environments and are therefore less likely to employ a male gaze subconsciously.

Drawing causal conclusions based on a limited data set, sampled from only five editions of a single competition, is not advisable. It is conceivable that the increase in female contenders—and consequently female jurors—is purely coincidental. As the global pandemic caused the cancellation of the 2020 and 2021 editions of the B-Jazz International Contest, it is impossible to observe if this upward trend continues or not.[15] However, it is clear that the current organizers are aware of the gender issue and, if need be, have been shown to allow changes in the procedural design of the contest, all the while safeguarding its identity and core mission (personal communication, January 20, 2021).

Conclusion

Jazz competitions know a fair share of detractors, as became evident from the heated debate on social and digital media that followed a provocative blog post in which pianist Ethan Iverson opined that "there is a dark side to getting judged for your art" (2011, 2012, Please the Committee Section). Yet, they can offer several opportunities not easily afforded elsewhere, such as instant visibility in the media or direct access to high-profile performers. In certain instances, these opportunities are particularly beneficial to women. According to Hope (2017), jazz musicians often rely

> on informal networks—and the networking habits of male jazz musicians do not always suit women. Deals and arrangements are often made at the post-gig bar "hang," not always seen to be the best place for women to do this work. (What Can be Done? section, para. 6)

Such networking opportunities arise at jazz contests, too, but here they can be designed to happen in a safe environment that does not easily allow for potential (sexual) harassment. For example, since 2015, Jazz Hoeilaart has offered all finalists a copious brunch on the day following the competition (but before the award ceremony, alleviating any possible sense of hierarchy among the participants). In this closed event, all contenders and adjudicators, in this particular instance joined by the esteemed guitarist Philip Catherine, who has acted as the contest's official "god-father," can share their post-contest experiences, exchange advice, and make connections for future collaborations. Indeed, some formal and informal associations have their origins in these competition brunches, for example, the guitar duo of Catherine and British guitarist Rob Luft (member of the Phil Meadows Project, a finalist of the 2017 edition), which was programmed to perform at the (aborted) festival Leuven Jazz in 2020 (personal communication, January 20, 2021). Generating this "sense of togetherness," as Verneert called it, is a crucial aspect of the competition, one that is perhaps even more important than the actual process of judging and ranking (personal communication, January 20, 2021).

While competitions hinge on the very idea of inclusiveness, this chapter has shown them to be even less hospitable to women than other fields of the jazz industry. I have considered some of the possible causes of this outspoken gender inequity and proposed some tentative solutions. For it is necessary that jazz contests become more gender-inclusive. After all, despite their inherent competitiveness, they provide an excellent site for offering young musicians, regardless of their gender or sex, visibility, community, and mentorship.

Notes

1 I would like to thank Leonard Brown, Patrick Clerens, Jan Dewilde, Alexander Dhoest, Pablo Smet, Filip Verneert, and the editors of this collection for their assistance and advice. This chapter's research has been made possible through a Fellowship by the Federal Research Organization – Flanders (FWO), project number 208720N.

2 At this point, I want to clarify that I am a middle-class cisgender and heterosexual male from a Western nation. This allowed me to pursue my professional ambitions, including participating in the 2011 edition of Jazz Hoeilaart, from a position of privilege, unhindered by the structural disadvantages experienced by women, minority groups, or others from social or economic disadvantageous milieus. Therefore, I cannot claim to write this chapter from a position of experience. To partly alleviate this lack, I have aimed to use sources by female or non-binary authors, primarily.

3 Within the context of this chapter, gender is understood in the limited sense of a person's assigned sex, adhering to a basic female/male binary. This is because data that reveals a broader spectrum of gender, including non-conforming and non-binary, is unavailable.

4 In the context of these two competitions, international should be understood in the limited meaning of attracting contenders from various countries.

5 For the sake of continuity, I use the designation "Jazz Hoeilaart" throughout this chapter, even when referring to the post-2015 editions.

6 In 2019, pianist Herbie Hancock, who has since long been a Board member, assumed the function of Institute Chairman, upon which the Thelonious Monk Institute of Jazz changed names to the Herbie Hancock Institute of Jazz. That same year, the competition was renamed accordingly. For the sake of continuity, I use the designation "Monk competition" throughout this chapter, even when referring to the 2019 edition.

7 See Abeles and Porter (1978) for a key study on the gender-stereotyping of instruments, and Wahl and Ellingson (2018, pp. 453-456) for a recent examination of the gendering of instruments in a jazz context.

8 See Pellegrinelli et al. (2021) for a study on gender in jazz polls and critics' year-end lists.

9 As data about who serves as a judge for the preliminary round is unavailable, I do not consider this. It is, however, important to note that this preliminary round is blind, with no information on any personal data of the applicants shared with the jury. Obviously, this doesn't apply to vocalists, whose voice typically reveals their gender. For an insider's perspective of the preliminary round of the 2018 piano competition, see Iverson (2017).

10 As Walker (2010) argued, the use of such "language of cutting and carving" leads to an "overstated characterization [that] undermines a whole dimension of this tradition that does not adhere to a narrow image of masculine aggression" (p. 187). Despite the violent images such metaphors recall, the "'cutting mentality' was one, not of anger and hostility, but of intimacy, love, and respect" (p. 187), according to Walker (2010). Also, see Ellis and Osmianski (2016) for an exploration of how women navigate the particular context of jam sessions. The Parker anecdote in question, whereby the saxophonist's fumbling resulted in a cymbal thrown at his head, is a critical element in Damien Chazelle's 2014 film *Whiplash*, where it is employed to justify the emotionally and physically abusive methods used by music teacher Fletcher (J.K. Simmons), one of the film's protagonists. See Wickman (2014) for a deeper analysis of this particular scene.

11 Wehr (2016) offered a model that shows how tokenism and stereotype threat contributes to a lowered self-efficacy, i.e., the "belief in one's own ability to be successful" (pp. 475-476).

12 One could argue for holding semi-blind auditions, with only the jury placed behind screens, but this would only partially alleviate the issue as a vocalist's gender would still be recognizable, as stated in note 9.

13 All translations from Dutch are by the author.

14 For more on the (historical) devaluation of singing, see Pellegrinelli (2008) and Wahl and Ellingson (2018).

15 Before the cancellation of the 2020 edition, the finalists' names were announced, but not yet of the jurors. Interestingly, there was one duo with a female vocalist/bassist and one all-female quintet among the six finalists. Perhaps this is indicative that the increase of female participants for this competition is indeed a trend.

References

Abeles, H. F. and Porter S. Y. (1978). The sex-stereotyping of musical instruments. *Journal of Research in Music Education*, 26(2), 65–75. https://doi.org/10.2307%2F3344880.

Annfelt, T. (2003). Jazz as masculine space. Retrieved from https://kjonnsforskning.no/en/2003/07/jazz-masculine-space.

Appadurai, A. (1986). Introduction: Commodities and the politics of value. In A. Appadurai (Ed.), *The Social Life of Things: Commodities in Cultural Perspective* (pp. 3–63). Cambridge: Cambridge University Press.

Ashton, K. (2013a, September 20). Saxophonist Melissa Aldana makes history at Thelonious Monk Jazz Competition. *Berklee College of Music – College News*. Retrieved from https://college.berklee.edu/news/melissa-aldana-win.

Ashton, K. (2013b, September 9). Three Berklee saxophonists compete for top international title. *Berklee College of Music – College News*. Retrieved from https://college.berklee.edu/news/berklee-saxophonists-compete-top-international-title.

Block, L. (Ed.). (2020). *Gender.macht.musik. – geschlechtergerechtigkeit im jazz*. Retrieved from www.deutsche-jazzunion.de/wp-content/uploads/2020/11/GENDER.MACHT_.MUSIK_.2020_digitalversion.pdf.

Caudwell, J. (2010). The jazz-sport analogue: Passing notes on gender and sexuality. *International Review for the Sociology of Sports*, *45*(2), 240–248. https://doi.org/10.1177%2F1012690209357120.

Data USA. *Jazz and Jazz Studies: Gender Imbalance for Common Institutions*. Retrieved from https://datausa.io/profile/cip/jazz-jazz-studies#demographics.

Derdeyn, S. (2019, June 26). Chile's Melissa Aldana Quartet to turn up heat at jazz festival. *Vancouver Sun*. Retrieved from https://vancouversun.com/entertainment/music/chiles-melissa-aldana-quartet-to-turn-up-heat-at-jazz-festival.

Ellis, Y. and Osmianski, A. (2016). Women and the jazz jam. In W. Knauer (Ed.), *Gender and Identity in Jazz* (pp. 146–161). Hofheim: Wolke Verlag.

Enstice, W. and Stockhouse J. (2004). *Jazzwomen: Conversations with Twenty-one Musicians*. Bloomington and Indianapolis: Indiana University Press.

Friedwald, W. (2017, March 29). Broadway, blues or jazz, singer Cécile McLorin Salvant makes us swoon. *Observer*. Retrieved from https://observer.com/2017/03/cecile-mclorin-salvant-concert-preview/.

Green, L. (1997). *Music, Gender, Education*. Cambridge: Cambridge University Press.

Heyman, M. (2020). The role and function of jazz competitions in Belgium, 1932–39. *Popular Music*, *39*(3–4), 439–458. https://doi.org/10.1017/S0261143020000422.

Hope, C. (2017, June 25). Why is there so little space for women in jazz music? *The Conversation*. Retrieved from https://theconversation.com/why-is-there-so-little-space-for-women-in-jazz-music-79181.

Iverson, E. (2011, April; 2012, August and September). Variants on a theme of Thelonious Monk (including guest post by Eric Lewis). Retrieved from https://ethaniverson.com/rhythm-and-blues/variants-on-a-theme-of-thelonious-monk-including-guest-post-by-eric-lewis/.

Iverson, E. (2017, October 12). Judge not, lest ye be not judged. Retrieved from https://ethaniverson.com/judge-not-lest-ye-be-not-judged/.

Lorge, S. (2019, February). Terri Lyne Carrington: Transform the culture. *DownBeat 86*(2), 24–29.

Martin, P. and Offroy, C. (2019). *Female-male representation in jazz and improvised music genres*. Retrieved from www.grandsformats.com/wp-content/uploads/2020/11/Etude-HF-diaporama-ENGLISH.pdf.

McCormick, L. (2015). *Performing Civility: International Competitions in Classical Music*. Cambridge: Cambridge University Press.

Mulvey, L. (1975). Visual pleasure and narrative cinema. *Screen*, *16*(3), 6–18. https://doi.org/10.1093/screen/16.3.6.

Pellegrinelli, L. (2008). Separated at "birth": Singing and the history of jazz. In S. Tucker (Ed.), *Big Ears: Listening for Gender in Jazz Studies* (pp. 31–47). Durham and London: Duke University Press.

Pellegrinelli, L., Effinger, S. J., Elizabeth, T., Grunenberg, K., Horn, R., Sebesky, G., and Weiner, N. (2021, January 12). Equal at last? Women in jazz, by the numbers. Retrieved from www.npr.org/2021/01/12/953964352/equal-at-last-women-in-jazz-by-the-numbers?t=1616578090496.

Raine, S. (2020). *Keychanges at Cheltenham Jazz Festival: Challenges for Women Musicians in Jazz and Ways Forward for Equal Representation at Jazz Festivals*. Retrieved from doi: 10.13140/RG.2.2.15390.15688.

Renz, T. (2016). *Jazzstudie 2016: Lebens- und Arbeitsbedingungen von Jazzmusiker/-innen in Deutschland*. Retrieved from http://jazzstudie2016.de/jazzstudie2016_small.pdf.

Robinson, C. (2019, March 9). A brief history of the origins of jazz's sexism. Retrieved from https://medium.com/@CRMusicWriter/a-brief-history-of-the-origins-of-jazzs-sexism-3ee4278bcff0.

Robinson, G. (2020, August 20). Grace Robinson: What is there to lose? Retrieved from www.attaboi.online/post/what-is-there-to-lose

Sinnenberg, J. (2019, December 4). Guitarist Evgeny Pobozhiy wins the 2019 Herbie Hancock Jazz Competition. Retrieved from www.capitalbop.com/HERBIE-HANCOCK-COMPETITION-EVGENY-POBOZHIY-GUITAR-2019/.

Tucker, S. (2000). *Swing shift: "All-girl" bands of the 1940s*. Durham and London: Duke University Press.

Wahl, C. and Ellingson, S. (2018). Almost like a real band: Navigating a gendered jazz art world. *Qual Sociol*, *41*, 445–471. https://doi.org/10.1007/s11133-018-9388-9.

Walker, K. (2010). Cut, carved, and served: competitive jamming in the 1930s and 1940s. *Jazz Perspectives*, *4*(2), 183–208. https://doi.org/10.1080/17494060.2010.506032.

Wehr, L. (2016). Understanding the experiences of women in jazz: A suggested model. *International Journal of Music Education*, *34*(4), 472–487. https://doi.org/10.1177%2F0255761415619392.

West, M. J. (2019, December 5). Evgeny Pobozhiy wins Hancock International Jazz Guitar Competition. *JazzTimes*. Retreived from https://jazztimes.com/blog/evgeny-pobozhiy-wins-hancock-international-jazz-guitar-competition/.

Whyton, T. (2010). *Jazz icons: Heroes, Myths and the Jazz Tradition*. Cambridge: Cambridge University Press.

Wickman, F. (2014, October 11). What *Whiplash* gets wrong about genius, work, and the Charlie Parker myth. *Slate*. Retrieved from https://slate.com/culture/2014/10/whiplash-charlie-parker-and-the-cymbal-what-the-movie-gets-wrong-about-genius-work-and-the-10000-hours-myth.html.

16

GENDERED INTERVENTIONS IN EUROPEAN JAZZ FESTIVAL PROGRAMMING: KEYCHANGES, STARS, AND ALTERNATIVE NETWORKS

Kristin McGee

Statement on Gender Terminology: The chapter's statistical analyses employ the terms female, male, non-binary, and mixed (gender). Female (musicians) refers to persons identifying as cisgendered women. Male refers to those identifying as cisgendered men. Non-binary refers to those who identify as trans men or women or explicitly referencing non-binary as their gender in artist bios. Mixed gender refers to musical groups with a variety of genders of musicians (male, female and/or non-binary). This author identifies as a cis-gendered white American women living in the Netherlands.

> If we understand identity as fantasy, we can comprehend how flipping the script does not have much purchase. For decades women will break stereotypes and yet each time still be described as groundbreakers. It would seem that the ground always encroaches around them to be broken again, as if for the first time. The stereotypes continually resurface because the Western epistemology that sets boundaries between self and other serves precisely to keep whiteness and maleness in privileged positions.
>
> (*McMullen 2019*, pp. 22–23)

Introduction

Jazz and its promotion within Europe via festival networks reflect long histories of cross-cultural exchange across the Black Atlantic (Gilroy, 1995; Gillett, 2013). As jazz's popularity diminished during the 1960s, European festivals provided one of a few dependable performance contexts for internationally touring musicians. Further, they provided prestigious platforms for local musicians to stage a uniquely European cosmopolitanism via intercultural improvisation and other performative modes of place making. Festivals also animated the artistic and entrepreneurial cross-cultural entanglements of local jazz artists and programmers who shared the stages with their 'heroes' of an oft-mythologized Black American jazz arts culture (McKay, 2004). In staging such collaborations, postwar jazz festivals offered artistic platforms for renegotiating cultural values in a period of economic and cultural reconfiguration. By participating in the cultural transmission of jazz, European musicians and festival directors updated the romanticized mythologies related to 'real' jazz and its exclusively male canon of 'great men.'[1] Such performative interactions created a space for aesthetic and cultural rejuvenation such as

DOI: 10.4324/9781003081876-18

through the promotion of hybrid jazz forms and especially those energized by popular musics, an interchange which Catherine Tackley describes as "vibrant and ongoing" despite attempts by jazz scholars to continually position jazz at the "cutting edge of musical development" (Tackley, 2018, p. 103).[2] Within these popular jazz festivals, jazz and pop came together within new styles of vocal jazz, jazz fusion, and later other hybrid constellations including electronic jazz, jazz rap, jazz pop, and neo soul.

Such channels of showcasing jazz reflected not simply monolithic, stable processes, but rather translocal, multidirectional interactions, always contingent upon the unique tastes and agencies of individuals involved. Moreover, particular patterns of convening cultural heritage in the United States have differed from the kinds of dialogical histories presented especially by European jazz festivals emerging during the 1960s and 1970s. In reality, these festivals' programs would partially adopt the 'great man' histories presented in preservationist performances, but they would also interject their own 'pluralist' visions for contemporary jazz in relation to their unique cultural disposition as European hosts and mediators of this modern international form. This aesthetic and cultural vision was intimately informed by emerging political and cultural currents from the counterculture to the student democratization movements in Europe and to the Black power and civil rights movements in the United States, in which Black musics occupied center stage (Street, 2015). Such cultural and political encounters afforded an eclectic space for hybrid experimentations such as jazz funk and rock fusion. From their origins in the 1960s and 1970s, the presentation of jazz alongside the vital popular music cultures of those decades, including styles sometimes disparaged as 'not jazz,' appeared not only unproblematic but as a desired aesthetic of these early jazz impresarios.

Yet such countercultural innovations failed to fully transform proscribed gendered expectations within jazz as a patriarchal or "hegemonic masculine" space (Connell and Messerschmidt, 2005), a space through which, according to Nicole Rustin, thinking and writing about jazz as difference has created "blackness, or race, as a metalanguage through which gender, specifically the feminine drops out of view" (Rustin, 2005, p. 446). As Lara Peregrinelli (2008) argued, the splitting of jazz genders into a feminized, sexualized, and commodified jazz vocalism and a masculinized, intellectual jazz instrumentalism appeared "separated at birth" and was prominently codified through jazz historiography and the gendering of popular music spaces through modernity. Sherrie Tucker too reminds us of the heterosexual economy to this split so that the boundaries of the bandstand maintain the construct of heteronormativity within jazz (Tucker, 2008, p. 11). Jazz's penning by male critics, European, and later American, seemed to authenticate such a gendered bifurcation, whose writings reproduced Frankfurt theorists' anxieties about the mass reproduction of music and its emasculating potential. Given the contingency of this gendered severing to jazz's origin narratives, that particular roles remained stubbornly sex segregated in contemporary performance spaces is therefore unsurprising (Istvandity, 2016; Rustin-Paschal and Tucker, 2008).

It is within this context of jazz's entrenched gendered ideologies and with a curiosity about the potential of modern festivals to disengage them that this study begins. In short, it seeks to examine to what extent European jazz festivals have challenged or perpetuated existing gendered paradigms through processes of cultural exchange as solidified within a European festival network. For this chapter, especially recent institutional initiatives are considered, mainly the EU Keychange pledge, developed to address gender imbalances within festival line-ups. In particular, the impact of Keychange upon the programming patterns of four European jazz festivals is examined: the North Sea Jazz Festival, Montreux Jazz Festival, JazzFest Berlin, and the Katowice JazzArt Festival. Through a general examination of these festivals' programming histories in comparison to a focused analysis of these festivals' programs over the period 2015–2019, this chapter reveals how Keychange in combination with related debates have stimulated alternative networks to the earlier and dominant *New York–based jazz star network*. Further, the chapter uncovers how such recent alternative networks are linked to festival programmers' ideological and aesthetic visions, impacting not only gender ratios of festival stages, but other intersecting criteria such as race, culture, and musical genre.

While a growing body of research on gender and jazz has emerged in relation to gender dynamics in the European jazz field, no studies have examined gender in relation to canonization and cultural valorisation within jazz festival performance roosters, and how these might impact the performative and gendered strategies of touring musicians. Yet failing to examine how intersections such as sexuality and race, or the gaps within European jazz culture where the 'feminine drops out of view,' would leave an account of European jazz festivals as sites of cultural heritage incomplete.

This chapter then considers various modalities of identity and especially gender, race, and nationality, acknowledging that bodies encounter obstacles differently as they navigate the spaces of public culture (Crenshaw, 1989). While women have participated in and been represented in European festival culture, more commonly they have been excluded or marginalized within European jazz performance spaces. Therefore, the chapter foregrounds the role of the *festival programmer* and festival programs more broadly to uncover how such staged and performative encounters have powerfully projected a predictably stable gendered script until only recently, while nevertheless providing opportunities for especially an exclusive network of *star female jazz vocalists*.

As will be seen, women celebrated as jazz vocalists and sometimes pianists persevered within EU festivals as complimentary to the 'great men' jazz histories, yet other female artists were continually excluded (mainly those instrumentalists not accommodating this expectation). Consequently, since the 1960s, festivals have fortified barriers for many women seeking participation in this transnational landscape. Further, European jazz festivals acted as prominent conduits for building networks and attributing prestige for touring musicians from abroad and at home. The New York–based star system of the American jazz industry has nowhere been more prominently enacted than on the stages of European jazz festivals since their emergence in the 1960s, and this network further solidified as festivals spread and expanded throughout Europe from the 1970s to today (Bares, 2015; McGee, 2011, 2016).

By collating and aggregating programs of four European jazz festivals, engaging in discussions with festival programmers, and finally analysing representative jazz festival media, this chapter uncovers ways in which European jazz festivals contributed to the hegemonic masculinity of jazz as a mobile, seasonal performative practice, while also considering how festivals altered the lineages of American jazz canons through their programming aesthetics and codification of a transnational star network. Further, the chapter reveals how such persistent patterns reinforced existing ideologies about jazz as masculine practice while forging a uniquely, and by no means homogenous, European 'aesthetic cosmopolitanism' (Regev, 2007).

Through its analysis of the data collected, the chapter reveals that while most women jazz musicians didn't achieve stardom within festival networks, some bolstered international careers because of their personal drive (against all odds) as well as the commitment of particular programmers such as Paul and Jos Acket (programming the North Sea Jazz Festival 1976–1992) and Claude Nobs (programming Montreux 1967–2013). More recently, the pioneering work of programmers Nadin Deventer (JazzFest Berlin) and Martyna Markowska (Katowice JazzArt Fest) and their daring strategies are intermittently explored.[3] Finally, the chapter highlights the powerful role performed by headlining *jazz singers* as critical and mobile representatives of the Black Atlantic, rather than side-stepping their contributions as merely feminized accompaniments to a more rigorous masculinized instrumental jazz framework. In fact, European jazz festivals have always highlighted the central role of vocal jazz for the genre's development and this vision of jazz history had afforded prominent positions for female jazz vocalists, young and old on festival stages.

Women in the (Jazz) Music Industry

In general, participation by women in various jazz music industry roles resembles the patterns exhibited in the popular music industry. For example, a recent study commissioned by the Annenberg Inclusion Initiative (Smith et al., 2019) found that women in the popular music recording industry accounted for 20 percent of recording artists, while as solo acts they represented 31 percent of recording artists.[4] Yet in record production, women were heavily underrepresented accounting for only 2 percent of all producers.[5] As songwriters, they fared slightly better, representing some 12 percent of the industry. Recipients of awards revealed that only 10 percent of Grammy nominees were women, yet 40 percent of nominees for 'Best New Artist' were women, betraying the 'leaky pipe' infrastructure of the popular music industry. Such statistics resemble patterns in the jazz music industry, where older male artists often outrank older women.

Within the jazz recording industry, a study by Pellegrinelli and others in 2021 examined the gender statistics in relation to the annual NPR Critics Jazz Poll between 2013 to 2020. They found that of the top 50 jazz recordings listed, only between 6 percent and 16 percent consisted of women-led projects, until 2019 when this figure rose to 30 percent.[6] The study referenced the perpetual influence of record labels upon critics' polls as well as the insular and homogenous cultural background of jazz critics. Further, it identified a secondary star system for 'exceptional' women jazz artists (Kernodle, 2014; Rustin, 2005) and simultaneously underscored forms of tokenism within such polls, which reward the same small group of female artists time and again.

Top-down initiatives such as Keychange in relation to grass roots campaigns such as WiMN (Women's International Music Network), shesaid.so, and We Have Voice, have only recently impacted jazz recording, performance, and criticism networks. As the #MeToo movement was reignited via social media in 2017, the sudden transformation in 2019 to 30 percent women artists in these polls seems less surprising, as social campaigns influence not only critics' tastes but the way that other gatekeepers consider nominations and key positions within performance contexts.

Gender Dynamics in the European Jazz Industry

Given the heterogeneity of the European music industry, few scholars have attempted European-wide gender analyses within the jazz industry, but some have considered jazz culture in specific national contexts. A recent study by Christa Bruckner-Haring (2012) examined patterns of enrolment in BA and MA jazz programs in Austria, revealing disparities between perceived ratios of women in the local jazz scenes and university student jazz performers, of whom only 4 percent to 21 percent were women. The curricular and instrumental choices of female students resembled patterns of participation long established within jazz education with the majority of women opting (or encouraged) to study voice and then piano, followed by saxophone with very few women performing other instruments. Other observations identified more women leading their own jazz groups and audiences becoming more diverse in terms of gender (Bruckner-Haring 2012, p. 136).[7] Finally, in 2020, a study in Germany by the Deutsche Jazz Union examined union members' attitudes regarding the gender dynamics in the German jazz field. Members consisted of 76 percent male and 22 percent female members (*Gender.Macht.Musik* 2020, p. 68).

Another gender-related study by Björck and Bergman compared the impact of two 'women in jazz festivals' in 2015. The study highlighted the differences in culture between Sweden and the United States, such as the social democratic and institutionalized initiatives of the Swedish government versus the more grass-roots oriented networks in the United States, including the Sisters in Jazz program established in 1997. In 2011, a new Swedish Agency, Musikverket, was set up to support projects working for greater gender equality in music. A more extreme policy in the Swedish context was to remove subsidies for those festival programs failing to meet a 25 percent ratio of female performers. After the Svensk Jazz festival lost their funding, heated debates regarding governmental 'meddling' and meritocracy ensued within the Swedish jazz field (Björck and Bergman, 2018, p. 44).

These studies' focus upon gender dynamics in performance and education contexts reveals how initiatives such as women's jazz festivals and networks could be useful in providing support as well as networking opportunities for women, but that the 'women in jazz' label was considered simultaneously problematic by artists trying to establish professional profiles (Björck and Bergman, 2018, pp. 49–50). One observable phenomenon is the tendency of women musicians to perform crossover genres rather than historically canonized instrumental jazz styles. In Sweden, many women avoid identifying themselves as jazz musicians (even if they had jazz training), and this self-designation often results in older, more traditional jazz clubs excluding them (Björck and Bergman, 2018, p. 10). Clearly the powerful mythologies and performative scripts of jazz as a hegemonic masculine practice could easily discourage women from adopting this label.

Myrtille Picaud's survey of jazz club and festival performances in Paris revealed similar yet more discouraging patterns, with women occupying only 10 percent of club performances, while for festivals in particular, their presence was virtually non-existent. The value of women's participation in the French jazz landscape had previously been studied by Marie Buscatto (2007) who found that women were not only more likely to perform as vocalists, but that these performances were often denigrated as "less than jazz" in comparison to their male instrumentalist peers. For Picaud and Buscatto, such unequal value attributions shored up established gender hierarchies in Paris, where "vocal jazz further appears socially constructed as a double periphery in the scene, the center being defined as male, and originating from Europe or the United States" (Picard, 2013, p. 134). Finally, Picaud found that male American musicians were the most highly valued in both symbolic and economic terms, concluding that Paris retains its intermediary position "as an ex-colonial capital, in international jazz circulations within which the United States remain dominant" (Picaud 2016 p. 140).

Keychange Pledge and Jazz Festivals

Recognition of the paucity of women in jazz festivals has precipitated various social and musical reactions within the history of jazz. During the 1970s, the women's liberation's and feminist movements drew attention to women's culture, offering collective platforms to ameliorate their marginalization in jazz, such as through the creation of the first women's jazz festival, the Kansas City Festival in 1978 (Brewer, 2017), followed by other women-centered festivals outside the United States such as the Melbourne Women's Jazz Festival in 1997 (Denson, 2014). Despite their value in fostering women's creativity and increasing their visibility, women in jazz festivals alone could not overcome the pernicious inequalities in live music performance arenas more broadly, with such inequalities persisting into the twenty-first century.

Current studies on gender dynamics within the live music industry have prompted both quantitative studies as well as new gender initiatives within Europe (Jutbring, 2016; Codrea-Rado, 2018). The most important is the Keychange Initiative established in 2015 by Vanessa Reed, CEO of PRS (Publishing Rights Society) Foundation in the UK. The foundation's first action was the composition and publication of a manifesto to the European Union, which highlighted the excessive sexism and disparities in economic opportunities for under-represented groups within the music industry. Keychange has since become an international platform supported by the Creative Europe Programme, which now aspires to be a "global movement working towards a total restructure of the music industry in reaching full gender equality" (About Us).

In 2015, Keychange initiated its 50/50 gender balance pledge for 2020 (and currently 2022). While the 50/50 pledge utilizes a binary gender frame, it offers festivals the option to flexibly interpret the scale based upon the "one women on stage" principle, claiming that even a single female artist provides important role models for girls and other women. As argued by Sarah Raine in relation to the Cheltenham Jazz Festival in the UK (having signed the pledge in 2019), Keychange provides "increased opportunities for women musicians in a male-dominated music scene" while also "shining a spotlight on gender imbalance." According to Tina Edwards of the *Guardian*, such a commitment could deliver immediate results, such as when Cheltenham's programme rose from 22 female musicians in 2017 to 63 in 2019 (Edwards, 2021). Yet as Raine and others acknowledge, this initiative cannot singularly resolve "pervasive issues of access, education, support and value within the jazz scene, and most likely the wider music industry" (Raine, 2020, p. 8–9).

Given the changing climate in the European music industry stimulated by such initiatives, in the following, the two smaller, festivals (Katowice JazzArt and Jazzfest Berlin) are compared to the two larger festivals (North Sea and Montreux) to delineate particular programming strategies undertaken to transform particular gendered ideologies first enacted during the late 1960s.[8]

Findings: Convening Gender in Four European Jazz Festivals (1964–2020)

Contextualizing recent transformations within longer festival histories enables an expanded perspective on moments of rupture and consistency within festival programming. This section therefore offers an overview of patterns discovered within the programs of these festivals over two periods: First, summaries of the genders and nationalities of 'stars' are presented over the festivals' entire histories. Second, the period from just before the emergence of the Keychange Pledge, or from 2015 to 2019, is studied with greater attention to the genders of 'all musicians on stage.'

The entire histories of these festivals range from 1964 to 2020. The first three festivals were established decades ago (JazzFest Berlin in 1964; Montreux in 1967; and North Sea in 1976) while the Katowice is relatively new with its first edition in 2012. Especially Montreux and NSJF are well-known in the international jazz industry and have acquired significant cultural capital for American jazz musicians; further, they are coveted festivals for both emerging and established international jazz artists.

To analyse programming patterns of these festivals' entire histories, four researchers (Nora Leidinger, Jasper Janssen, Andreea Dascalu, and myself) collated data related to perceived or stated gender of the lead artist of a group,[9] the stated nationality or country of residence of the performing group, the perceived or stated race or cultural background of a lead artist, the genre, and the numbers of years in which a particular artist or group performed for a festival.[10] In total we looked at 12,693 concerts within these four festivals. Both Montreux and the North Sea have increased dramatically in size since inception, from around 15 to 150 concerts a year, while the JazzFest Berlin has remained relatively stable with some 30 concerts per year. The Katowice, as a small-scale, city arts festival, programs between 10 to 20 unique performances/events a year.

Our second, more-detailed, analysis of the period from 2015 to the latest edition before the COVID-19 pandemic (2019 or 2020) considered a greater number of parameters. Here, we examined the total numbers of musicians and their genders on stage as well as their nationality or performance home-base. Information was retrieved from a variety of sources, such as programs provided by festival directors, personal artist pages, materials published on festival websites, Wikipedia artist entries, and live festival footage on YouTube. Since acquiring this data was so time-consuming, we limited our search of one of our parameters, 'all musicians on stage' to the last five years up to COVID-19 (2015–2019).

Festivals' Entire Histories (1964–2020): An American, Male Jazz Star Network

Our analyses uncovered star line ups of mostly African American, and later white, American male stars, who dominated the main stages as well as images presented in posters, marketing materials, and histories of the two larger festivals (Montreux and NSJF).[11] When considering artists with the most durable performing careers and star presence in these festivals, the top ten list betrays the important focus of festivals upon contemporary cross-currents in jazz with popular musics, and especially within jazz fusion. In order of prominence, this 'star' list features Herbie Hancock (performing during 30 different years), Chick Corea (25 years), Roy Hargrove (25 years), B. B. King (25 years), George Benson (22 years), Van Morrison (22 years), McCoy Tyner (22 years), John Scofield (21 years), David Sanborn (20 years), and Al Jarreau (19 years).

The majority are, not surprisingly, American (except Van Morrison), and most became musically active in the period of the 1960s, 1970s and 1980s (except B. B. King and McCoy Tyner). These musicians were praised for fusing commercially successful Black music genres such as funk, soul, and

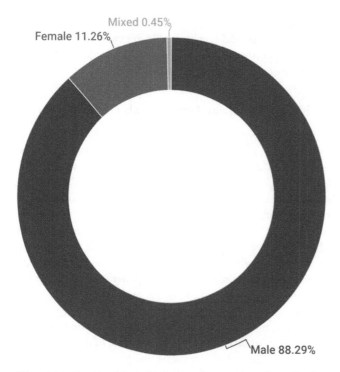

Figure 16.1 Combined festivals' gender representation of stars for their entire histories (1964–2020).

rhythm and blues with jazz, but also other genres including rock and pop. A prominent example of this transformation from older jazz styles to fusions of popular music with jazz is alto saxophonist David Sanborn, a staple of many pop and rock recordings of the 1970s and 1980s and an artist still occupying main stages at these two larger festivals. Unsurprisingly, none of these postwar jazz stars are women, although some have performed with leading male artists, especially as back-up singers. Of the top ten list, three are vocalists (Benson, Jarreau, and Morrison), but two of these artists, Benson and Morrison are also guitarists (and thus instrumentalists), which satisfies their performative expectations as 'bonified' masculine jazz musicians.

Many of the earlier so-called legends who headlined the festivals in the late 1960s and 1970s deceased or stopped performing in the 1980s and 1990s such as Dizzy Gillespie, Count Basie, Ella Fitzgerald, and Miles Davis. In our collated programming lists of the entire festival histories, Herbie Hancock emerges not only as reigning star having travelled to Europe more than 30 years, but he also occupied a dominant image in festival marketing. As the runner-up, Chick Corea, deceased in 2021, played all three festivals at various times from 1972 to 2019 with gaps of no more than three years between tours. Hard bop trumpeter, Roy Hargrove also played most years beginning in 1975 and last performing in 2018.

Women Stars in EU Festival Programs (< 15%)

The ratio of women performing over these festivals' duration corresponds with ratios determined by scholars in other jazz spheres. Our analyses lead to the obvious conclusion that women were gravely underrepresented and, when they did perform, they generally occupied expected roles as vocalists, and sometimes pianists. Moreover, many touring women vocalists crossed over into other genres or never identified as jazz artists, such as Aretha Franklin or more recently Jorja Smith, a Grammy-nominated English pop, soul, and contemporary R 'n' B vocalist. Here too, European jazz festivals supported other's view that women artists in jazz festivals never easily identified with the hegemonic masculinity of jazz performance practice.

In the top approximately 2.6 percent (or the top 222 of 6338 performing artists) of the most durable festival artists (the 'stars'), or those performing seven or more years, just 26 acts are led by or feature a woman. **In other words, women represent just 12 percent of star acts**. Women artists and especially jazz vocalists consistently performed in European jazz festivals as stars, yet their careers exhibited more touring gaps and therefore they acquired fewer spots in these superstar networks.

Of the top women performing nine or more years since the late 1960s, only three are non-vocalists: the multifaceted and virtuosic American pianist Dorothy Donegan (9 years), whose recordings and performances are often disregarded in dominant jazz histories; the experimental New York pianist and composer Carla Bley (10); and Dutch saxophonist Candy Dulfer (17 years), one of the top selling contemporary jazz artists (of all genders) since the 1990s, whose musical contributions receive little recognition in modern jazz polls and histories. The female stars in order of career longevity are:

1. Dee Dee Bridgewater (18 years, Black American soul jazz vocalist)
2. Candy Dulfer (17 years, Dutch saxophonist and vocalist)
3. Rita Reys (16 years, white Dutch jazz vocalist)
4. Dianne Reeves (15 years, Black American jazz vocalist)
5. Diana Krall (10 years, white Canadian pianist and vocalist)
6. Chaka Khan (10 years, Black American funk, fusion, and pop vocalist)
7. Carla Bley (10 years, New York pianist and composer)
8. Betty Carter (9 years, American jazz vocalist)
9. Etta James (9 years, Black American soul and rhythm 'n' blues singer)
10. Dorothy Donegan (9 years, Black American pianist)
11. Tania Maria (9 years, Brazilian pianist and singer)
12. Tuck and Patti (9 years, mixed-race American contemporary jazz duo)
13. Greetje Kauffeld (9 years, Dutch jazz vocalist).

Current Creative Director of North Sea Jazz, Michelle Kuypers stressed that these headlining, female jazz vocalists such as Dianne Reeves were a core facet of the festival and a main attraction for attendees (Kuypers, 2021).

Each of these performers secured prominent positions in the European jazz star network, yet few would figure in the many jazz histories written of either American or European jazz in the second half of the twentieth century. Others well-canonized in American histories include Carmen McRae, Nina Simone, and Ella Fitzgerald, who performed relatively often in earlier decades, yet these older (and eventually deceased) musicians stopped performing during the 1980s and 1990s. Despite the prominence of such star women in European festivals, as our analyses reveal, women tended to account for only between 5 percent to 15 percent of performers on stage, a figure mirroring the statistics of other facets of the jazz industry, at least until alternative strategies have been taken by the two smaller jazz festivals since 2018.

Of these female European festival stars, the majority are American (69%) and most, but not all are not surprisingly vocalists of contemporary as well as more traditional jazz styles. In addition to the vocal stars of jazz, both Etta James and Chaka Khan pioneered new forms of popular music in their decades of intense musical output (1960s and 1980s, respectively) such as combinations of rhythm 'n' blues, soul, and funk with rock and pop. Only Carla Bley, co-founder of the politically engaged Jazz Composers Guild in New York in the 1960s (Piekut, 2010), performed more avant garde jazz during the 1960s and 1970s. Of this network, seven are non-American, including Dutch vocalists Reys (the 'first lady' of European jazz), Kauffeld, and Jannah; Brazilian pianist and vocalist Tania Maria, Dutch saxophonist Tineke Postma, and Beninese vocalist Angélique Kidjo.

Also unsurprising was the prominent role of pianists as the second most common instrument. Given existing instrumental paradigms in jazz culture, very few brass or reed instrumentalists acquired career longevity, except saxophonist Candy Dulfer, who ranks number 19 in the overall top 100 list. Yet given Dulfer's continued popularity in both European festival stages, as well as within international contemporary jazz charts, she rarely features within jazz scholarship of the postwar period (McGee, 2013), while the recorded output of contemporaries Sanborn or Metheny are examined more extensively in contemporary studies (Fellezs, 2011; Nicholson, 2014).

Festivals Pre- and Post-Keychange (2015–2019): An Intersectional Analysis

The recent impact of Keychange and other ideological and political movements is hardly discernible in the composite festival lists which prioritized both male artists and instrumental genres associated with jazz fusion. Yet as we narrow our scope to the period after 2015, we begin to see not only modest transformations in the nationality and genders of performers on stage, but also changes in the performance practices and musical aesthetics of festival performances, changes reflecting the broader culture of DAW (digital audio workstation) driven musical styles as well as the aesthetic preferences of current festival programmers.

That a younger generation of programmers have differently impacted the aesthetics and ideologies of European jazz festivals is especially apparent in smaller and more locally based festivals. For example, Deventer and Markowska both commented upon the generational shift of their production teams in contrast to prior festival directors. With the entrance of these younger programmers, the design and promotional strategies too have undergone significant transformations. Such policies led these festivals to not only reposition established rosters and networks, but to critically anticipate the backlash against such strategies. Two techniques taken were to focus upon artists from the local and oftentimes, more experimental music scenes, such as represented by Polish electronic keyboardist and sample-based artist Joanna Duda (Keen), as well as programming under-represented artists outside the American or New York–based jazz star network. Further, both Deventer and Markowska sought to cultivate challenging projects with connections to other arts disciplines such as film, visual arts, and dance; such interarts connections became the driving feature of especially the Katowice JazzArt Festival since 2015.

Programming choices are often tied to forms of aesthetic curiosity in connection to the philosophies of admired exploratory jazz artists. To illustrate, for the Katowice festival, Markowska and her team adopted artist driven aesthetics about experimentation and border transgressions, such as 2020 motto "It's not jazz. For us, it's a process of transcending barriers" inspired by Abdullah Ibrahim. This motto aptly intimated the ways the festival attempted to re-integrate visual and corporeal arts such as dance into jazz festival culture in the virtual environment.

Comparing the entire festival histories with the period 2015–2019 reveals modest changes in programming patterns in relation to gender, race, and nationality. Interventionist feminist strategies, and now widely visible forms of digitally engaged political activism have presumably impacted programmers' philosophies as they support the rhetoric of freedom of expression, female empowerment, and racial justice in their programs and marketing campaigns. For example, Markowska argued that looking beyond established New York networks afforded her the flexibility to avoid the quality versus quota arguments, as locating excellent non-male musicians outside this narrow range was quite easy. Furthermore, by promoting the work of artists from under-represented regions such as Southern Europe, Africa or within Poland, a different kind of contemporary jazz network could materialize (Markowska, 2021). For Deventer, by prioritizing local musicians from Berlin as well as proactively contacting musicians from her team's network, altering the gender ratios was less challenging than expected. Finally, while the cultural and gendered identity was a main consideration, Deventer in particular claimed that because of environmental implications, flying musicians from North America every year was no longer tenable, and thus reinforcing local network's relation also to the current ecological crisis (Deventer, 2021).

When we examine programs only from 2015 to 2019, a few patterns emerge which indicate the impact of Keychange on festival line-ups. In terms of composite numbers, 166 artists (of 1189 total) have performed *at least two different years* between 2015 and 2019 within these four festivals; these artists represent the top 14 percent of total performances. In total, **21 percent of all festival acts from this period are female-led acts** (32 acts total), which reflects an increase of 9 percent from the 12 percent of prior decades. Further, an increasing number of mixed-gendered star acts appears, or acts *without* a clear featured artist, and these represent 3 percent of the top 14 percent of most durable acts.

Of these 32 female-led acts, the majority are vocalists (24) led by reigning star Cécile McLorin Salvant, a frequent favourite of critics polls in the United States (Pellegrinelli et al., 2021). Other established vocal stars include Dianne Reeves, Emeli Sandé, Melody Gardot, Somi, Diana Krall, and Dee Dee Bridgewater. Consistent with the entire histories of European jazz festivals, women continue to cultivate innovative vocal styles combining jazz and popular genres such as the jazz funk and neo soul of Hiatus Kaiyote (Australia), the international Caribbean and polygeneric jazz of Bokanté (with vocalist Malika Tirolien), the indie-driven neo soul of singer songwriter Lianne La Havas (UK), and the creative percussive and electronic vocal improvisations of the duo Ibeyi (France).

The increasing number of 'durable' female instrumentalists include pianists Kris Davis, Diana Krall, Eve Risser, Kaja Draksler; saxophonists Tineke Postma, Melissa Aldana, Angelika Niescier; guitarists Mary Halvorson, Ruthie Foster, and vocalist/guitarist Fleurine Verloop; and trumpeter Laura Jurd (of Dinosaur). The prominent positions of Polish alto saxophonist Angelika Niescier, Chilean tenor saxophonist Melissa Aldana, and Dutch tenor saxophonist Tineke Postma reflect the

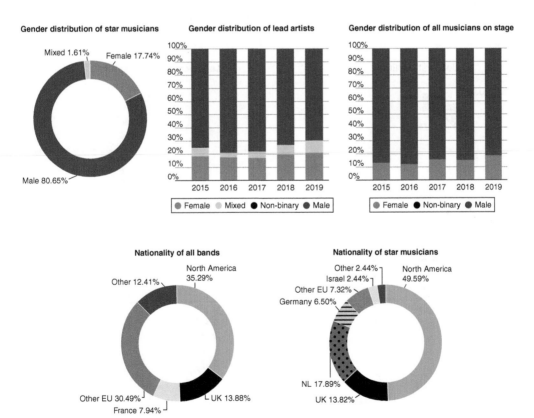

Figure 16.2 Cumulative festivals' gender distribution of micro-stars, lead artists, all musicians on stage, and nationality, 2015–2019.

growing internationalism of the jazz performance world, which increasingly attracts artists from outside of the United States whose profiles benefit from international digital promotion networks. Given the prejudices of ageism for mature women performers, mapping these performers' future performances will be necessary to ascertain if such initiatives aid in promoting sustainable careers such as of those patriarchs Hancock, Jones, and Corea, now the subject of countless tributes and birthday celebration concerts within festival programs. Of this list, only Bridgewater and Reeves appear as stalwarts of European festival stages.

If we take into account the possible impact of Keychange either indirectly or directly,[12] we find that individual ratios of star female acts averaged over the five-year period are 14 percent for Montreux, 19 percent for NSJF, 25 percent for JazzFest Berlin, and 26 percent for Katowice. However, since 2018, both Katowice and JazzFest Berlin have successfully programmed 50 percent acts which are either women-led or mixed-gendered, indicating that such initiatives can immediately transform the variety of gender representations on festival stages.

While the total number women-led acts accounted for around 21 percent on average in the last five years, **women musicians on stage** accounted for, on average, some 15 percent of all musicians, which means that the ratio of women-led star acts has risen some 9 percent (from 12%) while the number of women performing as backing musicians has likely increased even further as more women take up supporting instrumental roles.

While these festivals still feature a large percentage of American or US-based artists, the ratios have gradually diminished from the nearly 70 percent of American artists featured in earlier decades.[13] Each festival also currently features a higher proportion of home artists than in prior decades, ranging from 25 percent German artists for JazzFest Berlin, to 36 percent Polish artists for Katowice JazzArt Festival. A clear trend is a much wider diversity of artists from all over the world, but especially from

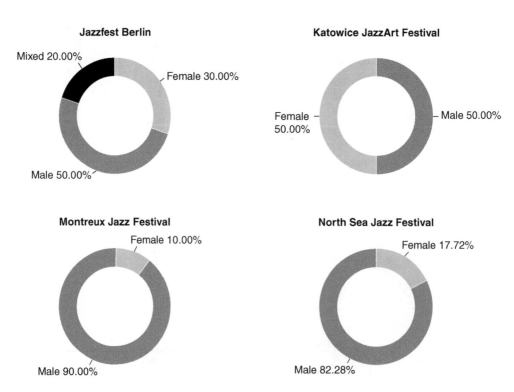

Figure 16.3 Individual festivals' gender distribution of micro-stars, 2015–2019.

Europe with steadily rising numbers from South America, yet low representation from Asia and Africa. The statistics of women-led acts resemble those of all genders on stage during this five-year period. Between 2015 and 2019, roughly 30 percent of women on stage came from the United States, and around 20 percent represented the home country.

As always, national and cultural identities are complex and often represent multiple cultural and national backgrounds, such as the self-identified multicultural backgrounds of artists like Somi (American/Rwandan/Ugandan) and Cécile McLorin Salvant who identifies as French Haitian but who was born in the United States. As Yoko Suzuki (2013) revealed, women jazz musicians maintain complex forms of identification in relation to jazz performance practice, at times expressing how their gender and race are experienced variously as assets in the acquisition of cultural capital to 'double negatives' in essentialist jazz lineages and performance expectations. Especially within European jazz festivals, the colonial and post-colonial histories are always already mapped onto the bodies and inform the strategies of performing jazz artists as they adapt and pioneer new performance scripts for the future.

Conclusion: An Invitation for Future Exploration

This gendered analysis of European jazz star networks revealed patterns of intense intercultural contact through the cultivation of a predominantly male network of New York–based jazz stars beginning during the late 1960s, one which coalesced around the sound of jazz fusion during 1980s and 1990s. Yet, claims to comprehensive representation in accounting for patterns of prestige and cultural heritage through Europe in the twentieth century cannot yet be established without further comparison to other European festivals. Moreover, that new genres would emerge as the center of European jazz festival culture such as jazz fusion and later electronic jazz and neo soul is unsurprising given the cosmopolitan and eclectic tastes of early festival programmers such as Nobs and Acket. Such genre couplings gave way to the new patriarchs of European jazz in the last decades of the twentieth century, especially through the persistent contributions and appearances of jazz explorers Hancock, Jones, and Corea. Yet that the ratios of non-male genders would appear largely unchanged belies the continued intersecting obstacles faced by women and other under-represented groups in the jazz festival economy. Nevertheless, women jazz vocalists forged their own star networks on European stages and were an important part of the emergence of new aesthetic styles and performance practices. The prominence of jazz stars Bridgewater, Reeves, and Reys, dominating the mainstages of European jazz festivals for decades speaks to the important role of vocal jazz for European jazz culture in the postwar period. Their spellbinding performances, documented in various concerts at Montreux are now the stuff of legends.

Keychange, when implemented by risk-taking programmers as a means to alter not only the genders of bodies on stage, but the very aesthetic and performative scripts of cross-cultural festival encounters, reminds us of Nicole Rustin's entreaty to complicate our ideas about genius and "blackness," allowing the possibility of " 'exiling' masculinity, or conventional notions of authority, authenticity, and brilliance, to the margins of race" (Rustin, 2005, p. 460). These invitations offer a springform to put aside star networks, familiar canons, and step outside our safety zones. The study of such a European jazz festival past endows us with a richer understanding of prior negotiations undertaken by such 'exceptional' female stars. This research is emboldened by this Keychange initiative as well as by the creativity and networking acumen of programmers such as Deventer and Markowska willing to navigate new territory in a time of precarity and market-driven imperatives. Their curiosity fueled by aspirations to enhance jazz careers and improve gender dynamics on festival stages aligns with contemporary debates about race and justice within the twenty-first century, and sets a new precedent for jazz in European festivals.[14]

Notes

1 See the widely cited critiques of French and German writers, including within Charles Delaunay and Hugues Panassié's magazine *Le Jazz Hot* during the 1930s, Joachim Berendt's *Das Jazz Buch* (1953), Hugues Panassié's *The Real Jazz* (1946), which maligned those popular jazz performers (and especially women) incorporating the more embodied aspects of jazz culture such as dancing and singing into theatrical entertainment contexts. In their studies of German jazz in the postwar period, William Bares (2012) and Uta Poiger (2000) would identify alternative and sometimes paradoxical modalities of intersecting identifications within Berlin's jazz milieu, such as the associations of jazz's perceived excesses with fascism, or of jazz's sexuality as threats to masculine respectability.

2 I'd like to thank Catherine Tackley for her useful comments and critiques of this chapter as well as Monika Herzog and the other editors of this edition for their helpful suggestions.

3 An article exploring the programming strategies, philosophies, and aesthetics of these two festivals in more detail is forthcoming.

4 This study looked at the Hot 100 Billboard charts from 2012 to 2018 (Smith et al., p. 7).

5 With the rise of the DAW (digital audio workstation), many more women are producing at home or in private studios and these artists often fall under the radar of official industry statistics. An excellent study on music production in relation to gender is Paula Wolfe's *Music in the studio: Creativity, Control, and Gender in Popular Music Sound Production* (2020), which offers ethnographic experiences of women producers while also highlighting the exclusionary gendered networks in the popular music field.

6 According to this summary, the NPR Music Jazz Critics Poll has been published by NPR Music since 2013, and it is the "largest annual jazz critics poll, drawing the participation of up to nearly one hundred and fifty critics who contribute to a range of media outlets" (Pellegrinelli et al., 2021).

7 Interviews too revealed similar ideologies replicated within prior studies regarding the perceived gendered capabilities of women, such as notions that men were more individualistic or rebellious, or that women had less stamina, and finally that women would drop out earlier to prioritize roles as mothers and wives. A pervasive myth was that men excelled at structured thinking and were therefore better improvisers. Some students recalled being discouraged from following jazz curricula in favour of classical music programs (Bruckner-Haring 2012, p. 13).

8 The larger and most established festivals, the North Sea Jazz Festival and Montreux are historicized in existing sources (Bares, 2015; McGee, 2016; Rentsch, 2010; Ténot, 1996).

9 In relation to gender binary limitations, we tried to incorporate a spectrum of gender identifiers, but this became challenging without in-depth study or sensitive disclosures by artists that would ostensibly objectify sexuality by "fixing jazz subjects as sex objects" (Tucker 2008, p. 2). A survey of promotional material however, revealed an increase in artists openly identifying as either trans or in non-binary terms in recent years. And this fact betrays the limitations of the gender binary and especially given the history of disavowing gender and sexuality diversity within jazz (Tucker, 2008). Nevertheless, we wanted to gain an overall view of how especially the featured artists related to prior gender ratios within festival programs and, further, how this has impacted the careers of (those perceived or identifying as) women.

10 I'd like to thank Leidinger, Janssen, and Dascalu for their time-consuming collation of these festivals. Leidinger provided one interview for the chapter as well as provided translations from German to English. Janssen also checked the figures and created useful graphics for the chapter.

11 For comparison, we collated statistics of both individual festivals and composite lists to gain a local versus international representation of the larger European festival circuit. Obviously, more studies of different festivals would be required to draw comprehensive conclusions about the stars (and resulting canons) of European jazz festival culture more broadly. Additionally, we mapped lists of artists who exhibited some level of durability, including those performing more than seven years during the entire festival histories. For the more recent period pre- and post-COVID-19, we measured artists performing more than two times to identify a newer generation of jazz stars. This last parameter was also meant to extrapolate the impact of Keychange and other gendered debates upon the recent jazz festivals programs.

12 Both JazzFest Berlin and Katowice signed the pledge in 2018 and 2019 respectively.

13 The national and cultural backgrounds of performing artists have always been complex and dependent upon prevailing cultural hierarchies such as those attempting to highlight or delimit the duality of national or cultural backgrounds, versus artists altering their cultural identification once immigrating to the United States to establish their careers in the centers of jazz production and valorization. Nevertheless, I felt it was important to include nationality, as it highlights the changing centers and peripheries of jazz booking and programming networks in relation to ideologies of national provenance and prestige.

14 To acquaint yourself with these artists, explore the Spotify playlist featuring "Women in European Jazz Festivals" at https://open.spotify.com/playlist/5vCdF9pWtl8TWakGApRSOY?si=CIIWJgOpSEiJ0Jk QXTa4QQ.

References

About Us. Keychange. Retrieved from www.keychange.eu/about-us.

Bares, W. K. (2012). Way out east: Cowboys and pioneer women on Berlin's jazz frontier. *Jazz Research Journal*, *6*(2), 170–200.

Bares, W. K. (2015). Transatlanticism as Dutch national spectacle: universalism and postpolitics at the North Sea Jazz Festival. *American Music*, *33*(3), 345–374.

Berendt, J. E. (1953). *Das Jazzbuch*. New York: Lawrence Hill.

Björck, C. and Å. Bergman. (2018). Making women in jazz visible: Negotiating discourses of unity and diversity in Sweden and the US. *IASPM@JOURNAL*, *8*(1), 42–58.

Brewer, C. G. (2017). *Changing the Tune: The Kansas City Women's Jazz Festival, 1978–1985*. Denton, TX: University of North Texas Press.

Bruckner-Haring, C. (2012). Women in contemporary Austrian jazz. In A. Arvidsson (Ed.). *Gender, Jazz, Authenticity: Proceedings of the 10th Nordic Jazz Research Conference*. Stockholm, Sweden.

Buscatto, M. (2007). *Femmes du jazz: musicalités, féminités, marginalisations*. Paris: CNRS Editions.

Codrea-Rado, A. (2018). 'There's still a big imbalance': how music festivals are working on gender equality." *The Guardian*, May 11. Retrieved from www.theguardian.com/music/2018/may/11/ music-festivals-agender-equality-wireless-green-man-slam-dunk-male-lineups.

Connell, R. W. and Messerschmidt, J. W. (2005). Hegemonic masculinity: Rethinking the concept. *Gender & Society*, *19*(6), 829–859.

Crenshaw, K. (1989). Mapping the margins: Intersectionality, identity politics, and violence against women of color. *Stanford Law Review*, *43*(6), 1241–1299.

Denson, L. (2014). Perspectives on the Melbourne International Women's Jazz Festival. *Jazz Research Journal*, *8*(1–2), 163–181.

Deventer, N. (2021). Online interview by Nora Leidinger via Google Meet. March 15.

Edwards, T. (2021). Female UK jazz musicians face sexual harassment and discrimination, says report. Feb. 16, 2021. *The Guardian*.

Fellezs, K. (2011). *Birds of Fire: Jazz, Rock, Funk, and the Creation of Fusion*. Duke University Press.

Gender.Macht.Musik. Geschlechtergerechtigkeit im jazz. (2020). Deutsche Jazzunion.

Gillett, R.A. (2013). Jazz women, gender politics, and the Francophone Atlantic. *Atlantic Studies: Literary, Cultural, and Historical Perspectives*, *10*(1), 109–130.

Gilroy, P. (1995). *The Black Atlantic: Modernity and double-consciousness*. Cambridge, MA: Harvard University Press.

Istvandity, L. (2016). Sophisticated lady: Female vocalists and gendered identity in the Brisbane jazz scene. *Journal of World Popular Music*, *3*(1), 75–89.

Jutbring, H. (2016). Festivals framed as unequal: Piggybacking events to advance gender equality. *Annals of Leisure Research*, *19*(4), 519–537.

Kernodle, T. (2014). Black women working together: Jazz, gender, and the politics of validation. *Black Music Research Journal*, *34*(1), 27–55.

Kuypers, Michelle. (2021). Online interview with Kristin McGee via Google Meet. April 6.

Markowska, M. (2021). Online Interview with Kristin McGee via Zoom, Feb. 15.

McGee, K. (2011). New York comes to Groningen: Jazz star circuits in the Netherlands. In B. Dueck and J. Toynbee (Eds.) *Migrating Musics: Media, Politics and Style*. London: Routledge.

McGee, K. (2013). Promoting affect and desire in the international world of smooth jazz. *Jazz Perspectives*, *7*(3), 251–286.

McGee, K. (2016). Staging jazz pasts within commercial European jazz festivals: The case of the North Sea Jazz Festival. *European Journal of Cultural Studies*, April 2016, 1–27.

McKay, G. (2004). 'Unsafe Things Like Youth and Jazz': Beaulieu Jazz Festivals (1956–1961), and the Origins of Pop Festival Culture in Britain. In A. Bennett (Ed.). *Remembering Woodstock*. Aldershot: Ashgate.

McMullen, T. (2019). *Haunthenticity: Musical Replay and the Fear of the Real*. Wesleyan University Press.

Nicholson, S. (2014). *Is Jazz Dead?: Or Has It Moved to a New Address*. London: Routledge.

Panassié, H. (1973/1946). *The Real Jazz*. Greenwood Press.

Pellegrinelli, L. (2008). Separated at 'birth': Singing and the history of jazz. In N. T. Rustin and S. Tucker (Eds). *Big ears: Listening for gender in jazz studies*. Durham/London: Duke University Press, 31–47.

Pellegrinelli, L., Effinger, S.J., Elizabeth, J., Grunenberg, K. Horn, R., Sebesky, G. and Weiner, N. (2021). Equal at last? Women in jazz, by the numbers. 12 Jan. 2021. Retrieved at www.npr.org/2021/01/12/953964352/ equal-at-last-women-in-jazz-by-the-numbers.

Picaud, M. (2016). We try to have the best: How nationality, race and gender structure artists' circulations in the Paris jazz scene. *Jazz Research Journal*, *10*(1–2), 126–152.

Piekut, B. (2010). "New thing? Gender and sexuality in the Jazz Composers Guild." *American Quarterly*, *62*(1), 25–48.piekut.

Poiger, U.G. (2000). *Jazz, Rock, and Rebels: Cold War Politics and American Culture in a Divided Germany*. Berkeley: University of California Press.

Raine, S. (2020). Keychanges at Cheltenham Jazz Festival: Challenges for women musicians in jazz and ways forward for equal gender representation at jazz festivals. 10.13140/RG.2.2.15390.15688.

Regev, M. (2007). Cultural uniqueness and aesthetic cosmopolitanism. *European Journal of Social Theory*, *10*(1), 123–138.

Rentsch, C. (2010). *Montreux Jazz Festival: Die emotionsmachine*. Rapperswil: Du Kulturmedien.

Rustin, N. (2005). 'Mary Lou Williams plays like a man!': Gender, genius, and difference in black music discourse. *South Atlantic Quarterly*, *104*(3), 445–462.

Rustin-Paschal, N., and Tucker, S. eds. (2008). *Big Ears: Listening for Gender in Jazz Studies*. Durham: Duke University Press.

Smith, S. L., Choueiti, M., Pieper, K., Clark, H., Case, A. and Villanueva, S. (2019). Inclusion in the recording studio? Gender and race/ethnicity of artists, songwriters and producers across 700 popular songs from 2012–2018. USC Annenberg. USC Annenberg Inclusion Initiative. Retrieved from http://assets.uscannenberg.org/docs/aii-inclusion-recording-studio-2019.pdf.

Street, J. (2015). Stax, subcultures, and civil rights: Young Britain and the politics of soul music in the 1960s. In D.G. Kelley and S. Tuck (Eds). *The Other Special Relationship: Race, Rights, and Riots in Britain and the United States*. Palgrave Macmillan: New York.

Suzuki, Y. (2013). Two strikes and the double negative: The intersections of gender and race in the cases of female jazz saxophonists. *Black Music Research Journal*, *33*(2), 207–226.

Tackley, C.J. (2018) Jazz meets pop in the United Kingdom. In: *The Routledge Companion to Jazz Studies*. Routledge, 97–104.

Ténot, F. et al. (1996). *Montreux Jazz Festival, 1967–1996*. Editions du Chêne.

Tucker, S. (2008). When did jazz go straight?: a queer question for jazz studies. *Critical Studies in Improvisation/ Études critiques en improvisation*, *4*(2).

Wolfe, P. (2020). *Women in the Studio: Creativity, Control and Gender in Popular Music Production*. Ashgate Popular and Folk Music Series. London: Routledge.

17

RESURRECTING MASCULINITY

Gender, Jazz Timbre, and the Afterlife of Dennis Irwin's Bass

ken tianyuan Ge

Context and Positionality Statement: This chapter critiques heteronormativity, a fiction about gender and sexuality whose expressions pervade jazz cultures. Using verbiage like "regendering," it calls attention to the cyclic, recursive ways in which people affix such notions to musical sounds. This filtering of jazz through heteronormativity supports an epistemological regime in which the music falls into lockstep with hypermasculinized and heterosexist ideals, effectively reinscribing rather than challenging patriarchy. I problematize this operation through the keyword of "resurrection." Resurrection conjures much more than masculinity: it is a complex nostalgia for what jazz was, and who its champions were. Jazz's heteronormative regenderings thus function intersectionally with other markers of difference, being powerfully informed by notions of class, race, ability, and geography in particular. My own position—summated here as heterosexual, cismale, second-generation Asian American, able-bodied, practitioner-scholar—reads alongside this chapter's critiques, yielding a project that attempts to leverage professional expertise and embodied knowledge into rigorous analysis, while advancing the ongoing self-work of understanding and divesting from white supremacist, heterosexist, and ableist paradigms of music that were never meant for me and the world I imagine.

Wincing as he stops down the strings of his mentor's double bass, New York jazz musician Neal Miner evinces an intriguing mixture of admiration and emasculation:

MINER: It's so incredibly … high, *high* action. The way Dennis played … and the tone that he would get … the way he pulled … It's the kind of action that you really have to manhandle to get a sound out of it. It's not set up quite easy. You really have to muscle every note … but if you can do it, it's going to give you back this amazing sound—which Dennis had … I definitely see why he did all those long tones, just to maintain that strength. He was a naturally big, strong guy anyways… But he was so graceful on it, like a bumblebee.

Miner is speaking to vocalist Aria Hendricks, who interjects from behind the camera:

HENDRICKS: Like a large, graceful … linebacker.
MINER: …Doing ballet!

DOI: 10.4324/9781003081876-19

Through this moment, taken from Miner's 2012 YouTube documentary, *Dennis' Bass*, I open the door to this chapter's dwelling place: within the afterlife of Dennis Irwin's instrument.[1]

This project is built from a place of care. Dennis Irwin (1951–2008) was a fixture in the New York jazz scene for over thirty years. A reliable sideman par excellence, incredibly prolific, and having performed on over five hundred albums, he was best known as the long-standing bassist of the Thad Jones-Mel Lewis Orchestra. His passing on March 10, 2008 left an audible void in the city's musical undergirding (Friedwald, 2008). *Dennis' Bass* documents the resonance of this loss, recording a moment of commemoration in which Miner and Hendricks, Irwin's partner, stir his instrument from dormancy. Because he mattered—deeply—in ways inaccessible to an author who did not know him personally, but was inspired by him nonetheless, this chapter does not directly interrogate Irwin's life. Instead, I analyze the reawakening that occurs in the film, following Irwin's instrument through its filmic geography of New York and attending to how it vibrates in the absence of its owner.

The premise that musical instruments have afterlives draws from a scholarly framework that complements my own interpretive and experiential lens. As the overtly gendered language of this opening vignette suggests, masculinity figures prominently in jazz bass praxis, which I conceptualize as a feedback loop informing how the double bass is set up, played, and heard. This gendered ideal lingers on when the original interface between a musician and their instrument is broken, such that Miner (the player), Hendricks (the witness), and Irwin's bass form an intimate triangle, resurrecting in its center a masculine image of Irwin's strength, endurance, and agility. Reminiscent of Muhammad Ali, who famously "floated like a butterfly" and "stung like a bee," Irwin is remembered here as a linebacker ballerina who delivered immense payloads of sound from the realm of grace. This reading builds from critical organology, which interrogates the connectivity of instruments, bodies, sound, and sociality through anthropological and ethnomusicological perspectives. Specifically, I draw from Maria Sonevytsky's "interpretive triangle" (2008) of hermeneutic possibility, which "extend[s] the performative act to include not only the dynamic between performer and audience, but among performer, *instrument*, and audience" (pp. 112–113, my emphasis). More generally, I acknowledge Eliot Bates's "social lives of musical instruments" (2012) by considering how basses take on new polyvalence after their owners have departed. Thus, in studying the afterlife of Irwin's instrument, I construct a care-ful epistemological frame while exploring the critical possibilities afforded by tri-angulating organology, jazz and gender studies, and studies of men and masculinities.[2]

From this intersection, I produce the chapter's central arguments. I argue that the double bass in jazz is doubly gendered: as a musical technology hypermasculinized by mainstream, "straight-ahead" jazz practices, and as a stylistically subjugated presence in the musical texture, whose labor is authenticated by heteronormative discourses. Masculinity invests in jazz's sounding practices and its historical processes, resurrecting itself through bass timbres while regendering and "straightening" epistemologies of the instrument. Irwin's bass, old but still ticking, thus resounds simultaneously with the social present and the imagined past. As we will see, the slice of New York's jazz scene appearing in the documentary—a mostly white, male cast of fellow bass practitioners—come to new understandings of Irwin, themselves, and their craft by proxy of Irwin's bass. Considered alone, the perspectives of this guild of men might yield a unidimensional critique of gender inequity and pro-vinciality in jazz. I instead follow a trajectory theorized by Nichole Rustin-Paschal, who advocates for a Black feminist rethinking of jazz scholarship that is "interested in more than decrying the absence of women or the misogyny of men in jazz or hagiography" (Rustin and Tucker, 2008, p. 5). Thus, I stake this chapter within a broader confrontation with jazz's historiographical and social investments in heteronormativity and masculinity, treating their latent, "mundane materiality" (Katz, 1995, p. 12) as absurd. Building from the testimony of Stephanie Greig, a lone basswoman appearing toward the end of the film, I wonder how masculinity has overdetermined the meanings emanating from Irwin's bass. Focusing on the dirt Irwin left behind on his fingerboard, I illuminate a material and symbolic connection to his sound praxis, which negotiated a "blue collar," white working-class identity alongside the tradition of African American embodied labor undergirding the musical textures of jazz history. By considering Irwin as not just a practitioner, but a sound theorist, I point toward a deep current of underexamined timbral politics that challenges the treble bias of jazz studies.

Reawakening

In the winter of 2011, Neal Miner's bass had been shipped away for an out-of-town gig, leaving him unable to fulfill a weekly local commitment in vocalist Annie Ross's band. He reconnected with Aria Hendricks, who was Irwin's partner in the final years of his life, and is now the keeper of his instrument. Hendricks had until then resisted the notion of loaning it out, but consented to Miner, who would have the honor of playing the bass for the first time since Irwin's passing. "I remember how she had recently mentioned feeling ready and wanting to have Dennis's bass played again," Miner recalls. "I thought this would be a great opportunity to borrow his bass from Aria's apartment for a night on the town—and, hopefully, show it a good time." He arrives at Hendricks's apartment, whereupon we enter the first act of *Dennis' Bass*.

Hendricks's camera hand closely attends as Miner turns the film's protagonist around from the corner, where it has been collecting dust. Irwin's battle-scarred bass—a tanky American Standard, crafted from blonde plywood sometime between 1937 and 1938—is a true relic.[3] The wear and tear from decades of hard use is unmistakable: gray duct tape, applied liberally to the upper bouts, presumably to cover up structural damage; the neck, shattered and consequently repaired; the wood body, checkered, pockmarked, and distressed.

It is an unforgiving, enigmatic instrument. Irwin had indeed set the suspension, or action, of his traditional gut strings "incredibly high," requiring a great deal of hand and arm strength to stop each note down onto the fingerboard. The height-adjustable, metal endpin had been replaced with a bar of thick, solid wood. Though it ostensibly enhanced the bass's resonance, extending Irwin's connection to the floor, there was a trade-off: the fixed height of the custom pin meant that anyone taller or shorter than Irwin could not play comfortably. The large hole drilled out to accommodate the pin also rendered the bass incompatible with "the wheel," a popular accessory that grants bassists the ability to roll onto subway cars, across boroughs, and into venues with relative ease. Noticing a mysterious string leashing the bridge to the rest of the instrument, Miner hypothesizes that for Irwin, no customization was without its purpose. Could Irwin's powerful *pizzicato* actually catapult the bridge off of his bass? Which represented the greater bother—maintaining an uncompromising string height and rigging the bass to explode, or retrieving the bridge from some far-flung corner of the bandstand? The string's presence, it seems, indicates the latter.

Even the case has its secrets. From the back pocket Miner removes a tangled nest of strings, organized inscrutably with painters' tape. The case itself is vintage, built for protection: at 20 pounds, the bulky leather almost doubles the weight of the instrument. But Irwin had addressed both weight and transportation by strapping his bass with bungee cords to an unwieldy luggage cart.

> HENDRICKS: So, the entire reason for sacrificing the wheel was for that peg.... I think he may have tried to explain that, but whenever he said something that he thought was kind of embarrassing, he would swallow it.... I would ask him, "Why don't you have a wheel?" Every bass player would have a wheel! And he was like [impression of Irwin muttering].

Despite Irwin's reticence, this much is clear to Hendricks: "He was the first to sacrifice convenience for a traditional sound."

Regendering

Double basses are notoriously challenging instruments to manage. Vulnerable to the elements, they expand and contract with the weather; cracks in the wood open during rainstorms, only to retreat into hibernation the following day. Professionals like Irwin often maintain two instruments: a quality, hand-carved boutique or antique, reserved for home use, recordings, or high-profile jobs, and an all-purpose, plywood "beater" for everyday gigs and outdoor use.[4] New technology has mitigated some of the working bassist's problems. Carbon fiber endpins exist for those who wish to shave grams. Reliable steel and synthetic materials render gut strings and their fickle intonation a thing of the past. Amplification, too, has become less backbreaking work: neodymium magnets, replacing heavy ceramic, can considerably reduce the weight of speaker cabinets.

Yet some bassists refuse these modern conveniences in the name of tradition and sound. I argue that Irwin's "sacrifice," deeply etched into the material form of his instrument, speaks to a culture of musical timbre that is at once specific to double bassists, and more broadly entangled with jazz's investments in technology, masculinity, class, and race. Here, I pause the film to reproduce a vivid example of how these contexts intersect around the bass in jazz. Critic Stanley Crouch wrote that Charles Mingus yearned to emulate

> the bebop horn players and worked on his facility until he could move across the instrument with a velocity and weighted force that are still far from common. The blessing of extremely large hands and powerful fingers allowed him to execute things that are still quite difficult for most bassists.... Unlike too many of those who came after him, Mingus never lost the thick, dark sound of the bass register or the strength of the long, heavy bass string. Even when the master bassist followed an idea into the extreme upper register, his instrument maintained its identity, never sounded like a cello. While Mingus increased the expressive possibilities of his instrument ... he didn't reduce the bass to a four-stringed extension of skittering castrati.
>
> *(2006, p. 101)*

Crouch lionizes Mingus as the ideal jazzman, a paragon navigating the aural tightrope of conditioned physicality, tempered emotionality, and tasteful virtuosity that all who follow must walk. This passage exemplifies the neotraditionalist discourses that Crouch and prominent musicians like Wynton Marsalis disseminated throughout the 1980s and 1990s, enshrining a golden age of mid-century jazz and, within its musical textures, heroic masculinity in the unamplified labor of African American double bassists.[5]

Crouch's Afrocentric model, deeply invested in the seminal, working Black bassists of bebop and hard bop, is situated within a broader dichotomy of classed masculinity that reinforces straight-ahead jazz ideals. Douglas Holt and Craig Thompson (2004) argue that the heroic ideal of American masculinity refracts into two "seemingly competing models": those of the breadwinner and the rebel (p. 427). While this dichotomy remains so ingrained in the imaginary that it might speak for itself, the breadwinner model significantly circumscribes my argument about jazz bass practices. Certainly, other classes of jazz practitioners—percussionists, vocalists, dancers, treble instrumentalists, other rhythm section players—also embody breadwinning sensibilities, which Holt and Thompson characterize as "reserved, dependable, and devoid of self-aggrandizing flamboyance," predicated on the "twin goals of earning social respect and earning money" (p. 427). And bassists are undeniably rebellious, too: following musicologist Brian Wright's work (2020) across the acoustic-electric divide, low-end players like Jaco Pastorius have flaunted their virtuosity in altogether bombastic ways.

However, the *historic challenge of accessing conventional models of virtuosity* that is unique to jazz double bassists has produced a framework of masculinized authenticity, based in a collaborative "will to succeed" (Holt and Thompson, 2004, p. 427), that takes precedence over rebellious individuality. Carrying over from the big band era, requiring enduring physicality and gruelingly high string action, these practices were authenticated by their blistering, bloodying labor, even as they foreclosed on dexterity. Notice that Crouch's Mingus is exemplary precisely *because* he reconciled his transcendent, horn-like melodicism with the patriarchal responsibility that weighed his bass to the ground (2006, p. 101). His anthropomorphized bass "maintained its identity, never sounded like a cello" whilst exploring its own upper tessituras, creating a "utopian resolution" (Holt and Thompson, p. 428) of the dialectic tension between rebel virtuosity and grounded conservatism. Indeed, Crouch dichotomizes even further, hearing a heroic equilibrium in how Mingus "triumphantly resolves the opposites of primitive intensity and high sophistication" (2006, p. 100).

In theory, Crouch's ideas have largely run their course. For three decades, jazz scholars have challenged neotraditionalism's exclusionary politics of history, canon, and American exceptionalism. Even before Crouch's passing in 2020, musicologist David Ake posited the birth of a "postneotraditionalist era" that saw "jazz's current leading lights embrace a broader array of musical practices and aesthetics than ever before" (2019, p. 77). Yet, in a contemporary jazzscape marked by the continued harassment, erasure, and exclusion of women, a sustained interrogation of jazz's complicity in reproducing gendered power difference, especially within instrumentalism, remains vital.

A closer look at Crouch's arguments grants a new level of insight into how basses/ists have weathered a kind of historiographic regendering, reflected in both musical practice and social inequity. In his framework, the "doubleness" of the double bass represents a fundamental split between Eurological and Afrological modes. "In European music," Crouch (2006) wrote, "the bass is almost always played with the bow and is never utilized with the freedom heard in jazz, where the *bull fiddle* is almost always plucked" (p. 100, my emphasis). Though his wording is ripe for psychoanalysis ("master bassist"?), I am more interested in the crisis of masculinity that Crouch staged, which serves to contextualize *Dennis' Bass* and the musical moment from which Irwin emerged. What do the shadowy, emasculated strawmen erected in this passage have to tell us? Who are these anemic cellists? These "skittering castrati"?

As I have argued elsewhere (Ge, 2018), the policing of jazz bass timbre remains a niche but crucially underexamined issue. Straight-ahead practices take a back seat in music histories of the American 1970s, which focus on the rise of hybridized, electric musics. While fusion and jazz-rock, underpinned by electric basses, certainly configured what Kevin Fellezs (2011) has called "agentive empowerment" for its practitioners, enabling "transgeneric" mobility beyond musical orthodoxy (p. 7), a parallel yearning for transcendence was being formulated by upright players working in "jazz proper." Beginning in the 1960s, with the introduction of steel strings, solid state amplifiers, piezo-electric pickups, and "direct" recording and amplification methods that reweighted the instrument's characteristic resonances, the sound of the bass dramatically changed. Practitioners seized upon these nascent technologies, sounding out in ways that were louder, busier, more heard than felt, and electrified in tone. According to bassist Buster Williams, "At one time, the bass just provided a thump, thump, thump, thump accompaniment, and you recognized it by its absence. Now, [it] is a voice to be reckoned with, a voice that helps form the music" (Berliner, 1994, p. 319).

Despite having hitched their wagons to jazz's pillars of individuality, virtuosity, and interactivity, these bassists' sounds aged poorly, resounding amidst a "tone war" which reached its nadir in racialized and gendered logics of marginalization. That white bassists like Scott LaFaro (who did not use steel strings or an amplifier) and Latinx bassists like Eddie Gomez (who did) were progenitors of this hyper-interactive, "vocal" style was not lost upon the neotraditionalists. For instance, Delfeayo Marsalis scored a stunning own goal during a blindfold-style listening test, after seizing an opportunity to take LaFaro and the white pianist Bill Evans to task:

> To me, [Scott LaFaro] was the one who did this. Bill Evans, knowing that he couldn't possibly compete with [Black pianists] Oscar Peterson and Wynton Kelly ... I think he said, "We're gonna go more to that European thing," which is like the symphony orchestra, where you don't have any string sound. You don't have anything that would be kind of aggressive.... Bill Evans was the guy who decided, "We're gonna play the acoustic bass more like a guitar—no string sound, nothing aggressive." And a lot of people have followed suit. Personally, I like, you know, you're playing bass. It's masculine. I don't like that feminine kind of a bass sound.
>
> (Odell, 2015)

After the performer on the recording was revealed to be the African American bassist Ron Carter, Marsalis had no choice but to walk back his statement.

Of course, such arguments require a forgetfulness toward African American bassists—like Carter, Williams, and Stanley Clarke, among many others—who sport an electrified tone. Regardless of his dubious ability to hear race and gender in bass timbre, however, Marsalis's binary pitting of Black, American heteromasculinity against white, European effeminacy echoes Crouch's model, which doggedly insists upon the "bull fiddle" as its totem. Here, basses become essentialized as powerful technologies of "real men," in danger of being co-opted into white, non-Black, or feminine modalities. This gendered division of musical labor, as Lara Pellegrinelli (2008) has argued, is inscribed in the "parentage of jazz" in dominant histories, which "can be read as symbolically gendered: the blues is a natural product of the untrained voice associated with the body and the sexuality of its performers, whereas ragtime is masculine, associated with instruments as tools and technical skill" (p. 34). The "liberation" model of bass playing, emerging from the late 1960s, thus tugs at a longer thread binding together jazz instrumentalism, technological mastery, and heteromasculinity—which some did not want to see unraveled.

The discursive campaigns I have deconstructed here were largely successful, despite their circular, deterministic, and "technoprimitive" logics. The electric mediations of both Black and non-Black bassists in the fusion era only garnered them limited capital as forward-thinking technologists. Their tinkerings, for some, only served to vocalize—and thus feminize—their efforts. Following gender and technology scholar Ruth Oldenziel (1997), this mixed reception of double bass timbres is symptomatic of an "intricate web" of institutional, discursive, and social forces that maintain heteronormativity in jazz cultures, corralling "boys and their toys" into a domain of masculine technicality while channeling women into the feminized work of singing (p. 62). By the turn of the century, this historiographic regendering of double bass sound was largely complete, causing the bright bass timbres of 1970s straight-ahead to gleam ambivalently, androgynously, in what Wynton Marsalis has dubbed jazz's "cultural dark ages"[6] (Dorfman, 1988).

Quietude

From this web, I resolve an image of Irwin's musical milieu. Amidst a technological and stylistic revolution among his peers in the early 1970s, Irwin began using gut strings exclusively. Though gut use had become anachronistic in less than a decade, for him the switch was nothing short of a revelation:

> When I started playing, steel strings were a foregone conclusion and pickups and amps.…
> When I changed to gut strings I realized that was part of the sound that I'd been hearing on records. It was different from what I was able to do with my hands on steel strings.
>
> *(Rosner, 2009)*

Determined to reconstruct and embody the sounds and kinetics of a bygone era, Irwin embarked on a lifelong pursuit of tone, steadily raising the tension of his strings to the point of collapse, transforming body and instrument into a historical technology of flesh, muscle, wood, and gut. Here, I unpause the film, tracing how Miner and his fellow bassists interface with this technology, meditating on how its sound resonates through Irwin's lifetime into the present moment of the film.

Miner is preparing to take Irwin's bass home to practice, cautiously rolling the luggage cart through Hendricks's and Irwin's kitchen.

HENDRICKS: You're going to get good practice right here [panning to the narrow entryway of the apartment] because this is a tight squeeze. It's a bit of an obstacle course … in the spirit of Dennis, and how difficult things were. And how he liked them that way.

210

As Hendricks walks Miner to the subway, the three reminisce on the "parade" of gawking passersby that Irwin, rolling his cart to performances, would deliberately avoid. Bidding farewell at the turnstile, the camera changes from Hendricks's hands to Miner's.

A brief, noisy shot follows, with neither bass nor human nor dialogue in frame, inviting us to experience Irwin's commute as he did.

In this second act, Miner begins to grapple in earnest with the instrument, sounding the entanglements I have thus far outlined. Back at his apartment, he splices together a series of quick cuts: with the instrument in center frame, cropping out all but Miner's hands, we hear a slow walking tempo, then a medium blues; the tuners groan from disuse; a side angle discloses how impossibly high Irwin's strings are set. In the final cut of the sequence, we see Miner's face consumed in stoic concentration just before he abruptly stops playing, shaking the pain out of his plucking hand. Yet the bass is hardly fatigued; Miner reclines it onto a chair and pans up and down his worthy adversary, seeming to understand that mastering it in time for his regular Tuesday night gig would be no easy feat. Producing thousands of *pizzicato* notes over the course of an evening now appears as daunting to Miner as it might have been unremarkable and routine for Irwin.

Miner invites two fellow practitioners to his home to experience the bass for themselves. Bassist Joanna Sternberg detects the odd, coppery smell of Irwin's strings and fingerboard, oxidized from years of use without cleaning. Bassist Michael Karn is impressed by the exceptional tone and volume of the instrument:

> KARN: It can really move some air.... Holding that F down is ... You can really feel the sound. It's huge. It's so clear. It's got a lot of definition.
>
> MINER: No wonder Dennis was always talking about long tones.
>
> KARN: He must have had a left arm like Popeye!
>
> MINER: I think he was pretty naturally strong.
>
> KARN: Plus, he did a lot of yoga, that helped.

Inspired by pain—in Miner's plucking hand and Karn's stopping hand, specifically—the two conjure a dialectic about Irwin's physicality that is simultaneously essentialized and habitually cultivated. On one hand, Irwin was "naturally strong," "had a left arm like Popeye"; on the other, his endurance was developed through years of self-discipline, long tone practice, and yoga.

Miner's directorial decisions also reinforce a double-sided masculinity. Juxtaposed are two complementary tropes: the meditative silence before battle, captured in Miner's taciturn, first-person shot on the train, and the quick-cut training montage, citational of every sports movie from *Rocky* to *Remember the Titans*. This explicit connection between music, sports, and masculinity deserves comment, for Crouch himself said: "The greatest pluckers and distance runners of the bass are jazz musicians." (2006, p. 101). As Ken McLeod (2011) has argued, Western sports and musics share the ancient Greek ideal "that the union of strength and beauty is the hallmark of the ideal man" (p. 8). Indeed, the image of Irwin as "graceful linebacker" closely follows how Christian McBride has theorized the bass's supportive role:

> In football ... [a]n offensive lineman is doing his job when nobody recognizes him ... They don't get the spotlight. But they are the most important part of the offense. They have to open the holes for the running backs; they have to protect the quarterback. Everybody follows the blockers. That's exactly what the bass player does in the band. We're protecting the harmony. We are making holes for the soloist out front.
>
> *(Cornish, 2015)*

In training, Miner thus articulates Irwin's praxis as a yearning for duty, taken up as a quiet, demurring, yet intensely tenacious crafting of sound and power.

Resurrection

Miner's preparations have paid off. In the third act, he takes the stage with vocalist Annie Ross. Irwin's bass resounds deeply underneath Ross, who introduces each bandmember and extends a separate acknowledgement to the special guest. Several local bassists have come out to support Miner and hear the instrument in action once more. After the concert, each plays the instrument for themselves. Miner asks them to share stories about Irwin, yet he hardly needs to make the request, for the bass seems to inspire these musicians to words. Doug Weiss deftly tosses off the busy melody to Oscar Pettiford's bass standard, "Tricotism," remarking that "it's easier to play fast than slow," before modestly recalling:

> WEISS: I remember the first time I ever touched this bass. [Irwin] asked me to sit in with the Vanguard Band.... I played some A-flat rhythm changes [snaps fingers, indicating a moderate walking tempo]. I was dead after the first chorus! ... I went to Small's with him one time and I forget who was playing [bass], but someone who played real guitar-style. [vocalizes gibberish, sliding hands up and down the fingerboard] Just playing all this shit on the bass. And he [Irwin] just started laughing uncontrollably. It wasn't like he was being mean or dissing the guy, but he was just so tickled.
>
> MINER: I can't understand this, Doug. He's got a rope connecting the bridge to the tailpiece. [Is it] in case it flies off?
>
> WEISS: Yeah! I actually saw that happen one time. He was playing a Joe Lovano gig and it just went *phew*—there's just so much tension [pointing down through the bridge] and he would pull so hard [gesturing laterally]. It's a safety wire.
>
> SPENCER MURPHY: I'm thinking of the way Dennis played—his facility and sound and grace— and then touching this instrument. It's intimidating. I feel like my fingers need to be twice as big.
>
> MINER: It makes me feel like a little boy.

Taken together, I argue that this male cohort shares an extended moment of "cultural intelligibility" (Butler, 1993, p. xii) as they enact a comparative project between themselves, Irwin, and the nexus of physicality and strength represented by his instrument. One imagines their hands and ears operating co-productively to process the stubborn tautness of the strings, the rattling of copper-wound gut against fingerboard that stronger hands might tame, and the aurality of what *could* emerge from a worthy player. Irwin's bass appears to be etched so deeply that, like a text, it resists disentanglement from both its inscriber and its gendered history of use. Therefore, I draw from Michel Foucault (1972) in considering how instruments, decoupled from their original owners and carrying on their own social afterlives, represent a preciously rare interface, a "vacant place that may in fact be filled by different individuals" (p. 95). Passed from hand to hand, Irwin "disappears" (Foucault 1984, p. 102) within the myriad inscriptions he left behind. Therefore, when I argue that *Dennis' Bass* has "resurrected masculinity," I am attempting not only to understand how intention is transduced from bodies into technologies, and from technologies to sound, but also how sound diffracts back into gendered understandings, which assemble within an aural and kinesthetic feedback loop, constellating in the sharing of multiple, embodied experiences.

Taken individually, I suggest that these anecdotes about Irwin perform the important work of testimony. As jazz scholar Tony Whyton (2010) has argued, anecdotes yield valuable insights into their tellers' subjectivities. Though scholars tend to find their "uncritical and less academic nature"

(p. 107) suspect, anecdotes nevertheless evidence the embodied experiences and motivations of their witnesses, such that "the witness is not simply an historian who documents things, but is someone who retains their own cultural baggage" (pp. 123–124). Accordingly, I ask: what dissonances surface as these witnesses, faced with Irwin's physicality and its material imprint, grapple with the instrument? What gendered "baggage" is shared by this guild of men? What do we make of this intriguing mixture of admiration ("his facility and sound and grace") and emasculation ("my fingers need to be twice as big," "it makes me feel like a little boy")? Where are those "skittering castrati" that Crouch fought to stave off? Are they those who attempt to walk Irwin's walk, and fail, or are they the "guitar-style" players that Irwin (and presumably Weiss) found so amusing?

I raise these dissonant questions in solidarity with jazz scholar Sherrie Tucker and a question she posed in 2008: *When Did Jazz Go Straight?* In her provocative article, Tucker critiqued the field of jazz studies for its complicity in historical methodologies that all but out queer jazz subjects while allowing the "historicity of straightness" to remain profoundly unexamined (p. 2). Building on Tucker's work, I turn a curious ear to the bass's heteronormative valences and ask a related question: *How straight is straight-ahead jazz?*

Consider, for instance, the foundational sound ideal of jazz and swing. Critic Ted Gioia (2016, p. 10) romanticized it this way:

> The locking together of the bass and drums ... may be the single most satisfying sound in all of jazz. The stars wouldn't shine so brightly if these partners at the back of the bandstand didn't possess such powerful musical chemistry.

But ethnomusicologist Paul Berliner, two decades before Gioia, archived this idea and its original, heteronormative connotation in his landmark study: "'For things to happen beautifully in the ensemble,' [jazz drummer] Charli Persip metaphorizes, 'the drummer and the bass player must be married'" (1994, p. 349).

What does it mean to conceptualize the quintessential relationship in jazz—the "hookup" between the bass and drums—as a sound metaphor for marriage? (Every quarter note an "I do"?) Should we entertain the notion that the linear swing feel of straight-ahead jazz has its best analogue in this historically heteropatriarchal institution, other compulsory roles and associations quickly fall into place. The drum kit, for instance, would metonymically represent Africa and the groom, with the bride, anthropomorphized in the curves of the bass, representing jazz's European parentage. What of the film's premise—a "night on the town" with the bass to "hopefully, show it a good time"? Is this a date? A prelude to wedding bells? Recalling this chapter's introductory quote: is "manhandling" the bass truly best practice? What of the fact that, precisely through the exclusion of women in jazz cultures, this marriage of musical technologies is most often configured between two men? Placing a "twist" (Tucker, 2008, p. 2) on this metaphor illustrates how heteronormativity maps down to the foundational elements of straight-ahead sound but collapses into absurdity under questioning. As Trine Annfelt (2003) has argued, jazz is a discourse of hegemonic masculinity in which "only heterosexuality qualifies for hegemony." This discourse erases queerness while elevating the possibility of (hetero)homosociality, for Irwin's bass does not "turn" these men; rather, it brings them together, resurrects masculinity, makes them into boys once again.

Just one woman bassist, Stephanie Greig, appears in the final gathering of the film. On the deserted bandstand, she strums a few notes on Irwin's bass.

GREIG: I'm tired already! It gets easier, I'm sure. If you played this bass every day, though, it would just be your bass. You'd learn to make it speak.... [Irwin said that] most of the time you have to be the floor. Sometimes you get to be a door or a window, but most of the time you're the floor.

Where the men in the film process Irwin's bass through masculinity, squaring their experiences against memories and inferences about Irwin's body and tone, Greig takes her experience of embodied dissonance in stride. Her comments point to what is lost in aural epistemologies of musical timbre and gender, reminding us that Irwin's relationship with his bass was painstakingly cultivated and irreducible to masculinity alone. The relationship with one's instrument is never static—like a friendship, it is negotiated through sustained emotional, social, and physical labor and care. "It gets easier": Miner's experience with Irwin's bass, though short-lived, was not unidimensional but grew from the initial encounter. Just as Miner adapted to the embodied sonic terms set by another, so too can corrective exposure to different ways of sounding reorient our own modes of self-representation, on and off the bandstand. Greig refuses to reproduce a heterosexist interpretation, instead positing an aesthetics of support, a timbre predicated on collectivity, which cites Irwin's physicality and endurance without reducing them to gendered essentials.

Greig also identifies an important component of Irwin's praxis: "being the floor" as a guiding metaphor for spatializing and embodying a sound role in jazz. Building on her testimony, I argue that "the floor" offers a rare opportunity to unfold Irwin's theory of sound, thereby contributing to the study of jazz and timbre writ large. I expand on the metaphorical obvious. Floors do not merely delimit space; they make space actionable. Reliable grounding enables walking, play, risk, and sometimes, flight. Resolute bassists have underwritten the efforts of jazz's most transcendent soundings: for every Thelonious Monk, a Wilbur Ware; every John Coltrane, a Jimmy Garrison. Indeed, Esperanza Spalding's transcendent vocals are supported by her own bass playing, embodying a microcosm of self-reliance. In what may be his only extant interview, Irwin told jazz writer Lora Rosner,

> I realize now part of my predilection for the Wilbur Ware, Jimmy Garrison kind of sound is the simplicity.... Those were the guys that I dug the hardest. I didn't realize 'til years later the urgency of making a few notes work for rhythmic effect is similar to what appeals to me about Wilbur, Jimmy Garrison, Henry Grimes, Larry Gales, as opposed to Niels-Henning [Ørsted Pedersen] or Scotty [LaFaro].
>
> *(2009)*

Irwin resonated with the depth of expression sounded in the musical labor of his favorite bassists. Though he does not elaborate, Irwin makes a clear distinction between African American bassists Ware, Garrison, Grimes, and Gales on one hand, and white bass virtuosi Niels-Henning Ørsted Pedersen and Scott LaFaro on the other. The interview, appropriately titled "Respect the Tradition," archives how Irwin, a white man, fashioned a genealogy of timbre, such that his body and instrument became technologies for housing and honoring his heroes' collaborative will in a project of cross-racial empathy (Davis, 2014).

Floors, like musical instruments, also accumulate dirt. Dirt is theoretically potent material: in *Men and Their Work* (1958), sociologist Everett Hughes argued that all occupations contain some form of "dirty work" which "in some way goes counter to the more heroic of our moral conceptions" (pp. 49–50). Writing long before the notion of jazz as "America's classical music," Hughes tellingly lists several "lowly occupations" containing dirty work: "apartment-house janitors, junk men, boxers, jazz musicians, osteopaths, pharmacists, etc." (p. 49). Thus, in a postneotraditionalist era where jazz enjoys a hallowed afterlife in the academy, I import a material and symbolic framework of dirt back into music studies to understand perhaps the most significant material trace that Irwin left upon his bass: the sediment accrued on his fingerboard[7] through decades of supportive musical labor. For Irwin disagreed with his more virtuosic peers in the 1970s, who hoped to level the sonic playing field with new technology. "Cats hated doing jam sessions, 'being a slave,'" he told Rosner. "But there's another way of looking at that." Unlike the bass liberators, who considered their traditional charge prescriptive, even stifling, Irwin ascribed dignity to the "dirty work" of bass playing. His answer, as Rosner puts it, was a "philosophy of playing with almost anybody and turning down almost nothing, assuming it has something good to offer."

ROSNER: What motivates you to do this?
IRWIN: Maybe it's some blue collar work ethic.

By embracing difficulty, choosing vibration over convenience, and seizing every opportunity to leave it all behind, night after night—the dirt, calloused skin, sweat, and oxidized copper—Irwin sounded his own truth.

Afterlife

HENDRICKS: This was her spot for eight years solid.... Just in that short period of time that she wasn't here, there was such an absence. It was a huge absence.
MINER: It was [only] twenty four hours!
HENDRICKS: It felt like two weeks! I'm thrilled on one hand that she's back, but on the other hand I feel really bad because ... I know that all she wants to do is be played.

This chapter has advocated for the study of musical instruments, particularly in the liminal spaces of their afterlives. Guided by the resonances of Dennis Irwin's bass, I have sought to critically deconstruct masculinity and heteronormativity as dominant epistemologies in jazz's historical and social soundings. In naming these pervasive ideals, which are latent in theory, pedagogy, and practice, yet intimately relational and affective, I have eschewed the cold language of "social construction" in favor of "resurrection." This metaphysically laden term reconceptualizes gender as socially invoked by vibrating matter, and critiques a timbral politics that, in summoning the violent hegemony of masculinity, elevates certain narratives while silencing others. In my case study, the resurrective function of heteronormative masculinity is ever-present, consolidating the raced and gendered logics of its own significance with common-sense ideals about the "right" way to sound the jazz tradition. Even in the film's conclusion (rendered above), Hendricks imbues her partner's instrument with gendered agency as it returns to dormancy, waiting to be resounded: *All she wants to do is be played.*

I redirect Hendricks's call to jazz studies. How does Irwin's bass want to be played? Are our teachers, practitioners, and critics willing to renounce "manhandling" as sound, *just* praxis? If resurrected masculinity is about nothing more than domination, control, and a symbolic wreaking of violence on musical bodies, then we must recall its use in classrooms and bandstands that, following the vision of Berklee's Institute of Jazz and Gender Justice, align with "the pursuit of jazz without patriarchy" (n.d.). The endgame epistemological project of the jazz tradition is not the continued reproduction of gendered hierarchy, or the reification of virtuosic power through ableist logics; rather, it begins by redressing those injustices through a capacious, inclusive reordering of musical, social, and historiographical value systems.

This chapter, focused intently on critiquing normative, heteropatriarchal ideals within straight-ahead jazz, can only be sustained within an ecology of reparative and deconstructive scholarship across a broad spectrum of practices and histories. Thus, I look forward to work that illuminates alternative imaginations, abilities, and soundings: celebrations of "otherwise possibility" (Crawley, 2020) that look back on the historical apparatus of "jazzmasculinity" (Rustin-Paschal, 2017) and move forward in a joyous abandonment. To imagine a jazz that sounds beyond patriarchy, that *provincializes masculinity*, I paradoxically return to Irwin. As a man who sought to "be the floor," who was quiet, humble, and rarely verbalized the decisions he made for himself and his instrument, his relationship to tradition was *made plain in sound*. This sound praxis—configured through material technology, articulated viscerally, through vibration—exceeded the language of gender. It imagined a dignity, an empathic connection with history, and a way of being in the world that put others first, sought to make them whole, and celebrated the collaborative work of improvisation. As the site where Irwin's embodied theory was placed into action, his bass vibrates on as a reminder of jazz's potential to realize its own dreams of justice.

Notes

1 Thanks to Mark Katz, Andrea F. Bohlman, David García, Elias Gross, Briana M. Nave, Destiny Meadows, and Kari Lindquist for their comments on this chapter, and to Anne Searcy and David Ake for their insights on earlier drafts.
2 "Care-ful" speaks to a methodology informed by caring, not wariness or what Paul Ricoeur termed "the hermeneutics of suspicion." Rather, I'm aligned with the reparative intellectual project notably articulated by Eve Kosofsky Sedgwick (2003, pp. 123–151).
3 This estimate is based on Miner's reading of the inside label (#207) and the serial number information provided by the H. N. White String Company's website.
4 Irwin owned a carved French bass, alongside the blonde plywood that is the subject of the film.
5 As Brian Wright (2014) has argued in his cultural history of the electric bass, the "supposedly acoustic, unamplified purity" of pre-fusion jazz presents a rhetorical "façade," as bassists had been amplified with microphones regularly since the 1940s (p. 293).
6 Thanks to David Ake for bringing this source to my attention. The subtitling of this section acknowledges a debt to "Regendering Jazz: Ornette Coleman and the New York Scene in the Late 1950s," which continues to inspire me (2002, pp. 62–82).
7 For more on Hughes and dirty sociological frameworks, see Simpson et al. (2016). I also recall the well-known quote attributed to Motown bassist James Jamerson, who was said to never clean his strings: "The dirt keeps the funk" (Licks, 1989).

References

Ake, D. A. (2002). *Jazz Cultures*. Berkeley: University of California Press.
Ake, D. A. (2019). After Wynton: Narrating jazz in the postneotraditionalist era. In N. Gebhardt, N. Rustin-Paschal, and T. Whyton (Eds.), *The Routledge Companion to Jazz Studies* (pp. 77–86). New York: Routledge.
Annfelt, T. (2003, July 17). Jazz as masculine space. *Kilden*. Retrieved from https://kjonnsforskning.no/en/2003/07/jazz-masculine-space.
Bates, E. (2012). The social life of musical instruments. *Ethnomusicology, 56*(3), 363–395.
Berliner, P. (1994). *Thinking in Jazz: The Infinite Art of Improvisation*. Chicago: University of Chicago Press.
Butler, J. (1993). *Bodies that Matter: On the Discursive Limits of "Sex."* New York: Routledge.
Cornish, A. (2015, November 18). Christian McBride on Ray Brown's bass and James Brown's appeal. *All Things Considered*. Retrieved from www.npr.org/2015/11/18/456540205/christian-mcbride-on-ray-browns-bass-and-james-browns-appeal.
Crawley, A. (2020). *The Lonely Letters*. Durham: Duke University Press.
Crouch, S. (2006). *Considering Genius: Writings on Jazz*. New York: Basic Civitas Books.
Davis, K. C. (2014). *Beyond the White Negro: Empathy and Anti-racist Reading*. Urbana: University of Illinois Press.
Dorfman, S. (1988). *Blues and Swing* [VHS]. Long Beach, CA: Geneon [Pioneer].
Fellezs, K. (2011). *Birds of Fire: Jazz, Rock, Funk, and the Creation of Fusion*. Durham: Duke University Press.
Foucault, M. (1972). *The Archaeology of Knowledge*. New York: Pantheon Books.
Foucault, M., and Rabinow, P. (1984). *The Foucault Reader*. New York: Pantheon Books.
Friedwald, W. (2008, March 14). Mourning and rejoicing for Dennis Irwin. *The New York Sun*. Retrieved from www.nysun.com/arts/mourning-rejoicing-for-dennis-irwin/72926/.
Ge, k. t. (2018). "Bright Bass Timbres in the "Dark Age" of Jazz: Eddie Gomez, Three Quartets, Transgression, and Transcendence" (Doctoral Thesis). University of Miami.
Gioia, T. (2016). *How to Listen to Jazz*. New York: Basic Books.
Holt, D. B., and Thompson, C. J. (2004). Man-of-action heroes: The pursuit of heroic masculinity in everyday consumption. *Journal of Consumer Research, 31*(2), 425–440.
Hughes, E. C. (1958). *Men and Their Work*. London: Collier-Macmillan.
Katz, J. (1995). *The Invention of Heterosexuality*. New York: Dutton.
Licks, D. (1989). *Standing in the Shadows of Motown: The Life and Music of Legendary Bassist James Jamerson*. Milwaukee: Hal Leonard.

McLeod, K. (2011). *We Are the Champions: The Politics of Sports and Popular Music*. Burlington, VT: Ashgate.

Miner, N. (2012). *Dennis' Bass* [YouTube Video]. Retrieved from https://youtu.be/WIVJ7cFPwys.

Mission, values, and vision. (n.d.). Retrieved from https://college.berklee.edu/jazz-gender-justice/mission-vision-values.

Odell, J. (2018, January 1). Before and after with Delfeayo Marsalis. *JazzTimes*. Retrieved from https://jazztimes.com/features/lists/before-after-with-delfeayo-marsalis/.

Oldenziel, R. (1997). Boys and their toys: The fisher body craftsman's guild, 1930-1968, and the making of a male technical domain. *Technology and Culture, 38*(1), 60.

Pellegrinelli, L. (2008). Separated at "birth": Singing and the history of jazz. In N. Rustin-Paschal and S. Tucker (Eds.), *Big Ears: Listening for Gender in Jazz Studies* (pp. 31–47). Durham: Duke University Press.

Rosner, L. (2009, April 28). Dennis Irwin: Respect the tradition. *All About Jazz*. Retrieved from www.allaboutjazz.com/dennis-irwin-respect-the-tradition-dennis-irwin-by-lora-rosner.php.

Rustin-Paschal, N. (2017). *The Kind of Man I Am: Jazzmasculinity and the World of Charles Mingus Jr*. Middletown, CT: Wesleyan University Press.

Rustin-Paschal, N., and Tucker, S. (Eds.). (2008). *Big Ears: Listening for Gender in Jazz Studies*. Durham: Duke University Press.

Sedgwick, E. (2003). *Touching Feeling: Affect, Pedagogy, Performativity*. Durham: Duke University Press.

Simpson, R., Hughes, J., and Slutskaya, N. (2016). White working class masculinities and dirty work. In *Gender, Class and Occupation*. London: Palgrave Macmillan.

Sonevytsky, M. (2008). The accordion and ethnic whiteness: Toward a new critical organology. *World of Music, 50*(3), 101–118.

Tucker, S. (2008). When did jazz go straight?: A queer question for jazz studies. *Critical Studies in Improvisation / Études Critiques En Improvisation, 4*(2).

Whyton, T. (2010). *Jazz Icons: Heroes, Myths and the Jazz Tradition*. New York: Cambridge University Press.

Wright, B. F. (2014). "A bastard instrument": The Fender Precision bass, Monk Montgomery, and jazz in the 1950s. *Jazz Perspectives, 8*(3), 281–303.

Wright, B. F. (2020). Jaco Pastorius, the electric bass, and the struggle for jazz credibility. *Journal of Popular Music Studies, 32*(3), 121–138.

18

JAZZ DANCE, GENDER, AND THE COMMODIFICATION OF THE MOVING BODY

Examining Patriarchal and White Supremacist Structures in Social and Commercial Jazz Dance Forms

Brandi Coleman

Often, jazz dance is embedded with cues that uphold socially and culturally determined gender norms that fall along the binary. Stereotypical movement tropes promoting hyperfeminine or hypermasculine movement aesthetics are ingrained and upheld by systems of patriarchy, White supremacy, and the commodification of the moving body. Some forms of jazz dance, specifically those that utilize Euro-American aesthetics, have become synonymous with highly gendered and hypersexualized movement for both men and women. In an art form that centers personal expression, communal inclusivity, and responsive improvisation as foundational elements of the genre, strict binary categorizations leave little room for gendered autonomy or nonbinary, gender-expansive expression. Narratives created and promoted by patriarchal and White supremacist systems—as evident in the structural ways in which race and gender were used as means of oppression and erasure of Black voices in jazz dance history—set up hierarchies, standards, and expected ways of being for jazz dance performers, choreographers, educators, and scholars.

Dance scholar and educator Dr. Takiyah Nur Amin (2014) stated, "Jazz dance is a uniquely American art form because of the amalgam of largely African and European cultural influences that blended—either by force or by choice—on this continent" (p. 42). However, the origin story of jazz dance is often told through a revisionist lens that centers the White male perspective as the defining voice of gendered movement aesthetics and the hierarchical positioning of jazz within the field of dance. This chapter explores the ways in which patriarchal and White supremacist systems inform and uphold stereotypical movement tropes, heteronormativity, and binary gender expression in jazz dance as well as the ways in which these systemic norms can be disrupted through gender-inclusive, human-centric pedagogy and choreography. These deep structures will be examined through the lens of authentic jazz dance, with roots in West and Central African cultures of music and dance and the African American lived experience in the United States, and through the commodification and colonization of the female body in Euro-American based commercial jazz dance.

Questions and topics that drive the research for this chapter include: What are the systemic structures in the history and continuum of jazz dance that uphold and perpetuate culturally constructed gender norms? How can we as performers, choreographers, educators, and scholars make space for

DOI: 10.4324/9781003081876-20

gender-inclusive or gender-expansive expression in jazz dance? What are the alternatives to binary, heteronormative movement aesthetics in jazz dance? Does the mode of presentation—jazz dance as entertainment, in social settings, or on the concert stage—affect the way gender expression is represented and promoted in jazz dance?

There is a great deal of scholarship on gender expression in dance and pedagogy, specifically in ballet and modern dance, and evidence of efforts to expand choreographic and pedagogical methods beyond heteronormative binary reflections. This is seen in the works of authors such as Wendy Oliver and Doug Risner (2017) and Gareth Belling (2017). Closer to jazz dance, there has been an increase in writing on equity and inclusivity for women in the business of musical theatre jazz dance as seen in writing by Bud Coleman and Judith A. Sebesta (2008), Pamela Cobrin (2011), Kerry Lee Graves (2001). And, most specifically to this chapter, there has been in-depth analysis of the hypersexualization of girls in competition dance with a focus on the cause and potential effects of this type of training on gender expression and presentation for young girls, choreographers, and the business models that promote these methods. This is seen in writing by Angela Russell, George Schaefer, and Erin Reilly (2018), Lisa Sandlos (2015), and Karen Schupp (2017). The research in this chapter looks at the field of jazz dance on a larger scope by investigating how socially constructed gender roles, gender expression, and gender constructs are present, upheld, or disrupted in jazz dance rooted in the Africanist aesthetics and the African American experience versus jazz dance that is infused with Euro-American aesthetics and movement ideals.

To note, I write from my perspective as a White, cisgender, queer woman whose gender expression in the jazz dance idiom transverses the stereotypical markers identified as feminine. My first professional job in the jazz dance-as-entertainment sector of the field required that I dress and perform a highly stylized version of gender that showcased feminine-assigned movement aesthetics. While dressed in high heels, fishnet tights, and revealing costumes and while performing hypersexualized movement and heteronormative choreographic narratives, my body in motion was used as a commodity to sell tickets and entertain attendees in a production-style variety show. Eventually, my performative, pedagogical, and choreographic work would be based in jazz dance that centers the Africanist aesthetics through kinetic and social elements and would use an egalitarian, gender-inclusive body alignment principle as the foundation for my performative, choreographic, and pedagogical work.

I recognize that I am a guest in jazz dance, an art form that is rooted in a culture that is not my own, and that Whiteness has informed, and still informs, my experiences and my writing. I do not wish to erase nor speak for Black voices. I have, and continue, to study and call upon scholars and authors such as Jayna Brown (2008), Brenda Dixon Gottschild (1998), Carlos Jones (2014), Jacqui Malone (1996), and Katrina Dyonne Thompson (2014), to name a few, in my research and my teaching. I aim to center the Black perspective and experience in order to honor the origins of jazz dance in West and Central African cultures and its roots in the African American experience, and to also acknowledge its evolution in response to the current socio-political and cultural climate.

Gender Detective

Lindy Hop icon Frankie Manning describes the intimate and inter-dependent relationship of jazz music and jazz dance when describing his experience dancing to his favorite big band, Chick Webb and His Orchestra. According to Manning, Webb would "focus on somebody doing a certain step, and he'd catch it" (Manning and Millman, 2007, p. 98). "Every time I kicked my leg out, Chick would say, 'DJBOOM!' If I did a little swing-out, Taft Jordan would play, 'BEOOOOWWW!'" (Manning and Millman, 2007, p. 99). Referring to trumpeter Taft Jordan, Manning said "He'd play a solo to the way we were dancing, and we'd respond by doing little rhythmic steps with the music" (2007, p. 99). This symbiotic relationship between the jazz musicians and the dancers of this era is further explained when author Jacqui Malone (1996) stated "the dancing was a visualization of the music and the musicians 'danced with sound' (p. 37). When describing the West and Central African cultural identity of the dancing-drummer as seen in the big band era she stated, "Rhythm tappers are jazz percussionists who value improvisation and self-expression. Jazz musicians tell stories with their instruments and rhythm tappers tell stories with their feet" (Malone, 1996, p. 95). Bodies in motion, seen in swinging and dancing musicians such as Cab Calloway, the rhythm tap drummers such as Philly Joe Jones and Buddy Rich, and in the explosive Lindy Hop dancers at the Savoy Ballroom, are a part of the origin story of jazz dance. No doubt, the aural sound of jazz music is infectious and deeply impactful for those who play it, listen to it, *experience* it. But, what happens when one begins to move to it? How do we *see* jazz in the body? How do socio-political and cultural constructs either constrict or make space for gender expression throughout the origin and evolution of jazz and jazz-adjacent dance?

The shared social elements of jazz seen in the embodied music of the dancing musicians—individual creativity within the community, improvisation, vocal encouragement, friendly challenges, call and response, and conversation—also translate to jazz dance, specifically jazz dance forms that honor the West and Central African and African American origins (Cohen, 2014). These elements, along with kinetic elements such as use of the flat foot, bent hip, knee and ankle joints, an inclined torso, isolation of various body parts, groundedness, angularity, and embodied syncopation and polyrhythms (Cohen, 2014) are not gender specific and are absent of indicators that are associated with socially-constructed movement stereotypes. Jazz dance that centers rhythm, percussive movement, and even scat-sung vocalizations prioritizes time-articulated, rhythm-specific energy performed in the "everyday" individual pedestrian body over the culturally-curated gender-specific body often present in the Euro-centric philosophy and aesthetic of commercial jazz dance. Billy Siegenfeld, founder and artistic director of Jump Rhythm® Jazz Project, affirms this when he stated, "[r]hythm is a phenomenon of energy and thus something sensed within the body. The verticality-asserting spine of ballet is a phenomenon of space and thus best appreciated by the eyes" (2009, p. 270). Rhythm-driven jazz dance eliminates the need to assign gender to the movement and instead puts rhythm, energy, emotion, and the inside-felt, outwardly-expressed individual identity at the forefront of the embodied relational conversation of jazz music and jazz dance.

Although the term jazz dance did not come about until the 1920s when it was used to describe dancing done to jazz music of the era (Amin, 2014, p. 35), early markers of embodied sexuality that would eventually become associated with jazz dance are specifically tied to the commodification of the body. It's not so much the hypersexualized movement present in multiple genres of jazz dance as seen in social forms (The Slow Drag, Boogie Walks) or commercial and musical theatre dance forms (television, music videos, competition jazz dance); it's the context in which the dancing is embedded that is to be considered: a social setting in which participants are dancing and responding to an in-the-moment felt sensation performed for the purposes of solo or shared enjoyment; or, in vernacular jazz which calls upon historical and cultural references of the integration of the pelvis and hips as a part of the full articulation of the body, along with other religious, communal, or cultural specifications; or, in commercial jazz dance that relies on the commodification of the female moving body, often while exploiting the naivete of young women who do not understand the complexities surrounding patriarchal narratives and systems of oppression and exploitation.

Jazz dance training that centers a Eurocentric perspective often upholds systems that normalize gendered cues from a young age, so much so that they become synonymous with or inseparable from jazz dance. Gendered cues are tightly woven into the personal and cultural fabric of one's identity as a jazz dancer—a naturalized movement signature that is a part of the social construct of jazz dance. Utilizing an upright spine, lifted sternum and protruding chest, and concerning themselves with controlled placement of the limbs in space, dancers working within a Eurocentric perspective of jazz dance follow expected movement traits according to assigned binary gender: for female-presenting dancers, this manifests in the body as slinky, highly sensual, fluid, hyperflexible movements performed with a steadfast come-hither, will you or won't you gaze while male-presenting dancers are expected to be powerful, athletic, and grounded while executing grand leaps, turns, knee slides, and dominant attention-grabbing tricks. To be sassy, sexy, and fierce means one is performing their gender at the highest level and these attributes are often affirmed by those in positions of power such as choreographers, teachers, and viewers. So deeply ingrained are these ideas in one's movement signature and subsequent self-identity as a dancer that they can become coupled with personal self-worth and authentic personal expression. And, these ideas are often modeled by teachers or older dancers, thereby instituting a kind of idolization of hyperfeminine or hypermasculine gendered dancing.

Cordelia Fine (2010), an academic psychologist and author, stated that "the gendered patterns of our lives can be so familiar that we no longer notice them" (p. 216). Fine's research on neurosexism addresses gender differences from a social and psychological perspective that pushes back against the area of neuroscience that positions gender differences as solely related to variances of the brain. In her book, *Delusions of Gender: How Our Minds, Society, and Neurosexism Create Difference*, she described the following:

> We start to think of ourselves in terms of our gender, and stereotypes and social expectations become more prominent in the mind. This can change self-perception, alter interests, debilitate or enhance ability, and trigger unintentional discrimination. In other words, the social context influences who you are, how you think, and what you do. And these thoughts, attitudes, and behaviors of yours, in turn, become part of the social context.
>
> *(Fine, 2010, xxvi)*

Binary gendered movement aesthetics that fall into categories of hyperfeminine or hypermasculine are often evident in the social context of jazz dance classes and choreography and often become a part of its pedagogical and creative DNA. When students are provided an opportunity to improvise, showcasing their personalized interpretations of the music and movement, it is common for them to instinctively revert to highly gendered stylizations in their movement choices. This in and of itself is not necessarily problematic except when the gendered movements are so deeply ingrained, so intimately connected that they become the accepted definition of jazz dance, overriding social and kinetic elements of jazz that are historically and culturally informed by its African and African American-derived origins. The outwardly expressed adoption of societally assigned gender markers—markers that are often inflated to "[impersonate] an ideal that nobody actually inhabits" (Butler, 1992, from Liz Kotz interview, para. 13)—supersedes foundational elements of rooted jazz dance such as polyrhythm and polycentrism, call and response, articulated and inclined torso, individuality within the community, and vocalizations, to name a few (Cohen, 2014, pp. 5–6). Subsequently, after years of training that features repeated pedagogical cues and choreographic narratives, *culturally predetermined* gender expression is institutionalized to such a degree that one's *personal* gender expression is actually more representative of systemic gender than of their own authentic self.

American philosopher and gender theorist Judith Butler (1988) explained that "[t]he ground of gender identity is the stylized repetition of acts through time" (p. 520). When considered through the lens of Euro centric jazz dance pedagogy and choreography, one can see how this applies in the expression of gender since dance training is often repetitive in nature and offers years of gendered movement, costuming, verbal reinforcement, cuing, and social affirmation through praise, encouragement, applause, priority casting, or advancement in one's career. However, it is not only the "doing" of these acts of gender through movement, costuming, pedagogy, and choreography that establishes a constructed identity but rather it is that the performativity of gender becomes intimately tied to one's own knowing of self. Butler (1988) stated that gender is "a constructed identity, a performative accomplishment which the mundane social audience, including the actors [dancers] themselves, come to believe and to perform in the mode of belief" (p. 520). Tune in to almost any popular television dance competition show and one can see examples of dancers performing gender under the auspice of jazz dance with a kind of embodied confidence, ownership, and personal believability that only comes with years of rehearsal and social conditioning in the studio classroom. In these cases, gender expression is not assumed or "put on" for an isolated occasion but rather is cultivated so much that it would take a conscious effort to move in any other way.

Race and the Commodification of the Dancing Body

How do hyperfeminine or gendered stereotypes and performance norms intersect with race and class? Systems of patriarchy, White supremacy, and commodification have narrated the Black dancing body for centuries from the period of enslavement through the early years of ragtime, blues, and the birth of jazz music and dance, and on through the evolution of jazz dance through the twentieth century.[1] In her book *Ring Shout, Wheel About: The Racial Politics of Music and Dance in North American Slavery*, author Katrina Dyonne Thompson (2014) discussed how travel narratives, a sort of European colonial travel blog, were written by White men whose intent was to "sculpt their [the reader's] personal ideals, aspirations, and imaginations" (p. 14) whether that be a vested interest in the slave trade or implementing and upholding religious ideology. In addition to observations of West African cultures, the writings offered critiques with the specific intent of supporting the author's interest in establishing themselves as the dominant culture. Using French enslaver and author Jean Barbot as an example, Thompson (2014) discussed how his travel narratives, written in the late 1600s to purposefully substantiate his slave trading business, were "constructed as a commodity, appealing to the longing for human labor, sexual desire, and power through the commodification and eroticization of African bodies" (p. 14). She discussed how these narratives served to "other" Africans and their cultures, including music and dance, in order to position and establish the European economy and culture as dominant. Thompson stated:

> Travel writers were not writing merely about music and dance; they were ascribing how blacks ought to be perceived and treated. The first stage of racial development in public ideology was to turn West African men, women, and children into commodities.
>
> *(Thompson, 2014, p. 32)*

White supremacist and patriarchal systems determined the representation of women in what would centuries later become jazz dance. These systems are present in early vernacular and social dance forms informed by Africanist aesthetics in comparison to vaudeville, musical theatre, and commercial dance driven by Euro-American perspective and aesthetics. Thompson (2014) explained how "[t]hrough their own Western gaze, these writers transformed African music and dance performances into sexualized scenes of intellectual and cultural inferiority for the consumption of a primarily white, male audience" (p. 23). Additionally, Brenda Dixon Gottschild (2003) explained how "[f]or centuries whites have seen the black body as a sexualized terrain—not because black people are sexually different from whites, innately or biologically, but because that is how whites chose to perceive blacks" (p. 41).

To this point, the Lindy Hop was considered by many to be "hot," sexualized, animalistic, raw, and savage when performed by Black dancers and viewed through a White lens. In fact, "[i]n the United States the dance was denounced...as a throwback to primitivism, a form of mass hysteria, and as leading to sexual deviation" (Crease, 1995, p. 211). Given the assignment of descriptors such as sexual and savage to Black-originated dancing, how do we reconcile the overtly and widely accepted sexualized connotations and situational choreographic narratives created and made popular by White male choreographers such as Bob Fosse or Jack Cole? What about the famous ballroom instructors, Irene and Vernon Castle, and their pedagogical approaches that erased the Africanist elements of Black-originated ragtime and animal dances in order to make the movements more appealing, easy to learn, and morally acceptable to White dancers and viewers? The colonization and codification of Black dances and dancing by the Castles, Cole, and Fosse are just a few examples of how systemic Whiteness affords White artists the ability to shape the narrative as to how Black dances are embodied and passed down and how Black dancing bodies are perceived, often reflecting cultural and socio-political ideals that are in direct contrast to the origins of the forms.

Systemic Narratives: Patriarchal Codification, and the Colonization of Women in Jazz Dance

There are distinct variations in training methodology and choreographic processes (the ways in which movement is passed down or taught to others) between jazz dance that originates from the Africanist aesthetic and that which is fused with, or centers, Eurocentric aesthetics. Dating back to colonial America, the Eurocentric perspective imposed guidelines that upheld and promoted societal norms of gendered behavior—how one should look, move, and interact socially based on their gender. With its erect, upright spine and highly controlled movements, all hallmarks of Eurocentric ideals, dancing was used as a vehicle for teaching manners and good morals with the intention that young, rich (White) girls learned to be good wives, good members of society, and good Christians (Malone, 1996, p. 38). While learning these danced-manners, the students were expected to follow the instructor exactly; to imitate the precise line and formation of the body in space without straying from the correct form or position. To make a personal choice or an improvised interpretation of a particular step that varied from what was dictated by the instructor would have been considered highly inappropriate and low class.

Conversely, the ethos of the Africanist aesthetic in learning and passing down embodied histories values personal expression and improvisation; one is not meant to follow the leader exactly or strive for rigid perfection in the teaching, learning, or performance process. For example, in referencing dancing of the plantation era, Malone (1996) shared how "slaves enjoyed a spontaneity, dynamism, and improvisational flair that reached back to their ancestors in central and western Africa, while the planters believed that a dance must be performed in a precise, unchanging way" (p. 49). When describing the ways in which the Lindy Hop dancers at the Savoy Ballroom passed around steps, Frankie Manning (2007) said, "[i]f another person learned your step, they might improve on it, which happened all the time. Then when someone else did it, it could spread, and the dance could advance" (p. 101) which reinforces the informal way (oral versus written and/or outside of the academy) in which the steps were taught in combination with the improvisatory nature of the learning process. One was expected to change the step and make it their own, allowing autonomous personal expression in dance without the constraints of gendered and social expectations for the dancer. The evolution of African-derived dance steps, especially jazz dance, is fundamentally based on cultural, social, and socio-political influences; personal interpretations of the movement and a reflections of one's true self are valued and affirmed in the movement.

In her book *Babylon Girls: Black Women Performers and the Shaping of the Modern*, author and scholar Jayna Brown discussed the training and performative institution of the chorus girl of the vaudeville era around the mid-nineteenth century and uses Englishman John Tiller's strict institutional training method as an example. Known as the "father of precision dance," his model was fundamental in establishing a "signature system for the formal training of chorus girl troupes" that were posited as "a welcome alternative to factory work and the dangers of poverty for young working-class girls" (Brown, 2008, p. 165). Brown explained how

> the meticulously rendered dance routines reflected the disciplinary training young girls should receive to become productive workers, as well as to avoid the temptations of the streets – the evils of sex, drink, and idleness – which they were seen as particularly vulnerable to

(p. 166)

While the Tiller girls did not necessarily fall under the jazz dance idiom, they made a formidable impression on the commercialized dance-as-entertainment industry featuring colonized female dancing bodies. The Tiller girls were a precursor to women working in shows produced by Florenz Ziegfeld who would come to represent the ideal chorus girls of the 1910s and 1920s. "Ziegfeld, the stage director Julian Mitchell, and Anna Held sensed the change in modern concepts of sexuality and designed a new ideal: the slim, athletic, and definitively Anglo-Saxon beauty" (Brown, 2008, p. 166). Morality-driven dancing structures in jazz-adjacent forms created race-based differentiation between Eurocentric and African-American movement and cultural philosophies surrounding the moving body, thereby continuing the practice of "othering" Black dance and the social dance origin of jazz dance. Noticeably, the whitened version of jazz dance of the era eliminated personal expression and any kind of undulation of the spine and incorporation of the rhythmic pelvis; decades later, the whitened version of jazz dance would be noticeably hypersexual, confidently embracing the sex-as-entertainment and sex-as-dancing commodity in a mainstream and culturally accepted way.

Around the turn of the twentieth century, socio-political and patriarchal themes were reflected onstage through the strict organization and machination of women's bodies in motion. The Eurocentric morality- driven unison dancing was intrinsically tied to good manners, follow-the-directions dancing, and Eurocentric aesthetics and standards of beauty and would set the standard for gendered stereotypes for women, specifically White women, in jazz-adjacent dance forms. One can see evidence of the industrialization of the female body in motion in the ways the "principles of uniformity, precision of routine, and efficiency of movement governing this period of industrial development were reflected in the codification of rigid dance training systems and increasingly regimented dance routines" (Brown, 2008, p. 164).

Issues of power and privilege were prevalent in the pre-jazz era of ragtime and blues music as White dance instructors Irene and Vernon Castle "whitened" ragtime dances to be more acceptable to White audiences and students. In her chapter "Just Like Being at the Zoo: Primitivity and Ragtime Dance" from *Ballroom, Boogie, Shimmy Sham, Shake: A Social and Popular Dance Reader*, Nadine George-Graves (2009) described how they "removed the African American influences on the movement styles that they considered lascivious because they were looser limbed" and "they emphasized the uprightness of the torso to be more in keeping with the European tradition" (p. 64). Moreover, Brown stated that the Castles determined that

> areas of the body, particularly the pelvis, the hips, and the chest, were hot zones, body parts that, when in full use, spoke undeniably of the natural urges that a civilized body should restrain. The expressive uses of these "zones" in dances were the language though which the gendered definitions of race and class were formed and contested in the body.
>
> *(Brown, 2008, p. 173)*

Jazz dance underwent a codified morphosis in the 1940s with the emergence and popularity of artists such as Jack Cole, Gus Giordano, Matt Mattox, Bob Fosse, and Luigi. Anointed with titles such as, "father of theatrical jazz dance" and "godfather of jazz," as in the case of Jack Cole and Gus Giordano, respectively, this group of choreographers and educators put forth narratives that erase and/or appropriate the roots of jazz dance. As White men, they had a platform of visibility, availability of resources, and masses of predominantly White students that allowed them the ability to redefine jazz dance according to *their* lived experiences. They took elements of African-derived jazz dance and inserted a Euro-American perspective to "legitimize" the work, elevate it, and make it high art that was acceptable to concert and commercial dance values and venues—a White savior perspective that assumes the art form needs to be made legitimate in order to be accepted by consumers. This was justified by the improvisatory nature of an evolutionary and culturally responsive art form as they used improvisation and personal expression as a vehicle to inserting their own Euro-American experiences and aesthetics into the work while erasing the origins in West and Central

African cultures and the African American experience. In his chapter "Jazz Dance and Racism" from *Jazz Dance: A History of the Roots and Branches*, author Carlos Jones explained that "the development of jazz dance as a codified technique during the latter half of the twentieth century has blurred or completely erased movement that does not emanate from white ideas of artistic value" (2014, p. 236). He went on to state:

> The marker for excellent artistry rejects the African aesthetic for the European idea of beauty. Dropping the pelvis, rolling through the hips, and rebounding up through an articulated torso are replaced by a rigidly controlled torso with elongated arms and a leg extension. The reason for raising one aesthetic over another emerges from racial privilege favoring a white choreographer over others.
>
> *(Jones, 2014, p. 236)*

Often, as was the case in the work of Cole, Giordano, and Fosse, their artistic point of view also assigned gender markers to the moving body, especially for women. Whether it was the masculine-leaning (read as strong, grounded, powerful) Giordano technique, the sultry, come-hither sensuality of Marilyn Monroe under the direction of Cole, or the hypersexualized movements of the quint-essential Fosse dancer, the jazz dance techniques harbored patriarchal determinations for the ways women performed gender that, because of their wide visibility in the theatrical and concert jazz dance arenas, had lasting implications for gender expression along the binary.

One part of the jazz dance continuum that became especially prevalent in the 1980s with the emergence of MTV music television was music video dance where "the emphasis was on contemporary movement styles to accompany new music ... [where] much of the choreography reflected a jazz dance sensibility" (George, 2014, p. 176). The music videos of this era used dance as a selling point for the artists' music and brand and the "choreography was characterized by kinetic, primal, often sensual movements, punctuated by punches, thrusts, and undulations" (George, 2014, p. 176). It was the dawn of an era of commercial dance that is still popular today. Defined as "any type of jazz dance that is associated with selling a product such as a car, clothing, or a song...or jazz-influenced dance performed in large, for-profit venues such as Las Vegas nightclubs, on television, or in film" (Guarino and Oliver, 2014, p. 28), commercial dance is most widely associated with popular music artists, commercials, music tours, dance television shows, and even musical theatre dance.

Commercial jazz dance inhabits a presentational body in that the dancing is meant for the visual consumption of others. The moving body is commodified and presented for the viewing pleasure and financial gain of others, often at the expense of the performer. Often, the movement aesthetics are highly gendered along the binary and because of the commercial nature of the genre, often center hypersexualized movements meant to attract viewers and reflect popular trends in current vernacular dances. This reinforces and perpetuates a system of gendered bodies as determined by patriarchal and White supremacist narratives that are normalized and accepted as the standard for all of jazz dance. Even when the movement is re-gendered (masculine-assigned movement aesthetics performed by female-presenting dancers or feminine-assigned movement aesthetics performed by male-presenting dancers), it still upholds stereotypes about the ways in which gender is expressed.

Rooted: Gender-Expansive Movement Aesthetics and Choreography

What would jazz dance look like in a culture that disrupts a system of heteronormative movement aesthetics that adhere to binary-aligning gender norms and are driven by patriarchal systems that uphold presentational and embodied stereotypes for women? An example of authentic jazz dancing that demonstrates kinetic elements that are separate from gender presentation can be found in the choreography and performance of Whitey's Lindy Hoppers. Whitey's Lindy Hoppers, assembled by Herbert "Whitey" White (a dancing waiter-turned-bouncer at the Savoy ballroom in New York

City) and led by Lindy Hop innovator Frankie Manning, are known as the greatest practitioners of Lindy Hop with their intense high-energy, incredibly rhythmic, and dynamic performances. During the 1920s, 1930s, and 1940s, the jazz swing rhythms and the accompanying dancing was representative of the symbiotic relationship between jazz musicians and jazz dancers, resulting in a simultaneous creation of music and movement. For the dancers, in response to the music, it was not about how the movement *looked* but rather how it *felt* which was not a gendered physical response but rather an emotional and musical response. It was a physical embodied expression of how the sound felt, how it pulsed through the body, how it elicited an undeniable human experience that was shared between the dancers.

Elements of the Lindy Hop, as seen in Whitey's Lindy Hoppers' performance in the 1941 movie *Hellzapoppin'*, showcase non-gendered movement in partnering mechanics and styled aesthetics. The dancing was performed in male/female couplings, adhering to traditional heteronormative partnering norms as well as upholding gender presentation models through costuming; but the *action* defied gender norms, as evidenced in the descriptive language used by author Robert Crease (1995) in his article, "Divine Frivolity: Hollywood Representations of the Lindy Hop, 1937–1942." When describing the dance scene from *Hellzapoppin'* (1941) featuring Whitey's Lindy Hoppers, Crease noted the way the dancers execute the steps when he states, "here the dancers are *thrown*, and without missing a beat—and not only do men throw women, but women throw men" (1995, p. 220). He went on to describe a moment between Al Minns and his partner, Willamae Ricker, where Minns "is held above the ground, upside down, by his partner" (1995, p. 220), demonstrating a partnering relationship that very much defies the traditional roles played by men and women.

Throughout the chapter, Crease described partnering relationships that were far from reminiscent of the rigid binary gender norms of the Eurocentric partnering of other forms of dance. Often in ballet, the woman is a passive participant (through appearance, not execution as women are anything but passive when in a partnering situation) while being lifted in the air, held above the man's head, and carefully carried through space as if on display. In contrast, Crease (1995) stated, "[i]n an air step, one partner lifted, flipped, tossed, or threw the other" and also described a moment in *A Day at the Races* with Snookie Beasely and Willamae Ricker where "Beasely picks Ricker up, tossed her through his legs, and throws her in the air so that her feet reach for the ceiling" (p. 214). Even when the narrative roles subscribe to heteronormative constructs of male and female partnering norms, the movement aesthetics do not. To this point, Billy Siegenfeld stated, "[i]nstead of emphasizing the outside-seen beauties of the body, the Lindy invites the eyes to feel-through beneath the body's surface to the energy shared by two people engaged in vigorously rhythmic, call-and-response relationships" (2014, p. 270).

A contemporary example of the social and kinetic elements of the Africanist aesthetic that disrupts societal gender norms assigned for women can be seen in the music video for Jon Batiste's "FREEDOM" which is set in New Orleans and features cultural markers of the African American experience. Interestingly, the dancing might be considered a commercial dance form since the dancing bodies are used as a vehicle for promoting and selling Batiste's music and personal brand. However, instead of subscribing to gender-assigned movement norms and heteronormative relational narratives driven by a commercialized Euro-American aesthetic commonly associated with commercial jazz dance, the movement aesthetics and visual cues maintain their cultural roots and social and kinetic elements of jazz dance while also serving the purpose of promoting the music of Batiste. Women-presenting dancers perform movements that highlight spinal undulations and pelvic isolations in choreography that harnesses communal elements of social dancing. Most notably, the intention of the choreography does not seem to present the body for visual consumption but rather to celebrate the embodied energy and felt sensation of the body in motion and in relation to the other performers, people, in the created environment. The dancers seem less concerned with performing for the viewer by highlighting and perpetuating feminine-assigned gender norms often used in entertainment to sell a product but instead are a part of the musical environment, reflecting cultural ties to African-American derived music and dance. A century after the Lindy Hoppers at the Savoy Ballroom, Batiste and the dancers are bringing social dance forms to the commercial dance arena while disrupting patriarchal or White supremacist systems, shifting the narrative from oppressive structures that typically produced stereotypical gender norms.

An example of a concert jazz dance form that makes space for autonomous gender expression and disrupts performative gender norms is Jump Rhythm® Technique (JRT), created by Billy Siegenfeld, founder and artistic director of Jump Rhythm® Jazz Project. JRT is a jazz rhythm-generated system of dance and theatre movement training that focuses on the expression of percussive energy rather than on the perfection of codified shapes. Based in the vernacular body, it calls upon functional alignment principles and emotion-driven instincts to fuel energy-specific jazz rhythms that are articulated in the expressive body. In both pedagogy and choreography, JRT directly contrasts the Euro centric philosophy and aesthetics of commercial jazz dance in that it prioritizes time-articulated, rhythm-specific energy performed in the "everyday" pedestrian self over the outward appearance (read societally and culturally approved) presentation of the body. According to Siegenfeld, "Rhythm is a phenomenon of energy and thus something sensed within the body. The verticality-asserting spine of ballet is a phenomenon of space and thus best appreciated by the eyes" (2014, p. 270). JRT eliminates the need to assign gender to the movement and instead puts rhythm, energy, and emotion at the forefront of the embodied relational conversation of jazz music and jazz dance.

Percussive vocalizations are an integral part of Jump Rhythm® Technique classes. Working to transform the moving body into a rhythmically accurate percussive instrument that "plays" jazz-influenced rhythms in the body by directing specifically timed bursts of energy to the extremities of the body, namely the hands, head, and feet, students learn exercises and choreography by articulating rhythm through scat-sung syllables, thus engaging both the voice and body in a simultaneous exploration of sound and movement. This approach is specifically designed to redirect their kinesthetic awareness towards an internally driven, externally realized movement aesthetic. Using the voice as an accompaniment to the movement clarifies the rhythm in the body and supports the emotional feel or narrative of the work.

Wendy Oliver and Doug Risner stated that "the messages that dancers receive and respond to regarding gender are deeply ingrained and affect their psyches, behavior, and creative output" (2017, p. 2).When asked how it felt to vocalize for the first time in a Jump Rhythm® class, students overwhelmingly responded that they felt weird, uncomfortable, and/or were afraid of being heard and subsequently judged for the sound of their voice, their choices in scat-sung syllabus, or of singing the wrong rhythm. Percussive movement and vocalizations are often perceived as ugly, awkward, aggressive, too direct, or assertive, especially when compared to the narratives regarding gender expression that have been normalized for women in jazz dance. Grammy-award winning jazz percussionist and jazz and gender advocate Terri Lyne Carrington noted that "women have not been socialized to play drums. It's not natural for us to hit things" (2020) which directly relates to the experiences of young women in percussive dance forms. The sharp, highly energized percussive movements and vocalizations of JRT and other rhythmic vernacular jazz dance forms are a distinct departure from the slinky, fluid, long, and lean stereotypes assigned for women in jazz.

Even though embodying percussive rhythms and vocalizing percussively goes against the hyperfeminine movement norms for women in jazz, students often express how good they feel after a class in which they were encouraged to channel their full emotional energy into the percussive "hits" in order to "play" the complex rhythms in the body. This action of using the hands, feet, and voice to drum the rhythms of the movement redefines the socially constructed gendered representation of women and offers agency and a platform to be heard, both literally and figuratively.

Conclusion

Jazz dance's embedded ethos of personal expression, communal inclusivity, and celebration of visceral energy make it a prime art form to experiment with non-binary gender performance. "Being free to speak one's inside voice requires taking a stand apart from what is conventionally approved of" (Siegenfeld, 2014, p. 275). As twenty-first century jazz dance practitioners, educators, choreographers, performers, and scholars, we have a responsibility to curate jazz-inspired work through a lens that is culturally and socially responsible, honoring the Africanist and African American roots and making space for gender inclusive movement aesthetics that affirm individual expression within the community.

To this, I send out a call to educators, choreographers, and practitioners that claim jazz dance and also to the young dancers who are passionate about jazz as future performers, practitioners, choreographers, scholars, and writers. How can we build a practice that honors, affirms, and centers the African roots and Africanist aesthetics? How can we adopt new pedagogies and choreographic structures and narratives that are truly inclusive to all and that move beyond the heteronormative binaries and patriarchal and White supremacist systems often seen in past and present-day jazz dance? How can we embody this change, especially given that jazz is, inherently, an embodied art form from its origins? Moreover, how will one's practice shift to reflect a twenty-first century awareness and make reparations to decades of erasure and racism by omission?

Based on my experience teaching jazz dance in higher education, my sense is that the current generation of young artists are curious—they have access to in-depth historical, cultural, and socio-political visual and written scholarship and archival information and can utilize social media as a platform for greater visibility and representation, especially for marginalized forms of dance such as jazz. This socially conscious curiosity, when considered in relation to gender and jazz dance, can be used to subvert societally constructed gender norms to make jazz more radically inclusive for all genders so that the music, dance, and lived experiences come to the forefront of this vibrant, culturally rich art form.

Notes

1 In her book, *The Black Dancing Body: A Geography from Coon to Cool*, scholar Brenda Dixon Gottschild denotes her use of the term "black dancing body" in reference to her exploration of the Africanist presence in black dance performance. She establishes this term as an expansion of the term "the dancing body" often used in contemporary dance.

References

Amin, T. (2014). The African origins of an American art form. In L. Guarino & W. Oliver (Eds.), *Jazz dance: A history of the roots and branches* (pp. 35–44). Gainesville, FL: University Press of Florida.

Belling, G. (2017). Engendered. In W. Oliver and D. Risner (Eds.), *Dance and Gender: An Evidence-Based Approach* (pp. 60–75). Gainesville, FL: University Press of Florida.

Brown, J. (2008). *Babylon girls: Black women performers and the shaping of the modern*. Durham, NC: Duke University Press.

Butler, J. (1988). Performative acts and gender constitution: An essay in phenomenology and feminist theory. *Theatre Journal*, 40, 519–531.

Cobrin, P. (2011). *From Winning the Vote to Directing on Broadway: The Emergence of Women on the New York Stage, 1880–1927*. Lewisburg, PA: Bucknell University Press.

Cohen, P. (2014). Jazz dance as a continuum. In L. Guarino & W. Oliver (Eds.), *Jazz dance: A history of the roots and branches* (pp. 3–7). Gainesville, FL: University Press of Florida.

Coleman, B. E., and Sebesta, J. (2008). *Women in American Musical Theatre: Essays on Composers, Lyricists, Librettists, Arrangers, Choreographers, Designers, Directors, Producers and Performance Artists*. McFarland.

Crease, R. (1995). *Divine Frivolity: Hollywood Representations of the Lindy Hop 1937–1942*. In Krin Gabbard (Ed.), (pp. 207–228). Durham, NC: Duke University Press.

Fine, C. (2010). *Delusions of Gender: How Our Minds, Society, and Neurosexism Create Difference of Gender*. New York and London: W.W. Norton.

George, M. (2014). Jazz dance, pop culture, and the music video era. In L. Guarino & W. Oliver (Eds.), *Jazz Dance: A History of the Roots and Branches* (pp. 174–183). Gainesville, FL: University Press of Florida.

George-Graves, N. (2009). Just like being at the zoo: Primitivity and ragtime dance. In J. Malnig (Ed.), *Ballroom, Boogie, Shimmy Sham, Shake: A Social and Popular Dance Reader* (pp. 55–71). Urbana and Chicago, IL: University of Illinois Press.

Gottschild, B. D. (1998). *Digging the Africanist Presence in American Performance: Dance and Other Contexts*. Westport, CT: Praeger.

Gottschild, B. D. (2003). *The Black Dancing Body: A Geography from Coon To Cool*. New York, NY: Palgrave Macmillan.

Guarino, L., & Oliver, W. (2014). *Jazz dance: A history of the roots and branches*. Gainesville, FL: University Press of Florida.

Jones, C. (2014). Jazz Dance and Racism. In L. Guarino and W. Oliver (Eds.), *Jazz Dance: A History of the Roots and Branches* (pp. 93–102). Gainesville, FL: University Press of Florida.

Kotz, L. (1992, November). The body you want: An interview with judith butler. *Artforum*. https://www.artforum.com/print/199209/the-body-you-want-an-inteview-with-judith-butler-33505.

Malone, J. (1996). Steppin' on the Blues: The Visible Rhythms of African American Dance. Urbana and Chicago: University of Illinois Press.

Manning, F., and Millman, C. (2007). *Frankie Manning: Ambassador of Lindy Hop*. Philadelphia, PA: Temple University Press.

Oliver, W., and Risner, D. (2017). *Dance and gender: An evidence-based approach*. Gainesville, FL: University Press of Florida.

Russell, A., Schaefer, G., and Reilly, E. (2018). Sexualization of prepubescent girls in dance competition: Innocent fun or "sexploitation"? Strategies (Reston, VA), 31(5), 3–7. https://doi.org/10.1080/08924562.2018.1490229

Sandlos, Lisa. (2015). Shimmy, shake, or shudder?: Behind the scenes performances of competitive dance moms. In A. Kinser, K. Freehling-Burton, and T. Hawkes (Eds.), *Performing Motherhood: Artistic, Activist, and Everyday Enactments* (99–120). Bradford ON: Demeter Press.

Schupp, K. (2017). Sassy Girls and Hard-Hitting Boys: Dance Competition Culture and Gender. In W. Oliver and D. Risner (Eds.), *Dance and Gender: An Evidence-Based Approach* (76–96). Gainesville, FL: University Press of Florida.

Siegenfeld, B. (2009). Standing down straight: Jump rhythm technique's rhythm-driven, community-directed approach to dance education. *Journal of Dance Education*, 9, 110–119.

Siegenfeld, B. (2014). "Performing energy: American rhythm dancing and the articulation of the inarticulate". In L. Guarino & W. Oliver (Eds.), *Jazz Dance: A History of the Roots and Branches* (pp. 268–278). Gainesville, FL: University Press of Florida.

Terri Lyne Carrington [Facebook page]. (October 15, 2020). Retrieved June 16, 2021, from www.facebook.com/TerriLyneCarrington.

The Tiller Girls. (n.d.). Retrieved from https://tillergirls.com

Thompson, K. D. (2014). *Ring Shout, Wheel About: The Racial Politics of Music and Dance in North American Slavery*. Urbana, IL: University of Illinois Press.

19

WOMEN'S ACCESS TO PROFESSIONAL JAZZ

From Limiting Processes to Levers for Transgression

Marie Buscatto

All around the world, jazz is a very "masculine" scene,[1] both numerically and symbolically, whether in France (Buscatto, 2007 [2018], 2021), in Great Britain (Raine, 2020), in Germany (Schulz, Ries, Zimmerman, 2016), in Sweden (Björck, Bergman, 2018) or in the United States (Jeffri, 2003), to name a few examples. While the invisibility and exclusion of female jazz musicians in past history is well documented (e.g. Dahl, 1984; Gourse, 1995; Tucker, 2002), no empirical contemporary study fully explores not only the scarcity of female jazz musicians in contemporary jazz worlds, but also social processes which enable some women to get access to professional jazz, sometimes at the highest level of reputation.

Based on two empirical long-term ethnographies conducted in France and in Japan, this chapter will both explain how female jazz musicians, as compared to their male colleagues, are limited in their ability to access, to maintain themselves and to get recognized as jazz musicians, and unveil how some women do get access to the jazz scene, and do maintain themselves over time, sometimes at the highest level of reputation. Through a systematic comparison of the trajectories of male and female musicians in both countries, this chapter will thus explain the strong numeric difference observed between both countries, since women represent around 30 percent of professional jazz musicians in Japan and less than 10 percent in France.[2]

Being a Professional Jazz Musician: A Strong Calling, A Tough Life Choice

In both countries, being a professional jazz musician is both a personal calling and a difficult life choice (Buscatto, 2004; Buscatto, 2022a). Both scenes are active and enable jazz musicians to make a living, but it comes at a high personal and economic cost.

Since jazz is a middle-upper class niche music whose popularity is quite limited, making a living as a jazz musician often requires working with others on different projects over time. One leads his or her own band, sometimes two or three bands at a time, but also plays with others as a side(wo)man. Moreover, if jazz in dedicated concert halls is what all dream to experience, most of jazz musicians have to develop multi-activity to make a living: teaching; performing in hotels, private parties or company events; participating in popular music recording sessions; arranging or composing popular music, children or movie tunes; accompanying musicians in other musical styles (salsa, folk, rock,

DOI: 10.4324/9781003081876-21

etc.); working as a cultural intermediary (for instance as a festival organizer, as a studio manager or a technician, as a music translator or as a recording technician); and, even, sometimes, working outside of jazz (such as for instance massaging, modelling or teaching French, Japanese, English or literature).

While a few renowned jazz musicians can make a living playing jazz only, most professional jazz musicians have to play different types of music in different settings and, in Japan even more so than in France, teach around half of the time. Moreover, Japanese and French jazz musicians have to spend a lot of time getting work and maintaining themselves as musicians: they have to do a lot of entrepreneurial and relational work with club managers, other musicians, potential club customers, students, jazz critics, jazz intermediaries or jazz agents.... Given all the work to be done in order to be able to make a living, their lives are quite flexible, precarious and they work long hours.

For the most renowned musicians, jazz keeps them busy (as teachers and as musicians) most of the time, but for most professional jazz musicians, jazz is almost a costly activity they engage in once they have taught music, played in other musical settings and/or worked outside of the music world to make a living. But whatever their professional situations, jazz is always defined as their calling, the music they are passionate about. While some are more into New Orleans, swing or bebop styles, others are devoted to hard bop, post-bop or improvised music, but all of them think of jazz as a passion, as a calling legitimating all the economic and personal hurdles they daily experience.

Jazz as a "Masculine" and Gender-Segregated World

This chapter is based on a systematic comparison between the French and the Japanese jazz worlds. In both countries, it appears that jazz remains quite a masculine and gender-segregated world, even if the Japanese scene has recently experienced a strong, even if partial, feminization process.

The study in France was led from 1998 till 2010, with recurrent updates up to now: interviews, observations, jazz press follow-up. The French jazz world is still a very masculine world both numerically and symbolically. First of all, around 8 percent of jazz musicians are women and no feminization has been observed since my first study.[3] Moreover, the French jazz world appears as a very segregated world, both horizontally and vertically. While around 65 percent of singers are women, around 4 percent of instrumentalists are women, some instruments being more feminine than others, such as the piano (around 6%), the harp (4 women) or the violin (around 9%), while others are very masculine such as the double-bass (less than 1%), the guitar (less than 2%), the trumpet (less than 2%) or the drums (less than 2%). And those few women tend to disappear over time, even more than men, even though most of them made it early on at the highest level of reputation.

The study in Japan has been conducted since November 2017 and has included interviews, observations, a daily Facebook follow-up with interviewed musicians, and jazz press follow-up (Buscatto, 2022a). I have listed around 654 musicians active in Tokyo and its surroundings.[4] Recently, the Japanese jazz world has been partly feminized: about 30 percent of jazz musicians are women, even more so among young musicians. As in France, it is quite a segregated, gendered world, both horizontally and vertically. Most singers are women (85%), some instruments are more feminine than others, such as the piano (47% of pianists are female), the koto (1), the clarinet (2 women), the flute (4 women, 3 men) or the violin (four women, four men) while others are very masculine such as the double-bass (98% of men), the guitar (95%) or the drums (92%). Wind instruments seem to have been partly feminized recently: saxophone (27% of women), trumpet (18% of women) and trombone (23%) with most women playing those instruments being under forty years old. And last but not least, women tend to disappear over time, more often than men, even though they made it early, as in France.

How to explain both the gendered horizontal and vertical segregations observed in France and in Japan as well as the recent feminization happening in Japan? How do some women happen to become female jazz musicians in France as well as in Japan? Here are the issues that will be addressed next in this chapter.

Limiting Social Processes: A Negative Cumulative Dynamic

The difficulties encountered by female jazz musicians are due to five main general processes which tend to accumulate over time, at different stages of women's potential careers—to develop musical practices at an early age, to choose to act as professional artists, to get trained, to get recruited, to experience art in favorable conditions once they have become professional musicians, to be able to make a living from jazz, to build up a reputation, to maintain oneself as a jazz professional musician over time.

Each of those five general processes varies in its specific form, from one person to another, from one country to another, and may also have an impact more or less powerful on women's abilities to act as artists, depending on the moment of their trajectory and their own resources to overcome those processes. But one is to understand that those processes do accumulate over time, one way or the other, to limit women's abilities to enter, to maintain themselves, and to get recognized as professional jazz musicians.[5]

Overrepresentation of Female Musicians in Devalued Singing

In all art worlds (Becker, 1982), women tend to be overrepresented in so-called "feminine" styles, genres or instruments, while men tend to be overrepresented in so-called "masculine" styles, genres or instruments. Those words ("feminine" and "masculine") are to be taken in two socially constructed senses here: practiced primarily by women/men and socially conceived of as feminine/masculine. And "feminine" activities tend to be devalued artistically (Buscatto, 2018). In jazz, the same phenomenon is observed when it comes to jazz singing which is both a "feminine" activity (numerically and symbolically) and is devalued musically as such.

On the one side, a strong proportion of female musicians are singers, and a vast majority of singers are women: 40 percent of Japanese female jazz musicians are singers and 80 percent of Japanese jazz singers are female while 65 percent of French jazz singers are female, and female jazz singers represent around 60 percent of French female musicians. On the other side, female singers are negatively hierarchized, and this affects their ability not only to play music and to remain as active singers over time, but also to be recognized by their colleagues and critics as worthwhile musicians when they remain as musicians, despite all difficulties.

Indeed, in Japan as in France, even if jazz singers find it easier than jazz instrumentalists to play music in commercial environments due to the audience's attraction to singers, they are not much invited as side-women by other instrumentalists and find it difficult to survive as jazz musicians over time, whatever their level of reputation:

> I play in jazz clubs once or twice a month. I have to get the customers come in. I am a singer, so, when I have a gig, I have to pay for the pianist, the drummer, the bassist, so I need to find the customers, the jazz clubs do not have any customers. Usually, in Japan, singers have to get the customers, especially the jazz clubs. So, it is very hard to play in jazz clubs for me. ... Sometimes musicians invite me to their gigs, but even then, I have to get the customers since I am singing on the stage most of the time!
>
> *(Female Japanese jazz singer, 40 years old)*

They either accept to lead their own band and develop multi-activity to make a living, or they drop out of the jazz music business, being tired of being on their own and not being able to make a living as their male counterparts. Therefore, unlike worldwide famous singers, such as Stacey Kent, Diana Krall or Cassandra Wilson, except for a few exceptions, even the most-renowned French or Japanese jazz singers never make a living with jazz. They mostly teach, lead choirs, do studio voices or have 'day' jobs outside their musical field. Jazz singing is indeed not considered as real jazz and tends to be associated with commercial work.

This is partly due—but not only, as I discuss later on—to the fact that instrumentalists and singers do not have the same conception of what characterizes music. In other words, while instrumentalists tend to share a "masculine" conception of jazz, female singers tend to share a "feminine" conception of jazz. This creates constant tensions and misunderstandings between those women and men when working together. Singers are often interested in interpreting songs and melodies. They focus on telling stories to the audience. Sounds and music, rhythmic and melodic ideas are important but only as long as they enable the singer to perform a melody in an emotional and personal way. The instrumentalist's main objective is to invent new songs, to create original music, to improvise creatively. Playing the melody is thus considered as secondary, whereas rhythmic, melodic or tonal creation comes first.

When playing together, these two differing conceptions of music, socially constructed as "feminine" and "masculine," make life difficult for everyone. On the one hand, singers complain about instrumentalists who do not respect the singing rhythms and specificities, are too talkative, or simply do not share their ideas. On the other hand, instrumentalists get tired of singers who are perceived as not being creative, autonomous, original. Singers tend to be associated with the discredited world of commercial jazz music—too easy to write, not at all original—which places them on the lowest rungs of the ladder of this musical world.

"Feminine" Negative Stereotypes Limiting the Recognition of Female Jazz Musicians as Real Artists

This leads us to the second key social process that makes it more difficult for female jazz musicians than male jazz musicians to remain in the jazz world; namely, the strength of "feminine" negative stereotypes. As already partly suggested above, this is quite damaging to women's long-term commercial, musical and professional access to jazz music. Whether the female stereotypes associated with women artists pertain to sexuality, seductiveness, motherhood, creative dependence, frailty or (lack of) virtuosity, they often go along with a disparaging attitude when it comes to assessing women's professional artistic abilities or the quality of the works of art they produce.

Let's see how this works out in Japan and France, since this process affects both singers and female instrumentalists, even if partly differently.

Regarding singers, even the ones who improvise and share instrumentalists' "masculine" conceptions of jazz tend not to be considered as real musicians and are thus not invited to work by the instrumentalists. Their performances are indeed not considered as "real" work, and are instead conceived as the "natural" expression of their true personality. On the one hand, their voice is not considered to be an instrument: as mentioned by a middle-aged French singer "for instrumentalists, a voice is natural, it does not need work. This explains the old cliché that singers are not musicians." On the other hand, while singing implies that one learns to work on one's physical posture on stage, this type of work is generally considered as the expression of one's natural capacities to attract the public. Their scenic work is quite invisible for instrumentalists and even for singers, who think of it as nothing but an expression of their true personality and their capacity to seduce, quite a disparaging vision of their professional scenic abilities.

Female instrumentalists, as well as female singers, are confronted with two more stereotypes which make it difficult for them to be considered as serious musicians.

On the one side, they tend to be sexualized by their colleagues. Women jazz performers radiate a strong seductive power, not only in the direction of the audience, but also for their music partners. Both female instrumentalists and singers tend to attract their colleagues' and the audience's sexual desire. While some degree of seductive power is required on stage (make-up, dress, expressions), that power seems like a permanent "danger" for jazz women who want to develop "healthy" relations with their colleagues, the cultural intermediaries or the audience. This is especially true for younger women players, but also affects the oldest ones. As they occasionally explained, "involuntary" mistakes are usually costly: collaborations that break off suddenly, a male musician, a jazz club owner or a producer who denigrates a female musician who rejected his advances, or a reputation that makes professional relations difficult. And in order to avoid such mistakes, they may avoid close relationships with their male colleagues, being then either considered as aloof or distant (and thus not interesting colleagues due to the lack of proximity) or dangerous women for the band (they may disturb the band if one musician falls in love or if a relationship develops with one of them). And sometimes those women do experience some kind of sexual harassment that leads them to stop the working relationship and feel quite pained and discouraged due to this difficulty to work in healthy relationships with male colleagues. This stereotype may get in the way by the accusation of their being put on the program because of their charm and seductive power and not for their musical qualities.

A second stereotype that strongly affects their ability to play as jazz musicians is the tendency of others to consider that women lack authority, making it difficult for them to be considered as legitimate leaders and to be accepted as such. Those, a minority, who have a strong reputation as leaders, tend to be considered by their male colleagues as difficult to play with. Their ability to lead and give orders is perceived as linked to their difficult personality, which is then denigrated as such, and which makes it difficult for them to be invited by colleagues. Those women, a majority, who try not to be considered difficult and to find ways to lead without hurting their male colleagues' feelings, tend not to be considered as strong-minded enough and thus also difficult to invite to play with.

"Masculine" Social Networks

Various research studies have demonstrated the importance of social networks for getting into and remaining in fluid, open art worlds, and for building-up a strong reputation (Becker, 1982). Co-optation is also facilitated by the intervention of close intermediaries: critics, agents, producers, and any other external sources of support. The fact is that artistic worlds are men's worlds, even when they are constituted of a majority of women, as theatre or dance, and they prove relatively unwelcoming to women. Women are more likely than their male colleagues to find themselves "naturally" marginalized and even excluded from networks of the sort that ensure co-optation (Buscatto, 2018).

French and Japanese female jazz instrumentalists as well as singers do not seem to belong to solid informal networks; their male colleagues in those networks do not seem to remember their presence or contributions when drawing up their own projects. When I ask men how they went about hiring musicians for their most recent projects, they mention people with whom they have worked in connection with different musical projects, or else people recommended to them by other musicians. And women are very unlikely to figure autonomously in these sets of potential collaborators.

For instance, when I asked one French instrumentalist if there were women jazz players working on his recent musical project, he answered,

> It's also who you meet by chance. There are the three or four people I've been working with now for around fifteen years already, I mean these guys are … And then there are the new people I met recently who I mentioned to you, two of them, people I've worked with regularly on other projects, and it just happened like that.
>
> *(Male French jazz instrumentalist, 43 years old)*

Women instrumentalists do not have this kind of sustained work relationship with men other than their life partners. And when they do work with men, the women themselves are the ones who took the initiative. Conversely, several women told me how being absent from the jazz scene for six months because they were working continuously on a project in another art world or had withdrawn temporarily for personal reasons—pregnancy, period spent abroad, temporary halt in their musical activities—was all it took for them to "disappear" from the list of "hirable" colleagues, even with people who had seemed their closest partners. When these women performers contact their former work partners, they say they are surprised to hear from them, claiming they were convinced they had too much work or were not playing anymore. They apologize for not being able to call them back in all cases, saying they simply do not have any projects under way themselves.

Impeding "Masculine" Social Conventions and Norms

Once they are 35 years old and above, female musicians—singers and instrumentalists—seem to find it more and more difficult to handle "male" conventions and norms that organize relationships among instrumentalists, despite the fact that they tolerated them fairly well in the early years, when they were becoming professional. Some of them even express the fact that they are "tired," either of the assertive, competitive behavior of some of their male colleagues, or of the self-assertion required for maintaining oneself in this professional arena. They are trying out other types of social relations, which they deem more satisfying, and abandoning what they consider excessively "virile," forceful, competitive behavior:

> When you've got six or seven guys on stage and you're the only woman, it's exhausting, really exhausting.
>
> Q: What makes it that way?
>
> Well, for them when they play, it's like being together on a soccer team—you've got to want to play soccer! I've been with bands on stage where I felt that the guys kept making a big deal of themselves, putting their balls up front. They wanted to wow the audience, that was important to them, and I have a hard time keeping up with them there. It may not look like it, but it gets pretty tiring after a while.
>
> *(Female French jazz instrumentalist, 38 years old)*

Many women over thirty say they "keep fighting" or "have a good sense of repartee." but that they are more and more "sick" of this type of relationship and of being too readily perceived as "moaners" because of it. They may develop other kinds of musical relationships in more mixed or entirely female contexts or outside jazz, or they may make a point of keeping moments experienced as "aggressive" to a minimum by only collaborating musically with musicians who treat them with respect. Being able to work with one's jazzman life partner seems to protect them from negative experiences. Some female musicians (though few of those I met with) go so far as to ask themselves whether they really have an artistic "vocation." This attitude is also found among some jazz men, usually those who have never attained any renown despite their efforts, rather than men who have tasted some type of success, like the women discussed here—the only ones who survive up to 35-40 years old anyway.

Articulating Professional Life and Family Life

The difficulty of combining professional and family life is often put forward to explain women's difficulty gaining access to managerial, scientific, political and leading activist positions or high, demanding social positions once they are getting older. This difficulty is indeed to be found in the lives of women artists in all art worlds once they reach their thirties and partly—but only partly—explains their tendency to withdraw from the artist life in their "career," as shown in all studies devoted to male and female inequalities in arts, even if some women do find ways to do differently (Buscatto, 2018).

When it comes to the French and the Japanese jazz worlds, the main issue, whether conscious or not, seems for those women whether to have children or not. In Japan, where women with kids are supposed to either become housewives or work part-time (White, 2013 [2011]), jazz instrumentalists or singers we met happen not to have kids. Only one female musician out of the eleven interviewed jazz female musicians had kids. This woman had her kid accidently early on and the kid was then raised partly by her husband's parents. Some of those women did say that having kids and being a jazz musician were not compatible and they had made this choice for this reason. Some women said they were too busy to think about it and then it was too late. One of them clearly stated that all her female musician colleagues who had had babies around her had stopped playing jazz seriously, or even completely, for the time being (she had at least ten examples to count). And it happens that all the Japanese jazz female musicians with kids I contacted, despite their very low level of activity in jazz as expressed on their Facebook page, never answered my request. But only one Japanese female musician expressed regrets not having kids despite her efforts late in life. Most of them seemed to think their life was more interesting overall even if their family and friends were putting high pressure on them (or had put high pressure on them when younger). Playing jazz definitely seemed more important than having kids, even if they "love children" and were not yet totally excluding this possibility for the ones below forty:

> My parents want me to get married and to have kids. Many of my friends are of course married and have kids. I love children, but I feel that if I have a baby, what would I do? … If I had a kid, I would have to quit everything! I could keep playing music of course, but I would have to stay at home with my kid, I could not play like now, so I do not see how to have kids, it would be too difficult, I don't see how.
>
> *(Female Japanese Jazz instrumentalist, 35 years old)*

Among French musicians, if half the women did not have kids for about the same reasons and along the same stories, the other half did have kids and their career management modes (highly variable) had proved innovative. Some women, helped by their own mothers, male partners, sisters or friends, managed to rear an only child while continuing along their chosen artistic path. A tiny minority of women artists shared both private and professional roles with their male jazz musician's partner. Yet others put their careers on hold for the time it took to raise children, or, either voluntarily or not, only had begun an artistic career after seeing their children through childhood. But, even if it made life more difficult for them to manage over time, kids were not the main reason for their difficulty to work and to get recognized as a jazz musician—feminine negative stereotypes, masculine conventions and networks being major processes to explain their difficulties as compared to their male colleagues.

Levers for Transgression

As just described, several social processes accumulate over time to ensure that men always fare better than women as jazz musicians. But even if they are not welcome, some women, in France and even more so in Japan, do find ways to get access, to remain and to be recognized at the highest level of reputation. We identify three key ways jazz gets feminized over time.

Long Institutional Training in Music

Access to art schools is key in explaining the feminization of most art worlds in contemporary democratic societies (Buscatto, 2018). Women's access to educational institutions has facilitated their entry into and maintenance within professional art worlds by making it possible to remove certain social barriers. And this explanation is key in explaining female musicians' access to the jazz world in France as well as in Japan. This is quite striking at first, since the jazz world does not set educational hurdles or pre-qualification rules that have to be overcome or complied with. How can we explain such a finding?

In France, while most jazz female musicians went through specialized jazz schooling to become professional musicians, usually starting at a young age, a majority of men engaged in formal studies as a kind of accompaniment at the time of their first musical experiences, and not all of them finished the music training programs they had enrolled in. Formal training institutions—conservatories and jazz schools—provided those women access to the technical know-how required for being evaluated (and evaluating themselves) as technically skillful. Thanks to those trainings, they also learnt how to deal with men in quite a masculine world: how to behave socially, on and off the stage, how to avoid seduction, how to create long-term relationships, how to set up a rehearsal without hurting male feelings—and they sometimes also met their first jazz male long-time partner. Last, but not least, they developed their first professional networks, with colleagues their age, but also with teachers who are also often active renowned jazz players and offer them opportunities to play in professional bands right from the beginning.

Regarding the Japanese situation, access to music training is even more important in order to explain the partial feminization of the Japanese jazz world (30% of musicians are indeed female).

On the one side, female and male pianists are at parity, so the Japanese feminization of jazz is partly due to the access of female pianists to the jazz scene. And musical education is key to understanding such a feminization. The piano, as well as singing or koto[6] playing, is a very "feminine" activity in Japan, both numerically and symbolically. Japanese girls are indeed enticed to learn the piano as part of their middle-class education, of their *okeikogoto* (Kowalczyk, 2018). Some middle-class women may also graduate in classical music universities or colleges as part of a suitable feminine education since, supposedly, it would help them meet a "good" husband and become a respectable housewife or part-time worker once married and having become a mother. They may even have become professional musicians as long as they were teaching classical music part-time to little girls while being respectable married women educating their kid(s) as "good wives, wise mothers" (White, 2013). And as it happens most female Japanese pianists I met did graduate in classical music and did not intend at first to become jazz pianists (Buscatto, 2022a). But graduating in classical music has opened the way to jazz. Most of them started to play jazz in university jazz big bands every day during their classical musical studies and started to learn and practice jazz with other male students this way. If jazz was not part of their official curriculum, their technical abilities developed in classical music while their access to those university big bands did open the way to the jazz life. They could then think of this track as a possibility and started to attend jam sessions and go to jazz clubs as part of their discovery and love for jazz. Two of them even went to the United States afterwards, one to study jazz, one to experience the jazz scene with her partner. Toshiko Akiyoshi, the famous Japanese jazz pianist born in 1929 and who has become famous both in the United States—where she lived most of her adult life—and in Japan, also opened the way to this possibility for some of those women and for the Japanese audience and critics even if their choice is still considered atypical and contrary to feminine middle-class behaviors and values (Buscatto, 2022a).

On the other side, still in Japan, the recent partial feminization of wind instruments is also to be explained thanks to women's access to education, even if it happened in quite a different way. Indeed, the first reason one finds more and more female trumpet players, saxophonists or trombonists in the jazz scene is mostly due to the current strong feminization of wind bands in high schools. As recently shown by Hebert, wind bands are indeed a very popular extracurricular activity in high-schools in Japan. According to him, "roughly 700,000 musicians in over 14,000 bands have typically performed in the three tiers of this annual contest [All-Japan Band Association National Competition]" (Hebert, 2012, p. 4), that is, a national contest prepared for all year long in high schools. And those wind bands, which play classical music and original Japanese tunes mainly, are 95 percent girl-composed. The saxophonist, the trumpet player and one pianist I interviewed started to play in such a wind band before turning to jazz later on in their life. They all attributed the recent feminization of wind instruments in jazz to this practice which was most exclusively feminine and gave them access to this instrument at early ages. The two youngest players also mentioned the viewing of a very popular movie, *Swing Girls*,[7] which was casting young high school girls playing in a wind band and discovering jazz in quite stimulating and seductive ways!

> When I was 5 years old, I started to play the piano at Yamaha. My mother liked music very much, she played the piano … So I started the piano. But I did not like music school much, I only liked playing! I was listening to the music from TV and I was playing the songs with my piano (…) When I was 12 years old, I joined a Wind Band in my Junior High School, and I started the X [her Wind instrument]. My mother had a X [Wind instrument] at home and I had watched *Swing Girls*, a jazz wind band movie which I had loved! So I really wanted to play the X!
>
> *(Female Japanese jazz instrumentalist, 25 years old)*

Develop Implicit Strategies to Overcome Negative Feminine Stereotypes

"Turning off the seduction" with colleagues

As already mentioned, female jazz players, singers as well as instrumentalists, radiate strong seductive power, not only towards the audience, but also for their music partners, and this seductive power not only tends to lead to the devaluing of their professional skills, but also makes it difficult for them to play with male colleagues and get recruited as side-women.

Over time, women jazz musicians learn how to do something fundamental: "turn off the seduction." This is the expression they often use in France in reference to an ability to prevent male desire from developing in a way they consider inappropriate. Some seem to have acquired this ability "naturally":

> If you're clear in your own mind, if you … if you're clear (and in this case I mean me), if there's someone important in my life, then nothing doing … it's not even a temptation. It's very clear for everyone, because all the people I mix with know me, and they also know me with my boyfriend. There's respect, there's … What I mean is, they let me be. And I don't get stuck in a corner either. There're never any problems, never any misunderstandings
>
> *(Female French jazz instrumentalist, 26 years old)*

In addition to adopting "clear" behavior, the presence of a stable life jazz partner who everyone knows or knows about seems a helpful means of protection, and it is one that female musicians often use in their exchanges with male colleagues. But it does not suffice, namely in moments of intense collaboration, such as tours, musical projects and music school studies, and they then have to be very "careful" to turn off seduction and ensure that their male colleagues, the audience, the club owners or the producers do not get seduced and start to flirt with them in inconsiderate ways. Japanese as French female musicians are aware that such seductive relationships may get in the way of becoming a legitimate jazz musician.

"Reversing the stigma"

One transgressive resource, often used unconsciously by some women, at least in the beginning, is their "feminine capital" which may help them get into and remain in art worlds. Those women may mobilize presumably unfavorable sexual stereotypes—emotion, elegance, seduction or weakness—to assert their "femininity" and thereby obtain recognition based on this supposed gendered difference. In this case we are dealing with an attempt at "reversing the stigma" (Goffman, 1963). Some female jazz musicians in France and Japan do appear as attractive women on their CD covers and on stage. This is more so for singers and pianists, who more often than other instrumentalists dress up, put make up on and jewelry and develop gracious gestures in order to sell their image as well as their music. It may also happen with some saxophonists or trumpet players. One should be aware that men, more so in Japan than in France, may also develop attractive figures to find gigs or to get recorded. Moreover, jazz is not pop or rock music, so when those women develop attractive images, they are generally not sexualized or overtly erotic as in pop music. One may speak of a discrete seduction strategy.

Another "feminine" resource mobilized by some women jazz musicians, again often unintentionally, at least at first, is to take advantage of the particular interest of critics, art program directors, and producers seeking to offer specific support to women. Those actors are favorable to programming "female" groups or leading musicians and to generating events that advantageously show women musicians. They are usually driven by a profit motive, as women artists are likely to have strong seductive power with audiences:

> After graduating from my University, I became a member of a jazz female Band. In Japan, many colleagues have Big Bands, so a producer looked for young female players, we played a lot of anime songs. It was very successful, sales were very good, we recorded maybe ten CDs. We played for more than 5 years. We even played on TV, we did a lot of promotion to sell the CDs! It was very successful!
>
> *(Female Japanese jazz instrumentalist, 40 years old)*

"Masculinizing" artistic practices

Another "strategy" might be to "masculinize" one's appearance, behavior, artistic skills in order to neutralize as far as possible the difficulties linked to the fact that they are viewed and experienced as women. Some women decide not only to refrain from any attempt to appear seductive but even to disguise or blunt their female identity. Though this behavior may close certain commercial doors, it may also enable these women to be perceived more as artists "like the others." If we did not observe this strategy much among Japanese singers and instrumentalists and among French singers, some French female instrumentalists were masculinizing their behaviors and physical appearance.

Those female artists do early on learn that being perceived as a woman will get in the way of being co-opted, valued positively and considered as a real colleague, and may learn to perform in "masculine" ways as far as possible. They intend not to be considered as passive, weak, dependent, poorly creative or overly sexual, and assert their creative artistic abilities. This was observed on the French scene only, and only a minority of women did masculinize their figures and gestures to get things done, quite successfully for the ones we observed.

Family "Over-socializations"

Women who succeed in entering and remaining in very masculine worlds and/or in getting recognized at the highest artistic level tend to benefit from what we have called "over-socializations" (Buscatto, 2018 [2007], 2021). In other words, as compared to their male colleagues, they tend to benefit from stronger family resources. More often than men, they tend to be raised in artistic families or privileged families. They tend to live with a partner (or successive partners) who belong to the jazz world—as an artist, a producer or an art critic for instance. And as already mentioned, they tend to attend high-level art schools, even if this is not officially needed for them to succeed.

In France as well as in Japan, some of the women jazz instrumentalists I spoke with also have fathers and in some cases mothers who are or were themselves professional jazz, traditional or classical musicians. The father or the mother may also be or have been a music aficionado or devoted concert-goer, and in some cases he or she organizes musical events. Some French jazz women have a brother or sister who is also a professional musician.

Another feature of several of these women's lives is having a close relative active in the music world. And they are likely to have men and women relatives who are active in one or another art world—poetry, painting, theatre—either professionally or as amateurs. In all these family configurations, art gets put at the center of daily life, and an artist career is a possibility. That possibility is hard to realize, as it is often a point of conflict and tension within the family circle at the beginning due to its negative image (even more so in Japan), but those women do benefit from such an "over-socialization." In such families, the fact that children choose an art practice, often one involving long, complex studies, is quite common, even in Japan, it is less jazz practice than music teaching, which is envisioned at first as already discussed.

Last but not least, French and Japanese jazz women singers or instrumentalists often live with professional jazzmen, usually musicians but in some cases jazz producers or program organizers. The fact is that the woman jazz musician's network is usually the same as her male partner's, which is first and foremost his—this is not an equally shared network. In such cases, when the love relationship comes to an end, the "network" disappears for the woman musician, who then has to rebuild both her personal and professional life from scratch. For the minority of women jazz musicians who do not have a male jazz-professional life partner, it is hard not only to stay in the jazz world but also to maintain professional work partnerships in the long run. The "natural" way these women develop is then to find relationships outside the jazz world, and in some cases even to withdraw entirely from that world.

Conclusion

Jazz worlds are not yet favorable to female jazz musicians' entry, nor to their maintaining themselves in those worlds or gaining artistic recognition. Depreciative "feminine" stereotypes, masculine social networks, "feminine" maternal roles, "masculine" conventions and norms, "feminine" socializations—all those social processes add up and work against women to become active professional jazz musicians, making life harder for them than it already is for male artists. But up against those difficulties specific to their position as women in men's worlds, some women artists use resources that enable them to partially defy or overcome this social reality. Access to musical training when teenagers as well as later in life is a major resource for women musicians. They also learn to either use "feminine capital" or "masculinize" their behaviors in order to be regularly hired and get recognized as artists. They are likely to be "over-socialized" and benefit from family resources—parents and partners—to learn informal skills, build-up efficient networks and feel confident in their artistic abilities.

Some female jazz musicians thus demonstrate a high ability to develop strategies in order to maintain themselves and/or to get recognized at the highest level of artistic recognition despite the "cumulative disadvantage" they face over time. Their ability to either overcome or make an efficient use of feminine stereotypes, or to develop collective actions to produce works of art in spite of it all do prove how individuals may act in contemporary art worlds to overcome obstacles and be able to create and to be valued as "real" artists. However, research studies do show, as for all other prestigious professions, that main resources which help women to overcome such a cumulative disadvantage are socially and collectively produced (Buscatto, 2018). On the one side, the more public institutions enable women to be trained, to be recruited and to be recognized in non-discriminatory ways, the more equality between the sexes one art world tends to promote. On the other side, if we look at those women who do overcome obstacles, one finds they tend to be "over-socialized" and benefit from specific individual resources that reinforce inequalities between men and women on other social grounds.

Jazz worlds do then appear as highly hierarchized worlds that are partly founded on social grounds that have nothing to do with artistic abilities, far from the myths of talent or genius. And this belief in the talent-only myth does reinforce jazz worlds' tendency to be as open and free of rules as possible, and thus produce and legitimize social and gendered differences, since most actors—critics, government, teachers, producers, audience or artists—who could act to help develop measures against discrimination do believe talent would be hindered by such actions and tend to fight against any kind of anti-discrimination measures—or denigrate them if they have to be part of them (Buscatto, 2018 [2007], 2021).

Notes

1 I based on my past epistemological work on the "sociologies of gender" (Buscatto, 2019 [2014], I will here define gender as a concept aiming to account for the social processes producing, legitimizing, transgressing, transforming and suppressing hierarchical sexed differences between women and men, between "feminine" and "masculine," according to principles aiming to ensure the primacy of the "masculine" in a "naturalized" way and to stigmatize any behavior contrary to, or abolishing these binary categorizations.

2 have extensively published on French female jazz musicians since my first paper in 2003. Therefore, part of this chapter is of course drawn from past publications on this topic when it comes to either describing the French situation, or stating general social processes affecting female jazz musicians (Buscatto, 2018 [2007], 2021). But the comparison between France and Japan has enabled me to generalize those findings to any jazz scene in the world.

3 When my 2007 book *Femmes du jazz* was reissued in 2018, I wrote an afterword titled "Eleven years afterwards … and (almost) nothing has changed." All the current indicators, whether quantitative or qualitative, indeed prove that the French jazz world remains a very masculine world as described in my initial study.

4 To know more about my methods, please read my article to be published end of 2022 (Buscatto, 2022a).

5 Please note that a similar reasoning has been exposed to explain the feminization of professional artists in all art worlds in "Western" countries (Buscatto, 2018).

6 The same observation applies for the experienced internationally renowned improvised koto player whose trajectory I analyzed from a sociological perspective (Buscatto, 2022b)

7 *Swing Girls* (スウィングガールズ *Suwingu Gāruzu*) is a Japanese 2004 comedy film directed and co-written by Shinobu Yaguchi. The plot follows a group of inept high school girls who form a big band. The film ranked 8th at the Japanese box office in 2004, and won seven prizes at the 28th Japan Academy Prize.

References

Becker, H. S. (1982). *Art Worlds*. Berkeley: University of California Press.

Björck, C., Bergman, A. (2018). Making Women in Jazz Visible: Negotiating Discourses of Unity and Diversity in Sweden and the US, *IASPM-Journal*, 8 (1), DOI 10.5429/2079- 3871(2018)v8i1.5en.

Buscatto, M. (2004). De la vocation artistique au travail musical: tensions, compromis et ambivalences chez les musiciens de jazz, *Sociologie de l'art*, 5, 35–56.

Buscatto, M. (2018 [2007]). *Femmes du jazz. Musicalités, féminités, marginalisations*. Paris, CNRS Editions.

Buscatto, M. (2018). Feminisations of artistic work. Legal measures and female artists' resources do matter, *Todas as Artes* Journal, 1 (1), 21–39.

Buscatto, M., (2019 [2014]). *Sociologies du genre*. Paris, Armand Colin.

Buscatto, M. (2021). *Women in Jazz. Musicality, Femininity, Marginalization*. London and New York: Routledge.

Buscatto, M. (2022a). Jazz as a way to escape one's social "destiny." Lessons from Japanese professional jazz musicians, *Jazz Research*, 50/51, forthcoming.

Buscatto, M. (2022b). Beyond Frontiers. From Japanese Traditional Koto to Transnational Improvised Music. In M.-O. Blin and P.-J. Castanet (Eds.), *Musique, Mondialisation et Sociétés*, Rouen, Presses Universitaires de Rouen, forthcoming.

Dahl, L. (1984). *Stormy Weather: The Music and Lives of a Century of Jazzwoman*. London: Quartet Books.

Goffman, E. (1963). *Stigma: Notes on the Management of Spoiled Identity*. Englewood Cliffs, NJ: Prentice-Hall.

Gourse, L. (1995). *Madam Jazz. Contemporary Women Instrumentalists*. New York: Oxford University Press.

Hebert, D. G. (2012). *Wind Bands and Cultural Identity in Japanese Schools*, Dordrecht and New York: Springer.

Jeffri, J. (2003). *Changing the Beat. A Study of the Worklife of Jazz Musicians. Volume 1: Executive Summary*. New York: National Endowment of the Arts.

Kowalczyk, B. (2018). *"Transnational" Art World. Career Patterns of Japanese Musicians in the European World of Classical Music*. PhD in Sociology, Varsaw University and Paris 1 Panthéon Sorbonne University.

Raine, S. (2020). *Keychanges at Cheltenham Jazz Festival. Challenges for Women Musicians in Jazz and Ways Forward for Equal Gender Representations at Jazz Festivals. Findings and Recommendations*. DOI: 10.13140/RG.2.2.15390.15688.

Schulz G., Ries C. and Zimmerman O. (2016). *Frauen in Kultur und Medien. Ein Überblick über aktuelle Tendenzen, Entwicklungen und Lösungsvorschläge*. Berlin: Deutscher Kulturrat.

Tucker, S. (2002). Big Ears: Listening for Gender in Jazz Studies, *Current Musicology*, 71–73, 375–408.

White, M. 2013 [2011] Change and diversity in the Japanese family. In V. L. Bestor, T. C. Bestor, and A. Yamagata (Eds.), *Routledge Handbook of Japanese Culture and Society*, 129–139. New York: Routledge.

20

"IT AIN'T WHO YOU ARE"

Authenticity, Sexuality, and Masculinity in Jazz

Ann Cotterrell

The trope of the highly charged, masculine, African American musician pervades jazz literature. British jazz composer and bassist Graham Collier had none of these characteristics, except masculinity, and even there he felt that as a gay man he was considered to be not fully masculine. In his seventh and final book, *The Jazz Composer* (2009), in a chapter he titled, "It ain't who you are (It's the way that you do it)," he wrote about his personal experience of prejudice as a result of "not being a (straight) man," as well as not being black, not American, and not "young and good-looking" (pp. 163–177). In this book, he argued that the key concept defining authenticity in jazz was not that it was music played by people with pre-defined characteristics who were members of a shared identity group, nor necessarily that it should swing, but that it should be improvised, and that would mean that "it was played in real time, once" (Collier, 2009, 30–41). It had to be true artistic expression by the musicians, and not necessarily conform to intersecting stereotypes of sexuality and gender, race, and nationality. This suggests that authenticity could be described, at least in part, in terms of artistic intent rather than as a genre imposed from above.

In examining the many-sided relationship between jazz and gender, questions arise concerning the relationship between sexuality and the making and perception of music, and the effects of discrimination in the whole jazz industry (musicians, promoters, record producers, jazz journalists, other writers and jazz audiences). While taking account of the wider context, this chapter focuses primarily on the identities and experiences of three openly gay jazz composers and improvisors: Americans Gary Burton and Fred Hersch through their autobiographies and reports of interviews, and Graham Collier through his biography, documents, and other writing. They have all been active musicians in the twenty-first century, and all three musicians found ways of dealing with prejudices against homosexuality while creating music that was authentic, coming out of their experiences, personalities and emotions. But they were affected by differences in the society and culture of the time and place in which they lived, and varied in their approaches to coming out as gay.

Being Gay

All three composers, Collier, Hersch and Burton, enjoyed long-term gay partnerships and spoke about them in interviews and autobiographies. Collier's partner, writer John Gill, discussed openness and concealment of gay orientation among musicians and publicized the role played by gay people

DOI: 10.4324/9781003081876-22

in all types of twentieth century music in his book, *Queer Noises*, published in 1995. Rather than claiming inclusiveness in the jazz world, Gill celebrated difference and, proud of the gay heritage, he did not want to see it hidden or dismissed. Graham and John met in 1976 and remained together until Collier's death in 2011, and Gill described the presentation of themselves as a couple, stating that "family, friends, colleagues and neighbours know about our sexuality." He also noted that they "kiss hello and goodbye at bus stops, stations and airports, and after all these years can only presume that our behaviour together in public must signify 'couple'. We couldn't pass for blokes if we tried." One such kiss provoked a homophobic reaction when they appeared in a television film of Collier's very successful "Hoarded Dreams" concert at the Bracknell jazz festival in 1983. At the end of the concert, following a standing ovation, Collier stepped offstage to receive congratulations, a drink, and a brief kiss on the lips from Gill. Such openness led to a homophobic reaction in one critic who saw the kiss on UK television, although it appeared to pass otherwise unnoticed amid the rapturous applause of the live audience (Gill, 1995, 69–72).

Overt homophobia may be rare, but it is an indicator of hidden attitudes to the sexuality of people and their relationships which, lying under the surface of polite society, can serve to devalue gay musicians and their work. The documentary film of "Hoarded Dreams" including the kiss incensed British jazz critic Jim Godbolt. Attempting to enliven his copy with a witty remark, he complained that the information that John was Graham's *inamorata* did not add to the music. He was, of course, insultingly using the feminine form of the noun. Godbolt also stated that a kiss between John Dankworth and Cleo Laine at the end of a concert "would be a lot more acceptable than the male osculation between John and Graham" (Godbolt, 1985, 9).

Godbolt was not unique among jazz writers for his homophobic views. Reviewer Steve Voce was challenged by Collier for the extremely disparaging homophobic remarks he made about gay men in a review of a record of "gay jazz," *AC/DC* (Voce, 1977), and in a subsequent article (Voce, 1978). In a letter to Voce's editor, Collier (1977) provided an insight into his ideas about categorisation of sexuality in jazz. He did not support the compilation of gay tracks, arguing that "[t]he homo- or hetero-sexuality of individuals is not important in jazz or life in general." Instead, he claimed that what is important is "personal freedom," an attitude which permeated his music.[1] Godbolt was born in 1922 and Voce in 1933 and perhaps they came from a generation that had grown up in a more homophobic culture when much homosexuality remained hidden. Probably referring to musicians rather than writers, in his book *Inside Jazz* (1973, 98), Collier had commented, "Homosexuality, like teetotalism, is not unknown though seemingly rare and is tolerated though largely ignored."

Homophobia appeared in a variety of other jazz-related contexts in the 1970s, and Collier encountered abuse in his role as a regular writer for *Gay News*. A catalogue of ECM records included a quote from a review of a Terje Rypdal record, written by Graham, and this ignited the wrath of some catalogue readers. Long, homophobic letters of complaint reached the record company in 1978 and 1979, angry at the inclusion of a quote from *Gay News*. They were duly rebuffed and the complaints were forwarded with wry humour to Collier, who was able to reply with a strong criticism of one of the letter-writers in his column in *Gay News* (Collier, 1979).

Collier recognized discrimination against people who did not fully belong to the hegemonic identity group, heterosexual masculinity, in jazz. He acknowledged the discrimination against women musicians, citing the Lincoln Center as an example at the time he was writing, and he was critical of the emphasis placed by the record companies on attractive female (and male) singers rather than instrumentalists. This was a matter that concerned him also in his earlier book, *Inside Jazz*, in which he acknowledged the significance of instrumentalists Lil Armstrong, Marian McPartland, and Melba Liston and, in England, Barbara Thompson and Kathy Stobart but noted that they were few in number at that time (Collier, 1973, 97–98). His personal concern however was with prejudice against gay musicians. He later stated, "I do have one advantage. I am male, although my being gay takes the edge off that for some observers" (Collier, 2009, 163). Being gay diminished his status in a hierarchical system based on prejudices about gender; he thought of his position in the system of power as lower than that of heterosexual men, and especially lower than that of straight African American men.

It is impossible to ignore the context of the time in looking at attitudes to homosexuality both in the UK and the United States (Ramsey, 2020). Hersch and Burton were both younger than Collier, who was born in 1937 and "came out" in the 1960s, before establishing his career, and before homosexual acts between consenting adult males were legal in England.[2] Burton (born in 1943) and Hersch (born in 1955) came out separately to the US public on National Public Radio in the early 1990s, but even at this time there were indications of homophobia (Gross, 1994). In a panel discussion at Columbia University in 2002, Burton said that he had experienced only one homophobic reaction since he came out (Davis, 2002a). He referred to a letter published in *Jazz Times* the previous week, headlined "Faggots in Jazz." The letter stated, Burton noted, that certain named musicians "couldn't swing," and "homosexuality was abnormal, etc. The usual kind of hate things." He was aghast that "one of our own magazines" had treated him so badly (Davis, 2002a). The issue of *Jazz Times* that published the offending letter included an article that criticized examples of homophobia (Gavin, 2001). But it also included, as pointed out by Sherrie Tucker, images that represented families as necessarily straight (2008, 10–11). In the nineteenth century, full masculinity as a middle-class social status required men to be heads of households supporting their families and asserting their status in the home (Brady, 2005, 28–29). This stereotypical association of family and domestic life with heterosexuality has been shown by Matt Cook (2013), writing about playwright Joe Orton in Britain, to have continued into the late-twentieth century in spite of changes in attitudes to sexuality.

Tucker (2008) has questioned the significance of asking homosexual musicians about their sexual orientation in a world where heterosexuals would not be asked the same question: To do so presumes that the norm is heterosexuality, and homosexuality is constructed "as particular and different" (p. 4). In the panel discussion in 2002, Burton commented that he is rarely asked questions relating to his sexuality, saying that "jazz people, interviewers, didn't bring [the question of sexuality] up. To this day, I don't think a jazz interviewer has ever asked about it. A couple of newspapers have, but not jazz people" (Davis, 2002a). When asked by an audience member whether he ever initiated such a line of questioning, he replied, "No, usually I leave the interviewing up to the interviewer." Sexuality seems to be a difficult topic for most interviewers, which may be because they think it would be an intrusion into the privacy of the interviewee. Francis Davis, who chaired the panel discussion, sought reasons for the reticence and said in an article in the *New York Times* published later in 2002, "this reticence seems disingenuous in light of the role that Miles Davis's reputed prowess with the opposite sex played in defining his appeal to many of his male fans. (Never mind the persistent rumors that Davis was bisexual.)" (Davis, 2002b).

Some jazz writers deem sexuality irrelevant and do not mention it. Dave Gelly's book about Stan Getz, for example, portrays Burton as a young man in his early twenties leading the band skilfully through airport hassles but does not mention his sexual orientation (Gelly, 2002, 138). Yet Burton's sexuality is relevant in Getz's biography as it reveals significant aspects of Getz's character and the relationship between the two men. Burton paints a less rosy picture than Gelly's account of the years in which Burton worked in Getz's band: The banter taken for granted in a macho environment can be uncomfortable for a gay person and, although Burton had not publicly identified as gay, Getz may have noted a feminine side to his character. According to Burton (2013, 115), Getz "made more 'faggot' remarks than anyone else," and a report in the *Miami Herald* (2013) claimed that Getz often called Burton "faggot" even though the latter had not come out as gay at that time. Hersch recollected his time touring with Woody Herman in 1977:

> Being a gay guy on a band bus is like torture; you couldn't really be out to those guys. They would have killed me. And everybody is talking about women, or sports, and into heavy

boozing. I was a pothead, not into alcohol, and I was not into women, and I was not particularly into sports, so it was kind of a non-starter.

(Iverson, 2020)

Ins and Outs

Musicians who are "out," deliberately and publicly, may object to being "inned." John Gill recorded that he felt offended (possibly unfairly) when a leading jazz writer and photographer, detailing the comments made by Jim Godbolt on the film that included Collier and Gill's kiss, cited it as an example of homophobia but without mentioning the names of the two men. He felt they had been "shoved back into the closet," when they were determined to be open about their relationship and their sexuality (Gill, 1995, 71–72). They did not mention any difficulties with friends and relatives but, after they moved to Spain in January 2000, they commented with irony that local people in the small mountain town of Ronda where they had settled walked past their house pointing out that "two men and no women live there."[3]

Gay musical life may be geographically situated, and ideals of masculinity vary over place as well as time. It may be more difficult in some areas and time periods to come out as homosexual. Both Burton and Hersch wrote in their autobiographies about the contrast between the lack of reference to homosexuality in the areas in which they grew up (Burton in Indiana, and Hersch in Ohio) and the jazz scene in late twentieth-century New York. Composer Billy Strayhorn grew up in Pittsburgh, moving to New York at the age of 23 in 1939. His biographer, David Hajdu (1996), commented that "in Pittsburgh, who he was had inhibited Billy Strayhorn from doing what he could do; in New York, what he could do enabled him to be who he was" (p. 65). Hajdu claimed a link between Strayhorn's musical success and the atmosphere in which he lived: He was open about being gay but was able to be so only by remaining in the shadow of Duke Ellington. Strayhorn's biography included a statement from his long-term friend, George Greenlee, "Duke didn't question his manliness. It wasn't like that for him back home" (Hajdu, 1996, 79–80).

Burton's musical abilities developed from an early age, and he has described how at 16 he decided firmly to become part of the jazz world, but also recognized that "being anything but heterosexual was incompatible with a career in jazz;" he had noted that "the scruffy, gritty jazz life was very masculine and hard-edged," and that to succeed he had to be welcomed into that community of players (Burton, 2013, 23). In his autobiography he also described not accepting, even to himself for many years, that he was gay; he married twice and had two children with his second wife, but in his forties he decided to live as a gay man with a male partner. Burton came out publicly on NPR in 1994 at the age of 51 although he had informed colleagues and friends in the five years before this. He had been apprehensive but was surprised by the lack of reaction from fellow musicians, colleagues in his academic role at Berklee, and audiences (Burton, 2013, 308–315).

Fred Hersch (2017) has described not wanting to be "pigeonholed," noting that "beauty and lyricism" in music "had traditionally been associated with male homosexuality in a restrictive and demeaning way." Although a straight man might "be praised for playing beautifully," he felt that "for a gay man to be described that way … it was almost like saying, 'Of course he plays beautifully – he's gay!'" (p. 152). He pointed out in an interview that many straight musicians "were able to play beautifully, emotionally, tenderly," and that there are jazz musicians "who are gay who play very aggressively" (Romero, 2020). He has also quoted the example of Stan Getz, a musician assumed to be heterosexual, whose music could be described as lyrical, as against Cecil Taylor, reputedly gay, who played in a far more aggressive idiom (Chinen, 2014).

Collier believed that technique and endurance were often emphasized in jazz education at the expense of sensitivity, and that this gave a macho bias to jazz and jazz players (Heining, 2018, 197). One piece from his *Symphony of Scorpions* particularly illustrates his sensitivity: The beautiful "Forest Path to the Spring," a duet for guitar and saxophones, was described by Graham as "the loveliest melody I ever wrote" (Gill, 2012). Not all of Collier's music was gentle and lyrical however – it covers a very wide emotional range proving the inappropriateness of the terms "feminine" and "masculine" when applied to music. Lisa Barg has pointed out that criticisms of Strayhorn's work as pretty, effete, or sentimental devalue the feminine aesthetic while linking "black masculinity" with "authentic jazz" (Barg, 2013, 814–815). In this context, it is not surprising that musicians might hesitate before coming out, stepping over the presumed binary divide into a permanent and inescapable musical identity of lower status as well as upsetting their work with other musicians, receptions by audiences, and the musician's personal relationships.

Hersch and Burton both deliberated carefully before coming out, and a concern that their music would be received as a different genre was one of the issues. Some musicians have been reluctant to come out because of the embarrassment this might cause to their families, and Burton was concerned about facing his ex-wife and two children with the news, but found they accepted it very well. He also wrote about his conversations with singer k. d. Lang, who was wondering how to break the news that she was a lesbian to her mother (Burton, 2013, 196), and Hersch recounted the support of his family, including two elderly grandmothers on telling them that he was gay (Romero, 2020). Both Hersch and Burton also worried about the effects on their careers; after telling family, friends, and colleagues that they were gay, they each delayed revealing it a wider audience.

Talking to Terry Gross on NPR in 2017, Hersch remembered that when Stan Getz was visiting his loft apartment in 1982 for a rehearsal, an otherwise trivial event occurred that changed his outlook:

> I realized that there were two toothbrushes in the bathroom, one for me and one for Eric. And as Stan was walking down the hall into my loft, I went and I hid Eric's toothbrush because I thought, oh, if he notices two toothbrushes, he'll think, oh, maybe there's somebody else here.

After Getz left, Hersch said to himself that, although he admired Getz for his amazing musicianship, "if he has a problem with me being gay, well, then it's his problem and it's not my problem." Following this, he began to think that there was a way of being less secretive. He later reflected that it might be hard for a young gay person of the twenty-first century to understand his perceived need for secrecy. In spite of the incident having an effect on his mental outlook, Hersch did not tell Getz that he was gay, and did not come out publicly until 1993 (Gross, 2017). He later explained his reticence by citing the intimacy of the relationship between musicians spontaneously composing music together, and concern that being open about his sexuality might disturb that relationship (Romero, 2020).

Martin Niederauer (2016) noted the significance of masculine hierarchies in jazz. Intimacy through music ensures unity, but this is complemented by competition. The relationships between musicians, in spite of the increase in the number of female musicians, remains that of a male hegemony with a "heteronormative structure" (p. 136). Niederauer drew in part on the work of Trine Annfelt (2003), who noted the strength of the hegemony of heterosexuality, the way in which jazz marginalizes women and homosexual men, and the difficulties for men in acknowledging homosexual feelings. Annfelt argued that jazz performance offers an intimacy that makes it less necessary for men to leave the closet. Hersch noted however that there was a cost to "keeping a closet…. Trying to compartmentalize yourself is not really a great recipe for good mental health" (Romero, 2020), and that in the twenty-first century there was a different attitude to gay men and gay couples.

Cecil Taylor appears to have been "outed" by Stanley Crouch without his consent (Crouch, 1982), and John Gill wrote that in 1985 Taylor "gave an interview to a Bay Area newspaper in San Francisco in which he discussed his career in terms of his race and sexuality being inextricably interlinked as issues" (Gill, 1995, 69). Although subsequent writers referred to Taylor's sexuality, his public statements were ambiguous. A 1991 interview drew attention to the complexity of his identity:

> I'm of American, Indian, African and English heritage, and I follow all these paths. Someone once asked me if I was gay. I said, 'Do you think a three-letter word defines the complexity of my humanity?' I avoid the trap of easy definition.
>
> *(Watrous, 1991)*

Coming out as gay may have been especially difficult for a black musician, given the pressure to maintain black heterosexual masculinity among men who had historically been deprived of power (Piekut, 2010, 36).

Taylor's interviewer in 1991, Peter Watrous, does not appear to have been the one who originally asked Taylor about his sexuality. For a critic to ask someone this question might seem over-intrusive and lead to a rapid curtailment of the interview, but avoidance of the question can be even more unacceptable than the question itself. A critic in the audience at the panel discussion in 2002 betrayed the complexity of polite behaviour hiding antagonistic views about gay musicians,

> I would never dream about asking any of you … about your sexual behaviour for an article…. Unless it has direct bearing on your music, I would ask that no more than I would ask somebody if they were a pedophile, if they beat their wives.
>
> *(Davis, 2002a)*

The implications of this statement would plainly deter anyone from revealing that they did not conform to the questioner's ideas of "normal."

Burton and Hersch defined themselves in a way that stressed normality. When Burton first came out he stressed that he was "a musician who happened to be gay." In an interview with Steve Rothaus (2013) he declared that he now felt that he was a gay guy who happened to be a jazz musician. "I am always aware that I am gay. I am always aware of my sexual identity…. I was gay all along." In his autobiography he later said: "Perhaps it's more accurate to say I'm just a guy who happens to be gay and happens to be a jazz musician. Ultimately I have no control over how the rest of the world sees me" (Burton, 2013, 355). It has been suggested that the fact of Hersch being gay and HIV positive has dominated media coverage about him. Jazz vocalist and pianist Patricia Barber has also commented on the extreme and repeated references in the press to her orientation as a lesbian (Tucker, 2008, 3–4). Gay musicians have sometimes been regarded as deviant from a norm, rather than part of a diverse world of musicians free to express themselves through art.

Authenticity

The connection between authenticity in life and in art has been noted by Cecil Taylor, Gary Burton, and Fred Hersch, among others. Even though Taylor may not have self-identified as gay, he described a need to free his mind of restrictions in order to create music. He had "put a lot of things into music that the music itself was not able to resolve" (Spellman, 2004, 4). After receiving help from an analyst he noted the freedom that was gained in his playing: "There was a definite change in the music, a change that was not, unfortunately, recorded." But there was hesitancy about his conclusion, "Of course I can't be too sure whether this change would have happened anyway" (p. 75).

Hersch appeared to have no doubts about the freeing of his mind following a health crisis which included time spent in a coma, followed by his coming out as gay and HIV positive: "I feel like my playing is, in every possible way, better. I think it's deeper…. I'm not … so self-critical or judgmental about what I play. I feel like my career has blossomed" (Gross, 2017). Burton thought that his playing was affected by feeling so much more free after he came out as gay: "Your state of mind and your emotional state [are] reflected in what you play" (Gross, 1994). Jazz singer and pianist Andy Bey came out in 1996, revealing that he was HIV positive and he too had suffered a serious health crisis. *Jazz Times* in 2001 reported Bey's view that the crisis helped him to make some of his best music, through feeling "like a free-er human being" (Gavin, 2001).

Being a composer can give greater freedom and personal control over lifestyle and music than being one of the members of a band. The composer/conductor is not necessarily "one of the guys" in a macho environment, and composition along with conducting or leading have formed part of the career of some women in jazz, notably Carla Bley, Maria Schneider, and Toshiko Akiyoshi, as well as gay musicians, including Strayhorn, Burton, Hersch and Collier. The status of outsider however can depend on a range of intersecting factors that are difficult to disentangle. Heining (2018) has attributed Collier's outsider status, at least in part, to his work that seems to be split between the avant-garde and the "more or less straight-ahead," working between freedom and structure, which is not easy to categorize (p. 162). Other jazz composers who have been regarded as outsiders have also defied categorization, including Ornette Coleman who resisted convention through his lifestyle as well as his music (Litweiler, 1992).

Heining (2018, 91) has additionally attributed Collier's feelings of being an outsider to his working-class origins but this can be exaggerated as, in some respects, his background was unexceptional. His education in a local grammar school was not untypical for young people in the British aspirant middle class in the 1940s and 1950s. Although he grew up in Luton, a fairly prosperous car-manufacturing town in southern England, he claimed an affinity with the culture of the north-east of England, where he was born, an area where deindustrialisation led to strong movements of protest and resistance.

There may have been other reasons for Collier's outsider status, his sexuality as an openly gay man made him an outsider in a world predominantly thought to be heterosexual and masculine for most of his career. Michael Rabiger, describing Collier's composition *Luminosity*, commented on

> a dynamic where the individual protests against the crowd, fights it, challenges it, then dies back gratefully into the arms of the ensemble, glad to become part of its community again. Here I sense something of Graham's history of creative protest, which is part of being working class, and gay when most of the artistic world had contempt for such as aspects of identity.
>
> *(Gill, 2014)*

The "individual protests against the crowd" and the sense of being an outsider led in Collier's music to "a distillation of solitude, a musical version of what it means to look inward and find beauty, anger, loss, regret, and kinship with those around you" (Gill, 2014).

Collier (1992) explored links between inward exploration and the creation of art in other media. He wrote that novelist Malcolm Lowry attached himself "to that personal, highly individual look at the world that a jazz musician expresses when he is soloing" (p. 244). In the same article, he linked Lowry's "moving from connection to connection in a kind of stream of consciousness" to jazz soloing, and wrote about the "hidden depths" in Lowry's writing that inspired his composition "The Day of the Dead" (p. 246).[4] Links between visual arts, literature and jazz have been explored by other musicians, but Collier was especially interested in the pursuit of art for art's sake: He was aiming to find his own art through music, sometimes inspired by literature and visual art (Collier, 2012). A Miró reproduction tile was kept on his desk to remind him to do his own thing "and be recognisable for that, rather than pursuing imitative work for commercial gain" (Collier, 2003).

Collier did not receive large financial rewards and felt that he had not received his due acclaim despite being the first British holder of a scholarship to Berklee in the 1960s where he studied under Herb Pomeroy. He was the first jazz musician to receive a British Arts Council bursary, was commissioned to produce music for Danish and German radio, set up a jazz school in Helsinki, and founded the first jazz department at the prestigious Royal Academy of Music in London where he became a professor. A member of the founding group of the International Association of Schools of Jazz, he co-edited the educational journal *Jazz Changes*. His workshop for young musicians created the group Loose Tubes, described as "one of the most creative and influential jazz orchestras founded in Britain" (Fordham, 2011). He also received an award from Queen Elizabeth, which he described as having pleased his mother, even though it provided no financial benefit (Collier, 2009, 173).

Financial success requires musicians to please a wide audience and the record companies. There are numerous examples of musicians, like Collier, who have adopted their own authentic approach to jazz and have failed to achieve a reasonable income. He was not a young and glamorous face to shine on the covers of magazines or CD sleeves, he was not an American bringing the self-confidence of the music they claimed to be theirs to Europe. In Britain, and possibly elsewhere, there is continuing adherence by many in the jazz audiences to the hard bop style of jazz, the competitive masculine style of music they enjoyed many years earlier.

"Authenticity" signifies for many jazz audiences, and for some musicians and writers, "the real thing": Music that is loyal to the traditions of jazz and conforms to a style thought to be historically associated with African American masculinity. This view of jazz is supported by the writings of Wynton Marsalis and Stanley Crouch, and reached Europe especially through the Ken Burns's television documentary *Jazz*, sometimes criticized for its neotraditional view of music. David Ake, for example, assessed changes in the "postneotraditional era" within changing cultural, gender, national and racial hierarchies (Ake, 2019). As pointed out by Tucker (2002, 395), "[j]azz authenticity has been constructed differently in different times and places." Developments in jazz have taken place outside America, and Haftor Medbøe (2013, 31, 86) drew an interesting distinction between "traditionalist" claims to authenticity, and locally and individually framed values of authenticity, and pointed out that authenticity in the perception of audiences may be different from authenticity viewed in personal terms by musicians.

Collier made an early decision to reject the neotraditional concept of jazz and to compose music he felt deeply, music that liberated instrumentalists in the orchestras to improvise as expressively as they could, individually and collectively. He believed that this type of authentic expression did not involve rejecting the history of jazz, in which he was deeply interested. There are many examples of this and, when he visited my home, I should not have been surprised to find that he sat enraptured listening to a recording by Pee Wee Russell. He also saw "C-Jam Blues" as "the epitome of the perfect jazz composition," and the entire history of jazz as "a continuum, that he was tasked with upholding and extending" (Gill, 2012). But he believed that, although jazz should be developed from the tradition, jazz compositions should always be reworked in performance, and this applied not only to the solos, but also to the whole structure (Cotterrell, 1985; Heining, 2018, 72–78, 162). Jazz critic Charles Fox quoted Hoagy Carmichael on one of Collier's early record sleeves: He "didn't mind what they did with jazz so long as they kept the deep, dark, blue centre." In the same sleeve, Fox pointed out that Collier wanted "the music to preserve its identity, its indigo flavour" (Fox, 1967).

While acknowledging the influence of Duke Ellington, Gil Evans, and Charles Mingus, Collier gave the examples of Australian composer Paul Grabowsky and Austrian Christian Mühlbacher, who "want to express themselves as what they are" (Collier, 2009, 167). American jazz pianist Bill Charlap has been quoted as saying, "a human being is a human being …. Art is not just about notes; it's about expressing some kind of experience. It's also about being yourself" (Gavin, 2001). New forms of composition may lead to greater fluidity in the music, and the balance of genders and sexualities of the musicians may change, but the identity of the music at its centre remains the same. Authenticity in this view of art requires freedom for musicians to present their individual view of the world, and, as argued by Collier, "nowadays, real jazz, authentic jazz, is in the playing, rather than the skin colour or gender alignment, in the sounds rather than in any specific country" (Collier, 2009, 176).

Notes

1 I am grateful to Duncan Heining for providing copies of Collier's documents.
2 The Sexual Offences Act, 1967, permitted homosexual acts in private between two consenting adults over the age of twenty-one in England and Wales. The achievement of full equality was a gradual process taking place over succeeding years.
3 Graham Collier and John Gill at their home in Ronda, 29 October 2001, in a conversation with Ann and Roger Cotterrell.
4 I am grateful to Mark Goodall for providing the *Firminist*, 3 (2012), dedicated to the life and work of Graham Collier.

References

Ake, D. (2019). After Wynton: Narrating jazz in the postneotraditional era. In N. Gebhardt, N. Rustin-Paschal, and T. Whyton (Eds.), *The Routledge Companion to Jazz Studies* (pp. 77–86). Routledge.

Annfelt, T. (2003). Jazz as masculine space. Kilden genderresearch *Newsletters* kjonnsforskning.no/en/2003/07/jazz-masculine-space

Barg, L. (2013). Queer encounters in the music of Billy Strayhorn. *Journal of the American Musicological Society*, 66(3), (771–824). https://doi.org/10.1525/jams.2013.66.3.771

Brady, S. (2005). *Masculinity and Male Homosexuality in Britain, 1861–1913*. Palgrave Macmillan.

Burton, G. (2013). *Learning to Listen*. Berklee Press.

Chinen, N. (2014, September 27). OutBeat Jazz Festival: Interview with Fred Hersch. *New York Times*. www.youtube.com/watch?v=OnT9zXSP_EQ

Collier, G. (1973). *Inside Jazz*. Quartet Books.

Collier, G. (1977). Correspondence with *Jazz Journal*.

Collier, G. (1979, June). Jazz. *Gay News*, 170.

Collier, G. (1992). Lowry, jazz, and the day of the dead. In S. E. Grace (Ed.), *Swinging the Maelstrom: New Perspectives on Malcolm Lowry* (pp. 243–248). McGill-Queen's University Press.

Collier, G. (2003). Sleevenote to CD: *The Third Colour*. Jazzprint.

Collier, G. (2009). *The Jazz Composer: Moving Music off the Paper*. Northway Publications.

Collier, G. (2012, October). Further Thoughts on the Malcolm Lowry Connection. *The Firminist*, 3, 9–12.

Cook, M. (2013). Homes fit for homos: Joe Orton, masculinity and the domesticated queer. In J. H. Arnold and S. Brady (Eds.), *What is Masculinity?* (pp. 302–323). Macmillan.

Cotterrell, R. (1985, April). *The Wire*, Graham Collier: Composer. 14, 43.

Crouch, S. (1982, March). *Village Voice*, March 30, 59. As quoted in John Gennari, *Blowin Hot and Cool: Jazz and its Critics*. University of Chicago Press, 2006.

Davis, F. (2002a, April). Talking Jazz: Live at the Village, Panel Discussion "Destination Out." www.columbia.edu/cu/najp/events/talkingjazz/transcript1.html

Davis, F. (2002b, September 2). Music: In the macho world of jazz, don't ask, don't tell, *New York Times*, C2, 19.

Fordham, J. (2011, September 14). Graham Collier Obituary, *The Guardian*.

Fox C. (1967). Sleevenote to LP: *Deep Dark Blue Centre*. (Reissued as Disconforme CD, 1999).

Gavin, J. (2001, December). Homophobia in jazz. *Jazz Times*, https://jazztimes.com/features/profiles/homophobia-in-jazz/

Gelly, D. (2002). *Stan Getz: Nobody Else but Me*. Backbeat Books.

Gill, J. (1995). *Queer Noises*. University of Minnesota Press.

Gill, J. (2012). Sleevenote to CD: *Relook: A Memorial 75th Birthday Celebration: Graham Collier, 1937–2011*. jazzcontinuum.

Gill, J. (2014). Sleevenote to CD: *Luminosity*. jazzcontinuum.

Godbolt, J. (1985, May/June). *Jazz at Ronnie Scott's*.

Gross, T. (1994). Interview with Gary Burton. NPR Fresh Air, January 5. https://freshairarchive.org/guests/gary-burton

Gross, T. (2017). Interview with Fred Hersch. NPR, Fresh Air, September 14. www.npr.org/2017/09/14/550966011/musician-fred-hersch-recounts-a-life-in-and-out-of-jazz-in-his-new-memoir

Hajdu, D. (1996). *Lush life: A Biography of Billy Strayhorn*. Granta.

Heining, D. (2018). *Mosaics: The Life and Works of Graham Collier*. Equinox Publishing.

Hersch, F. (2017). *Good Things Happen Slowly*. Crown Archetype.

Iverson, E. (2020). Interview with Fred Hersch, Do the M@th, https://ethaniverson.com/interviews/interview-with-fred-hersch/.

Litweiler, J. (1992). *Ornette Coleman: The Harmolodic life*. Quartet Books.

Medbøe, H. (2013). *Cultural Identity and Transnational Heritage in Contemporary Jazz: A Practice-Based Study of Composition and Collaboration"* [Doctoral Dissertation, Edinburgh Napier University]. www.napier.ac.uk/ ~/media/worktribe/output-182664/cultural-identity-and-transnational-heritage-in-contemporary-jazz-a-practice-based-study.pdf

Miami Herald. (2013, September 27). Vibraphonist Gary Burton: A gay guy who plays music. www.miamiherald. com/entertainment/celebrities/article1955601.html

Niederauer, M. (2016). Hegemony in jazz: Trying to understand one important element of jazz's gender relation. In W. Knauer (Ed.), *Gender and Identity in Jazz: Darmstadt Studies in Jazz Research*, 14, 125–146. Jazzinstitut Darmstadt.

Piekut, B. (2010). New thing? Gender and sexuality in the Jazz Composers Guild, *American Quarterly*, 62, 1, 25–48. https://doi:10.1353/aq.0.0123

Ramsey, G. P. (2020, March 13). Bebop, jazz manhood and "piano shame." *The Feminist Wire.* https:// thefeministwire.com/2013/03/bebop-jazz-manhood-and-piano-shame

Romero, D. (2020). Fred Hersch Interview. *New Orleans Review*, 44. www.neworleansreview.org/fred-hersch/

Rothaus, S. (2013). Interview with Gary Burton. www.youtube.com/watch?v=uP5hPmiKvJI

Spellman, A. B. (2004). *Four Jazz Lives*. University of Michigan Press.

Tucker, S. (2002). Big Ears: Listening for Gender in Jazz Studies, *Current Musicology*. 375–408. www.jstor.org/ stable/j.ctv1134ftp

Tucker, S. (2008). When did jazz go straight?: A Queer question for jazz studies. *Critical Studies in Improvisation*, 4, 2. https://doi.org/10.21083/csieci.v4i2.850

Voce, S. (1977, August). Gay jazz releases. *Jazz Journal*, 56.

Voce, S. (1978, February). Mincing with some barbecue? *Jazz Journal*, 24.

Watrous, P. (1991, May 10). Cecil Taylor, long a rebel, is finding steady work. *New York Times*, C14, 64.

PART 3

Society and Education

21

OPPRESSION AND HOPE

Students' Perceptions of Gender and Stereotypes in Jazz Appreciation and History

James Reddan

Clarifying Statement: In this chapter, the terms male and female are used in several ways. Participants' perceptions of male and female reference perceived gender based on physical representations related to the binary situated in the definition related to biological sex. Outside of this, male and female (unless specifically noted) are meant to include male-identifying and female-identifying individuals.

Introduction and Background

Often thought of as a male-dominated musical domain, both men and women have made significant contributions to jazz throughout its history. Gender perception and stereotypes have influenced the perception and trajectory of the jazz musician since its earliest beginnings including how instruments are selected for or by the player, questioning "where's the women," the "normalizing" of gender roles (Tucker, 2001) in ensemble participation, written documents, imagery, and sound recordings. Although individual experiences have differed, perceptions of gender in jazz music have been influenced by how gender was perceived historically, what and how gender has been documented, and perceptions of that documentation in relationship to gender stereotypes throughout jazz history.

Although there has been a demonstrable increase in the diversity of roles of both women and men in jazz music since the 1990s (Gourse, 1995, p. vii), there continues to be a sense of clear gender differences with how jazz is and has been portrayed and taught in higher education. Moreover, this has led to inconsistencies and perceived student biases on the part of the teacher about how and what is taught in jazz appreciation and history courses (Reddan, 2019). In recent years, there has been a movement to explore and expand the discourse around gender, gender disparity, and gender identity in the jazz world. Most recently, Terri Lyne Carrington founded the Institute of Jazz and Gender Justice at Berklee College of Music (Lorge, 2019, p. 25). As Tucker (2001) noted, it's not just about "where's the women." The importance of considering gender in jazz also requires us to consider how we can transform jazz culture by thinking about the issues of justice, oppression and perception while also considering what jazz would both look and sound like without the concept of patriarchy (Lorge, 2019, p. 25).

One of the ways we can think about transforming culture is to better understand how gender in jazz music is perceived and how it is taught. Jazz appreciation and history courses in higher education

DOI: 10.4324/9781003081876-24

are often the first places, and sometimes the only places that tertiary students experience jazz music. As educators, it is important to understand how tertiary students perceive gender in jazz through the examination of what they read, see, hear, and discuss in books, images, magazines, song lyrics and their personal experiences. Tertiary students can inform us about students' perceptions of how gender has been documented and portrayed, of perceived gender bias, and of how we can change this through the way that we teach jazz history and appreciation in a balanced and relevant way from this point forward. As Jorgensen (1996) noted, "if education is to grapple with the central issues of life, it ought to be vitally concerned not only with deconstructing and struggling against present realities but envisioning and celebrating realities" (p. 36).

Considerations of Gender

There have been a plethora of studies about music appreciation and jazz appreciation, and its definition, refinement, and redefinition, especially in higher education (Bares, 2020; Barrett, McCoy and Veblen, 1997; Enz, 2013; Pierce, 2012, 2015; Reimer, 2009; Small, 1998). The purpose of any type of education, especially music education (generally or jazz specifically), is to recognize and consider the power of music in our daily lives through consideration of and participation in active learning in addition to understanding our own passive participation outside of the classroom (Jorgensen, 2002; Pierce, 2015). Small (1998) noted that we should consider musicking, not just focusing on music as a product, but as a social process.

> Musicking is thus as central in importance to our humanness as is taking part in speech acts, and all normally endowed human beings are born capable of taking part in it, not just in understanding the gestures but of making it their own.
>
> *(Small, 1999)*

Therefore, part of our pedagogical consideration in teaching must be attention to personal relevance (Pierce, 2015). Bennett Reimer (2009) noted,

> [E]very subject worthy of study, including music, embodies a diversity of values, all deserving our attention.... One task of a philosophy of music education is to illuminate what those might be, so that in pursuing them, our effects on our students can be as beneficial as music is capable of making them.

Additionally, Doug Risner (2008) noted, "[E]ducation is never neutral, but rather a complex series of asymmetrical power relationships that are frequently hidden and unexamined" (p. 95).

Whether music major or non-major, Pierce (2015) posited that attention to personal relevance should be addressed in music courses taught under the guise of appreciation. Although Pierce's (2015) focus was on the issue of active learning and the dichotomy of practitioner versus spectator, the same dichotomy exists between teacher/student and gender in all forms of identification. In jazz appreciation and history courses in higher education specifically, the importance of personal relevance and social justice about perceptions of gender has become increasingly important and urgent. To do this, we must not just consider what information is taught. We must also consider how it is taught, who is teaching, the students' perceptions of what is taught and how it is presented by the instructor, textbook author, in supplemental materials, and all that is perceived, absorbed, and learned as part of the educational experience in our courses. The relevance perceived by the students as a result of our instruction as jazz appreciation and history educators could affect the importance and relevance placed on that information outside of the classroom (Reddan, 2014; Reddan, 2020). Therefore, it is important to consider critical pedagogy as a theoretical lens to understand issues of gender and students' perceptions of it in jazz appreciation education.

Critical Pedagogy and Gendered Teaching

Consideration of critical pedagogy continues to be important when addressing gender and teaching pedagogy in the arts. Risner (2008) noted that "critical pedagogy is an approach to teaching that seeks to help students question and challenge domination by exposing taken-for-granted assumptions and practices that limit, marginalize, and disenfranchise human agency and freedom" (p. 95). Jazz, as in most artistic studies, is couched in assumptions about gender and power relations that can produce "unjust educational and socio-cultural outcomes" (p. 94). This emphasizes a "silent conformity" that students subscribe to in terms of their perceptions of the binary male/female roles in jazz music and performance. As music educators and artists, we all bring our personal histories to teaching and if we are not careful, may "reproduce what it is we actually seek to change, especially in terms of gendered teaching" (p. 95).

Gendered teaching is often associated with the "banking method" of teaching (Risner, 2008, p. 95; Freire, 1970/1993). The teacher deposits information that is stored until it needs to be withdrawn for some purpose whether assessment or performance. It is the information that we as educators have been depositing that is both in question and requires further examination.

Freire's Oppression and Hope

Although the issue of gender in music (Koskoff, 2014; Magrini, 2003; McClary, 1991, 1994; O'Neill, 1997) and music education (Green, 1997, 2003, 2017; Hanley, 1998; Hargreaves, Marshall and North, 2003; Koza, 1993) and jazz (Monson, 1995; Prouty, 2010; Reddan, 2020; Tucker, 2001, 2008) has been explored extensively by multiple scholars, the issue of how gender has been represented and is taught in jazz education has become an increasingly important and substantive part of the larger discourse on this topic. The binary view of gender—men and women—has often led to the discussion of oppression in music and in education. In *Pedagogy of the Oppressed*, Paulo Freire (1970/1993) noted that "because it is a distortion of being more fully human, sooner or later being less human leads the oppressed to struggle against those who made them so." (p. 44). Furthermore,

> in order for this struggle to have meaning, the oppressed must not, in seeking to regain their humanity (which is a way to create it), become in turn oppressors of the oppressors, but rather restorers of the humanity of both.
>
> *(p. 44)*

All things being equal, exploring the perception of gender in jazz requires that we take an equal look at all sides of the issue, dealing less with the inclusion or exclusion of patriarchy and the binary definition of gender, but rather examining gender as a whole. It is not a question of who is responsible for oppression related to gender or how it is perceived. Rather, it is important to understand how, why, and consider how to change for the future.

Freire's (1970/1993) critical pedagogy is echoed by current scholars. Lind and McKoy (2016) noted that developing an understanding of how culture mediates learners' identity development is an important facet towards better understanding our student's definition of their individual identity. The perception of ourselves as "musicians" is significantly affected by our social and cultural environment (p. 49). This environment is directly influenced by what students are shown, see, listen to, and experience in the classroom and through the performance of our craft. Learners, whether in a lecture course or lesson, are in a constant state of identity development.

In addition to *Pedagogy of the Oppressed* (Freire, 1970/1993), it is also important for us to consider his *Pedagogy of Hope* (1994). As noted, regardless of his focus on literacy and silence about the arts, Freire's

> preoccupation with a people's culture, ... their historical and spiritual rootedness, [ability to] achieve self-respect[,] ... engage the political realities which they confront, and [their] struggle to create a more just, humane, egalitarian, and inclusive society" requires additional consideration.
>
> *(Jorgensen, 1996, p. 36)*

As artists, practitioners, and scholars, we must also consider "the tasks of critically examining [our] inherited beliefs and practices, determining whether or not [those] beliefs and practices should be changed, and undertaking changes [deemed] appropriate" (p. 38). As Jorgensen noted, "one's heritage cannot be accepted uncritically, because it carries the baggage of oppression within it. It validates some people and marginalizes others...It is often inhuman, sexist, classist and ethnocentric" (p. 38). If we subscribe to the points made by Freire in both *Pedagogy of the Oppressed* and *Pedagogy of Hope*, then as teachers, we must decide—based on our students' understanding, perceptions, and beliefs— what it is we believe and how that impacts how and what we teach. More importantly, we must also reflect on what our students' perceptions are about what we teach and how it is presented if we are to make pedagogical changes and upend the traditional "banking method" of teaching. Therefore, we must consider that students' perceptions of what they experience may have a profound impact on their understanding of the past. Their thoughts about a social theory of how to change provide a co-intentional transformation of reality for the future in the way gender is perceived and taught in jazz appreciation and jazz history in higher education.

Purpose of the Study

The purpose of this study was to understand how American undergraduate music students ($N = 30$) perceive gender in jazz music based on their examination of books, magazines, song lyrics, album and compact disc (CD) covers, and listening to jazz music in relation to the study of jazz appreciation and jazz history.

Research Questions

By completing this study, I hoped to answer two research questions:

(a) What differences, if any, do American undergraduate music students perceive about gender in jazz in relation to the educational materials they are presented?
(b) What factors, if any, affect American undergraduate music students' perceptions of gender and gender stereotypes in jazz music?

Participants

The participants in this qualitative study included 30 American undergraduate music majors who attend a public, state-funded university focused on liberal arts in the Pacific Northwest region of the United States. All participants were pursuing an undergraduate degree in music, including jazz and commercial music performance, music education, classical vocal or instrumental performance, and audio production. Participants included 15 males and 15 females. All participants chose to self-identify their gender, though their gender may not be the gender assigned at birth. All participants were between the ages of 20 and 26 at the time the study took place. Participants self-reported their race as either white (24), black (8), or Asian (2). Additionally, participants had a diverse range of experiences with jazz music, including playing or singing in a jazz ensemble, and taking coursework in improvisation, jazz history, and other courses. The average length of experience in jazz music was $M = 4.17$ years.

Methodology

To understand how American undergraduate music students perceive gender in jazz, a Focus group Research Method designed and articulated by Rosanna L. Breen (2006) was used. Focus group research is intended to generate ideas, present attitudes and opinions that are socially formed, provide a deeper understanding of the phenomenon, and help us understand how students will react to change in the future (Breen, 2006, p. 467). After recruiting a sample of 30 participants, the participants were placed into three groups of 10. Breen (2006) noted, groups larger than 10–12 will surpass theoretical saturation (p. 465). Each group of 10 participants met at different times and days based on the convenience of the meeting time to their schedules. The groups were not homogenous.

Each group was provided with a sample of books, articles, magazines, album covers, and song lyrics to examine for one hour. The time corresponded with the same amount of time participants would meet for a typical college course at their university. Participants were free to examine what they wanted and how much they wanted to examine within the allotted time. After the examination period, participants were brought together and sat in a circle. During each focus group interview, participants were asked five questions (see Figure 21.1).

The questions were designed for participants to share and compare their experiences with each other, develop and generate ideas, and explore issues of shared importance (Breen, 2006, p. 465). Following Krueger and Casey's (2000 p. 40–43) suggestions about focus group questions, the questions were all designed to sound conversational, clear, honest, stimulating, situational, and appropriate. This allowed for meaningful and non-intimidating conversation led by the participants with little interaction with the facilitator. The conversations were audio recorded and transcribed. The transcriptions were coded, themes were identified and summarized. The data were triangulated through rich narrative, member checks, and outside reader review.

Krueger's Categories (2000)	*Question*
Opening Question	What experiences have you had with jazz music prior to today?
Introductory Question	How did you feel about the different ways that gender was depicted in the different artifacts you reviewed?
Transition Question	Would you change anything about how gender is portrayed in jazz based on what you have reviewed?
Key Question	How do you think the documentation of gender in jazz could or should change in the future, if at all?
Ending Question	Finally, are there any other observations or ideas that we have not discussed related to gender and jazz that you would like to bring up now?

Figure 21.1 Focus group interview questions.

Themes

Based on coding and content analysis of the transcribed focus group interviews, five themes were identified. These themes were pervasive throughout the interviews and demonstrated consensus amongst the participants.

Theme 1: Participants' past experiences influence their perception of gender and jazz from an early age to present.

Participants' past experiences had an impact on their perceptions of gender and jazz from their earliest experiences to present. Many of the participants grew up listening to jazz and noted that "men were band leaders and played the loud instruments like trumpet, drums, and trombone while women played piano, flute, violin, or sang." Others did not start to participate in jazz until tertiary study. Several participants discussed jazz experiences back to grade 6 in middle school in extra-curricular or co-curricular jazz bands. Some experienced jazz for the first time at a general music or jazz music camp. One student's first experience with jazz music was watching the movie "Who Framed Roger Rabbit." Jessica Rabbit was his first exposure to a "jazz singer." Others noted that the first time they saw a "jazzer" that "looked like them," was in the movie *Dreamgirls*. Many (*n* = 19) participants noted that their past experiences, especially seeing someone "doing what they wanted to do who looked like them" had an impact on their early jazz experiences both as listener and performer. Participants who are primarily vocalists described coming to jazz study and participation much later either in high school or college.

Theme 2: There is a clear disparity in participant's perception of gender in jazz related to sexuality and emotion.

Participants in all the focus groups agreed that there is a clear disparity in the perception of gender in jazz related to sexuality and emotion. Specifically, participants noted how women (past and present) are depicted in images, album covers, magazines, and books compared to men. Generally, all participants agreed with each other that women are hypersexualized, noting:

> White women are thin and elegant with longer legs. Black women are bigger, bigger hair. Men are covered and in tuxes, long sleeves, or look like they should be taken seriously. Women show a lot of cleavage, tight outfits, legs, and look more "pretty."

Additionally, participants noted a variety of different song lyrics about love and loneliness. For example, participants noted that females very often sing of love and wanting a man to stay with them, loneliness, needing a man, and so forth. Contrarily, participants noted that males are often singing about love, but differently than the females singers. One participant explicitly noted how "their role as a male includes being able to cheat in relationships and 'know' they will be taken back, or other things that are much worse."

Sexuality and emotion were also important in the way gender is perceived in jazz when it comes to instruments versus singers. There was a clear disparity perceived as to what men and women can and cannot or should and should not do. Moreover, female instrumentalists were considered to emphasize more of the sexual nature of playing and holding an instrument, versus the talent of being a performer on that instrument. In books and magazines, participants noted that writing about women was primarily done by women and often seemed more objective. Books and articles by men written about women were perceived as being more critical and opinion-based rather than factual and objective. Finally, participants noted that, historically and presently, the depiction of gender in jazz seemed to be more about marketing than about the music and the true history. Participants perceived that, for both women and men, there was an exaggerated focus on the artist as object rather than artist as musician.

Theme 3: Stereotypical norms of the past are pervasive, if not exaggerated, in depictions of gender in jazz.

Participants perceived that stereotypical gender norms of the past are still pervasive, if not exaggerated in current representations of gender in jazz. This is true of both men and women, and non-binary persons. This includes both genders being hypersexualized and emotional disparities between genders. Participants noted gender norms in images and artwork on album covers. The participants perceived a clear difference in the emphasis and definition of masculinity and femininity in the images, with a disproportionate focus on masculinity. Additionally, participants noted an "age in" and "age out" related to jazz artists. Many are portrayed as youthful as possible, especially women. Participants noted that images of middle-aged women tended to be fewer, unless the artist was a big name. However, even then, it was clear that participants perceived that there was a focus on youth, or a strong career for older jazz musicians, especially male jazz artists. Participants noted that men didn't appear to age out at all.

One resource that participants emphasized as fighting back against stereotypes was the children's book "Little Melba and Her Big Trombone" by Katheryn Russell Brown (2014). Participants noted how this story demonstrated that anyone could do anything. Instruments, performance, and composing do not need to follow perceived gender norms, as participants noted that these areas were all primarily perceived to be male-dominated careers in jazz music. Participant W noted that the book "countered every single thing in all of the scholarly or real artifacts" that they were presented and familiar with, especially the concept that "women sing and men play" which was "all over in the artifacts" (Participant C). Participants were also very clear to note that the same disparity of perceived gender norms and stereotypes were just as pervasive in jazz as in classical music history. There was a clear desire for more balance in the literature and the teaching of both.

Theme 4: Gender and gender stereotypes in jazz are perceived to be related to racial bias.

When coding the data, a clear theme emerged that gender and gender stereotypes in jazz are perceived by participants to be related to racial bias. Participants noted the differences between the prevalence of white men versus black men, white females versus black females in written resources and in pictures. They also noted an emphasis on white males in many of the texts that they reviewed. They felt black females did not get enough recognition, nor was their entire story always being told accurately (i.e., Ella Fitzgerald wasn't just a singer, she was also the band leader). As noted by one participant, only one of the jazz appreciation textbooks even recognized the International Sweethearts of Rhythm and female instrumentalists of color.

One participant (a black female) told a personal story of the issue of gender, race, and stereotypes related to jazz and singing. Participant R noted that as a black female singer, everyone assumed she would be in the jazz ensemble or a gospel choir and sing at church. As she stated,

> I don't sing jazz or gospel, I'm studying opera. However, because I'm black and female with bigger hair and a bigger body, everyone assumes I must do jazz or gospel because I 'can't do' classical music. Whereas everyone assumes the reverse for white females (at least in my experience). If we are talking about gender in jazz, or in classical music, or in any type of music, it needs to be shown as something reflective of everyone. I'm tired of the damn stereotypes based on gender and race.

These sentiments were supported by many participants in all the focus groups.

Theme 5: The depiction and exploitation of gender in jazz should change for the future with a focus on non-binary stereotypes and focus on the music.

After analysis of the focus group data, it was clear that participants felt the documentation of gender in jazz should change in the future. Participants noted, based on their perceptions of how gender has been documented in jazz, a desire to think about jazz outside of gender norms with focus more on the music. As one participant said, "Let women be women, let men be men, let everyone be human. Why focus on the sexualization of anyone?" Moreover, this statement supported a consensus of thinking about gender and documenting gender emphasizing a more non-binary approach. As participant L said,

> Why worry about if it is a man or a woman? Both genders can do everything. We need to show more of the community and 'jazz for all' rather than focusing on binary genders. Does gender even need to matter anymore?

There was a clear desire not to document jazz based on the stereotypes that participants perceived being reflected in books, photos, literature and lyrics. There was a consensus to empower all and focus on what makes the individual, not what makes a gender a gender.

One clear desire of participants is for more female jazz composers and lyricists.

Participants noted that, in the documentation they reviewed (which was reflective of their experiences in public and tertiary jazz programs), male composers are greatly emphasized, and female composers, arrangers, and lyricists are often left out. This was true for contemporary female jazz composers and musicians. Overall, participants noted that the documentation of gender in jazz needs to be much more balanced, more up-to-date, and resourceful.

Conclusions and Implications

After coding and analysis of the data and identification and description of the themes, there are several conclusions based on this study. First, the participants in the study perceived that there are important issues and disparities in the representation of gender past and present that were causes of concern. The issue of balance between genders, more focus on music and less on binary gender, and less focus on gender stereotypes and norms were also clearly emphasized by participants. However, the other issue is that as a jazz community we need to be careful of gendering music and what we do with marketing in educational, scholarly and reference materials, images, and even in our lyrics. To quote a participant, the "old way" is not working for current tertiary students. Moreover, this has important implications for future jazz research, the development of a more balanced scholarly literature, composition opportunities, and both the K-12 and tertiary jazz curriculum. Jorgensen (1996) noted,

> It is important to distinguish between education and indoctrination. The former is liberating in its tendency toward facilitating individual growth, self-knowledge, a critical awareness of the world about us, and the willingness and wherewithal to engage in a struggle to remake that world a better place. The latter is repressive in its effect—apathy, malaise, disinterested-ness, existential wariness and hopelessness.
>
> (p. 39)

Furthermore, teachers have the responsibility to examine what they are teaching on an ongoing basis, even if it means shaking up the beliefs of others. This will be important if we are to more accurately reflect the roles all jazz participants can play regardless of gender both in current practice and historically.

Based on the findings from this study, it is clear that the focus-group participants thought of gender as a binary construct. This may have been a direct result of the preponderance of the binary construct of gender displayed in the materials presented and focus group questions asked. The materials presented as part of this study included peer-reviewed published research and textbooks in addition to images, lyrics, and recordings (current and historical) that are currently used in tertiary classrooms. These works are not produced, nor do they live simply in a vacuum. The lack of gender nonbinary materials available is not only evident, it is clear that they are simply nonexistent. As a result, there are implications for reconsidering how gender is presented within jazz history and in jazz generally representing all definitions of gender, including nonbinary. It is clear that students have presumptions about the definition of gender. Therefore, there are strong implications that additional discourse focused on how the construct of gender is both formed and defined in jazz generally and in jazz education specifically, is needed. Additional research about gender in jazz education is needed to understand how students understand gender, how we define the construct of gender individually and artistically both in jazz and jazz education, and why the discussion about gender in jazz (in all forms) is important.

Freire (1970/1993) noted:

> [T]he oppressed ... must find through their struggle the way to life-affirming humaniza-
> tion, which does not lie simply in having more.... In order to regain their humanity they
> must cease to be *things* and fight as men and women. They cannot enter the struggle as
> objects in order *later* to become human beings.
>
> *(p. 68)*

When considering gender in jazz, this means we cannot simply objectify gender; rather all sides participating in the discourse must work towards the humanization of all participants in jazz by thinking about how the humanization of the performance can be documented and transformed as a reflection of jazz—or more broadly—human culture. For this to happen requires an "intentionality ... in essence a 'way towards' something apart from itself, outside itself, which surrounds it and which it apprehends by means of its ideational capacity." (p. 69) Therefore, a comprehensive view of gender in jazz requires a co-intentional education where teachers and students, co-intent on reality, are both subjects coming to know it critically (p. 69). Based on participants perceptions, current literature, and consideration of both Freire's *Pedagogy of the Oppressed* (1970/1993) and *Pedagogy of Hope* (1994), it is of the utmost importance that educators teaching jazz appreciation and jazz history consider how the depiction and representation of gender in jazz impacts students and performers, and reflect on ways we can continue to improve this for them in the future.

References

Bares, W. K. (2020). A jazz history course for the information era. *Jazz Education in Research and Practice, 1*(1), 59–78. doi: 10.2979/jazzeducrese.1.1.06.

Barrett, J. R., McCoy, C. W., Veblen, K. K. (1997). *Sound Ways of Knowing: Music in the Interdisciplinary Curriculum.* Schirmer Books.

Breen, R. L. (2006). A practical guide to focus group research. *Journal of Geography in Higher Education, 30*(3), 463–475. doi: 10.1080/03098260600927575.

Brown, K. R. (2014). *Little Melba and Her Big Trombone.* Lee and Low Books.

Enz, N. J. (2013). Teaching music to the non-major: A review of literature. *Update: Applications of Research in Music Education, 32*(1), 34–42.

Freire, P. (1970/1993). *Pedagogy of the Oppressed.* Continuum.

Freire, P. (1994). *Pedagogy of Hope: Reliving Pedagogy of the Oppressed.* Continuum.

Gourse, L. (1995). *Madame Jazz: Contemporary Women Instrumentalists.* Oxford University Press.

Green, L. (2003). Music education, cultural capital, and social group identity. In M. Clayton, T. Herbert and R. Middleton (Eds.), *The Cultural Study of Music: A Critical Introduction* (pp. 263–273). Routledge.

Green, L. (2017). *How Popular Musicians Learn: A Way Ahead for Music Education*. Routledge.

Green, L. (1997). *Music, Gender, Education*. Cambridge University Press.

Hanley, B. (1998). Gender in secondary music education in British Columbia. *British Journal of Music Education*, *15*(1), 51–69.

Hargreaves, D. J., Marshall, N. A., and North, A. C. (2003). Music education in the twenty-first century: A psychological perspective. *British Journal of Music Education*, *20*(2), 147–163.

Jorgensen, E. (1996). The artist and the pedagogy of hope. *International Journal of Music Education*, *27*, 36–50.

Jorgensen, E. (2002). The aims of music education: A preliminary excursion. *Journal of Aesthetic Education*, *36*(1), 31–49.

Koskoff, E. (2014). *A Feminist Ethnomusicology: Writings on Music and Gender*. University of Illinois Press. Retrieved August 3, 2019, from Project MUSE Database.

Koza, J. E. (1993). The "missing males" and other gender issues in music education: Evidence from the music supervisors' journal, 1914–1924. *Journal of Research in Music Education*, *41*(3), 212–232.

Lind, V. R. and McKoy, C. L. (2016). *Culturally Responsive Teaching in Music Education: From Understanding to Application*. Routledge (Taylor & Francis Group).

Lorge, S. (2019). Transform the culture. *DownBeat*, *86*(2), 24–29. Elmhurst, IL: Maher Publications.

Magrini, T. (Ed.). (2003). *Music and Gender: Perspectives from the Mediterranean*. University of Chicago Press.

McClary, S. (1991). *Feminine Endings: Music, Gender, and Sexuality*. University of Minnesota Press.

McClary, S. (1994). *Cecilia Reclaimed: Feminist Perspectives on Gender and Music*. University of Illinois Press.

Monson, I. (1995). The problem with white hipness: Race, gender, and cultural conceptions in jazz historical discourse. *Journal of the American Musicological Society*, *48*(3), 396–422.

O'Neill, S. A. (1997). Gender and music. In D. J. Hargreaves and A. C. North (Eds.), *The Social Psychology of Music* (pp. 46–63). Oxford University Press.

Pierce, D. L. (2012). Rising to a new paradigm: Infusing health and wellness into the music curriculum. *Philosophy of Music Education Review*, *20*(2), 154–176.

Pierce, D. L. (2015). Redefining music appreciation. *College Music Symposium*, *55*. https://dx.doi.org/10.18177/sym.2015.55.sr.10871

Prouty, K. (2010). Toward jazz's 'official' history: The debates and discourses of jazz history textbooks. *Journal of Music History Pedagogy*, *1*(1), 19–43.

Reddan, J. M. (2014). "Effects of Presentation Mode on Community College Students' Perception of Performance Quality and Self-reported Level of Musical Engagement" (Doctoral Dissertation, Boston University).

Reddan, J. M. (2019, January). *Perceiving gender in jazz: Documenting the Past, Present, and Social Theorizing the Future* [paper]. Documenting Jazz, Dublin, Ireland.

Reddan, J. M. (2020, January 8–11). Un-gendering the Vocal Jazz Ensemble. Jazz Education Network 2020 Conference, New Orleans, LA.

Reimer, B. (2009). *Seeking the Significance of Music Education: Essays and Reflections*. National Association for Music Education.

Risner, D. (2008). The politics of gender in dance pedagogy. *Journal of Dance Education*, *8*(3), 94–97.

Small, C. (1998). *Musicking: The Meanings of Performing and Listening*. University Press of New England.

Small, C. (1999). Musicking—The meanings of performing and listening. A lecture. *Music Education Research*, *1*(1), 9–21.

Tucker, S. (2001). Big Ears: Listening for Gender in Jazz Studies. *Current Musicology*, *71*(73), 2. Columbia University.

Tucker, S. (2008). When did jazz go straight? A queer question of jazz studies. *Critical Studies in Improvisation*, *4*(2), 1–16.

22

PICTURING WOMEN IN JAZZ

An Analysis of Three Jazz History Textbooks

Ramsey Castaneda and Amanda Quinlan

Textbooks and the photographs contained within them are assumed by learners and professionals alike to be authoritative and accurate works that detail the facts and theories of their subject (Hornsley et al., 2005). While debates regarding the philosophical and historiographical approaches in textbooks are commonplace, the images reproduced in jazz textbooks remain uncritically examined and propagated despite their crucial role in socializing and enculturating learners to the norms and values of jazz communities. As arbiters of the music, particularly for novice musicians and students, textbooks illustrate through their photographs who has the privilege of entry to the pantheon of important jazz performers, and through their exclusion, who has had additional obstacles to overcome to gain legitimacy and acceptance in the world of jazz.

In this chapter we interrogate the ways in which jazz history textbooks represent jazz writ large by examining the frequency of, and the context in which, women are depicted photographically in three commonly utilized jazz history textbooks (Gridley, 2012; DeVeaux and Giddins, 2009; Bierman, 2015). First, we identified all the photographic images of performers that appear in these texts. The textbook, *Jazz Styles*, contains 100 photographs and 87 percent of them show only men, 5 percent include men and women together, and 8 percent photos were of women only. *Listening to Jazz* has a total of 87 photographs, 78.6 percent of those were of men only, while 7.1 percent of the photos were of both men and women, and the remaining 14.3 percent were of women only. Finally, *Jazz* included 218 photographs, 85.8 percent of which were only men, 11.9 percent are men and women, and 2.3 percent were photos of women only.

Our methodology for analyzing the photographic representation of women in these three texts consisted of scanning all the images (excluding album art, drawings, and graphics) and coding them according to gender, instrumentation, race, and genre. This data was used to create an interactive database to filter the photos according to any combination of coded criteria. Regarding the terminology of gender identification, jazz musicians in these photographs were categorized into either "man/men" or "woman/women," but we acknowledge that this binary is not representative of the population at large and perhaps not representative of our sample either. The identification of "woman" was used when the accompanying text used female pronouns, and in the rare cases where "she" was not used in descriptive text, we based our decision on the gendered presentation of how the musicians presented themselves and were likely to be interpreted by novice readers of an introductory jazz textbook.

DOI: 10.4324/9781003081876-25

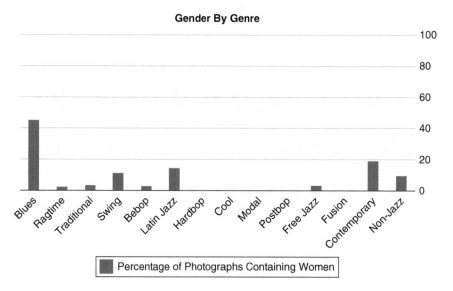

Figure 22.1 Percentage of images in all three textbooks that depict women, organized by genre. This figure includes non-musicians (fans or spectators, spouses, etc.) and duplicate images appearing in all three texts.

In general, gender representation by style was widely varied (see Figure 22.1). Within the entire database of images, we found that women were most likely to be featured in photographs of Blues performances, while there were no photographs of women performing Hard-Bop, Cool Jazz, Fusion, or Post-Bop. Women did appear in 45 percent of all Blues photographs across all three textbooks. Women were also most likely to appear in contemporary post 1990s styles of jazz. Still, of the total number of images of contemporary jazz musicians, just shy of 20 percent depicted women.

Our research clearly reveals a dearth of photographs in textbooks featuring women, a finding that reflects the long-standing erasure of women in jazz performance, recording, and education (Raine, 2020; Pellegrinelli et al., 2021; Wehr, 2016). Across all three textbooks we found that by a wide margin men appeared more often, followed by women alone, and finally by men and women appearing together, albeit less frequently. *Listening to Jazz* contained the highest percentage of photographs of women but the fewest number of photographs overall. Ed Berger's (2019) posthumously released review asserts that *Listening to Jazz* "shines the spotlight on some figures typically overlooked in introductory surveys [and] underscores the contributions of (and barriers faced by) women jazz musicians throughout the music's history" (p. 95).

Our data, empirical analysis, and interpretation suggests that the general lack of photographic representation of women is the result of a systemic dismissal of women's contributions to music and a traditionally unwelcoming or even hostile educational environment for women and girls' participation in secondary and post-secondary jazz education (McKeage, 2004; Russonello, 2017).

Jazz Textbooks

For students and teachers, textbooks have considerable influence. Sadker and Zittleman (2007) have noted that "students spend as much as 80 to 95% of classroom time using textbooks and that teachers make a majority of their instructional decisions based on the textbook" (p. 144). Hornsley et al. (2005) likewise found that even when texts are not used in the classroom, photocopying, reference, and teaching materials from textbooks often "delimit" the essential subject matter. Additionally, textbooks do not just present facts about a subject, they also enculturate their audience to the values and norms of its subjects, communities, and participants (including the authors of the text). In this way, textbooks act as a socialization guide to acceptance within a given domain (Brugeilles and Cromer, 2009, p. 16). When textual content in textbooks is combined with photographs, a medium that has been argued to be a knowledge gatekeeper in and of itself (Lyons, 2011), the potential for influence is even more potent. Together, textbooks and photographs convey to the novice a sense of incontrovertible truth. Photographs and textbooks inform and illustrate the next generation of jazz musicians and consumers about who are the legitimate and accepted members of the community.

Though jazz history textbooks are a relatively recent pedagogical development, DeVeaux (1991) noted 30 years ago that an "official" history of jazz was emerging through the narratives and canon observed in the collegiate jazz history textbook market (p. 525). The philosophical approach to jazz textbook writing can be divided into two simplified categories: jazz as autonomous music, and jazz music a socio-cultural influenced and reflective practice. Proponents of the autonomous approach to music treat music's value and import as stemming directly from the music itself, regardless of any perceived extra-musical influences, including social, political, and even biographical. Scholars whose work has included formalist and autonomous perspectives include Gunther Schuller, Mark Gridley, and Frank Tirro (Schuller 1958; Gridley, 2012; Tirro, 1993). Alternatively, jazz as a socio-cultural phenomenon includes proponents such as Scott DeVeaux, Tomlinson, Gabbard, and Harker, among others who detail non-musical aspects of the music and musicians' lives as formative influences (DeVeaux and Giddins, 2009; Tomlinson, 1992; Gridley, 2012; Gabbard, 1995; Heile et. al., 2016). For an example, see the back-and-forth between Gridley and Harker on jazz and civil rights in the *College Music Symposium*, volumes 47, 48, and 51.

Jazz textbooks tell and show their readers what jazz is all about, who shaped the genre, and who participates. Despite Gabbard's (1996) oft-cited observation that "part of what has made jazz so intriguing is the number of alternatives it has offered to conventional notions of masculinity and male sexuality." Whyton (2010) notes that the "African American masculine ideal continues to provide the standard by which authentic jazz performance is judged" (Gabbard, p. 7; Whyton, p. 36). And though various styles of jazz may have opened the doors for alternatives to masculinity, it must be simultaneously acknowledged that these alternatives are still nearly exclusively only available to the male performer. Indeed, throughout jazz history women report needing to perform masculinity to gain respect as well as work from their male peers (Russonello, 2017; For example, see Porter's 2002 writing on Abby Lincoln). Rustin and Tucker claim in *Big Ears* (2008) that "listening for gender in jazz studies shifts the contours of jazz history: the boundaries and definitions of what counts as jazz sounds and practices, our awareness of whose bodies are seen and not seen as jazz bodies" (p. 19).

It is also evident that jazz texts, while sharing a lack of space for female representation, are not necessarily similar in approach. For example, Prouty (2010) notes that Gridley's popular work, *Jazz Styles*, first published in 1978 (in its 11th edition at the time of this writing), exhibits a "lack of attention to social and historical context [that is] remarkable, especially considering its wide adoption as a standard text in the field" (2012, p. 32). Pellegrinelli also comments that Gridley ignores singers and that. while vocal jazz includes men as well as women, the suppression of vocal jazz artists eliminates a substantial amount of women's contributions to the music (Ruskin and Tucker, 2008, p. 42). In addition, Walser claims that Gridley "whitewashes" Miles Davis's career by ignoring the socio-cultural and biographical elements of his career (Wasler, 1993, p. 344).

While a formalist approach to music criticism and philosophy exists in any well-established tradition, it is disposed to ignore the potential impacts that non-music elements, such as photographs, may convey about the music and its associated communities (musicians, aficionados, industry professionals, etc.). However, even scholars who do not treat jazz as autonomous music are liable to under-recognize the potential influence of photographs in textbooks. Prouty remarks on DeVeaux and Giddins' *Jazz* (2009), that though it was published to tell the "story of jazz as it has never been told before" (DeVeaux and Giddins, 2009, backmatter), that it in fact offers "a narrative that is strikingly like the 'official version' that DeVeaux decried in 1991." Among Prouty's observations of *Jazz*'s limited non-canonical coverage was women, "a topic which is relegated mainly to an inset box discussion, aside from brief discussions of a few significant figures like Mary Lou Williams."

The representation of Mary Lou Williams is an interesting case. She was featured on the cover of Bierman's *Listening to Jazz*, the only woman to be featured on any cover of the three texts examined (the second edition, not analyzed for this chapter, features Sarah Vaughn on the cover). However, Williams herself has recently been described as a "token" (Tucker, 2001 p. 385) and "culture hero" (Teal, 2019, p. 2) of gender diversity in educational texts that merely disguises the problems of gender inequity. Teal, expanding on Sara Ahmad's work, *On Being* (2012), writes:

> If a lack of gender diversity in jazz is a problem, and celebrations of Mary Lou Williams are presented as a solution, Ahmed's line of thought encourages us to consider how uses of the Williams myth might obscure the relative absence of women's voices in jazz rather than solve the problem. As Ahmed goes on to argue, in an atmosphere in which institutions use statements on diversity as a form of public relations, "solutions to problems are the problems given new form." In considering gender imbalance and institutional sexism in jazz as a problem, I argue that holding up Williams as evidence that jazz represents diversity gives that original problem new form.
>
> *(p. 3)*

Similarly, we claim textbook photographs reveal an undercurrent in jazz history texts that espouses traditional and canonical ideals despite any authorial intent to the contrary.

Jazz History and Denial of Women

The absence of women in jazz textbooks does, in fact, reflect the reality of serious challenges, if not impediments, for women to receive recognition for their contributions to jazz. Indeed, jazz has its own history, which should be accurately represented, but not uncritically. The history of jazz covers an era in which women were systematically denied equal opportunities across social, political, and artistic endeavors. The roots of this structural sexism lay, in-part, in societal expectations during jazz's rise to an art music, and in the justifications for the formal acceptance of jazz in academia. In the post-swing era, when jazz began its ascent to highbrow music, jazz critics distanced themselves from the swing music of their youth. The wide-reaching popularity and entertainment value of swing seemed to betray the individualistic and genius tropes that pervade much of the Western art world. In contrast, the late-night, less accessible, small group jazz combos that helped define early bebop provided ample contrasts with which to prove the new jazz a high art. Among these differences between swing and bebop was the number of women performers as both instrumentalists and especially vocalists.

Part of the critics' distancing included a move away from theories of entertainment and popularity toward an autonomous and cerebral approach, common to classical musicological discourse, as a means of legitimizing the music by associating it with the highbrow art music of Western Europe and academic study in colleges and university. Furthermore, bebop, often argued to be the style that initiated jazz's acceptance as an art, was practiced and developed in after-hours clubs and was almost exclusively instrumental, rather than vocal, music. Both after-hours clubs and instrumental music were hindrances to non-male participation in the 1940s and 1950s when "traditional" societal gender roles were more prevalent. Pellegrinelli further notes that "if demanding art music is made by men for men as connoisseurs, then the elimination of singing as women's primary form of participation helps make jazz into a 'serious' (i.e., male) domain" (Pellegrinelli, 2008, p. 42).

Gennari also asserts that this shift in musicological approach was rooted in Cold War era ideals and linked to fears of feminized mass culture (Gennari, 2006, p. 181). The rise of mass mediated culture through new technology such as the radio and television resulted in an invasion of public discourse into the private, and domestic spaces. Radio and TV were seen as feminizing serious subjects, bringing the masculine and male-dominated public spaces into the feminized domain of the home (Laver, 2015, p. 14). McGee notes that the "parallel decline of jazz's mass popularity and its newly rising artistic status motivated contradictory representations within the medium of television," which included "feminized and nostalgic presentation of that that promoted commercial vocal jazz stars singing for mixed-gender television audiences," which contrasted with the serious and mostly male settings of jazz on television (McGee in Heile, Elsdon, and Doctor, 2016, pp. 74–75). The popularity and appeal of female spectatorship, McGee notes, caused resentment from less charismatic musicians. Gennari claims that one catalyst for "serious" critics and musicians to distance themselves from consumerism and mass culture was a "desire to foreground a sense of masculinist authority in the jazz criticism as well as the more cerebral, less popular jazz (McGee, 2016, p. 78; Gennari, 2006, p. 182). In "Separated at Birth," Pellegrani noted that although vocal jazz includes men as well as women, this suppression of vocalists (in any style of jazz) eliminates a substantial amount of women's contributions to the music in one fell swoop. Pellegrinelli (2008) adds that Gridley's work ignores singers all together, while the Porter and Ullmann text, *Jazz: From its Origins to the Present*, puts all vocalists in one chapter (Pellegrinelli, 2008, p. 44 n4; Porter et al. 1993).

The jazz critics' and historians' overall dismissal of women's contributions, and societal and musical challenges of participating in jazz performances, intentional or not, set the stage for a persistent headwind against non-male identifying jazz musicians. This headwind did not just make women's participation in jazz at the time more challenging but became embedded in the stories and photographs of the period that now illustrate educational textbooks. The effects of this can be observed, not just in our textbooks and education, but in the contemporary practices of jazz musicians. Pellegrinelli and colleagues' research on an NPR Jazz Critics Poll found that "the majority of band leaders, both male and female, fail to hire women for their recording projects, though women hire other women musicians at a higher rate than men do (Pellegrinelli et al., 2021). This finding bears witness to Terry Lynn Carrington's claim that while she does think [male jazz musicians] care about gender equality, she also "think[s] that there are plenty of guys who would vote for a woman president before hiring a woman in their band" (Lorge, 2019, p. 29).

The movement from swing to bebop, from entertainment to a style deemed worthy of high-art status, left women out of the picture due in part to societal fears and gender roles. The critics, historians, and academics who first detailed the birth of bebop and laid the groundwork for the early jazz history texts and textbooks, left women out of the picture.

How Photos Mean

Music photography bears an intriguing relationship to music studies. Music is an aural and temporal experience, while photography is a visual and static experience. Though a traditional jazz historiographic approach focuses primarily on the music itself, "new jazz studies" scholars have begun interrogating how the jazz images (among other extramusical elements) influence our experiences with the music. The visual and static medium of photography can therefore be argued to occupy a subordinate position in the primarily sonorous world of jazz and is thus easily brushed aside (or blindly accepted) in jazz historiography. Yet, photographs faithfully accompany music on album covers, texts, advertising, and videos, conveying details about the jazz "Art World" (Becker, 1982). Expanding Jed Rasula's notion of "The Seductive Menace," (Rasula, 1995, p. 134) Tony Whyton (2013) writes in *Beyond a Love Supreme*, that many of the problems surrounding jazz recordings also apply to photography:

> photographers … feed into the construction of jazz itself[;] … they frame the music in such a way that it invites a particular reading or has a connotative potential, their framing coming to stand for a whole series of cultural values.
>
> *(p. 36)*

Just as audio recordings hide many of the physical and social elements of music making that are representative of crucial dynamics of jazz, photographs too, by their careful selection by photographers and textbook editors (and lack of aural and temporal qualities) contribute to how learners and professionals conceptualize this music and its community and history.

In his influential semiotic essay, "The Rhetoric of the Image," in *Music Image Text*, Roland Barthes presented three ways that commercial images convey meaning through symbols: (1) the linguistic message, which include captions, labels, logos and any other textual information, (2) the symbolic message, the information that can be gleaned from visual cures in the frame or, (3) the literal message that is understood by the photographs index to something existing in the real world (Barthes and Heath, 1977). While the audience will have varied access to each of these messages based on their personal experience, it remains the intentional goal of the image producers to encode them. In his essay Barthes was specifically referring to images in advertisements, though these same principles can be applied to jazz photographs in textbooks. Textbook imagery functions much like advertisements by enticing, informing, and engaging an audience. Many of the jazz photographic images used in our study were not created in the context of advertisement but were created for a broader commercial use—for popularizing, reporting, and recording history. In some cases, the most popular jazz images were made for the explicit purpose of selling an image of jazz, such as Francis Wolff's employment by Blue Note Records. In others, documentary photographs, such as those by Herman Leonard were adopted and adapted by the media to convey meaning about jazz and jazz musicians. Like DeVeaux's observation of an "official" history of jazz emerging from the narratives in early jazz textbooks, a homogeneous collection of clothing, posture, smoke, expression, lighting, and gender, began depicting "authentic jazz."

This is not to say that jazz musicians are playing a character of themselves, but rather that as photographers planned their sessions and poured over contact sheets, there was an already existing idealization of the jazz aesthetic that they aimed to fulfil. Many of the surviving images have been catalogued, sold into estates and libraries, and made available for use within music textbooks, cementing their ability to imbue meaning and perpetuate cultural understanding through instruction. The vetting process that each iconic image has survived warrants consideration. How and why images survive the test of time and have come to represent jazz, and how they contribute to the image canon impacts the way jazz continues to be perceived. For an image to be selected for placement in a textbook, it must survive rigorous selection by a variety of parties. A photographer might be employed to take photographs for an album cover, promotional photos, editorial images or studio documentation, or a fan of the music could simply document the performance as they experienced it. Before the performer is in front of the camera, they or a manager may have decided how they would dress, or a stylist could have presented options. The photographer also makes aesthetic choices of angle, lighting, and choosing the decisive moment. One of the ways that we see this decision-making process is through contact sheets, which display thumbnail images of each on the roll of film. Photographers and editors use these sheets to determine which images warrant being printed in large size based on how well the images convey the desired effect. The decisions that are made about which photographs are printed, sold, and shared in part perpetuate specific narratives, mythologies, and stereotypes. The narrative suggested by an image, whether intentional or not, is the result of a vetting process between the medium (album art, textbook, advertisement, etc.), subject (musician[s], venue, performance, etc.), author (photographer), and extending to circumstantial factors such as agents, record labels, cover-art designers, copyright law, textbook-editors, art editors, and budget considerations.

The iconic jazz image contains a handful of tropes that have been adopted as signifiers for jazz by mass media. Heather Pinson notes that

> the general consensus of a mental picture of a jazz musician would be a well-dressed African American man playing an instrument, most likely a saxophone or a trumpet, with smoke wafting about the stage on which he is playing at a nightclub.
>
> *(Pinson, 2010, p. 16)*

The architect of this iconic jazz image is Herman Leonard, who's ubiquitous 1948 photograph of Dexter Gordon typifies Pinson's statement and adorns the cover of DeVeaux and Giddins' textbook, *Jazz*. Leonard's distinctive images typically feature a strong backlight, dark backdrops, portray a solitary person, extreme camera angles, portray a somewhat voyeuristic perspective, and are always in black and white. These tropes are situated firmly in the American 1940s and 1950s in style, environment, and camera technology, yet they continue to be reproduced to this day by contemporary photographers and musicians alike. These tropes reinforce notions of "the other," removing jazz from the experience of the everyday, and unify the image of jazz, cementing it into popular memory.

Additionally, Whyton has noted that jazz icons have

distinct categories of iconic codification [each] commanding their own distinct forms of adoration and worship. That could easily be categorised into narrative types such as spiritual master (Coltrane), majestic icon (Ellington), Faustian genius (Parker) or metamorphic prince of darkness (Davis).

(Whyton, 2010, pp. 36–37)

These narrative types are not just reflected in the ways in which we tell their stories, but also in how we photograph them, and in the images and tropes that we as scholars, musicians, and listeners choose to disseminate. Whyton's jazz-image archetypes can be observed throughout each of our selected textbooks as commonplace representations of specific styles of the music as well as depictions of jazz icons. Noteworthy is the omission of an archetypal "jazz-woman."

Women in Photographs: Musicians or Sex Objects?

Appearance, and certainly a woman's sexualized appearance, can be used to diminish as well as to distract from a woman's musicianship—or to even preclude inclusion. In conversation with Enstice and Stockhouse, for example, Diana Krall related this dilemma for women in jazz: "Lately I've had a problem[, either] I can't be a serious artist because of my looks, or I'm only successful because of my looks" (Enstice and Stockhouse, 2004, p. 188). Laver (2015) wrote that

race, gender, and sartorial sense, do influence media visibility.... Many critics, collectors, and even other musicians treat these traits as a priori evidence of a lack of musical substance.... their sexuality is understood to preclude the possibility of artistic excellence.

(p. 131)

As substantiated through numerous studies of women in jazz, and despite strides made in recent decades, the deeply rooted inequities in jazz persist across all levels (Pellegrinelli, 2021). Sherrie Tucker described the experience of women in the jazz world as this:

Women are invisible because they weren't good enough. Playing good enough meant playing like men. Women who play like men are "exceptional women," and exceptional women can enter the discourse without changing it. We can acknowledge the importance of an exceptional woman in jazz history while retaining the belief that women cannot play powerfully enough or women can't improvise. We can use her inclusion to argue that our historical vision of jazz is not sexist, but merit-based.

(Tucker, 2001–2002, p. 384)

Tucker asserts that the jazz world is structurally opposed to having successful women because in fact the success of a few "exceptional women" can function to ensure that the value of other women, of those who choose to play "like women," are discredited.

The year 2017 found gender diversity on the front pages of the jazz community, with the *New York Times* heralding it as a "Year of Reckoning" for women in jazz (Russonello, 2017). One catalyst was Ethan Iverson's now infamous, and since deleted, interview with Robert Glasper, "in which Glasper opines on why he believes women don't 'like a lot of soloing' and how groove is 'a musical clitoris' to women" (see Mercer, 2017 and Teal, 2019 for overview).

Response was swift, including the development of "We Have Voice," a collective of female and non-binary musicians taking a stand against sexual harassment in the professional and educational jazz communities. We Have Voice's open letter also pointed out that sexual violence is linked with gender inequity and invisibility:

> [W]e recognize that our present culture is the same one that minimizes and/or excludes artists of marginalized genders, ethnicities, sexual orientations, and so forth from venues, festivals, teaching jobs, newspaper and magazine reviews. When we bring awareness to sexual violence, we are also bringing awareness to this inequity and invisibility.
>
> *(We Have Voice, 2017)*

Saxophonist Camile Thurman, currently with the Jazz at Lincoln Center Orchestra, relayed that she nearly quit playing jazz in high school due to sabotage from male classmates, and that many of the women in her high school band did indeed quit all together (Roussonello, 2017). Thurman's experience proves Terry Lynn Carrington's point in a 2019 *DownBeat* interview in which she asserted this:

> "A large responsibility is with the band directors. A lot of them are problematic." Interviewer Lorge continued, "Bias among band directors shows up at the high school level, and even more critically, in middle schools, when children are learning to play.
>
> *(Lorge, DownBeat, 2019)*

Like jazz, photography too has traditionally been a male-dominated field. In examining Roy DeCarava's 1960 photograph of Ben Webster and John Coltrane embracing, Gabbard notes that DeCarava, as a black photographer, may have been more likely to capture intimate photographs of black musicians by being able to put them at ease (Gabbard, 2002, p. 338). Perhaps the same could be said of female photographers. Of the two known female photographers whose images are featured in the text, Carole Reiff was perhaps the most prolific and dedicated jazz photographer, and someone about whom very little is known.

Sex-Stereotyping, Girls in Jazz Education

Jazz education expands far beyond textbooks, but textbooks still provide unspoken "rules" for entry and inclusion. Among the rules implicitly encoded in jazz practice that are entangled with sexism is that of gender and instrument. Here, textbooks exert influence on readers as future music teachers that may encourage or dissuade jazz participation, listeners, or practitioners. There is a rich history of research on the sex-stereotyping of instrument choice, perception that instruments are either masculine or feminine, which leads to girls choosing feminine instruments while boys choose the masculine instruments (Abramo, 2011; Abeles, 2009; Sheldon and Price 2005; Conway, 2000). McKeage noted in her 2003 study that feminized instruments are mostly likely to be uncommon instruments in jazz education (flute, clarinet, etc.), or put another way, the bulk of jazz instrumentation is traditionally perceived as masculine (McKeage, 2003).

Interestingly, Barber's (1998) study showed that girls were just as likely to participate in jazz ensembles if they had already been playing instruments that happened to be used in jazz bands (e.g., if girls had already chosen to learn trumpet or drum set, for example, they were just as likely to join a jazz band as the boys). Kelley (2003) emphasized this relationship between early music education, instrument choice, and access to jazz education.

> Whether male or female, instrument choice, which occurs in the earliest contact points with public school music, has a deep impact on access to jazz learning, particularly when instrumentation of school jazz ensembles is limited to only big bands and big band instrumentation.
>
> *(p. 193)*

McKeage's (2003) work similarly shed light on the significant attrition of women's participation in jazz ensembles between high school and college: only 26 percent of women continued to play jazz in college while 62 percent of men continued to perform in college (p. 535). McKeage's work also revealed three common reasons for quitting jazz performance: (1) lack of connections between jazz and career aspirations, (2) institutional pressures to specialize in music areas other than jazz, and (3) comfort in the jazz environment (2004).

The discomfort women and girls reported in jazz ensembles was not limited to just educational settings. Esperanza Spaulding reported that when she played with an all-woman band for the first time, she realized that it was also the first time she could perform without having to guard against unwanted advances or sexist comments from male bandmates (Lorge, 2019, p. 27). Bassist Emma DayHuff echoed Spaulding's comment while speaking on the panel, "In Conversation: Gender Equity in Jazz," for Turn Up Her Mic, relaying how women are conditioned to "brace" for unwanted comments or assumptions when entering performance spaces, and preparing to say, "No, I'm not someone's girlfriend. No, I'm not a singer. I'm here to play" (Turn up Her Mic, 2020).

As with Kelley's conclusion (2003) that instrument choice in early education may impede access to jazz education in middle and high school, Wrape et al. (2016) showed that sex and gender stereotype of instruments may be "perpetuating disproportionate representations of women among professional musicians on an international scale" (p. 45). Wehr's study (2016) examined the experiences of women in jazz education and developed a model that shows how tokenism, stereotype threat, and low jazz self-efficacy leads to jazz avoidance (p. 477). Wehr wrote that

> Tokenism (stereotyped roles caused by being the only female, or one of a very few) contributes to stereotype threat (fear of confirming a negative stereotype), which contributes to lowered self-efficacy (belief in one's own ability to be successful) for jazz. Failure to have an expectation of success leads to avoidance of jazz participation.
>
> *(Wehr, 2016, p. 477)*

Indeed, women who have gained widespread acceptance in the jazz community have often needed to convey masculinity for acceptance. Dayhuff spoke of shaving her hair "into a mohawk to appear more aggressive … or less feminine… to trust that more of the musical interest that she was getting from men was genuine and not just empty flirtation" (Turn Up Her Mic, 2020, 40:00–40:28**).**

Photographic Data, Gender and Jazz Education

Jazz history textbooks should tell the ever-evolving story of jazz. However, there is a clear dearth of women in jazz texts. This corresponds to the well-known impediments of female participation in jazz as we've detailed above. In addition, this leads us to the related issue of non-binary gender identity as another aspect of diversity. Fumi Tomita, in his 2020 presentation, "*DownBeat Magazine* 1990–2019: A Study in Female Representation and Ethnic and National Diversity" at the inaugural Issues in Contemporary Jazz conference at the University of Utah (via zoom) emphasized the difficulty and challenges of identifying and categorizing gender via photographs. As did Pellegrinelli and colleagues regarding their analysis of women in the NPR Jazz Critics Poll, writing,

> Although the findings are currently limited to a gender binary, dividing artists into unequivocal categories for women and men, we acknowledge the presence of a broader spectrum of identities than our project was able to capture, including cisgender women and men, transgender women and men and those with non-binary, gender non-conforming and gender queer identities.
>
> *(Pellegrinelli, 2021)*

This is a vitally important issue closely related to our study, but it is beyond the scope of this chapter.

What we have done is to empirically examine the representation of women in recently published jazz history texts to bring to light the ongoing challenges to female participation in a musical form that has traditionally been male dominated. Our findings are based on photos from the three representative textbooks mentioned earlier, as these images provide a historiographical representation of jazz and its communities. It is clear from our database and analysis that women's roles in jazz, as conveyed in these photographs, are represented primarily by vocalists and pianists.

Our database includes photographs of women arranged into the following categories (see Table 22.1) of (1) piano players, (2) non-piano instrumentalists, (3) vocalists, (4) bandleader/composer, (5) non-musicians, and (6) International Sweethearts of Rhythm. Rather than counting the individual women within each photo, we choose to count each instance of a woman in a photograph as one (1) even if there were multiple women in the photos. We elected to base the percentages in the table on 63 photos rather than 62 to account for a photograph of Diana Krall at the piano with a vocal mic, counting her one photo twice: once as vocalist, once as pianist. Similarly, there are two identical photos of Esperanza Spaulding in *Listening to Jazz*, in which she is simultaneously playing bass and singing—we counted one of these photos as an instrumental photo and the other as a vocal photo. Most women pictured are either vocalists or pianists (over 75 percent of photos containing women), confirming Wehr's assertion that "jazz has long been recognized as a male-dominated field, with females traditionally having only limited acceptance, often in the roles of singer and pianist" (2016, p. 472).

An important note: In photographs in which women are performing, only the single photo of the International Sweethearts of Rhythm showed multiple women performing in the same shot, otherwise, women performers, such as Lil Harden, Billie Holiday, Mary Lou Williams were either entirely solo, or accompanied by men in the photographs. Contrary to this were photos that included

Table 22.1 Percentage of images in all three textbooks that depict women, organized by instrument, role, or band.

Women in all three textbooks combined	Photographic images including Women	As percentage of all photos (402)	As percentage of just women (63)*
Vocalists	32	7.96%	50.79%
Pianists	16	3.98%	25.40%
Non-musicians**	10	2.49%	15.87%
Non-piano instrumentalists	2	0.50%	3.17%
Bandleader/composer/arranger***	2	0.50%	3.17%
International Sweethearts of Rhythm	1	0.25%	1.59%

*   Only 62 photos in the three textbooks featured at least one woman, for these numbers we counted a photo of Diana Krall twice, as vocalist and instrumentalist

** Dancers, focused audience members

*** Both photos are of Maria Schneider

multiple women as either adoring fans, dancers, or audience members. Of the shots of women musicians, many were not playing nor even seen at their instruments, such as Alice Coltrane as an out-of-focus background to John Coltrane, and Lil Hardin standing behind the piano while Louis Armstrong posed seated at the piano bench.

Our analysis of photographs in jazz history educational texts illustrates the historical relationship between jazz and women. It also shines a light on current practices that inhibit equitable gender practices in the jazz community and in music education. The disproportionately low photographic evidence of women's contributions to the field can be seen in part as a reflection of the historical reality that jazz was, and continues to be, male dominated. But it is also the result of the early (and male-dominated) fields of academic jazz criticism that favored the autonomous and formalist philosophies of music, which by and large, for example, eschewed female jazz vocalists as lesser than their instrumentalist and male counterparts.

We believe, however, that these texts and their photographs tell a story that is not complete. In fact, our analysis is part of a larger movement in education, for example, as with ethnic studies, to ensure that people(s) who have traditionally been seen as inconsequential or unimportant in historical processes did, in fact, play vital roles, even if unrecognized or dismissed by "authorities." Therefore, the lack of equal and fair representation of women in authoritative texts wrongly conveys the idea that women were not significant participants in defining moments of jazz, contributing to stereotypes of gendered instruments and the "boys club" status of the jazz education and performance communities. Our examination of the photographic representation of women in authoritative textbooks reflects a social practice in which women are less likely to be hired for performances and recordings and are typically discouraged from participating in jazz-education programs. The corpus of jazz history textbook photography illustrates a story of systemic challenges and barriers that have often led to exclusion.

References

Abeles, H. F. (2009). Are musical instrument gender associations changing? *Journal of Research in Music Education, 57*(2), 127–139.

Abramo, J. M. (2011). Gender differences of popular music production in secondary schools. *Journal of Research in Music Education, 59*(1).

Barber, D. (1998). "A Study of Jazz Band Participation by Gender in Secondary High School Instrumental Music Programs." (Masters thesis, Rowan University).

Barthes, R., and Heath, S. (1977). *Image, Music, Text*. New York: Hill and Wang.

Becker, H. S. (1982). *Art Worlds*. Berkeley, CA: University of California Press.

Berger, E. (2019). Listening to Jazz. By Benjamin Bierman. *Journal of Jazz Studies, 12*(1), 92–98. https://doi.org/10.14713/jjs.v12i1.120.

Bierman, Benjamin (2015). *Listening to Jazz*. Oxford University Press.

Brugeilles, C., and Cromer, S. (2009). *Analysing Gender Representations in School Textbooks*. Paris: UMR CEPED.

Conway, C. (2000). Gender and Musical Instrument Choice: A Phenomenological Investigation. *Bulletin of the Council for Research in Music Education*, (146), 1–17. Retrieved April 4, 2021, from www.jstor.org/stable/40319030.

DeVeaux, S. (1991). Constructing the Jazz Tradition: Jazz Historiography. *Black American Literature Forum, 25*(3), 525–560. doi:10.2307/3041812.

DeVeaux, S., and Giddins, G. (2009). *Jazz*. New York: W. W. Norton.

Enstice, W., and Stockhouse, J. (2004). *Jazzwomen: Conversations with Twenty-one Musicians*. Bloomington, IN: Indiana University Press.

Gabbard, K. (1995). *Jazz Among the Discourses*. Durham, NC: Duke University Press.

Gabbard, K. (1996). *Jammin' at the Margins: Jazz and the American Cinema*. Chicago: University of Chicago Press.

Gabbard, K. (2002). Images of jazz. In Cook, M. and Horn, D. (Eds.), *The Cambridge Companion to Jazz*. (pp. 332–346). Cambridge: Cambridge University Press.

Gennari, J. (2006). *Blowin' hot and cool: jazz and its critics*. Chicago, IL: University of Chicago Press.

Gridley, Mark C. (2012) *Jazz Styles: History and Analysis* 11th ed. Boston: Pearson.

Heile, B., Elsdon, P., and Doctor, J. (2016). *Watching Jazz: Encounters with Jazz Performance on Screen*. New York, NY: Oxford University Press.

Hornsley, M., Knudsen, S. V., and Selander, S. (2005). *Has Past Passed?: Textbooks and Educational Media for the 21st Century*. Stockholm, SE: Stockholm Institute of Education Press (HLS Förlag).

Laver, M. (2015). *Jazz Sells: Music, Marketing, and Meaning*. New York: Routledge.

Lorge, Suzanne. (2019, February). Transform the culture. *DownBeat*, 82 (2), 24–29.

Lyons, S. (2011) "The identity of photography: exploring realism and the nature of photography in photojournalism," *Macquarie Matrix: Undergraduate Research Journal*, 1(1), 54–68.

Mercer, M. (2017, March 09). Sexism from two Leading jazz Artists Draws anger—and presents an opportunity. Retrieved April 5, 2021, from www.npr.org/sections/therecord/2017/03/09/519482385/sexism-from-two-leading-jazz-artists-draws-anger-and-presents-an-opportunity.

McGee, Kristin. (2016). Assimilating and Domesticating Jazz in 1950s American Variety Television: Nat King Cole's Transformation from Guest Star to National Host. In Heile, B., Elsdon, P., and Doctor, Jenny (Eds.), *Watching Jazz: Encounters with Jazz Performance on Screen* (pp. 73–102). New York, NY: Oxford University Press.

McKeage, Katherine M. (2004). "Gender and participation in high school and college instrumental jazz ensembles," *Journal of Research in Music Education*, 52(4), 343–356.

McKeage, K. (2003). "Gender and Participation in Undergraduate Instrumental Jazz Ensembles: A National Survey." (Doctoral dissertation, University of Wyoming, 2003).

Pellegrinelli, L., Effinger, S., Elizabeth, J., Grunenberg, K., Horn, R., Sebesky, G., and Weiner, N. (2021, January 12). Equal at last? Women in jazz, by the numbers. Retrieved April 5, 2021, from www.npr.org/2021/01/12/953964352/equal-at-last-women-in-jazz-by-the-numbers.

Pellegrinelli, Laura. (2008). Separated at "birth": Singing and the history of jazz. In N. Rustin and S. Tucker (Eds.), *Big Ears: Listening for Gender in Jazz Studies* (pp. 31–47). Durham and London: Duke University Press.

Pinson, K. (2010). *The Jazz Image: Seeing Music through Herman Leonard's Photography*. Jackson: University Press of Mississippi. doi:10.2307/j.ctt12f67g.

Porter, L., Ullman, M., & Hazell, E. (1993). *Jazz: From its origins to the present*. Englewood Cliffs, NJ: Prentice Hall.

Porter, E. (2002). *What Is this Thing Called Jazz?: African American Musicians as Artists, Critics, and Activists*. Berkeley, CA: University of California Press.

Prouty, Kenneth E. (2010). Toward jazz's "official" history: the debates and discourses of jazz history textbooks. *Journal of Music History Pedagogy*, 1(1), 19–43.

Raine, S. (2020). Keychanges at Cheltenham Jazz Festival: Challenges for women musicians in jazz and ways forward for equal representation at jazz festivals. Open Access Report.

Rasula, T. (1995). The media of memory: The seductive menace of records in jazz history. In Gabbard, K. (Ed.), *Jazz among the Discourses* (pp. 134–162). New York: Duke University Press.

Russonello, G. (2017, December 1). For women in jazz, a year of reckoning and recognition. Retrieved April 5, 2021, from www.nytimes.com/2017/12/01/arts/music/year-in-jazz-women-musicians.html.

Rustin, N., and Tucker, S. (2008). *Big Ears: Listening for Gender in Jazz Studies*. Durham and London: Duke University Press.

Schuller, G. (1958). Sonny Rollins and the Challenge of Thematic Improvisation. *Jazz Review* (November): 6–11. Reprinted in *Musings: The Musical Worlds of Gunther Schuller* (New York: Oxford University Press, 1986), 86–97.

Sadker D. and Zittleman K. (2007). Gender bias from colonial America to today's classrooms. In Banks, J. A. and Banks, C. A. M. (Eds.), *Multicultural education: Issues and perspectives* (pp. 138–158). Hoboken, NJ: Wiley.

Sheldon, D. A., and Price, H. E. (2005). Sex and instrumentation distribution in an international cross-section of wind and percussion ensembles. *Bulletin of the Council for Research in Music Education*, (163), 43–51. Retrieved from www.jstor.org/stable/40311594.

Teal, K. (2019). Mary Lou Williams as Apology: Jazz, History, and Institutional Sexism in the Twenty-First Century. *Jazz & Culture*, 2, 1–26.

Tirro, F. (1993). *Jazz: A History*. New York: Norton.

Tomlinson, Gary. 1992. Cultural Dialogics and Jazz: A White Historian Signifies. In Bergeron, K. and Bohlman, P. V. (Eds.), *Disciplining Music* (pp. 64–94). Chicago: University of Chicago Press.

Tucker, Sherri (2001). Big Ears: Listening for Gender in Jazz Studies. *Current Musicology*, 71–73, 375–409.

Turn Up Her Mic. (2020, September 9). Panel (9/08/2020) "In Conversation: Gender Equity in Jazz" [Video]. YouTube. https://youtu.be/bPpbbJKnxCg?t=2400.

Walser, R. (1993). Out of notes: Signification, interpretation, and the problem of Miles Davis. *The Musical Quarterly*, 77(2), 343–365.

We Have Voice Collective. (2017, December). Open letter. Retrieved April 5, 2021, from https://too-many.org/open-letter/.

Wehr, E. L. (2016). Understanding the experiences of women in jazz: A suggested model. *International Journal of Music Education, 34*(4), 472–487.

Whyton, T. (2010). *Jazz icons: Heroes, Myths and the Jazz Tradition.* Cambridge: Cambridge University Press.

Whyton, T. (2013). *Beyond a Love Supreme John Coltrane and the Legacy of an Album.* New York, NY: Oxford University Press.

Wrape, E. R., Dittloff, A. L., and Callahan, J. L. (2016). Gender and Musical Instrument Stereotypes in Middle School Children: Have Trends Changed? *Update: Applications of Research in Music Education, 34*(3), 40–47. https://doi.org/10.1177/8755123314564255.

23

DEGENDERING JAZZ GUITAR
Reimagining the Past—Realigning the Future

Tom Williams

Terminology: In the following chapter I have used both "woman" and "female" throughout. These are separated by use in abstract and contextualised settings (especially when considering the anatomy of the guitar and the often-used analogies about the female form), and significant care has been taken to not use either term pejoratively. In the interest of transparency and perspective, it feels pertinent to bring brief attention to my own background as a heterosexual male jazz guitarist, whose career and opportunities have not been affected adversely by my gender. Writing this chapter has required a level of introspection and reflection, and I would encourage all readers to consider their own experiences in light of the themes raised throughout.

Introduction

Discourse on gender in jazz is not new, nor is it when considering rock guitar, or popular music more generally. Unfortunately, research into female representation in jazz guitar is by comparison limited. Despite the rich lineage of female jazz guitarists (from Mary Ford to Emily Remler and beyond), pedagogy is still heavily organised around a male-centric hierarchy of jazz guitar (Teichman, 2020).

The guitar has been, and often still is, at the center of discussion surrounding issues of representation, gendered organology, misogyny, sexual imagery and gesture. The development of the form of the instrument has been guided, at least in part, by an objectification of the female form. There are also only a small number of female role models within the guitar community, and those who do exist tend to be marginalised. While these issues are at the forefront of other guitar-centered styles, there is an opportunity for further conversation here. As Dawe (2010) discusses when considering the male-dominant discourse surrounding the guitar more generally, there is significantly less attention given to women and the guitar.

The canonised history and scholarship surrounding guitar is also light on its emphasis on women. Boone's *The Guitar in Jazz* mentions only two female jazz guitarists (2003). As Dawe (2010) notes, many other texts such as Millard's (2004) include less than equal representation for women, and their contribution is often sidelined to the peripheries in chapters about women or gender specifically, thus problematically removing them from the central discourse. Dawe (2010) devotes an entire chapter to gender and the guitar and demonstrates a level of self-awareness of the issues present. Waksman (2001) drew attention to many of the gendered issues associated with the guitar and its community,

DOI: 10.4324/9781003081876-26

igniting the discussion surrounding guitar and gender, although again the ratio of females to males discussed is certainly not even. This is not meant to deride the work of these authors. While their work should be applauded, we should surely, now in the twenty-first century, be looking towards a discourse without separatist narratives. Many texts address the relationship between women and guitar objectively. Ackerley (1978) and Bayton (1997) are fixtures in gendered guitar scholarship and provide excellent perspectives. Lewis's doctoral thesis (2018) is perhaps one of the first in-depth analyses on three women considered to be the most historically important blues/jazz guitarists and is distinct from regular discourse, which can often be light on analysis, favouring instead sociocultural discussion alone.

Most importantly (when considering how access to jazz is carefully fostered), the idiom contains many of the fundamental skills required to compete in an increasingly competitive work market. Specifically, much of the contemporary music industry is inhabited by musicians who not only have strong fundamental abilities (instrument knowledge, applied theory, reading skills), but also have curated creative approaches through their engagement with improvisation, ensemble interaction, and community vernacular. Musicians who have attended prestigious jazz programs and schools are exposed to and interact with networks of musicians who form the corpus of leading idiomatically focused jazz ensembles and communities. These musicians also tend to be those who dominate sessional work, theatre, and other sought-after roles, not to mention also holding prestigious teaching posts.

It is imperative that we remove barriers inhibiting women from accessing these opportunities, so that community skills beyond the fundamentals can be equally developed.

The Gendered Guitar

The guitar itself, is often a gendered instrument as Dawe (2010, pp. 143–144) describes, especially in popular music. It is often discussed as an object of femininity, with the anatomy of the instrument analogised to that of a woman. Dawe is not the first to relate instruments to societal norms. Sachs (1962) separates masculine and feminine instruments, drawing specific attention to the flute and how it is perceived symbolically as a "love charm" (p. 94). Bayton (1997, p. 43) considers that the guitar is often seen as an extension of the male body.

Dawe (2010) interviewed luthiers who discussed the feminine nature of the instrument, analogising the shape of the guitar to that of a female's anatomy (p. 142). Some go further and discuss the instruments in even more explicit ways, describing them as if they were women, by hair colour— brunettes and blondes. Many male artists personify their instruments ascribing names and referring to them as "she." Sexual identity has been linked to guitar for over a century (Noonan, 2008, p. 96).

Vortex jazz club owner Dr. Hingwan believes that there is a clear perception surrounding those instruments suited to women and those suited to men (Stein, 2020, p. 114). Furthermore, gendered assumptions dominate instrument choice, with women often presumed to be singers. Many young women are guided as students towards instruments that are community facing (orchestral instruments being common), whereas instruments associated with individualism, autonomy, solo, and those considered more powerful are the preserve of young confident men, brave enough to assert their own voice.[1] Parents also reinforce gender stereotypes (Delzell and Leppla, 1992).

Gendering, and the issues caused by it, is exacerbated further in education, especially in secondary-school age students. In a recent study it was shown that the guitar is among the most gendered of all instruments (Hallam, Rogers, and Creech, 2008, p. 10). A combination of cultural, religious, stereotypes, role models, and peer-group factors are among some of the social barriers that may inhibit uptake of the instrument by women. The extent to which students are aware of the gendered natures of their instruments is less talked about and is certainly not a common consideration in pedagogical methods.

Idiom affects this, too. The classical guitar world has seen a huge shift in participation by women over the past century and is now light years away from the "sensual, feminine" (Noonan, 2008, p. 152) perception ascribed to the "first lady of guitar," Vadah Olcott-Bickford. If the gap is closing in Western classical guitar cultures, then why is it not in jazz guitar cultures?

Fender now suggests that 50 percent of their guitar purchasers are female (Mooney, 2017). The ubiquity of Fender's presence in the market also has an impact here, in that the ease by which someone can purchase an entry-level Stratocaster or Telecaster online likely far outweighs the ease of finding a suitable entry-level archtop guitar, without having to physically navigate the intimidating and masculine environment of a music retail store. Andy Mooney, Fender's CEO, lends context to this, recounting his own experiences of witnessing retail store employees automatically assume that women in the shop were there to buy for their husband or son (Mooney, 2017, p. 114).

The design of the guitar can also be problematic. Bayton (1997) considered that in the rock domain it is typical to hold the guitar at below waist level. The masculine and phallic imagery this connotes could be potentially off putting for a woman and is perhaps the only reason this might be done. Some women actively choose this way of holding the instrument, to subvert and challenge such imagery.

While ergonomically holding the instrument closer to the chest is far more accommodating, many women discuss that this might make them look stupid or indeed become uncomfortable because of their chests (Bayton, 1997, p. 44). For many, routes into jazz guitar come through post-rock explorations and inquisition, and so it is perhaps not unreasonable to surmise that many female rock players may be reluctant to transition to the chest held stance favoured in jazz guitar. The problem becomes amplified when you consider the difference between a solid body electric guitar and a large body archtop guitar. Interestingly, some of Bayton's respondents discussed the design itself, and pointed out the need for a better designed instrument to accommodate the female body (Bayton, 1997, p. 46).

Fender's CEO, detailed the company's intention to never offer a "woman's guitar" model and instead points to there being a "very real need ... to offer ... guitars that acknowledge that guitarists (male and female) come in all shapes and sizes physically" (Mooney, 2017). The point is admirable, but is left slightly moot, considering Fender has had nearly eighty years to address this which one might argue, given their market share, is their responsibility.

More recently Ernie Ball Music Man (EBMM), a household guitar brand, collaborated with Annie Clark (St. Vincent), to produce a design of her own that is ergonomic, lightweight, and well balanced. EBMM CEO Stirling Ball stresses that the guitar was not made with any gender in mind (despite contrary media reports), though it is clear how this might interest women guitarists, as Clark mentions, it is ideal for "smaller people and women especially" (Grant, 2016). Important here is having a designer who is a woman (one who is also a revered and established artist) create something that may be inspiring, relatable and address some of the ergonomic barriers discussed previously—especially in a marketplace driven by almost exclusively male signature models. There is also something striking about Clark's design. Gone are the smooth edges and round bottom common in electric guitar design, instead replaced by hard edges, symmetry, and geometric shapes. Perhaps the design here makes a subtle statement on the nature of the electric guitar design itself, focusing on utility and ergonomics, rather than aesthetics alone.

Male Centricity in the Jazz Guitarscape

Jazz has a long history of heteronormative dominance and participation (Ake, 2002; Caudwell, 2010; Dobson, 2010; Townsend, 2000). Women in jazz are often buried in the "footnotes" of history (Dahl, 1984, p. x). Jazz guitar is no exception. Its early history is built firmly in the image of Eddie Lang, Django Reinhardt, Charlie Christian and later Wes Montgomery. As Teichman discussed, many of the central components of jazz practice are built around masculine stereotypes and imagery and have been since the beginnings of jazz (2020, p. 203). The situation became more egregious as the masculine overtones of rock n' roll in the 1950s further widened the gender gap in the guitar community. The "Masculinist traditions" (Leonard, 2007, p. 39) that encapsulated rock music, the dominant popular music of the time, would inevitably affect the creative opportunities afforded to female jazz guitarists.

Historically, jazz emerged as a predominately male culture, at a time when women's rights were significantly less (Stein, 2020, p. 103). The associations of jazz culture—drugs, alcohol, sexual promiscuity—were diametrically opposed to the societal expectations placed on a woman at the time. Despite this, there were and have since been many all-women ensembles who remain a footnote to jazz discourse (Dahl, 1984, p. x).

Community plays a huge role in the development and nurturing of the identity of a jazz musician. As Reichman points out, "it's all about the hang." In a predominantly masculine community, it is certainly more difficult for women to navigate the community space. Again, it must be stated the climate is certainly in a state of flux at the moment. Jazz has recently received more attention in mainstream culture. In 2020's Disney Pixar release *Soul,* saxophonist Tia Fuller's incredible performance challenged the imagery of male gender dominance. She continues to be an excellent role model for new generations of jazz musicians, irrespective of gender, promoting an inclusive approach to jazz (Suzuki, 2013, p. 217).

Heteronormative male stereotypes are rife across the guitar community. While I hesitate to continually draw parallels with other idioms, discourse in other areas may help us understand the gender issues in the jazz guitarscape. Jennifer Batten, perhaps best known for her work with Michael Jackson, was frequently presumed to be a man: "It was easier to believe that the guitar player was a man who looked like a woman than that she was actually female" (Waksman 2001, p. 129).

Technology in the guitar community is also cast in masculine imagery. Waksman described the way guitarists would use the instrument as a "technophallus" (2001, p. 244). This presented a duality of issues for female guitar players. At once, it was incredibly difficult to break into a culture dominated by masculine sexuality, gesture, and embodiment. Furthermore, should female guitarists manage to permeate the culture, they risked abandoning their femininity for fear of being considered inauthentic and disrupting the patriarchal norms which afforded male guitarists a deeply integral part of their identity. Collier (1995) contextualises this: "The problem is something more than simply between women and men. Jazz is a macho thing, a power thing. . . . The gentler way of doing things is often ignored and regarded as effeminate" (p. 7).

Technical mastery on the instrument also became a highly gendered affair across all spectrums of popular music, despite there being no physical difference in the potential of skill acquisition across genders (Bayton, 1997, p. 39).

Bayton (1997, p. 40) argued that male musicians tend to be possessive of technical information and consider it a mark of masculine achievement. The guitar world is especially affected by this, considering the history of an instrument whose strong folk roots are often usurped by the pursuit of technical acrobatics in an attempt to lend legitimacy to players, and the instrument itself, through the development and preservation of virtuoso identities; identities that compete for dominance in their field. Put simply, "for a man, a good performance on the electric guitar is simultaneously a good 'performance' of masculinity" (Bayton, 1997 p. 43). Guitar hero/god complex is one of the core crests of male guitar culture, though glimmers of hope do exist as more women begin to pick up the guitar with an increased "dedication and commitment to technique" (Dawe, 2010, p. 137).

Certain performance modes are also dominantly masculine by their very nature. Improvisation can be risk laden, and in many instances those who are more daring—playing faster, harder, stronger, louder—are rewarded with praise. This high-octane environment may limit the expressive breadth of approaches available. In formative training, the opportunities to explore a range of approaches is essential in creating identity. As Teichman states, those who succeed in this kind of environment "may be perceived to confirm that they are 'doing' masculinity correctly according to dominant notions" (2020, p. 207).

In the UK instrumental tuition in pre-tertiary settings tends to fall into one of two categories: classical guitar pathway, popular music pathway. Long-established exam boards have a role in leading their candidates through highly specified repertoire, which indoctrinates and exposes students to certain practices and potentially limits others. Rock School Limited (RSL), for example, took the classical format favoured by Trinity and the Associated Board of the Royal Schools of Music (ABRSM) to model their own rock awards on. This typically consists of repertoire and technical knowledge, with skills commensurate with jazz practice, such as improvising, left circumventable in most instances. Repertoire does little to prepare students for navigating harmony in anything other than a rote way, which potentially ignores the rich history of rock/jazz/fusion that may help widen student perspectives. If instrumental teaching frameworks actively limit or ignore practices and musical fundamentals foundational to jazz, it becomes significantly more difficult to transition to jazz guitar, as doing so may represent a regressive step in students' learning journeys.

Gendered spaces, while useful at times, can also be detrimental. While features on female guitarists, all female groups, female festivals and other gendered spaces are helpful in rebalancing gender representations, there is a danger that segregation detaches the guitarists within from the wider community and culture. It is a common perception that those who are presented with their gendered prefix are likely to be judged before they ever hit their first note (Stein, 2020, p. 90). Some women actively avoid gendered spaces because they do not wish to become marginalised or thought of as separate within the jazz community. As Heble points out, many female jazz festivals struggle with exactly this issue (2000, p. 163). Rosie Frater-Taylor discussed her experience ambivalently,[2] giving a positive outlook on gendered jazz festivals, but also pointing to quality as the central issue, in that it should not ever be less, simply for inclusivity's sake.

Masculinity, power, virility, identity, virtuosity, technique have always been tied to gender of the idiom, and were certainly calcified during what we might now, in the twenty-first century, consider jazz's transition from adolescence into adulthood in the period 1920–1950. As Ake considers this normalised the competitive nature of jazz practice and with it the gendered norms (Ake, 2002, p. 30). The conquest of advanced harmonic practices, technical mastery, and dominance of voice are held dearly in the pedagogy of jazz, potentially limiting the time allowed to explore other modes of expression.

While the widening of gender discourse in the twenty-first century has helped to promote these kinds of curiosities, more work is needed to address the connectivity between abstracted discourse in academic research, and reality as seen in jazz clubs, festivals, schools and academies, which may be insulated from such discourse. In writing this chapter, I have had to negotiate the issues raised above, by the very nature of drawing focus on female jazz guitarists. It is my hope that the second half of this chapter will help address some of these issues and provide actionable steps to address the de-gendering of jazz guitar.

Finally, it must be noted that the issues herein can often be presented in factional or binary ways. This is not the case, and there is a whole spectrum to consider when navigating jazz, the guitar, and gender equality. The ebb and flow of tradition and modernity in jazz history provides many instances where proactive steps have been taken or encouraged to address these issues. Ake's (1998) discussion of Ornette Coleman's approach exemplifies this, for example, describing the many ways his approach challenged and undermined masculine tropes in jazz. The status quo is also slowly changing within the guitarscape. Women contribute to overall guitar cultures perhaps more than they ever have and continually challenge masculine ideologies returning the guitar to an instrument for making music instead of an appendage (Dawe, 2010, p. 129). The challenge lies in addressing jazz guitar cultures specifically, as progress is certainly not as quick there.

Misrepresentation in the Jazz Guitar Cannon

Jazz guitar has a long and rich history of female players. In early jazz, perhaps most focally, one might consider the work of Mary Osborne, a leading jazz guitarist of her time (Boone, 2003, p. 74), who featured in collaborations with jazz luminaries as diverse as Coleman Hawkins, Mary Lou Williams, and Billie Holiday. Osborne was one of the only female jazz guitarists to gain commercial success in the 1940s and 1950s and yet discussion surrounding her work and approach is still limited. Osbourne was raised in a musical family which nurtured her musical development. Playing in her father's ragtime band, having a mother who played guitar, helped create the right environment necessary for Osbourne to develop the tenacity needed to succeed as a woman in music. Rosie Frater-Taylor discusses a similar nurturing environment in her adolescence, as fundamental to her development.

Just as we include many early blues artists in the overarching pantheon of jazz, we can also consider the many incredible women of blues guitar who permeate jazz and guitar cultures. Players like Sister Rosetta Tharpe, Maybelle Carter, Memphis Minnie, and Mary Ford have all left more than a mere dent in the histories of guitar cultures. Kate Lewis, an expert in early blues guitarists, outlines the many aspects of style, technique, and approach that were developed by them and informed the approach of many who followed, irrespective of gender (Lewis, 2018).

An interesting case can be made when considering the perception of Mary Ford and her husband Les Paul. Despite the evidence of Ford's significant ability as a lead player, her position in history is firmly adjunct to that of her husband. Numerous promotional materials of the time presented Paul as the dominant, masculine, technical-minded half of the couple, with Ford often portrayed as an admiring onlooker.

It would be remiss to not mention Emily Remler (1957–1990), a guitarist who in her twenties, developed a mature approach that was simultaneously steeped in tradition and modernity. Remler went on to make a sizable impact on the tradition and trajectory of the jazz guitarscape and would have continued to, had she not passed away entirely too early.

The imagery on many of her album covers—*Firefly, Take Two (Emily Remler Quartet)*, does little to allude to the breathtakingly technical and fiery aspects of her music. These covers are a world apart from the introspective imagery on Riverside, Verve and Blue Note discs that had encapsulated jazz for some time. The cover of *Together* with Larry Coryell, showing Remler leaning adoringly on the shoulders of Coryell, paints a similarly submissive image that reflects that of Mary Ford and Les Paul. While the image suggests that Remler is in some way leaning on, or being held up by Coryell, Remler's dominant playing and approach on the album suggests the opposite.

Remler's most celebrated work, *East to Wes* (a tribute to Wes Montgomery), balances tradition with modernity well. The technical faculty demonstrated on the album is incredible and, yet, to the author's knowledge, is certainly not widely taught. On the rare occasions that Remler's music is brought up, it is usually to discuss her sonorous version of *Softly, as in a Morning Sunrise* and not the breathtaking solos on *Daahound, Blues for Herb, and Hot House*. Interestingly, while this album celebrates many of the approaches of Montgomery, it also points forward with a range of interesting and modern approaches (the use of fourths, harmonic superimposition, developmental ensemble interaction).

Remler's buoyant personality and approach is often softened, purging the intense, passionate and borderline avant-garde aspects in favour of a more acceptable patriarchal representation (Chapman, 2019).

Remler often discussed the issues that affected her as a woman in the music industry. Most pertinent was the commentary she faced off the stage: "I'm just playing the music. When I leave the stage, that's when people remind me that I'm a woman" (West, 2020). Remler was acutely aware of gender issues in jazz and eschewed the idea that her gender should define her: "Good compositions, memorable guitar playing and my contributions as a woman in music, but the music is everything, and it has nothing to do with politics or the women's liberation movement." (Chapman, 2019). While celebrated as a luminary, Remler's presence in the jazz guitar canon is still often only found through looking.

Since the 1980s, many female guitarists have made an impact on the jazz guitar community. The body of work produced by many—Sheryl Bailey, Mimi Fox, Mary Halvorson, Dierdre Cartwright,

Leni Stern, Felicia Collins, to name a few—is substantial and covers more than enough ground to form a comprehensive pedagogical framework for a guitarist without even having to mention the influential male guitarists and would arguably provide a wider spectrum of creative approaches than a male-only set of exemplars.

Excitingly, there are many women emerging as notable jazz guitar players who deserve a mention here. Stein (2020) highlights many young women guitarists—including Nora Bite, Rosie Frator-Taylor, Shirley Tetteh, and Sherika Sherard—who are making an impact in the British jazz community. During the course of this research, I interviewed emerging 'jazz' guitarist Rosie Frater-Taylor. Her music is hard to define, but there are many nods to a variety of influences. She discusses, among others, the effect Pat Metheny has had on her development. She states, "You could argue that some of Pat's playing is very emotional, so maybe that's why I'm drawn to a lot of the things that he plays," and also alludes to being driven by holistic aspects of music—the sounds, textures, layers, and meanings of songs—as much as she is by "interesting and complicated harmony." Despite this, she also acknowledges the importance of the tradition (learning standards, vocabulary, and canonical approaches), but hints at the importance of this not being prescriptive or limiting.

Importantly, she does not identify with the term "jazz," and instead thinks of the space she occupies as between genres and informed by a range of influences, singer-songwriters, formative experiences with rock guitarists, perhaps instead shaped and tempered with jazz vocabularies, harmony, and approaches. Like many others, she described an initial formative engagement with the guitar-learning rock pieces.

Her debut album features one solo on the track *Umami*. The solo demonstrates a mature approach, one which weaves a variety of well-curated harmonic and rhythmic approaches. There is a clear line of development and motivic explorations are common. The confidence Frater-Taylor demonstrated in her interview with me comes across in her approach, too, especially in the harmonic departures and superimpositions, which are every bit as engaging as approaches used by those who have dominated jazz guitar discourse in the past twenty years.

What struck me most in our conversation, was the depth of understanding she had of the subject, and the introspective maturity with which she navigated the, at times clumsy, interviewing. The formative environments available to her helped shape this confidence and maturity, as she discusses. A musically nurturing family set the precedent for what would then be developed in the National Youth Jazz Orchestra, the Royal Academy junior jazz program, and *Tomorrow's Warriors*.[3] Such a progression of educational environments was helpful to Frater-Taylor's development. Importantly, she considers herself lucky with the support she has had, and states that it "just takes one," when considering the importance of role models.

Frater-Taylor's personal experiences align with research into intersections of age and gender disparity, most notably less women in ensembles in the mid to late teenage years.

Furthermore, now studying for her jazz performance undergraduate, she discusses an ambivalence and alienation to some aspects, including being "encouraged to play with a degree of masculinity." She articulates that institutional settings are still somewhat detached from practice, echoing, in some ways at least, what many others have to say about being taught the male history of jazz with women presented as addendum. Frater-Taylor has a unique case because of the different learning environments she has been exposed to. Reflecting on this, she mentions "a huge divide, at least in British jazz ... between schools' jazz, which is predominantly white and male, and unschooled jazz, which is more diverse.[4]

Frater-Taylor points to both performative and education settings, where gendered commentary is the norm, discussing the "emotional and vocal-like" qualities of her approach. She makes reference to masterclasses, where her presence as a woman has led to assumptions that she was a singer. While she recognises that many might be phased and entirely put off by this behavior, her resilience stops her from caring so much, instead mentioning that many people will become offended on her behalf.

I would postulate at this point that her maturity of nature and understanding is perhaps necessary in navigating such a gendered idiom. The ability to do so without being phased or disabled when met with issues is too important. Frater-Taylor sees in herself the potential to be a role model because of these qualities and presents this without a flair of arrogance.

With such a rich and diverse canon of female guitar identities and works (as demonstrated above), it is then surprising that very little permeates pedagogy. As is powerfully expressed by Willis (2008), "The women who are playing, talking, signifying, and subverting need to be written into the jazz canon—as blue notes, these women need a new way to be transcribed and represented."

Gendering, Pedagogy and Barriers to Jazz Guitar

The first barrier is the uptake of the instrument. Gender differences in the choice of instruments has been discussed as part of the reason we see less women take up certain instruments and take part in jazz (Delzell and Leppla 1992; Hallam et al., 2008). Research and anecdotal evidence equally suggest that, while more females than ever are buying guitars, the drop-off rate is much higher. Frater-Taylor discussed a clear distinction between her time in NYJO compared to her time in the Royal Academy Junior Program which aligns with the idea that less women continue with the guitar into their mid to late teens. The perceptions and attitudes towards the instrument being in some way a male instrument and unsuitable for women is partly to blame but, equally, so are the conditions of jazz performance spaces, which may deter some from carrying on.

As Teichman discusses, jazz education has been affected by representation and discrimination for some time (2020, p. 205). Part of this systemic issue is due to academia itself, which has formalised and canonised jazz in such a way that it reflects the misrepresented history of the music, focusing mainly on the "greats," and not treating the outliers with as much importance. It is, however, a difficult position to navigate, given the historically low number of female jazz guitarists who have reached the same heights of public appreciation as the men who dominate the history currently. There is a danger in presenting female guitarists as "other," creating separate gendered sites in the canon for those guitarists to orbit. Pedagogy should actively present women early in the framework, and not simply as a footnote to satisfy inclusion.

Our overreliance on "standards" and the great American songbook can also be problematic. The thematic components of much early jazz lyrics carry with them a range of imbued gender stereotypes, male-gaze perspectives, and long since abandoned cultural perceptions. As much of the repertoire finds its way into instrumental jazz repertoire—one might argue that the gender disabling tropes embedded within them are carried over, too. It is not that we should abandon these artifacts, as their usefulness in outlaying the musical language of jazz practice cannot be understated, though we must be aware of "heteronormative assumptions permeating the original text," and that "the instrumental arrangement does nothing to challenge the underlying message of its content" (Teichman 2020, p. 206).

Equally an overreliance on standard practice jazz, is at odds with the developmental ethos of the music. As Teichman (2020 points out, there is still a reluctance to move away from the standards, even at the highest level of jazz education organisation. More generally, pedagogical practices that become cyclic and unchallenged perpetuate inherent issues for each new generation of students and teachers.

Performative spaces within the academy are potentially limited in their breadth of inclusion. In many instances, we tend to focus on the trial-by-fire method, where complex and personal approaches to improvisation and style are laid bare for others to critique, peers and tutors alike. This may "induce anxiety that hinders learning and creativity," (Wehr-Flowers, 2006, p. 339) especially for young women who are already dealing with finding the confidence to interact in a masculine space that carries many stereotypes. Many authors have also discussed the potential reluctance of young women to 'succeed' in such an environment for fears they place their feminine identity at risk.

Wehr (2016) postulates that women in jazz are susceptible to being trapped in 'token' roles (pp. 477–478). While it is hard to manipulate and directly challenge what happens in jazz performative spaces, we are not currently discussing how to manage these situations when presented with them. If we are to have hope of creating sustainable change in the equalities of jazz, we must model and critique both good and bad practices in formative settings.

Addressing the Issues: Degendering Jazz Guitar

Breaking the first barrier to jazz guitar, the instrument itself is essential here. While there is positive uptake in women exploring the guitar, and more role models than there have been historically, little attention is brought to modalities of jazz guitar. To move away from the archtop dogma, whose role models are predominantly male, we must champion the image of jazz guitar as something more malleable. Jazz can be played on a Telecaster, a Les Paul, a Stratocaster or any other "guitar." Bill Frisell, Marc Ribot, Wayne Krantz, and Mike Stern are just a few guitarists who navigate the jazz guitarscape with authentic voices, with no archtop in sight. We must not limit those who do not identify with larger body instruments, and a frank conversation needs to be had surrounding the physical affordance of a guitar in relation to its player, gender irrespective.

Providing a more balanced repertoire is also important. We might seek to allow students to critically appraise the idea of a linear history in jazz from the start of their development. Why, for example, is playing *All of Me* so important in the twenty-first century? If the answer is simply tradition, then that alone tells us we need to re-evaluate our priorities.

As the history of jazz music widens, the pressure on new students becomes greater in a model which prescribes tradition before development. There is simply too much to study. Where traditional standards are included in curriculum and repertoire, allowing students to challenge histories and continue to signify through the re-imagining of standards is also imperative.

Most pertinent to the jazz guitar, however, is a reimagining of the pantheon of jazz guitar. I would argue studying Emily Remler's playing on *East to Wes* is more than enough of an indoctrination to traditional vocabulary, community dialogue, style, and technical mastery. It should be encouraged— just as in other instrumental idioms, and especially if they might act as a precursor to a student's journey to jazz—that teachers ensure curriculum is designed with examples from genders other than male, and not simply those who meet traditional criteria for excellence. As we have discussed, many female jazz musicians simply have not had the same chances to excel or impact, as they are often absorbed by the masculine history. Curriculum and repertoire should reflect the practices imbued within jazz culture, that of the progressive, community-led, challenging, and emerging in respect to identity. It is easy to become complacent within institutionalised education, and many are reluctant to let go of what Teichman (2020) calls a "canon of treasured repertoire, narratives, and teaching practices." (p. 202) Ironically, to leave this unaddressed and continue perpetuating the myth of the great creators of jazz places the idiom in a similar hegemony to the European concert tradition from which jazz sought to emancipate itself at various times in its history.

Pedagogical methodologies favouring masculinity are endemic in instrumental jazz instruction, as has been discussed (McCord, 1996; McKeage, 2004). The prescriptive nature of what one learns on a jazz program needs to become more exploratory, and measured not against traditional exemplars but against wider (more inclusive) creative approaches.

Alleviating the performative pressures of performative jazz settings may also help here, especially when considering those aspects entrenched in heteronormativity: Broadly, improvisation, virtuosity, swing, historic repertoire, "spotlighting," "cutting contests." This again comes down to the protectiveness of those who may not wish to dismantle their own practices for fear of questioning their own utterances and identities. While these aspects should not be dismissed, they should at least be tempered with their opposites. Why, for instance, can someone not explore jazz practice through engagements with song writing, nuance of colour, technology, soundscape, minimalist, and other aspects? Where a more diverse range of techniques is being applied, we must ensure they are being portrayed with equality in relation to the "tradition."

We must provide educational spaces that do not facilitate "covering." Emulating good practice in education is more likely to impact real-world scenarios. Women should not feel that they need to conform, or to face demands on aspects of their identity to succeed. Bergonzi (2014) suggests including more material by homosexual composers to counter institutionalised homophobia and heteronormative tropes that dominate the jazz space. It stands to reason that simply rebalancing the role models to include a greater spread of perspectives from women would be a good start here. This should consider the staff, the repertoire, the guests, and approaches, which keep institutions aligned to historic masculine approaches.

Ensuring that women feel comfortable improvising is one of the biggest hurdles (Wehr, 2016). This is not to suggest that we should "soften" the performative environment but instead create effective spaces for cultivating resilience in risk taking processes. As Esperanza Spalding writes: "The price of impact in performance is vulnerability … It's not acting like you're vulnerable. It's having the courage to be [vulnerable]" (Spalding in Beuttler, 2019, p. 233). At the heart of this is improving self-efficacy in jazz practice (Wehr, 2016, p. 480).

Ensuring that we draw from a variety of role models is key here, too. In the same consideration as above, concerning pedagogy in and out of the academy, it is likely that with more visible women guitarists championed in the performative space, early career musicians would be less coloured by the historically masculine hierarchies in jazz performance. A concerted effort must be brought to all fronts, but special emphasis brought to pedagogy in the first instance, to ensure more women find their way into the academy and profession.

Conclusion

It is clear that many are incredibly passionate about the lack of gender equality in the jazz and guitar communities and wish for equal opportunities for those who share a love of the musical processes abundant in jazz: processes which give many the opportunity to express themselves at heights that other musical avenues may not reach. Perhaps through tackling a microcosm of the wider gender disparate humanities sector—namely the jazz guitarscape—we might hope to model ways of addressing the issue in other areas.

The intertwined issues of gender in respect to jazz and guitar combine to create a set of barriers that non-male students must progress through, as has been argued herein, to reach a level of professional competence. The instrument, the repertoire, the histories, the performative spaces, the role models and, importantly the pedagogies all contribute to these barriers. Disaggregation is necessary to begin to tackle some of the inherent issues.

Writing this chapter has allowed me to reflect on many experiences, not only as an educator, but as a student historically. My own experiences mirror many popular stereotypes and issue-laden scenarios. On one end of my experiences, I have distinct memories of secondary school guitar group lessons, in which we only had one female student, who was not given the same level of expectations of achievement or nurturing as the rest of us, and soon gave up. On the other end, as an undergraduate I have memories of classes where certain tutors often analogised narrative in improvisation in ways relating to masculine notions of sex. While my memory is fragmented with many experiences like this, it is concerning to think of how many times I encountered similar issues and was ignorant to the fact that it was problematic. I do wonder if a more aware pedagogy might help avoid this ignorance for others.

As Teichman (2020) argues, it is the responsibility of educators to depose archaic discourses and pedagogies in favour of a more reflexive model which seeks to address the issues presented herein (p. 211). This can be uncomfortable and require self-reflection on one's own practice in the first instance.

It is hoped that this chapter will serve as a platform for exploration, further research, and practical solutions to many of the problems outlined. If we genuinely want an equal and fair representation for all in jazz and guitar cultures, we must start to reimagine the definitions, practices, histories, and pedagogies that still persevere despite a growing public awareness of the importance of gender issues in our communities.

Notes

1 There is an abundance of research that discusses gendered instrument preferences in a range of contexts. See Griswold and Chroback, 1981; Delzell and Leppla, 1992; O'Neill, 1997; O'Neill and Boultona, 1996.
2 During an interview conducted in January 2021.
3 An inclusive UK organisation that aims to foster vibrant communities of jazz artists, audiences, and communities.
4 An analogy is made here between HE setting jazz education as the former and an organisation like Tomorrow's Warriors as the latter.

References

Ackerley, C. (1978) Women and guitar in Ferguson, J. (ed.) *The Guitar Player Book*. New York: Grove, pp. 259–261.

Ake, D. (1998). Re-Masculating jazz: Ornette Coleman, "Lonely Woman," and the New York jazz scene in the late 1950s. *American Music* 16 (1) (Spring, 1998): 25–44.

Ake, D. (2002). *Jazz Cultures*. Berklee: University of California Press.

Bayton, M. (1997). Women and the electric guitar in Whiteley, S. (ed.) *Sexing the Groove: Popular Music and Gender*. London: Routledge.

Bergonzi, L. (2014). Sexual orientation and music education: continuing a tradition. *Music Educators Journal* 100 (4): 65–69.

Beuttler, B. (2019). *Make It new: reshaping jazz in the 21st century*. Lever Press.

Boone, G. M. (2003). The guitar in jazz. *The Cambridge Companion to the Guitar*, 67–86.

Caudwell, J. (2010). The jazz-sport analogue: Passing notes on gender and sexuality. *International Review for the Sociology of Sport* 45 (2): 240–248

Chapman, C. (2019). Arts remembrance: Emily Remler—The short life and sad death of a jazz guitarist—The Arts Fuse. Retrieved 28 March 2021, from https://artsfuse.org/188483/arts-remembrance-emily-remler-the-short-life-and-sad-death-of-a-jazz-guitarist/.

Collier, J. L. (1995). *Jazz: The American Theme Song*. New York: Oxford University Press.

Dahl, L. (1984). *Stormy Weather: The Music and Lives of a Century of Jazz Women*. New York: Pantheon Books

Dawe, K. (2010). *The New Guitar Scape in Critical Theory, Cultural Practice and Musical Performance*. Aldershot: Ashgate.

Delzell, J. K., and Leppla, D. A. (1992). Gender association of musical instruments and preferences of fourth-grade students for selected instruments. *Journal of Research in Music Education* 40 (2): 93–103.

Grant, K. (2016). St Vincent: musician who helped produce female-friendly guitar. Retrieved 21 March 2021, from www.independent.co.uk/news/people/profiles/st-vincent-profile-musician-who-helped-produce-guitar-sympathetic-female-form-a6878021.html.

Griswold, P. A., and Chroback, D. A. (1981). Sex-role associations of music instruments and occupations by gender and major. *Journal of Research in Music Education* 29 (1): 57–62.

Hallam, S., Rogers, L. and Creech, A. (2008) Gender differences in musical instrument choice. *International Journal of Music Education* 26 (1): 7–19.

Heble, A. (2000) *Landing on the Wrong Note: Jazz, Dissonance, and Critical Practice*. New York. Routledge.

Leonard, M. (2007). *Gender in the Music Industry: Rock, Discourse and Girl Power*. Aldershot: Ashgate.

Lewis, K. (2018). *Mothers and Sisters: Instrument and Idiom in the Music of Maybelle Carter, Memphis Minnie and Sister Rosetta Tharpe*. University of Surrey, Guildford, UK.

McCord, K. (1996). The state of the art today. jazz women: Sung and unsung: Symposium and Concerts, October 19 and 20, 1996. N.P: Smithsonian Institution: 28–33.

McKeage, K. M. (2004). Gender and participation in high school and college instrumental jazz ensembles. *Journal of Research in Music Education* 52 (4): 343–356.

Millard, A. (Ed.). (2004). *The Electric Guitar: A History of an American Icon*. Baltimore: Johns Hopkins University Presss.

Mooney, A. (2017). Women and the Guitar. *Music Trades*, Feb. 2017.

Noonan, J. (2008). *The Guitar in America: Victorian Era to Jazz Age*. Jackson: University Press of Mississippi.

O'Neill, S. A., and Boulton, M. J. (1996). Boys' and girls' preferences for musical instruments: A function of gender? *Psychology of Music* 24 (2): 171–183.

O'Neill, S. A. (1997). Gender and music. In D. J. Hargreaves and A. C. North (Eds.) *The Social Psychology of Music* (pp. 46–63). Oxford: Oxford University Press.

Sachs, Curt. 1962. *The Wellsprings of Music*. The Hague: Martinus Nijhoff.

Stein, S. (2020) *Gender Disparity in UK Jazz—A Discussion*. Amazon KDP.

Suzuki, Y. (2013). Two strikes and the double negative: The intersections of gender and race in the cases of female jazz saxophonists. *Black Music Research Journal* 33 (2) 207–226.

Teichman, E. (2020). Pedagogy of discrimination: instrumental jazz education. *Music Education Research* 22 (2): 201–213.

Townsend, P. (2000). *Jazz in American Culture*. Edinburgh: Edinburgh University Press.

Waksman, S. (2001). *Instruments of Desire: The Electric Guitar and the Shaping of Musical Experience*. London: Harvard University Press.

Wehr, E. L. (2016). Understanding the experiences of women in jazz: A suggested model. *International Journal of Music Education* 34 (4): 472–487.

Wehr-Flowers, E. (2006). Differences between male and female students' confidence, anxiety, and attitude toward learning jazz improvisation. *Journal of Research in Music Education* 54 (4): 337–349.

West, M. (2020). The rise and decline of guitarist Emily Remler–JazzTimes. Retrieved 28 March 2021, from https://jazztimes.com/features/profiles/emily-remler-rise-decline./

Willis, V. (2008). Be-in-tween the spa[]ces: The location of women and subversion in jazz. *The Journal of American Culture* 31 (3): 293–301.

24

"MUSIC SAVED MY LIFE"

Jennifer Leitham on Life, Music, and Gender

Joshua Palkki, Carl Oser, and Jennifer Leitham

> Usually, when I tell people that I'm interested in gender and jazz, they think that means that I am interested in reclaiming the "lost" histories of women who played jazz. And I am. Or in exposing the ways that sexism affects women who play jazz today. And I am. But in addition to these interests, and in part because of them, I am also interested in gender as an analytic category for understanding how power is organized, maintained, and challenged, and how change occurs.
>
> *(Tucker, 2002a, p. 386)*

Introduction

In 2017, Sasha Berliner penned a blog post overtly identifying and critiquing the patriarchal underpinnings of the jazz world—putting into stark terms a fundamental truth: that jazz and jazz education is just as vulnerable to sexism as any other part of society. Berliner's (2017) post did what scholar Sherrie Tucker has oft implored the jazz world to do: invoke gender, not as a quota to be filled, but as a framework to understand the interactions of jazz and jazz-adjacent persons of all genders (Tucker, 2002a, 2002b). As Tucker (2002a) intimates in the opening quote, the notion of gender studies as something that only applies to women, or to women's interaction with men, has changed in recent years as the visibility of trans and gender-expansive persons in the United States has increased dramatically (e.g., Henig, 2017).

This chapter explores the life of Jennifer Leitham (b. 1953), a professional jazz bassist who happens to be a transgender woman. In sharing Jennifer's story, we hope to not only add one more "lost" history to the jazz narrative, but to contemplate the power dynamics inherent in this narrative and ask how the jazz community might use this story to support people of all genders who wish to engage in the world of jazz.

Vocabulary for Common Ground

Not unlike jazz, gender is a framework whose definitions are contextual, fluid, and ever-evolving. By the time this book goes to print, many gender-related definitions likely will be outdated. Nevertheless, we endeavor to define key terms, with the hope that the curious reader might take to the Internet (e.g., Gender Minorities Aotearoa, n.d.) to monitor the transformation and evolution of these ideas over time.

DOI: 10.4324/9781003081876-27

Gender is a set of socially constructed and context- and culture-dependent ideas regarding what behaviors and physical attributes are considered "masculine" or "feminine." The term *transgender* is "an umbrella, or broadly encompassing term of many gender identities of those who do not identify or exclusively identify with their sex assigned at birth" (Trans Student Educational Resources, n.d.). *Transgender* (or *trans*) as a term is used quite broadly and may now include a diverse group, including people who identify in myriad ways, and who utilize many terms to describe their gender identity (Beemyn and Rankin, 2011). *Cisgender* denotes a person whose gender identity and sex assigned at birth match.

Method

This chapter is not an attempt at a "traditional" music education research study.[1] This project is unique in that the focus of the chapter, Jennifer Leitham, is a co-author driving how her story is conveyed (Arvay, 2002), not merely a subject masked behind a pseudonym. In describing collaborative narrative work, Arvay (2002) states, "I envision my participants as co-investigators and co-actors in this research performance, not as respondents answering upon request, nor as informants merely imparting information. As a performance, the conversation is complex on many levels" (p. 213). The use of "performance" here seems apropos as Jennifer's life has been full of performances: both on and off the stage.

The process of recording one's lived experiences in writing is complicated—and inevitably reductive (Arvay, 2002). Nevertheless, we endeavor to paint a portrait of Jennifer's life that may shed light on the gendered power dynamics of the jazz world and the world at large (Tucker, 2002b). We first recount Jennifer's life and story with interjections from Joshua and Carl. From there, we explore Jennifer's music/jazz education and what jazz education might learn from her experiences—what Patton (1990) calls *applied research*.

Positionality

Power dynamics and inequalities are inherent in collaborative research and writing projects (Shdaimah and Stahl, 2012). All three authors have unique vantage points and lenses through which they view this work. Joshua identifies as a white, cisgender, gay, educated, privileged, able-bodied man who works as a college professor and a researcher on queer issues in music education. Carl identifies as an able-bodied, white, cisgender, straight, upper-middle class male who works as a vocalist, pianist, and music educator. Jennifer identifies as a white, transgender, bisexual, self-educated, privileged, able-bodied woman who works as a professional musician, composer, vocalist, and educator. Our hope is that in combining these three perspectives, we may amplify Jennifer's story, bringing it to an even broader audience.

One of the major tenets of transgender theory (Nagoshi and Brzuzy, 2010) is for trans persons to speak for themselves and to speak their own truth. Thus, all sections labeled "Snapshots" contain Jennifer's own words compiled from interviews. The sections marked "Aside" contain reflections and connecting material by Joshua and Carl. In this way we (Joshua and Carl) attempt to disrupt the power relations inherent in cisgender people "studying" trans topics/persons. Additionally, we strongly encourage the curious reader to supplement this reading with audio recordings from Jennifer's extensive musical catalogue, as this is, perhaps more than anything, where Jennifer expresses herself in the way that only music can.

In doing this work, we draw on writing by Vijay Iyer who explores the intersections of jazz improvisation and narrative. Iyer (2004) refers to the notion of

> "changing up all the stories": it implies a shift in emphasis from top-down notions of overarching coherence to bottom-up views of narrativity *emerging* from the minute

laborious acts that make up musical activity. ... In short, the story is revealed not as a single linear narrative, but as a fractured, exploded one. ... It is only through this process of examining the puzzling shards of these exploded narratives that we may reveal a mosaic with a discernable underlying pattern.

(p. 395, emphasis in original)

Jennifer Leitham's life—like the journey of so many creative artists—is a collection of "puzzling shards of ... exploded narratives" (Iyer, 2004, p. 395).

Jennifer Leitham

Leitham's personal and musical journey has been documented in the popular media/mainstream press (Doyle, 2007; Heckman, 2009; James, 2016) and in academic circles (Drake, 2011). A 2003 story by *Los Angeles Times* journalist Lynell George was one of the first interviews for which Leitham sat after her 2001 transition (George, 2003). Leitham cites this article as a particularly sensitive treatment of her story, especially for its time. Articles from various print sources since this 2003 story are consistent in terms of content while varying in sensitivity to norms surrounding gender diversity. The bulk of the press regarding Leitham, however, consists of press reviews associated with the release of *I Stand Corrected* (Meyerson, 2012), a documentary on Leitham's career, before and after and transition (e.g., Murray, 2012).

Jennifer's Life

Snapshots, Part 1

I always had musical tendencies when I was young. I would sing a lot and always be noodling around on whatever—I'd play on the swing set and sliding board at the playground with sticks. I'd bang on things at home, but my parents discouraged me. In school, I tried to learn the clarinet[;] ... I actually played pretty well for someone in the fourth grade, but I wouldn't stop improvising. The band director didn't like that because it meant that I wouldn't be disciplined enough to play in the marching band. *[laughs]* Even at that age he could tell that my instincts were in jazz.

There's something about singing music in that I could lose the feeling of gender, even though I was singing tenor parts. That communal thing of being with guys and girls at the same time and just not caring which one you were, *[chuckles]* that was really attractive to me. *[pause]* I made good friends in the chorus. At the same time, I was a jock. I loved playing baseball and it helped deflect some of the bullying and taunts because I looked like a girl. But I still got a lot of flak for singing in the choir and being so girly looking. It held me back in sports, but with the choir I could excel, and it didn't matter how big I was, or that I didn't play football. Those things weren't held against you in the choir.

I sang the high parts in the barbershop quartet, and that gave me a sense of pride ... Maybe they were gendered parts that I was singing, but I was [on] the highest note and I was isolated. Inside, I knew I could sing the girls' parts in the choir, but I never felt comfortable enough to come out—to tell people what I was going through.

I started to get noticed by rock bands because of my voice. So, I was asked to be in bands more because I could sing than play. I worked in a fast-food joint at night and skipped school to work in a car wash, saved up and procured an electric bass, thinking it was going to make me a more valuable band member[;] ... I thought it'd be really easy, you don't have to play chords—it's just one note. *[laughs]* When I was younger, I played along with my records on a toy guitar, then all the strings fell off but the bottom two, so I could only play melodies or bass lines. I played both … not really knowing what I was doing, just played what I heard. Later, that worked well on electric bass, and once I had an instrument my music career started to take off. I could play just about anything I heard on a record once I had that electric bass.

Aside

Trans vocality, the relationship between one's voice and one's gender identity, is a new, complex, and fascinating area of study (e.g., Meizel, 2020). Some trans singers feel that the voice plays a role in affirming their gender identity, while others feel little or no connection (Palkki, 2020). The fact that Jennifer says, "Maybe they were gendered parts that I was singing" may refer to the experience of viewing tenor and bass vocal parts in a choral context as "masculine." While in her twenties, Jennifer was recruited to play in a Top 40 band because of her voice, which she describes as "higher than Jon Anderson."

Snapshots, Part 2

Dysphoria hit me very hard during my senior year in high school. I lived in fear and tried to deflect any clues as to what I was going through. Once I graduated and eventually played in a commercial band, I had the experience of being encouraged to express my gender by a few women I met. But fear won out again and I went back in my cocoon. I stopped singing because my voice was so high. I was embarrassed by my voice: I thought it was giving me away. I got very paranoid about being outed. This was 1973–1974—different times. It could be fatal. Didn't sing in public for 30 years. So, I was terrified about people knowing my real story. *[pause]* When I left that band, I began to study music. And studying music was what enabled me to deal with the dysphoria. Otherwise, I probably would have killed myself. I think applying myself to music saved my life.

Think of the times. It was the seventies. How many people were open about who they were—even if they were gay, let alone trans? That wouldn't be something you'd bring up in a conversation. You certainly didn't want to get that reputation—your professional career would be over—especially then. It was life-threatening. I was very careful to keep it under wraps. There were a few women that I confided in who I felt I could trust. But it wasn't like I was raging "out," you know? It wasn't like that. It was really secretive. And like I said before, there was always something about music that let me put the dysphoria aside. Playing music—I lost any kind of feeling of gender in the act of playing the music anyway. In dealing with the politics and dealing with trying to get the gig you had to be gendered. *[chuckle]* I mean, I would do all kinds of things to disguise myself.

I was lucky in those years that it was cool to grow your hair out and be a rockstar type—that I could, in some ways, realize my physical being as being somewhat feminine. But I disguised myself by being a jock. I was really good at certain sports, which I'm still good at to this day. Around that time, I started to consciously try to talk in a lower voice. I worked really hard getting my voice to go *[speaking in a low range]* deep "into my diaphragm" and speak really low. So, in a way it was a disguise. Although—while I was in the rock band and out there in the world, I had some encounters where— I don't know if "coming out" is the right word—but some women that I met were basically encouraging me to join their tribe. They were reading me before I even knew what it was—I was getting read and encouraged. But I couldn't dare let anybody know about that in my professional circle.

I was quite dysphoric. When I had to revert at the end of playing the summer of 1973 at the Jersey Shore where I really lived the life and had to go back to living the way I was normally, I was quite sullen. I'm sure I wasn't socializing well at that point; it was dangerous to be open. When word of my escapades that summer were made known to the guys in that band, I was fired for it.

A few years later, after some study, while I was playing shows in the Poconos, I was recruited to play in Buddy Rich's band, but I turned it down. I had a bassist friend that played for him and at the end of the third gig, he had a cymbal thrown at his feet and was fired on stage. [*chuckle*] I was young. I looked like a girl. I figured I'd be easy prey for somebody who was that mean and macho. I was too afraid and paranoid. I didn't know what the word "transgender" meant, but I had those feelings. I still had that dysphoria. I met a woman while I was playing at Palumbo's nightclub in Philadelphia, and after we became close, I confided to her about my gender identity, and we hit it off over that.

Things had really progressed well in Philadelphia and, in 1983, after I toured with Woody Herman and married, we moved to Los Angeles in 1983. [Four years later], in 1987, I got the call in the middle of the night to play for George Shearing. In the morning I flew to San Jose airport—drove out in a limo to the Paul Masson Winery in Saratoga. I had no idea about this when George called, but Mel Tormé was also on that gig. That weekend was recorded by Concord Records, an album called *A Vintage Year* (Tormé and Shearing, 1988). Mel won the Grammy for best male jazz vocalist, and he hired me to be his bassist. [*pause*] So, that's where my modern-day career really started.

Aside

Jennifer's journey exemplifies how the gender landscape of the United States has drastically changed since the 1970s. The increasing modern presence of "out" trans and gender-expansive people in popular culture has ushered in a new and resilient generation of trans individuals (Beemyn and Rankin, 2011; Henig, 2017). At the same time, transphobic legislation, including, but not limited to, "bathroom bills," Trump's ban of trans people in the US military, recent legislation prohibiting health care for transgender children and prohibiting transgender participation in sports, have served to further oppress trans people. Jennifer's narrative beautifully illustrates that being an "out" trans individual was not a socially viable option until well beyond the 1970s.

In Philadelphia, Jennifer played with Larry Coryell, Jon Hendricks, Gloria Lynne, Shirley Scott, and Jimmy Bruno, along with other artists, and in a Lambert, Hendricks, and Ross-inspired trio called Tuxedo Junction. Once in Los Angeles she played with well-known artists, including Eartha Kitt, Bob Cooper, Bill Watrous, Ed Shaughnessy, Tommy Newsome, Snooky Young, Peggy Lee, Benny Carter, Take 6, k.d. lang, and many others. She recorded her first solo record in 1988 and, from 1987 to 1996, served as the bass player for jazz vocalist Mel Tormé. Following Tormé's stroke in 1996, Leitham began touring with Doc Severinsen. In 1999, while Jennifer was playing with Severinsen, she was inadvertently "outed" to him. At a Halloween show in Phoenix, she dressed as Audrey Hepburn and subsequently ran into Doc outside of the hotel bar....

Snapshots, Part 3

I say, "Doc, I'm very discreet about this. Nobody's ever gonna find out. It's not gonna be in the *National Enquirer*." And his first words to me were, "there's no such thing as bad publicity." From that point I knew it was going to be okay—at least as far as other people knowing about me. I knew that it wasn't a death sentence. I said, "This isn't going to be the end of my career, is it?" And Doc says, "It could just be the beginning."

After my ex had made nefarious calls to everyone I worked for about my plans to transition, outing me, Doc and I had a real long heart to heart. He counseled me for a couple hours and he basically told me, "I hired you as a bass player, not as a man or a woman. As long as you play as good as you do, you'll always have a job with me." Didn't really work out that way in the long run, but at the time it gave me a lot of—I don't know if security is the right word—but just realizing that I'd have an income. If I hadn't had Doc's encouragement—if I didn't have that knowledge that I would have an income, I'm not sure I would have had the courage to go ahead.

So, Doc came in before the rehearsal started and stood in front of the band and said "Gentlemen, I have an announcement, "our bass player, John Leitham is going to be known from now on as Jennifer Leitham. And I don't want any remarks or jokes from anyone. He's our bass player and she's now Jennifer." Boom. That was it.

After my transition none of the symphonies we played for made any kind of negative comments … everybody seemed pretty supportive. I sent notices about my transition to all the jazz festivals I was contracted to play as a leader or individual, and to a couple of schools that I had contracted with to do some clinic work. I had a nice picture made and sent a cover letter: "I'm going to be transitioning. This is how things are going to be, and there will be no change in my approach to playing or performing or teaching. It's about the music." Everybody I had a contract with was great. They were all fine with having me play there at least once. A lot of these festivals I had played every year. They all honored that first year. But the school in Wisconsin, where I was going to be artist-in-residence, they turned me down flat and they said they didn't want their kids exposed to that kind of thing.

Aside

After her 2001 transition, Jennifer continued to work with Doc Severinsen and also as a freelance musician. While she had cultivated her own musical projects since the 1980s, it was during this post-transition period that she increasingly pursued work with her trio, performing original compositions and penning original lyrics. During this period, Jennifer describes having a "surge of creativity." When we talked with Jennifer in late 2020, she described how, in recent years, she has focused more on her own music—recording albums, including *The Real Me*, *Future Christmas*, MOOD*(S)WINGS*, and *Remnants of Humanity* (Leitham, 2006, 2014, 2015, 2019).

Snapshots, Part 4

After my surgery, because of complications, I needed time to recover, and I wrote a lot of songs and put lyrics to old songs during that time. That's the music I eventually recorded on *The Real Me* (Leitham, 2006). All the time I was playing with Doc, I was leading my own band here in L.A.

Since then, I've concentrated more on playing my own music. I made a Christmas record, *Future Christmas* (Leitham, 2014) that's done well. *Jazz Times* magazine listed one of the tunes as one of the "Top 50 Jazz Christmas Songs of the Last 50 Years" (*JazzTimes*, 2020). There's a standout tune "Future Christmas (The Global Warming Winter Holiday Blues)." I've become a musical satirist. It's very wry holiday music. I made an album called *MOOD(S)WINGS* (Leitham, 2015) … I'm always writing and there's more original stuff on that record. "Stick It in Your Ear," from my *The Real Me* CD has become a bona fide hit tune on Spotify! *Left Coast Story* (2008). My protest CD, *Remnants of Humanity* (Leitham, 2019) came out last year. Lately my focus has mostly been on my own music. The prestige level of bookings has been rising. I don't work that often, but when I do, it's generally on a pretty big stage.

Aside

Today, Jennifer continues to pursue her own musical ventures while serving as a role model and mentor for younger trans musicians. Role models can be influential for trans and gender-expansive people as they navigate their gender identity, as was the case for Jennifer. While she was playing with Mel Tormé, she met composer Angela Morley, an "out" trans woman. This was influential for Jennifer, as it was an indication that she could continue to have a career in music while staying true to her identity—that her transness did not need to be a barrier to musical success.

Snapshots, Part 5

Angela Morley was the first transgender person I ever met. I was so impressed by her— general way of living life. The fact that her talent was what she put forward. She didn't talk about being transgender. Although musicians were joking about her all the time—she let it all roll off her back. I was very observant of how Mel Tormé and his management and the various people who in the studio related to Angela. I saw a glimmer there that, "Hey, maybe I can really be who I am," you know?

Some musicians would be making snide remarks—talking about what she wore, generally phobic comments, but what impressed me was how Mel and Angela had a lot of good laughs. Everything was so matter of fact—there was no attention paid to her gender. In the booth, nobody made references to it, nobody did anything untoward or questioned her presentation. I'd never met a trans person before, so it was all very enlightening to me—very eye-opening.

She found out about my transition not long after I'd made a public splash over it in the press while playing with Doc Severinsen's band. She called and offered some counsel. We talked maybe four or five times on the phone, she was very helpful to me, basically telling me everything's fine and she was very proud of me. She transitioned in 1972—she was a trailblazer—her friends and colleagues celebrated her transition and threw her a big party. That was the end of the public display for her and, from then on, she was strictly about the music.

As to being public, Angela was a big influence in dealing with it—I was getting some strange press coverage in the beginning of my transition, and I shut it down. I didn't want to become a spectacle, or tabloid folly. Somebody had written a tabloid wire-service story titled "Jazzy Crossdresser Becoming a Real Woman." Calls came from gotcha afternoon television talk shows, you could see where it was going if I played along, so I didn't do interviews for a while.

Trans folk often ask me for advice and counseling—somebody sent their website, "transgender cellist," and I say, "stop that!" Nobody puts "man cellist" or "woman cellist,"—you're a cellist! Are you good or aren't you?! So, I've always been very wary of putting my being transgender in my resume. Other people do it to me constantly.

Nowadays I seem to get more attention because I'm transgender than for my music. You guys wouldn't be talking to me *[chuckles]*—if I was just talking about my bass playing or my singing. When I get press attention, when the jazz publications come to me now—they want to hear about transgender stuff. They don't ask about my music. I fought it for a long time. I didn't want to be a transgender oracle, but that's my lot—that comes with the territory. So, when asked, I speak about it and will continue to.

Nowadays, there are some younger jazz musicians who are beginning the journey and some who've transitioned and are in the public a bit. They ask me for advice, and I give it. I pass along what Angela Morley told me: Try to make it about the music. She was a much more private person than I am. She didn't want to talk about transgender issues, but now I feel that I need to. There are so many forces aligned against us these days that there has to be more authentic representation of trans people to help other people to see us as equals.

Aside

In an ideal world, gender would not be a liability for anyone in their music-making. But unfortunately, that is not the reality of the current state of American society nor of the music/jazz world. Musicians' bodies are part of what is evaluated in live performance—and in hiring decisions. For better, and sometimes for worse, various identity markers (e.g., race and gender) become salient. Furthermore, while some aspects of identity are easily or always read by others, queer people have the unique burden of continually needing to "navigate the closet door" as they decide to whom to be "out"—and why (Jackson, 2007).

Post-transition, Jennifer has wrestled with a desire to be seen simply as a "musician," not necessarily as a "transgender musician." Identity theory proposes that each of us has various "role identities" that make up who we are (Charng, Piliavin, and Callero, 1988). This may be a helpful tool in understanding Jennifer's desire to be seen as a musician first and foremost. Jennifer gives more salience to her identity as a professional jazz musician than as an "out" trans woman and/or trans advocate. Thus, Jennifer continues to hope that her peers in the jazz world will continue to see her as a musician despite her gender identity.[2]

Navigating a jazz community known to be patriarchal, cisgender-centric, and homophobic can be difficult for anyone who is not a cisgender straight man. As an enterprise mired in various layers of privilege related to socioeconomic status, gender, race, ethnicity, and sexuality, the jazz/music education communities are in desperate need of narratives from underrepresented and historically marginalized groups (e.g., Garrett and Palkki, 2021; Talbot, 2017). Music educators and jazz educators in particular may glean lessons from Jennifer's story. To that end, we continue by chronicling her experiences and thoughts surrounding music education.

Before we proceed with Jennifer's thoughts about education, it is important to clarify what we mean when we use the term "education," which often is conceived of in relation to an academic institution. Here we draw upon the conception of education versus schooling proposed by Kruse (2014): "[E]ducation happens everywhere for all people in all settings, whereas school and schooling refer to a specific location and organization of sanctioned knowledge and skills" (p. 8).

Focus on (Music) Education
Snapshots, Part 6

Back in 1973, I found a guitar teacher who was instrumental in helping me learn how to practice and get a basic knowledge of harmony: Start to realize what a triad is, how to alter that triad, and learn to read music—those elemental things. There was a string bass teacher who taught downstairs, and my guitar teacher taught upstairs. I would listen to the string bass teacher teach while I was waiting to take my lesson upstairs. I could hear how much clearer his method was—how un-mystical. I started taking string bass lessons, and that's when I became a musician—studying with Al Stauffer.

Back then there weren't many university jazz programs. Eastman School of Music and Berklee were the two big jazz schools that I was aware of at the time. I could never have come close to affording either one. I don't think I was at a level that could have achieved a scholarship at that time. I took private lessons and learned on the bandstand, learned by doing—learned from playing with players better than me. I don't think I'd be the player I am now had I come up in a classroom environment. I think I profited by that apprenticeship, one-on-one type of learning. Nowadays it's practically passé. You have to have a shingle for people to think you're a player or teacher. You have to have that connection with your classmates, they become your circle for life, you're true to your school, play with your fellow alumni, it's a different way of doing things now. Back then it was more private study.

I don't come from money, couldn't have afforded tuition. I left home when I was 17 and my high school grades weren't good enough to get me admitted to a school. I had a terrible bout with gender dysphoria when I was a senior in high school and skipped all of my classes except choir. So, I didn't have the grades or the money. I attended Montgomery County Community College for a semester. Then I hooked up with that commercial band and got so busy I couldn't go to class anymore. There was no time to study—I had started to travel. I dropped out of college.

When I left that band, I began lessons with Al, and as I progressed, he started to recommend me— first to rehearsal bands—there were several within a 50-mile radius of Philadelphia. Al had played with Bud Powell. When famous artists would come through Philadelphia and use local players, Al would often be the bass player. He had a huge reputation in Southeastern Pennsylvania. He was recommending me to these big bands so I could learn how to swing. *[pause]* Some of those guys had played in Ellington's band, and Count Basie's, and with the Nat Pierce Elliot Lawrence Big Band in New York City. They were really experienced players. Some of them had traveled in the big band era with famous dance bands. Because Al Stauffer had such a good reputation, they cut me some slack in the beginning when I couldn't read that well, or didn't swing that well. They stuck with me for a while until—in about four months time, I was swinging. I was reading and I was swinging. It was a great experience playing with these older players who were better than I was, who knew how it should feel and could in turn show me how it felt. And were so nice about it, so encouraging. That's something that kids in schools often miss out on. Almost everyone you play with is teaching you something. To this day, I still consider myself a student of music.

Aside

Jennifer's work with Al Stauffer exemplifies a pivotal juncture in her jazz/music *education* versus *schooling* (Kruse, 2014). In helping her gain foundational knowledge, Stauffer set Jennifer on a path to a professional career in music. Later in her career, she found teachers in artists like Slam Stewart, Mel Tormé and Doc Severinsen. In describing her experiences taking classes at a community college (but not having time to attend class because of her professional gigs) and discussing the programs at Eastman and Berklee, Jennifer is discussing jazz *schooling*.

It is ironic that so much of Jennifer's story is essentially unprecedented relative to mainstream jazz histories, while other parts of her musical journey are exceedingly well-aligned with traditional jazz narratives, including the process of musical apprenticeship (Jones and Brenton, 2015). This apprenticeship model of education was the primary mode by which jazz flourished for nearly half a century. As Jennifer alludes to them, university jazz programs were far from mainstream at the time and were, by their very design, restricted to those who could afford to be there. On top of this, these institutions, like most of academia, have been the domain of white, upper-class, straight, cisgender men. In this way, we can appreciate the intersectionality of all of this: Jennifer, as a white trans woman (pre-transition), had the opportunity to grow as a practitioner of Black[3] music through an apprenticeship model. However, it was through classism that she was ultimately dissuaded from participating in jazz "schooling" as such.

Snapshots, Part 7: Jennifer's Advice for Jazz Educators

There's no favored type of person who is better at music. We all start from the same place, and everyone needs to be encouraged. You can't brush aside somebody because they're different. It's that way in life—it's that way with everything. And, what I'd like to see music education become better at, is giving women and LGBT or queer people an equal opportunity. You can't let internal prejudices color your teachings. Also, be truthful. It's hard to talk to students and be real about what obstacles they may have in front of them, but they need to hear it. Maybe if we who are different keep sticking our necks out there, ten or fifteen years from now we won't be talking about things like this. Educators have to become proponents of equality and truth.

Final Aside: What Jennifer's Story Might Mean for Jazz Education

The Quandary of being "Out"

One of the most perplexing parts of Jennifer's story is her intense desire to be seen as a professional musician—not a "trans professional musician." In our follow-up interview, Jennifer said this:

> If my music helps get that message out to people, that's good. I mean, I'd love for people to see me as a musician first and to understand that I'm trying to be a serious artist. And I like to think my product that I put out there has value. But if that doesn't happen and they just want to talk about the trans stuff, I'll talk to you about the trans stuff.

It was very clear in our interviews that Jennifer was very committed to this idea that "it's about the music." But she also has been very public about her transition. When asked about this dichotomy, Jennifer said

---

Snapshots, Part 8

In being open about who I am, especially in the time that I came out, I hope that it had a positive effect or caused people to do some research. Think outside of their own existence—think differently. Hopefully it helped open some doors for people. When I finally transitioned in 2001, I was 48 years old. I'd had a career, had some notoriety. In order to continue a career, there was no way I could hide where I had been, especially since I play left-handed, a very rare thing. So, I had to be open. My life became more about educating people about gender than it was playing music. It wasn't something I volunteered for; it just came with the territory. I've learned a lot in the time since I've transitioned. I know I wasn't perfect in trying to educate, [and] know I had things wrong some of the time, but I think I'm a lot better at it now than I was in 2001. People have asked me for advice over the years and I've freely given it, but I always say I am not the end all, everyone's experiences are unique. I teach the best when I teach from my experiences.

In the trajectory of her career, unfortunately, Jennifer did not have much of a choice about being "out." In order for her to benefit from the clout of her previous professional accomplishments, she needed to retain some connection to her previous identity. As she says, "I had to be open." This notion of negotiating one's level of "outness" is context-dependent and complex (Jackson, 2007; Tucker, 2002b). Furthermore, the phrase "I know I wasn't perfect in trying to educate" illustrates the construct that Jennifer was, in some ways, expected to share the experiences of *all* trans people—an impossible task. Here Jennifer highlights the absurd idea that persons from marginalized populations often are forced to educate those who wield more power—a unique burden to navigate.

Resisting the "Old Boys Club"

In the documentary *I Stand Corrected*, Jennifer and other interviewees described the jazz world as "macho," "rather homophobic," and "male-dominated"—assertions very much in line with writings by various jazz scholars (e.g., Tucker, 2002a). Jennifer's story spans many decades in which she was forced to navigate highly gendered spaces in making a career as a professional jazz musician. After a long career playing behind successful (presumably) cisgender straight men, she became a band leader "out of necessity," but now says it's "what I live for" (Meyerson, 2012).

So, what influence might Jennifer, as an "out" trans woman, have on the larger jazz world? What impact does her visibility and work have on the jazz "Old Boys Club"? Might her presence in the jazz world disrupt normative, long-held notions about gender in jazz? Viewing these questions in the context of larger societal issues, it is important to note that "[trans] visibility cannot simply be equated with social acceptance" (Koch-Rein, Yekani, and Verlinden, 2020, p. 3). In other words, Jennifer's ability to thrive amid a transphobic jazz community, does not exempt this community from the need for self-reflection. What systems and structures can the jazz community put in place so that future would-be trans jazz musicians do not have to face the transphobia that Jennifer endured and continues to endure? Jennifer's cisgender male colleagues never have to "come out" as anything—they can be simply "jazz musicians" (Tucker, 2002b). How might the jazz community work to make cisgender women and transgender people feel included? How can we expect trans women to be *seen* in a jazz world where cisgender women still are marginalized? Perhaps in identifying problematic, old fashioned, gendered aspects of the jazz world, jazz educators can begin to work and advocate for change.

A pertinent question for jazz education might be: What role can jazz educators play in helping to create a more diverse, equitable, and inclusive culture? Jazz educators can hire mentors from diverse backgrounds and to mentor similarly diverse students beyond cisgender, straight, white men.[4] The discussion of various intersecting identities (race, socioeconomic status, gender identity, sexuality) into jazz education may help to open up space for difficult, messy, and necessary conversations around issues of diversity, equity, inclusion, and access. Jazz educators could partner with educators beyond the world of jazz to tackle some of these issues and advocate for change.

Education versus Schooling

The notion of education versus schooling seems apropos when applied to Jennifer's experiences and to the jazz world more broadly. In our first conversation, she described how jazz education had moved "from the street to the academy." Too often, the academy has meant educational institutions as a space for white, straight, cisgender (often financially privileged) males. What has incorporating jazz into the academy done to exclude would-be trans jazz musicians, and what can we do to make this a more inclusive and affirming space? Jennifer advises jazz educators to remain equity-minded. Jazz education is rife with possibility in terms of social justice lessons on race, socio-economic status, sexuality and, of course, gender. Equity-minded jazz educators can draw upon notions of critical pedagogy to frame educational experiences in a way that challenges tropes, stereotypes, racism, heterosexism, and transphobia. Jazz can be a tool to help students understand equity and justice for trans and gender-expansive persons.

As Jennifer notes below, her life is indeed "in the notes." That being the case, we once again implore you to explore her recordings as another opportunity to engage with her musical life.

Snapshots, Part 9

Trans people are here. *We've always been here, and we will continue to be.* We're a part of the human experience and you're not going to legislate us away or try to put us behind bars or keep us from playing sports or keep us from representation. That's just not going to happen. Why not be open and let people that aren't familiar with the subject see you and see that we're just like everyone else? We want the same chances, the same normal things. All LGBT people: We're just out here trying to live our lives, and we're not trying to hurt anybody. And if you would embrace us, you would be a lot less fearful. *[chuckles]* There's nothing to be afraid of here.

There are so many instances in my life, I say it all the time—I don't know if I'd be here, if not for people who stepped up and helped me. From patrons to crowdfunding, my teachers and mentors, people have so often been there for me. I am filled with gratitude. Why have I been so blessed to have such support? Maybe it's because of who I am, where I've been, and that I am an authentic person, I like to think that some of it comes to me because I am so immersed in the music—I live in the notes.

Notes

1 While this is true, standard qualitative research protocols were observed. Because the authors prefer to spend more of this chapter highlighting Jennifer's words, research method details are available in writing upon request.
2 Role identity even played into the creation of this chapter. Joshua was sought out because of his role as a scholar on queer issues in music (education); he brought on Carl because of his experience as a jazz musician. Through a mutual colleague of Carl and Jennifer, she was brought on and agreed to share her story as an "out" trans jazz musician.
3 While a thorough unpacking of jazz and race is beyond the scope of this chapter, we would like to acknowledge the inherent problematic nature of three white authors writing about a music birthed and developed by Black Americans.
4 There may be a parallel and potential model here in the increased attention to, and mentorship of, cisgender women in STEM fields.

References

Arvay, M. J. (2002). Putting the heart back into constructivist research. In J. D. Raskin and S. K. Bridges (Eds.), *Studies in Meaning: Exploring Constructivist Psychology* (pp. 201–223). Pace University Press.

Beemyn, G., and Rankin, S. R. (2011). *The Lives of Transgender People*. Columbia University Press.

Berliner, S. (2017, September 21). An open letter to Ethan Iverson (and the rest of jazz patriarchy). www.sashaberlinermusic.com/sociopoliticalcommentary-1/2017/9/21/an-open-letter-to-ethan-iverson-and-the-rest-of-jazz-patriarchy.

Charng, H.-W., Piliavin, J. A., and Callero, P. L. (1988). Role identity and reasoned action in the prediction of repeated behavior. *Social Psychology Quarterly, 51*(4), 303–317.

Doyle, J. D. (2007). Transgender Music Special, Part 4. www.queermusicheritage.com/aug2007s.html.

Drake, R. M. (2011). *An Exploration of Transgender Identity and Jazz: The Liberation of Jennifer Leitham* (Publication No. 1493115); ProQuest Dissertations and Theses database.

Garrett, M. L., and Palkki, J. (2021). *Honoring Trans and Gender-expansive Students in Music Education*. Oxford University Press.

Gender Minorities Aotearoa. (n.d.). *Trans 101: Glossary of trans words and how to use them.* https://genderminorities.com/database/glossary-transgender/.

George, L. (2003, August 31). Going solo in a man's world. *Los Angeles Times.* www.latimes.com/archives/la-xpm-2003-aug-31-ca-george31-story.html.

Heckman, D. (2009). Jennifer Leitham: Transamerican music. *JazzTimes, 39*(3), 46–50.

Henig, R. M. (2017, January). Rethinking gender. *National Geographic, 231*(1). www.nationalgeographic.com/magazine/2017/01/children-explain-how-gender-affects-their-lives/.

Iyer, V. (2004). Exploding the narrative in jazz improvisation. In R. G. O'Meally, B. H. Edwards, and F. J. Griffin (Eds.), *Uptown Conversation: The New Jazz Studies* (pp. 393–403). Columbia University Press.

Jackson, J. M. (2007). *Unmasking Identities: An Exploration of the Lives of Gay and Lesbian Teachers*. Lexington Books.

James, F. (2016, May 4). An acclaimed bassist overcomes jazz's transphobia. *LA Weekly*. www.laweekly.com/an-acclaimed-bassist-overcomes-jazzs-transphobia/.

JazzTimes. (2020, December 21). What are the best jazz Christmas songs in the *JazzTimes* era? 50 Years, 50 Jazz Christmas Songs. *JazzTimes*. https://jazztimes.com/blog/50-years-50-jazz-christmas-songs-a-jazz-holiday-playlist/.

Jones, E., and Brenton, H. (2015). Using social media to revive a lost apprenticeship model in jazz education. In L. Steels (Ed.), *Music Learning with Massive Open Online Courses (MOOCs)* (pp. 177–194). IOS Press.

Koch-Rein, A., Haschemi Yekani, E., and Verlinden, J. J. (2020). Representing trans: Visibility and its discontents. *European Journal of English Studies*, *24*(1), Online First Publication. https://doi.org/10.1080/13825577.2020.1730040.

Kosciw, J. G., Greytak, E. A., Palmer, N. A., and Boesen, M. J. (2014). *The 2013 national school climate survey: The experiences of lesbian, gay, bisexual, and transgender youth in our nation's schools*. GLSEN.

Kruse, A. J. (2014). *"They wasn't makin' my kinda music": Hip-hop, schooling, and music education* (Publication No. 3633607) ProQuest Dissertations and Theses database.

Leitham, J. (2006). *The Real Me*. Sinistral Records.

Leitham, J. (2008). *Left Coast Story*. Sinistral Records.

Leitham, J. (2014). *Future Christmas*. Sinistral Records.

Leitham, J. (2015). *MOOD(S)WINGS*. Sinistral Records.

Leitham, J. (2019). *Remnants of Humanity*. Sinistral Records.

Meizel, K. (2020). *Multivocality: Singing on the Borders of Identity*. Oxford University Press.

Meyerson, A. (2012, April 3). *I Stand Corrected* (Documentary, Biography, Music).

Murray, L. (2012, November 13). Review: "I Stand Corrected," Jennifer Leitham's transgender journey in the transphobic world of jazz. *BERKSHIRE ON STAGE*. https://berkshireonstage.wordpress.com/2012/11/13/review-i-stand-corrected-jennifer-leithams-transgender-journey-in-the-homophobic-world-of-jazz/.

Nagoshi, J. L., and Brzuzy, S. (2010). Transgender theory: Embodying research and practice. *Affilia*, *25*(4), 431–443. https://doi.org/10.1177/0886109910384068.

Palkki, J. (2020). "My voice speaks for itself": The experiences of three transgender students in American secondary school choral programs: *International Journal of Music Education*, *38*(1), 126–146. https://doi.org/10.1177/0255761419890946.

Patton, M. Q. (1990). *Qualitative evaluation and research methods*. Sage.

Shdaimah, C., and Stahl, R. (2012). Power and conflict in collaborative research. In B. Flyvbjerg, T. Landman, and S. Schram (Eds.), *Real Social Science: Applied Phronesis* (pp. 122–136). Cambridge University Press.

Talbot, B. C. (Ed.). (2017). *Marginalized Voices in Music Education*. Routledge.

Tormé, M., and Shearing, G. (1988). *A Vintage Year*. Concord Records.

Trans Student Educational Resources. (n.d.). Definitions—Trans Student Educational Resources. Retrieved from www.transstudent.org/about/definitions/.

Tucker, S. (2002a). Big Ears: Listening for Gender in Jazz Studies. *Current Musicology*, 71–73. https://doi.org/10.7916/cm.v0i71-73.4831.

Tucker, S. (2002b). When subjects don't come out. In S. Fuller and L. Whitesell (Eds.), *Queer Episodes in Music and Modern Identity* (pp. 293–310). University of Illinois Press.

25

CAN E-FLAT BE SEXIST?

Canonical Keys as Marginalizing Practice in Jazz

Wendy Hargreaves and Melissa Forbes

Throughout this chapter we use the term *gender* to refer to both gender and sex whilst acknowledging that, strictly speaking, sex is designated by biological differences, and gender is socially constructed. Both Wendy and Melissa are females biologically who identify and live as females.

Introduction

If we placed *The Real Book* (2004) and *The New Real Book* (Sher, 1988) in front of a group of jazz musicians and asked whether females are marginalized in these books, what might they identify? They may point out the discriminatory gender roles in the lyrics of "Black Coffee." They may detect that the photographs in *The New Real Book* show 30 male instrumentalists but no female instrumentalists. They may note that female composers are barely represented. Some may even observe that the captions beneath the photographs of the five female singers misspell Carmen McRae's name once (McCrae) and Sarah Vaughan's name twice (Vaughn). But would anyone point to a key signature?

The marginalization of women in jazz can take both overt and covert forms. Indeed, it can be so subtle that it is not seen as such but, rather, regarded as "just the way things are." Tucker (2001) implores readers to listen vigilantly with "big ears" for the subtle ways issues of gender permeate jazz. Her argument invites us to consider whether something as utilitarian as a choice of key might be a gendered theme in jazz, and, if so, are our ears big enough to hear it?

This chapter arose from the first author's (Wendy's) reflections on personal experiences in jazz education. During her first year at university, Wendy participated in a jazz ensemble class as the vocalist in a seven-piece band, where she grappled with performing with an authentic jazz sound. One challenging song was the standard "Gone with the Wind," which the ensemble performed in the key of E-flat. Wendy had no difficulty with swinging, phrasing, following the harmonic changes, or communicating lyrics, and her soprano voice floated easily over the top F5 in the melody. She was acutely aware, however, that no matter how she tried, she sounded the least authentic in the ensemble. While her classmates began to sound like jazz cats, her high-pitched attempt sounded more like she stood on its tail!

The experience poses interesting questions when revisited using Tucker's (2001) "big ears." Somewhat unquestioningly, Wendy sang in E-flat rather than A-flat, like Sarah Vaughan and Ella

DOI: 10.4324/9781003081876-28

Fitzgerald. Was the key responsible for creating Wendy's sense of reduced authenticity compared to other students? Can a key wield a subtle discriminatory power that can potentially marginalize female vocalists from the community of practice experienced by jazz musicians?

Or, to ask it another way, can E-flat be sexist?

To answer this question, we begin by exploring the ways in which keys have been absorbed into canon through the performance of jazz standards, print music and fake books, and are perpetuated through jazz practice and culture. We then present an analysis of 40 well-known standards recorded by prominent female vocalists and compare the recorded keys to printed keys. This analysis shows that the keys used by female jazz singers seldom match the keys in the influential fake books. This is followed by a discussion of jazz voice style and function to outline why performing in a key other than the canonical key is usually necessary to achieve an authentic jazz vocal sound for female jazz singers. We conclude by outlining the implications for jazz practice and education and make recommendations on ways to foster inclusivity regarding female vocalists and key choice.

The Performance of Jazz Standards and Canonical Keys

To provide context, the journey begins by examining the use of songs known as jazz standards, that have been performed and recorded frequently by jazz musicians over the genre's history. While an exact list of standards varies among sources (e.g., Aebersold, 1992; Crook, 1999; Levine, 1995), standards are considered essential knowledge for professional jazz musicians (Gioia, 2012) and a prerequisite for participating in ensembles (Monson, 1996). As Levine (1995) quips when highlighting core songs in his recommended repertoire, "Don't move to New York without knowing most of them" (p. 419).

Jazz performance convention allows musicians to demonstrate individuality and innovation by altering various musical elements of standards (Berliner, 1994; Friedell, 2020). However, a strange, almost contradictory practice arises in relation to keys: musicians may perform standards in *any* key (Bowen, 2015), and there is an emphasis on being skilled sufficiently to play them in *all* keys (Berliner, 1994), yet each standard is associated conventionally with *one* particular key (Bowen, 2015). Jazz musicians refer to it as the usual, standard, original or normal key (e.g., Aebersold, 2003, p. ii; Rufus Reid in Berliner, 1994, p. 293; Gioia, 2012, p. xiv; Spradling, 2007, p. 51). Calling tunes in their "original" key on the band stand demonstrates a jazz musician's knowledge of and respect for jazz traditions.

The existence of "usual keys" is explained by Friedell's (2020) theory of performance rules as traditions that are "granted normative significance by social practices" (p. 807). This accounts for Bowen's (2015, p. 263) observation that "most players can identify the 'usual' keys ... for most standards." It shows that just as a knowledge of jazz standards exists and a freedom to change their key, so too does a knowledge of their conventional key.

Of the terms that describe the conventional key, the most misleading is "original." The authoritative overtones of "original" suggest that the song's key was drawn from its first publication or public performance. To the contrary, Bowen (2015) shows how Coleman Hawkins's 1939 instrumental recording was the catalyst for the social practice of performing "Body and Soul" in D-flat rather than the originally published key of C, or any of the variety of keys used prior to Hawkins. Tracing how the key of each standard became common practice is beyond the scope of this chapter. Suffice to say, an association exists between a standard and one specific key, and this knowledge has become part of the jazz canon. Consequently, we prefer the term "canonical key" (as used by Bowen, 2015, p. 274) rather than "original" key, as it acknowledges the contribution of social practice, rather than replicating a creation myth without verification. "Canonical key" also usefully denotes the embedded, assumed, or authoritative nature of the keys of jazz standards within jazz practice and culture.

Canonical Keys in Fake Books

While in theory instrumentalists have creative license to perform standards in a variety of keys, beginners necessarily start by learning them in one key. That key is often the canonical key by virtue of teachers, mentors and performers directing students towards recordings and notations respected by the jazz community (e.g., Aebersold, 1992; Levine, 1995). As a result, the canonical key is often by default at the forefront of the beginner jazz instrumentalist's experience with a song. Berliner (1994, p. 66) observes that the first key a novice encounters can leave such a strong impression that students often experience a "shocking revelation" when they discover that songs may be performed in keys *other* than "the first printed version they encounter."

Berliner's observation connects experiences of learning repertoire with reading print music. He notes that despite a reliance on learning aurally, most beginners "eventually learn to read music in order to gain access to additional material" (Berliner, 1994, p. 64). Today, reading skills are a normal part of formal jazz education (Prouty, 2006), which is significant given that these institutions contribute markedly as the training grounds for new generations of jazz musicians (Berliner, 1994, pp. 55–57).

The emphasis on reading music at university invites inquiry into exactly what jazz students are reading, and how those sources may affect their knowledge of repertoire and associated conventions. This is not to minimize the substantial and frequently lauded contribution of listening to recordings when learning jazz. Rather, it acknowledges that print music is not without its own capacity to influence acquired knowledge and to perpetuate canonical or unexamined practices.

One category of print resources that is widely used by developing jazz musicians is jazz fake books (Berliner, 1994, p. 64; Kernfeld, 2006; Monson, 1996, p. 184). These books provide a large compilation of lead sheets of jazz standards, giving ready access to repertoire and captured conventions. They denote a key and time signature, melody and chord changes for each standard. Unlike recordings, fake books can also supply a clear presentation of a composer's original idea from which musicians develop their personal interpretation. This circumvents the difficulty of separating which musical ideas in a recording emanate from a performer and which are part of the composer's original intent (e.g., Konitz in Hamilton, 2007, p. 200).

One particularly influential fake book is titled, ironically, *The Real Book* (2004). Described in the *New York Times* as "the bible of jazz fake books" (Lydon, 1994), *The Real Book* was compiled originally in 1975 by two jazz students at Berklee College of Music who wanted to create a book for jazz musicians that had greater relevance and accuracy than anything accessible at that time (https://officialrealbook.com/history/). Their book was sold surreptitiously as it did not observe copyright laws, yet its popularity grew quickly and spread internationally (Kernfeld, 2006). Another four illegal editions followed until it was transformed by Hal Leonard Corporation in 2004 into the legal, sixth edition.

Publisher Sher Music produced its own fake book, called *The New Real Book* (Sher, 1988). Despite the similarity in titles, this legal publication was not associated with *The Real Book*, but likely rode on its popularity to generate success (Kernfeld, 2006, p. 140). Together, both Sher Music's and Hal Leonard's fake books are staple resources in jazz education, often appearing in university libraries (e.g., University of Sydney, Australia; Leeds Conservatoire, UK; University of Michigan, United States), and in the resource list in instructional jazz texts (e.g., Crook, 1999; Levine, 1995; Weir, 2005). Librarian Koblick (2013) argues for the inclusion of *The Real Book* (2004) and *The New Real Book* (Sher, 1988) in public libraries. She notes that many libraries already have fake books servicing the community and argues that these two particular sources should be included based on their superior accuracy and accessibility.

For professional musicians, *The Real Book* and *The New Real Book* may function as performance suggestions for standards (e.g., Kernfeld, 2006, pp. 142–143) and as fodder for disputes over authentic chord changes (e.g., Berkman, 2009, p. 33). For students, however, their notation captures and partially stabilizes some mystifying elements of jazz repertoire, creating a level of authority, and ultimately canonization (Kernfeld, 2006, p. 138). Musician and educator Steve Swallow observed this institutionalizing effect at Berklee College of Music in 1975. In an interview with Kernfeld (2006), Swallow recalls the hilarity of walking through the college hallways hearing "flagrant harmonic violations just spewing out" of the practice rooms (p. 136). In contrast, one month after *The Real Book* was in circulation, he recalls suddenly "hearing the right changes to tunes that had [previously] been butchered" (Kernfeld, 2006, p. 136).

Not only did *The Real Book* unify, rightly or wrongly, the harmonic changes of the printed songs for students, but it also institutionalized their keys (Bowen, 2015, p. 263). Consequently, the process used to select keys for print is central to determining whether gender discrimination affected the choice. Unfortunately, only one of the two influential fake books overtly states their selection process. *The Real Book's* method is not provided, beyond a reference by the publisher of the legal edition to changing some keys at the copyright holder's request (https://officialrealb ook.com/history). Kernfeld's (2006) research, however, describes how the text was first developed using advice and proofreading from instrumental musicians, the viewing of band scores, and the copying from lead sheets provided by instrumental composers. All of these suggest there was an emphasis on instrumental sources which may have influenced the creators' perspective in editorial decisions, such as the choice of key. Whatever the key selection process, *The Real Book* (2004) has the same keys as *The New Real Book* (Sher, 1988) for 56 of the 64 songs that appear in both books (89.4%).

In contrast to *The Real Book*, the process for selecting keys for *The New Real Book* is revealed by the musical editor, Bauer, who writes:

> The key of the standards reflect common practice. Ignoring vocal renditions (which are transposed to suit a singer's range), there was usually general agreement concerning the key among various instrumental recordings … At other times more than one valid key emerged … In these cases we looked to the most well-known recording or used our own best sense of contemporary practice.
>
> *(Sher, 1988, p. ii)*

Bauer's bias towards instrumental versions over vocal versions is likely a symptom of a social divide between instrumentalists and singers in the jazz community, with instrumentalists attributed greater authenticity as jazz musicians than vocalists (Pellegrinelli, 2005, pp. 2–4). Both the legal (2004) and the illegal (1975) editions of *The Real Book* also show evidence of considering instrumentalists more prominently than singers. The preface of both editions states that the book is "designed, above all, for practical use," yet the omission of lyrics suggests that vocalists' usage was either not considered or it was deemed less important than instrumentalists' usage.

Superficially, Bauer's ignoring of vocal renditions appears to be a gender-neutral directive, applicable to both male and female singers. In application, it erased more women from the assessment of "common practice" than men. The evidence for this lies in the appendix (Sher, 1988, pp. 421–426), which cites the "major sources" consulted when scoring each chart. Here, multiple examples can be found where the printed key does in fact match the key of the cited *male* vocal recording (e.g., Sinatra's "Angel Eyes" in C minor; Nat King Cole's "Nature Boy" in D minor; Joe Williams's "Come Sunday" in B-flat). This aligns with Barnes's (in Aebersold, 2003, p. ii) experience that standards suit male vocal ranges, and with Berkman's (2009, p. 39) comment that "most standards are written in keys that favor male voices." Regardless of whether Bauer's term, "vocal renditions," was intended to mean both male and female vocalists, the final product is a book that notates songs in keys that better suit male voices.

In his foreword, Bauer explains that vocal renditions are renditions of songs that are "transposed to suit a singer's range" (Sher, 1988, p. ii). This practice is sometimes referred to by instrumentalists as performing songs in "singers' keys" (e.g., Bowen, 2015, p. 278). Singers' keys (or a singer's key) describe a key, other than the canonical key, that accommodates a vocalist's "practical use," as will be discussed later. Publisher Jamey Aebersold Jazz used the term as a selling point for the 107th play-a-long volume entitled *Singers! It Had to be You: 24 Standards in Singer's Keys* (Aebersold, 2003). The book's intention to "cater to the needs of singers" (p. ii) manifests in selecting keys "that enable most female vocalists to sing in a more comfortable range" (p. ii). Again, we see the use of a term, singers' keys, that appears to be gender-neutral but in application distinguishes females only. The contradiction is also visible in the claim that the book addresses the needs of "vocalists" (gender-neutral) by lowering the key of standards by a third or fourth, yet noting that "many male vocalists have the ability to sing standards in the original written key" (p. ii). In other words, male singers may not have needed these singers' keys in the first place.

The explanation for commonly associating singers with females is simple. Females occupy the role of jazz singer more frequently than males (Cole in Grime, 1983, p. 81; Hargreaves, 2014, p. 287; Pellegrinelli, 2005, p. 6). There are two relevant, significant consequences of this social composition. First, any practice that delineates on the basis that a jazz musician is female is likely to impact on the majority of singers. Second, any practice that delineates on the basis that a jazz musician is a singer will likely impact on a greater number of females than males. Consequently, an editor's practice of excluding singers when selecting keys for print potentially impacts more women than men. Before exploring the implications of this delineation, we will first verify that the keys of the two fake books do in fact differ frequently from the key choices of renowned female vocalists.

Method and Analysis

Sixteen renowned female jazz vocalists were selected as a representative sample of respected female vocal practice in performing jazz standards across many decades. Each singer is named in four books that catalogue famous jazz artists (i.e., Carr, Fairweather and Priestley, 2000; Crowther and Pinfold, 1997; Friedwald, 1992; Yanow, 2008). An exception was made for Dianne Reeves, who appears in three of the sources. Her absence from Friedwald (1992) is understandable given that her reputation was still growing at the time of publication. Recordings of these 16 singers were readily accessible in digital format from Spotify, Apple Music or iTunes. Accessibility was essential because listening to exemplar renditions is a recommended practice for vocal jazz students (e.g., Madura, 1999, p. 29; Weir, 2005, p. 6).

Next, 20 jazz standards in *The New Real Book* (Sher, 1988) were chosen randomly for analysis. Each song was checked to ensure it (a) included lyrics; (b) was identified as a standard by a minimum of three of five nominated sources (i.e., Complete Jamey Aebersold Jazz Play-a-long Book Index, n.d.; Crook, 1999; Gioia, 2012; Levine, 1995; www.jazzstandards.com); and, (c) had digitally accessible recordings by a minimum of five of the 16 selected female jazz singers. Any song that did not meet all three requirements was discarded and replaced with another random choice. The process was repeated until a quota of 20 compliant songs was reached. In cases where multiple recordings of a song from a single artist existed, one version was selected randomly for analysis.

A similar process was used for selecting 20 songs from *The Real Book* (2004). Each song from *The Real Book* was examined to ensure it (a) was identified as a standard by a minimum of three of the five previously mentioned sources; and (b) had digitally accessible recordings by a minimum of five of the 16 selected female jazz singers. Three additional criteria were applied during selection. First, songs that had already been examined in *The New Real Book* were eliminated. Second, due to the continued widespread use of both the illegal and legal editions of *The Real Book*, the song had to be replicated in the same key for both iterations. Third, lyrics for the songs were required to be readily available, either online or in other printed anthologies, as neither iteration of the book printed them. If a song did not meet any of the requirements it was discarded and another random choice was made. The process was repeated until the quota of 20 songs was met. The final tally of renditions by 16 selected female singers of each of the 40 songs from the combined list from *The Real Book* and *The New Real Book* generated a total of 248 recordings for analysis[1] (see Appendix 1).

Analysis began with listing the key of the print music of the 40 songs. Next, each recording was played until the first entry of the female voice at the chorus, at which point the recorded key of the female singer was noted.[2] Modulations that occurred later in the song were not listed. Songs where the recorded key matched the key in the print version were further analysed to determine if the vocalist sang the melody's lowest notes in the first chorus, or whether the notes were replaced with other melodic ideas at a higher pitch. If at any point during the first chorus, the vocalist sang pitches as low or lower than the notated score, they were considered as having capacity to sing in the notated key for the recording.

Findings

The findings of key analysis for *The New Real Book* are provided in Table 25.1. It shows that four of the 122 recordings of renowned female jazz singers (3.28%) are in the same key as the notated keys. Of the four songs that match keys, one singer uses melodic alteration to replace the lowest notes of the notation with higher options when performing the first chorus. Thus, the total of recorded songs that match keys and where the artist sings the lowest notated pitches in the first chorus is three of 122 recordings (2.46%).

Table 25.2 presents the findings of key analysis for *The Real Book*. It shows that 12 of the 126 recordings of renowned female jazz singers (9.52%) are in the same key as the notation. Of the 12 songs that match keys, three singers use melodic alteration to replace the lowest notes of the notation with higher options when performing the first chorus. Thus, the total of recorded songs that match keys and where the performer sings the lowest notated pitches in the first chorus is 9 of 126 recordings (7.14%).

The results demonstrate clearly that the sample of 40 printed songs from *The New Real Book* and *The Real Book* do not represent the common practice of 16 renowned female jazz singers. Of the 16 recordings that did match notated keys, four singers remain within the tonality by altering the lowest notated pitches. The final combined total of recordings where female singers remain within the notated tonality without melodic alteration at the lowest notes is 12 of 248 recordings (4.84%).

Jazz Vocal Style and Voice Function

These findings demonstrate that in approximately 95 percent of recordings analysed, prominent female singers recorded songs in keys *other than the canonical key*. To understand why this is necessarily the case, we now turn to a discussion of the stylistic and functional characteristics of female jazz singing. This section will provide a brief overview of two salient factors affecting female singers and key choice in jazz: (1) singing style in jazz and (2) singing voice function, particularly as it pertains to registration and vocal range.[3] Jazz singing is broadly characterized by stylistic complexity, comprised of unique rhythmic, tonal, emotive, melodic and improvisatory qualities (Crowther and Pinfold, 1997; Friedwald, 1992; Yanow, 2008). Within this complexity, our discussion here is concerned with one facet of jazz singing style, namely how the voice functions physiologically to perform melodic lines that are stylistically authentic.

Female jazz singers generally favour the lower pitch range of the voice to convey a conversational delivery of the lyric (Shapiro, 2016).[4] Berkman (2009, p. 39) observes that jazz singers tend to "exploit their lower range more, singing as altos." This stylistic preference is based on myriad contributing factors. First, communicating the lyric and storytelling is of vital importance in the singing of jazz standards (Hargreaves, 2014; Shapiro, 2016; Weir, 2005). This is easier to achieve when using the same pitch range and acoustic properties of speech.[5] Second, the use of amplification in jazz singing (Shapiro, 2016; Spradling, 2007) means that jazz singers (unlike their classical counterparts) can

Table 25.1 A Cross-reference of Printed Keys from 20 Songs in *The New Real Book* (1988) with the Recorded Keys of 16 Female Jazz Singers.

Song Title and Printed Key in The New Real Book	Anderson, Ernestine	Carter, Betty	Christy, June	Clooney, Rosemary	Dearie, Blossom	Fitzgerald, Ella	Holiday, Billie	Horn, Shirley	Horne, Lena	McRae, Carmen	Merrill, Helen	O'Day, Anita	Reeves, Dianne	Vaughan, Sarah	Washington, Dinah	Wilson, Nancy
"All of Me" in C						G	F	G						G	F	F
"All or Nothing at All" in C			Ab			Ab	G	G						Bb	G	
"All the Things You Are" in Ab	Eb					Db				Eb	Db			Eb		C
"But Beautiful" in G	C			Db		Bb	C		Db	C					C	
"Darn that Dream" in G			C			Db	C		C					D		Bb
"Do Nothing 'Til You Hear From Me" in Bb			C	Db		C	C		C	Bb [a]	C			Eb		
"Don't Get Around Much Anymore" in C	C [a,b]		F			F			G					G		
"Everything Happens to Me" in Bb		Eb		C		Eb	Eb		Db	Db	D					
"Gee Baby Ain't I Good to You" in Eb				Ab		C	Db	Bb							Db	Db
"Gone With the Wind" in Eb	F	F				Ab	F	F			G			Ab		
"I'm Old Fashioned" in F				Bb	C	Db		C		Bb	C			Eb		
"If I Were a Bell" in F				Eb	C	Bb		A		Bb	A			F		
"Like Someone in Love" in C					E	G		F	Gb							Gb
"Misty" in Eb	Ab	Bb		Bb		Bb			G	G		Ab	C	C		
"Moonlight in Vermont" in Eb			A			C	A					Bb	Bb	Db		
"Skylark" in Eb	Eb [a]			Gb		Ab			C	Ab		Bb	Bb	Db	Db	
"Speak Low" in F						Ab	Bb			C		Ab	C	Db		
"Tenderly" in Eb				Bb		Bb	G		C	G		A			Bb	
"There Will Never Be Another You" in Eb	F			A		Bb				Ab		Ab		Bb		Bb
"Wave" in D				B	B	D [a]				C				Eb		C

a The first chorus is recorded in the same key as the printed notation.

b The singer replaces the lowest notes of the melody with higher notes.

Table 25.2 A Cross-reference of Printed Keys from 20 Songs in *The Real Book* (2004) with Recorded Keys of 16 Female Jazz Singers.

Song Title and Printed Key in The Real Book	Anderson, Ernestine	Carter, Betty	Christy, June	Clooney, Rosemary	Dearie, Blossom	Fitzgerald, Ella	Holiday, Billie	Horn, Shirley	Horne, Lena	McRae, Carmen	Merrill, Helen	O'Day, Anita	Reeves, Dianne	Vaughan, Sarah	Washington, Dinah	Wilson, Nancy
"April in Paris" in C	Bb			F		F	F							F		
"Autumn in New York" in F						C	Bb		B					C		F
"Easy to Love" in C			Eb			D	Eb			Eb		Db		Eb		
"How High the Moon" in G						Eb						Db	C	Eb		
"I Can't Get Started with You" in C				F		Ab	G			F	F	F		Ab	G	
"I Could Write a Book" in C		G				F					F	F		F		
"I Got it Bad" in G	**G**[a,b]			Bb		Bb	Bb			C				C	Eb	
"It Don't Mean a Thing" in Gm	**Gm**[a]	Am		Bbm		Dm	Bb		C	C		**Gm**[a]		C		
"Lush Life" in Db					**D**[a]	Bb			Db	C			C	C		
"Mood Indigo" in Ab				Bb		Bb				Db			Eb	Eb		
"My Funny Valentine" in Cm						Gm		Fm	Gm	Gm		Fm	**Cm**[a]	Gm	Bb	**Db**[a]
"My Ship" in F	Ab		C	Bb		G			Bb	Bb		G		C		C
"Prelude to a Kiss" in C			Ab			F			G	F				Ab		Ab
"Round Midnight" in Ebm		Bbm	Am			Bbm	Db			Am	Gm			Bbm		Am
"Sophisticated Lady" in Ab	**Ab**[a,b]			Ab[a,b]		C	B			**Ab**[a]			C	C		
"Stompin' at the Savoy" in Db		C				**Db**[a]						**Db**[a]	**Db**[a]	**Db**[a]		Db
"There is No Greater Love" in Bb	C	F					F							Eb		
"When I Fall in Love" in Eb	C	C								Bb			Eb		Bb	
"When Sunny Gets Blue" in F	C	C		D	D					C		Bb		Bb		D
"You Don't Know What Love is" in Fm						Bbm	Am			Bbm		Gm	Gm		Bbm	Cm

a The first chorus is recorded in the same key as the printed notation.

b The singer replaces the lowest notes of the melody with higher notes.

employ this conversational delivery and do not need to physically "project" their voices to be heard. Third, the historical and cultural roots of jazz can, in part, be found in the blues, which, together with other African American vocal styles from the nineteenth century (such as shouts, field cries, work songs and spirituals) are characterized by an energetic, speech-like quality in the singing.[6] The preference for female jazz singers to sing in the lower pitch or alto range contrasts with singing in the Western classical tradition (such as art song and opera), which, at least for female singers such as sopranos and mezzo-sopranos, favours a higher pitch range.[7] As we will see below, these pitch ranges (low or high) are associated with the concept of singing voice *registers*. A singer's ability to navigate vocal registers plays a vital role in their ability to present a stylistically and artistically authentic jazz performance.

To understand how a singer navigates pitch, it is necessary to briefly examine the underlying mechanics of vocal registers. Due to their complexity and multi-faceted nature, vocal registers have recently been described by one preeminent voice scientist as "the snake pit of voice pedagogy" (Herbst, 2020). With this warning in mind, we take *register* to refer to a series of homogenous tones within which most voices (male and female) tend to function in accordance with a particular mechanical principle (paraphrased from Garcia, 1847; see also McCoy, 2012 and, McKinney, 2005). We use the terms "head register" and "chest register" for the voice functions which relate to higher and lower pitches respectively.

The primary *passaggio* or "break" between the two registers for females who sing commercial styles such as jazz can be anywhere from around D4-G4 up to top C5 in some cases (McCoy, 2012). If chest and head registers can be thought of as "gears" for the voice, then a primary aim of much singing voice pedagogy is concerned with developing the singer's ability to skilfully sing through the break in registers to fully exploit their vocal range and timbral possibilities (Sundberg, 1987). "Mix" register (another highly complex concept and a contentious term in singing voice pedagogy) can refer to many things, but for current purposes let us take mix as the ability of a singer to move between chest and head registers, creating a seamless vocal "blend."[8] Gaining these skills (for those who do not have the innate or intuitive ability) can be a long and slow process, requiring high levels of expertise relating to the indirect control of laryngeal musculature in response to breath pressure whilst understanding the influence of vocal tract shaping (resonance) on laryngeal behaviour.

The psychoacoustic perception of these registers, namely, how they sound to the listener, is of relevance to our discussion in terms of achieving an authentic jazz style. As noted above, female jazz singers predominantly use chest register in a lower pitch range to achieve a conversational, speech-like quality. Jazz singers will also use "mix" register on higher pitches in the lower range to maintain speech-like quality (rather than using head register, although again there are exceptions) (see Kochis-Jennings et al., 2012).[9] A singer producing (predominantly) higher pitches in head register (which sounds much less speech-like) will lose the conversational quality of most jazz singing. In female voices the pitch range for chest register can be anywhere from around E3 to Bb/B4, whilst mix can enable singers to maintain a speech or chest-like quality at higher pitches. Commercial music female singers may begin to "mix" anywhere from approximately Eb4 or the primary *passaggio* through to Bb4/B4/C5 (and beyond), also known as the second *passaggio*. Whilst there are undoubtedly jazz singers with tremendous vocal range who use chest, mix and head registers skilfully (such as Ella Fitzgerald, Sarah Vaughan, Dianne Reeves, and Nancy King), the "bread and butter" of the jazz sound for singers is maintaining a speech-like or conversational quality in the lower pitch range associated with chest and mix registers, particularly when delivering the melodic head of a jazz standard. It is also important to note that, due to differences in the size of the vocal folds, the male voice generally has a lower fundamental frequency than the female voice (Titze, 2000).[10]

How are these issues brought to bear on key choice for female jazz singers? By way of example, the canonical key of "All the Things You Are" is A-flat and Tony Bennett's recording in 1962 in that key demonstrates the characteristic conversational quality of jazz singing. However, consider the scenario in which a female singer is introduced to the tune via a fake book during an ensemble class. The printed melody is too high—Eb5 at its highest (The Real Book, 2004). If the singer is experienced enough to recognize that the written key will not sound authentic when sung, they may be able to adjust and sing down the octave or improvise the melody to suit her range.[11] For developing jazz singers, however, such ingenuity may not be an option. Singing down the octave and staying true to the melody will take the tune beyond the reasonable range of chest register for most female singers. In the case of "All the Things You Are," the canonical or male key is around a fourth or fifth away from a more suitable key for female singers. As Berkman notes, male keys may in fact suit "true" soprano voices, but singing jazz standards in the soprano range is stylistically inappropriate. Some developing or inexperienced female singers may attempt to sing "All the Things You Are" as written in A-flat using head register. This will result in a loss of conversational quality and an "inauthentic" sounding performance, as was the case with the example described in the introduction of singing "Gone with the Wind" in E-flat. In any of these scenarios, when confronted with the canonical key, the developing female singer—particularly those inexperienced in jazz and improvisation—is marginalized from the outset because none of the available options is ideally suited to accommodating the female voice.

There are many conceivable scenarios in which a novice, developing or inexperienced jazz singer may feel obliged to or have no choice but to sing in a canonical key. They may be placed under pressure (subtle or overt) to do so from instrumentalists, band leaders or educators, for whom the canonical key is familiar and/or convenient. Many developing jazz singers will not have the music literacy skills to transpose charts or perhaps more fundamentally, the awareness of the implications of key on their voice.[12] It goes without saying that it is incumbent upon vocal jazz educators to make this latter lesson one of the first for developing singers. As noted above, when a developing jazz singer has no option but to sing in the canonical key, this will generally force them to either sing up the octave using head register (if they have access to it) resulting in an inauthentic sound, or, in chest register, but with an inability to sing the lowest pitches in a tune. In either scenario, the jazz singer sounds "inauthentic," thus committing perhaps one of the gravest "sins" in jazz culture. It is also important to note that age is a factor in determining keys for female singers (Spradling, 2007, p. 51). Whilst older female singers—with years of experience, a lower voice, and mastery of vocal technique—may be able to perform in canonical keys with octave displacement and improvisation as necessary,[13] such a feat is usually beyond the younger singer who may be new to jazz style, possess a higher vocal range and rudimentary vocal technique.

In summary, jazz vocal style favours a conversational delivery associated with chest and mix vocal registers, which are associated with the lower to medium pitch range in the female singing voice. Due to the difference in size of vocal folds based on sex, males generally have access to lower pitches than females. Canonical keys favour the vocal range and registration of the male voice where it is easy to maintain a conversational tone. These same keys are (generally speaking) too low for a female singer to achieve the same desired vocal quality for jazz singing. Usually only experienced jazz singers with well-developed vocal technique possess the improvisatory skills to perform in canonical keys.

Implications and Recommendations

The analysis presented in this chapter together with consideration of the stylistic and functional requirements of jazz singing demonstrates that canonical keys, as presented in fake books and perpetuated through practice, are not well suited to female jazz singers, particularly those in the early stages of development. Bowen (2015, p. 284) states that "[s]ingers are more eager ... to personalize the key than instrumentalists." For female jazz singers, personalization of key is more than a matter of "eagerness" —it is one of stylistic and functional necessity. Adjustments to keys for female singers occur at macro and micro levels. At the macro level, the key must be transposed to bring the melody within the physical capabilities of the singer to convey the style. This usually involves transposition of the tune by approximately an interval of a fourth away from the canonical key. At the micro level, a singer may then choose to make further adjustments (by a semitone or tone) to suit tonal "sweet spots" of the voice. Generally speaking, male singers do not need to make the significant macro adjustment to key (transposing by a fourth) that their female counterparts must make. They can and do make micro adjustments. For example, in 2015 Tony Bennett sang "All the Things You Are" in the key of A (up a semitone from the canonical A-flat). For physiological and stylistic reasons, the adjustment to canonical keys at the macro level is usually necessary for the female jazz singer.

Any female singer who has heard the collective groan of the band when requesting to transpose the canonical key to a suitable key will understand that the pressure on singers to conform to canonical keys can result in feelings of marginalization and sometimes even exclusion. These feelings can have an adverse impact on the developing female jazz singer, particularly when attempting to perform with and in front of others (who are usually mostly male). Music performance anxiety can affect singers of all levels of experience (LeBorgne and Rosenberg, 2021). Emotional distress is likely to have a negative impact on the physical systems used for singing (LeBorgne and Rosenberg, 2021). The developing singer under pressure to sing in an inappropriate canonical key is disadvantaged both physically and psychologically, compared to instrumentalists. This makes the job of singing the melody during the head difficult, and, by the time solos come around, the task of improvisation especially daunting. The ability to improvise is an important marker of expertise in jazz (Hytonen-Ng, 2013; Madura, 1996). Expert jazz singers describe how successful improvisation occurs in a state of flow where they feel psychologically safe to experiment and make mistakes (Forbes, 2021; Forbes and Cantrell, 2021). Music performance anxiety and flow are generally considered to be antithetical (Csikszentmihalyi, 2002; see also Cohen and Bodner, 2021). For the developing female jazz singer, performing in a stylistically inappropriate canonical key may increase the likelihood of experiencing performance anxiety and diminish access to flow. Thus, performing in unsuitable keys may have multiple and ripple effects for female singers: they may experience immediate physical discomfort and anxiety; the ability to improvise and experience flow may be hindered; and the overall result may be stylistically inappropriate. It seems reasonable to hypothesize that such effects may contribute to the perception that (female) singers are regarded as deficient jazz musicians (Hargreaves, 2013).

It is incumbent upon jazz instrumentalists and educators to understand and support female singers to perform in stylistically and functionally appropriate keys; to do anything else is to bar the authentic participation of female singers in jazz. To achieve stronger inclusion of female jazz vocalists, jazz educators would benefit from receiving some basic training in vocal function—this could be as simple as jazz voice educators collaborating with their instrumental counterparts to build mutual understanding of jazz traditions and vocal considerations, thus better placing educators to accommodate the practical implications of including female singers in instrumental ensembles (see also Eade, 2021). Jazz educators might also make students aware that the canonical keys enshrined in fake books can marginalize singers. We suggest educators discuss with and encourage instrumentalists to challenge an uncritical acceptance of canonical keys. By intervening early and often in the ensemble setting, jazz educators could better represent the interests of developing female vocalists who are in the process of acquiring the necessary assertiveness or music literacy skills to identify their needs and provide their own alternative resources. Finally, female jazz singers must be educated in the implications of key choice as well as lead sheet preparation, band leading skills and the ability to advocate for their own musical needs.

It would be prudent to recommend a suitable alternative resource to the existing fake books; however, the current market lacks an option of a book with suitably transposed charts *and* the critical combination of attributes that made *The Real Book* the de facto textbook of jazz education: that is, an extensive anthology of jazz lead sheets with authentic jazz harmonies, collated in a single, bound, affordable songbook, with alternative B-flat and E-flat versions for a collaborative jazz ensemble experience. Current resources are deficient on one or more accounts, such as insufficient repertoire (e.g., Rawlins, n.d.-a); full scored accompaniments (e.g., *Jazz Divas*, n.d.); or high/low voice or men's/women's editions but no parallel editions for B-flat and E-flat instruments for full ensemble participation (e.g., *The Real Vocal Book*, n.d.; Rawlins, n.d. -b). Digital solutions such as the iReal Pro app have enabled quick and easy transposition of chord changes into any key, but as yet do not include a song's melody or lyrics.

Printing two editions for voice types appears to be a step forward, or ironically backwards to 1939, when the fake book's predecessor, *Tune-Dex*, originally provided this (Kernfeld, 2006). Segregating editions by voice type, however, is less likely to normalize alternative keys and more likely to replicate a hierarchy where the male edition is preferred. Consider, for example, whether impoverished instrumental students would prioritize purchasing both male and female editions when one book alone could meet their need for repertoire?

One defence against a biased hierarchy of male over female editions is to print the second, transposed version of each song on every second page of a book, as *The New Real Book* did for "Boogie Down" (Sher, 1988, pp. 29–33), only this time with different keys rather than instrumentations. All musicians would then be presented repeatedly with two options of keys and have equal, ready access to perform both. This integrated approach, along with additional E-flat and B-flat editions containing the dual keys, has a greater chance of re-educating jazz musicians to include and consider female vocal keys for ensemble use, normalize the practice and stimulate positive change for inclusivity.

Conclusion

In this chapter, we have shone a light on canonical keys as a gendered practice with the aim of encouraging all in jazz to listen harder and look closer at how something as seemingly objective as key can operate discriminatorily. Canonical keys are generally naturally suited to the male voice. Female singers must transpose jazz standards to bring them within an achievable vocal range and appropriate vocal register to produce a stylistically authentic performance. At the least, female singers are inconvenienced by canonical keys; at worst, when faced with situations in which they must sing in canonical keys, female singers (particularly those in the early stages of development) are at risk of producing inauthentic performances, which has the effect of marginalizing these singers as unskilled within jazz culture.

This chapter has not focused on the role of jazz tradition (including performance and recording practices), social dynamics and gender norms in negotiating keys within a jazz ensemble. We acknowledge that these are all potential factors in the marginalization of female singers and would be a worthy subject of future research. Moreover, the longer-term effect of the marginalization of female singers due to canonical keys is beyond the scope of this chapter. Future research might consider how experiences like the one described in the introduction may have negatively influenced female singers' level of participation and/or contributed to singers' reputation as lesser jazz musicians.

Can E-flat be sexist? Yes. When presented as a canonical key, something as simple as key can be gendered and discriminatory. It is a simple reality that voice function and achieving authentic female vocal jazz style are not compatible with most canonical keys. It is time for the jazz canon of standards to be more empathetically, readily, and consciously transposed to respect the undeniable physical and personal presence of female singers in the jazz story.

Appendix 1: Discography

Anderson, E. (1960). It don't mean a thing [Song]. On *My kinda swing*. UMG Recordings.
Anderson, E. (1960). Moonlight in Vermont [Song]. On *My kinda swing*. UMG Recordings.
Anderson, E. (1993). Don't get around much anymore [Song]. On *Great moments with Ernestine Anderson*. Concord Jazz.
Anderson, E. (1993). Skylark [Song]. On *Great moments with Ernestine Anderson*. Concord Jazz.
Anderson, E. (1997). My ship [Song]. On *Jazz singing 1: The jazz vocal collection*. Polygram.

Anderson, E. (1998). There is no greater Love [Song]. On *Isn't it romantic*. TMD Jazz.

Anderson, E. (2011). Autumn in New York [Song]. On *Hot cargo*. Fresh Sound Records.

Anderson, E. (2015). Gone with the wind [Song]. On *Ernestine Anderson swings the Penthouse*. HighNote Records.

Anderson, E. (2015). There will never be another you [Song]. On *Ernestine Anderson swings the Penthouse*. HighNote Records.

Anderson, E. (2020). Stompin' at the Savoy [Song]. On *Autumn in New York*. M.D. Music.

Basie, W. J., & Vaughan, S. (1996). If I were a bell [Song]. On *Count Basie & Sarah Vaughan*. Parlophone Records.

Bennett, T. (1962). All the things you are [Song]. On *Tony Bennett at Carnegie Hall: June 9, 1962*. Columbia Records.

Bennett, T., & Charlap, B. (2015). All the things you are [Song]. On *The silver lining: The songs of Jerome Kern*. Columbia Records.

Brown, C., & Washington, D. (1989). Darn that dream [Song]. On *Brownie: The complete EmArcy recordings of Clifford Brown*. UMG Recordings.

Carter, B. (1993). All the things you are [Song]. On *Betty Carter at the Village Vanguard*. Verve.

Carter, B. (1993). There is no greater Love [Song]. On *Inside Betty Carter*. Blue Note Records.

Carter, B. (2005). 'Round midnight [Song]. On *'Round midnight*. Warner Strategic Marketing.

Carter, B. (2005). When I fall in love [Song]. On *'Round midnight*. Warner Strategic Marketing.

Carter, B. (2009). But beautiful [Song]. On *I can't help it*. LMG.

Carter, B. (2012). Gone with the wind [Song]. On *Precious and rare: Betty Carter*. Le Chant du Monde.

Carter, B. (2012). I could write a book [Song]. On *Precious and rare: Betty Carter*. Le Chant du Monde.

Carter, B. (2012). It don't mean a thing [Song]. On *Betty Carter's finest hour*. Universe Remasterings.

Carter, B. (2012). Moonlight in Vermont [Song]. On *Precious and rare: Betty Carter*. Le Chant du Monde.

Christy, J. (1956). 'Round midnight [Song]. On *The misty Miss Christy*. Capitol Records.

Christy, J. (1957). When Sunny gets blue [Song]. On *Fair and warmer*. Capitol Records.

Christy, J. (1995). Don't get around much anymore [Song]. On *Great ladies of song: Spotlight on June Christy*. Capitol Records.

Christy, J. (1995). Everything happens to me [Song]. On *Day dreams*. Capitol Records.

Christy, J. (2002). Stompin' at the Savoy [Song]. On *June Christy sings the standards*. EMI Records.

Christy, J. (2005). Do nothing 'til you hear from me [Song]. On *Ballads for night people*. Capitol Records.

Christy, J. (2005). My ship [Song]. On *Ballads for night people*. Capitol Records.

Christy, J. (2006). Misty [Song]. On *The intimate Miss Christy*. Blue Note Records.

Christy, J. (2009). Prelude to a kiss [Song]. On *Duke Ellington: It don't mean a thing if it ain't got that swing*. Discmedi.

Christy, J. (2009.). All or nothing at all [Song]. On *BD Music presents June Christy*. BD Music.

Christy, J. (2012). How high the moon [Song]. On *Big band divas of the 1940s*. Delta.

Clooney, R. (1956). I got it bad (and that ain't good) [Song]. On *Blue rose*. Sony Music Entertainment.

Clooney, R. (1956). Mood indigo [Song]. On *Blue rose*. Sony Music Entertainment.

Clooney, R. (1956). Sophisticated lady [Song]. On *Blue rose*. Sony Music Entertainment.

Clooney, R. (1958). Do nothing 'til you hear from me [Song]. On *Swing around Rosie*. UMG Recordings.

Clooney, R. (1977). I can't get started with you [Song]. On *Everything's coming up Rosie*. Concord Jazz.

Clooney, R. (1987). Skylark [Song]. On *Rosemary Clooney sings the lyrics of Johnny Mercer*. Concord Jazz.

Clooney, R. (1989). My ship [Song]. On *Show tunes*. Concord Jazz.

Clooney, R. (1992). Wave [Song]. On *Girl singer*. Concord Jazz.

Clooney, R. (1993). Gee baby ain't I good to you [Song]. On *Do you miss New York?* Concord Jazz.

Clooney, R. (1998). Like someone in love [Song]. On *The Concord jazz heritage series*. Concord Records.

Clooney, R. (2004). April in Paris [Song]. On *Rosie solves the singing riddle*. BMG Music.

Clooney, R. (2004). But beautiful [Song]. On *From Bing to Billie*. Concord Records.

Clooney, R. (2004). Moonlight in Vermont [Song]. On *The Rosemary Clooney show: Songs from the classic television series*. Concord Records.

Clooney, R. (2004). There will never be another you [Song]. On *The Rosemary Clooney show: Songs from the classic television series*. Concord Records.

Clooney, R. (2005). Everything happens to me [Song]. On *Ballad essentials*. Concord Records.

Clooney, R. (2014). I'm old fashioned [Song]. On *Mostly Mercer*. Harbinger Records.

Clooney, R. (2014). It don't mean a thing [Song]. On *100 plus jazz lounge ballads and songs*. Play.

Clooney, R. (2014). Tenderly [Song]. On *100 plus jazz lounge ballads and songs*. Play.

Cobb, A., & Washington, D. (2000). I got it bad [Song]. On *Cobb and his mob in concert featuring Dinah Washington*. High Note Records.

Cole, N. K. (2000). Nature boy. [Song]. On *Unforgettable*. Capitol Records.

Dearie, B. (1994). Lush life [Song]. On *Me and Phil: Blossom Dearie live in Australia*. Australian Broadcasting Corporation.

Dearie, B. (1998). I'm old fashioned [Song]. On *May I come in?* Blue Note Records.

Dearie, B. (1998). When Sunny gets blue [Song]. On *May I come in?* Blue Note Records.

Dearie, B. (2013). If I were a bell [Song]. On *The jazz collection 1957-1961*. Marmot Music.

Dearie, B. (2013). Like someone in love [Song]. On *The jazz collection 1957-1961*. Marmot Music.

Dearie, B. (2020). Wave [Song]. On *Blossom's planet*. Daffodil Records.

Diva Jazz Orchestra & Wilson, N. (2014). All of me [Song]. *Swingin' life*. MCG Jazz.

Ericson, R., & Anderson, E. (2009). I got it bad [Song]. On *Rolf Ericson and the American all stars*. Dobre Records.

Fitzgerald, E. & Armstrong, L. (1957). Autumn in New York [Song]. On *Ella and Louis again*. UMG Recordings.

Fitzgerald, E. & Armstrong, L. (1957). Stompin' at the Savoy [Song]. On On *Ella and Louis again*. UMG Recordings.

Fitzgerald, E. & Armstrong, L. (2011). Moonlight in Vermont [Song]. On *Ella and Louis*. UMG Recordings.

Fitzgerald, E. & Pass, J. (1983). Speak low [Song]. On *Speak love*. Fantasy.

Fitzgerald, E. & Pass, J. (2011). My ship [Song]. On *Easy living*. Concord Music.

Fitzgerald, E. (1958). April in Paris [Song]. On *Ella Fitzgerald, Billie Holiday and Carmen McRae at Newport*. Verve.

Fitzgerald, E. (1958). I got it bad [Song]. On *Ella Fitzgerald, Billie Holiday and Carmen McRae at Newport*. Verve.

Fitzgerald, E. (1962). All of me [Song]. On *Ella swings gently with Nelson*. UMG Recordings.

Fitzgerald, E. (1962). Darn that dream [Song]. On *Ella swings gently with Nelson*. UMG Recordings.

Fitzgerald, E. (1962). I can't get started with you [Song]. On *Ella swings gently with Nelson*. UMG Recordings.

Fitzgerald, E. (1975). Wave [Song]. On *Ella Fitzgerald at the Montreux jazz festival 1975*. Fantasy.

Fitzgerald, E. (1978). All or nothing at all [Song]. On *Lady time*. Fantasy.

Fitzgerald, E. (1989). Round midnight [Song]. On *Clap hands, here comes Charlie*. UMG Recordings.

Fitzgerald, E. (1991). Everything happens to me [Song]. On *Like someone in love*. UMG Recordings.

Fitzgerald, E. (1991). Like someone in love [Song]. On *Like someone in love*. UMG Recordings.

Fitzgerald, E. (1994). My funny valentine [Song]. On *Essential Ella*. UMG Recordings.

Fitzgerald, E. (1997). Easy to love [Song]. On *Ella Fitzgerald sings the Cole Porter song book*. UMG Recordings.

Fitzgerald, E. (1997). I could write a book [Song]. On *Ella Fitzgerald sings the Rodgers and Hart song book*. Verve.

Fitzgerald, E. (2007). All the things you are [Song]. On *Gold*. UMG Recordings.

Fitzgerald, E. (2007). How high the moon [Song]. On *Live at Mister Kelly's*. UMG Recordings.

Fitzgerald, E. (2007). Misty [Song]. On *Gold*. UMG Recordings.

Fitzgerald, E. (2007). You don't know what love is [Song]. On *Live at Mister Kelly's*. UMG Recordings.

Fitzgerald, E. (2013). There will never be another you [Song]. On *North Sea jazz legendary concerts*. Bob City.

Fitzgerald, E. (2016). Gee baby ain't I good to you [Song]. On *Live in Cologne 1974*. Jazzline.

Fitzgerald, E. (2016). Gone with the wind [Song]. On *Ella Fitzgerald sings sweets songs for swingers*. UMG Recordings.

Fitzgerald, E. (2016). If I were a bell [Song]. On *Ella swings lightly*. UMG Recordings.

Fitzgerald, E. (2017). Do nothing 'til you hear from me [Song]. On *Ella Fitzgerald sings the Duke Ellington song book*. UMG Recordings.

Fitzgerald, E. (2017). Don't get around much anymore [Song]. On *Ella Fitzgerald sings the Duke Ellington song book*. UMG Recordings.

Fitzgerald, E. (2017). I'm old fashioned [Song]. On *Ella Fitzgerald sings the Jerome Kern song book*. UMG Recordings.

Fitzgerald, E. (2017). It don't mean a thing [Song]. On *Ella Fitzgerald sings the Duke Ellington song book*. UMG Recordings.

Fitzgerald, E. (2017). Lush life [Song]. On *Ella Fitzgerald sings the Duke Ellington song book*. UMG Recordings.

Fitzgerald, E. (2017). Mood indigo [Song]. On *Ella Fitzgerald sings the Duke Ellington song book*. UMG Recordings.

Fitzgerald, E. (2017). Prelude to a kiss [Song]. On *Ella Fitzgerald sings the Duke Ellington song book*. UMG Recordings.

Fitzgerald, E. (2017). Skylark [Song]. On *Ella Fitzgerald sings the Johnny Mercer Song Book*. UMG Recordings.

Fitzgerald, E. (2017). Sophisticated lady [Song]. On *Ella Fitzgerald sings the Duke Ellington song book*. UMG Recordings.

Fitzgerald, E., & Armstrong, L. (2011). Tenderly [Song]. On *Ella and Louis*. UMG Recordings.

Holiday, B. (1957). Darn that dream [Song]. On *Body and soul*. UMG Recordings.

Holiday, B. (1957). Moonlight in Vermont [Song]. On *Body and soul*. UMG Recordings.

Holiday, B. (1958). All or nothing at all [Song]. On *All or nothing at all*. UMG Recordings.

Holiday, B. (1958). Everything happens to me [Song]. On *Stay with me*. UMG Recordings.

Holiday, B. (1958). Sophisticated lady [Song]. On *All or nothing at all*. UMG Recordings.

Holiday, B. (1958). Speak low [Song]. On *All or nothing at all*. UMG Recordings.

Holiday, B. (1991). Gee baby ain't I good to you [Song]. On *Lady in autumn: The best of the Verve years*. UMG Recordings.

Holiday, B. (1991). Prelude to a kiss [Song]. On *Lady in autumn: The best of the Verve years*. UMG Recordings.

Holiday, B. (1992). April in Paris [Song]. On *Billie's best*. UMG Recordings.

Holiday, B. (1992). Gone with the wind [Song]. On *Billie's best*. UMG Recordings.

Holiday, B. (1997). But beautiful [Song]. On *Lady in satin*. Columbia Records.

Holiday, B. (1997). You don't know what love is [Song]. On *Lady in satin*. Columbia Records.

Holiday, B. (2008). I got it bad [Song]. On *50 best blues favorites*. Ba–Ba Music.

Holiday, B. (2010). All of me [Song]. On *The essential Billie Holiday*. Sony Music Entertainment.

Holiday, B. (2010). I can't get started with you [Song]. On *The essential Billie Holiday: The Columbia years*. Sony Music Entertainment.

Holiday, B. (2011). Autumn in New York [Song]. On *Billie Holiday: Amazing collection*. Play.

Holiday, B. (2011). Do nothing 'til you hear from me [Song]. On *Billie Holiday: Amazing collection*. Play.

Holiday, B. (2011). Tenderly [Song]. On *Billie Holiday: Amazing collection*. Play.

Holiday, B. (2011). There is no greater Love [Song]. On *Billie Holiday: Amazing collection*. Play.

Holiday, B. (2014). Easy to love [Song]. On *100 plus essential jazz ballads*. Play.

Horn, S. (1986). I got it bad [Song]. On *A lazy afternoon*. SteepleChase.

Horn, S. (1991). Gee baby ain't I good to you [Song]. On *Violets for your furs*. SteepleChase.

Horn, S. (1995). All or nothing at all [Song]. On *The main ingredient*. UMG Recordings.

Horn, S. (1995). I'm old fashioned [Song]. On *The main ingredient*. UMG Recordings.

Horn, S. (1998). My funny valentine [Song]. On *I remember Miles*. UMG Recordings.

Horn, S. (2005). But beautiful [Song]. On *But beautiful: The best of Shirley Horn*. UMG Recordings.

Horn, S. (2009). Like someone in love [Song]. On *Intimate Shirley Horn*. Wnts.

Horne, L. (1962). But beautiful [Song]. On *I have dreamed*. Jazz Arena.

Horne, L. (2002). Don't get around much anymore [Song]. On *The Jubilee shows: No. 19, No. 20*. Jubilee.

Horne, L. (2004). Like someone in love [Song]. On *It's love*. BMG.

Horne, L. (2005). My funny valentine [Song]. On *Lena: A new album*. Copyright Group.

Horne, L. (2005). My ship [Song]. On *Lena: A new album*. Copyright Group.

Horne, L. (2007). Autumn in New York [Song]. On *The best of Lena Horne*. EMI Records.

Horne, L. (2007). Darn that dream [Song]. On *101 – The best of Lena Horne*. AP Music.

Horne, L. (2007). Do nothing 'til you hear from me [Song]. On *The best of Lena Horne*. EMI Records.

Horne, L. (2007). Prelude to a kiss [Song]. On *The best of Lena Horne*. EMI Records.

Horne, L. (2010). When I fall in love [Song]. On *Gone but not forgotten*. X5 Music.

Horne, L. (2012). Speak low [Song]. On *Summertime*. Puzzled Records.

Horne, L. (2017). I got it bad [Song]. On *Love Lena*. SRI Jazz.

Horne, L. (2018). Mood indigo [Song]. On *Once in a while*. Nagel-Heyer Records.

King, N. (2006). There will never be another you [Song]. On *Live at the Jazz Standard*. MAXJAZZ.

McRae, C. & Carter, B. (1996). Sophisticated lady [Song]. On *The Carmen McRae – Betty Carter duets*. Verve.

McRae, C. (1986). Prelude to a kiss [Song]. On *Any old time*. LCR.

McRae, C. (1990). My ship [Song]. On *Live and kickin'*. KEM Enterprises.

McRae, C. (1994). You'd be so easy to love [Song]. On *Carmen McRae*. Bethlehem Music.

McRae, C. (2001). Round midnight [Song]. On *Carmen sings Monk*. BMG.

McRae, C. (2003). Tenderly [Song]. On *Sarah – Dedicated to you*. BMG.

McRae, C. (2003). Wave (Take 32) [Song]. On *Sarah – Dedicated to you*. BMG.

McRae, C. (2004). My funny valentine [Song]. On *The best of Carmen McRae: The millennium collection*. Hip-O Records.

McRae, C. (2004). Speak low [Song]. On *The complete Ralph Burns sessions*. Lone Hill Jazz.

McRae, C. (2004). When I fall in love [Song]. On *The best of Carmen McRae: The millennium collection*. Hip-O Records.

McRae, C. (2005). I got it bad [Song]. On *The sound of silence*. Atlantic Recording.

McRae, C. (2005). When Sunny gets blue [Song]. On *Bittersweet*. Atlantic Recording.

McRae, C. (2009). Do nothing 'til you hear from me [Song]. On *New York state of mind*. Cugate.

McRae, C. (2009). Everything happens to me [Song]. On *New York state of mind*. Cugate.

McRae, C. (2009). I can't get started with you [Song]. On *Give me the simple life*. Dazzling Dames.

McRae, C. (2010). If I were a bell [Song]. On *Secret love*. Entertain me.

McRae, C. (2011). Skylark [Song]. On *Bye bye blackbird*. Ornithology Rec.

McRae, C. (2012). But beautiful [Song]. On *Speak low*. Crates Digger Music.

McRae, C. (2012). Lush life [Song]. On *Blue moon*. Ap Music.

McRae, C. (2013). All the things you are [Song]. On *Carmen McRae sings great American songwriter*. Universe Remasterings.

McRae, C. (2013). Duke Ellington: Satin doll/ Mood indigo [Song]. On *Time after time*. One Media iP.

McRae, D. (2003). Misty [Song]. On *Sarah – Dedicated to you*. BMG.

Merrill, H. (1961). April in Paris [Song]. On *Parole e musica*. Ricordi S.P.A.

Merrill, H. (1961). Everything happens to me [Song]. On *Parole e musica*. Ricordi S.P.A.

Merrill, H. (1961). You don't know what love is [Song]. On *Parole e musica*. Ricordi S.P.A.

Merrill, H. (1994). Gone with the wind [Song]. On *Brownie*. Decca Records.

Merrill, H. (2000). If I were a bell [Song]. On *Christmas song book*. Merrill Music.

Merrill, H. (2001). I got it bad [Song]. On *No tears no goodbyes*. Decca Records.

Merrill, H. (2001). Round about midnight [Song]. On *Music makers*. Decca Records.

Merrill, H. (2009). All the things you are [Song]. On *American songbook series: Irving Berlin and Jerome Kern*. Helen Merrill.

Merrill, H. (2009). I'm old fashioned [Song]. On *American songbook series: Irving Berlin and Jerome Kern*. Helen Merrill.

Merrill, H. (2012). My funny valentine [Song]. On *Live at Nalen (with Jan Johansson)*. Riverside Records.

Merrill, H. (2012). When I fall in love [Song]. On *Best of Helen Merrill*. Klub Music Publishing.

O'Day, (1999). Gone with the wind [Song]. On *The complete Anita O'Day Verve & Clef sessions*. UMG Recordings.

O'Day, A. (1952). Speak low [Song]. On *The lady is a tramp*. UMG Recordings.

O'Day, A. (1955). I can't get started with you [Song]. On *Anita*. UMG Recordings.

O'Day, A. (1955). You don't know what love is [Song]. On *An evening with Anita O'Day*. UMG Recordings.

O'Day, A. (1957). Tenderly [Song]. On *Anita sings the most*. UMG Recordings.

O'Day, A. (1958). My funny valentine [Song]. On *Anita O'Day sings the winners*. UMG Recordings.

O'Day, A. (1960). I could write a book [Song]. On *Anita O'Day and Billy May swing Rogers and Hart*. UMG Recordings.

O'Day, A. (1962). Do nothing 'til you hear from me [Song]. On *All the sad young men*. UMG Recordings.

O'Day, A. (1999). My ship [Song]. On *The complete Anita O'Day Verve & Clef sessions*. UMG Recordings.

O'Day, A. (1999). Stompin' at the Savoy [Song]. On *The complete Anita O'Day Verve & Clef sessions*. UMG Recordings.

O'Day, A. (1999). There will never be another you/Just friends [Song]. On *The complete Anita O'Day Verve & Clef sessions*. UMG Recordings.

O'Day, A. (2000). When Sunny gets blue [Song]. On *Anita O'Day's finest hour*. UMG Recordings.

O'Day, A. (2005). Misty [Song]. On *Angel eyes: Live in Tokyo*. Kayo Stereophonic.

O'Day, A. (2010). It don't mean a thing [Song]. On *There's only one*. Essential Media.

O'Day, A. (2013). Easy to love [Song]. On *Verve Ultimate Cool*. Decca.

O'Day, A. (2014). How high the moon [Song]. On *Your birthday present: Billie Holiday and guests*. Mag Music.

O'Day, A., & Krupa, G. (2007). Skylark [Song]. On *The essential collection: Hoagy Carmichael*. Avid Entertainment.

Reeves, D. (1987). I've got it bad [Song]. On *Dianne Reeves*. Blue Note Records.

Reeves, D. (1996). Tenderly [Song]. On *The ground encounter*. Blue Note Records.

Reeves, D. (2001). Speak low [Song]. On *The calling*. Blue Note Records.

Reeves, D. (2002). Misty [Song]. On *The best of Dianne Reeves*. Blue Note Records.

Reeves, D. (2003). Darn that dream [Song]. On *A little moonlight*. Blue Note Records.

Reeves, D. (2003). Skylark [Song]. On *A little moonlight*. Blue Note Records.

Reeves, D. (2005). How high the moon [Song]. On *Good night good luck*. Concord Music.

Reeves, D. (2007). Lush life [Song]. On *Billy Strayhorn: Lush life*. Blue Note.

Reeves, D. (2007). My funny valentine [Song]. On *Music for lovers*. Blue Note Records.

Sinatra, F. (2018). Angel eyes [Song]. On *Frank Sinatra sings for only the lonely*. Capital Records.

Vaughan, S. (193) My funny valentine [Song]. On *All time favorites by Sarah Vaughan*. UMG Recordings.

Vaughan, S. (1958). Like someone in love [Song]. On *After hours at the London House*. UMG Recordings.

Vaughan, S. (1977). Stompin' at the Savoy [Song]. On *The complete Sarah Vaughan on Mercury Vol. 4*. UMG Recordings.

Vaughan, S. (1986). All of me [Song]. On *The complete Sarah Vaughan on Mercury Vol. 2*. UMG Recordings.

Vaughan, S. (1991). Tenderly [Song]. On *Live in Japan Vol. 2*. Mainstream Records.

Vaughan, S. (1991). There is no greater Love [Song]. On *Live in Japan Vol. 2*. Mainstream Records.

Vaughan, S. (1991). There will never be another you [Song]. On *Live in Japan Vol. 1*. Mainstream Records.

Vaughan, S. (1991). Wave [Song]. On *Live in Japan Vol. 1*. Mainstream Records.

Vaughan, S. (1992). My ship [Song]. On *The essential Sarah Vaughan*. UMG Recordings.

Vaughan, S. (1997). Misty [Song]. On *Ultimate Sarah Vaughan*. UMG Recordings.

Vaughan, S. (1999). Lush life [Song]. On *The no. 1 jazz vocals album*. Polygram Records.

Vaughan, S. (1999). Moonlight in Vermont [Song]. On *The no. 1 jazz vocals album*. Polygram Records.

Vaughan, S. (2002). Autumn in New York [Song]. On *The definitive Sarah Vaughan*. UMG Recordings.

Vaughan, S. (2005). Easy to love [Song]. On *Sarah Vaughan the collection*. Parlophone Records.

Vaughan, S. (2005). Round midnight [Song]. On *Sarah Vaughan the collection*. Parlophone Records.

Vaughan, S. (2005). Sophisticated lady [Song]. On *Sarah Vaughan the collection*. Parlophone Records.

Vaughan, S. (2006). All or nothing at all [Song]. On *The very best of Sarah Vaughan*. Parlophone Records.

Vaughan, S. (2006). When Sunny gets blue [Song]. On *Sarah plus two*. Parlophone Records.

Vaughan, S. (2009). Gone with the wind [Song]. On *Don't worry be happy Vol. 2*. Wnts.

Vaughan, S. (2012). Darn that dream [Song]. On *100 the lady is a tramp: 10 x 10 best female jazz singers of all time*. Play.

Vaughan, S. (2013). I could write a book [Song]. On *200 jazz greatest hits ever*. Digital Remasterings.

Vaughan, S. (2013). How high the moon [Song]. On *200 jazz greatest hits ever*. Digital Remasterings.

Vaughan, S. (2013). I can't get started with you [Song]. On *Vocal jazz giants Vol. 1*. Firefly Entertainment.

Vaughan, S. (2013). I got it bad [Song]. On *Sophisticated lady: The Duke Ellington songbook collection*. Concord Music.

Vaughan, S. (2013). Mood indigo [Song]. On *Sophisticated lady: The Duke Ellington songbook collection*. Concord Music.

Vaughan, S. (2014). All the things you are [Song]. On *Whole lotta classic hits Vol. 4*. Suburban Squire.

Vaughan, S. (2014). April in Paris [Song]. On *100 plus essential jazz ballads*. Play.

Vaughan, S. (2014). Prelude to a kiss [Song]. On *100 plus essential jazz ballads*. Play.

Vaughan, S. (2015). Speak low [Song]. On *BD Music presents Sarah Vaughan*. BD Music.

Washington, D. (1962). Mood indigo [Song]. On *Tears and laughter*. UMG Recordings.

Washington, D. (1963). Don't get around much anymore [Song]. On *The good old days*. UMG Recordings.

Washington, D. (1988). If I were a bell [Song]. On *The complete Dinah Washington on Mercury Vol. 4*. UMG Recordings.

Washington, D. (1995). There is no greater Love [Song]. On *Blue gardenia: Songs of love*. UMG Recordings.

Washington, D. (1995). When I fall in love [Song]. On *Blue gardenia: Songs of love*. UMG Recordings.

Washington, D. (2000). I could write a book [Song]. On *Dinah Washington's finest hour*. UMG Recordings.

Washington, D. (2003). I can't get started with you [Song]. On *The most beautiful jazz voices ever Vol. 3*. MasterSong.

Washington, D. (2006). Do nothing 'til you hear from me [Song]. On *The very best of Dinah Washington*. Parlophone Records.

Washington, D. (2012). All of me [Song]. On *Gold*. The Island Def Jam Music.

Washington, D. (2012). You don't know what love is [Song]. On *For those in love*. Hot Record Society.

Williams, J., Jones, T., & Lewis, M. (1995). Come Sunday [Song]. On *Presenting Joe Williams and Thad Jones, Mel Lewis, the jazz orchestra*. Blue Note Records.

Wilson, N. (1990). But beautiful [Song]. On *But beautiful*. Capitol Records.

Wilson, N. (1996). Wave [Song]. On *The best of Nancy Wilson: The jazz and blues sessions*. Capitol Records.

Wilson, N. (2005). Darn that dream [Song]. On *The great American songbook*. Capitol Records.

Wilson, N. (2005). Gee baby ain't I good to you [Song]. On *Save your love for me: Nancy Wilson sings the great blues ballads*. Capitol Records.

Wilson, N. (2005). Lush life [Song]. On *The great American songbook*. Capitol Records.

Wilson, N. (2005). My ship [Song]. On *The great American songbook*. Capitol Records.

Wilson, N. (2005). Sophisticated lady [Song]. On *The great American songbook*. Capitol Records.

Wilson, N. (2005). When Sunny gets blue [Song]. On *Guess who I saw today: Nancy Wilson sings songs of lost love*. Blue Note Records.

Wilson, N. (2005). You don't know what love is [Song]. On *The great American songbook*. Capitol Records.

Wilson, N. (2007). I can't get started with you [Song]. On *The very best of Nancy Wilson: The Capitol recordings*. Capitol Records.

Wilson, N. (2007). Like someone in love [Song]. On *The very best of Nancy Wilson: The Capitol recordings*. Capitol Records.

Wilson, N. (2007). Prelude to a kiss [Song]. On *The very best of Nancy Wilson: The Capitol recordings*. Capitol Records.

Wilson, N. (2007). There will never be another you [Song]. On *The very best of Nancy Wilson: The Capitol recordings*. Capitol Records.

Wilson, N. (2012). Round midnight [Song]. On *Sixties sweethearts Vol. 4*. AP Music.

Notes

1 "Sophisticated Lady" (McRae and Carter, 1996) was analysed twice to examine the approach of each singer individually as they performed different sections in this duet.

2 "Wave" (Fitzgerald, 1975) and "There is No Greater Love" (Vaughan, 1991) were listened to in full because the songs are presented as scat solos with significant variation to the melodies.

3 For the sake of brevity and simplicity the following sections contain generalizations whilst acknowledging that when discussing singing voice style and function there will always be exceptions to the rule.

4 Examples abound in Tables 25.1 and 25.2 but for specific reference see Billie Holiday's "But Beautiful" and Carmen McRae's "Everything Happens to Me."

5 See Spradling (2007) for a discussion of these properties in jazz singing.

6 See Pellegrinelli (2008) for a discussion of the ways in which the evolution of jazz from blues has been coded distinctly as embodied, vocal, and therefore as gendered.

7 See Spradling (2007) for further information on some of the physical and acoustic differences between jazz and classical singing.

8 For an in-depth discussion of mix see Herbst (2021); see also Kochis-Jennings et al. (2012)

9 For example, Blossom Dearie's improvised opening to "Wave" and her singing of the melody at the beginning of the bridge.

10 Again, this is a generalization and there are always exceptions, such as singer Jimmy Scott, who was credited as a female singer on Charlie Parker's "Embraceable You" (Shapiro, 2016), or Nancy King who can access a very low range for a female singer.

11 For example, see Ernestine Anderson's "Don't Get Around Much Anymore" in the canonical key, where she interprets the melody liberally to avoid the lower reaches of the melody.

12 Inexperienced singers are also unlikely to understand the implications of certain keys for instrumentalists (e.g. "preferred" keys for pianists, transposing instruments, etc.).

13 Nancy King's version of "There Will Never Be Another You" in the canonical key of E-flat is a master class in jazz vocal technique and improvisation.

References

Aebersold, J. (1992). *How to Play Jazz and Improvise*. (6th ed., Vol. 1). Jamey Aebersold Jazz.

Aebersold, J. (Ed.). (2003). *Singers! It Had to be You*. (Vol. 107). Jamey Aebersold Jazz.

Berkman, D. (2009). *The Jazz Singer's Guidebook: A Course in Jazz Harmony and Scat Singing for the Serious Jazz Vocalist*. Sher Music.

Berliner, P. F. (1994). *Thinking in Jazz*. University of Chicago Press.

Bowen, J. A. (2015). Who plays the tune in "Body and Soul"? A performance history using recorded sources. *Journal of the Society for American Music, 9*(3), 259–292. https://doi.org/10.1017/S1752196315000176.

Carr, I., Fairweather, D., and Priestley, B. (2000). *Jazz: The Rough Guide* (2nd ed.). Rough Guides.

Cohen, S., and Bodner, E. (2021). Flow and music performance anxiety: The influence of contextual and background variables. *Musicae Scientiae, 25*(1), 25–44.

Complete Jamey Aebersold Jazz play-a-long book index. (n.d.). www.jazzbooks.com/mm5/merchant.mvc?Screen=free.

Crook, H. (1999). *Ready, Aim, Improvise: Exploring the Basics of Jazz Improvisation*. Advance Music.

Crowther, B. and Pinfold, M. (1997). *Singing Jazz*. Miller Freeman.

Csikszentmihalyi, M. (2002). *Flow: The Classic Work on How to Achieve Happiness* (Rev. ed.). Rider.

Eade, D. (2021). Jazz school: Singing with the band. *DownBeat, January*, 58–61.

Forbes, M. (2021). Giving voice to jazz singers' experiences of flow in improvisation. *Psychology of Music, 49*(4), 789–803. https://doi.org/10.1177/0305735619899137.

Forbes, M., and Cantrell, K. (2021). Choose your own adventure: Vocal jazz improvisation, conceptual metaphor, and cognitive embodiment. *Musicae Scientiae*. Advance online publication. https://doi.org/10.1177/10298649211062730

Friedell, D. (2020). Why can't I change Bruckner's Eighth Symphony? *Philosophical Studies, 177*(3), 805–824.

Friedwald, W. (1992). *Jazz Singing: America's Great Voices from Bessie Smith to Bebop and Beyond*. Da Capo Press.

Garcia, M. (1847). *Mémoire sur la voix humaine présenté à l'Académie des Sciences en 1840*. Duverger.

Gioia, T. (2012). *The Jazz Standards: A Guide to the Repertoire*. Oxford University Press.

Grime, K. (1983). *Jazz Voices*. Quartet Books.

Hamilton, A. (2007). *Lee Konitz: Conversations on the Improviser's Art*. University of Michigan Press.

Hargreaves, W. (2013). Profiling the jazz singer. *British Journal of Music Education, 30*(3), 383–396.

Hargreaves, W. (2014). *Jazz Improvisation: Differentiating Vocalists* [Doctoral dissertation, Griffith University]. https://research-repository.griffith.edu.au/handle/10072/366673.

Herbst, C. T. (2020). Registers—The snake pit of voice pedagogy part 1. *Journal of Singing, 77*(2), 175–190.

Herbst, C. T. (2021). Registers—The snake pit of voice pedagogy part 2. *Journal of Singing, 77*(3), 345–358.

Hytönen-Ng, E. (2013). *Experiencing "flow" in Jazz Performance*. Ashgate.

Jazz divas. (n.d.). Hal Leonard.

Kernfeld, B. (2006). *The Story of Fake Books: Bootlegging Songs to Musicians*. Scarecrow Press.

Koblick, R. (2013). *Jazz Fake-books as a Resource in the General Library. Collection Building, 32*(4), 139–144.

Kochis-Jennings, K. A., Finnegan, E. M., Hoffman, H. T., and Jaiswal, S. (2012). Laryngeal muscle activity and vocal fold adduction during chest, chestmix, headmix, and head registers in females. *Journal of Voice, 26*(2), 182–193.

LeBorgne, W. L. and Rosenberg, M. (2021). *The Vocal Athlete* (2nd ed.). Plural Publishing.

Levine, M. (1995). *The Jazz Theory Book*. Sher Music.

Lydon, M. (1994, April 10). Flying below the radar of copyrights. *The New York Times*. www.nytimes.com/1994/04/10/arts/pop-music-flying-below-the-radar-of-copyrights.html.

Madura, P. D. (1996). Relationships among vocal jazz improvisation achievement, jazz theory knowledge, imitative ability, musical experience, creativity, and gender. *Journal of Research in Music Education, 44*(3), 252–267.

Madura, P. D. (1999). *Getting Started with Vocal Improvisation*. MENC.

McCoy, S. (2012). *Your Voice: An Inside View*. Inside View Press.

McCoy, S. (2016). Singing jazz and voice science. In J. Shapiro, *So You Want to Sing Jazz? A Guide for Professionals* (pp. 17–34). Rowman & Littlefield.

McKinney, J. C. (2005). *The Diagnosis and Correction of Vocal Faults*. Waveland.

Monson, I. (1996). *Saying Something: Jazz Improvisation and Interaction*. University of Chicago Press.

Pellegrinelli, L. V. (2005). "The Song is Who? Locating Singers on the Jazz Scene." [Unpublished doctoral dissertation]. Harvard University.

Pellegrinelli, L. (2008). Separated at "birth": Singing and the history of jazz. In N. Rustin and S. Tucker (Eds.), *Big Ears: Listening for Gender in Jazz Studies* (pp. 31–47). Duke University Press.

Prouty, K. E. (2006). Orality, literacy, and mediating musical experience: Rethinking oral tradition in the learning of jazz improvisation. *Popular Music and Society, 29*(3), 317–334. https://doi.org/10.1080/03007760600670372.

Rawlins, S. (n.d.-a). *Singer's Book of Jazz Standards: Women's Edition*. Hal Leonard.

Rawlins, S. (n.d.-b). *Jazz Tracks for Singers: Women's Edition*. Hal Leonard.

Shapiro, J. (2016). *So You Want to Sing Jazz? A Guide for Professionals*. Rowman & Littlefield.

Sher, C. (Ed.) (1988). *The New Real Book: Jazz Classics, Choice Standards, Pop-fusion Classics*. Sher Music.

Spradling, D. R. (Ed.) (2007). *Jazz Singing: Developing Artistry and Authenticity*. Sound Music Publications.

Sundberg, J. (1987). *The Science of the Singing Voice*. Northern Illinois University Press.

The Real Vocal Book. High Voice. (n.d.). (2nd ed., Vol. 1). Hal Leonard.

The Real Book. (2004). (6th ed.). Hal Leonard.

Titze, I. (2000). *The Principles of Voice Production*. National Centre for Voice and Speech.

Tucker, S. (2001). Big ears: Listening for gender in jazz studies. *Current Musicology, 71–73* (Spring), 375–408.

Weir, M. (2005). *The Jazz Singer's Handbook. The Artistry and Mastery of Singing Jazz*. Alfred.

Yanow, S. (2008). *The Jazz Singers: The Ultimate Guide*. Backbeat Books.

26

INCLUSIVE JAZZ HISTORY PEDAGOGY

Sonya R. Lawson

Statement: Because I view gender as a sociocultural construct on a spectrum that can differ from the biology of a person, I use the terms woman/women and man/men in my chapter unless the author of a work I discuss uses other terms such as female/male or masculine/feminine. I am a cishet woman.

Introduction and Background

Although many jazz histories' treatment of the complexities in the development of jazz are sophisticated, many textbooks about jazz are not. They continue to be structured around genres and promote a jazz canon that is mostly populated by African American men. Because most students first learn about subjects through textbooks, this often leads them to categorize jazz as a cultural art form with a central prototype that is narrowly defined instead of wonderfully chaotic and vibrant. Essay anthologies, documentaries, general histories, biographies, and articles all enhance readers' and viewers' perception of the breadth and depth of jazz and engage with relationships among gender, race, sexuality, authenticity, and meaning.

One goal of pedagogy in music history is to lead students to a deeper and richer understanding of musical styles and forms. Another goal is to encourage students to think critically about the production and consumption of music both synchronically and diachronically. An obstacle that prevents the teacher from attaining this goal lies in the cognitive tendency of people to categorize cultural phenomena in highly restricted ways. Focusing on the role of gender in jazz discloses a basic problem with the categorization of jazz. This involves the question of "What is jazz?" The answer to this question depends on the type of categorization involved in answering it. The fact of the matter is that what counts as jazz has undergone significant changes in the last hundred years and has been a major topic of analysis and discussion by recent scholars of jazz, including David Ake (2002), Andrew Clark (2001), Scott DeVeaux (1999), Robert G. O'Meally (O'Meally et al., 2004), Charles Hiroshi Garrett (Ake et al., 2012), Eric Porter (2002), Nichole Rustin (Rustin and Tucker, 2008), Sherrie Tucker (2000), and Tony Whyton (2006).

All the above scholars in their work show that the debate about what is considered jazz has raged for decades, and people approach the issue from a variety of viewpoints about what the important aspects of jazz are. For some the most important aspect is improvisation, for others it is rhythm, and for others it is race and ethnicity. Until recently, gender as an important factor has been neglected. The fact of the matter is that in this musical tradition there has been too much change in what counts

DOI: 10.4324/9781003081876-29

as jazz and too much variety to satisfy the search for rigid criteria. Structuring jazz history around concepts other than genres and biography benefits students by exposing them to the enormous variety of music contained under the umbrella term "jazz"—a term that defies simple categorization.

Unfortunately, textbooks often present music as a set of these rigid criteria, perpetuating stereotypes about who performs jazz, who consumes jazz, and who decides what counts as jazz, all of which misinform students about the diversity in the jazz world. Women, particularly those who perform on any instrument other than piano, are often marginalized as not being as significant as male musicians. Musicians who do not play standard rhythm section instruments or trumpet, trombone, or saxophone are also often overlooked, as are male vocalists and vocal jazz groups. Given this, the question that is often asked by pedagogues is: How can we include these overlooked people without destroying the value of starting with a textbook? Instead of spreading stereotypes often contained in these texts, why not try supplementing a textbook with other materials that render the history of jazz more inclusive? By choosing to supplement textbooks with artifacts such as articles, essays, and documentaries that employ descriptive techniques, instructors can address many neglected musicians and open a dialogue about the music and performers who were considered mainstream and those who defied conventions. Furthermore, descriptive approaches can teach how cultural concepts such as "mainstream" and "marginal" are constructed. Instead of a simple presentation of famous people and famous music, a descriptive approach to jazz history can become a gateway to teaching students more sophisticated concepts about categorization, the canon, and how academics and others discuss music. This chapter is an overview of various categories of supplemental materials and a discussion of some specific sources that will help instructors on jazz history to be more inclusive in their pedagogy.

Edited Anthologies of Essays

Integrating edited anthologies of essays into classes is the easiest way of broadening students' perceptions of jazz, with the greatest "bang for the buck." By looking at the chronology of these publications, instructors and students can learn how they influenced each other and how the gaps regarding gender in the earlier anthologies are filled by later anthologies. Starting in the late 1990s and continuing into the present, numerous anthologies that explicitly grapple with the jazz canon have been published. Essays contained in *The Jazz Cadence of American Culture* (O'Meally, 1998), *Riffs and Choruses* (Clark, 2001), and *Uptown Conversation: The New Jazz Studies* (O'Meally et al., 2004) explore jazz from new angles and methodologies. The authors are from a wide variety of disciplines, most often viewing jazz through sociocultural and political lenses and not focusing primarily on the sounds. Anthropologists, archivists, cultural historians, journalists, film scholars, literary critics, musicologists, musicians, poets, and visual artists all write about jazz in these anthologies. This represents a departure from earlier writings that often focused on the sounds and on myths about players and disregarded broader cultural features. Writing in accessible language that does not presuppose sophisticated understanding of cultural concepts, these authors provide a firm foundation for understanding the various ways scholars investigate jazz.

Out of the 200 essays in these three anthologies, only three explicitly confront gender: Hazel V. Carby's "It Jus Be's Dat Way Sometime: The Sexual Politics of Women's Blues" (O'Meally, 1998, pp. 469–482), Farah Jasmine Griffin's "When Malindy Sings: A Meditation of Black Women's Vocality" (O'Meally et al., 2004, pp. 102–125), and Linda Dahl's (2004) "Preface, *Stormy Weather.*" However, just because these anthologies do not address gender does not mean they should be ignored. Characterized by interdisciplinary approaches to the sociocultural study of jazz, combined with a willingness to look beyond established narratives that center around male African American instrumentalists, they epitomize an excellent starting point in understanding the musicological philosophy now called New Jazz Studies.

Big Ears: Listening for Gender in Jazz Studies (Rustin and Tucker, 2008) and *Jazz/Not Jazz: The Music and Its Boundaries* (Ake et al., 2012) build upon the styles, theories, and methodologies from the previous anthologies by focusing specifically on gender intersecting with race, class, and space. *Big Ears* stands out as the first and only anthology specifically constructed around gender. As Rustin and Tucker write in the introduction,

> One common thread is that none of the articles finds it imperative to prove that gender is an important category of analysis, or that jazz is worthy of academic study, or to prove that women played jazz, or that men have gender.
>
> *(Rustin and Tucker, 2008, p. 9)*

Further, in this introduction they chronicle the history of jazz and gender studies, which is valuable to anyone who wants to know where, when, and how this field evolved.

The text itself is laid out in three sections. The book starts with historiography in "Rooting Gender in Jazz History," moves to examinations of gender and performance in "Improvising Gender: Embodiment and Performance," and ends with an investigation of jazz subjects outside of performance or composition in "Reimaging Jazz Representations." I have chosen three representative examples from the book to showcase the diversity of approaches to gender in the field of jazz studies.

Lara Pellegrinelli's (2008) "Separated at 'Birth': Singing and the History of Jazz" argues that singing has long been ignored within jazz scholarship as secondary to the study of instrumentalists and sets out to explain why that has happened. Her article is clear and persuasive and explores how biases toward women's bodies and toward African Americans devalue vocal jazz. As Pellegrinelli writes,

> Indeed, the marginalization of singers by scholars of women in jazz may very well occur because the singers' mainstream popularity complicates or perhaps even eclipses altogether the 'stories of devaluation and absence' with which such scholars have primarily been concerned.
>
> *(p. 31)*

Pellegrinelli's essay historicizes why this has happened by focusing on how early jazz history is centered around singing—the blues, spirituals, and work song—yet, as soon as men entered the picture, the focus shifted to instrumental music, because singing was women's work and therefore not as worthy of critical attention. This contributes to the erasure of women singers from early histories of jazz and continues today. Pellegrinelli ends her article with a call to action: "Contemporary historians must continue to challenge dominant discourse for the ways in which they embed gender and impact the representation of women" (p. 44).

Tracy McMullen's (2008) "Identity for Sale: Glenn Miller, Wynton Marsalis, and Cultural Replay in Music" investigates questions of masculinity in jazz by first discussing how a wildly popular reenactment of a 1940s Glen Miller radio broadcast by the mixed-race, mixed-gender Yale Concert Band broke the social mores during the time of Glen Miller. Miller did not allow women or people of color in his band. McMullen writes, "Indeed, the Miller reenactment presents a unique opportunity to undress the cross-dressing and racial-traversing that often attends such nostalgic performances of identity" (p. 130). She contrasts the Yale performance with how Wynton Marsalis, in his work with the Jazz at Lincoln Center Orchestra, highlights Black masculine hipness, the flip side of Miller's whiteness. Marsalis is portrayed as someone who espouses "Jazz as Democracy" but who constructs jazz as male and African American centered. In his way, he comes across as limited in his view of who should play jazz as Miller was. As a result, the Yale Miller reenactment is problematic for dissimilar audiences. The tone of this essay is seriocomic, employing ideas of nostalgia, homogeneity, and democracy to challenge readers to grapple with complex ideas about representation and authenticity.

João H. Costa Vargas's (2008) "Exclusion, Openness, and Utopia in Black Male Performance at the World Stage Jazz Jam Sessions," combines ethnography with political studies. Based on 26 months of ethnography in and around the jam sessions at the World Stage in South Los Angeles's Leimert Park neighborhood, Costa Vargas's essay investigates the gendered space of these sessions. His focus is on community spaces and how local discourses shape the views of those spaces. Costa Vargas makes the case that the democratic environment at the World Stage is a space primarily reserved for African American men, and therefore questions of representation within a larger community need to be asked. Costa Vargas bluntly writes, "Intolerance toward race, gender, class, and age differences as well as marked suspicion toward those who lived in areas considered degraded were some of the most readily available traits of Leimert's social life" (p. 342). He ends his essay on a hopeful note, stating that the jam sessions, even with all their faults, are passionate calls for social justice and change that refuse to accept easy answers.

These three articles grapple with the intersection of gender, the body, and authenticity, opening up opportunities for engaging students in discussions about the politics of embodiment. Pellegrinelli focuses on how biases against women's bodies leads to devaluing vocal jazz as authentic jazz as instrumental jazz, McMullen focuses on how men's bodies are seen as the most authentic way of performing big band jazz, and Vargas describes how the intersection of race, gender and community spaces problematizes accurate representation within a diverse community.

Like *Big Ears* before it, the anthology *Jazz/Not Jazz: The Music and Its Boundaries* (Ake et al., 2012) interrogates music and musicians that lie outside the canon, populating the periphery of what has traditionally been counted as jazz. As the authors write, "the book takes as its basic premise that genre designations play a fundamental role in shaping how we teach, learn, create, access, and assess music" (p. 3).

> The belief that genre powerfully influences how audiences and critics consume music and talk about it drives each of the essays in the book, as the authors grapple with "what is at stake when people construct, maintain, cross, and challenge the boundaries designed to separate one genre from another—in this case, jazz from, well, everything else."
>
> *(Ake et al., 2012, p. 3)*

Like *Big Ears*, the book is organized into three sections. Part 1 considers categorization, Part 2 ponders practices, and Part 3 spotlights jazz education. I have chosen four examples from this book to show how these authors build upon the sophisticated theorizing about gender in jazz established by *Big Ears*.

John Howland's (2012) "Jazz with Strings: Between Jazz and the Great American Songbook" is the most musicological chapter in the book, complete with helpful music notation and formal outlines. He discusses the marginalization of popular jazz-with-strings albums of the 1940s and 1950s by examining them through a lens of class politics. In most jazz histories, these string-infused albums (if mentioned at all) are often classified pejoratively as "middlebrow" music that was solely commercial and not jazz at all. This is problematic for many reasons. As Howland writes, "we must recognize that jazz emerged as a *marketing* category distinct from popular music only *after* jazz was no longer a popular music for the dancing and youth markets of the swing era" (p. 141).

Jessica Bissett Perea's (2012) "Voices from the Jazz Wilderness: Locating Pacific Northwest Vocal Ensembles within Jazz Education," tackles not only the disparities between vocal and instrumental jazz educators but the odd place vocal jazz occupies in the history of jazz—simultaneously revered by many and vilified by others. Bissett Perea charts the emergence of vocal jazz ensembles and the challenges they have presented to jazz educators in terms of balancing jazz style with choral technique. These are often tangled up in gendered ideas of who should be making what types of jazz. She writes,

> Although vocal jazz ensembles and jazz choir culture have made enormous strides over the past four decades, their accomplishments continue to be marginalized in favor of

conforming to the aims of dominant jazz narratives and discourse: 'real jazz' is the sole province of (male) instrumentalists, and as a mixed gender enterprise, 'vocal jazz' remains marginal to jazz history.

(p. 233)

Bissett Perea is uniquely qualified to write about this, drawing on her experiences as a vocal jazz performer, director, and researcher.

David Ake's (2012) "Crossing the Street: Rethinking Jazz Education" contends that the importance of college programs in the sustaining and development of jazz has been considerably diminished in histories of jazz, partially because of four myths that undermine the role of educators in the development of the music. This mythology weakens the role of women, educators, suburban and rural geography, and market forces in histories of jazz, because they do not fit the yearned-for narrative of the self-taught, hip, urban (and urbane) man of jazz. Ake skillfully describes and then skewers these myths, ending his essay with a clarion call to be hopeful and aware of the myriad ways performers, students, and listeners learn jazz.

Jazz/Not Jazz closes with an inspiring essay by Sherrie Tucker (2012), "Deconstructing the Jazz Tradition: The 'Subjectless Subject' of New Jazz Studies." This article's purpose is twofold. On the one hand, Tucker articulates the impact and influence of DeVeaux's (1991) seminal "Constructing the Jazz Tradition: Jazz Historiography" on the emerging field of gender and jazz studies in the 1990s. On the other hand, she asks, what kinds of narratives do scholars and educators want to tell about the New Jazz Studies? One of the compelling attributes of Tucker's article is the way she peppers it with questions for readers to ask themselves—which can easily translate into classroom questions. For example, she asks,

Is jazz a genre, a culture, a discourse? Without the jazz tradition as stable ground, what do we teach in jazz studies classes? If there is no stable subject or object of study, is jazz studies in crisis, or is it developing exciting, new directions—theories and methods—as is sometimes argued about other fields such as women's studies, black studies, and American studies?

(Tucker, 2012, p. 269)

The questions that Tucker articulates encompass the thread that runs through all the anthologies and, by looking at the history of the publications, we can see how these articles interact and influence each other. Taken together, the essays in these anthologies make it easier for teachers to show their students a variety of ways of thinking musicologically instead of simply presenting jazz as a linear evolution of styles that were propelled by great soloists who were most often African American men. Each of these anthologies embraces the New Jazz Studies; interrogating the position of author, audience, performer, and consumer in sophisticated and highly focused ways. Teachers can choose the perspectives that they are most comfortable exploring, while questioning the agendas of the textbooks they often must use in the classroom. The narrow focus of the essays in these anthologies is broadened out to encompass far-ranging socio-political ideas in the general histories that will be discussed next.

General Histories

The four general histories I have chosen all take as their starting point the uneasy relationship between popular culture and jazz. Musicians, cultural critics, and historians tend to downplay this relationship for various reasons, including the myth of authenticity, the desire to have jazz be taken seriously as an art form, and the discomfort with juxtaposing popular music and jazz because of the common pejorative view of commercial music.

Sherrie Tucker's (2000) *Swing Shift: "All-Girl" Bands of the 1940s* is an engaging book that chronicles the careers of all-girl swing-era bands such as the International Sweethearts of Rhythm, the Darlings of Rhythm, the Prairie View Co-Eds, Sharon Rogers All-Girl Band, and Phil Spitalny's Hours of Charm. Based on oral interviews, trade periodicals, Black newspapers, and her own analysis of what few films and recordings exist, Tucker situates her research within the larger context of American views of race and gender. As she says in the introduction,

> Finally, I make interventions whenever possible that work toward explicitly gendering jazz and swing history. In other words, recognizing that talking in a non-gendered, universal way, as many dominant swing narratives claim to do, is actually to talk about men's history. To press women into these so-called general frames will reliably render them inauthentic. Instead, I will strive toward presenting a history that looks at ways in which women and men were both present and that recognizes swing culture as a field on which specific gender constructions were affirmed, contested, performed, and consumed.
>
> *(Tucker, 2000, p. 29)*

Published in 2000, Tucker's book was groundbreaking. Her skillful use of primary sources, interviews, and reclamation history, combined with lenses from women's studies and American studies, provided a model for future scholars to follow.

David Ake's (2002) *Jazz Cultures* is a noteworthy contribution to the growing body of New Jazz Studies. He addresses topics of current interest to jazz scholars, including race, class, and gender in jazz culture; the embodiment of music; modernism and jazz education; historiography; and the construction of tradition. Ake's argument is constructed around six case studies. As he writes in the introduction,

> rather than a broad-based survey of stylistic innovation, each of the book's chapters concentrates on a specific moment or institution, focusing on the historical cultural, technological, and musical phenomena that gave rise to different ways of playing and understanding jazz.
>
> *(Ake, 2002, p. 3)*

These phenomena include the omission of Louis Jordan from jazz history; gender analysis of Ornette Coleman's controversial New York debut; and the problems with reifying John Coltrane's Giant Steps in college jazz education programs. Ake's book raises thought-provoking questions that are still being answered today.

Kristin McGee's (2011) *Some Liked It Hot: Jazz Women in Film and Television, 1928–1959* borrows its title from the 1959 film *Some Like It Hot*, which offers contextualization for the growing presence of women in audiovisual media from the 1920s to the 1950s. McGee specifically addresses racial issues, focusing on the commonalities and differences between White and Black women in film and television. For example, in the first chapter, McGee contrasts swing-era bands The Ingénues (a White band) and the Harlem Playgirls (a Black band):

> By examining the differing performance contexts of the Ingenues and the Harlem Playgirls, I reveal that the theatrical and mass-mediated contexts, in which the most commercial and successful of the white all-girl bands honed their professional skills, was as responsible for their eventual exclusion from the jazz canon as it was for their popular acceptance and durability during these two decades.
>
> *(p. 35)*

By drawing upon the recent work of feminist performance scholars and cultural jazz scholars in her analyses of film and television, McGee prompts her readers to think about the masculinist orientation of the jazz canon.

Like Ake's *Jazz Cultures*, Tony Whyton's (2013) *Jazz Icons* is organized around case studies firmly grounded in New Jazz Studies. By means of these case studies, he examines the influence of jazz icons through different forms of historical artifacts, including recordings, language, image, and myth. Whyton argues that jazz icons not only provide musicians and audiences with figureheads and mythology to venerate but also represent values and attitudes that shape the view of the music itself. Referring to the opening "Jazzman" scene of the 2004 movie *Collateral*, Whyton writes,

> I suggest that jazz icons occupy a complex place within contemporary culture that is evidenced through film and media representations such as this, and I have therefore adopted a multifaceted approach to understanding icons. When referring to icons, I use the word with all of its dominant definitions in mind and suggest that it is this conflation of meanings that makes jazz discourse particularly interesting and unique. Whereas conventional discussions of iconic jazz stars revolve around visual imagery, my work seeks to develop the study of icons to include the ways in which they have become symbols for the jazz life and reflect the values of the neo-traditionalist mainstream.
>
> *(p. 6)*

Among the ideas Whyton confronts in these case studies are jazz education, the essentialist myth of Duke Ellington, and the controversy of Kenny G performing cover versions of Louis Armstrong.

Although these general histories might seem dissimilar, all are steeped in the ideas of the New Jazz Studies. Tucker and McGee focus on women in their histories, drawing upon primary sources and explicitly gendering their narratives to reclaim authenticity for these women. Their writing serves as a potent antidote to the narratives employed in textbooks that present men's histories as authentic. Ake and Whyton write case studies that focus on men, but that investigate the intersections of culture, commercialism, and masculinity through the lens of gender discourse. All four of these authors employ innovative media representations of their subjects, educating students in new ways of framing jazz musicians instead of simply duplicating old tropes.

One of the oldest tropes found in jazz histories is the biography of the great man, and in this age of influencers and celebrities many students already are primed to want to know about the lives of the people in their textbooks. The next section will help teachers match the type of biography with their students' interests.

Biographies

Biographies are, at their simplest, the story of a person's life. However, there are diverse ways to structure biographies, each with its own conventions that influence the reader's perception. According to Ed Sharrow (2020), biographies fall into four categories: *historical fiction, academic, fictionalized academic,* and *prophetic*. Typically, easily accessible biographies of female jazz musicians are historical fiction, academic, or fictionalized academic biographies, whereas the biographies of male jazz musicians often fall under the fictionalized academic or prophetic biography type. Why such variance? Perhaps, as evidenced by the New Jazz studies proponents, it is because until recently, women jazz musicians were not considered worthwhile spending time researching.

In this section I focus on female musicians whose biographies are rarely included in academic texts because, as shown in the preceding sections, women have always been a part of jazz, they just haven't always been written about. Including a variety of biographies of women jazz musicians as supplements to a class enhances students understanding not only of the women under consideration, but the sociocultural context of their lives. Additionally, young women can see their own struggles and triumphs mirrored in these stories. Representation matters.

Historical fiction is generally a creative account of a person's life that tells a good story and often is based around a sociocultural idea. These are often written when there is a dearth of facts, or the person is somewhat shrouded in mystery, and they often use interviews with others. Examples of historical fiction are biographies of Billy Tipton (Middlebrook, 1998), Lil Harden Armstrong (Dickerson, 2002), Valaida Snow (Allen, 2005), and Peggy Gilbert (Pool et al., 2008).

Academic biography relies greatly on documented facts and noted accomplishments and is often heavily footnoted. Generally, these biographies are more about the minutiae of someone's life and less concerned with lessons learned or sociocultural ideas. Examples of this type are biographies of Betty Carter (Bauer, 2003), Marian McPartland (de Barros, 2012), Mary Lou Williams (Dahl, 2001), Dinah Washington (Cohodas, 2004), and Ella Fitzgerald (Nicholson, 1995).

Fictionalized academic biography contains the best elements of the previous two categories—a strong, entertaining story combined with factual accuracy and quotes from people who knew the subject. Often these biographies explore sociocultural aspects of the subject's time. These are analogous to the "biopic" film genre, which requires heavy dramatization to appeal to an audience. Examples of this type of biography are works on the lives of Mary Lou Williams (Kernodle, 2004), Hazel Scott (Chilton, 2010), Valaida Snow (Miller, 2007), and Billie Holiday (Clarke, 2002). Farah Jasmine Griffin's (2001) *Harlem Nocturne: Women Artists and Progressive Politics During World War II* is a triple biography of novelist Pearl Primus, choreographer and dancer Ann Petry, and jazz pianist Mary Lou Williams. Set against the backdrop of the struggle for social justice during World War Two, the intertwining of their lives in Harlem is enthralling.

Prophetic biography combines the academic approach of considering facts with a spiritual goal or ideal theme. Often this theme is discovered by the author of the biography, and carefully chosen facts are used to promote the thesis and uplift and inspire the reader. Examples of this are biographies of Alice Coltrane (Berkman, 2010) and Billie Holiday (Griffin, 2001).

Choosing selected parts of these biographies to compare writing styles, the construction of identity, the intersection of race and class, and the sociocultural context helps students understand that there is more than one way to tell the story of someone's life, and that the choices an author makes affect their audience's perception of that person. And, if a student really wants to do a deep dive or meta-analysis into how biographies are constructed, they can choose a biography about a jazzwoman and contrast it with a biography about a jazzman.

Compilations of Interviews

Jazzwomen: Conversations with Twenty-One Musicians (*Enstice and Stockhouse, 2004*)

In this compilation, written in 2004, Wayne Enstice and Janis Stockhouse interview women jazz musicians about their basic biography and gently ask these women to reflect on the culture in which they live and work. These thought-provoking interviews are handled so skillfully that it feels as if the reader is sitting in on a wonderful conversation between friends. Each interview is preceded by a short introduction to the artist and followed by a brief discography. This simple structural device is potent, giving the reader immediate context about the musician and then enabling them to find (and hopefully purchase) recordings, without having to bother flipping to endnotes. *Jazzwomen's* interviewees address everything from career development and musical influences to questions of racism and sexism. Through this multiplicity of voices, readers learn how not only gender but also race has marginalized many jazz women. Established musicians such as Sheila Jordan, Clora Bryant, Shirley Horn, and Abbey Lincoln are side by side with younger musicians including Regina Carter, Ingrid Jensen, Diana Krall, Virginia Mayhew, and Maria Schneider.

Freedom of Expression: Interviews with Women in Jazz (*Becker, 2015*)

I have included this book because the interviewees are mostly musicians currently working in the twenty-first century who are lesser known. That is the strength of the book. The weakness is that author Becker does not have a good grasp of the history of women in jazz as presented in the introduction, and this lack of understanding permeates the interviews. He prefaces the book by writing,

> So while some men, and more than a few women believe a book about women in jazz is unnecessary, from my (male) perspective, I do not believe the book is going to do any musician a disservice, not from where I sit, and not at this point in history.
>
> *(Becker, 2015, p. 25)*

Becker prompts his subjects to discuss the present challenges of being a working musician in an ever-changing music business, choosing to avoid any questions about struggles they have encountered because of race, gender, or sexuality. Usefully, many of the women comment on the current state of the recording industry and talk about how they market and finance their music through avenues of crowdfunding, licensing, and self-released albums. Thirty-seven women are interviewed, including well-known musicians Dee Dee Bridgewater, Terri Lyne Carrington, Eliane Elias, Midi Abair, and Jane Ira Bloom. Lesser-known musicians include violinist Mazz Swift, trumpeter Ellen Seeling, cellist Nioka Workman, bassist Iris Ornig, and harpist Brandee Younger.

Journals of Interest

To find current articles of the type collected in the abovementioned anthologies, the *Journal of Music History Pedagogy, Jazz Research Journal, Jazz and Culture,* and *Jazz Perspectives* are valuable resources. Collectively these journals publish authors who write from a variety of perspectives that come under the heading New Jazz Studies. They include early-, mid-, and late-career perspectives. The focus and lens of each journal is different, so it is easy to find content that guides instructors to a more inclusive pedagogy.

The *Journal of Music History Pedagogy* (JMHP) is a biannual, peer-reviewed, open-access online journal committed to the publication of original articles and reviews connected to teaching music history at all levels and disciplines. In addition to articles devoted to innovative pedagogy, this journal has special issues devoted to topics of diversity and inclusivity. These have included the following:

- **Decolonization:** challenging issues of whiteness and Euro-American-centered perspectives.
- **Information Literacy and the Music History Classroom:** addressing how to approach issues of authority, expertise, and the limits and bias of the Western European canon.
- **Ecomusicology:** positioning notions of natural sound in relation to other historically constructed categories such as race, gender, sexuality, and national origin.

Examples of recent articles include Heli Reimann's (2012) "Jazz Education and the Jazz Periphery: An Example from Estonia," and Nathan Bakkum's (2015) "A Concentric Model for Jazz History." The JMHP is a publication of the Pedagogy Study Group of the American Musicological Society.

Jazz Research Journal is a biannual, peer-reviewed journal that explores a range of cultural and critical views on jazz, focusing on many disciplines including musicology, cultural studies, film studies, sociology, and cultural studies. According to their website, "the editors particularly welcome articles that challenge traditional approaches to jazz and encourage writings that engage with jazz as a discursive practice" (*Jazz Research Journal*, n.d.). Examples of recent articles include Myrtille Picaud's (2016) " 'We Try to Have the Best': How Nationality, Race and Gender Structure Artists' Circulations in the Paris Jazz Scene" and Louise Denson's (2014) "Perspectives on the Melbourne International Women's Jazz Festival." *Jazz Research Journal* is an Equinox Publication based in the United Kingdom, associated with Leeds University.

Jazz and Culture is a biannual publication devoted to publishing cutting-edge research on jazz from multiple perspectives. The homepage for the journal explicitly states, "Drawing upon recent trends in music scholarship, we (the editors) further seek to interrogate a range of issues connecting music, race, class, gender, and other realms of social practice" (Jazz and Culture, n.d.). The articles vary, including oral histories, typical research articles, poetry, sound–text artworks, and reviews. A sampling of recent articles includes Kimberly Hannon Teal's (2019) "Mary Lou Williams as Apology: Jazz, History, and Institutional Sexism in the Twenty-First Century," Eric Lewis's (2018) "This Ain't a Hate Thing: Jeanne Lee and the Subversion of the Jazz Standard," and Ofer Gazit's (2020) "Passing Tones: Shifting National, Social, and Musical Borders in Jazz-Age Harlem." *Jazz and Culture* is a collaboration between the University of Pittsburgh's Jazz Studies Program and the University of Illinois Press.

Jazz Perspectives is an international, peer-reviewed triennial publication whose focus is on the cultural and musical study of jazz from an international perspective. On their website they state, "As a refereed academic journal with an international editorial board of renowned jazz scholars, *Jazz Perspectives* provides a broad forum for promoting cross-disciplinary scholarly dialogue across the academic jazz community" (*Jazz Perspectives*, n.d.). They cover recent literature, new recordings, and media, as well as traditional jazz. Recent articles include Sarah Caissie Provost's (2017) "Bringing Something New: Female Jazz Instrumentalists' Use of Imitation and Masculinity," Kevin Fellezs's (2010) "*Deracinated Flower:* Toshiko Akiyoshi's 'Trace in Jazz History,'" and Jennifer Griffith's (2010) "Mingus in the Act: Confronting the Legacies of Vaudeville and Minstrelsy." *Jazz Perspectives* is a Taylor & Francis (Routledge) publication, based in the United Kingdom.

As seen above, there finally exists a wide variety of journals that focus on jazz studies from multiple perspectives and with degrees of nuance. People just discovering jazz studies or who have been steeped in it for years will find articles to tantalize and rouse if they want to become more inclusive in their pedagogy.

Documentary Films

Film is one of the most visceral and potent tools for building an inclusive pedagogy. Four documentaries that portray various aspects of jazz through a women-centered lens are *In Her Hands*, *Girls in the Band*, *Lady Be Good*, and *International Sweethearts of Rhythm*. Each of these films illuminates an inspiring story that not only uncovers and reclaims the history of women in jazz but seeks to persuade viewers that women are an ineffable part of jazz performance and history. The filmmakers compellingly combine photo montages, interviews with jazz musicians, interviews with audience members, interviews with cultural critics, video of sociocultural events, and video of performances.

To expose audiences to numerous women often left out of jazz history textbooks, I have chosen to highlight three documentaries that focus on groups of women, as well as a recent one on Mary Lou Williams. I start with the most recent because it highlights mid-career women who are generally ignored, as well as young women currently studying jazz. This is a good way to engage students in inclusive pedagogy because these are musicians they potentially can see perform live! I then travel backwards, ending with a Mary Lou Williams film because she is one of the only women depicted in all the jazz textbooks. It is important to note that all these documentaries confront the intersection of race and gender head on, whether that be by recounting the trials and tribulations of travelling and performing during the Jim Crow Laws days or by reporting how performers could not get recording contracts or festival gigs because they were "too dark" or "too ethnic" looking.

The 2019 documentary *In Her Hands*, by Kay D. Ray (2020) , revolves around the second tour of Monika Herzig's all-women jazz band Sheroes and the obstacles they faced as women jazz instrumentalists. The film interspersed concert footage and filmed school clinics with interviews of women musicians from around the United States. One area that sets this documentary apart from the previous ones mentioned is its emphasis on education, including role models and mentors, and on opportunities for young girls and women to play jazz. Interviews with middle schoolers, high schoolers, and young women in their 20s are at the heart of the film. These clips are interspersed with interviews with women in their 40s and older who discuss the lack of role models and educational opportunities they had. This leads into a moving section about the fight for blind auditions at Jazz at Lincoln Center—as orchestras have been doing since the 1970s—in order to have a more equitable band, and the various ways organizations like Jazz Girls Day, New Orleans Center for Creative Arts, Seattle Women's Jazz Orchestra Middle School girls' jazz workshops, and Women's Jazz and Blues Camp in Berkeley provide stellar opportunities for young women to experience and experiment with jazz. Anat Cohen, Grace Kelly, Ingrid Jensen, Naomi Moon Seigel, the Seattle Women's Jazz Orchestra, Marge Rosen, the Montclair Women's Big Band, Ellen Seeling, Jean Fineberg, the DIVA Jazz Orchestra, and Sherrie Maricle are featured.

The 2013 documentary *Girls in the Band* (Chaikin, 2013) frames its storytelling by referencing how few women were present in the historical photo *A Great Day in Harlem* (Kane, 2021), which brought together a pantheon of legendary jazz musicians. The film closes with a 2008 re-creation featuring several generations of women jazz musicians. Unlike *In Her Hands*, this documentary focuses on women jazz instrumentalists of the 1930s and 1940s, contrasted with women who have been performing since the 1970s. Roz Cron, Clora Bryant, Peggy Gilbert, Billie Rogers, Carline Ray, Marian McPartland, and others discuss the peak of their careers playing mainly in all-female groups during the jazz and swing golden age and how many of those opportunities disappeared in the 1950s and 1960s. This is contrasted with interviews and clips of women who came of age in the 1970s during the second wave of feminism and women active today, including Geri Allen, Terry Lyne Carrington, Ingrid Jensen, Tammy Kernodle, Sherrie Maricle, Patrice Rushen, Esperanza Spalding, and Hiromi Uehara.

International Sweethearts of Rhythm: America's Hottest All Girl Band (Schiller et al., 2007) is a reissue of three separate documentaries created by Greta Schiller and Andrea Weiss in the 1980s: *International Sweethearts of Rhythm* (1986), *Tiny and Ruby: Hell Divin' Women* (1987), and *Maxine Sullivan: Love to Be in Love* (1988). Presented as a trilogy concerning women in jazz who were active in the 1940s, these were some of the first documentaries to reveal the implications of race, gender, and sexuality issues for this community of musicians. *International Sweethearts of Rhythm* chronicles the career of the band of the same name from its formation at the Piney Country Life School in Mississippi in the late 1930s through its evolution into a highly popular professional band. The film includes historical footage of women, clips of the band from some of their appearances in feature films, and interviews from the late 1980s with surviving band members. The focus of the film is how difficult it was to be taken seriously as female instrumentalists during the swing era, how racial prejudices shaped band members' lives, and how they coped with these ordeals. One of the most moving parts of the film is when Anna Mae Winburn, Tiny Davis, Rosalind "Roz" Cron, Helen Jones, Helen Saine, and Evelyn McGee speak about all the things they had to do to hide that they were a mixed-race band. This included perming hair, putting on blackface, living on a bus because they could not chance a hotel, and running away from the police.

Tiny and Ruby covers the 42-year friendship and intimate relationship of two Sweethearts alumnae, Tiny Davis and Ruby Lucas. This film is less of a historical telling than *Sweethearts* and more of a biographical homage to Davis, who, billed as the Female Louis Armstrong, was the star performer of the Sweethearts band. The film takes place mostly within their home, interspersed with photos and video clips. This short film is moving because it shows women in their retirement years who still have a full, musical life. Too often representations stop focusing on women once they hit middle age and lose track of what they accomplish in their later years.

Maxine Sullivan: Love to Be in Love is the anomaly in this trilogy because Sullivan has no connection to the Sweethearts of Rhythm. Sullivan was a famous crooner in the 1930s, known for swinging traditional songs such as "Loch Lomond." This documentary focuses on the benefits of being a singer during the swing era (there is much more film footage of her than of female instrumentalists of the time) contrasted with the problems of being a woman managed and controlled by men.

The 2018 film *Mary Lou Williams: The Lady Who Swings the Band* (Bash, 2018) is the most recent of several documentaries that spotlight Mary Lou Williams, the most scrutinized woman jazz musician found in the textbooks. Carol Bash's documentary reflects the celebrity and artistry of Williams in its superb use of archival photos, recordings, and interviews to reframe a biography that many people already know the broad outlines of. Actress Alfre Woodard provides the voice of Mary Lou Williams, reading from her letters and memoirs—providing a more visceral reaction to words full of emotion than a photograph of her writing does. The result is a film that serves as an introduction to an extraordinary woman and also connects to the ongoing discussion of the struggles faced by women jazz musicians present in the abovementioned documentaries. This film also foregrounds commentary from Black women historians and biographers, still a rarity in many jazz documentaries.

Corresponding to the general histories by Tucker and McGee, and the biographies from the previous section, these documentaries skillfully employ archival footage, compelling narrative voiceovers, and interviews to engage and delight the viewers, raising questions about representation and gaze while educating their audience about the lives and music of jazzwomen.

Conclusion

The recent Oscar Award winning Pixar movie *Soul* (Docter, 2020) offers a captivating image—a woman-led jazz band at the center of the film. Disney's Pixar movies epitomize popular culture, and merely having a female saxophonist as a pivotal character is cause for celebration. Protagonist Joe Gardner desperately wants to be a professional jazz pianist instead of a middle school band director. His big chance comes when he auditions for a gig with saxophonist Dorothea Williams and her band at the world-famous Half Note Jazz Club. What happens after the audition is the basis for the whole rest of the movie. I don't want to spoil it—so find it and go watch it!

Astonishingly, Dorothea is not the only woman in the band. Her group consists of female bass player Miho and Curley, a male drummer. Moreover, it is not just the animation that shows women— the actual musicians on the soundtrack are women too: saxophonist Tia Fuller and bassist Linda May Han Oh. In addition, Teri Lyne Carrington was one of several music consultants. Such a simple thing as this animated representation normalizes women as compelling jazz musicians. Therefore, it behooves educators to have material ready to answer questions about women jazz musicians. Why is this important? Perhaps this movie is the first time a young person has encountered jazz, and they want to know more. What are you going to give this person to read or to watch? Textbooks are cumbersome, and difficult to quickly change to reflect current developments in research. However, they do serve the purpose of introducing students to a subject they may know very little about, albeit in a constrained way. Employing a range of sources discussed in this chapter—such as essays, articles, films, and interviews to supplement and challenge—a textbook teaches students the benefits (and the pitfalls) of relying on a monolithic source, engaging them in inclusive pedagogy that has space for musicians of all genders.

References

Jazz Research Journal. (n.d.). Retrieved February 14, 2021, from https://journal.equinoxpub.com/JAZZ/about.

Ake, D. (2002). *Jazz Cultures.* University of California Press. www.jstor.org/stable/10.1525/j.ctt1ppshp.

Ake, D. (2012). Crossing the street: Rethinking jazz education. In D. Ake, C. H. Garrett, and D. Goldmark (Eds.), Jazz/not Jazz (pp. 237–263). University of California Press.

Ake, D., Garrett, C. H., and Goldmark, D. I. (2012). *Jazz/Not Jazz: The Music and Its Boundaries.* University of California Press. https://muse.jhu.edu/book/25946.

Allen, C. (2005). *Valaida.* Little, Brown.

Barros, P. de. (2012). *Shall We Play That One Together?: The Life and Art of Jazz Piano Legend Marian McPartland* (1st edition). St. Martin's Press.

Bash, C., Mary Lou Williams Project (Firm), and Kanopy (Firm). (2018). *Mary Lou Williams: The Lady Who Swings the Band*. http://[institution]. kanopy.com/node/2018407.

Bauer, W. R. (2003). *Open the Door: The Life and Music of Betty Carter* (Illustrated edition). University of Michigan Regional.

Becker, C. (2015). *Freedom of Expression: Interviews with Women in Jazz* (First Edition). Beckeresque Press.

Berkman, F. J. (2010). *Monument Eternal: The Music of Alice Coltrane*. Wesleyan University Press.

Chaikin, J. (2013, May 10). *The Girls in the Band* [Documentary, Biography, History, Music]. Artist Tribe, One Step Productions.

Chilton, K. (2010). *Hazel Scott: The Pioneering Journey of a Jazz Pianist, from Café Society to Hollywood to HUAC*. University of Michigan Press.

Clark, A. (2001). *Riffs and Choruses: A New Jazz Anthology*. Continuum.

Clarke, D. (2002). *Billie Holiday: Wishing on The Moon* (First Thus edition). Da Capo Press.

Cohodas, N. (2004). *Queen: The Life and Music of Dinah Washington* (1st Edition). Pantheon.

Costa Vargas, J.H. (2008). Exclusion, openness, and utopia in Black male performance at the World Stage Jazz Jam Sessions. In N.T. Rustin and S. Tucker (Eds.), *Big Ears* (pp. 320–347). Duke University Press.

Dahl, L. (2001). *Morning Glory: A Biography of Mary Lou Williams*. University of California Press.

DeVeaux, S. (1991). Constructing the jazz tradition: Jazz historiography. Black American Literature Forum, 25(3), 525–560. https://doi.org/10.2307/3041812

DeVeaux, S. (1999). *The Birth of Bebop: A Social and Musical History*. University of California Press.

Dickerson, J. L. (2002). *Just for a Thrill: Lil Hardin Armstrong, First Lady of Jazz*. Cooper Square Press.

Docter, P. (2020). *Soul*. Walt Disney Pictures, Pixar Animation Studios.

Enstice, W., and Stockhouse, J. (2004). *Jazzwomen: Conversations with Twenty-one Musicians*. Indiana University Press.

Griffin, F. J. (2001). *If you Can't be Free, be a Mystery*. Free Press.

Howland, J. (2012). Jazz with strings: Between jazz and the Great American Songbook. In D. Ake, C. H. Garrett, and D. Goldmark (Eds.), *Jazz/Not Jazz* (pp. 111–147). University of California Press.

Kane, A. (2021). A Great Day in Harlem *(photograph)*. https://en.wikipedia.org/w/index.php?title=A_Great_Day_in_Harlem_(photograph)&oldid=1004774944.

Kernodle, T. L. (2004). *Soul on Soul: The Life and Music of Mary Lou Williams*. UPNE.

McGee, K. A. (2011). *Some Liked It Hot: Jazz Women in Film and Television, 1928–1959*. Wesleyan University Press.

McMullen, T. (2008). Identity for sale: Glenn Miller, Wynton Marsalis, and Cultural Replay in Music. In N. T. Rustin and S. Tucker (Eds.), *Big Ears* (pp. 129–154). Duke University Press.

Middlebrook, D. W. (1998). *Suits Me: The Double Life of Billy Tipton*. Houghton Mifflin Harcourt.

Miller, M. (2007). *High Hat, Trumpet, and Rhythm: The Life and Music of Valaida Snow*. Mercury Press.

Nicholson, S. (1995). *Ella Fitzgerald: A Biography of The First Lady of Jazz* (Reprint edition). Da Capo Press.

O'Meally, R. G. (Ed.). (1998). *The Jazz Cadence of American Culture* (p. 576 pps). Columbia University Press.

O'Meally, R. G., Edwards, B. H., and Griffin, F. J. (Eds.). (2004). *Uptown Conversation: The New Jazz Studies* (p. 544 Pages). Columbia University Press.

Pellegrinelli, L. (2008). Separated at "Birth": Singing and the history of jazz. In N. T. Rustin and S. Tucker (Eds.), *Big Ears* (pp. 31–47). Duke University Press. https://doi.org/10.2307/j.ctv1134ftp.5.

Perea, J. B. (2012). Voices from the Jazz Wilderness: Locating Pacific Northwest Vocal Ensembles within Jazz Education. In D. Ake, C. H. Garrett, and D. Goldmark (Eds.), *Jazz/Not Jazz* (1st ed., pp. 219–236). University of California Press; JSTOR. www.jstor.org.scroll.lib.westfield.ma.edu/stable/10.1525/j.ctt1pnrks.15

Pool, J. G., Tomlin, L., and Wagner, J. (2008). *Peggy Gilbert and Her All-Girl Band* (Illustrated edition). Scarecrow Press.

Porter, E. (2002). *What Is This Thing Called Jazz?: African American Musicians as Artists, Critics, and Activists*. University of California Press.

Ray, K. D. (2020). *In Her Hands—A Kay D Ray Film*. Retrieved February 5, 2021, from http://kaydray.com/InHerHands/index.html.

Reimann, H. (2012). Jazz education and the jazz periphery: An example from Estonia. *Journal of Music History Pedagogy*, 3(2), 183–185.

Rustin, N. T., and Tucker, S. (2008). *Big Ears: Listening for Gender in Jazz Studies*. Duke University Press.

Schiller, G., Weiss, A., Reitz, R., Reita, R., Gordon, D., Sullivan, M., Davis, T., Lucas, R., Clarke, C., International Sweethearts of Rhythm, Jezebel Productions, Rosetta Records (Firm), and Agat Films (Firm). (2007). *International Sweethearts of Rhythm: America's Hottest All girl Band*.

Sharrow, E. (2020, February 4). *Know the Four Types of Biographies*. Medium. https://medium.com/@edsharrow1129/know-the-four-types-of-biographies-57c0053b1939.

Tucker, S. (2000). *Swing Shift: "All-Girl" Bands of the 1940s*. Duke University Press.

Tucker, S. (2012). Deconstructing the jazz tradition: The "subjectless subject" of new jazz studies. In D. Ake, C. H. Garrett, and D. Goldmark (Eds.), Jazz/not Jazz (pp. 264–284). University of California Press.

Whyton, T. (2006). Birth of the school: Discursive methodologies in jazz education. *Music Education Research, 8*, 65–81. https://doi.org/10.1080/14613800600570744.

Whyton, T. (2013). *Jazz Icons: Heroes, Myths and the Jazz Tradition*. Cambridge University Press.

27

NEGOTIATING HEGEMONIC MASCULINITY IN AUSTRALIAN TERTIARY JAZZ EDUCATION

Clare Hall and Robert Burke

Introduction: Jamming on Gender in Jazz

Against the backdrop of global movements to combat gender-based injustices and local expressions of demand for change against sexual abuse (e.g., #metoo,[1] #March4Justice[2]), this case study of Australian jazz performance students' experiences of gender equality is timely. The field of jazz studies has long demonstrated that masculinity presents a particularly problematic and persistent set of gender-based inequalities for both female-identifying and male-identifying musicians (Rustin and Tucker, 2008). These inequalities run in parallel with seemingly intractable gender inequality across the Australian music industry (Hall and Burke, 2020; Hope, 2018). Edmond (2019) explains that, at least from a policy perspective, the explanations for gender inequality in music are well known and consistently have to do with: "motherhood; boys' club; confidence gaps; a lack of women in leadership positions; segregation along lines of gender with women overrepresented in traditionally feminized roles[;] … sexist and hostile working environments" (p. 74). Men more often mentor other men than women (McSweeny, 2013), women composers often hide their gender if possible (Bennett et al., 2019), and some music instruments are 'gendered' by teachers and students alike (Green, 2002).

Despite such comprehensive understandings, gender injustices in jazz music remain a point of contention in public discourse. This study aims to illustrate that jazz is not yet an inclusive or safe space for all participants, and doing so by documenting the experiences of a group of emerging jazz musicians. In order to examine the challenges female-identifying jazz musicians encounter at the undergraduate level of university studies, we set out to reevaluate the durability of the 'jazzman' as an idealised musical identity. Notwithstanding the limitations of binary conceptualisations of gender, for the purposes of the following discussion, our references to females and males henceforth denote those who identify their gender as female or male regardless of their biological body. Whilst our study did approach trans- and non-binary identifying students, they declined to participate.

Despite decades of feminist interventions to encourage more females to participate in jazz, from festivals to educational contexts, female musicians continue to struggle for inclusion, illustrating a persistent immutability in regard to gender relations in jazz (van Vleet, 2021). Heteronormativity and resultant gender-based exclusions are well-researched in jazz studies and historiography (Ake, 2002). We expand on these by engaging the seldom-heard voices of young Australian musicians who are learning how to navigate their way into professional jazz work in contemporary times. Academic studies about gender impacts in the jazz field in Australian higher education are rare, and

DOI: 10.4324/9781003081876-30

they provide a valuable opportunity to investigate why female jazz musicians continue to experience inequalities, as do other female jazz musicians around the world, particularly instrumentalists (Björk 2016, Buscatto 2018; Raine, 2019; Rustin and Tucker, 2008). There are more studies available about gender difference in Australian creative culture more broadly, for example, Edmond (2019) suggests that "Australia has struggled to close the cultural gender gap, and in many creative fields the situation has deteriorated" (p. 75), a claim demonstrated in music more specifically (Hope, 2018). Our research seeks to redress this through the study of undergraduate university musicians' experiences of jazz education in respect to gender as the means to instigate change.

Jazz Identities and Hegemonic Masculinity

In both the social and musical realms of learning to be a professional jazz musician, there are particular patterns of gender relations that we found students to be both reproducing and contesting. While a growing body of historiographic and ethnographic studies redresses the exclusion of female musician's stories in jazz scholarship (Brown, 1991; Monson, 1995; Rustin and Tucker, 2008), there remains a paucity of empirical research on female, and particularly young females', experience of jazz culture during their studies. As Tucker (2012) explains, the traditional cultural narrative of jazz history has centered around the veneration of "great men" and their achievements (p. 264). The 'jazz hero' narrative is central to the gendered performances of the 'jazzman' as the 'genius improviser' (Early and Monson, 2019). This is exacerbated when the notion of musical genius is almost exclusively ascribed to men (Battersby, 1989).

Rustin-Paschal (2017) describes the jazzman's masculinity, embodied in the gender performances of Charles Mingus, across an extensive array of signifiers, including, innovation, collaboration, expertise, exceptionality, emotionality, genius, non-conformity, authority, freedom, creativity and competition. It also represents a position of power (Connell, 2000). Rustin-Paschal also argues 'jazzmasculinity' can be performed by both male and female bodies, and suggests Celia Mingus is an example of a female 'jazzman' in the way her involvements as record company leader also displayed "expertise, discipline, and the mastery of self, others, and the music" associated with jazzmasculinity (p. 98). Despite arguments about gender diversification, including queer delineations in jazz (Björck and Bergman, 2018; Teichman, 2018, 2020), the kinds of isolated examples of 'regenderings' marked by the performative turns made in the late 1950s mentioned above do little to help us understand why gender delineations in jazz continue to be such a battleground, especially where female-identifying musicians are concerned.

The stereotypical 'jazzman' identity presents challenges on and off the stage for many of the students we interviewed. These include a demonstration of the acquisition of the embodied dispositions, attitudes and musical approaches known to delineate the successful jazz musician. Female jazz instrumentalists throughout history have been denied access to the resources for becoming a 'jazzman', access that is restricted by race, sexuality, and class as well as gender (Monson, 2008; Rustin-Paschal 2017). Nevertheless, many professional females perform jazz masculinity to some extent, in that they occupy the position of power accustomed to males through their embodiment of dispositions associated with masculinity in jazz, such as virtuosity, authority, and innovation.[3] This reveals the hegemonic form of this sociomusical space. Understanding the impact of gender in jazz performance requires researchers to examine the complex interplay between these social positions and the concomitant power that they each occupy. We argue that no study of gender in jazz can ignore the interplay between masculinity and femininity as inter-relational concepts. MacDonald and Wilson (2006) emphasise both the material and discursive elements of hegemonic identities in understanding music identity-formation in jazz.

Whether a hegemonic archetype of a jazz musician is externally available, or simply represents a range of ostensibly similar constructions by individuals, the idea of a characteristic jazz musician is an important device in jazz musicians' accounting for their practice. In descriptions of what "you" do as a jazz musician, musicians at least affirm the idea of a typical musician, whether they are referring to the same ideal or not.

(p. 75)

Reconciling the idealisation of the 'jazzman', and what he and his music represents across time, continues to be the subject of much fascination. By reflecting on how gender through jazz has been previously understood across different times, places and spaces, it ought to be acknowledged that jazz, as much as gender, is ever-changing and that masculinities and femininities are plural (Connell, 2000). We are, however, ever more troubled by the patterns of domination that subordinate anyone without access to the material-discursive resources of a gender considered most desirable and valuable. In this regard, we see an apparent cultural reproduction of certain kinds of jazzmen as the most legitimate across time and place. Rustin-Paschal's (2017) seminal work on the particular kind of jazzman that Charles Mingus's masculinity performs is in contrast to our interest in the continuum of multiple masculine and feminine constructions we observe students encountering as they negotiate which kind of musician they want to become. We sought to examine aspects of gender that appear to be most and least open to change in regards to jazz music performance and reception. Viewing gender relations in jazz through the lens of Connell's concept of hegemonic masculinity (2000) enables a renewed conversation about not only what dispositions and practices are socioculturally exalted in the field of jazz, but how the structure of gender relations plays out in the musical lives of young musicians.

We deploy the concept of hegemonic masculinity to examine students' attempts to negotiate their musical identities within jazz cultures in Australia. Connell and Messerschmidt (2005) explain that, "Hegemony works in part through the production of exemplars of masculinity (e.g., professional sports stars), symbols that have authority despite the fact that most men and boys do not live up to them" (p. 846). Within jazz culture, the authoritative position of the jazzman continues to dominate as an exemplar of the most desirable gender performance, despite diverse masculinities existing in the field of jazz (Burke, 2006). Whilst the criticisms of hegemonic masculinity theory have pointed at the tendency for its usage to promote masculinity as a fixed, transhistorical construct (Connell and Messerschmidt, 2005), our study examines how some elements of jazz masculinity do indeed appear to be durable across time. Who and what is the 'jazzman' today?

Fast forwarding to the present day, we see vestiges of this "masculine assertion" enmeshed with current practices, in addition to the continued idolisation of the 'new' jazzmen that abound. This may explain why the majority of jazz practitioners are still male. As the starting point for addressing why change in gender disparity continues to be an immutable problem, we interrogate the nature of a 'jazzman' in contemporary culture as the basis to gain insight into the gendered hierarchies of power evident in Australian jazz culture more broadly. We examine whether some of the 'old' masculinities continue to be 'rehearsed' in and outside the jazz ensemble through the hegemonic jazz masculinity we observe in that context. To begin the work of reinterpreting and reconfiguring gender in jazz today, we pursue the important first question: How do students in an Australian university understand and negotiate gender in learning to become a jazz musician?

Methodology

This study is part of a groundswell of renewed interest in gender diversity in jazz, particularly in Australia (Burnett, 2021; Denson, 2014; Hall and Burke 2020, Hope, 2017; Keller, 2020), which has developed a more detailed understanding of the extent of contemporary gender inequities in jazz. Applying a narrative case-study methodology (Stake, 2005), we investigate the role of gender identity in the complex sociomusical space within the jazz ensemble learning environment. The study compares jazz and improvisation students' negotiation of jazz cultures whilst performing music in Australian higher music education. We use gender as a lens to understand some of the tensions and challenges resulting from the gendered power relationships that exist in the sociomusical spaces inhabited by these students.

As musician-educator-researchers with in-depth experiences of the inner workings of jazz ensembles and improvisation, the team is well placed to analyse the findings. As audience/educator (author 1), and improvising practitioners/educators (authors 2 and 3), we investigate the experiences of 15 music students who are enrolled in a Bachelor degree in jazz and popular music in an Australian university. The participants were recruited using convenience sampling, and included 10 females (8 vocalists, 1 pianist, 1 drummer), and 5 males (2 guitarists, 1 trombonist, 1 saxophonist, 1 vocalist) aged between 19 to 30 years of age in 2019. We have replaced their names with fictional ones, for the purpose of this chapter. Single case studies can be criticised for providing findings that are not easily generalisable (Salkind, 2010). However, consistent with qualitative case study and narrative methodologies, the purpose of the research design is to produce verisimilitude, not generalisability, so that likeness to other similar cases can be compared (Clandinin, 2006). The small scale of the study and participant group provides depth rather than breadth in the responses. This depth offers valuable detailed insights about the quality of individual experiences.

Students were invited to volunteer to be involved in a 60-minute group or individual interview where they would share stories of their gendered experience in music making and any vision they may have for developing greater gender diversity in the jazz and popular music industry. The student group were interviewed during an intensive study period, where they were working together in close quarters over a two-week period.

Narrative methodology produces stories of experience (Clandinin, 2006) that incorporate both the textual (linguistic) and textural (embodied, sonic) elements of musical narratives (Hall, 2015, 2018). Gendered stories interconnect with broader discourses, leading us beyond the realm of the personal, creating stories that can, in turn, shape identities (Tamboukou, 2003). As Andrews (2004) points out, the internalisation of dominant cultural narratives come to represent normative experience and can be reproduced as 'blueprints' for the stories we live and tell. Therefore, "we will be trying to situate our work culturally and politically; we will also want to pay attention to the micro-contexts of research through which these broader issues are lived and clarified" (Squire, 2013, p. 67). To do this we analysed the interviews in a six-stage process to generate emergent themes and organise significant narratives, as outlined below:

Stage 1: Affective personal reactions of the authors.
Stage 2: Identify thematic resonances and associated verbatim quotes.
Stage 3: Highlight narrative repetition/patterns, metaphors, silences.
Stage 4: Compare/contrast similarities and differences across narratives.
Stage 5: Refined emergent themes into 4 main thematic categories.
Stage 6: Extract story excerpts as exemplars of the main themes.

From these six stages, four main thematic categories were identified in the students' experience: discrimination and exclusion of females, male gender threat and fragility, female emotionality, and aversion to feminist identities. This chapter focuses on an exploration of the first theme, that of discrimination towards females, and the forms this takes. The term 'ensemble space' will be used to describe the space that is inclusive of the band room, rehearsal room, teaching room and the concert platform. A key activity in these ensemble spaces is jazz jamming, which is at the heart of jazz improvisation practice, and occurs in all jazz ensemble spaces to some degree. The next section discusses the tensions between the various gendered jazz identities students negotiate within these spaces.

'Jazzcats' Playing against 'Crazy Feminist Ladies'

The students' experiences demonstrated a continued idolisation of 'the jazzman'. But who is the jazzman, and how and what does his music communicate today in the Australian context? Notwithstanding the range of gender identities available to these students, our deliberate questioning of this particular musical masculinity in a unitary sense stems from our aim to understand if the jazz world these students inhabit is dominated by particular gender performances, how and why. The students describe a musical masculinity reminiscent of the 1950s jazzmen in the way they identify musicians with the most cultural cachet. This is articulated by a number of students who use the term 'Jazzcat' to describe the 'top' jazz musicians. We suggest 'Jazzcat' embodies hegemonic jazz masculinity as the most desirable position of power that all students strive towards in some way, and that the gender of the 'Jazzcat' is definitively male. Regardless of whether students aspire to be 'like him', it is to be expected that musicians of all genders desire the recognition of excellence that his position affords. But who are 'Jazzcats' and what do they do? Students describe 'Jazzcats' as the musicians whose high musical calibre is rewarded with the best gigs, front lining the best bands, and many opportunities to play. He is highly visible, self-assured, desirable and part of an elite class of musicians. But there are distasteful dimensions to his identity. One female student describes this jazz masculinity as a "big egotistical arrogant guy," whereas others describe the "classic jazz guy" as being a member of a heterosexist "boys club" fraternity. Some students almost dismiss inappropriate behaviour with comments such as "Oh, you know how jazz guys are, especially at that age," and "they're just like that. It's just a classic jazz guy."

The 'Jazzcat', as a hegemonic form of masculinity, is reserved for a particular kind of successful male musician. While top female musicians may reach the musical heights of their male colleagues when they perform jazz masculinity, often better than males do, according to Rustin-Paschal (2017), they can never be 'cats'. The students in our study clearly align this identity with the heterosexual male body, and establish that there is no female equivalent to the male 'Jazzcat'. Any cat-like musical performance from a jazzwoman is only symbolically ever an imitation of jazzmen, because while her sound may be able to mimic the qualities of jazz masculinity,[4] her body cannot transcend the gender codes inscribed in the 'Jazzcat'. These codes require a male body to perform the homosociality associated with this hegemonic masculinity (Annfelt, 2003). To be a 'cat' also has discursive roots in American cultural history of hipness (Ford, 2013).

Regardless of what label these students use to describe the dominant form of masculinity they encounter, we gain a sense of the female students' attempts to resist being controlled and affected by jazzmen's aggressiveness. A jazz vocal student, for instance, describes with indignation the resolve required to withstand the challenge jamming with male peers often demands. She says, "I'm gonna take a solo, following the melody, and jump in before the saxophonist just comes and fucking pushes me off the bridge!" The female students describe a kind of musical double-standard, where their male colleagues apply different levels of pressure towards them than their male peers that they must learn how to overcome. Kylie explains, "I need to look over my charts like crazy and make sure every hit is there because the second they see one weakness in the chart, they're like, 'She's useless'." Whereas the same weaknesses in her male colleagues' charts do not attract the need for the same defense. When presented with her male peers' work she says,

> they're not charts, they're scribbles. But it's cool because it's improv for them and it's experimenting and it's growth, but if we do it, it's like, "Oh, I don't have time for your shit. Why don't you know what you're doing?"

Female musicians' need to constantly uphold their musicianship against the inherent inferiority some are made to feel, which requires intense emotional labour. Nadine explains, "It's just my experience, but I am used to being seen as inferior because I am a woman." This battle against denigration plays out in the rehearsal room, where males can "flex on other people that make them feel like they're lesser," as Lisa describes. While males do also compete with other males, Bethany's defensiveness illustrates the form this 'flexing' against females can sometimes take:

> I've brought in a chart of an original before and I got completely ripped into....It was something so fucking stupid. I hadn't put like the double bar line at the end. Literally insane and they were like, "This chart is wrong," and I was like, "What do you mean?... But I think just my personality lends itself to working with men. I would hope everyone would not take shit, but that's just not the reality because shit is going to get thrown at you whether you take it or not, however, you deal with it. But I've always been able to stand up for myself.

Females describe frequent microaggressions embedded in musical interactions, such as being musically pushed around and humiliated, which can be linked back to the ruthless competitive nature of the cutting session. This jazz culture continues in the sense that inherent within it is the musical 'fight' to be the one who plays the best solo, who is the leader and who claims a creative space of their own. The hero of these battles, as previously mentioned, has historically been male, but this is a situation true to the present day due to the struggle female jazz musicians continue to encounter with hostility, which makes participation in ensemble settings more challenging for females than males. Although the male students do not describe a need to 'stand up' for themselves in the same way as the females, they report some awareness of hegemonic jazz masculinity. For instance, John explains,

> There's a lot of male ego in the jazz scene, particularly in bebop, which is very central to at least the pedagogy here. But I think most jazz pedagogy is pretty bebop central. And I think that bebop is a system that lends itself to a bit of that ego, that whole—it sort of can be somehow competitive .... [T]he virtuosic requirements and fast tempos can lead themselves to a certain sort of toxic masculinity ... where the music becomes very much about showing off virtuosic capacity. I guess it becomes easier to present some egotistical display as opposed to where it's more about sensitivity and dynamics and interaction.

According to John, the egoism of jazz masculinity tied up with the virtuosic requirements of bebop are antithetical to a more sensitive, interactional kind of musician. John goes on to explain that the socialisation of what makes jazz masculinity toxic—arrogance and ego—is also fundamental to the 'make-up' of the successful improvising musician.

> I think that sometimes just because of the way that men are raised, there's a certain level of arrogance that goes with that, and I don't think that that's necessarily conducive to good music-making, but it's also part of what makes them take initiative, I guess, for things like improvisation.

Here, male egotism is aligned with the competitive and virtuosic approach to improvisation so integral to the bebop tradition. The reliance on the bebop tradition in jazz education discussed above, makes it difficult to diverge from the jazz canon when 'real' jazz to students is seen to originate and align with bebop heroes. Harry comments that he was lucky to have had an early education in "actual jazz tunes like Charlie Parker" because his father is a jazz musician. His father provided him "an example of what a musician looked like ... 'cause I always knew it was an actual viable option. So it wasn't that scary" However many of the female students question this canon, and search for a way to find a space within it. A venture not always welcomed. For instance, Catherine confirms the resistance to change is about a desire for 'authentic' jazz:

> So much of the history of jazz is male-dominated apart from like, maybe, vocal jazz as a genre and so therefore, when we are told to diversify or encouraged to diversify, a lot of people just sort of, "I don't want to do that, that's not the tradition." Like, this is so boring, this isn't really jazz.

Investments in 'real' jazz wed students' aspirations to particular embodiments and sonic expressions. The picture portrayed so far is a continuum of gendered subjectivities that places egotism, arrogance, self-assuredness, virtuosity, competitiveness and the authority to discriminate at the top of the musical hierarchy. However, some students demonstrated a willingness to attempt change. John's suggestion that playing with "sensitivity and dynamics and interaction" is more complex than a virtuosic display might represent something of a counter-hegemonic jazz masculinity within the hierarchy. Particularly refreshing is that this stance is reflected in his own playing, where some of the key harmonic, melodic and rhythmic elements are taken from bebop, but bypass the more competitive and pattern-based elements to integrate with diverse cultural influences through multiple genres outside jazz. Recent examples of a cross pollination approach can be found in the music of Jane Ira-Bloom and Herbie Hancock, as well as Australian artists and educators Paul Grabowsky and Sandy Evans. This contemporary divergence from the bebop canon reinforces the need for institutionalised jazz and its pedagogy to also diverge, and reflect the diversity of post-bop artistic practice that is inclusive of a variety of improvisational paradigms and educational epistemologies, such as Indigenous knowledges (Saraydarian, 2021) and hybridised diasporic jazz (Gioia, 2011; Johnson, 2019). It is here within increasingly diverse intersectionality in jazz that the spaces to reinscribe symbolic gendered meanings exist.

It is worthwhile noting that the conversations with males consisted of considerably more discussion about actual music making than the females, the latter being focused more on the sense of injustice and the emotionality surrounding their experiences despite being asked the same interview questions. This reflects the distribution of emotional labour around gender inequity. For instance, the males' view of the masculine toxicity is, primarily, confined to its effects on their musical practice. This is in contrast to the forms of social oppression and symbolic violence that the females emphasise. One of the main pressure points for the females is the anger they feel about the forms of exclusion they experience. Exclusionary practices are often applied in the formation of ensembles at an elite level, and experienced by all musicians, not just jazz. The female students perceive being excluded from ensemble selection more often than their male peers and as a result find negotiating jazz ensemble spaces more challenging. While male students describe finding supportive peers to jam with as challenging for them also, being actively excluded from opportunities is rarely a feature of the males' storytelling. For instance, Peter deploys what he understands to be his 'ego' to succeed in managing who is in and who is out of his ensembles.

> And so where the ego comes into it, is when certain people say, "Do you wanna jam? I'll make an assessment on how hard I think they're working or how good I think they are, but if I just feel like they're faffing about, I just think they're not gonna take it anywhere, then I'd go, "no," and that's it. To me, that's ego. That's me flexing my ego, and going "No, I think I'm better than this person."

Peter's position of certainty and authority to be the decision-maker in the jam session is linked to his competitiveness and sense of entitlement to make value judgements about his colleagues' standard of musicianship. He is purposely including musicians who are not better than him. Unfortunately, for the females, their gender is often tied to perceptions of ability, and they describe being overlooked as if invisible by their male peers. Bethany's viewpoint is one of many such stories from the females about the struggle to be seen.

> Nobody wants to jam with a jazz vocalist, that's not a thing that happens. I literally was standing there with a group of guys and I was the only other person with them and they were like, "Cool. So do you guys wanna go and have a jam?" and didn't look at me and left, and I was like I'm literally a jazz musician and I have way more experience than you guys[;] … I think if it was man—I feel like if it was a male vocalist, it probably wouldn't be as common.

The females' struggles to be regarded as legitimate jazz musicians is another parallel with times past where jazzwomen were subjected to overt discrimination based on their gender (Provost, 2017; Rustin and Tucker, 2008). In the study, females' perception of worthiness was diminished by the need to require permission from males to have their playing heard. As Melissa comments, she feels "you need permission from the men to show my skill or demonstrate what I have to offer or be myself, but I think I'm starting to realise I don't have to do that." Lisa is more animated about her opposition to the tensions she faces, which she describes as a "mob mentality" amongst the males:

> I get passionate about things like whenever I hang out with mates. I'm shut down, I'm silenced, because, "Ugh, you're going on a misogynist rant. She's going on her feminist rant," and even my closest friend who's in this course would say, "Just stop talking about these issues because it gets annoying. It takes away from the fun…. And that's always shaking me up, and I feel that often when I do get into those rants, I'm often silenced and brought down. And even in an ensemble setting, I always find myself sitting to the back because I get brought down by stronger personalities and I'm quite animated, but I don't want our personalities to collide, so that's why I identify that and I sit to the back.

Peter reiterates he has found the communication style of males problematic and frustrating:

> I just find that with females in general they're a lot more willing to just stop talking and listen rather than yell over the top, whereas with all their discussions previously, for a man who wants to be over the top, they can and they do.

Females tolerate 'over the top' behaviours and gender discrimination out of concern about upsetting their male colleagues. It is evident that confronting their peers about troubling behaviours is difficult because of the discomfort it would cause males. A sense of threat and male fragility is also another key theme amongst the male and females' narratives that is beyond the scope of this discussion. What is pertinent here is that conversations about gender justice in jazz is risky business for both males and females, as Melissa explains:

> I think there're so many people out there who have such a negative attitude towards feminists because there's some really strong-minded ones, which I think is really helpful. But then everyone is always like, "Oh, patriarchy," But I'm like but that stuff actually exists. For me, harmony in relationships is a really important thing and I think I often tend to put myself second in order to avoid conflict…. I feel like the [males'] jokes are the way that they interact because they're not comfortable to interact on it on another level. I feel like that's very judgmental of me to say that…. Emotional intelligence is a big thing and we really need to be able to speak maturely or just like speak about emotions without feeling insecure about your identity as a man.

The risk for females speaking up about gender discrimination in music is being further stigmatised, as Lana explains, "There's such a stereotype of 'crazy feminist lady', but when a male calls it out, 'Oh, that's a very valid point'." When the females do speak up about gender injustices in jazz they can experience double denigration, the first being objectification as 'only women' the second for being "called bitch or intense or dramatic or crazy" when they challenge this objectification, as Kylie explains.

> I've had guys, they had never heard me sing before at all or I could be horrible, and they came up to me and were like, "Let's jam sometimes." I was like, "Oh, okay, why?" and then later on, they asked me out for a drink.... You don't care what I sing like. You're doing it for what I look like.... I just ignore it and try to keep going. Well, I do keep going and I try. Sometimes, I do get really irritated though and then when I do, when I turn around and I'm out of the room, I'd be like, "Is this why you wanna jam with me? Is this what's going on?" Then they straightaway turn around and go, "You don't have to be crazy." I get that very often, that, "You don't have to be so intense." It's like, "Well, I do, because I need to defend myself."

Despite the durable and pervasive behaviours of the 'Jazzcat', a palpable sense of the females' efforts to both tolerate and push back against the many challenging aspects of negotiating their jazz music-making was experienced in all female participants. Some females sense the need to defend themselves against a contestational, hostile and exclusionary culture, despite the further scorn this can generate for them. We suggest this is indeed a heterosexist carryover from historical jazz cultures that are transported by gendered practices enmeshed with the bebop tradition. We gain a clear view of the emotional labour required by female jazz musicians to navigate the challenges of undertaking an undergraduate jazz course. But what we lack, besides narratives of female-championing jazzmen, is clarity around if and how they manoeuvre themselves into more powerful positions of decision-making on their own terms and how they find ways to sustain this labour.

Conclusion

This chapter discussed a group of students' experiences of jazz ensemble performance that indicate the depth of entrenched gendered power imbalances at play in Australian jazz students' education. We propose that it is critical to contextualise emerging jazz musicians' identities within the historical jazz cultures they inherit, and the study found that the hegemonic masculinity associated with these cultures is still present. The student jazz musicians alternately experience and display trace elements of jazz masculinity from the past in the way that they negotiate their music education and performance activities. Therefore, we were led to question the durability of some of the jazzman's historical symbolic power and how that has transferred to today's jazz gender relations. We see evidence of this in some of the challenges this generation of musicians face in aspects of higher music education and their attempts to negotiate productive relationships through jazz ensembles. Hegemonic masculinity theory has given us an insight into the jazz masculinity most powerful in this context, which we suggest is constituted by virtuosity, egotism, leadership, hostility, authority to be heard, and competitiveness, contributing to an exclusionary culture. Some musicians are reproducing a gendered pattern in bebop masculinity through the 'Jazzcat' identity. This acclaimed identity position appears to flourish in a conservative understanding of jamming culture that continues to idolise the jazzman hagiography, resulting in the exclusion of those musicians who do not conform to this musical masculinity.

Focusing on the sociomusical exclusions reported by undergraduate musicians, we gain a clear view of how discrimination plays out for female-identifying students through their encounters with contemporary jazzmen, also named 'Jazzcats'. These include females' experience of a sense of invisibility, self-doubt, lack of being heard, requiring permission, verbal and musical denigration, emotional threat, personal risk and lack of engagement with gender justice more broadly. A narrative method of analysis has enabled us to portray a picture of the female students' dismay and indignation at the seeming intractability of gender inequality in jazz. While this single case study is not generalisable, we suggest is it indicative of a broader culture that, as Edmond (2019) describes in relation to the gender gap across the music industry, presents "a gnawing, inescapable sense of Déjà vu" (p. 74).

This chapter has identified some effects of hegemonic jazz masculinity—however, to take this discussion further, a more comprehensive profile of the relationship between modern jazzmen and jazzwomen is required. A more complete examination of the source of the durable 'jazzman' characteristics from within all elements of jazz education programs would also be useful. This carries on the unfinished work started by many before us that refreshes what we regard are critical avenues for future study from our position, which are; the impacts of binary gender categories in jazz, the essentialisation of jazz as inherently masculine, how female performances of jazz virtuosity can be reinscribed as more than merely performances of masculinity, and how bebop's harmonic, melodic, rhythmic and stylistic attributes can be disassociated from the identity of the jazzman into a process that offers knowledge, freedom and safety in jazz improvisation.

Our aspiration is for the term 'Jazzcat' to denote a musician of any gender who cultivates welcoming safe spaces where all musicians are able to participate equally in the making of music that reflects the diversity of today's society.

Notes

1 Tarana Burke started the #Metoo movement in 2006: https://en.wikipedia.org/wiki/Tarana_Burke.
2 Janine Hendry was initiator of the #March4Justice in 2021 that involved 47 marches across Australia in protest of sexual assault within Australia's parliament: www.janinehendry.com/.
3 Examples of artists that could be considered performing jazzmasculinity are Melissa Aldana (Tenor Saxophone), Geri Allen (Piano), Roxy Cos (Tenor Saxophone), Terri Lyn Carrington (Drums), Angela Davis (Alto Saxophone), Ella Fitzgerald (Singer), Ingrid Jensen (Trumpet), Melba Liston (Trombone), Linda Oh (Bass), Hazel Scott (Piano) and Marylou Williams (Piano). With the exception of Hazel Scott, the foundation of these female musicians' performance lies in the bebop tradition.
4 See Provost (2017) for a full discussion on the gendered sonic imitation of jazz women.

References

Ake, D. (2002). *Jazz Cultures*. University of California Press.
Andrews, M. (2004). Counter-narratives and the power to oppose. In M. Bamberg and M. Andrews (Eds.), *Considering Counter-narratives: Narrating, Resisting, Making Sense* (pp. 1–6). John Benjamins.
Annfelt, T. (2003). *Jazz as Masculine Space*. https://kjonnsforskning.no/en/2003/07/jazz-masculine-space.
Battersby, C. (1989). *Gender and Genius: Towards a Feminist Aesthetics*. Indiana University Press.
Bennett, D., Hennekam, S., Macarthur, S., Hope, C., and Goh, T. (2019). Hiding gender: How female composers manage gender identity. *Journal of Vocational Behavior, 113*, 20–32.
Björk, C. (2016). *In Search of Good Relationships to Music: Understanding Aspiration and Challenge in Developing Music School Teacher Practices*. Åbo Akademi University Press.
Björck, C., and Bergman, Å. (2018). Making women in jazz visible: Negotiating discourses of unity and diversity in Sweden and the US. *International Association for the Study of Popular Music Journal, 8*(1), 42–58.
Burnett, F. (2021). *Play like a girl: How does historical underrepresentation of women in the field of jazz and improvised music impact women musicians in 2021?* (Conference presentation). Australasian Jazz and Improvisation Research Network (AJIRN) Conference 2021.
Burke, P. (2006). Oasis of swing: The Onyx Club, jazz, and white masculinity in the early 1930s. *American Music*, 320–346.
Buscatto, M. (2018). Trying to get in, getting in, staying in: The three challenges for women jazz musicians. In J. A. Halley and D. E. Sonolet (Eds.), *Bourdieu in Question: New Directions in French Sociology of Art* (pp. 338–360). Brill.
Brown, E. B. (1991). Polyrhythms and improvisation: Lessons for women's history. *History Workshop, 31*, 85–90.
Clandinin, D. J. (Ed.). (2006). *Handbook of Narrative Inquiry: Mapping a Methodology*. Sage Publications
Connell, R. W. (2000). *The Men and the Boys*. Allen and Unwin.

Connell, R. W., and Messerschmidt, J.W. (2005). Hegemonic masculinity: Rethinking the concept. *Gender and Society*, *19*(6), 829–859.

Denson, L. (2014). Perspectives on the Melbourne International Women's Jazz Festival. *Jazz Research Journal*, *8*(1–2), 163–181.

Early, G., and Monson, I. (2019). Why jazz still matters. *Daedalus*, *148*(2), 5–12.

Edmond, M. (2019). Gender, policy and popular music in Australia: 'I think the main obstacles are men and older men'. In *Toward Gender Equality in the Music Industry: Education, Activism and Practice* (pp. 73–87). Bloomsbury Academic.

Enstice, W., and Stockhouse, J. (2004). *Jazzwomen: Conversations with Twenty-one Musicians* (Vol. 1). Indiana University Press.

Ford, P. (2013). *Dig: Sound and Music in Hip Culture*. Oxford University Press.

Gioia, T. (2011). *The History of Jazz*. Oxford University Press.

Green, L. (2002). Exposing the gendered discourse of music education. *Feminism and Psychology*, 12(2), 137–144.

Hall, C.A. (2015). Doing sociology with musical narratives, *UNESCO Observatory E-Journal Multi-Disciplinary Research in the Arts*, *5*(1), 1–27.

Hall, C.A. (2018). *Masculinity, Class and Music Education: Boys Performing Middle-class Masculinity*. Palgrave.

Hall, C. A. and Burke, R. L. (2020). Talking all that jazz: Unsilencing gender in music. https://lens.monash.edu/@politics-society/2020/09/15/1381258/talkin-all-that-jazz-unsilencing-gender-in-music.

Hope, C. (2017). Why is there so little space for women in jazz music? *The Conversation*, *26*.

Hope, C. (2018). Limelight in-depth: Cat Hope: All music for everyone. *Limelight Magazine*, www.limelightmagazine.com.au/features/limelight-in-depth-cat-hope-all-music-for-everyone/.

Johnson, B. (2019). *Jazz Diaspora: Music and Globalisation*. Routledge.

Keller, A. (2020). Andrea Keller on jazz and gender. *Soundscapes. Melbourne Recital Centre* https://soundescapes.melbournerecital.com.au/explore/andrea-keller.

MacDonald, R. A., and Wilson, G. B. (2006). Constructions of jazz: How jazz musicians present their collaborative musical practice. *Musicae Scientiae*, *10*(1), 59–83.

McKeage, K. (2003). Gender and participation in undergraduate instrumental jazz ensembles: A national survey. *Journal of Research in Music Education*, *52*(4), 343–356.

McKeage, K. M. (2004). Gender and participation in high school and college instrumental jazz ensembles. *Journal of Research in Music Education*, *52*(4), 343–356.

McSweeny, E. (April 10, 2013). The power list: Why women aren't equals in new music leadership and innovation. *New Music Box*. www.newmusicbox.org/articles/the-power-list-why-women-arent-equals-in-new-music-leadership-and-innovation.

Monson, I. (1995). The problem with white hipness: Race, gender, and cultural conceptions in jazz historical discourse. *Journal of the American Musicological Society*, *48*(3), 396–422.

Monson, I. (2008). Fitting the part. In N.T. Rustin and S. Tucker (Eds.), *Big Ears: Listening for Gender in Jazz Studies* (pp. 257–287). Duke University Press. http://hdl.handle.net/10400.21/11249.

Provost, S. C. (2017). Bringing something new: Female jazz instrumentalists' use of imitation and masculinity. *Jazz Perspectives*, *10*(2–3), 141–157.

Raine, S. (2019). Keychanges at Cheltenham Jazz Festival: Issues of gender in the UK jazz scene. *Towards Gender Equality in the Music Industry: Education, Practice and Strategies for Change*. Bloomsbury Academic. pp. 187–200.

Rustin, N. T., and Tucker, S. (2008). *Big Ears: Listening for Gender in Jazz Studies*. Duke University Press.

Rustin-Paschal, N. (2017). *The Kind of Man I am: Jazzmasculinity and the World of Charles Mingus Jr.* Wesleyan University Press.

Salkind, N. J. (2010). *Encyclopedia of Research Design*. Sage Publications.

Saraydarian, G. W. (2021). 'Space is the place': Thinking through a place-based pedagogy for jazz improvisation. *Jazz Education in Research and Practice*, *2*(1), 154–162.

Squire, C. (2013). From experience-centred to socioculturally-oriented approaches to narrative. In M. Andrews, C.Squire, and M. Tamboukou (Eds.), *Doing Narrative Research* (pp. 47–71). Sage.

Stake, R. E. (2005). Qualitative case studies. In N. K. Denzin and Y. S. Lincoln (Eds.) *The Sage Handbook of Qualitative Research* (pp. 443–466). Sage Publications.

Tamboukou, M. (2003). *Women, Education and the Self*. Macmillan.

Teichman, E. (2018). Something's missing from my jazz band's bulletin board: An autoethnographic reflection on making space for girls and women in jazz education. *The Canadian Music Educator*, *59*(4), 8–12.

Teichman, E. (2020). Pedagogy of discrimination: Instrumental jazz education. *Music Education Research*, *22*(2), 201–213.

Tucker, S. (2012). Deconstructing the jazz tradition: The 'subjectless subject' of new jazz studies. In D. Ake, C.H. Garrett, and D. Goldmark (Eds.), *Jazz/Not Jazz* (pp. 264–284). University of California Press.

Van VleetK. (2021). Women in jazz music: A hundred years of gender disparity in jazz study and performance (1920–2020). *Jazz Education in Research and Practice*, *2*(1), 211–227.

Wehr-Flowers, E. (2006). Differences between male and female students' confidence, anxiety, and attitude toward learning jazz improvisation. *Journal of Research in Music Education*, *54*(4), 337–349.

28

JAZZWOMEN IN HIGHER EDUCATION

Experiences, Attitudes, and Personality Traits

Natalie Boeyink

Recent dismissals of jazz faculty members from institutions of higher education due to allegations of sexual harassment or discrimination have brought a focus to problems that have long been discussed in privacy, but rarely shared publicly. In November of 2017, the Canadian Broadcasting Corporation published an account of the release of a Berklee College faculty member after University of Manitoba students informed Berklee of their experiences being harassed by the former faculty member. Six women filed allegations, the extent to which were not publicized except for statements saying they felt that they were physically in danger and were mentally traumatized. They reported a decrease in self-worth and that their passion for music had been lost (Nicholson, 2017).

When jazz departments and colleges are slow to take corrective action for sexual harassment and discriminatory behavior, the binary female students of the jazz programs suffer academically, personally, and professionally. The actions, words, and atmosphere established by faculty in male-dominated fields such as jazz, directly affect their female students—shaping their views of jazz as a viable career path and their success in the degree program (Lawson et al, 2018).

Collegiate jazzwomen want the respect of their peers and faculty. They want to be included in student "hangs" and informal jams, and to be taken seriously by faculty and administrators when they raise an issue about harassment within the jazz program. Perhaps most importantly, they want to be held to same standard as their male peers and not be underestimated in their abilities as jazz musicians.

This chapter explores numerous aspects of the experiences of collegiate jazzwomen—with a focus on instrumentalists. The nature of sexual harassment and forms of discrimination described by collegiate jazzwomen will be examined, as well as their attitudes toward the jazz field and jazz improvisation, confidence, and common personality traits. Ideas for improving the experiences of jazzwomen and cultivating a more equitable learning environment are provided.

Attitudes Toward the Jazz Field

Group Status

The attitudes of instrumental jazzwomen toward being in the jazz field are shaped by numerous factors. One factor is being a member of a skewed minority group (Kanter, 1977). In collegiate jazz programs, a 20-piece big band comprised of 18 males and only two females, is a prime example of a

DOI: 10.4324/9781003081876-31

skewed population. According to Kanter's definition, these two women are "tokens" who are often treated and viewed as *the* representatives of their group. In the case of the one or two women in a big band, their token status is defined by their sex.

Women in skewed minority groups often feel they are extremely visible and overly observed. Their heightened visibility contributes to a disproportionate sense of performance pressure, particularly because they feel they are the sole representatives of their group, the female sex (Spangler, Gordon and Pipkin, 1978). Collegiate jazzwomen know that balance between the sexes in an ensemble leads members to be more relaxed around each other, the number of sexist jokes decreases, and there is a stronger focus on playing music (Boeyink, 2015).

Isolation is a recurring theme in the collegiate jazzwoman's experience. Sometimes they sit apart from their male peers because they do not feel comfortable or welcome to join the other male musicians. As a result, the women are perceived as aloof or as know-it-alls. Though women want to be part of the jazz circle, they are often excluded from group invitations or the "hang" because having a girl around "kills the vibe" (Alexander, 2011, p. 17; Berliner, S., 2017) This has a negative effect by narrowing the peer group of jazzwomen, and stifles musical development because the women do not benefit as much from jam sessions, informal practice sessions, or listening sessions initiated by their peers (Alexander, 2011). Often, the female population in a jazz degree program is so small that there are too few women to be considered "one of the guys" and included in activities off campus (Boeyink, 2015).

Career Connections

The ability of jazzwomen to connect studying jazz at a university to their career aspirations is important, though McKeage (2003) found that at the university level, female students could not make that connection. Unintentional institutional barriers such as degree requirements and instrument choice negatively impact women's participation in jazz. Stringent degree requirements governing the types of ensembles that count toward required credits often limit women's access to and participation in collegiate jazz ensembles, unless they are majoring in jazz (McKeage, 2003).

Playing the "right" instrument—meaning a standard jazz instrument (saxophone, trumpet, trombone, piano, bass, guitar or drum set) usually factors into being able to fully participate in jazz, and as a result, also affects attitudes toward the jazz field (Storb, 1996; Rizzi, 2000). The sex-stereotyping of musical instruments has long-term effects on career aspirations for women, and it usually happens during a player's formative years, when they first pick their instrument in middle school. Abeles and Porter (1978) found that three instruments strongly associated with jazz performance were sex-stereotyped as masculine: drums, trombone, and trumpet.

Beyond connecting a jazz degree to career aspirations, the realities of pursuing a career as a jazz musician may deter some women from going for the degree. Musicians in popular genres, including jazz, have high levels of anxiety and stress, which Kemp (1996) theorized was due to job insecurity, separation from home and family, a risky lifestyle, and other factors. Kemp's theory is echoed in similar assertions about factors contributing to the small number of instrumental jazzwomen (Storb, 1996; McKeage, 2003; Carroll, 2007).

School Environment

There is a strong relationship between the environment created by jazz faculty and how female students in the degree programs are valued and treated. Faculty members' actions, words, and behaviors shape male student attitudes and behavior toward the female students. With silence, faculty may tacitly or implicitly condone the sexist attitudes, and discriminatory or harassing behavior of male students. If sex is a factor in how students and teachers interact, as asserted by

P.F. Berliner (1994), it may also contribute to the small number of female instrumentalists in jazz degree programs.

The expectations of faculty play a role in how collegiate jazzwomen perceive their place in the program. Women often believe they are being treated with kid gloves or held to a different (lower) standard than their male peers (Berliner, S. 2017). When treatment or leniency differs for female and male students, it can lead to male students altering their expectations or underestimating their female peers.

Microaggressions in the band room or classroom may not be malicious, but negative comments undermine a jazzwoman's confidence. As educational institutions are striving for more gender-inclusive language, comments such as "man up" or "grow a pair" have no place in the educational sphere. Women balk at being qualified by their sex and referred to as the "chick [insert instrument here]," or hearing comments such as, "You don't see a lot of good girl drummers out there," (Boeyink, 2015). Jazzwomen describe offensive conversations between band mates who complain about their girlfriends or wives, band members touting the benefits of a "traditional woman" as a partner, and listening to degrading stereotypes of women that made them uncomfortable during combo and big band rehearsals (Alexander, 2011; Boeyink, 2015).

Mentorship

Also contributing to attitudes toward the field is the lack of female role models. Collegiate jazzwomen have considerably more access to male mentors than to female mentors. Results from Payne's (1996) analysis of music faculties in the United States and Canada demonstrated that females constituted only 24 percent of full-time faculty which was below the 33 percent found for women in academia across the United States. Not only are there disproportionately fewer females on music faculties, but an even smaller percentage of participants who were ranked at the professor level were female. Through examining the distribution of female tenure-track music faculty members by area, Payne found females were .8 percent and .5 percent of jazz ensemble and jazz studies faculties, respectively. Overland (2016) cited data from 2015 in which the ratio of female faculty reported by NASM-accredited institutions had increased to 32 percent, up from 29 percent in 1996.

The lack of female role models has been cited by instrumental jazzwomen for many years. In a 2003 study by McKeage, the three female participants were not able to name any women in jazz when ask about role models. Though today there are instrumental jazzwomen with national and international visibility, they still are not household names, and female collegiate musicians struggle to name them (Boeyink, 2015).

Attitudes toward Jazz Improvisation

Confidence

Studies have shown that women are significantly less confident jazz improvisers, have higher levels of improvisation anxiety, have a less positive attitude towards learning jazz improvisation than their male peers, and they take fewer solos (McKeage, 2003; Steinberg, 2001; Wehr-Flowers, 2006). Collegiate jazzwomen describe their attitudes toward jazz improvisation in negative terms, using words such as "hesitant," "timid," "devastating," "struggle," "disappointed," and "avoid" (Boeyink, 2015). Negative attitudes and low confidence in their improvisation skills lead many women to avoid improvisation and step aside in combo rehearsals because they do not want to take the first solo. Despite negative feelings on improvisation, jazzwomen who feel their peers respect their abilities as a jazz player are more confident and competent improvisers. They tend to worry less about embarrassing themselves while improvising, and their nerves do not interfere with their ability to improvise (Boeyink, 2015).

Improvisation Anxiety

Improvisation anxiety is a big obstacle for jazzwomen. Often, the level of anxiety is situational, dependent on the setting of the performance. If a performance or situation is perceived as high stakes, the level of anxiety increases. This anxiety can increase over time and gets worse the longer she has to wait for the performance or the solo during the performance. The ability to recover from a bad solo is critical for long-term success, and those who experience high levels of improvisation anxiety have difficulty recovering and focusing on what comes next in a performance (Boeyink, 2015).

Curriculum and Repertoire

Jazz History

The lack of representation in jazz history and jazz appreciation texts also contributes to female jazz instrumentalists having few female role models. University jazz studies courses and textbooks tend to focus on male instrumentalists, which gives the impression that women instrumentalists rarely existed, and that their contributions were not worth being written into history. Though there is a growing body of literature on jazzwomen and their contributions, research on women in jazz has largely taken the form of historical retrospectives and biographies. Lil' Hardin Armstrong, Mary Lou Williams, Ella Fitzgerald, and Billie Holiday are the women most frequently included in jazz textbooks, and occasionally an all-female big band of the 1940s, the International Sweethearts of Rhythm, is cited.

Jazz Pedagogy

Jazz pedagogy classes offer an opportunity to shift jazz education to be more inclusive of contributions by women; however, pedagogy books are lagging. While excelling in the mechanics of jazz education, pedagogy books neglect the skills needed to cultivate an environment that embraces all students, regardless of sex. In addition, those texts provide few resources for including jazzwomen in jazz education. As jazz is still viewed a domain of binary men, pedagogy classes should address specific ways to support and encourage young jazzwomen and provide students with information and the tools that will keep young women involved in jazz ensembles.

Jazz Ensembles

Most collegiate jazz ensemble libraries are filled with compositions and arrangements by men. Research on selecting ensemble repertoire and jazz pedagogy books emphasizes the musical mechanics behind repertoire choices (Dunscomb and Hill, 2002; Ghiglione, 2007; Kearns, 2011; Warnet, 2018). While those are important, diversity in composers is as well. An inclusive way of diversifying repertoire is to regularly program music by women composers. In doing so, they become part of the jazz cannon instead of a footnote in the jazz ensemble experience.

Personality Traits and Sexuality

Personality

The personality traits of women in male-dominated fields may be key to identifying and supporting women who want to pursue a career in such fields, whether jazz or structural engineering. A study of 40 instrumental collegiate jazzwomen revealed the ranked personality traits of reliable, independent, and imaginative as the most common and strongest traits (Boeyink, 2015). The finding on independence aligns with Lemkau's (1979) assertion that women in male-dominated fields are independent and high in competency traits that complement the masculine ideal, and that women in atypical professions have higher levels of "tough-mindedness" and assertiveness than women in sex-typical professions (Lemkau, 1983).

Being a risk-taker and imaginative are traits of jazzwomen who not only enjoy improvising, but consider themselves successful improvisers (Boeyink, 2015). If a jazzwoman is risk-averse or considers herself low on the imaginative scale, she is far less likely to put herself in a situation—such as a jam session—in which she will be judged solely on her improvisation.

Sexuality

Female jazz instrumentalists often face rumors of their sexual preference and assumptions about their sexuality. This may be attributed to the masculine personality traits they exhibit. Assumptions could also be a result of a jazzwoman's perceived "aloofness" for not expressing overt sexual interest in male colleagues. Sexual androgyny plays a role in the perception of instrumental jazzwomen and their personalities (Kemp, 1985). It also helps explain their ability to better relate to males than females, contributing to the number of jazzwomen who have more male than female friends. Kemp's studies have shown that music majors and professional musicians have patterns of sex differences that do not align with sex differences in similar groups of non-musicians (Kemp, 1982, 1985, 1996).

Stereotyping

Stereotypes about women jazz musicians and the debate on whether or not women can or should play jazz date at least back to an article published in *DownBeat* magazine in 1938. In the unsigned article entitled, "Why Women Musicians are Inferior," the author wrote, "Outside of a few sepia females, the woman musician never was born capable of sending anyone further than the nearest exit" (McCord, 1986, p. 135). Lorraine Cugat, wife of band leader Xavier Cugat, wrote in a 1951 *DownBeat:*

> A girl, no matter what she's got just can't be a glamorous creature with the mouthpiece of a saxophone between her pretty red lips, or while blowing her lovely face all out of shape playing a trumpet or trombone. Girls who want to be musicians should stick to piano, violin, harp, or even accordion; any instrument the playing of which doesn't detract from their feminine appeal.
>
> *(McCord, 1985, p. 129)*

Roles

Beyond questioning the ability of female jazz instrumentalists and issues stemming from sex-stereotyping musical instruments, stereotypes of women in jazz exist on other levels: their ability to appreciate or understand jazz, and their roles in a jazz ensemble. Wehr (2018) captures the roles available to jazzwomen who usually end up being "the only one" in their ensembles. Borrowing from Kanter (1993), Wehr describes their options as: (1) mother, (2) kid sister, (3) seductress, or (4) iron maiden.

According to Wehr, the mother is a caretaker, someone in the band whom the members go to for advice or emotional support. The kid sister is a female friend within the group who does not bring sexual tension nor is perceived as being in competition with the men. The seductress is a romantic prospect or woman who is paired with a male member of the group. The perception of seductress or potential love interest often leads to misinterpretation of a jazzwoman's actions (Boeyink, 2015). Jazzwomen eager to "talk shop" or get the phone number of a male colleague for professional reasons, are often perceived by men as having a romantic ulterior motive. Sexual politics add a layer to interactions between jazzwomen and men. The "iron maiden," who is "unsocial and possibly unfeminine," presents no sexual tension (Wehr, 2018).

Stereotype Threat

Stereotype threat arises for collegiate jazzwomen because they usually constitute a very small minority in their school's jazz program (McKeage, 2003; 2004). In *Whistling Vivaldi*, social psychologist Claude M. Steele (2010) describes stereotype threat as an "identity contingency" that stems from the knowledge that we, as members of our society, "have a pretty good idea of what other members of our society think about lots of things, including the major groups and identities in society (p. 5)." Steele (2010) describes this "collar" of stigma as powerful because the individual knows that one misstep may cause the outside group to whittle the individual down to the stereotype. The individual may be viewed as an exemplar of the negative stereotype and be treated accordingly.

Collegiate jazzwomen feel the burden of being the only representative of their sex in the ensemble or rehearsal room (Boeyink, 2015; Berliner, S., 2017). They experience a type of anxiety stemming from stereotype threat and the worry that a bad solo or poor performance will lead their male peers and faculty to associate the errors with being female, thereby confirming a negative stereotype associated with their sex—women cannot or should not play jazz. In her open letter describing her experiences as a young jazzwoman, vibraphonist Berliner (2017) recounts the humiliation she experienced in a school ensemble rehearsal when a substitute director asked if she could play an F blues, a skill usually taught to beginners. Berliner writes, "I could hardly say anything because his words felt so condescending and shocking and I didn't want to show him emotional vulnerability.... I am standing there humiliated because I have worked extremely hard at my craft." Berliner continues to describe the confidence it takes to be a young woman working to prove herself to men: "[impressing them] every single time . . . is not only wildly nerve wracking, but it is unrealistic because nobody can be that perfect . . . yet, women are still subjected to it because they are expected to prove it 100 percent of the time without fault. If they don't, they are fulfilling their stereotype." Though the male students in the combo witnessed the rehearsal, none stood up for her or would acknowledge what they had seen.

As in the studies cited by Steele (2010), the further women progress in the jazz field, the harder it is for them to persist. He theorizes that the conditioning of women for particular sex roles, general discrimination against them, or low expectations of their abilities contribute to an exit from their chosen field. The women who persist in jazz encounter these scenarios and are among the few who stay the course despite discrimination and harassment, and conditioning into particular sex roles.

In Steele's (2010) research, when participants in an experiment were explicitly told their task did not in any way measure the trait associated with the negative stereotype of their group, they performed better and their anxiety levels measured lower. Women who felt the stereotype threat performed worse than the women participants who did not (Steele, 2010, p. 40). Stereotypes about binary females and women musicians impact their experiences as jazz majors, from the expectations of their binary male peers and faculty, to sexual harassment and discrimination.

Experiences in the Jazz Field

Expectations

Collegiate instrumental jazzwomen experience audience members and clinicians at jazz festivals expressing surprise at their presence and their ability. Suzuki (2013) found that forms of praise for jazzwomen demonstrated an intersection between race and sex. Janelle Reichman recalled someone yelling from the back of a club that she sounded, "like an old black man!" (Suzuki, 2013, pp. 211–212). Reichman interpreted the compliment as validation of authenticity because she was a young white woman. Ingrid Jensen recalled Bobby Shew telling her at age 14 he thought she was, "an old black guy playin' like that up there. What a surprise to see a young white chick" (Enstice and Stockhouse, 2004, p. 156).

Glasper and Iverson Controversy

In 2017, pianist and former member of The Bad Plus, Ethan Iverson, published his interview of Robert Glasper on his blog (Iverson, 2017). When the interview turned to a discussion of groove-based music, Glasper stated:

> I've seen what that does to the audience, playing that groove. . . . Getting back to women: women love that. They don't love a whole lot of soloing. When you hit that one groove and stay there, it's like a musical clitoris.
>
> *(para. 47)*

Insinuating women lack the intelligence to appreciate complex or lengthy jazz solos, and reducing them to a sexual organ for him to stimulate with his music, is demeaning to jazzwomen and women who enjoy attending shows.

Iverson's interview elicited responses from collegiate and professional jazzwomen—attempts to explain to Iverson it was not only Glasper's statements, but Iverson's response and defense of the statements that were sexist and offensive. Berliner (2017) described lowered expectations from her jazz faculty, gave a candid description of sexual harassment at jam sessions and having her playing denigrated by men in retaliation for rebuffing their advances. Following Michelle Mercer's (2017) National Public Radio report recommending discourse on the gendered nature of jazz, drummer Terri Lyne Carrington expressed that sexism in jazz has been long discussed, though there has never been true dialog with the perpetrators. Carrington (2017) called for men to acknowledge their privilege in the jazz world and to reframe jazz to not oppress, stereotype, or objectify.

Sexual Harassment and Discrimination

Sexual harassment and discrimination are indisputable barriers to having a career in jazz. Fitzgerald, Shullman, et al. (1988) devised a system for categorizing sexual harassment into five levels: (a) sex harassment, (b) seduction, (c) sexual bribery, (d) sexual coercion, and (e) sexual imposition or assault. Both Carroll (2007) and Alexander (2011) found that sexual harassment is a factor that negatively impacts the career trajectories of jazzwomen. Microaggressions in the classroom and rehearsal room include lewd and sexually suggestive comments that contribute to hostile learning environments and negative experiences. They range from inappropriate references to female body parts, to sexually charged comments such as "lick that reed" (Carroll, 2007). When a professor equates the ability to understand music to sex, doing so in a classroom full of men and only a single woman, she is made to feel uncomfortable (Innis, 2017). Such comments make women just as uncomfortable as unwanted physical contact, and are sometimes more insidious.

Enduring putdowns of a non-sexual nature during rehearsal is also problematic. As recounted in Alexander (2011), "a tenured member . . . said during a big band rehearsal . . . that women didn't have the 'bravado' necessary to take impassioned solos or to be lead trumpet players" (p. 21). They have also been told they are too small to play their instrument or that they cannot put enough air into their horn. While discrimination is often discouraging, Alexander also found that it can serve as a catalyst for jazzwomen to cultivate a jazz scene in which they can be leaders and thrive.

Female students have been the target of teasing and "that's what she said" jokes, and forced to listen to degrading jokes about women or women in jazz. Alexander (2011) placed discriminatory behavior into two categories: sexual harassment or exclusion. Jazzwomen reported they felt uncomfortable when their peers made sexual gestures or requests of a sexual nature; and made demeaning jokes about women, all-female jazz groups, or female band leaders. Few reported the sexual discrimination to their faculty leadership or university administration, and some felt the behavior worsened after reporting.

Indirect forms of verbal harassment and discrimination include faculty using pet names and overt interest in a female student's sexual life. Faculty using pet names for only their female students suggests a level of familiarity or intimacy that is not always welcome. Intrusion into a female student's personal life by showing interest in her sex life is another form of harassment. In Boeyink (2015), one student relayed that she knew a teacher was asking a male student for details about their intimacies and for descriptions of her body. It was an open secret within the jazz department and, although her peers found it funny, she was uncomfortable being around the teacher.

Sexual harassment and discrimination can lead to a student dropping out of her collegiate program, leaving behind a full scholarship (Boeyink, 2015). After three years of feeling overlooked, neglected, and simultaneously harassed by jazz faculty and guest artists, one student went to the head of her department to discuss how she felt she was not getting the same educational and professional support the men in the program were receiving. He did not believe her and only a year from graduating, she left the school and her full scholarship.

Solutions

Solutions for improving the experiences and success of collegiate jazzwomen include improvements in (1) access to role models, (2) pedagogy, (3) curriculum and repertoire, (4) guest artists and festivals, and (5) hiring practices.

Role Models

A recurring theme in the experiences of collegiate jazzwomen is lack of female role models (McKeage, 2003, 2004; Rizzi, 2000; Steinberg, 2001; Alexander, 2011; Boeyink, 2015). Whether in the form of exemplars studied and transcribed, performing compositions by women composers, having female faculty members and guest artists, or including jazzwomen in the curriculum, having female role models is critical for collegiate jazzwomen.

Pedagogy

Our approach to jazz pedagogy—*how* we teach—is just as important as *what* we teach. As educators, it is incumbent upon us to recognize how societal expectations and stereotypes affect our students—especially jazzwomen. Acknowledging stereotype threat can help educators better equip jazzwomen to enter the professional realm.

Updating jazz pedagogy courses to equip jazz educators to teach and encourage jazzwomen of all ages will have an effect on keeping women involved. Pedagogy students need to learn to be mindful of their language and examine the importance of the musicians held up as examples and role models. Future jazz educators should have access to a pedagogy text that contains materials and musical examples by women.

Curriculum and Repertoire

Curriculum for a jazz degree needs revision to be more equitable, diverse and inclusive. Reconsidering the curriculum to include music and content from marginalized voices benefits all students.

Improvisation and jazz history courses offer few, if any, instrumental examples by women (Steinberg, 2001). In improvisation or styles and analysis classes, examples by jazzwomen should be studied, transcribed and played. Inclusion in the curriculum establishes women as authorities. Existing jazz history and appreciation textbooks often group jazzwomen into a single chapter rather than presenting them as part of the history of jazz. Instead of making women a footnote in jazz history, textbook authors and editors should be writing them into history, incorporating their contributions with those of the great male musicians. Educators can give students supplemental readings, articles and customized playlists to support curriculum that includes the contributions of jazzwomen.

Gagne's (2021) research on gender disparities in programming collegiate jazz ensemble concerts found that of 1,474 total compositions or arrangements listed on programs, about 93 percent were by male jazz composers or arrangers, while works by women comprised almost 6 percent. Negative comments from jazz faculty about female jazz composers illustrate one reason collegiate jazz ensemble libraries are dominated by male composers: "[One] professor made 'an offhand joke … saying my composition was not so organized because I am female'" (Alexander, 2011, p. 21). Jazz ensemble libraries should include compositions and arrangements by Mary Lou Williams, Christine Jensen, Maria Schneider, Carla Bley, Melba Liston, Patty Darling, Ellen Rowe, Sherisse Rogers, Toshiko Akiyoshiki and Rebeca Mauleón. Jazz directors can explore commissioning works by women composers. Gagne (2021) highlights the challenge given the paucity of repertoire by women composers and arrangers available through popular publishers and distributors. In surveying the J. W. Pepper jazz catalog of 2020–2021, of the 1,197 jazz works listed, about 3 percent were by woman composers or arrangers (Gagne, 2021).

Guest Artists and Festivals

Guest artists offer opportunities to enhance diversity and inclusion efforts on campuses. Due to the small number of women on jazz faculties, bringing jazzwomen to give master classes, or to perform with faculty and student ensembles, begins to normalize the presence of jazzwomen, demonstrates the high level of achievement women have attained, and helps female students envision a path forward for themselves. University jazz festival coordinators have the opportunity to highlight jazzwomen as adjudicators, clinicians and performers.

Hiring Practices

Studies of hiring practices have shown that institutions tend to replicate gender inequality, as gender is a "fundamental part of the structure of organizations" (Britton, 2017, p. 10). Most jazz departments do not have a woman on faculty, and for those that do, often the women are vocalists or adjunct. Trish Colter, a professional jazz vocalist and former head of the vocal department in Humber College's jazz program, described her experiences in higher education (Kearns, 2011). As a leader, she made it part of her mission to ensure that vocalists, female students and faculty got the respect of administrators and her colleagues. Colter acknowledged that she sometimes found it easier to "just roll with the punches" (p. 156), balancing being collegial with aggressively advocating for her students. To increase diversity on faculties, search committees need to mitigate implicit biases and consider recruiting committee members from outside the music department.

The actions, words and the atmosphere established by faculty directly affect female jazz students—shaping their views of jazz as a viable and desirable career path, and their success in the degree program. Faculty set the tone and are the model for how male students will treat their female peers, and modeling bad behaviors and using discriminatory language is detrimental to all students.

Conclusion

What collegiate jazzwomen want is clear. They want to be respected and included by their peers and be treated by faculty as serious musicians with the same potential as male students. Knowing they are being held to the same standards as their male peers is important. Jazzwomen need female mentors so they know there is a path forward, and they want faculty to prepare them to be leaders themselves—whether on future jazz faculties, performing or composing, or leading their own ensembles. Collegiate jazzwomen want a harassment-free, gender-neutral educational environment, and also to be heard by faculty and administrators who will take appropriate actions if jazzwomen raise an issue of harassment or discrimination. When the music, scholarship, and voices of women within the field of jazz are heard, we will see an increase in the presence and acceptance of jazzwomen in colleges and universities.

References

Abeles, H. F. & Porter, S.Y. (1978). The sex stereotyping of musical instruments. *Journal of Research in Music Education*, 26(2), 65–75.

Alexander, A. (2011). *Where Are the Girls? A Look at the Factors that Limit Female Participation in Instrumental Jazz* (DMA Thesis). Retrieved from www.arielalexander.com/live/.

Berliner, P. F. (1994). *Thinking in Jazz: The Infinite Art of Improvisation.* Chicago: The University of Chicago Press.

Berliner, S. (2017). An open letter to Ethan Iverson (and the rest of jazz patriarchy). Retrieved from www.sashaberlinermusic.com/sociopoliticalcommentary-1/2017/9/21/an-open-letter-to-ethan-iverson-and-the-rest-of-jazz-patriarchy.

Boeyink, N. (2015). *A Descriptive Study of Collegiate Female Jazz Instrumentalists* (Doctoral Dissertation).

Britton, D. M. (2017). Beyond the chilly climate: The salience of gender in women's academic careers. *Gender and Society* 31(1), 5–27.

Carrington, T. L. (2017). Sexism in jazz: Being agents of change. Retrieved from www.huffpost.com/entry/sexism-in-jazz-agents-of-change_b_58ebfab1e4b0ca64d9187879.

Carroll, D. W. (2007). Sisters in Jazz: A five-year study of career paths and barriers. *Jazz Research Proceedings Yearbook* (pp. 39–47). Manhattan, KS: IAJE Publications.

Dunscomb, J. R. and Hill, W. L. (2002) *Jazz Pedagogy: The Jazz Educator's Handbook and Resource Guide, Book and DVD.* Miami: Warner Brothers.

Enstice, W. and Stockhouse, J. (2004). *Jazzwomen: Conversations with Twenty-one Musicians.* Bloomington: Indiana University Press.

Fitzgerald, L.F., Shullman, S.L, Gailey, et al. (1988). The incidence and dimensions of sexual harassment in academia and the workplace. *Journal of Vocational Behavior*, 32: 152–75.

Gagne, C. (2021, January). "Addressing gender disparities within jazz ensemble literature and programming at the collegiate level." Poster presented at the meeting of the Jazz Education Network JENX Conference, online.

Ghiglione, B. (2007). Choosing quality jazz band repertoire. *The Canadian Music Educator, Summer* 48(4), 61–62.

Innis, C. (2017). Students report sexist encounters at the New School for Jazz. Retrieved from www.newschoolfreepress.com/2017/05/15/students-report-sexist-encounters-new-school-jazz/.

Iverson, E. (2017). Interview with Robert Glasper [blog]. Retrieved from https://ethaniverson.com/interview-with-robert-glasper/.

Kanter. R. M. (1977). Some effects of proportions on group life: Skewed sex ratios and responses to token women. *American Journal of Sociology* (82), 965–990.

Kanter, R. (1993). *Men and Women of the Corporation.* New York: BasicBooks.

Kearns, J. M. (2011). "Thinking about Jazz Education in Canada: A Comparative Case Study of Collegiate Educators Regarding Pedagogy, Administration, and the Future of Jazz Education." (Doctoral Dissertation). Retrieved from www.proquest.com/.

Kemp A. E. (1982). The personality structure of the musician: III. The significance of sex differences. *Psychology of Music* 10(1), 48–58.

Kemp, A. E. (1985). Psychological androgyny in musicians. *Bulletin of the Council for Research in Music Education* (Late Fall), 102–108.

Kemp, A. E. (1996). *The Musical Temperament: Psychology and Personality of Musicians.* Oxford: Oxford University Press.

Lawson, K. M, Kooian, L. Y., and Kuchta, O. (2018). Professors' behaviors and attributes that promote U.S. women's success in male-dominated academic majors: Results from a mixed methods study. *Sex Roles 78,* 542–560.

Lemkau, J. P. (1979). Personality and background characteristics of women in male-dominated occupations. *Psychology of Women Quarterly 4*(2), 221–240.

Lemkau, J. P. (1983). Women in male-dominated professions: Distinguishing personality and background characteristics. *Psychology of Women Quarterly 8*(2), 144–165.

McCord, K. (1985). The conceptualization of women in jazz. *Proceedings from National Association of Jazz Educators National Conference* (pp. 128–139). Kansas City: National Association of Jazz Educators Publications.

McCord, K. (1986). All-women jazz groups. *Proceedings from National Association of Jazz Educators National Conference,* (pp. 134–140). Kansas City: National Association of Jazz Educators Publications.

McKeage, K. (2003). "Where Are all the Girls?" Women in Collegiate Instrumental Jazz. *Gender Education Music and Society.* Retrieved from www.queensu.ca/music/links/gems/past/No.%201/KMarticle.htm, accessed October 19, 2009.

McKeage, K. (2004). Gender and participation in high school and college instrumental jazz ensembles. *Journal of Research in Music Education 52*(4), 343–356.

Michelle Mercer's report, National Public Radio, (March 9, 2017).

Nicholson, K. (2017). Jazz prof Steve Kirby fired from Berklee College after U of M students share harassment complaints. Retrieved from www.cbc.ca/news/canada/manitoba/steve-kirby-fired-berklee-college-harassment-complaints-1.4404394.

Overland, C. (2016) Gender composition and salary of the music faculty in NASM accredited universities. *College Music Society, Vol. 56.*

Payne, B. (1996). The gender gap: Women on music faculties in American colleges and universities, 1993–1994. *College Music Symposium 36,* 91–102.

Rizzi, M. C. (2000). The Education of Women Jazz Musicians: Insights into Effective Teaching (Doctoral Dissertation). Retrieved from www.proquest.com/

Spangler, E., Gordon, M. A. and Pipkin, M. (1978). Token women: An empirical test of Kanter's hypothesis. *American Journal of Sociology 84*(1), 160–170.

Steele, C. M. (2010). *Whistling Vivaldi: How Stereotypes Affect Us and What We Can Do.* New York: W. W. Norton.

Steinberg, E. N. P. (2001). "'Take a solo': An Analysis of Gender Participation and Interaction at School Jazz Festivals" (Doctoral Dissertation). Retrieved from www.proquest.com/.

Storb, I. (1996). Women in jazz. *Proceedings from the International Association of Jazz Educators Annual Conference* (pp. 134–141). Kansas City: International Association of Jazz Educators Publications.

Suzuki, Y. (2013). Two strikes and the double negative: The intersections of gender and race in the cases of female jazz saxophonists. *Black Music Research Journal 33*(2), 207–226.

Warnet, V.M. (2018). "An Investigation of the Music Literature Being Performed at Jazz Band Music Performance Assessments in Florida." (Master's Thesis). Retrieved from www.proquest.com/.

Wehr, E. (2018). Jazz, Gender, and Iowa's all-female jazz orchestra. Retrieved from https://jazzednet.org/resources/jazz-gender-iowas-female-jazz-orchestra/.

Wehr-Flowers, E. (2006). Differences between male and female students' confidence, anxiety, and attitude toward learning jazz improvisation. *Journal of Research in Music Education 54,* 337–349.

29

THE GENDER IMPERATIVE IN JAZZ

The Role of Intercultural Maturity in Jazz Curricula

Lenora Helm Hammonds

Gender Context Statement: I am using the terms woman/women or jazzwoman/jazzwomen instead of female. My personal preference stems from the accuracy of the use of female, considered as an adjective, for example, female plug, female dog, versus woman, a noun. Only a human can be a woman. I support and include any person who identifies as woman in my reference to women in my writing. As for my personal orientation: I am a cisgender, straight woman who uses the personal pronouns she/her/hers.

Background

Prouty (2012) discussed how jazz has long been deemed a metaphor for globalization, reflecting a tension between global influences and America, and representing in sound America's identity in the world (p. 151). Following two world wars, jazz music experienced rapid expansion around the world, culturally impactful in unabetted scope and momentum. It is said to be a global music because of this diffusion:

> Extending around the world, the jazz community is cosmopolitan: while jazz originated in the United States, members of the transnational jazz community can be natives of almost any land, and while many of them belong to the middle or upper classes, they can belong to any class.
>
> *(Austerlitz, 2005, p. xiv)*

It seems counterintuitive then to have a need to examine if jazz musicians are interculturally competent, or if a set of activities exist in the pursuit of jazz skills to engender intercultural maturity. Jazz music is a worldwide phenomenon, and jazz audiences exist all over the globe (Austerlitz, 2005; Baraka, 2009; Berliner, 2009; Heath, 2010; Horne, 2019). Prouty (2012) posited that jazz music has become recognized as a link connecting threads of many cultures, and jazz musicians engage with audiences through these global connections. The gender biases in jazz are global issues, have been discussed in global texts and examined in global research, but not yet resolved in global contexts (Impey, 1992; Payne, 1996; Cion, Ray and Helm, 2000; Soules, 2011; Kernodle, 2014; Herzig and Baker, 2014); Boeyink, 2015; Carrington, 2021; Helm Hammonds 2021).

DOI: 10.4324/9781003081876-32

Contextualizing the Gender Imperative

Intercultural maturity is a complex set of behaviors and perceptions requiring many developmental stages of cultural understanding, self-awareness, and knowledge. Monson (2009b) stated, "the interactive creation of music and cultural heterogeneity and identity are viewed as interrelated" (p. 192). The ability to successfully engage with different others in jazz environments is highly dependent upon many factors, including the culture of the setting, background of the persons interacting and group dynamics. We must first frame what a jazz culture might engender with regard to gender biases. Researcher Crenshaw (2016) stated an idea pertinent to our conversation:

> Communications experts tell us that when facts do not fit with the available frames, people have a hard time incorporating new facts into their way of thinking about a problem. Without frames that allow us to see how social problems impact all the members of a targeted group, many will fall through the cracks of our movements, left to suffer in virtual isolation.
>
> *(Crenshaw, TED Talk 2016)*

Crenshaw further elucidated introducing the term in social justice research of intersectionality, to discuss problems concerning gender that overlap to create multiple levels of social injustice. A frame matters so that we may understand what the problem is exactly and begin to ferret out possible solutions.

Our current problems concerning jazz gender justice point to exactly that which Crenshaw discussed; a lack of frames describing the intersection of jazzwomen and jazz gender justice. There are few frames clarifying the multi-pronged nature of the problems jazzwomen encounter. Some of the viewpoints expressed about a lack of gender justice in the jazz culture demonstrate the inability to think of the biases as a problem. These viewpoints include: As long as women are playing jazz, for whom is the lack of integration with male players on the bandstand an issue? Or views attacking character including (I was actually asked this by the parent of a friend), "What kind of woman wants to hang around a tour bus with men all of the time?"

Understanding Intercultural Maturity

For what I have learned of intercultural maturity, and my lived experience as a jazzwoman impacted by jazz gender justice, I am enthused to find answers for my jazz peers. An answer to ending biases must include an approach to addressing the behavior and perceptions of individuals so that subsequent group interaction is affected. There are no utopian circumstances, but it is at least on these two points my discussion continues: how to foster change in individuals to effect group interactions in jazz, and how to better serve jazzwomen. I will now further unpack both the efficiency and efficaciousness of utilizing intercultural maturity as an approach to impact gender biases.

The work of researchers Bennet and Bennet (2001) and King and Baxter Magolda (2005) distinguished two important concepts in the complex set of social behaviors in which to orient our understanding of how intercultural maturity develops. The first is that intercultural maturity is the term of choice to refer to the combination of concepts, attitudes and skills necessary for effective cross-cultural interaction. Further, intercultural maturity occurs when knowledge, attitude and behaviors come together cognitively for the individual. An indicator of how one matures includes how a given individual's awareness affects behavior within the group. The second area distinguished from popular intercultural maturity models is the perception of interpersonal and intrapersonal development. As individuals' personal interactions mature, an understanding unfolds in group interactions of the impact on the collective group, resulting in cultural awareness amongst the group. Intercultural competence definitions congealed as researchers gained more clarity and consensus. These concepts became the cornerstones of intercultural maturity models. Developmental behaviors as markers for intercultural competence are thus categorized as cognitive, interpersonal and intrapersonal traits in individuals.

Notable nuances of difference are illustrated in several theoretical frameworks of intercultural maturity in the literature among researchers (Deardorff, 2009; King and Baxter Magolda, 2005; Perez, Shim, et. al, 2015; Reid, 2013; Taylor, 2016). Emerging from the frameworks were situational changes based on individuals' capacities to achieve intercultural maturity. Models of intercultural competence in which intercultural maturity is measured are often parsed into categories based upon how individuals traverse the paths to affect traits, behaviors, or cognition. These models generally are parsed into frameworks aligned in the following categories: Adaptational (a process of mutual adjustments of interdependent interactants); Developmental (stages of maturity in acquiring intercultural maturity); Co-orientational (shared meanings and mutuality of communication); Compositional (lists of relevant traits, skills and characteristics of competency); and Causal (theoretical linear system of mediating variables) (Reid, 2013).

King and Baxter Magolda (2005) argued that achieving this set of competencies required a holistic approach through a conceptual, multi-dimensional framework with a focus on progress toward intercultural maturity. To understand how one comes to function as interculturally competent, an in-depth consideration is necessary regarding what comprises maturity in intercultural contexts. Research into this learning outcome suggested the capacity for intercultural maturity *develops over time*. King and Baxter Magolda (2005) synthesized a conceptual model from studies with college students, coalesced from aspects of Bennet's (1993) intercultural development model, and from student development and holistic theories of self-authorship from Kegan (1994) and Baxter Magolda (2001). King and Baxter Magolda proposed a multi-dimensional framework of intercultural maturity over a developmental trajectory of dimensions. Their Intercultural Maturity (IM) model (2005, p. 576) portrays intercultural maturity in three dimensions: cognitive, intrapersonal, and interpersonal maturity on a continuum from initial, intermediate and mature levels. The IM model of King and Baxter Magolda called for educators to use multi-dimensional approaches rather than a one-dimensional approach. The three-levels of initial, intermediate and advanced maturation, across three domains of cognitive, interpersonal and intrapersonal, comprising a nine-stage matrix. Moving through each of the three levels, across the stages of maturation denotes how intercultural maturity develops through stages over time. A breakdown of the nine stages is as follows: initial/cognitive, initial interpersonal, initial intrapersonal; intermediate/cognitive, intermediate/interpersonal, intermediate intrapersonal; and, advanced/cognitive, advanced/interpersonal, advanced/intrapersonal. A core tenet of the King and Baxter Magolda IM model is that *increased engagement across cultural orientations* advances an individual through the developmental domains toward intercultural maturation.

A deeper dive into the qualities of each dimension in the King and Baxter Magolda (2005) IM Model is useful for our discussion here. The IM model is characterized by capacities for an individual to *communicate or behave as a result of maturity in cognitive, intrapersonal, and interpersonal dimensions*. Competence in the interpersonal dimension determines choices an individual makes while comparing how one views oneself in relation to others (p. 574). Self-development or identity-development, as described in the model, is specific to competence in the intrapersonal dimension (p. 577) and understanding how people think about themselves is specific to development in the cognitive dimension (p. 575).

Jazz and Intercultural Maturity

Recent research in musicology offers interesting connections to all three of these domains. Jazz musicologists (Berliner, 2009; Monson, 2009b; Prouty 2012) suggested that jazz settings with peers may provide the context in which students move beyond their comfort zones and develop skills to negotiate management of intercultural interaction. Barrett (2012) recounts a story told by National Endowment for the Arts (NEA) jazz master, drummer/composer/bandleader Max Roach from a performance with trumpeter Dizzy Gillespie on *Night in Tunisia*. At one point in the song, the players were a bit lost:

> When the beat got turned around, it went for about 8 bars. In such a case, someone has to lay out. You can't fight it. Dizzy stopped first because he heard what was happening quicker than the rest of us, and he didn't know where "one' was. Then it was up to Ray Brown and [Walter] Bishop and myself. One of us had to stop, so Bishop waved off. Then it was up to Ray Brown and myself to clear it up. Almost immediately, we found the common "one" and the others came back in without the public realizing what had happened.
>
> *(p.33)*

What drummer Max Roach intimated in this account were several competencies across the King and Baxter Magolda (2005) intercultural maturity model firing through the band all at once. Within the performance moment described above, the jazz musicians had to have what Barrett (2012) calls an "implicit yes allowing everyone to move forward even in the midst of uncertainty" (p. xi). The nature of jazz improvisation requires musicians to anticipate a constellation of knowledge skills, where observation, analysis, discovery and curiousness are skills needed to master for effective performances. Each band member had characteristic markers for cognitive, interpersonal and intrapersonal domain maturity engaging one another—all within seconds during the performance—and the resilience of each band member in front of a live audience. Inherent in their interactions were proof of a culture to embrace a psychological comfort zone to embrace errors as a collective responsibility. Taking cues from the first dissenting voice—in this example Dizzy Gillespie halting further playing— the improvisation "changed hands" so to speak to relinquish control in the moment. With the prospect of a musical train wreck formulating, what might have been harrowing to musicians in another genre of music was seemingly all in a night's work for these jazz veterans. Demonstrated among the players was self-awareness (cognitive), willingness to trust others and integrating aspects of oneself (intrapersonal), and the interdependence everyone on the bandstand had to surrender (interpersonal) in order for the music to work.

Here are some overarching ideas to guide our conversation forward from this point:

1. Intercultural maturity develops over time in initial, intermediate and advanced stages and over three domains, cognitive, interpersonal and intrapersonal traits.
2. Increased engagement across cultural orientations with different others progresses an individual over the developmental continuum of traits.
3. Cognitive traits are how people think of themselves, Interpersonal traits are how one views themselves and makes choices in relating to others, Intrapersonal traits are one's self-identity and self-development views affecting choices with others.

There is much to unpack if we turn our discussion to jazz culture through a lens of intercultural maturity. Ethnomusicologist Monson (1994) interviewed fourteen notable jazz musicians about their lived experiences in jazz and provided a look at what jazz musicians felt about public opinion of jazz culture:

> Musicians stressed their fundamental disdain at being cast in the image of a jazz musician as untutored, instinctual, nonverbal, and immoral rather than knowledgeable—an image that has been transmitted, in a wide range of historical writings. This image has pervaded jazz discourse in both obvious and subtle ways and has been tied to what (quoting Monson)

Ted Gioia has titled the Primitivist Myth. In it the jazz musician is constructed as a "noble savage" who maintains a pure emotional and unmediated relationship to his/her art.

(Monson, 1994)

The importance of an awareness of perceptions held by laypersons about jazz musicians is a key to using the personal development approach of intercultural maturity as a vehicle to exact change affecting gender biases. Jazz musicians have distinct ideas about who they are; self-identity and cultural orientations are generally strong and well established (Taylor, 1977; Crouch, 2006; Horne, 2019). Intercultural maturity is exemplified in how an individual behaves and communicates in intercultural settings. Culture is a contested term with respect to group interactions, and intercultural competence has many variants influencing individual behaviors. Spitzberg and Changnon (2009) defined intercultural competence as:

> The appropriate and effective management of interaction between people who, to some degree or another, represent different or divergent affective, cognitive, and behavioral orientations to the world. These orientations will most commonly be reflected in such normative categories as nationality, race, ethnicity, tribe, religion, or region. To a large extent, therefore, intercultural interaction is tantamount to intergroup interaction.
>
> *(p. 7)*

However, it is crucial to remember that amongst sociocultural groups in which individuals have membership, it is the *individuals* who interact. We want individuals to take responsibility to address personal behaviors in circumstances when discriminatory actions are happening. Wise (2012) aptly stated, "Guilt is what you feel for the things you have done, responsibility is what you take because it is the person you are (p. 89)." Collective voices from 'woke' jazz musicians may guilt individuals to change behaviors. What is more impactful is the shift that occurs if individual responsibility is taken to unroot personal biases. Then, group dynamics may change. Awareness is a first step in each of the initial stages of all three developmental categories along the King and Baxter Magolda Intercultural Maturity Model continuum. Significant maturity changes in the cognitive; interpersonal and intrapersonal domains of an individual's growth must be activated by outside factors. Factors affecting intercultural maturity changes are brought about from interactions with individuals through outside instigation. A jazz orientation to the King and Baxter Magolda (2005) Intercultural Maturity Model (IMM), could be used as a tool to give jazz educators a concrete example of a holistic approach. A new developmental model will be discussed shortly. It contains cognitive, interpersonal, and intrapersonal examples of aligning jazz pedagogy tested to identify what activities instigate a continuum of development toward intercultural maturity. Used with college students, the model shows promise as a tool to address gender issues.

Prouty (2012) voiced concern about educators' disconnect and "how jazz education history has been written in a way that distances it from its non-academic roots" (p. 58–59). The importance of this statement is the implication that, for jazz education to be authentic to its non-academic roots and serve as a healthy platform to foster global citizenry, many voices need to be heard and understood. Getting to non-academic roots may involve the personal development of individuals—students and faculty—in the academy to facilitate a set of concepts upon which to reorient deeply ingrained personal and cultural biases, including gender biases.

Using Intercultural Maturity to address jazz gender justice

Separate from the sex of a person, gender is an understanding of socio-cultural and historical forces, including spheres of activity—men working in the world and women at home—ingrained in our cultures. Soules (2011) discussed concepts about women and gender and asserted that gender is a cultural construct. Intercultural maturity frameworks go to the heart of a cultural construct such as gender as an idea about self-identity, perceptions about right and wrong with respect to self and others, and impositions of these perceptions on group behavior.

"Traditional gender roles are now so ingrained in culture that men and women accept them without questioning their legitimacy" (Soules, 2011). If gender is an idea that is socially constructed, then the perceptions about gender are open for shifts of change, and therein lie a possibility for jazz educators to effect these changes. How gender is experienced in jazz settings is dependent on both the individual perceptions and collective culture created by persons interacting. Spitzberg and Changnon (2009) defined intercultural maturity as the ability to effectively manage behavior and communication with those who have different or divergent orientations in normative realms of race, ethnicity, gender, nationality, religion, or tribe (groups). Though the idea of roles and abilities of jazzwomen may come from the outer culture, and many of these ideas engendered outside of jazz settings, they exist inside of jazz settings as normalized and expected.

If as educators we lean toward inculcating our students and peers to be interculturally competent— and, in being so skilled, demonstrate intercultural maturity—changes in the interactions with jazzwomen may be fostered toward respect and equality. New pedagogical approaches coupled with socio-cultural learning may result in students learning more than how to play their instruments. King and Baxter Magolda (2005) discussed how interculturally mature individuals demonstrate adaptability, flexibility, openness, empathy, relationship development, and curiousness. Empathy might be a highly misunderstood human characteristic, but is powerful in formulating changes in individual and group interactions. Hendricks (2018) salient definition of empathic behavior is useful for intercultural maturity frames:

> What can empathy do—and why we perceive it as a worthy quality—is that it helps us take on the perspective of another person, so much so that we can imagine or even feel what it would be like to be that person or to live that person's life. In a general sense, then, empathy has the potential to motivate us to treat others as we would want to be treated ourselves—but only if we choose to act upon those empathetic thoughts and feelings in kind and noble ways.
>
> *(p. 55)*

As educators, we would not want our students to say we did not prepare them for a multiversed world or to ignore the signals emanating from voiced concerns of jazzwomen that biases were engendered from our jazz culture. "Empathy, cooperation, and music belong together. Meanwhile, settling our sights on performing better than others may steer us away from relationships of trust" (Hendricks, 2018, p. 70).

Helm Hammonds (2021) reported findings on instigation of intercultural maturity through jazz curricula highlighting the awareness and understanding demonstrated by individuals in the study. The qualitative case study comprised jazz students as participants in geographic cohorts from three universities on three continents (United States, South Africa, and Denmark) in a globally networked learning environment. Findings from the study are significant to our discussion on the efficacy of jazz curricula on students' intercultural maturity. The assignments in the study included: (a) creating a video bio as a self-introduction to the class, (b) writing a blues using thematic material from a folk song from each participant's own culture, (c) collaborating on a song with a classmate in the cohort from another school, (d) discussing jazz history, (e) creating a song as a contrafact, and (f) studying the work and contributions of a woman jazz composer. The data revealed observable changes in behavior and communication of the participants across the three stages of initial, intermediate, and advanced development in cognitive, interpersonal, and intrapersonal domains. Emerging from the data as observed behavior of participants were themes of *Adaptability, Curiousness, Empathy, Identity (Personal and Cultural), Openness, Self-Awareness.* The tactile and visual artifacts demonstrating these themes were from the submitted assignments, included videotaped autobiographical essays, written essays, mp3 recordings, lyric sheets, social media posts of career achievements, and videotaped presentations from assignments.

The jazz student responses in the Helm Hammonds (2021) study provided several instances of the developmental threads in interpersonal and cognitive domains—namely how students understood and perceived the actions and behaviors of peers. An interesting behavioral phenomenon that emerged from the students was the quality of self-awareness and resilience in jazz learners, particularly the tasks involved in jazz composition and improvisation. These topics require reflexivity in creative expression and variances of musical experience, inculcating an expectation of judgment in a jazz socio-culture. The resulting emotional and psychological repercussions of students engaged in jazz improvisation and jazz composition are a veritable 'Petri dish' to observe behavioral outcomes. Students' expressions of personal opinions and beliefs with peers facilitated through jazz topics elicited an observable range of intercultural maturity.

At the crux of the reasoning for incorporating intercultural maturity as a learning outcome for jazz settings is the ability to use a research-based approach to address gender biases. The desired outcome would be for individuals to develop awareness, understanding and knowledge of individual behaviors' and perceptions to mitigate gender biases from occurring. Helm Hammonds (2021) reported significant observations relatable to the developmental traits in cognitive, interpersonal, and intrapersonal domains in response to jazz composition and jazz history activities. Here are findings from the Helm Hammonds study useful for jazz educators to effect change in gender biases:

1. Performing and/or composing jazz does not automatically instill an ability to develop competency in effective and successful communication with others. However, performing and/or composing jazz *does* involve developing skill in improvisation. Individuals who are interculturally mature exhibit qualities of adaptability, flexibility, openness, empathy, amicability, and curiousness—all traits that are encountered on the pathway in learning to improvise (Monson 1994; Berliner, 2009; Kelly, 2013; Bromley, 2019). And further, these qualities are needed in mastering an instrument and performing with others (Wiggins, 1997; Dunscomb and Hill, 2002; Wehr-Flowers, 2006; Helm Hammonds and Ortisejafor, 2015). Jazz educators could embed improvisation and composition tasks factored for intercultural maturity outcomes to instigate students' development in the initial, intermediate, and advanced levels of cognitive, interpersonal, and intrapersonal domains.

2. The growing international expansion of jazz and the ever-expanding global jazz community practically guarantees practitioners will have bandmates who are culturally different—and with whom they have no cultural connection other than the music they will play together. In some regions, the cultural norms are that men and women may not perform together or socialize together. However, many countries have well-established jazz artists and communities of jazz professionals interconnected with commercial entities that function as economic powerhouses for those regions, (e.g. jazz festivals, jazz radio stations, jazz, music and trade conferences, cultural organizations), emerging from the work and careers of the artists, both men and women. (Prouty, 2012). As a matter of practicality, it seems prudent to prepare jazz students for successful navigation in the global expanse of cultural norms that has evolved.

3. A range of attributes in the initial, intermediate and advanced stages of intercultural maturity were represented in study participants' attitudes, skills, behaviors and knowledge as a result of interaction with different others, and were observed in cognitive, interpersonal and intrapersonal traits.

4. The findings supported the ability for instigative activities to elicit growth in intercultural maturity domains. If educators design activities to discuss and bring awareness, understanding and knowledge of the impact of jazz gender justice, and embed into jazz composition, jazz

improvisation and jazz history activities, pedagogy can be cultivated in the jazz curricula as a catalyst for change.

5. Program outcomes and course outcomes can be transformed so curricula designers can support the conversation for educators' needs, consider pedagogical enhancements, and facilitate student development in intercultural maturity domains.

A Jazz Orientation of the Three-Dimensional Developmental Trajectory of the Intercultural Maturity Model

Perceptions about roles of men and women in jazz settings as right/wrong are valid competencies to address as learning outcomes. Such competencies could be considered as important as the fundamentals of instrument instruction, or pedagogy of improvisation and composition. Kernodle (2014) addresses the ideas about women breaking norms of how to work and with whom to work, resonating this concept about "appropriate roles" of jazz women. Kernodle rejects these tenets:

> The exceptional woman becomes the rationale for the exclusion of other women and lends support to a narrative of invisibility that occurs in jazz histories as it relates to women musicians. Most important is how this narrative of the exceptional woman has defined common misunderstandings of how these women worked and created art.

Being misunderstood, misnamed and unframed allows continuation for gender biases to exist in jazz culture. The issues of not being respected, seen or heard reverberate in absences of women in jazz discographies and in recorded audio and video documentation of the lives of jazzwomen. Identity and cultural perceptions of jazzwomen perpetuated in this menagerie of frames disallows the wholeness of the person, their creative artifacts and the artistic contributions.

The developmental traits germane to jazz subjects are outlined in the new intercultural maturity model. A diagram of the model is below.

The model is intended to clarify subtleties in participant behavior and communication across the developmental continuum elicited by jazz particularities. The Helm Hammonds (2021) conceptual model, *A Jazz Orientation to the Three-Dimensional Developmental Trajectory of the Intercultural Maturity Model*, is an explanation of how jazz topics were used as jazz college students constructed meaning and communicated perspectives and behaviors along the developmental continuum of the IMM. These were also important distinctions in the findings as it relates to the ability of jazz subjects to activate personal development in cognitive, interpersonal, and intrapersonal domains.

On the farthest left column of the chart are the three domains of development, Cognitive, Intrapersonal, and Interpersonal. The second from the left column are the three stages an individual traverses in each domain of development in initial, intermediate, and advanced stages. Each jazz topic is divided into the activities that elicited reactions or observable changes for participants as they moved across the continuum of the three stages or three domains. The activities were in topics of jazz composition, jazz improvisation, and jazz history.

In each of the intercultural maturity domains, there are aspects of an overlap of factors evidenced in how an interactant responds to the behavior of a peer. No isolated activity was responsible for the total movement from one level to the next. As the sessions progressed, I observed conversations and assignment submissions evidencing perceptions different from the initial statements or beliefs expressed by the students. Emergent themes from their interactions evolved, and my journal notes and jottings were important resources from which to weave together a full picture of study participants' developmental processes. To the extent *an individual allowed themselves to engage*, the influence of the peer-to-peer interaction created a simultaneous momentum of changed behaviors from the students of many of the domain factors.

A Jazz Orientation of the Three-Dimensional Developmental Trajectory of the Intercultural Maturity model.

Domain of Development	Stages of Development	Jazz Activities: Composition	Jazz Activities: Improvisation	Jazz Activities: Jazz History
Cognitive	Initial	Categorizes knowledge about composition devices or concepts as blanket "right" or "wrong"; Lacks empathy or respect for others' creative ideas and unable to receive feedback on work. Minimizes other's ideas and efforts in compositional processes or outcomes.	Categorizes pathways in jazz knowledge about improv strategies and methodologies as right or wrong; Lacks resilience to attempt after failures in performance and eschews encouragement, even to the point of being self-effacing; Lacks hardiness to receive feedback on work.	Believes cultural practices and values of different others' jazz histories are right/wrong/absolute. Resists one's own beliefs and cultural perspectives could be wrong and instead see's other's beliefs about jazz history is wrong.
	Intermediate	Evolving resilience and acceptance of the compositional uncertainty and development of compositional ideas and perspectives; Some capacity to have empathy for personal processes and embracing progress as a possibility for one's self.	Evolving awareness of multiple perspectives about the improvisational process and the ability to shift perspectives. Some capacity to adopt a personal process to embrace the hardships and resilience needed to progress in improvisational skills. Improvisation achievement seen as a growing as a possibility with a distinct self-authorship.	Evolving awareness and embracing of knowledge claims of others' contributions to jazz history. Some capacity to have construct knowledge process to embrace different others historical cultural journey as valued.
	Mature	Ability to conceptualize and adopt cultural framing of compositional ideals and shift perspectives and behaviors into an alternative worldview allowing review and conceptual input from multiple cultural compositional strategies.	Ability to shift and embrace new and emerging improv concepts and ideas. Able to engage alternative improv ideas while in performance and recall and embrace ideas in mid-performance of others' strategies.	Ability to shift historical perspectives and espouse on thoughts of a transnational jazz worldview allowing multiple narratives. Embrace and adopt cultural re-framing of jazz histories,
Intrapersonal	Initial	Lacks respect of one's own creative ideas. Differences viewed as identity threat and creative ideas of others devalued; Self-identity is narrowly defined and used as the lens to guide choices regulating interpretation of experiences during the composing process.	Lacks respect of one's own improvisational efforts or ideas. Has trouble making connections to improv ideas and identifying one's own voice within a group of different others. Differences viewed as identity threat and creative ideas devalued; Self-identity is muddied in group and band settings.	Lacks understanding of other cultures, with respect to one's own jazz history. Unable to adapt to idea of shared histories in cultural contexts. Narrow lens for historical narratives and denies global contributions as derivative. Thinks of jazz as extractive if not referential to their own identity.
	Intermediate	Evolving sense of identity as a jazz composer and an ability to compose as distinct from external others' ideas about own abilities; this tension creates increased self-examination of Identities in own cultural setting; recognizes legitimacy and value of other composers' culture, ideas and contributions. Developing hardiness and resilience about self-identity to incoming feedback.	Evolving sense of self-authorship and awareness of identity as a jazz improviser and an ability to function with different others as valid contributors. Identity as distinct from external others' ideas about own abilities; this tension creates increased self-examination of identities in own cultural (band) setting; recognizes legitimacy of contributions and ideas of other jazz improvisers. Hardiness and resilience improve for incoming feedback as jazz improvisation skills develop leading to adaptability of outside ideas.	Awareness of identity and personal place within the reflected jazz history as a performer and contributor; Evolving self-authorship as distinct from external others' ideas about own identity as attached to local, regional, national jazz history; this tension creates increased self-examination of identities in own cultural setting; recognizes legitimacy of other jazz historical cultures, ideas and contributions.
	Mature	Capacity for self-authorship that openly engages challenges to one's views and beliefs about the jazz compositional process and that considers social identities embedded in jazz compositions (race, class, gender, etc.) in a global and national context as valid and necessary; Embraces and integrates these aspects of others and self into one's identity as a jazz composer.	Capacity for self-authorship that openly engages challenges to one's views and beliefs about the jazz improvisational process and that considers social identities embedded in improvisations (race, class, gender, etc.) in a global and national context; Embraces and integrates these aspects of others and self into one's identity as a jazz improviser.	Recognizes contributions of iconic jazz improvisers of other cultures. Capacity increases for openness that accounts for and considers social identities embedded. In jazz historical narratives (race, class, gender, etc.) in a global and national context; Embraces and integrates these aspects of others and self into one's world-view about jazz history
Interpersonal	Initial	Lacks understanding of intersection of other cultures' creative contributions to compositions. Identity lacking in compositional ideas and primarily sourced from others. Affirmation desperately needed from others. Lacks desire to collaborate with others. Lacks ability to be accepting of diverse others (gender, race, ethnicity, instrument) in concept as group or band members.	Cannot demonstrate empathy or respect for others' journey of development of improv skills. Rejects others' participation in sessions. Disrespects bandmates time in trading choruses or selfishly takes inordinate amounts of choruses. Rejects compositional ability/input of diverse personnel/group members/band members.	Believes different others appropriate one's own cultural history instead of legitimately creating distinct contributions to jazz history and rejects embracing narrative and interactions with diverse others. Narrow lens for diverse others' jazz history and invalidates historical input from other cultures.
	Intermediate	Evolving desire to compose with diverse others and engage from judgment; Prefers free-agent orientation in group/bands/ensembles but likes being involved in collaborative creative settings where multiple perspectives exist; still a strong need for others' approval and support. Some adaptability to consider impact of socio-cultural norms on intergroup relations.	Willingness to embrace as necessary improvisational settings with diverse others and shifts toward ability to engage and interact; Can "share the bandstand" but stays removed as lone soldier in ideas; the need for others' approval allows some interaction. Some adaptability to socio-cultural norms creating input of value for improvisational perspectives during intergroup sessions.	Evolving awareness of others' historical jazz narratives as authentic instead of "stolen" and a developing desire to discuss and receive opinions with diverse others and refrain from judgment; Likes being involved in group examination where multiple perspectives exist; still a strong need for others' support of ideas. Exploration of how social systems impact norms of the historical narrative group in jazz glocales.
	Mature	Capacity to teach and support the compositional process and engage in meaningful, interdependent relationships with diverse others that are grounded in an understanding and appreciation for human differences; An understanding of ways social systems impact individual composers' choices in collaborative settings; willing to work for the rights of others to freely express compositional ideas/directions. May be inclined to admonish others who are judgmental and culturally insensitive.	Capacity to teach and support the improvisational process and engage in meaningful, interdependent relationships with diverse others that are grounded in an understanding of ways social systems impact individual improvisers' choices in collaborative settings; Some adaptability to socio-cultural norms creating input of value for improvisational ideas/directions. May be inclined to freely express improvisational ideas/directions. May be inclined to admonish others who are judgmental and culturally insensitive.	Capacity to teach and support the oral and cultural histories and narratives of different others as core to the jazz lexicon. Able to engage and lead meaningful, interdependent collaborations and relationships with diverse others that are grounded in an understanding and appreciation for human differences; A understanding of how social systems impact individual perspectives on jazz history in collaborative settings; willing to work for the rights of others to express and document jazz legacies ideas/directions. May be inclined to admonish others who are judgmental and culturally insensitive.

Figure 29.1 Jazz and Intercultural Maturity

Jazz educators can look at the options offered in the *Jazz & Intercultural Maturity Model* below to situate conversations about gender biases in the activities embedded in curricula.

The following are parallels from the findings of the Helm Hammonds (2021) study, as outlined in the Jazz Intercultural Maturity Model and pedagogical ideas to address gender discrimination issues.

Jazz Composition. Jazz composition is largely taught as a pedagogical next step to jazz improvising in academic settings, and jazz history as a necessary core requirement in the jazz curriculum (Dunscomb and Hill, 2002; Goodrich, 2007; Kelly, 2013). The canon of jazz composers is highly gendered and largely missing the contributions of jazzwomen. Jazz composition activities were interesting in participants' reflexes toward the vulnerability of being judged. The faculty encouraged discussion about the mental and psychological stressors of the compositional process. Students saw themselves in each other's reflections and sharing about the disparities of women composers' omissions in the jazz canon, of not being aware of choosing "mostly male composers and arrangers" and how to program a mix-gendered set of music. The domains of interpersonal and intrapersonal development were activated as students' concerns over how their creative ideas would be judged and discussed publicly were noted. Students were empathic to classmates when it was their turn to share the ideas with classmates or teammates.

Jazz Improvisation. Some students demonstrated empathy and hardiness in discussing the creative ideas of peers, while others were adaptable and resilient in giving way to the challenges of "trading fours," a common musical context of jazz improvisation where students share the spotlight "giving their solo" within four bar sections of the form (Herzig and Baker, 2014). Emphasis was on listening and supporting students with comments to validate the ideas of peers' efforts for the jazz improv assignments. Students are amenable to look at their own behavior and perceptions once an understanding of the impact on gender biases of belittling comments, peer pressure and sharing the bandstand during soloing.

Jazz History. Activities on the subject of jazz history discoveries in each country of the participants and faculty encouraged conversation revealing students' nationalistic group orientations in a way that was not necessarily evident in jazz improvisation activities. Jazz history activities elicited intrapersonal and cognitive domain behaviors and communications amongst participants, especially when discussing the absence of documented histories of jazzwomen. Persistent stories in movies and books, both fiction and non-fiction accounts; these should be discussed to address why there is a focus on drug and aberrant behaviors of jazzwomen icons like Billie Holiday, Anita O'Day and Mary Lou Williams. The focus of the conversations in the study addressed how jazzwomen's trauma often overshadowed and eclipsed their musical contributions. A focus on identifying and highlighting musical innovations of jazzwomen like Holiday, O'Day and Williams help to facilitate identities for which jazzwomen and girls can embrace with confidence.

It is my hope that educators are inspired to look toward intercultural maturity development as a potential tool to address jazz gender justice. The activities-as-instigators to elicit gradations of the dimensions in each domain of initial, intermediate and mature development can be embedded in jazz pedagogy. Distinctions arose from this research which may also influence the conversation at the heart of the transnational jazz discourse, particularly how we can become increasingly capable of hearing and respecting the many voices of our jazz communities, as well as collective identities in the jazz culture. Imagine if it could be deduced that adding jazz education may offer avenues—not a panacea, but a research-based approach—in the general education curriculum to contribute to students becoming interculturally mature enough to reject gender biases.

Conclusions

A multi-dimensional approach is suggested for eradicating the many layers of discrimination and bias existing in jazz settings and, especially, in jazz education curricula. Adopting a mindset of a gender imperative could show support for jazzwomen and girls and galvanize a new paradigm in jazz. Many paradigms in jazz education research have been explored for efficacy of instruction, not only for the potential impact of interventions but also for complex, structural curricula reform. The Helm Hammonds (2021) and Helm Hammonds and Oritsejafor (2015) studies provided indication that jazz can be used as a vehicle of development toward intercultural maturity, and thus affect jazz students becoming interculturally competent. If jazz improvisation and composition have this power to influence who is deemed "worthy" amongst musicians in the jazz culture, they can be used for personal development of individuals. It will be interesting to employ this mindset as a tool for developing intercultural maturity through jazz education curricula to address gender biases, gendered instrument choices and gender justice.

Recommendations from the Helm Hammonds (2021) findings for infusing jazz pedagogy with intercultural maturity traits are inclusive of the following:

1. Jazz improvisation is a necessary skill set for all jazz musicians. Be aware of how the culture is developed to encourage community and empathy to allow for an enjoyable process of development and growth for all students.

2. Language about gender and ability, implications of playing at a level of strength to prove oneself would not assist intercultural maturity of the participants.

3. Environment influences a socio-culture and the leadership in a given environment—be it classroom or bandstand—could change a culture wrought with gender biases. Empathy, self-awareness and identity are crucial traits in interculturally mature individuals, and these traits can be developed under the careful tutelage of a compassionate educator who embeds the activities and conversation to develop these traits.

4. Group cooperation is a socio-cultural construct; a result of environments where intercultural maturity is the agreed social currency—a decision made by the group to interact with respect for everyone. Hendricks (2018) provided relevant research for music educators with insights for developing empathic mindsets and compassionate teaching and learning environments. "Empathy, cooperation and music belong together" (p. 70). The socio-culture among jazz musicians engaged in improvisation is often one of competitiveness, which can create a sense of separateness. Intercultural maturity skills can mitigate this element of the jazz socio-culture.

There is promise in social activism toward jazz gender justice currently taking hold in jazz circles led by noted jazzwomen. Two recent platforms I want to mention are especially exciting. The first is an initiative embraced by NEA Jazz Master and drummer, Terri Lyne Carrington at Berklee College of Music and the newly created Berklee Institute of Jazz and Gender Justice.[1] Terri Lyne is the founder and artistic director of the institute with a formidable and long-historied successful career in jazz. On a recent webinar on the topic of racism in jazz education for which we both were speaking, Terri stated simply of her denunciation of common mistropes in jazz that women should endeavor to "play as hard as the men" to prove excellence or belonging. Indeed!

The second initiative is The Haven Hang with Camille Thurman—Young Lioness Musician Q&A Advice Hour[2] on YouTube. It is coined by Thurman as a live-streamed Q&A virtual mentorship platform for young women musicians (lionesses) to ask questions and talk one-on-one with internationally acclaimed, Jazz at Lincoln Center's tenor saxophone chair and vocalist, educator Camille Thurman and guests." I love this excellent, free resource for the jazz community for the breadth of topics and its array of guests, including violinist Regina Carter, bassist Mimi Fox, vocalist Rene Marie, pianist Bertha Hope and others. Thurman also includes women artists of other disciplines like journalism, dance, communications and related arts disciplines. A laudable undertaking, this video series is important for the access it affords listeners to the documented stories and life lessons from world-renowned jazz and arts professionals. I hope you have a chance to visit this dynamic series, which at this writing is 15 hour + long sessions. Examples like these were a result of activities from the outcomes outlined in the Jazz Intercultural Maturity Model.

As an example, one young woman student, being emphatic about discussing/presenting the history of women's contributions to jazz history in her country, initiated a conversation in the class about jazz and gender. This could be perceived as maturity in the Empathy factor and/or a recognition of a responsibility to work on behalf of others (final stage of interpersonal domain maturity). Given the understanding that pre-seminar, the interactants in the study did not all hold the same beliefs and understandings about any specific topic (evidenced by the pre-study survey), the ability for their engagement to influence or change opinions could reveal themselves in their subsequent choices in songs, assignment topics or career decisions (in post-survey study answers).

The moniker for the Berklee College of Music's Berklee Institute for Jazz and Gender Justice is, "What would jazz sound like in a culture without patriarchy?" I think this says it all. I venture to dream of this world.

Notes

1 https://college.berklee.edu/jazz-gender-justice.
2 www.youtube.com/playlist?list=PLaOa12r61_SBKOB--RkVFJrobzGwkH6jt.

References

Austerlitz, P. (2005). *Jazz Consciousness: Music, Race and Humanity*. Middletown, CT. Wesleyan University Press.

Baraka, A. (2009). *Diggin: The Afro-American soul of American Classical Music*. Berkeley. University of California Press.

Baxter-Magolda, M.B. (2001). *Making Their Own Way: Narratives for Transforming Higher Education to Promote Self-development*. Sterling, VA.

Barrett, F. J. (2012). *Yes to the Mess: Surprising Leadership Lessons from Jazz*. Boston. Harvard Business Review Press.

Berliner. P. F. (2009). *Thinking in Jazz: The Infinite Art of Improvisation*. Chicago: University of Chicago Press.

Bennett, M. J. (1993). Towards Ethnorelativism: A Developmental Model of Intercultural Sensitivity. (pp. 21–71). In R. M. Paige (Ed.), *Education for the Intercultural Experience*. Yarmouth, ME. Intercultural Press.

Bennett, J. M and Bennett, M. J. (2001). Developing intercultural sensitivity: An integrative approach to global and domestic diversity, 3rd ed. In D. Landis, J. Bennett & M. Bennett (Eds.), *Handbook of intercultural training*, pp. 147–164. Thousand Oaks: Sage.

Boeyink, N. (2015). A Descriptive Study of Collegiate Female Jazz Instrumentalists. (Doctoral Dissertation, Indiana University 2015).

Bromley, K. (2019). "Person Centered Learning in a Collegiate Jazz Combo." (Doctoral Dissertation, Boston University, 2019). ProQuest Dissertations Publishing. 13425317.

Carrington, T. (2021). *Dismantling Patriarchy is a Daily Practice*. Library of Congress; Accessed: https://blogs.loc.gov/music/2021/04.

Cion, S. J., Ray, C. and Helm, L. Z. (2000). When women band together: Three jazz artists share their stories. *The Women's Review of Books*, 18(3), 8–9

Crenshaw, K. (2016). *The Urgency of Intersectionality*. TED Talk.

Crouch, S. (2006). *Considering Genius: Writings on Jazz*. Cambridge, MA. Civitas Bookss.

Deardorff, D. K. (2009). Synthesizing conceptualizations of intercultural competence: A summary and emerging themes. (pp. 66–83). In D. K. Deardorff (Ed). *The SAGE Handbook of Intercultural Competence*. Los Angeles. Sage.

Dunscomb, J. R. Hill, W. (2002). *Jazz Pedagogy: The Jazz Educator's Resource Guide*. Van Nuys. Alfred Music Publishing.

Goodrich, A. (2007). Peer mentoring in a high-school jazz ensemble. *Journal of Research in Music Education*. 55(2), 94–114.

Hammonds, L. H. (2021). "A Jazz Orientation of the Three-dimensional Developmental Trajectory of the Intercultural Maturity Model." (Doctoral Dissertation, Boston University) ProQuest Dissertations Publishing 28770684.

Helm Hammonds L. Z., and Oritsejafor, E. (2015). Navigating the performing arts in a globally networked classroom (pp. 145–164). In P.C. Layne and P. Lake (Eds.), Global Innovation of Teaching and Learning in Higher Education: Transgressing Boundaries. In *Professional Learning and Development in Schools and Higher Education*. Vol. 11, C. Day and J. Sachs (Series Eds.). United Kingdom. Springer.

Heath, J. and McLaren, J. (2010). *I Walked with Giants: The Autobiography of Jimmy Heath*. Philadelphia. Temple University Press.

Hendricks, K. S. (2018). *Compassionate Music Teaching: A Framework for Motivation and Engagement in the 21st Century*. London. Rowan & Littlefield.

Herzig, M., Baker, D. (2014). Beyond jamming: A historical and analytical perspective on the creative process. *Journal of the Music and Entertainment Industry Educators Association, 14*(1), pp. 183–217.

Horne, Gerald. (2019). Jazz and justice: Racism and the political economy of the music. New York. *Monthly Review Press*.

Impey, A. M. (1992). *They Want Us with Salt and Onions: Women in the Zimbabwean Music Industry*. Indiana University. ProQuest Dissertations Publishing. 9310214.

Kegan, R. (1994). *In Over Our Heads: The Mental Demands of Modern Life*. Cambridge, MA: Harvard University Press.

Kelly, K. B. (2013). "A New Cartography: Learning Jazz at the Dawn of the 21st Century." (Doctoral Dissertation, Arizona State University, 2013).

Kernodle, T. (2014). Black women working together: Jazz, gender, and the politics of validation. *Black Music Research Journal, 34*(1), 27–55. doi:10.5406/blacmusiresej.34.1.0027.

King, P. M. and Baxter Magolda, M. B. (2005). A developmental model of intercultural maturity. *Journal of College Student Development, 46*(6), 571–592. doi:10.1353/csd.2005.0060.

Monson, I. (1994). Doubleness and Jazz improvisation: Irony, parody and ethnomusicology. *Critical Inquiry, 20*(2), 283–313.

Monson, I. (2009b). *Saying Something: Jazz Improvisation and Interaction*. Chicago: University of Chicago Press.

Payne, B. (1996). The Gender Gap: Women on Music Faculties in American Colleges and Universities 1993–1994. *College Music Symposium, 36*, 91–102. Retrieved June 17, 2021, from www.jstor.org/stable/40374286.

Perez, R.J., Shim, W., King, P.M., and Baxter Magolda, M.B. (2015). Refining King and Baxter Magolda's Model of Intercultural Maturity. *Journal of College Student Development, 56*(8), 759–776. doi:10.1353/csd.2015.0085.

Prouty, K. (2012). *Knowing Jazz: Community, Pedagogy, and Canon in the Information Age*. Jackson, MS: University Press of Mississippi.

Reid, E. (2013). Models of Intercultural Competencies in Practice. *International Journal of Language and Linguistics, 1*(2), 44–53. doi: 10.11648/j.ijll.20130102.12.

Soules, K. (2011). *Playing Like a Man: The Struggle of Black Women in Jazz and the Feminist Movement*. B.A. in Music Senior Capstone Projects. 2. http://digitalcommons.cedarville.edu/music_and_worship_ba_capstone/2.

Spitzberg, B. H. and Changnon, G. (2009). Conceptualizing intercultural competence. (pp. 2–52), In D. K. Deardorff (Ed.). *The SAGE Handbook of Intercultural Competence*. Los Angeles: Sage.

Taylor, A. (1977). *Notes and Tones: Musician to Musician Interviews*. New York: Perigree Books.

Taylor, K. B. (2016). How prepared are students for global citizenship? A qualitative, holistic approach to assessing intercultural competence. *The Journal of Student Affairs Inquiry, 2*(1), 1–21.

Van Vleet, K. (2021). Women in jazz music: A hundred years of gender disparity in jazz study and performance (1920–2020). *Jazz Education in Research and Practice, 2*(1), 211–227. doi:10.2979/jazzeducrese.2.1.16.

Wehr-Flowers, E. (2006). Differences between male and female students' confidence, anxiety and attitude learning jazz improvisation. *Journal of Research in Music Education, 54*(4), 337–349.

Wiggins, I. (1997). *An assessment of the state of jazz music education in the public high schools of North Carolina: A foundation for curriculum revision in higher education* (Doctoral dissertation, University of North Carolina at Greensboro, 1997).

Wise, T. (2012). *Dear White America: Letter to a new minority*. City Lights Books. San Francisco.

30

IN HER OWN WORDS

Documenting the Current Realities of Women-in-Jazz

Kiernan Steiner and Alexandra Manfredo

I remember specifically not lifting my head from my notebook. Being the only woman in the classroom, I felt every man's eyes looking at me. My face felt red and hot, warmth creeping up from my neck to my cheeks. I remember being unsure of how to react to the sexual comment made in class. Every muscle was telling me not to move. I pretended I had not heard what was said. It was a helpless feeling. I counted down the minutes until I could bolt from the room.... If I felt isolated and unsafe in the classroom, how was I supposed to find freedom in the music that is jazz?

Introduction

Since the recent resurgence of the #MeToo movement, first coined and created by Tarana Burke, women from various disciplines and backgrounds have been courageously sharing their stories of sexual harassment and assault, and the jazz community is no exception. The #MeToo movement is rooted in empathy (Get to Know Us, 2021), using social media hashtags to provide an outlet for women to use their voice to join millions of people around the world speak up against sexual violence and discrimination. In recent music-related publications, there have been dozens of articles written by female-identifying jazz musicians discussing issues of sexual harassment and assault during their studies at music conservatories and universities (Healey, 2016; Sevian, 2017; Mercer, 2017; Schmalenberger and Maddox, 2019). These articles sparked conversations and raised many concerns. Van Vleet (2021) wrote: "Despite there being research on the topic of female underrepresentation in jazz, resources are not so current as to address the impact of the '#MeToo' movement on gender inequality in jazz" (p. 212). Burke (2021) started the #MeToo movement in response to her work with young women and girls, especially Black women and girls, who had experienced sexual violence and systemic oppression (Get To Know Us, 2021). Burke's (2021) philosophy, "empowerment through empathy," grounds the #MeToo movement in values of community and trust. On the #MeToo Movement website it said,

> Tarana has used her platform to share her long-standing belief that healing is not a destination, but a journey. This philosophy has inspired millions of survivors who previously had to live in isolation to deal with the pain, shame and trauma of their experience.
>
> *(Get To Know Us, 2021)*

DOI: 10.4324/9781003081876-33

Through personal interviews, a review of jazz scholarship, and gender studies, we have unearthed stories of women-in-jazz to demonstrate the importance of documenting their lived experiences, in order to address difficult realities, such as sexual discrimination and harassment, within the jazz community.

Online articles written by leading female jazz musicians, such as Lauren Sevian (2017) and Biddy Healey (2016), have brought to light many of the issues of sexual harassment and violence women-in-jazz have experienced for decades. Sevian (2017) described a moment when she reported an objectifying comment made by a male professor, and her female senior administrator replied with: "Lauren, do you want to have a career?" Unfortunately, this response is all too common and widely accepted as a way to cope with these experiences. Sevian (2017) concluded, "Still, what had the greatest impact on me was what happened in school: someone I thought I could trust, who was supposed to be in my corner, turned out to be just another card-carrying member of The Old Boys' Club." In another article, Healey (2016) writes:

> Among the women I interviewed as well as in the literature, women seem to feel socially excluded in male-dominated ensembles. As a freelance, ensemble-based industry, jazz is a social art. Women I interviewed reported being excluded from banter and not invited to the "post-gig hang." One interviewee called her bandmates out on it, and they openly told her they'd rather hire other men because "they could joke around and they didn't have to censor themselves."

The literature concerning the lived experiences of women-in-jazz on and off the bandstand is limited. For too long, the jazz community has ignored and erased the contributions of women-in-jazz. In W. Knauer's *Gender and Identity in Jazz* (2016) it says:

> Jazz used to be a predominantly male music. Not only were most of the musicians male, but its aesthetics and social environment was dominated by male ideals and male players as well. In the public perception of this music women as well as other groups or identities not compliant with the male orientation of jazz's origins played only a minor role.
>
> *(p. 7)*

Efforts to document women-in-jazz have begun, however; this work has been, and continues to be, led by women. Tucker (2001/2002) wrote:

> In jazz studies, "gender" is still often taken to denote inclusion of women, and "women's work" at that. In other words, it is the prerogative of women and pro-woman men to gather information on women musicians and compile it for dissertations and for articles and books intended for women readers. In this viewpoint, work on gender and women is seen as benevolent, as a special interest, as useful for women interested in women, but is not considered crucial for jazz scholarship as a whole.
>
> *(p. 384)*

After recognizing the exclusion of women-in-jazz in the publication *Jazz Spoken Here* (1992), Enstice and Stockhouse (2004) interviewed female leaders in jazz, in hopes to uncover the breadth of experiences of female jazz musicians. In the introduction of *Jazzwomen*, Enstice and Stockhouse (2004) wrote:

> Still, for those of us who look beneath the pervasive topcoat of pop culture, the male jazz player is available for discovery. Reigning as countercultural heroes since at least the inception of bop, the men of the music have seen their work spawn a satellite industry, complete

with independent labels and a specialized press. But what of the heroines? How about the talented women who have had the courage to enter the predatory waters of the jazz life? Where is the comparative historical conscience, the equivalent critical corpus, in relation to their work?

(p. xiv)

Their documented interviews include inquiries of gender politics and sexism, which served as a foundation for this investigation into female representation in jazz programs in higher education (see Enstice and Stockhouse, 2004). Enstice and Stockhouse (2004) acknowledged other ways women-in-jazz are "othered" (p. xv):

The twenty-one women featured in this book were chosen to represent a cross-section of styles, career stations, and instruments. ... Instrumentalists were favored over vocalists in our selection of interviews, because women playing jazz on a horn or drums have had a much higher glass ceiling to shatter. ... Nonetheless, we are mindful of the irony that our format, with its exclusive focus on women, mimics the gender-imposed ghettoization that many of these fine performers have chronically suffered in their careers.

(p. xv)

Here, Enstice and Stockhouse (2004) briefly described his methodology in selecting jazz-women to interview and how instrumentalists were favored, in order to make sure those voices were heard. Throughout the book, many of the interviews discuss the need for more representation, but few self-identified as "feminist" (Enstice and Stockhouse, 2004).

Within jazz history, a darker side of American culture has spread its influence. This is apparent today even in the age-old question of "what 'is' and 'is not' jazz?" a damaging question designed to exclude. Similarly, Tucker (2016) questions this conundrum of women-in-jazz:

How do we get out of this conundrum? To consider women musicians, especially women as instrumentalists who play instruments associated with men and masculinity—drums, for example—in jazz discourse, they still must be added in. And to add women in, means they are not already in. Subtract them and you still have jazz. Women jazz musicians go missing unless the framework is explicitly: *woman-in-jazz*. But *woman-in-jazz* depends on the assumption that "Jazz" does not already have women in it—a frustrating premise for women who play jazz and the people who write about them.

(p. 247)

Furthermore, in *Gender and Identity in Jazz* (2016) it addressed how societal pressures have caused female instrumentalists to question their gender identity:

Andrea Beall, another Benson drummer from the 1960s band, personally felt conflicted with being female playing this instrument. She jokingly described that playing the drums made her fall into the gender category of "other." ... Gender assumptions about instruments appear to be so deep-rooted in society that even a musician like Beall, who was playing the drums from a very early age, struggled with her own sense of gender identity specifically because of her instrument.

(p. 185)

This quotation shows how societal biases, expectations, and norms have influenced women-in-jazz, regardless of explicit experiences of sexual discrimination and harassment, and it is time for the jazz community to acknowledge and address these concerns.

Wehr-Flowers (2006) conducted a study on the differences between male and female students' confidence, anxiety, and attitude towards learning jazz improvisation. While this does not expose information directly related to our concerns about sexual discrimination or harassment, it is interesting to see how young women, in comparison to young men, react to questions about a critical part of jazz studies. Wehr-Flowers (2006) reported, with the completion of 137 surveys,

> results indicate females are significantly less confident, more anxious, and have less-efficacy (attitude) towards learning jazz improvisation. The mean score for females was lower than the mean score for males on every statement ... which further reinforces the differences between males and females on the dependent variables.
>
> *(p. 345)*

These findings are in alignment with many of the stories shared by the interviewees, which is a feature of most creative industries (Hennekam and Bennett, 2017).

The book *Modern Sexism: Blatant, Subtle, and Covert Discrimination* by Benokraitis and Feagin (1994) is an important resource for understanding various forms of sexism. It is organized using the "Blatant, Subtle, and Covert Discrimination" framework, which outlines the complexities of sex discrimination and why it has been difficult to detect, identify, strategize, and remedy:

- **covert:** the unequal and harmful treatment of women that is hidden, purposeful, and, often, maliciously motivated;
- **subtle:** the unequal and harmful treatment of women that is typically less visible and obvious than blatant sex discrimination;
- **blatant:** the unequal and harmful treatment of women that is typically intentional, quite visible, and easily documented (pp. 39–43).

Benokraitis and Feagin (1994) illustrate (p. 43) other dimensions of the framework on sex discrimination, such as intent, degree of harm, documentation, and remedies (p. 45). The authors acknowledged there are areas of overlap in these types of discrimination, but all types of discrimination cause some degree of harm (p. 43). Moreover, in cases of sexual harassment it is usually intentional (Benokraitis and Feagin, 1994, p. 72). This framework was critical to our understanding of the complexities of sexual trauma which contribute to the importance of this work.

In preparation for this study, scholarship concerning jazz history, gender and jazz, and sexism in the workplace shaped the scope and focus for the interview questions. The interviews focused on these four concepts: assimilation, tokenism, sex discrimination, and sexual harassment (see Pasque and Nicholson, 2011; Blackstone et al., 2014; Hennekam and Bennett, 2017). For the purpose of this chapter, please refer to the following definitions from the *American Psychological Association Dictionary of Psychology* (2020):

- **assimilation:** the process of absorbing, incorporating, or making similar. In making judgments, for example, it refers to finding similarities between the target being judged and features of the context in which it is judged.
- **tokenism:** the making of a perfunctory or symbolic gesture that suggests commitment to a practice or standard, particularly by hiring or promoting a single member of a previously excluded group to demonstrate one's benevolent intentions.
- **sex discrimination:** differential treatment of individuals on the basis of their biological distinction as male or female. Although such treatment may sometimes favor women relative to men, in contemporary society, most sex discrimination favors men over women; common manifestations include unfair hiring and promotion practices, lower wages paid to women

doing the same type of work as men, and a tendency to undervalue characteristics and interests associated with women.

- **sexual harassment:** conduct of a sexual nature that is unwelcome or considered offensive, particularly in the workplace. According to the U.S. Equal Employment Opportunity Commission, there are two forms of sexual harassment: *quid pro quo* and behavior that makes for a hostile work environment.

Additional terminology, such as intersectionality and positionality, allows us to be critical of sex and gender power dynamics in the workspace (see Blackstone et al., 2014; Pasque, 2011; Crenshaw, 1991). Blackstone et al. (2014) further explains how intersectionality and positionality may influence individual perceptions and experiences, "Although few studies have asked how age affects perceptions of sexualized workplace interactions, there is good qualitative evidence that such perceptions vary by gender, race, and sexuality" (p. 316). Intersectionality and positionality are helpful in understanding the nuance and complexities found in each individual woman's account of their experiences in jazz. Hennekam and Bennett (2017) discuss how sexual harassment has been "normalized" in workplace environments, which makes self-reporting a complicated process (p. 418). Blackstone et al. (2014) continues:

Age represents a less commonly examined dimension of power in the study of perceptions and experiences of harassment. Nevertheless, age appears to operate together with gender to shape experiences across diverse school and work settings. … In sum, prior research shows that the meaning of sexualized interactions at work varies with workplace and historical context as well as cultural dimensions of power such as gender and sexuality.

(pp. 316–317)

Literature Review

Historically, women-in-jazz have been marginalized greatly due to societal expectations placed on women and female-identifying individuals. Dahl (1984) wrote:

The public, entrepreneurs claimed, just wouldn't accept women on the concert stage, unless they were opera singers. The American woman, like music itself, was thought best kept in the parlor. … Thus, budding female musical talents most often remained unformed, while skilled women musicians printed and performed unknown quantities of music for private consumption.

(p. 8)

Furthermore, women-in-jazz have not been adequately represented in historical documents and jazz scholarship. Robinson (2019) writes:

Other than singers and pianists, jazz magazines throughout most of the twentieth-century rarely covered women jazz musicians. This led to the widespread belief that women who play jazz were exceptions to the norm and that there must not be very many female jazz musicians, because if there were many of them, they would receive media coverage.

This lack of representation and social pressure has made it challenging for women to thrive in jazz spaces. In *Jazz: A History*, Tirro (1993) addresses this disparity:

Women have played a significant role in the history of jazz from its earliest days, but the popular stereotype unfairly restricts the female contribution primarily to vocal music: the classical blues singers, the "girl vocalists" of the swing and bebop eras, and an occasional pianist. Women jazz musicians have achieved much more, but they have not found it easy to acquire full citizenship among the instrumentalists of jazz for many of the same reasons they have had to struggle for equal rights in the corporate world: Victorian notions about a woman's "place"; Puritanical views about men and women working together on the road, after hours, and in venus of pleasure and entertainment; stereotypical ideas about wind instruments for men and string instruments for "ladies"; the threat of unemployment for working males as a large outsider group attempts to gain entrance into a monopolized profession; "old boy" networks; male booking agents and club owners; hostile, cute, and ignorant music critics; and more.

(p. 189)

Tirro (1993) recognizes the gender disparities in the re-telling of jazz history, but does not appear to address this inequity beyond pointing out this disparity in his publication. Although there have been attempts to include and "add-in" women-in-jazz to textbooks and other historical documents (see Tucker, 2016, p. 247), it is necessary for us to take a more critical perspective on this issue. Additionally, Kernodle (2014) explained how the trope of the exceptional woman can also cause challenges towards achieving gender equity: "The exceptional woman becomes the rationale for the exclusion of other women and lends support to a narrative of invisibility that occurs in jazz histories as it relates to women musicians" (p. 29).

Across the United States, gender disparity continues to be an ongoing issue in jazz studies programs and it is important to document the lived experiences of current women and female-identifying jazz musicians to reflect upon the needs of the jazz community (see Van Vleet, 2021). Van Vleet (2021) wrote: "Presently, women are still underrepresented in jazz, with only around 10% of jazz academics being female. In a college jazz band, it is common that out of 20 or more musicians, one to four are female" (p. 212). This gender disparity leads young female jazz musicians to struggle with self-esteem and confidence (see Wehr-Flowers, 2006). Schmalenberger and Maddox (2019) described the experiences of jazz instrumentalists:

Experiences of sexual harassment and gender are important to consider in understanding the work environments of female brass players. Sociological literature on workplace climate, though not specific to musical organizations, confirms a correlation between individual perceptions of discrimination and job satisfaction.

(p. 3)

With many factors attributed to the absence of female leadership in these programs, sexual discrimination and harassment must be brought to the forefront as a possible contributor to this current state of academia (see Pasque, 2011). A critical study on the gender disparity in jazz by Van Vleet (2021) concluded:

While my research demonstrated the existence and impact of discrimination and sexualization of women in jazz music historically, the interviews demonstrated that discrimination continues to create a barrier between male and female musicians. This discrimination, which stems from over a century of sexism, can be obvious, subtle, or even accidental. Modern discrimination can be so subtle, in fact, that women do not even know that it is happening.

(p. 224)

Documenting the narratives of female jazz musicians is an integral step in identifying patterns of violence, due to systemic sexism and misogyny (see Benokraitis and Feagin, 1994). Benokraitis and Feagin (1994) addressed the insidious ways sexism is upheld in society:

> Whether the behavior is conscious or inadvertent, intentional or unintentional, many people reinforce sexism (1) by not being aware of sex discrimination; (2) by internalizing sex stereotypes; (3) by ignoring sexism because they seek acceptance by male peers or bosses; and (4) by not doing anything about sex discrimination because they are afraid of rejection or reprisal. Since women are products of and participants in their culture, it is not surprising that they often collaborate in sexist behavior.
>
> (p. 52)

Similarly, Van Vleet (2021) reported that some women-in-jazz say they do not experience any sexism "as far as they can tell" (p. 225).

The effects of this exclusive jazz environment have infiltrated the university and conservatory, resulting in individual, organization, and institutional discrimination. According to Benokraitis and Feagin (1994), "Educational institutions illustrate the pervasiveness of sex discrimination. Treating girls (and women) as inferior starts in the lower grades and continues throughout professional education. Throughout the educational process, girls and boys have very different experiences" (p. 46).

While gender disparities continue in many areas across campuses, jazz departments are greatly unbalanced (see Van Vleet, 2021). In jazz history courses, we learn about the impact of male leaders in jazz and their contributions in this field, but have very few discussions on the experiences of women-in-jazz. To pinpoint why jazz departments are not representative of the greater jazz community, it is necessary to document the stories and narratives of current female jazz musicians in higher education to archive their personal and professional experiences in the jazz community. Throughout the interviews, common threads of discrimination and isolation were prevalent within academic and performance settings (see Hennekam and Bennett, 2017).

Williams (2016) wrote, "The Othering of female jazz musicians has taken several forms since the music's origins, all of which contribute to a disparaging and demoralizing opinion of women's ability to perform at the same level as men" (p. 58). In attempts to reconcile the representation of women-in-jazz with the reality of their participation in its history, scholars have added biographies and anecdotes of women-in-jazz to the textbooks, however, Tucker (2016) explained, it is not enough to simply "add-in" (p. 247). Robinson (2019) wrote, "Equality in jazz will not come to pass until patriarchy itself is erased from our society."

As an example of how the talents of these women have been disregarded throughout history, it is common to learn about women-in-jazz through their relationships with men-in-jazz, rather than their musical contributions or achievements. In one of our conversations with a jazzwoman, she stated she had been repeatedly referred to as the partner of another jazz musician, being recognized for her relationship status, rather than her own standing as a jazz musician, which she said happened often. Benokraitis and Feagin (1994) described what happened to this participant as subjective objectification, "Women are often not seen as able and intelligent people but as possessions or conduits for male accomplishments" (p. 97).

The findings from the Wehr-Flowers (2006) study concluded that the self-perceptions of female players are not as confident as their male counterparts and females do not feel capable of competing with their male peers. This lack of self-confidence can continue throughout a female musician's career and work environment causing many more challenges for these individuals throughout their careers. One result of self-doubt in survivors of sex discrimination is withdrawal (Benokraitis and Feagin, 1994, p. 166), as evident in the testimony of Participant A who stated, "I gotta stop worrying about what people think and start being myself. So, yes, for years, I felt like I've had to reserve parts of myself. Keep it under wraps." As described by this participant, emotional and psychological distress is a common part of being a woman-in-jazz (see Benokraitis and Feagin, 1994).

The power of the #MeToo movement came from the overwhelming volume of women's voices that spoke to their experiences with sexism and misogyny. From this collective sharing of individual women's stories, women-in-jazz were also inspired to share stories of their own (see Sevian, 2017; Healey, 2016). Further research compiled for this study was supported by the definition of sexism by Benokraitis and Feagin (1994), which helped us deepen our understanding of the complexities of sexism within the jazz community. The literature on the "othering" of women-in-jazz (Williams, 2016) and the participation of women-in-jazz (Tucker, 2016) supports our argument that the lack of documentation contributes to the silencing of their voices.

Methodology

To gain a diverse and broad perspective for our study, a list of names and contact information of current female jazz professors at universities across the United States was compiled. From our initial list of 40 names, 10 individuals accepted the invitation to participate, 3 individuals opted out of the study, and 27 individuals did not respond. We had an initial response rate of 25 percent. Due to the intimacy of the study, it was a challenge to get individuals to respond or participate. Other factors specific to the nature of the jazz discipline, such as scheduling, traveling, touring, as well as personal conflicts, made it difficult to complete interviews with each participant. While beginning our interview process, it became indisputable that the participants had similar concerns about job safety which is another indicator of the importance of this work. To protect the identity and safety of the participants, all names of individuals, institutions, and locations remain anonymous. Each participant has been assigned an alphabetical letter for individual protection, as well as acknowledge the unique experiences of being a woman-in-jazz. Presently, conversations that focus on experiences of women, especially sexual discrimination and harassment, continues to be threatening to a woman's career and livelihood. Furthermore, the direct quotations and paraphrased accounts address each situation from the perspective and reality of the individual. We received consent from our participants to utilize direct quotations in order to accurately document their individual experience. This study is not an interpretation or an analysis of the content and information discussed in the interviews. All of the interviews were conducted by phone or with online video communication technology in the fall of 2018. Every participant approved their transcription and all direct quotations that have been included in this document. Finally, this study largely utilizes gendered terms, such as male/female and man/woman. This decision was not meant to exclude any member of the jazz community that may not identify with these binary labels, but to examine these gender roles that have historically marginalized women-in-jazz. All of our participants (i.e. Participant A; Participant B; Participant C; etc.) self-identified as a woman-in-jazz.

In Her Own Words: Our Study

As the #MeToo movement continued to empower women to share their stories, we began to seek guidance from women-in-jazz to better understand the current reality of sexism and sexual harassment within the jazz community beginning in the fall of 2018. By telephone and video conference calls, we conducted interviews with participants who volunteered their time and energy to this project. The importance of this study became evident when asking our participants, 'Have you experienced sexual discrimination and/or harassment as a student, teacher, or while performing?' and their answers were unanimously "Yes."

Throughout each of the interviews, the participants described their educational background and what academic life was like as a jazz student. Without hesitation, each participant had stories of being tokenized in their jazz programs because they were "the only" or "one of a handful" of women in their undergraduate programs, and "the only one" in their master's and/or doctoral programs. By being tokenized, women feel the need to prove their talents and musicianship to their male peers and teachers. Participant B explained one aspect of her academic experience:

> Usually if you did something really well—it was always noted. Because everyone didn't expect you to do really well. So if you really excelled at something, or you scored really high on a test or something, they would make a big deal of it. But, then again, you always feel like you have to do a super good job, instead of just passing. That isn't quite good enough.

According to Benokraitis and Feagin (1994):

> Tokens often recognize that they are different but must pretend that the differences do not exist to preserve a cooperative work environment. Although they are the most noticeable performers, they are often in the organizational backstages. They rarely relax because they are not really equal to their peers. They often feel lonely and alone.
>
> *(p. 125)*

These experiences of being the only woman in an academic setting, especially in music schools and conservatories, can be defining for a young woman's career and create feelings of self-doubt and anxiety (see Wehr-Flowers, 2006; Schmalenberger and Maddox, 2019; Benokraitis and Feagin, 1994). Furthermore, Benokraitis and Feagin (1994) write, "Even when there is no immediate bodily injury, job discrimination and hostile workplaces produce real illnesses in victims… Victims' behaviors may also change. Some may try to overcompensate by working harder or longer" (p. 165). This can cause long-term effects on the physical body, as well as the emotional and spiritual health of the musician (Van der Kolk, 2015).

In our interviews, the questions addressed the impacts of being a woman-in-jazz in higher education. For many of our participants, they described scenarios when male students and colleagues alike would regularly comment on their behavior and teaching style as being too "feminine." Benokraitis and Feagin (1994) wrote:

> We teach women to safeguard relationships, to be nurturant, and to help others feel good about themselves. This learn-to-please behavior sets up competitions between women or the praise of others, especially men. Even in the workplace, some women may sabotage other women to be liked or promoted by men.
>
> *(p. 137)*

Participant C mentioned that it is an expectation for female jazz teachers to act maternally toward their students, and be someone who nurtures and cares for students' emotional well-being, instead of their musicianship. In our conversations, a common discussion point was about the dominant presence of men as chairs or directors of music departments in higher education, while women in higher education are consistently viewed as "motherly" or "nurturing."

While teaching in K-12 settings is generally deemed feminine, higher education, especially jazz music, tends to be male dominated. Benokraitis and Feagin (1994) further explained,

> They expect women bosses to be more friendly, more accepting of tardiness, and to show a greater personal interest in the employees. These and other double standards free men from work and responsibility, reinforce sex stereotypes, and dilute women's authority.
>
> *(p. 116)*

Participant A stated: "I'm the caring one. I'm in a sea of all men in the jazz department. … [Students say] she's the sensitive one, she is the one I can cry in front of." Participant D also shared:

> I've had young men tell me that they wished I would yell at them more, because their high school band directors yelled at them and boy, did that get results, and that's what they need and that's what they want, and I'm a bad director because I'm not yelling at them. I tried once, I tried yelling but I mean, I'm not a yeller, it's not what I do. I would yell if I saw someone hurting a child or animal, I would jump right in. I'm not a yeller when it comes to pedagogy and education.

This patriarchal point of view in jazz poses major physical, emotional, and spiritual dangers for women-in-jazz. If a woman is too strong, her teaching can be deemed "mean," "unnecessary," and ultimately, disregarded. Participant D continued,

> It's really tough because there's this idea that especially in jazz, it's male oriented and the whole idea of leading a big band or whatever is that you need to use macho gestures and count off in a certain way. You know, it's kind of an aggressive and patriarchal type of thing and to do it differently makes some people uncomfortable.

Overall, our participants explained they were frustrated by the amount of time they have to address their gender in professional spaces, while their male counterparts rarely have their gender brought up in a work setting.

In the classroom or rehearsal setting, many of our participants had experienced discrimination and harassment by their professors, mentors, and peers while studying their craft. Examples of this discrimination was a common topic throughout our interviews, ranging from comments made about their playing style to having their personal space being invaded while playing. Participants also described instances of being dismissed as an authority on their instrument in a variety of settings. Participant E explained how she was dismissed as the leader of her band,

> I think a lot of gender discrimination is subliminal. It isn't necessarily so overt. But it's things like arriving to a gig with my band where I have been the contact person, and the sound engineer will check-in with someone else before me. Because they don't assume I am in charge of production or have knowledge of it.

Unknowingly, this participant explained her experience with sexism within the Benokraitis and Feagin framework (see Table 3.1, p. 43) of covert–subtle–blatant discrimination. She continued: "I have had engineers mansplain how to use a microphone. I know how to use a microphone." Over time, these gendered microaggressions, which can be intentional or unintentional (see Table 3.1), are harmful to a woman's health. More specifically, it undermines a woman's expertise and disrespects their training, experience, and education.

Benokraitis and Feagin (1994) also assert that women are judged on their appearances, whereas men typically are judged on their accomplishments (p. 26). Many of the stories expressed concern towards societal expectations placed on female jazz musicians and academics, including issues of clothing, body image, playing styles, pedagogical practices, as well as rehearsal and/or gig environments, and are blatant experiences of sexism (Benokraitis and Feagin, 1994). In this patriarchal society, physical appearance is still emphasized (see Benokraitis and Feagin, 1994; Feagin, 2013). From the many interviews conducted, instances of sexual harassment and discrimination, such as unwanted advances and inappropriate commentary from other musicians and professionals in the music industry. Many of our participants explained they confronted sexual harassment in performance arenas as well as educational settings. After a particular incident occurred, Participant F said they felt required to make a choice: to ignore the assault or minimize the assault. Participant C said it is these types of interactions that make it difficult to let guards down and trust bandmates of the opposite sex,

> I think that there's a huge, protective barrier that women put up in a professional setting because especially in jazz there's a predatory aspect to the interactions and over time you learn to put up a wall unless somebody proves otherwise that you can let them in.

Through the sharing of these stories, women-in-jazz are able to break their silence and amplify this call for change by documenting their experiences.

Her Story: A Call for Collective Healing

Women-in-jazz cannot continue to be silenced any longer. The importance of these interviews is to center women's perspectives that have otherwise been silenced (Tirro, 1993; Enstice and Stockhouse, 2004). After conducting these interviews, it has become evident to us that there is a major emotional and spiritual crisis in the jazz community, due to sexual discrimination and violence, and it is time to tend to the community. Across disciplines and professional spaces, women continue to be vilified for their courage when they choose to report sexual misconduct or discrimination (see Benokraitis and Feagin, 1994). Benokraitis and Feagin (1994) write:

> Many women say that when they report sexual harassment and other forms of discrimination, the responses by both individuals and organizations are frequently hurtful and disappointing. Organizations are slow to react and often blame the victim. The accused may falsify data or deny that they have received complaints by the victim.
>
> *(p. 168)*

This type of response has conditioned many women to not report their experiences, which creates more distrust and reasons for concern (Benokraitis and Feagin, 1994, p. 168).

As female-bodied and female-identifying musicians with many years of experience in the American higher education system, the inspiration and reasoning behind this research and study is personal. For us, stories of sexual discrimination, harassment, and violence are not just those of the "other," but stories of our own. After finding the courage to share these experiences with each other, we wanted to connect with more women-in-jazz who were willing to share their stories. Through conversation and an open dialogue with our participants, our experiences as music students and educators were affirmed, validated, and welcomed.

These interviews demonstrated the complexities and nuances of sexism and misogyny in American society, at large. Within individual university and collegiate jazz programs, women continue to be a minority demographic. Women-in-jazz who have overcome these barriers have not done so without their share of negative experiences and trauma. For young jazzwomen in undergraduate jazz programs, especially, this lack of community and support can be greatly discouraging (see Healey, 2016; Sevian, 2017). For too long, women have been dismissed and ignored when sharing their experiences, whether it be about their personal or professional spheres. Tucker (2001/2002) wrote listening for gender as a way to be

> helpful not only to those of us wanting to understand sexism and the experiences and contributions of women in jazz, but also to anyone wishing to develop more frameworks for addressing the histories, sounds, functions, and meanings of this fascinating and multi-faceted music.
>
> *(p. 377)*

This ability to listen for gender in jazz must be taken up by the whole jazz community in order for women-in-jazz to be seen for their full contributions to jazz, and to help readers listen for gender, we address how the othering of women-in-jazz has contributed to the acceptance of and complicity with sexual discrimination and harassment in the jazz community. Online publications concerning first-hand accounts of sexual discrimination, harassment, and violence, supported by interdisciplinary research in gender studies, jazz history, and music education provide evidence for more research concerning sexism in the jazz community.

For women-in-jazz who have had continuous exposure to sexual discrimination, harassment, and violence, significant changes in behavior can occur. Benokraitis and Feagin (1994) list potential consequences for survivors of sexual discrimination:

- General depression, as manifested by changes in eating and sleeping patterns, and aches and pains that prevent women from attending class or completing course or work assignments.
- Dissatisfaction with work, college, major, or a particular course.
- A sense of powerlessness, helplessness, and vulnerability.
- A loss of self-confidence and self-esteem and a decline in academic or job performance.
- Changes in attitudes or behaviors toward sexual relationships.
- Irritability with family, friends, or coworkers.
- A general sense of anger, fear, or anxiety.
- An inability to concentrate, even on routine tasks.
- Alcohol and drug dependency. (p. 166).

Benokraitis and Feagin (1994) further explain how survivors of sexual discrimination may show similar traits of, or development of post-traumatic stress disorder (p. 166). In *The Body Keeps the Score: Brain, Mind, and Body in the Healing of Trauma* under "Breaking the Silence," Van der Kolk (2015) writes:

> Silence about trauma also leads to death—the death of the soul. Silence reinforces the godforsaken isolation of trauma. … As long as you keep secrets and suppress information, you are fundamentally at war with yourself. Hiding your core feelings takes an enormous amount of energy, it saps your motivation to pursue worthwhile goals, and it leaves you feeling bored and shut down.
>
> *(p. 234)*

Currently within our jazz history textbooks and literature, there is a narrative that does not identify sexism, sexual assault, or harassment within jazz. By documenting these individual experiences of sexual discrimination and harassment in this study, our participants have furthered the conversation by breaking their silence and grounding our research in reality. These are the stories that must be included in order for current and prospective women-in-jazz to fully experience the freedom that is foundational to the music of jazz. As we continue to look for more opportunities to be inclusive of women and non-binary musicians within jazz, these courageous conversations are necessary for destigmatizing sharing personal stories of sexual discrimination and harassment.

Burke (2021) explains the #MeToo Movement is committed "to help every individual find the right point of entry for their unique healing journey." For the jazz community to move forward, we believe it is time to focus on healing and repairing relations with current women-in-jazz and other marginalized identities. Women and underrepresented communities must be listened to and heard when speaking about their experiences in jazz. Today, women continue to have legitimate concerns about their job safety and livelihoods if they choose to speak about or report on incidences of sexual discrimination, harassment, and violence, which speaks to the sexist nature of jazz in higher education. We must be able to share our stories without fear. We must be heard. We must acknowledge the pain and trauma that has been, and is currently being, held by so many women-in-jazz. Now is the time to have open and honest conversations about the present conditions for women-in-jazz and reimagine jazz education for the next generation of women-in-jazz.

Appendix A

Interview Questions

- What is your primary instrument?
- Are you currently teaching in academia?
- When were you first exposed to music, in general? When were you first exposed to jazz?
- Who was your first favorite jazz musician or what was your first favorite jazz album?
- Have you always known you wanted to be in academia? Was performing your first love? Or, where do you see yourself wanting to be in the future?
- Would you use the term feminist to describe yourself and why?
- Have gender stereotypes played a role in your education? Personal life? Professional life?
- Have gender stereotypes ever affected your relationship with your instrument?
- In your own opinion, do you feel like there is a lack of female inclusion in higher education? If so, what do you think are the causes for this?
- Where have you previously studied? How many women were in your program at the time?
- When/where did you receive your first job in higher education?
- Have you experienced sexual discrimination and/or harassment as a performer? When booking gigs? Collaborating with other musicians?
- Have you experienced sexual discrimination and/or harassment as a student or when teaching? From previous/current supervisors? Peers? Students?

References

APA Dictionary of Psychology. (2020). *American Psychological Association.* https://dictionary.apa.org/.

Benokraitis, N. V. and Feagin, J. R. (1994). *Modern Sexism: Blatant, Subtle, and Covert Discrimination* (2nd ed.). Englewood Cliffs, NJ: Prentice Hall.

Burke, T. (2021). History and Inception. *Me too.* https://metoomvmt.org/get-to-know-us/ history-inception/.

Blackstone, A., Houle, J., and Uggen, C. (2014). "I didn't recognize it as a bad experience until I was much older": Age, experience, and workers' perceptions of sexual harassment. *Sociological Spectrum, 34*(4), 314–337. https://doi.org/10.1080/02732173.2014.917247.

Crenshaw, K. (1991). Mapping the margins: Intersectionality, identity politics, and violence against women of color. *Stanford Law Review, 43*(6), 1241–1299.

Dahl, L. (1984) *Stormy Weather: The Music and Lives of a Century of Jazzwomen.* New York: Pantheon Books.

Enstice, W. and Stockhouse, J. (2004). *Jazzwomen: Conversations with Twenty-one Musicians.* Bloomington, IN: Indiana University Press.

Feagin, J. (2013). *The White Racial Frame* (2nd ed.). New York: Routledge.

"Get To Know Us." (2021). *Me too.* https://metoomvmt.org/get-to-know-us/tarana-burke-founder/.

Healey, B. (2016, August 1). *Be Good or Play Like a Man: Why Women Aren't Getting into Jazz. Biddy Healey,* www.biddyhealey.com/blog/2016/6/18/ be-a-good-girl-or-play-like-a-man.

Hennekam, S., and Bennett, D. (2017). Sexual harassment in the creative industries: Tolerance, culture and the need for change. *Gender, Work, and Organization, 24*(4), 417–434. https://doi.org/10.1111/gwao.12176.

Kernodle, T. L. (2014). Black Women Working Together: Jazz, Gender, and the Politics of Validation. *Black Music Research Journal, 34*(1), 27–55. https://doi.org/10.5406/blacmusiresej.34.1.0027

Mercer, M. (2017, March 9). Sexism from two leading jazz artists draws anger and presents an opportunity. *National Public Radio.* www.npr.org/sections/therecord/ 2017/03/09/519482385/sexism-from-two-leading-jazz-artists-draws-anger-and-presents-an-opportunity.

Pasque, P. A., and Nicholson, S. E. (Eds.). (2011). *Empowering Women in Higher Education and Student Affairs: Theory, Research, Narratives, and Practice from Feminist Perspectives*. ProQuest Ebook Central. Sterling: Stylus Publishing.

Robinson, C. (2019, March 9). A brief history of the origins of jazz's sexism. *Medium*. https://medium.com/@CRMusicWriter/a-brief-history-of-the-origins-of-jazzs-sexism-3ee4278bcff0.

Schmalenberger, S., and Maddox, P. (2019). Female brass musicians address gender parity, gender equity, and sexual harassment: A preliminary report on data from the brass bodies study. *Societies* (Basel, Switzerland), *9*(1), 1–15. https://doi.org/10.3390/soc9010020.

Sevian, L. (2017). Sexism in Jazz, from the Conservatory to the Club: One Saxophonist Shares Her Story. *WBGO*, www.wbgo.org/post/sexism-jazz-conservatory-club-one-saxophonist-shares-her-story#stream/0.

Tirro, F. (1993). *Jazz: A History*. New York: Norton.

Tucker, S. (2001/2002). Big ears: Listening for gender in jazz studies. *Current Musicology*, *71/73*, 375–408.

Tucker, S. (2003). Women in jazz. *Grove Music Onlines*. www.oxfordmusiconline.com/ grovemusic/view/10.1093/gmo/9781561592630.001.0001/omo-9781561592630-e-2000730100.

Tucker, S. (2016). A conundrum is a woman-in-Jazz. In W. Knauer (ed.), *Gender and Identity in Jazz* (pp. 241–262). Darmstadt: Jazzinstitut Darmstadt.

Van der Kolk, B. (2015). *The Body Keeps the Score: Brain, Mind, and Body in the Healing of Trauma*. New York: Penguin Books.

Van Vleet, K. (2021). Women in jazz music: A hundred years of gender disparity in jazz study and performance (1920–2020). *Jazz Education in Research and Practice*, *2*(1), 211–227. https://doi:http://dx.doi.org.ezproxy1.lib.asu.edu/10.2979/jazzeducrese.2.1.16.

Wehr-Flowers, E. (2006). Differences between male and female students' confidence, anxiety, and attitude toward learning jazz improvisation. *Journal of Research in Music Education*, *LIV/4*, 337–349.

Williams, K. (2016). 'Alright for a Girl', and other jazz myths. In W. Knauer (ed.), *Gender and Identity in Jazz* (pp. 57–70). Darmstadt: Jazzinstitut Darmstadt.

31

CALL AND (HER) RESPONSE

Improvisation and The Myth of Absence

Dana Reason

Introduction

I would like to start this chapter with a game. The first prompt is a warm-up: Write down the names of 20 female musicians in jazz. Look at your list. Was it hard or easy to name these musicians? For the second prompt: Name 5 females who are involved in significant or emergent public jazz scholarship, education, or perhaps developed a jazz method, jazz history book, jazz curriculum, or hosted a jazz radio program. How did you do? Was it hard or easy to identify females? For the third and final prompt: Name 5 genius improvisers who also identify as female. If you were able to name between 5–10 females in jazz, bravo. Reflect on how long it took you to identify these females in these various roles within the field of jazz.

In this chapter, I examine how past and current institutionalized forms of jazz study, post-genre improvisation, research, and practice continue to disadvantage efforts for the inclusion and representation of female practitioners, innovators, and educators. Current frameworks of jazz study and progeny often do not involve intersectional and critical gender studies or teach interventional notions of improvisation; thereby enabling frameworks that promote and normalize exclusionary behavior and bias towards female practitioners. The field of jazz must be reformed through a systemic re-evaluation of critical intersections, formative pedagogy, recorded histories, ethnographies of females in jazz musics, and post-genre practices of improvisation.

Additionally, in the spirit of ethnographic practices, I draw extensively from my own experience as a female who, as a graduate student, simultaneously developed intersectional research on female improvisers and entered motherhood. As a result, my graduate research remained somewhat dormant (not published as a book) due to the significant pause I took in my scholarship to raise my children.

To holistically address a paper on gender and jazz at this time in our socio-historical reckoning, I must include the following:

(1) I must acknowledge that I am a white woman (she/her/hers) who has benefitted where others have suffered from institutionalized racism.
(2) I must acknowledge that I cannot speak for others, but I can actively listen, learn, and be an aligned activist.

DOI: 10.4324/9781003081876-34

Improvisation: Radical Revisions

Institutionalized forms of music study that utilize improvisation and real-time music-making are often earmarked as jazz methods, and thus considered a codified and vetted practice. The subject area allotted within the music academy (from middle school to college) for "making-things-up" has historically been delegated to those working in jazz studies, which gained more momentum with "the first college degree in jazz ... offered in 1947 at North Texas State Teachers College in Denton, now the University of North Texas. M.E" (Worthy, 2011, n.p.). This is evidenced by curriculum programming in most college campuses, publications, and textbooks, which provide a narrow view of the history of jazz, performance, and education.

Furthermore, examining research about the use of improvisation in academic settings may prove helpful in understanding how approaches to teaching improvisation are implemented. For example, Anna Song points to the discrepancy of understanding the importance of improvisation for education in music. What her research survey found was not surprising—improvisation is most prevalent within the jazz idiom, as 73 percent of jazz-related courses use improvisation more than 15 percent of the time, compared to only 18 percent of all non-jazz-related courses (Song, 2013, n.p.). Improvisation was seemingly more widespread in jazz band/ensemble than in jazz choir (Song, 2013, n.p.). In a different study on improvisation by Bridget Rinehimer (2012), specifically for music educators, she remarked that while the pedagogy was not a jazz-centric methodology, improvisation amongst this study centered on the use of Orff-Schulwerk (Rinehimer, 2012). While neither Song nor Rinehimer's studies address the issue of gender, it is still valuable to study how improvisation is taught. Additionally, these studies do not mention or demonstrate evidence that non-idiomatic improvised approaches to real-time music-making are considered within curricular pedagogies, nor do they address whether females teach courses with improvisational techniques.

With the increase of popular music studies throughout the globe—which approaches music-making from a post-genre and integrated sensibility, embracing amateur skills, DIY attitudes, singer-songwriter aesthetics, and digital musicianship—we are experiencing a revolution in how real-time music-making (i.e., improvisation) is central to teaching and practice (Kluth, 2018). This current musicking continues to evolve and grow out of the African American Diaspora, global aural traditions, the peer-to-peer pedagogy of the social media generation, online learning resources, and more (Kluth, 2018). Much of this musicking takes place inside the laboratory of social engagement, cultural and populist practice, and what George Lewis posits, "creole," elements of American society (Lewis, 2017). And yet, the creolization of music is still far from operational and institutionalized pedagogy.

A 2021 study on *Females in Jazz Music: A Hundred Years of Gender Disparity in Jazz Study and Performance* by Kaitlyn Van Vleet (1920–2020) concluded that while the participation of females in jazz has improved, the discrimination for females participating in the field started a hundred years ago, and there is more to rectify (Van Vleet, 2021). The disputes over essentialist and gendered attitudes towards females are often a footnote in jazz and improvised music scholarship and pedagogy. Daphne Brooks's (2021) new book, *Liner Notes for the Revolution*, brilliantly and fiercely exposes these problems as trenchant in popular forms of Black feminist musical contributions, talents, spaces, production and sound, and, in particular, "listening," that serves as an important framework:

> Doing this kind of work, getting down to this kind of *labor in listening*, requires grappling with a history that has no hall of fame, no landmark biopics, no Graceland pilgrimage sites, no *Hamilton*-sized musical to memorialize the depth of its lasting impact. Such absences, blind spots, and silences—cultural manifestations of what [Toni] Morrison famously refers to as "the disremembered and unaccounted for."
>
> *(Brooks, 2021, p. 8)*

Brooks (2021) goes on to suggest it is time to revolutionize the ways in which Black feminist thought and radical traditions, and the various artists who created theses musics, be (re)discovered (Brooks, 2021, p. 8).

> In her seminal work, musicologist Marcia Citron notes that "Critical reception is the next marker on the professional path. Unfortunately, females have been subjected to gender-linked evaluation, placing them in a 'separate but not equal' category that has widened the gulf between themselves and the homogeneous canon.
>
> *(Citron, 1990, p. 106)*

Additionally, Franzisaka Schorder points out:

> Improvisation is a type of musicking that is evidently marked by a very sensual, tactile engagement with one's tools, on the one hand—it specifically brings into being the body and instrument relation to the playing musician as a highly tactile and intimate relation marked by constraint and resistance.
>
> *(Schroder, 2014)*

Thus, reimagining the female body in jazz and improvised modes of music re-engages systems of knowledge that the performing body disseminates and relies on the memory of sound to enact a real-time performance strategy. Such a discussion is nonetheless critical for addressing the under-representation of female creatives in fields requiring real-time music practices and engagement. There are still so many personal, professional, and musical experiences of females who improvise that have yet to be researched, discovered, and listened to. Writing in a collection that traces the evolution of feminism in ethnomusicology, Ellen Koskoff and Suzanne Cusick (2014) traced the first, second and third waves of feminism, into the 2010s and beyond. Their collection recounts the imbalance of feminist music scholarship within the larger discourse on women and gender; which is helpful for our discussion on gender and jazz:

> In the late 1990s, I began to feel a sense of frustration with mainstream ethnomusicology. Wonderful new monographs and anthologies were appearing, as well as countless articles documenting various gendered musical practices cross-culturally. Why, then, had this literature remained largely on the margins of the field? Why had the obvious (to me) benefits of feminist music scholarship based on fieldwork been so slow to integrate into mainstream discourses?
>
> *(Koskoff and Cusick, 2014)*

How might educators connect these promising equitable systems of making with the knowledge of improvised forms and practices from jazz? I believe that educators—such as myself—who are actively teaching the next generation of students in the field of music have a tremendous responsibility. A responsibility to not only challenge and question historical and pedagogical training (including our own), but to seek out and integrate new and diverse voices in their classroom teachings.

Listening for Change: A Brief Ethnography

My early experience as an improviser involved making things up at the piano—starting at the age of 3—and learning music from the radio, the television, and my parents' record and tape collections. However, two very important things were missing from my elementary and high school music training in Canada: I never played or learned a *single* piece of piano music by a female; and the only music I ever performed by black composers were two pieces by Scott Joplin—*Maple Leaf Rag* (Joplin, 1960) and *The Entertainer* (Joplin, 1971)—and Stevie Wonder's *You Are the Sunshine of My Life*

(Wonder, 1972). In my early teens, through listening to college radio from the University of Toronto, I started to hear new sounds and styles of music and became highly influenced by African American music—a sharp contrast to my formal training at the Royal Conservatory of Music, an institution founded in 1886 and that focused on Western Classical Music traditions.

High school at Interlochen still perpetuated classical music from the Western Art music perspective as the standard. Composition was from the experimental (e.g. David Cope's *New Music Composition*) perspective, and the jazz piano studies used Billy Taylor's piano method book. Billy Taylor (1921–2010) was a remarkable educator, and his method demystified approaches to playing jazz standards on the piano. It was through Billy Taylor's pedagogy method book that I discovered the sounds of Duke Ellington, Billie Holiday, Bessie Smith, Bill Evans, Horace Silver, Oscar Peterson, and Miles Davis, learning the musicality of their voices, phrasing and profound sound, but most importantly, about the canonization of "Jazz Standards" (Taylor, 1982). I was made aware of jazz female singers, but never any female composers, instrumentalists, arrangers, and certainly no band leaders.

During my undergraduate training at McGill University, I returned to radio, but this time as a broadcaster with my own show, *Soundings* on CKUT 90.3 FM. On the show, I highlighted innovative practices in music, especially the work of female improvisers such as Miya Masaoka, Marilyn Crispell, Ikue Mori, Amina Claudine Myers, Carla Bley, Cassandra Wilson, and more. A few years later, in graduate school, I would go on to interview many of the female improvisers whose work I played on CKUT 90.3.

Throughout my undergraduate studies, I was frequently denied the mentorship necessary to develop a rigorous grasp of jazz music by the exclusionary class content and educational attitudes—that included being told that "there were no women participants or no women worth studying in jazz"—throughout any of my undergraduate courses (e.g. jazz history, jazz theory, jazz arranging and jazz piano performance). Subsequently, all of my undergraduate jazz courses were taught exclusively by white males. The disappearance of females and BIPOC was also perpetuated in my Western classical, popular music, composition, world music and music technology undergraduate courses. Clearly, the lack of gender balance was not just limited to jazz, but prevalent in all genres.

There were only two other females in my jazz classes. Unfortunately, the hostile, competitive, and macho environment caused one talented female, a saxophonist, to quit, and the other, an equally gifted female singer, to change her major to philosophy, abandoning the formal study of music altogether. I, too, eventually receded from jazz studies to focus entirely on classical music instead because my jazz piano teacher regularly did not show up for my lessons.

My story is not unique. Ingrid Monson, writing about her experience in the instrumental sectional as a trumpet player states, "over and over, I felt publicly disrespected and I dreaded going to the rehearsals. By the end of the semester, I thought that maybe I just was not good enough to be entitled to basic courtesy" (Tucker, 2008 p. 275–276). Later on in her story, Monson details another incident with the same band and band director. This time, a female singer came to sing with the band, and the male director "fell all over himself being chivalrous with this woman, who, unlike the horn players, was considered to be filling a gender-appropriate role" (Tucker, 2008, p. 276). The band director was sending a gendered message: that females are welcome as singers or piano players—never instrumentalists (Tucker, 2008, p. 276).

Jayna Brown (2021) writes about the problematic repercussions of patriarchy in relation to the overlooked music of pianist, organist, and harpist, Alice Coltrane, in her book *Black Utopias*. Although both Alice Coltrane and John Coltrane were innovative musicians, the enculturated systems of the patriarchy in both domestic and musical spheres meant that his career had the opportunity to move forward while Alice's career diminished in order to assist his ascent to fame (Brown, 2021). Brown theorizes that it is extremely likely for Alice Coltrane to have carried more weight of influence than she has been credited for regarding the musical legacy of John Coltrane. Essentially, she continued his sonic legacy, taking measures to incorporate his approaches—rather than her own—to jazz. Brown concludes that,

[t]here are many reasons why Alice Coltrane has not received the kind of scholarly attention her music and life merit. Musically, her greatness is overshadowed by her role as John Coltrane's wife. ... Alice's innovative work on the piano, and her place as one of the very few jazz harpists, are not taken seriously by mainstream jazz scholarship, which feminizes these instruments, relegating them to supporting positions and evaluating their players as less capable of innovation.

(Brown, 2021, p. 62–63)

From Alice Coltrane's story we are reminded that playing the piano does not guarantee a female's recognition or acceptance in jazz music either. If you cannot find a place to belong, perhaps you have to create your own community. This notion inspired me, a graduate student at the University of California San Diego, to conceive of and (with the help of graduate student colleagues Michael Dessen, Jason Robinson, Sean Griffin, and others) develop a symposium called "Improvising Across Borders" under the mentorship of George E. Lewis (Lewis and Piekut, 2016, n.p.).

This symposium, which was amongst the earliest of its kind in the U.S., sought to challenge the ways in which improvisation and improvised strategies, together with critical inquiry, could move beyond simple reified and inscribed categories in the field of music towards an inclusive humanities-based and interdisciplinary discourse about jazz, gender, race, social justice, and improvisation (Lewis and Piekut, 2016, n.p.).

"Improvising Across Borders" brought together over a hundred participants, including many seminal thinkers and practitioners of improvised practices from several artistic disciplines. Critically aware of the lack of females in roles of leadership and pedagogical influence, my vision in creating this conference was to highlight a variety of diverse practitioners and scholars, including keynote speaker Pauline Oliveros, and additional speakers such as George E. Lewis, Anthony Davis, Vijay Iyer, Eleanor and David Antin, Ed Sarath, Alvin Curran, Eddie Prevost, Jann Pasler, Ajay Heble, Catherine Sullivan, Douglas Ewart, Mchaka Uba, Chris Williams, Alvin Curran, and more. By bringing this community together, it became evident that critical issues around and within improvisation was not only a collective theme, but an emerging field that included jazz, but that was not beholden to a narrow, canonized understanding of it.

In the words of Ingrid Monson, "good jazz improvisation is sociable and interactive just like a conversation." (Monson, 1996, p. 84). At "Improvising Across Borders," our interest was precisely this: How could modular and generative thinking through improvisation and discourse navigate this field through the personal, the political, the equitable, and the sonic?

Musician-improvisor La Donna Smith (1999) reflected on the importance of the "Improvising Across Borders" symposium:

The collective of panelists, artists, skeptics, and practitioners merged their minds and hearts in one of the most important meetings of the decade to break down barriers and create dialog acknowledging improvisation as the true process to the imagination, the common thread in all music.

(Smith, 1999)

"Improvising Across Borders" was part of a groundswell of collective activities and conversational attitudes with rigorous research practices taking place in the early 2000s through the intellectually pioneering and cross-disciplinary research of George E. Lewis and other practitioners such as Ajay Heble, Daniel Fischlin (University of Guelph, Canada), Eric Lewis (McGill), Georgina Born (UK), and others (Lewis and Piekut, 2016, n.p.).

"Improvising Across Borders" also laid the conceptual and theoretical groundwork for my dissertation, *The Myth of Absence: Representation, Reception, and the Music of Experimental Women Improvisors* (2002). In this dissertation, I defined a new theory, "The Myth of Absence," wherein female-identified creative musical voices are not a central part of curriculum offerings, historical narratives, the genius canonical speak, or proffered as models to imitate (Reason-Myers, 2002). "The Myth of Absence" questions systematic disenfranchisement and the patriarchal misconception that women remain grossly marginalized from jazz discourses, pedagogies, and practices because they are simply not considered integral to the field of jazz, improvised, or innovative musical intelligences. To revisit "The Myth of Absence" is to examine its consequences for females creating real-time in a variety of fields. My dissertation (and all subsequent work) intentionally highlights—and names—females at the margins of multiple-genre frameworks, boundary-pushing sound practices, research methodologies, real-time explorations, and musical languages.

Part of my dissertation included researching five festivals that took place between 1968 and 2000. I found that only 28 females total had ever performed at the annual, international festival *Total Music Meeting* (Berlin, Germany) during this 26-year span. Of these 28 females, not a single musician was a black, and only 3 were Asian. The highest percentage of females programmed at *The Total Music Meeting* in a single year was in 1995 and it featured 5 percent female musicians (Reason-Myers, 2002, p.155–158).

Additionally, I interviewed a diverse group of female musicians about their experiences as females working in the field of improvised music, who had been active since 1950 in North America, Asia, and Europe. They included American pianist, arranger, and composer Amina Claudine Myers; French classical and experimental bassist Joëlle Léandre; Scottish vocalist, improviser, dancer, and performer Maggie Nicols; UK bassoonist and composer Lindsay Cooper; American drummer Susie Ibarra; American accordionist, composer, and improviser Pauline Oliveros; kotoist, performance artist, and electronic musician Miya Masaoka; pianist Marilyn Crispell; Swizz pianist Irene Schweizer; British cellist and anthropologist Georgina Born; American violinist India Cooke; Japanese drummer and electronic musician Ikue Mori; American actress and singer Maia Axe; Canadian percussionist Gayle Young; American harpist Susie Allen; American harpist and composer Anne LeBaron; Spanish-German composer and singer Maria DeAlvear; and American flutist Jane Rigler (Reason-Myers, 2002). I included all of their names here because this was an early attempt in my research to archivally document a dynamic range of female improvisers practicing in innovative, interdisciplinary ways that directly challenged institutionalized and patriarchal forms of what constitutes jazz and improvisation (Reason-Myers, 2002).

Although this chapter is too short to detail the interview responses, it is important to note that they represent a wide variety of approaches to real-time and improvised music forms and practices. Additionally, there was a core collection of readings that shaped my interview questions. These seminal writings include Ruth Solie's (1995) *Musicology and Difference*; Susan McClary's (1991) *Feminine Endings: Music, Gender, and Sexuality*; Ellen Koskoff's (1987) *Women and Music in Cross-Cultural Perspectives*; Judith Butler's (2006) *Gender Trouble: Feminism and the Subversion of Identity*; Neuls-Bates's (1996) *Females in Music: An Anthology of Source Reading from the Middle Ages to the Present (Cross-Cultural Perspective)*; Lucy Green's (1997) *Music, Gender, and Education*, and many others.

The redefining of the canon of both music genres and practices is a distinct form of activism to redress the gender and intersectional imbalances in music. Examples of this include Tara Rodgers's (2010) *Pink Noises: Female on Electronic Music and Sound*; Tracy McMullen's (2019) *Hauthenticity: Musical Replay and the Fear of the Real;* Nicole Rustin and Sherri Tucker's (2008) *Big Ears: Listening for Gender in Jazz*; Tammy L. Kernodle's (2004); *Soul on Soul: The Life and Music of Mary Lou Williams*; Daphne A. Brooks's (2021) *Liner Notes for the Revolution: The Intellectual Life of Black Feminist Sound*; and Jayna Brown's (2021) *Black Utopia: Speculative Life and the Music of Other Worlds*, and many others.

Over the past five years, a growing number of journals and seminal research collections have expanded the discussion on gender and intersectionality in improvisation as well, including *The Journal of Popular Music Education* (founded in 2017); *The Oxford Handbook of Critical Improvisation Studies, Vols. 1 and 2* by George E. Lewis and Benjamin Piekut (2016); and the emergence of Berklee's

Institute of Jazz and Gender Justice by Teri Lyn Carrington (founded 2018), a program with a tag line of 'jazz without patriarchy' (https://college.berklee.edu/jazz-gender-justice). Additional alliances for the inclusion of discussions for gender, improvisation and jazz also include: *International Alliance for Women in Music* (IAWM) (https://iawm.org/), and *Critical Studies in Improvisation/Études critique en Improvisation* (Guelph University, (www.improvcommunity.ca/publications/journal), among others.

While we have made some strides around inclusivity over the past 20 years, scholarship about jazz, improvisation, race and gender, the inclusion and centralization of females in this field remains problematic. Females who utilize improvised frameworks in their musical practices remain marginalized or rendered invisible by not being named in print or public reviews or as participants in creative projects. For example, a 2019 retrospective concert at the Armory in New York City with the NEA Jazz Master and brilliant composer, Roscoe Mitchell, curated by Jason Moran, was reviewed in the *New York Times*. The musical program featured solo performances and original compositions by Mitchell, and ensemble pieces with and without Mitchell. This *Times* review, *Roscoe Mitchell Jackhammers a New Musical Funhouse*, by Seth Walls (2019), does not reflect the incredible intentionality, awareness, and gender-sensitive balance that Mitchell achieved in the ensemble personnel for this retrospective concert. Additionally, Walls's review does not include the name of a single female performer from this concert, of which there were 5 (out of the 14 total performers, including Mitchell).

In addition to the much-deserved attention in the review towards Roscoe Mitchell, Walls names only a few, very established male musicians from the ensemble. Even when reviewing Mitchell's works that utilize female performers, such as "Cutouts for Woodwind Quintet" (Roberta Michel, flute; Christa Robinson, oboe; Carlos Corddeio, clarinet; and Sara Schoenbeck, bassoon; and John Gattis, french horn), there are no female performer names mentioned: "In the second concert, a collection of players drawn from the Wavefield Ensemble showed off a lovely group blend when navigating the sympathetically swirling melodic motifs in 'Cutouts for Woodwind Quintet'" (Walls, 2019). The ensemble players remain anonymous, which is deadly for female musicians who are already seemingly invisible in the field despite the relatively favorable response to the music played.

Even "Nonaah" by Roscoe Mitchell, one of his most well-known solo works (Steinbeck, 2016), now rewritten for a trio, was only mentioned by its title. There was no reference to the trio performing it, which included two females, and one male—Catherine Lee, oboe, John Savage, flute, and myself on piano (Walls, 2019). Walls writes: "At the second show on Wednesday, his stridently strutting 1970s 'Nonaah' was played in a more lyrical later arrangement for piano, oboe, and flute" (Walls, 2019). This awkward and glaring failure to name specifically female performers *at all* perpetuates the patriarchal assumptions that either (1) there were no female performers, or (2) the female performers were not worth mentioning (either due to their obscure careers or the perceived level of quality). Regardless of what caused the absence of female names in the article, the result is the same: the perpetuation of "The Myth of Absence."

Each one of us has a social and historical responsibility to name female musicians, scholars, composers, improvisers, and so forth. Consistently. Repeatedly. In reviews, in journals, in books, in our oral histories, and in our classrooms. Otherwise, the "Myth of Absence" continuously perpetuates, and with it, the erasure of females, their creativity, and their labor in improvisation, jazz music, and scholarship.

The Textbook Remains the Same

In 2019, I taught an introductory undergraduate survey Jazz History course at Oregon State University. The latest jazz anthology we used featured a black woman on the cover of the textbook, but once inside the book, one was met with the same kinds of prescribed roles that females have played throughout jazz history: that of a blues songstress or piano player. There was no information on female trombone players, drummers, or saxophonists, for that matter. There was one female bass player included, Esperanza Spalding, with a full-page photograph featured in the text (Deveaux and Giddins, 2019, p. 346). The textbook, a staple of the course, did not examine the ways in which this music stretched and morphed stylistically and cross-pollinated with other kinds of music experiences, identities, and practices. Furthermore, we did not learn about females challenging historically gendered ways in which females made things up (as soloists or band members), and we certainly did not encounter female band leaders or lead composers and arrangers, as Sherri Tucker's (Tucker, 2000) research in *Swing Shift*, a book about the 1940s all-female bands points to (Tucker, 2000). The history of all-female bands of the twentieth century remains largely ignored in the textbook arena.

Instead, we can contrast how females are compared to male musicians: David Yaffe (1999) discussed the music of drummer Susie Ibarra: "many devoted jazz fans would have difficulty naming any female jazz drummers on the scene, essentially besides Ibarra" (Yaffe, 1999)—it should be noted that just this year, 2021, drummer Terri Lyne Carrington was awarded an NEA Jazz Masters Award, a sign of slow progress. Fast forward to today, do we find a similar sexist treatment of female artists? In a blog post, writer Gian Paolo Galasi (2016) asked: "Is the Avante-Garde sexist?" He discusses how he had been wondering about this problem for several years after a concert with a friend. He explains:

> I was going to a concert with a friend, a trumpet player, who told me that females cannot play saxophone because their rib cage is smaller than a man's. Curiously enough, in that period, a woman saxophone player was emerging, Matana Roberts and the media dedicated to improvised music were praising her for the freshness of her sound and vision.
>
> *(Galasi, 2016, n.p.)*

Through the evolution and stabilization of the study of jazz in schools, we have codified a particular approach to improvisation. An approach that privileges the theoretical organization of the music into forms, functions, and structures within the pedagogical framework of jazz. An approach that historically aligns with various masters and genius improvisers who are readily available on recordings, jazz scholarship and textbooks. An approach that is still primarily centered around male composers and musicians. This codified practice also seems to suggest that particular sonic structures are the preferred and accepted standard of artistry. Perhaps a feminist response to this musical standardization is to question: How does one measure a standard of excellence in a musical practice that values the individual sonic autonomy and experience of each practitioner *rather* than a singular form of "accepted" expression or excellence?

Individual creative choices in an improvised context constantly reassert the interconnectedness of life, identity, and artistic expression. Improvisation problematizes the notion of reproducing a work "only for the standard" that is to be mastered and reproduced (Attali, 1985, p.101). How might we, in music, re-examine the creative process itself as having great artistic value rather than exclusively championing and evaluating the final product based on pre-existing standards? Expanding and legitimizing what constitutes an authentic or original sound when creating real-time music is necessary to examine in the context of improvisational biases. How do we move beyond the tropes of jazz vocabulary at the outset or carry the methods into the practice without bringing along the big band charts or the "Real-Book" as evidence and permission to start making something up in the first place? In fact, what about challenging the limitations of the Real-Book in the first place, like Terri Lyne Carrington (2021) has done, by creating a revised version of the Real-Book, titled *The New Standards*, which now includes more female charts by musicians such as Esperanza Spalding, Marina Schneider, and Geri Allen (www.loc.gov/item/webcast-9771/?loclr=eamdce). As the original Real-Book had only included a single chart by a female, Carrington felt it was important to change this paradigm:

> "I noticed that when we play standards, old or new, most often there are no women represented as music composers. I feel this book will address that, offering a large, curated

group of songs for students, professionals, and educators to access and add to their repertoire," says Carrington. "This highlights our philosophy that the music will only live up to its full potential when gender equity is a guiding principle."

(Ahn, 2020)

The discussion and practice of scholarly standards and evaluations in jazz and improvised music continue to shape who is—or is not—included in the musical canons, references, or histories. The enforcement of a standardized practice is not a new development. Don Heckman's 1967 article *The New Jazz: A Matter of Doing* focused on whether or not it is possible to determine if the people playing freely improvised music are competent; he is concerned with "Where are the standards of excellence" (Reason-Myers, 2002, p. 192). However, if females are playing freely improvised music that defies a codified practice and historically expected sounds of "jazz," the musicians are subject to not only gender bias, but also gendered conceptions of how "good" music "ought to sound."

To develop transformative approaches to improvised music, curriculums, and practices, I suggest we turn to the Feminist Improvising Group (F.I.G.) as a preliminary example. Founded in 1977, F.I.G's interdisciplinary improvised performances included music, dance, theatre, movement, spoken word, social, feminist and critical approaches. The music of F.I.G. posed significant challenges for listeners or critics who want to know what to expect from improvised music in order to have a standard to compare it with. As a result, the group's music was heavily criticized and at times devalued.

The Swiss pianist in the group, Irène Schweizer, was recognized as a virtuoso because of her stylistic range and facile technique, but there were others in F.I.G. that chose more theatrical elements, for example, humor (Reason-Myers, 2002), that were dismissed or questioned as not belonging to the music in a real way. Ajay Heble, a F.I.G. member, remarks that "perhaps our own inability to see past culturally produced notions of innovation make it difficult to recognize when a woman is being innovative" (Heble, 2000).

The music performed by the women in F.I.G. was vastly different from what the majority of men were playing at the *Total Music Meeting*, in Germany (1977). For many of the attending European performances (male and female), mastery of the instrument was one of the hierarchical standards by which performances were measured, as is demonstrated by Schweizer's remarks:

We were not that serious, like men, they play that thing and they think they are the greatest[;] they take it so seriously but for us it was more fun but I think it was still good music, but we presented it differently. It was the humor that men couldn't take. The kind of humor we presented was too much for them.

(Reason-Myers, 2002, p. 77)

To join F.I.G., one did not necessarily have to be a trained musician. Maggie Nichols, one of the core members, talked about the original concept for F.I.G. as being open to all women, and even for women who had never improvised. Nichols remarked "I was excited about bringing in women from all different levels, in a truly feminist way. … I wanted it to be accessible to women at all different levels of musicianship" (Reason-Myers, 2002, p. 78).

Today, we are at the place where a force like multi-Grammy award winner, Terri Lyne Carrington, has set up a new institution "Jazz and Gender Justice" at Berklee College of Music in Boston, to address the areas of inequity for females in jazz and improvisation (https://college.berklee.edu/jazz-gender-justice). This new institute is a place to start collectively rethinking the jazz canon and, in particular, she and her cohort want us to question "what would jazz without patriarchy sound like?" (Lorge, 2019, n.p.)

At a recent conference titled: "Return to Center: Black Women, Jazz, and Jazz Education" (https://college.berklee.edu/events/return-to-the-center-black-women-jazz-and-jazz-education), put on by Berklee Institute of Jazz and Gender Justice in June, 2021, in the opening remarks Terri Lyne Carrington discussed how she was not personally affected by gender bias as a female drummer, but that once she started to open her eyes, and listen to more stories from other female musicians in jazz, she recognized female musicians had experienced these issues repeatedly. (https://college.berk lee.edu/events/return-to-the-center-black-women-jazz-and-jazz-education).

The belief that there are no females to select from in the first place, and therefore no geniuses, are representative of this problematic "Myth of Absence." Larry Blumfeld, one of the early editors in chief of *Jazziz* magazine, remarked "that the presence of female musicians (and journalists) is still rather scarce." He states,

> I've gone to a lot of conventions and a lot of panels and a lot of festivals, and I've had female writers come up to me and ask, 'How come there aren't more female writings about jazz?' I've had female musicians come up to me and lament how there are no female leaders on a given festival's program, or maybe just one.
>
> *(Reason-Myers, 2002)*

You may be thinking: *Blumenfeld's comments were from 21 years ago. Surely, things have changed.* At that time, there were no females identified as "masters" or "young lions" whom female and male students could learn from, identify with, or imagine becoming—the jazz-genius woman has yet to be introduced into history (McMullen, 2019).

So how many women journalists are writing and examining female jazz and improvised-based artists today? A Google search for female journalists generates a very small percentage of names. In my own search, I learned of a female jazz journalist from Spain: Mirian Arbalejo. Her writing includes a variety of gender-balanced, stylistic practitioners, and offers an opportunity to veer away from the exceptionalism narrative when it comes to females in jazz: so that newer names arrive alongside more established artists like pianist Aki Takase; Miho Hazama; Tomeka Reid; and Caroline Shaw. Arbalejo blurs genre distinctions in her writing to widen the stylistic approaches, attitudes, and accepted borders of practices, too (Arbalejo, 2021). And yet, as recently as 2021, Arbalejo wrote about her disappointment around issues of jazz coverage of women:

> By reason of this commitment to my profession and especially to my community, when a poll about the best pianists of the last 100 years published by a Spanish magazine— focused on classical music and jazz—came to my attention, I found myself disheartened seeing how the 26 polled people were all men. I honestly thought we got over this kind of behavior, but here I was again writing an email to this magazine and sharing with them the conclusions from the piece published by my colleagues just before the NPR Jazz Critics Poll was out: *Equal At Last? Women In Jazz, By The Numbers*, so the publishers could have a fresh reference to the impact of women's absence in the results of said poll.
>
> *(Arbalejo, 2021)*

Similarly, in the United States, the National Endowment for Arts (NEA): Jazz Masters Awards tells the limited story of females and (recognized) female mastery in jazz (National Endowment for the Arts, 2021).

Out of the 46 people awarded The NEA Jazz Masters Award between the years 2011–2021, only 10 were allotted to females in jazz, which is equivalent to 21 percent (National Endowment for the Arts, 2021). The 10 female award recipients were: Terri Lyne Carrington (drummer, composer, educator, producer); Dorthaan Kirk (jazz advocate); Maria Schneider (composer, arranger, bandleader); Joanne Brackeen (pianist, composer, educator); Dianne Reeves (vocalist); Dee Dee Bridgewater (vocalist, producer, broadcaster); Wendy Oxenhorn (musicians' advocate);

Table 31.1 National Endowment for the Arts Jazz Masters Awards, 2011–2021

2021 (Year)	3 (Males)	1 (Female)
2020	3	1
2019	3	1
2018	2	2
2017	4	1
2016	3	1
2015	3	1
2014	4	0
2013	3	1
2012	3	1
2011	5	0

Carla Bley (composer, arranger, bandleader, keyboardist); Lorraine Gordon (jazz club owner, awarded for jazz advocacy); Sheila Jordan (vocalist, educator) (National Endowment for the Arts, 2021).

It is clear that our musical canons are replete with absences, and much of the work that has been done by early female scholars in jazz, improvised, and general music histories, have not been integrated with other advances in music research. This work still tends to reside outside dominant scholarship, existing in a vacuum, or possibly viewed as a *female-only problem*, and not a *music or jazz music or improvised music* problem.

Call and (HER) Resounding Response

The goal of this chapter was to revisit the developments and recent history of inclusion of females in jazz and improvised music practices since the early 2000s in order to identify areas of oversight of females involved in improvisation, real-time composition, jazz practices, and education in order to foster consolidation, community, and solidarity with other researchers and practitioners in the fields of jazz and improvised music study. I would like to propose that we utilize George E. Lewis's definition of improvisation that is not necessarily jazz-centric but rather encompasses a wide range of improvised and oral traditions and practices:

> Improvised music is a social location inhabited by a considerable number of present-day musicians, coming from diverse cultural backgrounds and musical practices, who have chosen to make improvisation a central part of their musical discourse. Individual improvisers are now able to reference an intercultural establishment of techniques, styles, aesthetic attitudes, antecedents, and networks of cultural and social practice.
>
> *(Lewis, 1996, p. 110)*

Improvisation is not prescriptive, but rather a set of musical strategies that can be applied to *any* music or sound that resonates with each practitioner to embolden personal identities and inclusive forms of musical expression. By questioning the ways in which knowledge is framed, coded, and adopted, it is my hope that we continue to interrogate systemic biases that limit and silence the diverse voices and practices of women in jazz and improvised music.

I started this chapter with a game, and I would like to end it with one. This time, there is only one prompt: How many of the female practitioners, scholars, or musicians' names referenced in this chapter were new to you? None? Some? All? Say their names. Share their ideas. Listen to their music. Collectively, we can improvise our way out of "The Myth of Absence."

References

Ahn, E. (2020) Institute of Jazz and Gender Justice Celebrates *New Standards* by Female Composers. January 21, 2020 (www.berklee.edu/news/berklee-now/terri-lyne-carrington-kris-davis-linda-may-han-oh-perform-red-room-cafe-939-berklee).

Arbalejo, M. (2021). *I Do Write. So Let Me Write.* https://jazzineurope.mfmmedia.nl/2021/04/i-do-write-so-let-me-write/. Oct. 22.

Attali, J. (1985). *Noise: The Political Economy of Music.* Minneapolis, MN: University of Minnesota Press.

Brooks, D. (2021). *Liner Notes for the Revolution: The Intellectual Life of Black Feminist Sound.* Cambridge, MA: The Belknap Press of Harvard University Press.

Brown, J. (2021). *Black Utopias: Speculative Life and the Music of Other Worlds.* Duke University Press. https://college.berklee.edu/events/return-to-the-center-black-women-jazz-and-jazz-education https://www.berklee.edu/news/berklee-now/terri-lyne-carrington-kris-davis-linda-may-han-oh-perform-red-room-cafe-939-berklee.

Butler. J. (2006). *Gender trouble : feminism and the subversion of identity.* Routledge.

Citron, M. J. (1990). "Gender, professionalism and the musical canon," *Journal of Musicology, 8*(1), 102–117.

DeVeaux, S. K., and Giddins, Gary. (2019). *Jazz: Essential Listening* (Third edition.). W. W. Norton.

Gabbard, K. (1995). *Jazz among the Discourses.* Durham: Duke University Press.

Galasi, G. (2016). Is the Avante Garde Sexist? Blog Oct. 13. http://completecommunion.blogspot.com/2016/10/is-avant-garde-sexist.html.

Green, L. (1997). Music, Gender, Education. Cambridge: Cambridge University Press.

Heble, A. (2000). *Landing on the Wrong Note Jazz, Dissonance, and Critical Practice.* New York, NY: Routledge.

Joplin, S. (1960). *Maple Leaf Rag* (Encore series). New York: Larrabee Publications.

Joplin, S., L., Vera B., and Jackson, R., (1971). *The Collected Works of Scott Joplin* (Americana Collection Music Series; 1). New York: New York Public Library.

Kernodle, T. (2004). *Soul on Soul: The Life and Music of Mary Lou Williams.* Boston: Northeastern University Press.

Koskoff, E. (1987). *Women and Music in Cross-cultural Perspective.* Westport, CT: Greenwood Press.

Koskoff, E., and Cusick, Suzanne. (2014) *A Feminist Ethnomusicology: Writings on Music and Gender.* Champaign, IL: University of Illinois Press.

Lewis, G. (2017). The situation of a Creole: In "Defining Twentieth-and-Twenty First-Century Music." *Twentieth-Century Music, 14*(3), 442–446.

Lewis, G. E., and Piekut, B. (2016). *The Oxford Handbook of Critical Improvisation Studies, Vol. 1.* Oxford: Oxford University Press USA—OSO.

Lewis, George E. (1996). Improvised music after 1950: Afrological and Eurological perspectives. *Black Music Research Journal, 16*(1), 91–122. https://doi.org/10.2307/779379.

Lorge, S. (2019). Terri Lyne Carrington Transforms the Culture *DownBeat Magazine* I, Jan. 25, (https://downbeat.com/news/detail/terri-lyne-carrington-looks-to-transform-the-culture).

McClary, S. (1991). *Feminine endings : music, gender, and sexuality.* University of Minnesota Press.

McMullen, T. (2019). *Haunthenticity: Musical Replay and the Fear of the Real* (Music/culture). Middletown, CT: Wesleyan University Press.

Mieszkowski, S., Smith, J., and De, V. M. (Eds.). (2007). Sonic Interventions. ProQuest Ebook Central https://ebookcentral.proquest.com.

Monson, I. (1996). *Saying Something: Jazz Improvisation and Interaction* (Chicago Studies in Ethnomusicology). Chicago: University of Chicago Press.

National Endowment of Arts: Jazz Award 2021 recipients. (2021). www.arts.gov/honors/jazz.

NEA Jazz Masters Awards: www.arts.gov/honors/jazz/list?title=&field_year_value=All&page=0.

Neuls-Bates, C. (1996). *Female in Music: An Anthology of Source Readings from the Middle Ages to the Present* (Revised ed.). Boston: Northeastern University Press.

Reason-Myers, D. (2002). "Myth of Absence: Reception," (Doctoral Dissertation). www.jazzstudiesonline.org.

Rinehimer, B. (2012) "Teaching Improvisation within the Gender Music Methods Course: University Teacher Experiences, Approaches, and Perspectives." (Masters Thesis), Indiana University: (https://scholarworks.iu.edu/dspace/handle/2022/19673/browse?value=Rinehimer%2C+Bridget+Dawn&type=author).

Rodgers, T. (2010). *Pink Noises: Female on Electronic Music and Sound.* Durham, NC: Duke University Press.

Schroder, F., and Haodha, M. Ó. (2014). *Soundweaving.* Newcastle upon Tyne: Cambridge Scholars Publisher.

Smith, L.D. (1999). Improvising Across Borders. UCSD, La Jolla, California. https://intuitivemusic.dk/iima/isy.htm

Solie, R. (1995). *Musicology and Difference: Gender and Sexuality in Music Scholarship.* Berkeley: University of California Press.

Song, A. (2013). Music Improvisation in Higher Education, Published online: 11 November 2013. *College Music Symposiums, 53.*

Steinbeck, Paul. (2016). Talking Back. *Music Theory Online*, 22(3). https://doi.org/10.30535/mto.22.3.8.

Taylor, B., *Jazz Piano: History and Development* (1982). Dubuque, Iowa: C. Brown Publication.

Tucker, S. (2008). *Big Ears: Listening for Gender in Jazz Studies. Current Musicology*, (71–73), 375.

Tucker, S. (2000). *Swing Shift: "All-girl" Bands of the 1940s*. Durham: Duke University Press.

The Royal Conservatory of Music, Toronto. (2020). Retrieved from https://en.wikipedia.org/wiki/The_Royal_Conservatory_of_Music.

Van Vleet, K. (2021). Female in Jazz Music: A Hundred Years of Gender Disparity in Jazz Study and Performance (1920–2020). *Jazz Education in Research and Practice*, 2(1), 211–227.

Walls, S. (March 7, 2019). Review: Roscoe Mitchell Jackhammers a New Musical Funhouse www.nytimes.com/2019/03/07/arts/music/review-roscoe-mitchell-park-avenue-armory.html.

Wonder, S. (1972). *Talking Book*. Tamla. Detroit MI: University Music Group.

Worthy, Michael D. (2011). Jazz Education. In *New Grove Dictionary of Music and Musicians*. Oxford University Press. https://doi.org/10.1093/gmo/9781561592630.article.A2093226.

Yaffe, D. (1999). Holding Her Own Among All the Guys. *New York Times*. May 30, sec. 2:22.

PART 4

Policy and Advocacy

32

VICTIMS NO MORE

How Women and Non-Binary Musicians Are Collaborating for Gender Justice in Jazz

Beatriz Nunes and Leonor Arnaut

Author's Statement

In this chapter we use the terms female, male and non-binary. In the terms female (women, girls) and male (men, boys) we address cisgender identities, whose gender identity and biological sex assigned at birth are the same. The term non-binary refers to gender identities that are neither male nor female, that are in between or beyond the gender binary. Non-binary is a term that covers all gender identities outside the gender binary. Both authors identify as cisgender women.

Introduction

In the last decade, women and non-binary jazz musicians have been collaborating in structured organizations to address gender disparities in jazz. These organizations implemented strategies to overcome the lack of non-male musician representation in jazz. They have also been addressing imbalanced power dynamics, such as sexual harassment and abuse, that still hinder women musicians in performative contexts.

Academics have demonstrated how gender is a socially constructed and performative category of human differentiation (Butler, 1990). Philosophers and sociologists have already exposed the patriarchal system as a normative social construction, where women are presented as an 'other' to a normative male self (Beauvoir, 1953). In this patriarchal system, normative males profit from unbalanced power relationships, where androcentric narratives prevail as dominant (Bourdieu, 2001). Contemporary theories observe gender as a multifaceted issue that intersects race, social class, sexuality, and other identities. These dynamics create layered experiences of privilege that also determine power relationships (Crenshaw, 1990).

Even though scholars agree that jazz is historically a heteronormative male environment, questions remain on how to achieve gender equality. What strategies need to be initiated towards achieving gender inclusion in the near future? The actions taken by women and non-binary jazz feminists and activists address these lingering questions.

Along with the feminist movement of the 1970s, the first advocates for jazz women's rights emerged in the United States. Although second-wave feminists led critical social shifts towards equal pay and job opportunities, feminist movements of the twentieth century struggled to converge and address various circumstances of privilege. It was in the late 1980s that third-wave feminists embraced

DOI: 10.4324/9781003081876-36

the concept of intersectionality, arguing that social identities can suffer from layers of oppression caused by gender, race and class (Crenshaw, 1990).

At the same time, postmodernist theories explained gender as a socially constructed, performative and fluid category, problematizing the gender binary system as an incremental hierarchy between men and women (Butler, 1990). The contribution of gender non-binary perspectives became fundamental in contemporary feminist movements in jazz, such as We Have Voice (WHV) and the Women in Jazz Organization (WIJO). These organizations identify themselves as groups of women and gender non-binary with different sexual identities that advocate an intersectional perspective. Following the #MeToo movement in 2017, the discussion of female vulnerability in male-dominated environments was accelerated, and it influenced the activism for non-patriarchal representation in jazz.

This chapter provides a historical perspective of feminist activism in jazz in the United States since the 1970s with a focus on the strategies of three contemporary organizations. This study will focus on the experiences of three activists from different generations in the United States, trumpeter/big band director Ellen Seeling, saxophonist/composer Roxy Coss and vocalist/composer Sara Serpa.

Framing Women's Struggle for Gender Justice in Jazz

It is not uncommon to associate jazz with political activism, the struggle for racial equality or even with freedom itself. If we consider racial and social struggles as foundational aspects of jazz music, political activism and jazz have been historically connected. However, it is necessary to criticize how the narrative of freedom and empowerment in jazz made it difficult to deconstruct subtexts of masculinity in a predominantly male and heteronormative musical territory.

According to trumpeter Ellen Seeling, the act of surviving as a woman jazz instrumentalist in the 1970s was a huge act of activism in itself:

> There was a small number of women jazz instrumentalists in the 70s, primarily pianists and guitarists. … There were no organized groups or activities that were seen as activists or practicing gender activism in jazz that I was aware of. But you can bet these women were living under the jazz patriarchy, and knew they were under the thumb.

Seeling was the first woman to graduate with a degree in jazz studies from Indiana University, in 1975, and led several initiatives, from all-women big bands to legal organizations defending women's rights.

Influenced by the second-wave feminism arising in the United States at the same time, the first women's jazz festivals were held in Kansas City and in New York City. In March 1978, Carol Comer and Dianne Gregg founded the Kansas City Women's Jazz Festival, the first US festival created to address women's representation in jazz. The first edition featured three days of workshops, jams and concerts with performances by Betty Carter, Toshiko Akiyoshi's big band, an all-star female group led by Marian MacPartland, culminating with the performance of Mary Lou Williams.

Inspired by the festival in Kansas City, Cobi Narita, founder of the Universal Jazz Coalition (UJC) in New York City, started the New York Women's Jazz Festival, also in 1978. This festival premiered as the 'Universal Jazz Coalition Salute to Women' in the Casablanca Club in New York City, and was transferred to Carnegie Hall in the following editions. The New York Women's Jazz Festival also had concerts, workshops and jam sessions.

Several musicians recognize Cobi Narita's contribution to the jazz community in New York, particularly as an advocate for jazz women. Narita founded the Jazz Center of New York, recalled by Seeling as a critical place for her integration in the jazz community:

> There was a small number of women jazz instrumentalists in the seventies, primarily pianists and guitarists. Carla Bley, Joanne Brackeen, Marian McPartland, Mary Osborne, Dottie Dodgion, Janice Robinson, Paula Hampton, Jean Davis, Willine Barton, Carline Ray,

Sharon Freeman, Bertha Hope, Ann Patterson, Melba Liston and Jean Fineberg were all active and performing with different groups and as freelancers. As a newly arrived New Yorker in 1975, I was lucky enough to have played with many of these musicians. We were members of Cobi Narita's Universal Jazz Coalition, which in its day was seen in part as a feminist jazz organization.

(Ellen Seeling, interview, April 12, 2021)

Narita also founded the UJC Big Apple Jazzwomen featuring 17 women with Ellen Seeling running it. This band performed at the Lincoln Center Jazz Festival, the UJC Jazz Festival, and more.

The feminist movement of the 1970s provided an important theoretical background for these initiatives:

Because of the new Women's Movement in the 1970s, there was a lot of new awareness and consciousness-raising about women and our condition in the workplace. This also helped women jazz players to begin to recognize that we had a history, and that it had mostly been ignored by the jazz establishment. We saw that there was serious gender discrimination in our field. Women jazz artists were starting to be noticed, and there was a resurgence of older women artists like Melba Liston, Marian McPartland, Sarah McLawler and others.

(Ellen Seeling, interview, April 12, 2021)

In the same period, all women jazz orchestras with an early feminist background began to flourish in the East and West Coast. Examples are Straight Ahead, a Detroit based quintet formed in 1987 with Cynthia Dewberry, Regina Carter, Eileen Orr, Marion Hayden and Gayelynn McKinney; Alive!, a San Francisco Bay Area quintet active from 1975 to 1985 with original members Barbara Borden, Carolyn Brandy, Susanne DiVicenzo and Rhianon; and Ann Patterson's Maiden Voyage, an all-female orchestra founded in Los Angeles in 1981 that was active until the 2000s. This band reached wider recognition after performing on the Johnny Carson Show. Another influential all-women orchestra established in the early 1990s is DIVA, founded by Stanley Key in 1992 and headed by drummer Sherrie Maricle. DIVA has been providing role models for several jazz female instrumentalists until the present: "DIVA is often called "No Man's Band," and has blown myths of "women can't play" out of the water for decades. The group has toured the world and has released eleven recordings to date." (Ellen Seeling, interview, April 12, 2021). There was also New York city-based Kit McLure's Band, an all-female big band formed in 1982. In 2004, saxophonist Kit McLure released the "Sweethearts Project," a tribute to the all-women orchestra of the 1940s, the International Sweethearts of Rhythm. Although all-women groups have existed since the early 1920s, with all-girl bands having a particularly active period during World War II, all-women bands of the 1940s were not perceived as authentic as their contemporary all men-bands, which hampered women's recognition, visibility and historical documentation (Tucker, 2000).

According to Ellen Seeling, jazz women became more vocal about gender discrimination stating in the mid-1990s:

Women's advocacy groups began to spring up around the country. The International Women in Jazz grew out of a seminar on Women in Jazz organized by Pastor Dale Lind and held at Saint Peter's Church in New York City in September 1995. The Women in Jazz Association, based in Austin, Texas, was founded in 1994, and the Women in Jazz, Inc., based in NYC was formed in 2009. Regional women in jazz organizations have also popped up in Seattle, South Florida, and New York City in recent years. But the only organization employing legal solutions to gender discrimination in jazz is my own group, Jazzwomen and Girls Advocates, founded in 2015 in the San Francisco Bay Area.

(Ellen Seeling, interview, April 12, 2021)

In 2015, Seeling co-founded Jazzwomen and Girls Advocates (JAGA) with attorney Sara Sanderson. JAGA addresses gender disparities in jazz through legal advocacy: "We look at the gender distribution among members of large jazz organizations and their signature ensembles, festival and concert programming, music education programs and jazz faculties from middle school through college." (Ellen Seeling, interview, April 12, 2021).

Seeling credits Lara Pellegrinelli's article "Boy dig boy" in the *Village Voice* in 2000 as one important piece to deconstruct the myth of jazz meritocracy: "Pellegrinelli focused on the absence of women in the band during her interview with artistic and executive director Wynton Marsalis. It was pretty clear that the hiring process then was closed." (Ellen Seeling, interview, April 12, 2021). After several protests organized by Ellen Seeling addressing the exclusion of female members in the Jazz at Lincoln Center Orchestra, the organization successfully negotiated new hiring policies in 2016. After consulting with Ellen and JAGA, Jazz at Lincoln Center adopted blind auditions, the first official blind audition process in jazz. JAGA also negotiated a wider percentage of presenting women at the Monterey Jazz Festival increasing the programming from 7 percent women instrumentalists to about 30 percent by 2018.

In the 2010s, novel women's festivals and associations appeared in the United States, such as the Washington Women in Jazz Festival (WWIJ) organized by pianist Amy K. Bormet in 2011, the We Create Jazz Festival presented by Laura Gentry from Cincinnati in 2019. Further examples are the Seattle Women in Jazz Festival premiered in 2013, Knoxville Women in Jazz Festival in 2016, Alabama Women in Jazz Festival in 2014, among others.

These initiatives share a common strategy of creating performative opportunities for female jazz musicians. These organizations also share a common perspective about the importance of role models and female musicians' visibility as a needed inspiration for new generations of jazz women. Most of these festivals present workshops and female mentorship programs along with their programming strategy.

More recently, the Berklee Institute of Jazz and Gender Justice (BIJGJ) founded in 2018 by artistic director Terri Lyne Carrington, demonstrates a systematization of activism for gender equality in jazz education. The institute's mission is "to recruit, teach, mentor, and advocate for musicians seeking to study jazz with gender equity as a guiding principle."[1] In a presentation by advisory board member Dr. Farah Jasmine Griffin, intersectionality of gender identities was highlighted as one main issue for the institute. The principle of intersectionality, approaching gender-diverse identities, including transgender and non-binary, represents one of the main perspective shifts from previous activist organizations for women's rights such as JAGA. The BIJGJ leads an advocacy approach that considers not only cis-women, but also transgender and non-binary musicians as underrepresented in the heteronormative patriarchal system: "Gender justice implies a politic where boys and girls, men and women, cis- and transgender, gender non-conforming and non-binary persons-everyone is valued equally and shares in the equitable distribution of power, knowledge, and resources."[2]

The institute commits to addressing gender disparities at the college through curriculum, recruitment, residencies, performances, research, and community engagement. The organization shows a profound intersectional consciousness, recognizing deep-rooted struggles against patriarchy through gender and racial justice.

European Movements for Gender Balance in Jazz

Since the 2000s, women's jazz festivals have been emerging in Europe. That is the case of Women in Jazz in Halle, Germany, founded in 2006, recognized as a cultural best-practice in the Digital Conference on Gender Equality in December 2020; the Women in Jazz Festival in Gothenburg founded in 2015; and the Stockholm Women's International Jazz Festival established in 2019. In 2021, the Stockholm Women's International Jazz Festival hosted a live stream conference on Gender Balance in Jazz, organized in collaboration with Europe Jazz Network. In Italy, in 2015 the community Women in Jazz Network set up the first WinJazz Festival in Rome. This project is funded by the Ministry of Culture of Italy with the main goal of promotion and mobility of young women jazz musicians in Europe. In 2019, the festival Feminajazz was also founded in Spain. This festival held workshops and masterclasses and also a round table about the future of jazz and women's participation.

It has also stimulated educational jazz programs such as Tomorrow's Warriors Female Collective founded in 2011 in London. The TW Female Collective is a jazz educational program committed to offering educational opportunities for female musicians in a safe space.

The 2010s saw the rise of the first European initiatives pledging parity in the music industry. One example is Keychange, founded in 2015 in the UK. This organization is funded by the Creative Europe Programme of the European Union and works in partnership with music festivals in 12 different countries from Europe, the United States and Canada. The Keychange Gender Balance Pledge was established in 2017, aiming to attain 50/50 gender balance in music festivals by 2022. Hull Jazz Festival and Cheltenham Jazz Festival are examples of festivals committing to this pledge (Raine, 2019). Although Keychange recognizes that the five-year framework to achieve 50/50 gender balance in music festivals might be ambitious, it argues that setting specific goals is extremely important towards achieving change.

In Europe, organizations are also signing Manifestos for gender balance. In September 2018, at the 5th European Jazz Conference in Lisbon, 93 members of the Europe Jazz Network (EJN) signed the Manifesto on Gender Balance in Jazz and Creative Music. This Manifesto is the result of the EJN "Europe Jazz Balance" initiative, that has examined diversity and discrimination in jazz since 2014, with financial support from the Creative Europe Programme of the European Union. The Manifesto raises awareness toward gender balance, and encourages its members to "put in place policies and action plans to involve more women as artists, artistic directors and producers, staff and board members and audience members in our work." The Manifesto also invited EJN members to complete a survey regarding their work over the past three calendar years to inform the formulation of future strategies.

The Contributions of We Have Voice and WIJO

In 2017, the social media impact of the #MeToo movement triggered an increased awareness about sexual harassment and forms of abuse that women endure in the workplace. This initiated an urgent discussion about consent, unbalanced power dynamics and violence against women. The #MeToo movement was founded in 2006 primarily by social rights activist Tarana Burke. Burke's #MeToo aimed to empower young women, especially young women of color, survivors of sexual assault. In 2017, actress Alyssa Milano used twitter to suggest that every woman victim-survivor of sexual assault use the hashtag #MeToo in their social media status. Milano's viral #MeToo reached substantial mediatic attention that credited the actress for launching the movement on social media. As media coverage failed to acknowledge Burke's previous work, the movement's appropriation was discussed by Burke and other activists. As the hashtag gained publicity, Burke remobilized her commitment to focusing the conversation on power and privilege, contextualizing #MeToo as part of a wider movement to counter the white-supremacist patriarchy (Rodino-Colocino, 2018). The #MeToo entered all social and cultural environments, including the art form jazz.

As a reaction to the #MeToo movement, in 2017 a group of female and non-binary musicians founded the We Have Voice collective. The collective was created by 14 musicians from "different generations, races, ethnicities, cultures, abilities, gender identities, economic backgrounds, religious beliefs and affiliations,"[3] These musicians are Fay Victor, Ganavya Doraiswamy, Imani Uzuri, Jen Shyu, Kavita Shah, Linda May Han Oh, María Grand, Nicole Mitchell, Okkyung Lee, Rajna Swaminathan, Sara Serpa, Tamar Sella, Terri Lyne Carrington, and Tia Fuller. As a co-founder of the WHV collective, vocalist, composer, and producer Sara Serpa agreed to share her personal perspectives as an activist for gender balance in jazz. These contributions are personal and do not represent the collective.

According to Sara Serpa, the collective was created spontaneously as a reaction to the articles and stories about harassment of women and abuse of power, in the jazz and creative music world inspired by the #MeToo movement. The collective introduced two main initiatives, an Open Letter and a Code of Conduct (CoC). The collective's Open Letter was the result of a series of conversations regarding news of violence and gender discrimination in the art industries in 2017. The Open Letter emerged after the publication of a *Boston Globe* article by Kay Lazar titled "Berklee let teachers quietly leave after alleged sex abuse, and pushed students for silence," and other news about sexual violence and gender discrimination in the music industry. These articles denounced a patterned practice of sexual misconduct, enabled by a pervasive culture of tolerance in institutions and from peers. WHV positioned as an organization against the culture of tolerance and silence about sexual harassment in the performative arts: "We will not be silent. We have voice. We have zero tolerance for sexual harassment."[4] On the collective's website, the group invites others to add their names to the Open Letter as an act of support, solidarity and commitment to create a culture of equity in the professional artistic world. The Open Letter is available in WHV's website with 1216 signatures at the time of writing:

> The first initiative was the Open Letter, where we show solidarity (with the survivors who came forward with their stories of abuse). Many people signed it, men, women, of every generation, from outside and inside the music community. It was an attention call to bring awareness to what had been happening for decades in our professional world. At the time the letter had a strong impact. The idea of a Code of Conduct came after. Because many professional institutions have codes of conduct, but for us, musicians, our workplace is very fluid, in which boundaries are not clear. Relationships in the music field do not operate in the same way as in an office for example. There are many connections between people that are co-dependent, but it is not in a contractual way, it is in a much more psychological and emotional way.
>
> *(Sara Serpa, interview, March 9, 2021)*

The WHV Code of Conduct for the Performing Arts is a pioneer document in jazz, creative music and the performing arts, a document that defines consent, abuse and safe space in the context of music as a workplace. For Sara Serpa, the definition of the concept "workplace" was one of the most important exercises.

On the website of the collective, sexual harassment is defined as "a type of personal or institutional abuse that uses sexual behavior to alarm, control, demean, intimidate, bully, belittle, humiliate, or embarrass another person."[5] As it states, sexual harassment is usually not related to sexual desire. It is mostly an abuse and misuse of power, a predatory behavior to assert dominance. In their Code of Conduct, the WHV Collective defines the following conditions: What is a safe(r) space? How is sexual harassment defined by the law? What is a workplace? What is consent? What impacts consent?

The use of the term safe(r) is an acknowledgement of the group's intersectionality, understanding that "what is "safe" shifts depending on one's various identities and positionalities."[6] The code clarifies the concept of consent considering the impact of power dynamics, such as between a teacher and a student, a band leader and a collaborator, a festival promoter and an artist. Unbalanced power dynamics associated with female numeric disadvantages in jazz put females in a particularly vulnerable situation. For Sara Serpa, the creation of the Open Letter and the Code of Conduct initiated a shift away from the position of victim:

> For me it was a reaction of not wanting to absorb these stories and not accepting the position of the victim. ... [T]he Code of Conduct was an empowerment tool, to name

situations. By giving name, we are able to identify when abuse happens and take a different position about it, while not accepting to be victims.

(Sara Serpa, interview, March 9, 2021)

The WHV collective promoted, encouraged and invited musical institutions to adopt the document. This process included a public announcement on the institutions' website and social media, and a guarantee that all of the institution's collaborators understood the commitment. The institutions were also advised to display the document in their performance spaces, such as rehearsal/dressing rooms, offices, classrooms, studios, and so forth. Sixty-one institutions from the United States, Canada and Italy committed to the *We Have Voice Code of Conduct* for the performing arts. These institutions are record labels, music collectives, jazz festivals, schools and universities such as Winter Jazzfest, The New School: School of Jazz and Contemporary Music, SF Jazz, Monterey Jazz Festival, Biophilia Records, among others.

Along with the CoC, We Have Voice has led several roundtable discussions in 2018 and 2019. Although a primary focus was given to sexual harassment, the collective was also invested in a discussion about female representation.

The *We Have Voice Code of Conduct* earned significant public attention and media coverage in *The New York Times*, NPR and other newspapers and blogs. In 2019, *The New York Times* considered the WHV collective to be one of the ten definitive moments of the decade in jazz. The media coverage helped raise awareness on sexual harassment in the context of jazz (Mercer, 2018).

Sara Serpa acknowledges how traumatic these experiences are for victims, and she observes that there is an absence of structured response for incidents of sexual harassment in music, such as legal organizations and mental-health assistance. Although some women musicians reached out to the group for counseling, WHV's does not have the ability nor the intention to mediate conflicts, as it states on the website.

Serpa added that one of the main achievements of the Code of Conduct was to offer clarity and tools for people working in the performing arts. It was important not only for victims, but also for bystanders who, in her opinion, have exceptional power to change situations of abuse:

> Just the fact that the CoC is there (displayed on the New School's walls) makes people much more conscious. And people can consider if they can help others when there is a situation of abuse or humiliation. They can have an active role. ... Actually, that is the most challenging part. There are so many bystanders who have witnessed so many situations and were never able to say something. Enablers have as much power as active perpetrators.
>
> *(Sara Serpa, interview, March 9, 2021)*

Serpa added that it is very difficult, and that it will take a long time to achieve structural change. Sometimes male allies will display what Serpa calls a "performative alliance," that does not result in effective and consistent change in their practices. Performative allies will engage in the conversation about gender balance from a position of established power and will not consider women's experiences as different. Regarding how challenging it is to change systems of male normativity, Serpa considers that it is important for women to take up their own narratives, spaces and create their communities. Serpa is committed to "normalize powerful women and non-binary musicians." During 2020, she developed a mentorship program with Jen Shyu and Jordannah Elizabeth called M3-Mutual Mentorship. This project aims to provide gendered diverse models and settings where people can learn with each other without the regular educational hierarchy.

According to Sara Serpa, advocacy is "invisible work." Musicians who lead these organizations are not paid and need to spend their time researching, planning, working without any financial compensation. Women jazz musicians who engage in activism thus take on an additional burden. They often sacrifice time for creating to conduct research, talks, conferences, meetings and other non-paid activities.

Serpa observes the contribution of the *We Have Voice* collective as a legacy for younger generations. The Code of Conduct created a previously non-existent language about abuse and consent, deconstructing naturalized practices. Through this empowering language, Serpa includes "cis-women, cis-men, trans-women, trans-men, non-binary people, and those who are otherwise marginalized musicians" into the advocacy initiative enabling them to "say no" to situations of abuse.

Another New York city–based organization is WIJO (Women in Jazz Organization), also created in 2017. Members include over five hundred professional performing jazz musicians who identify as women or gender non-binary. The first monthly meeting of the collective was organized by Roxy Coss and Aubrey Johnson. Coss recalls the political and sociological environment in the United States after the presidential election of 2016 as one precipitator for the creation of the collective:

> I realized the need for a network of women in jazz, and wanted to create a productive outlet
> to channel my frustration about the election results, as well as my own personal day-to-day
> treatment and experiences of being a woman in New York City, and a jazz musician.
>
> *(Roxy Coss, interview, April 13, 2021)*

WIJO is led by Coss as president, Tahira Clayton as vice president and Allegra Levy as secretary. The organization pursues three main goals: to empower individuals in the organization; to foster inclusivity and solidarity, and strengthen the intersectional community of women and non-binary people in jazz; to address inequalities in jazz culture and on the jazz scene through activism.

As a female jazz saxophonist, Roxy Coss experienced jazz through profound gender isolation, experiences of sexual harassment, a lack of access to opportunities and a lack of equal treatment regarding education and performance. Coss also acknowledges a lack of community and support during her musical journey:

> I began to realize how important it was for women in jazz to connect and share their
> experiences with one another, both to help, support and educate each other, and to reflect
> on our shared experiences, rather than carrying the weight of being "alone" and feeling
> like your experiences were your own fault, or that you were the only one going through
> them. Playing and touring with the DIVA jazz orchestra gave me a glimpse into this type
> of community and support system of women in jazz.
>
> *(Roxy Coss, interview, April 13, 2021)*

In order to foster a female and non-binary jazz community, WIJO organized a collegiate mentorship program. The WIJO Mentors program aims to provide role models to up-and-coming jazz musicians and composers in a safe and supportive environment with professionals from around the world. Coss believes that mentorship is one efficient way to connect and empower young female jazz students:

> [T]hey don't feel as alone, even if they're the only girl in their jazz program, because they
> know twenty other young women studying jazz around the country, so they feel connected
> and empowered. And, they have access to information from their Mentors that they would
> not have otherwise.
>
> *(Roxy Coss, interview, April 13, 2021)*

Alongside the mentorship program, WIJO leads monthly meetings, concerts, hang and jam sessions. These events have successfully facilitated a professional and personal community of women in jazz. The organization also facilitates professional opportunities for women jazz musicians through Apple playlists, podcasts and a recurring radio show on WKCR NYC. These initiatives aim to increase the number of role models and to break through female invisibility in jazz.

The group also leads discussions, clinics and lectures in several countries. In 2019, WIJO participated in Jazzahead with an open table presented at the Jazzahead! Conference. The committee presented WIJO artists to labels, promoters, and other industry professionals in order to help festivals and labels achieve 50/50 gender parity in the industry.

As previously stated by Sara Serpa, in Roxy Coss' opinion female musicians' activists struggle to balance their artistic careers with their activist initiatives: "It is extremely challenging to balance a career in jazz, and to add the work of running these programs is strenuous." (Roxy Coss, interview, April 13, 2021).

It is also challenging to foster an intersectional gendered diverse community in jazz considering the multitude of issues to be addressed. Contemporary groups that focus on intersectionality struggle to address all the different needs, backgrounds and perspectives of its members. As feminist movements of the twentieth century battled to unify and address male privilege, contemporary feminist organizations in jazz are more aware of individual experiences of layered privilege:

> Every woman has a different set of experiences, and therefore a different idea of how to solve the issues we face – this is at the core of intersectionality. We as a leadership team try our best to figure out what all of these needs are, and which ones we can reasonably address. It feels like steering a huge ship, with many conflicting currents.
>
> *(Roxy Coss, interview, April 13, 2021)*

One of the myths frequently found in jazz history narratives is the depiction of women as competitive and antagonistic (Kernodle, 2014). As male competitiveness in jazz is perceived as a creative force, for women however, it tends to be seen with statutory purposes, in order to be the one that earns peer and historical validation. This tokenism prevents unified collaboration towards a shared goal:

> [W]e are pitted against one another, thinking that there is only space for one woman in any given situation. … We all have internalized this patriarchy, and sometimes that is a self-inflicted wound that gets in the way of real progress for the individual or for the collective.
>
> *(Roxy Coss, interview, April 13, 2021)*

Since validation is rooted in a masculine system, women have contradicting experiences in defining identity. Some musicians do not acknowledge individual experiences of gender discrimination in jazz, but actually perceive the masculine canon as natural.[7] There are still successful jazz women instrumentalists who deny gender discrimination in jazz, who consider the issue of gender overrated and disregard it as political, believing in a merit system where competent women musicians have the same chances to succeed as their male peers.[8]

For activist Ellen Seeling, denial of gender discrimination in jazz from other women instrumentalists sabotages the needed advocacy efforts. Sara Serpa also finds it challenging to congregate every woman's perception about issues of gender disparity in jazz: "Sometimes it is not because we are women that we are aligned in the same goals. It is hard to find consensus. It is hard, people have their own agendas." (Sara Serpa, interview, March 9, 2021).

Despite the challenges facing activists, these organizations have been instrumental in facilitating action towards a more balanced music industry and jazz community. Through their initiatives, they have provided spaces for gender minorities in jazz that facilitate networking as well as have created educational programs and role models for future generations.

Conclusion

Several informal and formal networks of musicians were created over the last decades as spontaneous reactions to gender discrimination in jazz. Building after the several contributions of feminist movements and Feminist Studies concepts, activists and musicians in the United States and Europe have engaged in initiatives towards gender balance, such as jazz festivals programming gender minorities, mentorship programs, pledges towards parity in festival programming, blind auditions, declarations regarding sexual harassment and misuses of power in the workplaces, fostering a diverse jazz community through jam sessions, educational programs and networking. However, according to the testimonials of various activists, it is difficult to change a system deeply rooted in patriarchy. Most leaders acknowledge that it will take a long time to achieve a completely gender-balanced music industry. Nonetheless, their actions have been critical in raising awareness and facilitating action against gender discrimination in jazz.

Some of these organizations directly collaborated with other institutions to promote their initiatives. Targeted requests and advocacy towards leading jazz organizations and institutions, such as universities and festivals, were successful strategies towards introducing specific policies in these environments.

Regarding cases of sexual abuse and harassment, it will be critical to create legal structures for protection of victims and for mental health assistance in schools, universities, festivals, and other institutions offering musical programs. The pioneering creation of the CoC provides a framework that offers victims justification of their experiences. However, adequate support resources are not necessarily implemented and offered.

We also found that the creation of a community can support confidence and self-efficacy of women and non-binary jazz musicians. The network established by WIJO as well as their mentorship programs is an important empowerment tool for underrepresented gender identities.

We also understood that European organizations often benefit from funding resources through the Creative Europe Programme of the European Union. However, US organizations such as WIJO and WHV do not have federal funding resources and are mainly led by female musicians themselves. Volunteer advocacy becomes an additional burden on time and resources for musician activists, often in conflict with their professional life.

This chapter documents the leadership of women and non-binary jazz musicians towards raising awareness of gender disparities in jazz. Their advocacy facilitates implementation of new policies at institutions and in industry organizations. It will remain critical to engage the whole jazz community and beyond towards deconstructing the lingering structural bias against gender minorities in jazz.

Acknowledgements

We would like to acknowledge the contribution of Ellen Seeling and Roxy Coss sharing their experiences as female jazz musicians and activists in the United States. We would also like to acknowledge the contribution and support of Sara Serpa who shared critical bibliography resources about this subject and was available to discuss issues about the project beyond her interview.

Notes

1 Berklee Institute of Jazz and Gender Justice website, available at: https://college.berklee.edu/jazz-gender-justice.
2 Griffin, 2018, available at: www.youtube.com/watch?v=ZWkLg8wWCrw.
3 We Have Voice website, available at: https://too-many.org/who-we-are-2/.
4 We Have Voice, Open Letter, available at: https://too-many.org/open-letter/.
5 WHV website, available at: https://too-many.org/sexual-harassment/.
6 WHV Code of Conduct, available at: https://too-many.org/sexual-harassment/.
7 Mary Lou Williams claimed that she was never rejected because of her gender, but at the same time her discourses denote internalized canons of masculinity as natural: "And in a world where playing strongly was everything, it happened that all successful women jazz pianists played like men" (Soules, 2011, p. 22).

8 Aki Takase considers that gender does not have any influence in someone's opportunities in music:

> "This description [UNESCO's definition of jazz as standing for the eradication of discrimination] is meant well, but has more to do with politics than with music. In this sense, the issue of women is also overrated. A good female musician will always prevail!"
>
> *(Schmidt, 2017, p. 83)*

References

Beauvoir, S., (1953). *The Second Sex*. Vintage Publishing

Bourdieu, P. (2001). *Masculine Domination*. Stanford University Press.

Butler, J. (1990). *Gender Trouble*. Routledge.

Crenshaw, K. (1990). Mapping the margins: Intersectionality, identity politics, and violence against women of color. *Stan. L. Rev.*, 43, 1241.

Europe Jazz Balance. (2018). "EJN Manifesto on Gender Balance in Jazz and Creative Music" available at: www.europejazz.net/sites/default/files/EJN_Manifesto_on_gender_balance.pd.

Griffin, F. J. 2018. Speech for Berklee Institute for Jazz and Gender, 30 of October. Available at: www.youtube.com/watch?v=ZWkLg8wWCrw.

Kernodle, T. L. (2014). Black women working together: Jazz, gender, and the politics of validation. *Black Music Research Journal*, 34(1), 27–55.

Mercer, M. (2018). "A map to the line and how not to cross it: a code of conduct for the performing arts" in NPR. Available at: www.npr.org/sections/therecord/2018/04/30/607142770/a-map-to-the-line-and-how-not-to-cross-it-a-code-of-conduct-for-the-performing-a?t=1620664010251.

Raine, S. (2019). Keychanges at Cheltenham Jazz Festival: Issues of Gender in the UK Jazz Scene. In: Strong, C. & Raine, S. (eds.) *Towards Gender Equality in the Music Industry: Education, Practice and Strategies for Change* (pp. 187–200). Bloomsbury.

Rodino-Colocino, M. (2018). Me too,# MeToo: Countering cruelty with empathy. *Communication and Critical/ Cultural Studies*, 15(1), 96–100.

Schmidt, K. (2017). Money and a Room of One's Own?! A Feminist Deconstruction of the Situation of Female Jazz Musicians 1960–1980. *European Journal of Musicology*, 16(1), 81–93.

Soules, K. (2011). "Playing Like a Man": *The Struggle of Black Women in Jazz and the Feminist Movement*. B.A. in Music Senior Capstone Projects. 2.

Tucker, Sherrie. (2000). Swing Shift: "All-Girl" Bands of the 1940s. Duke University Press

WHV. (2017). "Code of Conduct." Available at: https://too-many.org/black-and-white-2/.

WHV. (2017). "Open Letter." Available at: https://too-many.org/open-letter/.

33

WOMEN IN JAZZ

A Failed Brand

Rebecca Zola

Statement on Gendered Terms: I use the term "women" for all people who identify as a woman. In the case of the term "man" or "men" in this chapter, I am referring to cis-gendered men, or men who benefit from patriarchal systems of power. I prefer not to use the terms "female" and "male" as I find them to highlight sex rather than gender identity. I include trans and non-binary members of the jazz community as sharing struggles of gender equity with women in jazz. I identify as a woman in the jazz community, both as a musicologist, and as a woman jazz musician.

Introduction

At the 2018 Newport Jazz Festival, a newly formed supergroup performed, and caught the attention of Blue Note record label president, Don Was. This group, named Artemis, is an all- women jazz supergroup, and is the first of its kind to be featured on the Blue Note record label. The concept of *Jazz Supergroups* is something that has been a tradition at Blue Note as early as 1984, when Blue Note created the supergroup, "Out of the Blue" to showcase Blue Note's top young jazz talents. Supergroups are curated bands comprised of successful individual jazz musicians—put together in bands—but whose careers may not have otherwise overlapped. These bands get together to record an album, which is then promoted with some touring. Blue Note has continued producing supergroups and, in the past 10 years, multiple new supergroups have been assembled, including "The Blue Note Seven," and "Our Point of View." Supergroups have generally been created for their commercial and touring value. The supergroup model is built not only to promote the record label, but also to boost the career of each individual involved. For example, with "Out of the Blue," the breakup of the supergroup was the result of the increased success of each band member's solo career.[1] In the case of Artemis, what were Don Was' intentions for signing them to this iconic jazz label? Their gender makeup inherently categorizes them under the *Women in Jazz* brand. Moreover, their generational, cultural, international and ethnic diversity (Jurkovic 2020) makes Artemis an ideal display of diversity in today's neoliberal capitalism. Neoliberal capitalism aims to manipulate identity politics into a marketing ploy to turn a profit. For example, the media's reception of Artemis consistently takes the gender, ethnicity and age of each woman in the group into account in their reviews and promotions of the band's music and concerts,[2] something that would rarely be seen in promotional materials for an all-men jazz band. At a time when the history of gender discrimination and sexual harassment in

412

DOI: 10.4324/9781003081876-37

the jazz genre has entered the public debate, Artemis presents a perfect representation of the *Women in Jazz* brand for the Blue Note label.

Women in Jazz is a brand that has increasingly entered the programming of jazz venue and festival rosters over the past decades. What started with the 1978 *Kansas City Women in Jazz Festival* as a way to showcase many of the talented women in jazz who had dealt with various barriers of inclusion (Brewer 2017), has turned into a neoliberal marketing tool used to promote music businesses. With the rise of the *#MeToo* movement in other areas of the entertainment industry,[3] music industry professionals as well as individuals in the jazz community have commercialized the movement by implementing the *Women in Jazz* brand to promote individual careers and organizational fiscal growth. But this commercial exploitation of the brand *Women in Jazz* does little to change the gender dynamics in jazz at large, favoring the neoliberal model of individual success in its capitalist system. Combined with second-wave feminism, the branded idea of *Women in Jazz* has provided industry professionals with a new marketing opportunity fashioned by identity politics. This relationship between feminist movements and neoliberalism created a new form of feminism known as neoliberal feminism. Breaking down the main tenets of neoliberalism and its relationship to contemporary feminism in America will help define the resulting concept of neoliberal feminism. It will also help to understand how it has spurred the gender-branded movement of *Women in Jazz*, creating opportunities for ensembles such as Artemis to thrive.

Neoliberal Feminism and *Women in Jazz*

Neoliberalism centers around the belief in the free market as a self-correcting system that allocates resources efficiently and serves the public interest well (Stiglitz 2008). It puts the production and exchange of material goods at the heart of the human experience. As a government mechanism, neoliberalism is rooted in values of free enterprise and entrepreneurialism. With a focus on individual entrepreneurship, neoliberalism departed from principles of collective welfare. This focus on individualism has been followed by a surge in identity politics.

Identity politics at its most basic is when the concept of identity is

> used by political entrepreneurs to persuade people to understand themselves, their interests, and their predicaments in a certain way, to persuade certain people that they are (for certain purposes) "identical" with one another and at the same time different from others, and to organize and justify collective action along certain lines.
>
> *(Brubaker and Cooper 2000, pp. 4–5)*

This combination of entrepreneurship and identity politics requires individuals to market themselves as a unique and worthwhile participant in the capitalist society that they contribute to. In contrast to the radical feminism of the 1960s and 1970s that focused on abolishing hierarchies of power and advocated for solutions towards gender equity and equality through the power of large group activism, here, a new feminism puts women in competitive battles for individual economic success. The neoliberal feminist is essentially coerced, or even trapped into working within the patriarchal structures as an entrepreneur, stretching herself thin to "have it all," instead of fighting for structural change for her peers.

Through the lens of neoliberal feminism, the jazz scene presents itself as a microcosm of the inherently capitalist apparatuses. Women in Jazz is a neoliberal feminist brand that only supports a limited number of careers. This brand benefits the jazz business while maintaining a patriarchal hierarchy in the community. It does so by continuing to frame women as the exception, and in this case forcing them to become competitive individual entrepreneurs in order to succeed in an environment that is built to exclude them. This argument will be exemplified with two case studies: Jazz at Lincoln Center (J@LC), and The New York City Winter Jazz Fest (WJF).

Jazz at Lincoln Center (J@LC)

J@LC is well known in the eyes of the jazz community, both for their flagship home base in the center of Manhattan right next to Lincoln Center, as well as their high-end sponsorships and affiliations. Through the brand they have cultivated, J@LC's relationship with capitalism, corporate America, and even neoliberalism becomes immediately apparent. In *Freedom of Choice: Jazz, Neoliberalism and Lincoln Center*, Laver writes on how J@LC's brand identity attracts sponsors and generates profit. He explains how much American corporate and cultural interests have become intertwined: "freedom of consumer choice [is how] Americans have come to understand political freedom" (Laver 2014, p. 549). The idea of consumer choice is a key tenet of neoliberalism, giving the consumer "a powerful means of fashioning one's self in an era of heightened consumption" (Taylor 2016, p. 4). Defining "freedom" as consumer choice dilutes the meaning of democratic freedom. As a result, the consumer creates identity through the brands they associate themselves with in a process supported by a market-centered government.

Large arts institutions like J@LC benefit from sponsors whose brands represent high-class and luxury. Some of J@LC's most well-known corporate sponsors include Altria, Bank of America, Cadillac, Brooks Brothers, and of course, Coca Cola. J@LC's creative director, Wynton Marsalis, works hard building relationships with these sponsors and finding new funding opportunities for the organization. His role in building the successful brand of J@LC, and as a businessman, has been so successful that he has been recognized as a leader and invited to speak at the World Business Forum (Chinen 2006). On top of their wealth of corporate funding, J@LC receives millions of dollars in public funding from the New York City Mayor's Office, City Council, the National Endowment for the Arts (NEA), the New York State Council for the Arts (NYSCA), the City Department of Cultural Affairs, and more.[4] J@LC is one of the wealthiest jazz organizations in the world, with 2019 reports of $47 million in revenue, and $236 million in assets. In 2019 alone, they received over $25 million in grants and contributions, and Marsalis's salary caps off at over $1.7 million annually.[5]

J@LC has been publicly criticized for not including women in their jazz orchestra and in their general concert programming. In a 2000 interview, Marsalis spoke directly to the fact that the touring orchestra, one of the most prominent ensembles worldwide, included no women members (Pellegrinelli 2000). He claimed that while he is "trying to incorporate women" in J@LC and the J@LC orchestra, it is not his priority nor his primary responsibility. Pellegrinelli notes that J@LC accepts (at the time of the article) $18 million annually in public funding. Some of the public foundations and organizations that give funding to J@LC have specific guidelines for hiring employees which receive their funding. While the NEA, for example, writes in their guidelines that their grant recipients must support "access to the arts for all," NYSCA's grant contains more specific language:

> The contractor will not discriminate against any employee or applicant for employment because of race, creed, color, national origin, sex, age, disability, or marital status and will undertake or continue existing programs of affirmative action to ensure that minority group members and women are afforded equal employment opportunities without discrimination.[6]

Whether J@LC is actively ignoring these guidelines from the grants they receive, or whether they somehow think this does not apply to them is perplexing and baffling. But it is important to note that in public grants, grant recipients are typically required to abide by the policies of the benefactor organizations.

In the over 15 years since J@LC incorporated, they still have not hired a single woman for their full-time orchestra personnel. A very small percentage of annual J@LC concert programming includes women musicians, and while they have attempted to create some *Women in Jazz* oriented programming, it continues to fit into the model of treating women in jazz as the exception from the norm. For example, the educational wing of J@LC created a program called "Are You the Next Mary Lou Williams," a piano competition for girls under 15 years of age. Profiled in *Mary Lou Williams as Apology* (Teal 2019), Teal writes about how J@LC uses Mary Lou Williams as a "culture hero."

Viewing someone as a "culture hero" means that they become exceptionalized, or treated as an exception from the norm, because they are too paradoxical to be perceived as real; they stand outside of life because of the contradictions they embody (Teal 2019, pp. 2–3). When Mary Lou Williams is used in programming as "culture hero," she continues to embody the notion that women in jazz are anomalies, rather than common, or achievable phenomena. Her history reflects a woman who managed to succeed in jazz despite the discrimination and apprehension against her. Her talent and ability to overcome obstacles in order to succeed in the genre therefore becomes an exceptional model for women in jazz. In essence, not all women can do what Williams was able to do; one must have to be *exceptional* in order to achieve a level of success as a woman in jazz. As a result, Williams as a successful woman in jazz has become a role model for what women who strive to be jazz musicians must compare themselves to. This Mary Lou Williams "culture hero" model also diverts responsibility from the majority gender in this history, men in jazz. By placing the task on women to overcome obstacles of gender discrimination on their own, rather than tasking the jazz community at large with deconstructing these gender power dynamics, women continue to be isolated in their mission to try and break into the jazz scene. Teal summarizes this notion beautifully in referring to the Mary Lou Williams piano competition for girls at J@LC:

> When we suggest that girls follow Williams' lead, are we suggesting that jazz today has room for diverse voices? Or that women who put in extra effort of not only mastering their instruments but also mastering the skills necessary to thrive in a male-dominated culture should continue to be the handful of people who ease that culture's collective conscience by making jazz appear diverse?
>
> *(Teal 2019, p. 4)*

In addition, it's important to question why J@LC chooses to use a deceased Black woman to represent a majority of their *Women in Jazz* events, rather than employing more women musicians living and performing in New York City. Using a Black woman's image from a completely different historical context in the present brings up issues of tokenism.[7] Taking into account how J@LC manipulates the image and memory of Mary Lou Williams to mask a problem of gender diversity, we now can draw parallels to the previously discussed concepts of neoliberal feminism. Williams' legacy at J@LC is essentially "obscure(ing) the relative absence of women's voices rather than solve(ing) the problem" (Teal 2019, p. 3). In this sense, Williams is a model for the entrepreneurial woman in neoliberal feminism. Rather than attempting to change the conditions for all women in jazz, the entrepreneurial woman in jazz—she who may try to follow Williams's legacy, works to tackle obstacles on her own in isolation to succeed for herself. Her success is not defined by her gender identity, but rather despite it, and any other woman who wishes to achieve that same success must battle those same obstacles. Neoliberal feminism puts the responsibility of success on the individual, rather than on the collective.

Laver points to the same model of entrepreneurship in neoliberalism functioning in the context of achievement for Black Americans. He writes that J@LC is "a monument to what African Americans can ostensibly achieve through the neoliberal alignment of individual, government, and corporate interests and efforts" (Laver 2014, p. 552). As is the case in neoliberal states, groups defined by a particular identity, in this case, Black Americans are stuck attempting to progress and gain rights and equity as a community within a capitalist, entrepreneurial framework that favors the individual over the collective. Marsalis, the successful Black musician and business icon became an entrepreneurial figure, one others can look to in attempting to achieve their own individual success. Neoliberalism takes the idea of identity and capitalizes on it, creating individual models for each successful possibility marked by identity politics, but it does not produce an opportunity for collective progress. J@LC is steeped in this neoliberal rhetoric.

Taking into account what has been discussed thus far with regards to J@LC and neoliberal feminism, the following is an analysis of the J@LC *Diet Coke Women in Jazz Festival*. Looking at the lineup of this annual festival,[8] it becomes clear that only about half of the musicians playing at the festival are even women. Instead, they are mainly women-led bands, and/or tribute bands to a well-known woman in jazz of late. The music curated from the festival continues to represent the conservative model of jazz that J@LC promotes, one that fits specific musical guidelines for compositional period and improvisational style. Dale Chapman describes the musical style presented at J@LC as neoclassical jazz, which promotes "a music that emphasizes straight-ahead swing feel, adherence to conventional blues-based and popular song forms, the use of primarily acoustic instrumentation, and the privileging of a stylistic vocabulary that extends roughly from New Orleans polyphony through to 1960s postbop" (Chapman 2018, p. 6). Jerome Harris writes about the idea of the "canon" verses "process" approaches in jazz, and describes the canon approach as focusing on the continuity of jazz's past historical practice, and consequently, "its concern is with the preservation, proper interpretation, and accurate transmission of this practice. It also stresses the art form's rootedness in a specific social context" (Harris 2003, p. 118). J@LC therefore fits into the "canon" approach in jazz.

The festival itself is sponsored by Diet Coke at a venue whose primary jazz club space is sponsored by regular Coca Cola. "It is hard to think of a single other product that bears its marked, attenuated, 'feminized,' and shadow-self image more precisely than Diet Coke, particularly in its once-a-year presentation on a stage described as Coca-Cola" (McMullen 2008, p. 144). McMullen highlights the fact that the very branding choice of the festival by one of J@LC's primary sponsors, Coca Cola, capitalizes on gendered marketing, and uses their *lite* version of their product to cater to what they assume to be a more feminine audience. As McMullen states beautifully, "J@LC and its sponsors sell jazz as a sophisticated masculine accessory" (McMullen 2008, p. 142).

In each event at J@LC, whenever *Women in Jazz* is attached, so too are the sponsors associated with the J@LC brand, and the few women who are included in that space automatically come to be represented by that brand. Marsalis and J@LC as an organization have made few strides in adjusting their programming to include more women jazz instrumentalists into their regular concert calendar. For an example from their concert programming season, January 2019 at Dizzy's[9] included 22 bands in their main time slot, four of which were women-led by Queen Esther, Michela Marino Lerman, Tatiana Eva-Marie, and Sharon Clark. Of those four women-led bands, three of them were vocalists (meaning there was only one band in the entire month led by a non-vocalist woman and in this case was tap dancer Marino Lerman, not an instrumentalist). The majority of women performers on their stages are vocalists, which reinforces the image for the general public that the vast majority of women in jazz are singers.

In J@LC's other programming, the same can be said for representation of women instrumentalists. For example, for their Spring 2021 term of "Swing University," a series of virtual classes for jazz students and fans of all levels, only one class (out of ten classes offered) is taught by a woman, and it is their course on "The Life and Music of Ella Fitzgerald," with instructor Carmen Bradford. Their 2021 virtual fundraising gala was hosted by vocalist Dee Dee Bridgewater, with special guests Anna Deavere Smith (actress) and Veronica Swift (vocalist), besides all men instrumentalists on the lineup. Similarly, the 2020 virtual fundraising gala featured vocalists Cecile McLorin Salvant, Catherine Russell, and Dianne Reeves, with the exceptional inclusion of saxophonist Karolina Strassmeyer representing Germany as part of the gala's theme of worldwide jazz. Besides Strassmeyer, all instrumentalists in the almost two-hour long presentation of global jazz by J@LC included only male instrumentalists.

Again, the sparse programming that includes women often uses women vocalists rather than instrumentalists, pigeonholing women at J@LC into a particular role. Of course, this is not to say that there have not been concerts including women instrumentalists at all—the 2021 concert program included performances by the Helen Sung Quartet, as well as Lakecia Benjamin performing a tribute concert to the music of the Coltranes. But it is important to note the way in which J@LC chooses to present their brand to the public. Scrolling through the J@LC website, images of men jazz musicians fill the pages of each and every section of their programming media. One can easily find both images of deceased men jazz musicians and members of the J@LC orchestra, sprinkled here and there with promotional images of women jazz vocalists, many of whom shown in the image, again, are no longer living. The way in which J@LC presents their brand prioritizes the visual representation of men jazz musicians—it is rare to find a picture of a woman instrumentalist throughout their sprawling, intricately designed website.

In a time when most entertainment industries have responded to the *#MeToo* movement, addressing the pay gap for women in these industries, and eliminating male industry professionals who displayed discriminative or abusive behavior, J@LC as one of the world's leading jazz organizations is not participating in the conversation. Instead, they reinforce stereotypes of presenting women performers as vocalists and use branding to accentuate masculine perceptions of jazz. When they do include inclusive programming similar to the Mary Lou Williams piano competition, concepts of tokenism and competition are apparent. The few women who do find their way into J@LC programming are often used as tokens for all women in jazz, thus limiting the spaces available for women's entry into the patriarchal system, and therefore isolating women rather than providing spaces where women can be welcomed into jazz together.

Winter Jazzfest (WJF)

In contrast with J@LC, Winter Jazzfest (WJF) is an annual jazz festival with a focus on social justice in their marketing. WJF was founded as a side project to the annual gathering of the Performing Arts industry during the annual Association of Performing Arts Presenters (APAP) conference in New York City. Concert promoter Brice Rosenbloom saw an opportunity to present artists for industry professionals and further their career (Laban 2017). Rosenbloom initially presented the first WJF during the same week as APAP in order to facilitate attendance and career opportunities for jazz artists. Essentially, WJF was founded as a capitalist mechanism of convenience to provide financial opportunities to individual jazz musicians in New York City. Seventeen years later, WJF has transformed into an 11-day festival with events in Manhattan and Brooklyn at a range of venues and galleries, many of which do not usually present jazz. Hundreds of artists from all around the world are featured, from new artists to veteran performers.

In 2017, several new concepts were added to the WJF model: a festival theme, and *"Winter Jazzfest Talks."* The theme was social justice and was presented with panel discussions and multimedia lectures (West 2017). Since 2017, the social justice theme has remained a consistent addition to WJF with a special focus on current events. Topics in these talks have included conversations surrounding race and the civil rights movement, international borders and citizenship, health, and gender and jazz. The gender and jazz talks have become more frequent and prominent in the festivals since 2017 and have included panels with prominent artists who also perform throughout the festival.

As the *#MeToo* movement gained traction with extensive media coverage, particularly in the entertainment industry,[10] conversations surrounding gender discrimination in jazz extended to various online platforms and academia.[11] As a result, WJF included the narrative into concert programming and talks.[12] Since 2017, there have been annual talks specifically centered around gender and jazz co-sponsored by The New School and Berklee College's *Institute of Jazz and Gender Justice*.

In 2018 the WJF focus on the subject was featured in a TV segment on PBS News Hour called, "Female Jazz Musicians Raise their Voices Against Sexism."[13] The clip features Terri Lyne Carrington, Esperanza Spalding, and Sasha Berliner, three women jazz instrumentalists who had performed at that year's festival. Unlike in the festival programming, where the language used in programming titles and marketing for the festival focuses more on *gender* and jazz, this segment specifically refers to sexism against *women/females* in jazz. This shift in language from "gender and jazz" to "women/females in jazz" identifies a conceptual discrepancy between the two entities. While WJF chooses to maintain a gender-neutral language and therefore a less provocative stance on the topic, the TV segment attaches the feature to the larger issue of the #*MeToo* movement, and sexual harassment against women in the entertainment industry.

This TV segment focuses on the exceptional career of Carrington, a child prodigy who started performing professionally at 10 years of age. In the segment, Carrington mentioned not having many women peers, and being an "exception in the boys club." She is the first and only woman instrumentalist to win a Grammy for best jazz instrumental album. "Her win defied the traditional stereotype of women in jazz" (quoted from the segment). This TV Segment brands Carrington similarly to Mary Lou Williams as a "culture hero" (Teal 2019). While Mary Lou Williams is a historic icon, Carrington is a current artist with a prominent career. Her success despite her gender has made her a model for what successful women in jazz can achieve if they overcome the obstacles of gender discrimination. We need more current models like Carrington, but the question remains on how to brand these success stories without labeling them as exceptions, or "others."

As a result of her successful career, Carrington was able to found and lead the *Institute of Jazz and Gender Justice* at Berklee College of Music. This separate center in the school focuses on jazz curriculum in an "integrated and egalitarian setting."[14] In return, Berklee is able to capitalize on Carrington's reputation as the leader of this new institute. But a question that remains is how creating a separate institute, rather than integrating ideals of egalitarianism and gender equity in the entire college curriculum, can facilitate the needed changes. Usually, academic departments each focus on a specific topic of research or pedagogy. Since Berklee already has a jazz department, why is a second department for jazz study necessary that focuses on gender justice—shouldn't this be part of the vision of the main jazz department? I posit that Berklee should rethink their choice of creating a department distinct from the jazz department, rather than implementing the *Institute of Jazz and Gender Justice's* goals and pedagogical practices into the main jazz department.

The TV segment on WJF also mentions that more than a third of the acts at the 2018 WJF had women as bandleaders, and this ratio would continue to increase thanks to WJF signing onto the *Keychange Pledge*.[15] This pledge, now acknowledged by 45 international music festivals, aims to implement a 50/50 gender balance in lineup and conference panels by 2022. *Keychange* aims to change gender disparities in the music industry primarily by changing gender representation ratios at music events. While this may help create more of a physical presence of gender balance, a critique of this method would claim that this does not change the conditions of the patriarchal structure in which this industry continues to exist. Ahmed writes, "to be included can [thus] be a way of sustaining and reproducing a politics of exclusion." (Ahmed 2012, p. 163) When music festivals and organizations focus solely on the numbers of gender diversity, they are not changing the conditions of how the discriminated-against gender operates within the community. Festivals and organizations need to find additional ways to support more women in their careers so that more and more women will be qualified to perform and present their work.

One controversial article that criticized *Keychange's* goals as unrealistic wrote, "Only one in 20 jazz instrumentalists now being female, how do we get half the performers in festivals to be women virtually overnight without compromising standards?" (Shriver 2018). If the conditions of the jazz community do not change, how do we expect there to be a change in the number of women jazz instrumentalists at the same standard of performance as men? Perhaps these festivals and organizations can provide more educational opportunities, such as workshops, mentorships, and even scholarship opportunities for more rising women students of jazz to feel supported, which will in turn encourage more of these women to continue to enrich their musicianship and careers.

Additionally, this television segment mentions WJF signing on to another initiative, an open letter written by the *We Have Voice* collective, which provides a code of conduct for "promoting safe(r) spaces in the performing arts."[16] This code of conduct outlines many standard concepts from corporate human resources departments, which are often not formally addressed outside of these corporate environments, such as fostering a workplace environment, defining sexual harassment and consent, and tools for "fostering diversity." While this letter has now been signed by hundreds of individuals and arts organizations, and can also be found in multiple languages, it is tricky to pinpoint if and how this code of conduct is implemented, and whether there is any process or consequence for mandating or disciplining those who do not follow the code of conduct they have signed on to. Similar to human rights legislation for women that have come up in the past decades with the feminist movement,[17] without a solid plan of action for implementing it in institutionalized art spaces, it is nearly impossible to guarantee these feminist ideas are put into effect.

WJF has made the effort to include social justice as a visible topic in the marketing of their festival (on their website and in press and media coverage) with the addition of panels on gender and jazz, and by signing on to *Keychange* and the *We Have Voice* initiatives. But WJF is ultimately a for-profit festival that benefits individuals performing at the festival, and its corporate sponsors.[18] If individual women gain opportunities to perform at this festival, and it furthers their careers in the jazz scene by boosting recognition and adding to their resume, that is surely a benefit to each of those individual women. But, again, the fact that individual women will gain financial and professional success through this festival falls under the model of neoliberal feminism—promoting individual entrepreneurship rather than success of the collective and facilitating structural change. It would be optimistic and perhaps naïve to think that panels on gender and jazz will change the dynamics of gender and jazz, as the panel is a voluntary event that is most likely attended by a supportive audience. Consequently, the conversation stays isolated, similarly to Berklee's *Institute for Jazz and Gender Justice*.

Conclusion

The case studies in this chapter have outlined two different business models in the contemporary jazz industry and their branding of *Women in Jazz*. Jazz at Lincoln Center's programming implies that *Women in Jazz* is a very narrow category branded by corporate sponsors that stereotype the feminine (Diet Coke) and presents *Women in Jazz* as an exceptional phenomenon (Mary Lou Williams). Winter Jazzfest has taken great efforts towards including topics of "social justice" in their marketing and programming, and their sponsored Gender and Jazz Talks fit into this expansion. But these talks are confined to an already supportive audience and fail to initiate the needed change in the wider jazz community. Furthermore, as exemplified with the supergroup Artemis, the presentation of a few highly successful women reinforces concepts of tokenism.

WJF seems to have genuine intentions to change the conditions for gender dynamics and equity in jazz—they just haven't quite figured out how to implement the ideas they care about outside of a marketing context. The *We Have Voice* collective's letter for creating safer spaces in jazz provides guidelines for how to change the toxic masculine environments common within the jazz scene. Now, WJF needs to figure out a set of procedures to carry out *We Have Voice*'s suggestions. Jazz organizations and jazz educational institutions must take the guidelines of the *We Have Voice* collective, and the conversations taking place in these panels on gender and jazz, and implement them in their organizations, and they must enforce these workplace safety guidelines with consequences for those who do not comply. It may even be beneficial for jazz institutions and organizations to look at how other institutions in the entertainment industry have succeeded in creating more intersectionally equitable workplaces. From changing hiring practices, creating human resources procedures and educational tools for promoting secure and supportive workspace practices, and maintaining open dialogue between musicians, music organizations and venues, the jazz scene can use the same models for equitable change that already have been in practice in other industries.

In a similar vein to WJF, Berklee's *Institute for Jazz and Gender Justice* is in a separate wing from the rest of the school. How will this institute create change for jazz and gender justice if the only people involved are those voluntarily applying for the programs? Educational institutions, such as Berklee College must integrate their curriculum and programming from the *Jazz and Gender Institute* throughout the entire school's programs, rather than keeping the institute a separate wing in the school—keeping it separate will once again not create change in the jazz community at large.

Women in Jazz bands, such as Artemis, have the opportunity to provide a supportive collective space for musical creation among women in jazz, without marking the space simply by gender. Women should be welcome to perform and work together without feeling that there is not enough space for everyone, that they are competing for the slim opportunities in the exceptional model of successful women in jazz that exists in spaces such as J@LC. Feminist scholar and activist bell hooks wrote, "abandoning the idea of Sisterhood as an expression of political solidarity weakens and diminishes feminist movement" (hooks 1984, p. 44). Intersectional[19] solidarity among women is vital for creating more supportive spaces and opportunities for women to participate and be included in jazz. This means providing collaborative spaces for women, such as mentorship programs and educational programming, rather than competitions that pit women against each other. Another idea is to create spaces for open dialogue in jazz venues and organizations that ask women what they need in order to feel more welcome in the community.

Those in leadership positions at institutions such as J@LC that receive funding, especially from public organizations such as NYSCA, should not only realize that their funding comes with a responsibility to support diversity in their programming and hiring methods, but that they need to follow the guidelines of diversity, equity, and inclusion written into the funding requirements. Direct communication between women in the jazz community, funding sources, and jazz organizations can streamline efforts in what needs to be changed in hiring practices and workplace models. Opportunities for women in jazz shouldn't exist in a vacuum. Opportunities should be integrated into regular seasonal programming to show young women students of jazz that they are not simply the exception, but a part of the norm in jazz performance and education. A new egalitarian culture of jazz must be adopted and enforced in all jazz spaces, so that women can participate openly in jazz, rather than just as a part of the *Women in Jazz* brand.

Notes

1 This information is taken from the Blue Note website's artist page on "Out of the Blue." www.bluenote.com/artist/out-of-the-blue/.

2 The following are some examples of the way different media articles have represented Artemis in their writing:

> "It cuts across all generational, cultural, international, and ethnic planes." (Jurkovic 2020).
> "Multigenerational, multicultural, all-female" (Hynes 2020).
> "The lineup spans generations, backgrounds and styles" (Layman 2020).
> "They all just happen to be women … of all ages and from around the world" (Bentley 2020).

3 The *#MeToo* movement has infiltrated Hollywood, the popular music industry, and even politics in the United States. For a cross-section timeline of the rise of the *#MeToo* movement since its inception, please refer to Nicolaou and Smith 2019.

4 This is a considerable amount of the public arts funding available in New York and federally, and most public arts funding are going to arts NGOs fitting the size and scope of places like J@LC.

5 Public funding amounts are publicly available information, and are available on multiple websites, including these:

> https://nonprofitlight.com/ny/new-york/jazz-at-lincoln-center-inc.
> www.causeiq.com/organizations/jazz-at-lincoln-center,133888641/#:~:text=Jazz%20at%20Lincoln%20Center%20is,and%20%24236%20million%20in%20assets.

6　These examples are taken from research in Pellegrinelli (2000). She has since continued to expand her research on representation of women in jazz and policies that either support or prevent gender equity in her article for NPR (Pellegrinelli 2021).

7　Tokenism is a theory originally coined by Rosabeth Moss Kanter which describes recruiting a small percentage of people from an underrepresented group (i.e., gender or racial group) in order to give an appearance of equality or diversity in that space. To read on Kanter's original theory: Kanter (1977).

8　While not all of the annual lineups have been archived in an accessible location, the 2009 festival lineup can be viewed at the following link: www.jazzcorner.com/news/display.php?news=757.

　　In this festival, I noted 16 women musicians, 13 men musicians, and something around 18 musicians whose gender is not discernible from the lineup description.

9　www.jazz.org/dizzys/events/calendar/january-2019/

10　Here are some of the instigating events that snowballed the *#MeToo* movement:

January 21, 2017, the first day of Donald Trump's presidency, millions of people march in the Women's March in Washington DC and other cities around the world.
October 2017, multiple women make public claims of sexual harassment against Harvey Weinstein.
October 16, 2017, the *#MeToo* hashtag gains traction on twitter, and becomes an international phenomenon.
For a comprehensive timeline of more events in the *#MeToo* movement, Nicolaou and Smith (2019).

11　Here are a few of the popular articles written either by or about women in jazz, especially about their experiences with gender discrimination in jazz: Vandever (2018); Berliner (2017); Sevian (2017).

12　Specific "Winter Jazzfest Talks" that have focused on gender and jazz include "Jazz and Gender: Challenging Inequality and Forging a New Legacy" (2018) with Angela Davis, Lara Pellegrinelli, Arnetta Johnson, and Vijay Iyer, moderated by Terri Lyne Carrington; "Jazz and Gender: Finding Solidarity" (2019) with Toshi Reagon, Roxy Coss, Vanessa Reed, Maria Grand, Fay Victor, John Murph and co-moderated by Sarah Elizabeth Charles and Nate Chinen; "Jazz and Gender: A Discussion of Community, Culture and Participatory Allies" (2020) with Aja Burrell Wood, Chloe Rowlands, Naomi Extra, Jerome Jennings, Ben Williams and co-moderated by Sarah Elizabeth Charles and Nate Chinen; "An End to Norms: WJF Jazz and Gender Talk Series, In partnership with The New School and The Berklee Institute of Jazz and Gender Justice" (2021) with Terri Lynne Carrington, Maureen Mahon, Samora Pinderhughes, Fay Victor and hosted by Sarah Elizabeth Charles; "Jazz, Gender and Black Feminism: What We Can Learn" (2021) with Toshi Reagon, Aja Burrell Wood, Darius Jones, hosted by Sarah Elizabeth Charles.

13　www.youtube.com/watch?v=4Xo8BYRXOOA&feature=emb_logo.

14　Quoted from jazz and gender institute website: https://college.berklee.edu/jazz-gender-justice.

15　Quoted from *Keychange*'s website: www.keychange.eu/what-can-i-do.

16　Quoted from *We Have Voice*'s website: http://wehavevoice.org/.

17　One such article that talks about new human rights legislation for women, and the challenges facing the attempt to create more women's rights legislation is in the writing of Bunch (1990).

18　Some of WJF's corporate sponsors and partners include: Steinway & Sons, Bowers & Wilkins, Dayglo Ventures, and East Village Moxy. A list can be found at the bottom of the website: www.winterjazzfest.com/.

19　When I use the term "intersectional" here, I intend to reference intersectionality in the context of Kimberle Crenshaw's writings on intersectional feminism. I do not mean to be reductive of Crenshaw's work on this topic, and therefore suggest further reading from Crenshaw (1989).

References

Ahmed, Sara. (2012) *On Being Included: Racism and Diversity in Institutional Life*, Duke University Press.

Berliner, Sasha. (2017) "An Open Letter to Ethan Iverson (And the Rest of Jazz Patriarchy)," sashaberlinermusic.com www.sashaberlinermusic.com/sociopoliticalcommentary-1/2017/9/21/an-open-letter-to-ethan-iverson-and-the-rest-of-jazz-patriarchy.

Bentley, Alison. (2020) "Artemis," *London Jazz News* https://londonjazznews.com/2020/09/28/artemis-artemis/.

Brubaker, Rogers; Cooper, Frederick. (2000) "Beyond 'Identity,'" *Theory and Society*, Vol. 29, No. 1, pp. 1–47, Springer.

Bunch, Charlotte. (1990) "Women's Rights as Human Rights: Toward a Re-Vision of Human Rights," *Human Rights Quarterly*, Vol. 12, pp. 486–498.

Brewer, Carolyn Glenn. (2017) *Changing the Tune: The Kansas City Women's Jazz Festival, 1978–1985*, University of North Texas Press.

Chapman, Dale. (2018) *The Jazz Bubble: Neoclassical Jazz in Neoliberal Culture*, University of California Press.

Chinen, Nate. (2006) "Wynton Marsalis: The Once and Future King of Jazz at Lincoln Center," New York Times. www.nytimes.com/2006/08/27/arts/music/27chin.html.

Crenshaw Kimberle. (1989) "Demarginalizing the Intersection of Race and Sex: A Black Feminist Critique of Antidiscrimination Doctrine," *Feminist Theory and Antiracist Politics*, The University of Chicago Legal Forum, Vol. 1989, No. 1, p. 139.

Harris, Jerome. (2003) "Jazz on the Global Stage" in Monson, Ingrid, ed., *The African Diaspora: A Musical Perspective*, Routledge.

hooks, bell. (1984) *Feminist Theory: From Margin to Center*, South End Press.

Hynes, Jim. (2020) "All-Female Jazz Supergroup Artemis Makes Its Blue Note Debut with Tenacious Self-Titled LP" (Album Review), *Glide Magazine* https://glidemagazine.com/248013/all-female-jazz-supergroup-artemis-makes-its-blue-note-debut-with-tenacious-self-titled-lp-album-review/.

Jurkovic, Mike. (2020) "Artemis: Artemis," All About Jazz www.allaboutjazz.com/artemis-artemis-blue-note.

Kanter, Rosabeth Moss. (1977) "Some Effects of Proportions on Group Life: Skewed Sex Ratios and Responses to Token Women." *American Journal of Sociology* Vol. 82, No. 5, pp. 965–990.

Laban, Linda. (2017) "Jazz Legends Explore their Social Justice Legacy," The Observer https://observer.com/2017/01/social-justice-winter-jazzfest-2017/.

Laver, Mark. (2014) "Freedom of Choice: Jazz Neoliberalism and Lincoln Center," *Popular Music and Society*, Vol. 7, No. 5, pp. 538–566, Taylor & Francis.

Layman, Will. (2020) "Artemis is the Latest Jazz Supergroup," Pop Matters www.popmatters.com/artemis-jazz-review-2648532914.html.

McMullen, Tracy. "Identity for Sale: Glenn Miller, Wynton Marsalis, and Cultural Replay in Music" from Eds. Rustin, Nichole T.; Tucker, Sherrie. (2008) *Big Ears: Listening for Gender in Jazz Studies*, Duke University Press.

Nicolaou, Elena and Smith, Courtney E. (2019) "A #MeToo Timeline to Show How Far We've Come—and How Far We Need to Go," Refinery 29 www.refinery29.com/en-us/2018/10/212801/me-too-movement-history-timeline-year-weinstein.

Pellegrinelli, Lara. (2000) "Dig Boy Dig," The Village Voice www.villagevoice.com/2000/11/07/dig-boy-dig/.

Pellegrinelli, Lara. (2021) "Equal at Last? Women in Jazz, By the Numbers," NPR www.npr.org/2021/01/12/953964352/equal-at-last-women-in-jazz-by-the-numbers.

Sevian, Lauren. (2017) "Sexism in Jazz from the Conservatory to the Club: One Saxophonist Shares her Story," WBGO.org www.wbgo.org/music/2017-10-20/sexism-in-jazz-from-the-conservatory-to-the-club-one-saxophonist-shares-her-story.

Shriver, Lionel. (2018) "Jazz is Dominated by Men. So What?," The Spectator www.spectator.co.uk/article/jazz-is-dominated-by-men-so-what-.

Steger, Manfred B.; Roy, Ravi K. (2010) *Neoliberalism: A Very Short Introduction*, Oxford University Press.

Stiglitz, Joseph E. (2008) "The End of Neoliberalism?," Project Syndicate www.project-syndicate.org/commentary/the-end-of-neo-liberalism?barrier=accesspaylog.

Taylor, Timothy D. (2016) *Music and Capitalism: A History of the Present*, University of Chicago Press.

Teal, Kimberly Hannon. (2019) "Mary Lou Williams as Apology: Jazz, History, and Institutional Sexism in the Twenty-First Century," *Jazz and Culture*, Vol 2. Pp. 1–26, University of Illinois Press.

Vandever, Kalia. (2018) "Token Girl," medium https://medium.com/@kaliamariev/token-girl-564457c86f13.

West, Michael J. (2017) "WJF Artists Address Social Justice," DownBeat https://downbeat.com/news/detail/wjf-artists-address-social-justice.

34

ACCESSING JAZZ'S GENDERED PLACES AND SPACES

Sarah Caissie Provost

Note on terminology: In this chapter, I (a straight cisgender woman) speak about queer, trans- and cisgender women and queer cis- and transgender men as a group or multiple groups, but always set apart specifically from straight cisgender men. A straight cisgender man is one who was assigned male at birth, continued to identify as male throughout his life, and sought opposite sex relationships. In this chapter, I uncover the reasons why all people who do not fit into this straight cisgender group of men experienced exclusion from jazz. I use "queer" or "LGBTQ" as shorthand to describe the group of people distinct from straight cisgender women (though, as I discuss, it is difficult to recover the experiences of LGBTQ musicians, and there is considerable overlap between all of these groups that remains hidden).

Billy Tipton's life has become the prime example of the lengths to which women will go in order to be accepted by the jazz world. Assigned female at birth in 1914, Tipton became a jazz musician and, according to a biographer (Middlebrook, 1998), he began dressing and acting as a man to facilitate this career. He had several common-law wives and was father to three adopted sons, all of whom insisted that until after his 1989 death, they did not know he was born and lived his early life as female. "Billy" began as the stage name of "Dorothy" but eventually became his full-time identity, purportedly because the jazz world was so difficult to enter as a woman (Middlebrook, 1998, p. 55).

Tipton's gender identity was surely more complicated than the story of his entry into jazz can reveal.[1] For example, Halberstam (1998, p. 150) notes that the popular reading of Tipton's transition is another example of the common erasure of transgender stories. Tipton's "reveal" set off a "transphobic media circus," and the narratives that ensued, including the Middlebrook work cited above, have only recently begun to be corrected (Gardner, 2020). While transmasculine erasure is the main force in Tipton's posthumous story, the easy acceptance of his origin story by the cisgender world—*of course* he would masquerade as a man to play jazz; a woman jazz musician would never have been successful, regardless of her musical ability—also tells us that access into jazz's spaces has long been problematic. As more stories from jazz's early days have surfaced, we have also begun to understand the ways that queer, trans- and cisgender women and queer cis- and transgender men navigated the primarily cisgender male jazz world.

How did these musicians access spaces that were closed to them, through social barriers or musical ones? I consider "access" to refer to several concepts. Firstly, it refers to the physical places of jazz, which were often hostile or perceived as unsavory to women and non-cisgender

DOI: 10.4324/9781003081876-38

or non-heterosexual musicians. These places may have barred these musicians outright, or, more often, they may have simply discouraged them from entrance through social pressures. Secondly, access requires musical acceptance; this type of access is achieved through playing the right instrument or in the right musical style for entry into jazz's musical spaces. Finally, access refers to social opportunities; even if one plays a jazz instrument and can enter the venue, the musician must still be given musical space in which to perform. By identifying and detailing the historical construction of jazz's barriers to access, we begin to delineate a future jazz world built on equity and diversity of perspective.

I acknowledge and build upon the legacy of the word "access" within disability studies, as well as the similar issue of access that has recently been realized in the form of transgender "bathroom bills" of the mid-2010s. Bathroom access for transgender people brings up issues of belonging and safety that are similar to the problems that women and non-hetero- and cis- men have experienced in jazz. The framework of these jazz obstacles as "access" allows us to view queer, trans- and cisgender women and queer cis- and transgender men as possessing the skills and constitution necessary for jazz performance, instead of emphasizing their differences from the dominant musicians. Delineating access reveals the ways in which the jazz world can undergo the institutional and cultural changes necessary for non-cis-hetero male musicians to contribute fully. These concepts are similar to the "social mode" of disability, which deemphasizes the body itself, turning instead to the barriers and solutions of the environment (Williamson, 2015). Just as accessibility in planning and design benefits more than the disabled, increasing access to jazz's spaces and places will lead to a more robust and vibrant jazz community. Increasing access to jazz spaces is not solely about rectifying long-standing injustices; it also has the potential of expanding jazz language, creativity, and audience.

Difficulties abound in tracing historical barriers to access in jazz. Rarely were these musicians barred outright from the places of jazz making; instead, they were simply not chosen to play, an act which is rarely documented. As saxophonist Jane Ira Bloom says, "It's the phone calls that you don't get. … It's the sin of omission, and that's what's so deadly about it." (Enstice and Stockhouse, 2004, p. 9) And even when these musicians were admitted to jazz's places and spaces, their contributions to the field largely go unrecognized, as they suffer further omissions from the texts and recorded histories of jazz. There also exists a tradition of silence surrounding the intimidation methods utilized for maintaining jazz's barriers to access. Therefore, we must recognize that the instances of exclusion, harassment, and violence documented were likely a tiny proportion of the true number of such occurrences.

If jazz's accessibility for women is difficult to trace, accessibility for LGBT musicians is even more complex and fraught. Gay or queer men were able to pass as straight to access jazz performance spaces, though most lesbian, queer, and bisexual women were still excluded from these same spaces along with straight women. Additionally, as Tucker notes, explorations of queer involvement carry the danger of outing or mis-identifying queer musicians (Tucker, 2008, p. 4). If the aforementioned Billy Tipton was indeed a transgender man, historians have outed him harmfully by revealing the biological features which he clearly wished to hide—and further compounded the damage by insisting upon a narrative that hinged upon women's career options. Queer musicians are doubly hidden; first, by a jazz community that has historically wished to prevent their participation, and secondly, by a historical community that rightly chooses not to out them.

I identify several different aspects of gendered jazz spaces, detailing examples of musicians who adapted to access these spaces: (1) Women and queer musicians were dissuaded from participation by the overtly cisgender and heteronormative masculinity of jazz's performing spaces. In jazz's early days, these spaces included brothels, bars, and the street; in later days, the concept of jazz as an individualized art form set artistic barriers for women, whose creative prowess was questioned. These homosocial spaces were maintained by harassment and violence toward nonconforming bodies, experiences that came to be ritualized. (2) Gendered musical instrument specialization—influenced by the association of brass and percussion instruments with parades and the streets—meant that women, at the onset of their musical training, were dissuaded from participation in jazz. Jazz communities often dismissed the possibility of women's performance on the simple basis of what instrument they played. Feminized roles such as pianist and vocalist provided acceptable entrance points for women into jazz spaces, yet these roles were denigrated or their impact reduced. (3) Jazz's musical practices often disadvantaged the non-cisgender male and non-heterosexual; cutting contests, for example, required both physical access (to the nightclub stage) as well as musical assertiveness that women were not socialized to perform. Women-only jazz spaces existed, but these spaces were considered inferior by both women and men. Later, some women and queer musicians found places in avant-garde jazz communities, which were perceived by both men and women as open musically and socially (and for some, coded specifically feminine in practice, if not physicality). Others found continued barriers to accessing these same spaces.

The Spaces of Jazz Masculinity

Jazz's masculinity was not born with jazz, but rather developed. Women were vital in the propagation of early jazz and related styles such as the blues. For example, New Orleans-based jazz of the early twentieth century included many women, though these women were restricted to certain spaces in which their presence was acceptable. Histories of jazz often begin in Storyville, the famed red-light district centered around Basin Street in New Orleans and the only one of its kind in the United States. Jazz did not actually begin in Storyville, but the popularity of the area ensured that many people who would not otherwise come into contact with this burgeoning musical style did in fact hear its practitioners.

Lara Pellegrinelli (2008) argues that women singers were prevalent in the spaces of early jazz, notably the brothels and dance halls of Storyville and the traveling theater circuits. However, historiographers focused on instrumental jazz, and the history of jazz became inextricably bound to the history of recorded jazz, contributing doubly to the erasure of these foundational jazz singers. Pellegrinelli cites the careers of several women, including singer and cornetist Miss Antonia Gonzales, singer Ann Cook, and singer and pianist Mamie Desdoumes. Since these women were also sex workers, whites as well as middle-class Blacks viewed jazz as a sexually corrupting force, led by women. She writes, "Eliminating women from the discourse gives exclusive control over the music and sexuality to men, enabling them to contain the singing body" (p. 43). Notably, most of these women were transcribed into history by mentions from famous jazz men; for example, Jelly Roll Morton describes "chippies in their little-girl dresses … standing in the crib doors singing the blues" (Ramsey and Smith, 1939, p. 35). Thus, it was the jazz men who took the women's music and achieved musical sophistication by removing the music from its association with sex work—and, as Pelligrinelli notes, by changing the music's association from the voice, and by extension the female body, to instruments and "potential legitimization in the white world" (2008, p. 34). These forces of respectability politics moved the site of creative power from the Black female body to the White male. Storyville was closed in 1917, and many of its buildings demolished by the 1930s, but it was not the only place that jazz proliferated. Sherrie Tucker notes that the existence of jazz performances as dances sponsored by "Catholic churches, social clubs, lawn parties, fish fries, and other settings" complicates the idea that jazz was "born in brothels" (Tucker, 2008, p. 5).

Even when separated from its associations with Storyville, jazz retained its seedy reputation, mainly through jazz musicians' drug use from the 1930s to the 1960s. The drug most associated with jazz in the 1930s was cannabis, evidenced by the many songs about "vipers" (including "If You're a Viper," "A Viper's Moan," "Song of the Vipers," and "The Viper's Drag," among others). Several of jazz's most famous performers were arrested for possession, including Louis Armstrong and Gene Krupa. By the late 1940s and into the 1960s, jazz's disrepute was enabled through many musicians' use of heroin, a drug that Ben Sidran calls a "shortcut to the presence of a masculine 'front'" (Sidran, 1981, p. 120). This "front" was created in part by the effect the drug had on the voice, causing a "drag" and contributing to the increasingly common persona of the jazz musician as a passive man.

The jazzman himself was presumed to be Black—despite the legion of white appropriators. According to this presumption, the Black jazzman stereotypically had a "natural" penchant for performing an improvised style, particularly one that prioritized the Black sounds of the blues. White men, while lacking the connection with the natural form of jazz, were assumed to be competent and could study and learn the style. Women of both races were assumed to lack both natural creative prowess as well as the ability to learn, and therefore it was perceived that women needed extraordinary abilities and circumstances to even be considered part of the jazz world. As a result, many women encouraged comparisons with men, which indicated cachet in jazz's hierarchy (Suzuki, 2014). This hierarchy prevents women (both Black and White) from success in jazz; they are threatening forces that disrupt the "symbolic and concrete proof of African American manhood" (Porter, 2002, p. 28) that jazz provided. Suzuki also notes the financial incentives of jazz participation in the 1940s ceased to exist after the 1960s, giving Black women more reason not to spend the considerable financial resources necessary to purchase instruments and training, particularly considering the move of jazz studies into the expensive field of higher education (Suzuki, 2014, p. 222).

Jazz's relationship with the recording industry contributed to the erasure of women from jazz history. For many, the history of jazz is synonymous with the history of recorded jazz despite that recorded jazz, particularly prior to long-playing records, poorly represents the practices of jazz. Preventing women from recording jazz has had the effect of preventing their entrance into the narratives of jazz history. The first women to record jazz were initially white singers (beginning with Marion Harris in 1916), then Black singers (with blues musicians, including Mamie Smith). The stylistic overlap between jazz and blues results in a confusing list of which Black musician made the "first" record, with both W. C. Handy (1914) and King Oliver's Creole Jazz Band (1923) variously cited.[2] Women jazz instrumentalists were particularly slow to be recorded, with Lil Hardin (Armstrong) performing on sessions in 1925, but trumpeter Dolly Jones being called the first to record on jazz trumpet in the startlingly late year 1938. The large gap between 1916– 1938 spanning the earliest days of recorded jazz women reflects the dearth of these musicians, particularly instrumentalists, from the history of audio recordings. Many women, including those cited by Pellegrinelli (2008) were never offered recording sessions. Even in the 1940s, few of the many "all girl" bands recorded, contributing to the erasure of these women from jazz history (Tucker, 2000).

One potential avenue to inclusion was to perform in a masculine manner, even if one could not present physically as male. The most successful of jazzwomen were almost always described as having masculine playing styles (Provost, 2017). Mary Lou Williams "played like a man" (Rustin, 2005), Lil Hardin Armstrong played "hard" like Jelly Roll Morton (Taylor, 2008), and trumpeter Valaida Snow was often compared (by herself as well as others) to Louis Armstrong (Miller, 2007). Clora Bryant, bebop-era trumpeter, notes that at first, she was told she played "like a woman," but as she became more accepted, "played like a man" (Schudel, 2019). Bryant indicates that she did not consciously decide to play in a masculine manner, but her description shows the way that male musicians and critics rationalized her presence among them eventually allowing access because of her masculine style, even if that masculinity existed solely in the minds of the men hearing her.

The very notion of a feminine musical style in which Bryant could perform is itself fraught. Marcia Citron (1993), in her study of classical music's women and femininity, details the inherent problems with developing a consciously feminine musical style. Women have little female culture to draw from, and are thus left with only two choices, as enumerated by Virginia Woolf: to protest her gendered self by calling herself "only a woman," or to reject her femaleness by asserting herself to be "as good as a man" (p. 68). Citron analyzes the latter:

Only by marking herself as different from what patriarchy considered inferior or by being perceived that way could she hope to gain acceptance. Symbolically this might resemble an inverted Oedipal killing: woman gilling the female culture she came from.

(p. 77)

Thus, women jazz musicians separate themselves from any notion of femininity by performing hardness, assertiveness, or notable markers of a famous man's style. Queer musicians, too, were often typecast as being "soft"; Jelly Roll Morton himself describes developing a hard style to distinguish himself from other male pianists, who were assumed to be queer (Taylor, 2008, p. 50), which Lil Hardin then borrowed in turn to sound masculine.

While some women consciously utilized masculine playing styles in order to access musical spaces and subvert the notion that women lack creative prowess, Nichole Rustin-Paschal (2017) argues that, like Halberstam's female masculinity, jazzmasculinity (as coined by Rustin-Paschal) is a quality that women as well as men can cultivate. In her work on Charles Mingus, she details the jazzmasculinity of Mingus as well as several women, including Hazel Scott and Billie Holiday. Scott in particular utilized similar notions of Black masculine anger (notably, while maintaining a feminine, sexualized appearance onstage). For Rustin-Paschal, jazzmasculinity often resulted in (or was a result of) political and racial involvement.

Jazz Relationships and Gender-based Violence

A primary deterrent to women and queer participation in jazz has been the violence enacted upon them by jazz men. Scholars have largely neglected to historicize the role of violence in the careers and lives of jazzwomen, despite examples of women who experienced physical, sexual, and musical violence as major forces in their jazz careers. By collecting and analyzing these stories, we can reveal the ways that such violence props up the gendered power structures of jazz performance, the role of hegemonic masculinity in jazz culture, and the ways that jazzwomen have accepted, utilized, or endured violence in order to access jazz spaces.

For both men and women, the violence enacted upon the musicians in jazz culture is sometimes presented as crucial to the development of a jazz artist. Consider the 2014 film *Whiplash*, a story about a young man subjected to an abusive jazz instructor named Terence Fletcher. Fletcher rationalizes his violence by citing the history of jazz and the necessity of violence to developing jazz performers by recounting an (apocryphal) story of Jo Jones "nearly decapitat[ing]" Charlie Parker with a cymbal, which he cites as the most formative moment of the young Parker's career. The aim of violence, Fletcher argues, is greatness: "I was there to push people beyond what's expected of them. I believe that is an absolute necessity. Otherwise we're depriving the world of the next Louis Armstrong, the next Charlie Parker" (Chazelle, 2014). Fletcher makes apparent that violence is a price—one cannot perform at the highest level without paying this price. With a similarity to hazing rituals, enduring violence is a way of proving that one is dedicated to jazz. Anecdotes abound of men attacking other men in jazz groups, with Charles Mingus's fights with Jimmy Knepper, Juan Tizol, and others serving as the most famous. Yet violence is far more often the price that women, not men, pay to be afforded access to jazz performance. *Whiplash* avoids this issue by featuring a single woman performer, who is dismissed after playing just three notes ("You're in the first chair. Let's see if it's just because you're cute … yep, that's why"). Including women in the story or, alternately, making the protagonist Black, would alter the story from one focused specifically on jazz and violence to one complicated with gender- and race-based violence.

Since gender-based violence abounds, it can be difficult to tease out the strands that are unique to jazz. Several of jazz's early women have detailed the effects of violence on their careers. The idea of violence as a price that a performer pays in exchange for an exceptional jazz career is made clearest by bebop singer Sarah Vaughan. In 1977, an interviewer asked Vaughan about her experiences performing with Billy Eckstine's big band. After calling Eckstine her "father," Vaughan chose to recount her time with Eckstine's big band thusly:

> But all the fellows really looked after me—they would beat me if I didn't listen to them! One time, I was late going to Indianapolis, where the band was playing a dance; I was having so much fun in Chicago, I decided to stay: "I'll see you guys later." When I got there, the dance was just over; I walked in and said: "Hi, guys. Sorry I'm late." So they all formed a circle round me, and beat me to death! After getting hit on the arm by fifteen guys, when I left there both my arms were down by my sides—I couldn't move. And I was never late anymore. Yes, I could do no wrong in that band—if I did, I would do it no more. I was very fortunate, compared with other girls I've seen in orchestras.
>
> *(Tomkins, 1977)*

Similarly, Mary Lou Williams reports that musicians and managers would routinely beat women for "not doing it right," and in her case, they would also withhold food from her. About both examples, Williams expresses gratitude, saying, "it was good for me" (Dahl, 1999, p. 47). These anecdotes show the way that violence was expected and casual; like for the protagonist of *Whiplash*, learning to endure violence was part of learning to be a jazz musician. Vaughan and Williams also show the fraught relationship between violence and jazz women; both described feeling grateful for the experience of violence, describing it as formative forces in their careers. Vaughan's word choice, "fortunate," is also ominous. Does it indicate that other women were not "cared for" enough by their band members to be hit, or that these women suffered more terrible violence? Vaughan didn't elaborate. Thus, violence in jazz could be considered gatekeeping by men dissuading women from entering jazz to maintain the homosocial space or alternately, hazing. A woman could access jazz space if she proves her worth through endurance of violence, not entirely through the meritocracy.

Even if not directly condoned, as with Vaughan and Williams, the women of early jazz tended to minimize the effects of violence or omit it entirely. This is most common with sexual violence, the instances of which must be exponentially more common than are their mentions. Occasionally, a woman speaks somewhat frankly about her experiences. Singer Anita O'Day, for example, detailed being raped by actor John Boles, but joked about it. She called it "gentle," wondering "whether it had been his way of thanking me" for helping him get to a performance on time. She does qualify that she would have preferred flowers, candy, or cognac, particularly considering the rape resulted in her fifteenth pregnancy, which was ectopic and caused severe pain as it ruptured her fallopian tube (O'Day and Eells, 1981, p. 174).

O'Day's willingness to talk in detail about her experiences is unusual. Other women minimize sexual violence as being part of the life of a woman, particularly one touring with groups of men. Mary Lou Williams, for example, reported a sexual assault, her second within two days, while traveling on a train, but does so in such vague terms that one might miss it (Dahl, 1999, p. 76). Trombonist Melba Liston too spoke about the violence she experienced traveling with groups comprised entirely of men, including, "rapes and everything." The interviewer calls her experiences "hard dues" (O'Connell, M. H., and Tucker, S., 2014, p. 142). Liston then speaks vaguely about abortion: "I'd just go to the doctor and tell him, and that was that" (O'Connell, M. H. and Tucker, S., 2014, p. 143). O'Connell and Tucker analyze Liston's balance between openness and reluctance in detailing such traumatic events as survival skills particular to Black women; dissemblance that allowed Black women to hide their inner selves from those who dominate them (2014, p. 144). Similarly, other women created alternate explanations for the violence they suffered. Mary Lou Williams entered the hospital ostensibly for a "nose job," but biographer Linda Dahl reports, not that dissatisfaction with her original appearance was the reason for the operation, but instead that bassist Al Lucas broke her nose (1999, p. 156). Dahl calls Lucas "a brawler," but also notes of Williams that a relative was "surprised that somebody hadn't killed her" because of the frank feedback she gave to her male colleagues (1999, p. 156).

These gatekeeping and hazing activities might be considered the price that women paid in order to access jazz spaces, like Liston's "hard dues." One of the ways women tried to avoid paying this price yet maintain access to jazz performance spaces was to engage a male supporter namely, but not always, a husband. While they met performing, Mary Lou Williams's marriage to guitarist John Williams and Lil Hardin's marriage to Louis Armstrong allowed them entrance to higher-level jazz performing groups than they might have had access to otherwise, particularly during their early careers. In later years, Alice Coltrane's entrance into her husband John's group launched a career that persisted past his death. Williams, too, sustained a fruitful career after her initial marriage ended. Yet a jazz marriage was not as protective as it might seem. Mary Lou Williams frequently appeared with scars from her second husband, Harold Baker (Kernodle, 2004, p. 90), and Sarah Vaughan reported domestic violence by her manager-husbands as well (Hayes, 2018). Several of jazz's legendary men were also notoriously violent toward their non-jazz wives; Miles Davis's wife Frances describes life-threatening abuse, while Stan Getz's wife reports that he attempted to throw her out of a sixth-floor window. In the most egregious example, pianist Al Haig was accused of strangling to death his third wife, Bonnie. His second wife, Grange Rutan, recounts the domestic abuse she suffered from Haig, connecting it specifically with the bebop scene, in her book *Death of a Bebop Wife* (Rutan, 2007).

Marriages were not the only way women accessed the homosocial spaces of jazz. The few women that were able to enter jazz performance spaces were often nurtured by more famous men; for example, pianist JoAnne Brackeen noted that Art Blakey considered her "his adopted daughter" (Enstice and Stockhouse, 2004, p. 25), and Sarah Vaughan also refers to Billy Eckstine as a father figure. Trumpeter, singer, and dancer Valaida Snow marketed herself as "Little Louis" following an encounter with Louis Armstrong, allowing her to capitalize off of Armstrong's career. Snow's actual interaction with Armstrong was brief and apocryphal, but simply invoking Armstrong's supposed approval was enough for her to create a full marketing strategy for her musical career. Similar to the woman who "played like a man," these women utilized their relationships with famous men or created relationships where little existed in order to gain access to these masculine spaces.

More recently, the price of admission to jazz spaces has changed from enduring violence to enduring sexual harassment, resulting in similar gatekeeping and hazing as well as the silence that masked episodes of violence in bop and pre-bop jazz. The #MeToo movement of 2017 brought forward stories of harassment from many fields—yet jazz was not immediately one of them. Jazz scholar Lara Pellegrinelli (2017) bemoaned this, writing:

> Watching as the women of Silicon Valley came forward to expose the men who have harassed them. Watching as the women of Hollywood came forward to detonate rumors of the casting couch spectacularly. Watching as women in the media came forward, ending the careers of powerful hosts. Watching as women have righteously assailed our politicians. Watching as the women—and men—of classical and new music[—]articulated how their realms have felt the oppressive effects of gender. But the women of jazz have not come forward as I have long hoped and imagined they would.
>
> I do not think they are coming.

One of the few jazz musicians to speak during the height of #MeToo, vibraphonist Sasha Berliner highlighted the harassment that young women in jazz suffer. In a 2017 blog post, Berliner stated the transactional nature of harassment outright, noting that she was harassed by a more-established male performer, finally realizing that "these were sexual advances, and if I didn't submit to them, I would lose some of my gigs I had planned that summer that he was also on." Berliner also reports that the jam session remained the same homosocial space as in the 1940s, calling it a "testosterone fueled wank fest." Most poignantly, she notes the silence and complicity of the male-dominated jazz scene and its effects on her engagement with jazz: "the more my male friends and colleagues who witnessed me being a victim of sexism time and time again and did absolutely nothing to interfere, the harder it became to maintain strength" (Berliner, 2017).

One important group working to improve working conditions and access to jazz spaces is the collective We Have Voice. Established in response to #MeToo and comprised of leading musicians and scholars from jazz and related fields, most of whom identify as women, We Have Voice developed a "Code of Conduct" defining key concepts and action items to aid in creating equitable performing spaces. Institutions and individuals are invited to sign on to the Code of Conduct, which emphasizes the intersectionality of harassment and how to recognize and thwart it (https://too-many.org/). Widespread adoption and implementation of such initiatives may be key to reducing the barrier to access that sexual harassment creates.

Gendered Instrument Specialization

A foundational barrier to women's participation in jazz, particularly early jazz, were the instruments deemed appropriate for women to play. At the turn of the century, women were still dissuaded from playing most wind instruments, except for the flute, since they required unseemly contortions of the mouth (Macleod, 1993, p. 295). Brass and percussion instruments related to another homosocial space: the military. These instruments found their way onto the parades and streets of New Orleans and other turn-of-the-century cities, eventually becoming the instruments of jazz. Gendered associations have been slow to change; by the 1980s, only 15 percent of orchestra members in brass, percussion, and string bass were women (Macleod, 1993, p. 302). Moreover, women sometimes choose their instrument specifically because it has been rejected by male players; for example, the soloistic properties of the electric guitar led many men to choose it over the bass, creating an opening for women (Clawson, 1999). The fear of taking attention or power from men dissuades women from assuming leadership roles; similarly, men dissuade women from taking jobs that they view as "belonging" to the men. In the pre-bebop economy, this was marked; jazz jobs were vital and were possible points of social mobility for Black and Latino men (Suzuki, 2014). Therefore, few were willing to cede these jobs to women.

The feminized and hyper-visible role of the vocalist was one access point for women. Despite that the biggest jazz hits in the Swing era were vocal numbers, and jazz singers were some of the most publicly recognizable musicians. However, the jazz world managed to minimize the impacts of singers and eventually all but eliminated the role itself. The vocalist's job was often decorative, in both physical appearance and musical content. Even the vocalists with the most famous and lucrative bands at the height of their popularity were considered decorative. Will Friedwald, for example, describes Martha Tilton, Benny Goodman's vocalist during his most popular period between 1937–1939, as "filling out pretty gowns, decorating bandstands, and giving gal jitterbugs reason to get sore at their pubescent boyfriends" (Friedwald, 1996, p. 95). Yet women in non-feminized roles were expected to conform to male dress; Tracy McMullen notes of her time playing saxophone in big bands that she was expected to wear a "faux tux" while the woman singer wore a beaded gown, underlining the gendered expectations of instrumentalist versus singer (McMullen, 2008, p. 131). And the existence of women singers could be threatening for male musicians. Benny Goodman notoriously switched vocalists often, which prevented anyone from challenging his supremacy as leader. By changing singers every year or two, no one could be conclusively identified as the voice of the Goodman orchestra (Magee, 2005). These Swing-era vocalists were often called "canaries," connoting the light and flighty, another manner of denigrating women's contributions to jazz—and insinuating that they could be caught by the men, or "cats/hepcats" in the parlance of the day.

While many early jazz women were vocalists, the piano was also an obvious entrance point into jazz for women. The instrument had a long-standing association with femininity. Improvements in piano manufacturing increased access to the instrument in the nineteenth century, and many middle- and upper-class homes owned one. As the piano became a central item in nineteenth-century in-home entertainment, many girls and women learned the instrument in the course of preparing themselves for marriageability. The late nineteenth century also saw the advent of the professional woman pianist, women's first major inroad into the world of instrumental art music. Thus, the instrument became so linked with femininity that, by the late nineteenth century, men who played piano were assumed to be queer (Lomax, 1973, p. 7). Both Lil Hardin (Armstrong) and Lovie Austin spoke about being encouraged to study piano because of its connection with home entertainment rather than its career possibilities, and Jelly Roll Morton initially expressed ambivalence to taking up the piano because of its association with queerness (Taylor, 2008, p. 50).

Women instrumentalists were expected to support the men in many ways. Pianists Lovie Austin and Lil Hardin Armstrong were both known as accompanists, not soloists; this may have placated the men they performed with, who were assured their dominance over the female players. Both pianists also assisted the groups through tedious work that the men preferred not to do: Austin notated Morton's music, and Hardin wrote out many of the lead sheets from King Oliver and Louis Armstrong's bands for their famous 1920s recordings. This behind-the-scenes work was even more pronounced for some gay men. As Lisa Barg notes, Billy Strayhorn lived as an openly gay Black man, but all of his work was hidden from public view and enabled by the "safe haven" of Duke Ellington (Barg, 2013).

Gendered Musical Practices

With early bebop came the famous cutting contests, which caused access to jazz in the 1940s and 1950s to become competition-based (Ake, 1998, p. 29). Now more gently referred to as a "jam session," the cutting contest of the 1930s and later featured several soloists who would attempt to outplay one another in a battle with instruments instead of knives but clearly conjuring up the violent image. Sometimes considered a model of democratic process, as everyone in a jam session gets their "say," the jam was also an area for elitism and exclusivity to proliferate. Ake notes that cutting contests added a new layer of virility and power into the mix (1998, p. 29). Still, examples exist of women participating in jam sessions during the bebop period. Mary Lou Williams recounts an episode when she awoke at 4am to saxophonist Ben Webster at her window: "He was saying, 'Get up pussycat. We're jamming and all the pianists are tired out now. [Coleman] Hawkins has got his shirt off and is still blowing. You got to come down'" (Williams, 1954, p. 11). In this example, however, Williams is the last resort, invited only when "all the pianists" were finished. More concerningly, despite being included in jam sessions, women were almost always neglected on records. As previously mentioned, jazz grew up with the recording industry and was, for many listeners, defined by records, so women's omission had the profound effect of almost complete erasure from the developing jazz canon.

Even forms of jazz that were considered open and accepting could exclude women. David Ake connects Ornette Coleman's free jazz groups of the late 1950s with a decrease in the assumed heteronormative masculinity of jazz, noting the inability to perform a cutting contest over the fluid forms of free jazz. "There are no chord changes to run," he asserts, "nothing here to 'conquer'" (Ake, 1998, p. 33). Coleman himself rejected the aura of sexuality that clung to jazz musicians, finding it distracting. However, even if the music's tether to masculinity had been frayed, this did not result in an influx of women, who found continued barriers to access. Tucker writes:

> Yet many improvising women will tell you that free jazz, in social practice, has not exactly been known for its gender equity. In 1997, The Women's Avant Fest was held in Chicago, by composers Maura Bosch and Kitty Brazelton. Brazelton, as well as composer, flutist, and performance artist Janice Misurell-Mitchell, both of whom performed at the festival, told me that they felt that the avant-garde field was more open to women in classical music

than in jazz. According to Brazelton, the 'downtown' experimental jazz world is extremely male-dominated, as well as instrumentally dominated (which leads to gender segregation).

(Tucker, 2004, p. 260)

The barriers to women's access of jazz spaces were even more pronounced prior to free jazz, yet one small but significant space persisted: the all-woman group. Barred from recording, paying gigs, or both, many women turned to the "all-girl" bands of the 1930s and 1940s, detailed in Sherrie Tucker's influential work, *Swing Shift* (2000). These "girl bands" were financially and sexually exploitative, and women revealed conflicting feelings about playing in them. Having a jazz community made entirely of women could be affirming, yet Tucker notes that these same women often cited their collaborations with famous male musicians as their most significant experiences. Tucker also notes that in her study of women's experiences in all-girl bands, the women largely rejected the ideal of all-female community and the lifting up of women by other women that second-wave feminists seek in their histories. Tucker says about the romanticized notion of female community, "I find [it] rather seductive but I also want to punch [it] in the nose" (Tucker, 2004, p. 245). Nostalgia for these communities misrepresents them as idylls of escape from mainstream gender and race constructs.

The "women-in-jazz" phenomena persisted after the girl bands of the 1940s; since the exclusion of women from jazz spaces continued, so did the need for all-women events and the raising of awareness of these performers. Enter the "women-in-jazz" label, which has been applied to festivals, workshops, histories (of which this work is admittedly a part), conferences, and media events. Intended to right the exclusion of women, the "women-in-jazz" event has largely perpetuated the problem, giving women one place to gather musically while continuing to exclude them from most other jazz spaces. The term "women-in-jazz" is problematic because it creates a unified community where none exists and limits women professionally, even though the term is useful because it draws together support and collectivizes resentment at the experiences of improvising women. It is, as Heble writes, "an awkward antisexist jazz strategy" (Heble, 2000, p. 88). Women-in-jazz delineates women as an addition to jazz, not an integral part of the whole; they are not integrated into the concepts and practices (Tucker 2004, p. 255). In a 2001 interview, saxophonist Jane Ira Bloom expressed surprise at the persistence of all-women events, saying, "Isn't it something that there still *are* women's jazz festivals? I thought they would be gone by now ... we would be fully integrated into the jazz world by then as women have been in other fields" (Enstice and Stockhouse, 2004, p. 10). These concerns are echoed by groups that are consciously all-women, including the free jazz collectives Les Diaboliques, Feminist Improvising Group, and European Women's Improvising Group (which are connected through a series of alumni). Smith notes, "Les Diaboliques continues to struggle with the representation 'woman,' as well with the class consciousness, soulful creation, and the issues that continue to exist for women in the traditionally male-dominated sphere of free improvisation" (Smith, 2008, p. 185).

Conclusion: Building Accessible Jazz Spaces

Initiatives like We Have Voice's Code of Conduct are promising, but they are useless if women, non-cisgender, and LGBTQ musicians are not already occupying the spaces that have adopted them. We cannot time travel to record neglected musicians. Giving beginning musicians unbiased access to instrument choices and musical styles requires a sweeping change of attitudes surrounding gender and sexuality. Fixing these barriers to access is a formidable task, but a surmountable one. While the willing women of jazz can break the silences that surround them, men are the main force that will change these barriers. Rectifying longstanding historical omissions will require that the primarily male instructors of jazz history courses commit to including queer, trans- and cisgender women and queer cis- and transgender men. Moreover, these musicians must not be relegated to "special topics" sessions but must be presented as formative forces in historical record. One barrier to proper inclusion is the method of jazz instruction; jazz students often study history by transcribing and memorizing famous recordings. Since many women and queer cis- and transgender men were never recorded, instructors must incorporate descriptions of these musicians' playing and lives or, in rarer cases, available sheet music. Studying arrangements can also be a powerful tool working towards inclusion, since women and queer cis- and transgender men tended to take supportive roles such as arrangers. Scholars can recognize the intersectionality of jazz's barriers to access and work to detail and dismantle them by reframing and redefining the parameters of jazz history to include not only neglected demographics, but also the contributions of those who supported the more famous performers and those whose contributions are not available on audio recordings.

Breaking down gendered barriers may require large societal changes (which are slowly happening), but educators may enact change through schooling. Gendered instrument specialization has proven tough to change, but educators can encourage girls and women to explore different methods of expression. Doubling instruments may be an easy entrance into jazz; while saxophonists are expected to double on the more feminized flute and clarinet, flutists and clarinetists are less often encouraged to pick up the saxophone. Inviting young flutists and clarinetists to develop saxophone skills may increase numbers from underrepresented groups. Allowing instruments not traditionally associated with jazz in both youth ensembles as well as professional ensembles will diversify both the ensemble demographics as well as musical content and creativity. Similarly, the structures and behaviors of jazz, including the jam session, can be improved with welcoming and stabilizing formats.

As I worked on this chapter, I discovered that my citation management software recognized the words "jazzman" and "jazzmen" but not "jazzwoman" or "jazzwomen." Jazzwomen: unrecognized even by AI. Perhaps this is an easy next step toward jazz's future gender parity.

Notes

1 I deliberately avoid speculation on Tipton's specific gender identity here, as Halberstam notes that investigation of gender identity following a person's death is an act of outing.
2 Some note that Black instrumentalists could have been recorded earlier than King Oliver's Creole Band: the first Black band offered a contract seems to have been The Creole Band (not King Oliver's) in 1916, who reportedly turned down the session because they were afraid of others stealing their music, a common problem experienced by vaudeville musicians at the time (Gushee, L., and Carr, H., 1988, p. 90).

References

Ake, D. (1998). Re-masculating jazz: Ornette Coleman, 'Lonely Woman,' and the New York jazz scene in the late 1950s. *American Music, 16*(1), 25–44.

Barg, L. (2013). Queer encounters in the music of Billy Strayhorn. *Journal of the American Musicological Society, 66*(3), 771. doi:10.1525/jams.2013.66.3.771.

Berliner, S. (2017, September 21). An open letter to Ethan Iverson (and the rest of jazz patriarchy). www.sashaberlinermusic.com/sociopoliticalcommentary-1/2017/9/21/an-open-letter-to-ethan-iverson-and-the-rest-of-jazz-patriarchy.

Chazelle, D. (Director) (2014. *Whiplash* [Film]. Los Angeles, CA: Bold Films and Blumhouse Productions.

Citron, M. J. (1993). *Gender and the Musical Canon.* Cambridge: Cambridge University Press.

Clawson, M. A. (1999). When women play the bass: Instrument specialization and gender interpretation in alternative rock music. *Gender and Society, 13*(2), 193.

Dahl, L. (1999). *Morning Glory: A Biography of Mary Lou Williams* (1st ed.) Berkeley: University of California Press.

Enstice, W., and Stockhouse, J. (2004). *Jazzwomen: Conversation with Twenty-one musicians.* Bloomington: Indiana University Press.

Friedwald, W. (1996). *Jazz Singing: America's Great Voices from Bessie Smith to Bebop and Beyond.* New York: Da Capo Press.

Gardner, C. M. (2020, December 23). A Portrait of Trans Masculinity in the Story of a Jazz Musician. https://hyperallergic.com/606218/no-ordinary-man-billy-tipton-documentary/.

Gushee, L., and Carr, H. (1988). How the Creole Band Came to Be. *Black Music Research Journal, 8*(1), 83–100.

Halberstam, J. (1998). *Female Masculinity.* Durham and London: Duke University Press.

Hayes, E. M. (2018). *Queen of Bebop: The Musical Lives of Sarah Vaughan*. New York: Ecco.

Heble, A. (2000). *Landing on the Wrong Note: Jazz, Dissonance, and Critical Practice*. New York: Routledge.

Kernodle, T. L. (2004). *Soul on Soul: The Life of Mary Lou Williams*. Boston: Northeastern University Press.

Lomax, A. (1973). *Mister Jelly Roll; the Fortunes of Jelly Roll Morton, New Orleans Creole and Inventor of Jazz* (2d ed.). Berkeley: University of California Press.

Macleod, B. A. (1993). "Whence comes the lady tympanist?" Gender and instrumental musicians in America, 1853–1990. *Journal of Social History*, 27(2), 291–308.

Magee, J. (2005). *The Uncrowned King of Swing: Fletcher Henderson and Big Band Jazz*. New York: Oxford University Press.

McMullen, T. (2008). Identity for sale: Glenn Miller, Wynton Marsalis, and cultural replay in music. In N. T. Rustin, and S. Tucker (Eds.), *Big Ears: Listening for Gender in Jazz Studies* (pp. 129–154). Durham, NC: Duke University Press.

Middlebrook, D. W. (1998). *Suits Me: The Double Life of Billy Tipton*. New York: Houghton Mifflin Company.

Miller, M. (2007). *Hi Hat, Trumpet, and Rhythm: The Life and Music of Valaida Snow*. Toronto: Mercury Press.

O'Connell, M. H., and Tucker, S. (2014). Not one to toot her own horn(?): Melba Liston's oral histories and classroom presentations. *Black Music Research Journal*, 34(1), 121–158.

O'Day, A., and Eells, G. (1981). *High Times, Hard Times*. New York: Putnam.

Pellegrinelli, L. (2008). Separated at "birth": Singing and the history of jazz. In Nichole T. Rustin and Sherrie Tucker (Ed.), *Big Ears: Listening for Gender in Jazz Studies* (pp. 31–47). Durham, NC: Duke University Press.

Pellegrinelli, L. (2017). *Women in Jazz: Blues and the Objectifying Truth*. https://nationalsawdust.org/thelog/2017/12/12/women-in-jazz-blues-and-the-objectifying-truth/.

Porter, E. (2002). *What Is this Thing Called Jazz? African American Musicians as Artists, Critics, and Activists*. Berkeley, CA: University of California Press.

Provost, S. C. (2017). *Bringing something new: Female jazz instrumentalists' use of imitation and masculinity*. *Jazz Perspectives*, Vol. 10(2–3), 141–157.

Ramsey, F., Jr., and Smith, C. E. (1939). *Jazzmen* ([1st ed.] ed.). San Diego: Harcourt Brace.

Rustin, N. (2005). "Mary Lou Williams plays like a man!" Gender, genius, and difference in Black Music Discourse. *South Atlantic Quarterly* 104(3), 445–462.

Rustin-Paschal, N. (2017). *The Kind of Man I am: Jazzmasculinity and the World of Charles Mingus Jr*. Middletown, CT: Wesleyan University Press.

Rutan, G. (. H. (2007). *Death of a Bebop Wife*. Redwood, NY: Cadence Jazz Books.

Schudel, M. (2019, September 4). Clora Bryant, barrier-breaking jazz trumpeter, dies at 92. www.washingtonpost.com/local/obituaries/clora-bryant-barrier-breaking-jazz-trumpeter-dies-at-92/2019/09/04/6889da0a-ce5b-11e9-8c1c-7c8ee785b855_story.html.

Sidran, B. (1981). *Black Talk* (1st ed.). New York: Holt, Rinehart and Winston.

Smith, J. D. (2008). Perverse hysterics: The noisy *cri* of Les Diaboliques. In N. T. Rustin, and S. Tucker (Eds.), *Big Ears: Listening for Gender in Jazz Studies* (180–209) Durham, NC: Duke University Press.

Suzuki, Y. (2014). Two strikes and the double negative: The intersections of gender and race in the cases of female jazz saxophonists. *Black Music Research Journal*, 33(2), 207–226.

Taylor, J. (2008). With Lovie and Lil: Rediscovering two Chicago pianists of the 1920s. In N. T. Rustin, and S. Tucker (Eds.), *Big Ears: Listening for Gender in Jazz Studies* (pp. 48–63). Durham, NC: Duke University Press.

Tomkins, L. (1977). *Interview Two: A Beautiful Session*. https://nationaljazzarchive.org.uk/explore/interviews/1634231-sarah-vaughan-interview-2?.

Tucker, S. (2000). *Swing Shift: 'All-girl' Bands of the 1940s*. Durham: Duke University Press Books.

Tucker, S. (2004). Bordering on community: Improvising women improvising women-in-jazz. In D. Fischlin, and A. Heble (Eds.), *The Other Side of Nowhere: Jazz, Improvisation, and Communities in Dialogue* (1st ed.). Middletown, CT: Wesleyan University Press.

Tucker, S. (2008). When did jazz go straight?: A queer question for jazz studies. *Critical Studies in Improvisation / Études Critiques En Improvisation*, 4(2).

Williams, M. L. (1954, May 1). Battle of the tenor kings. *Melody Maker*, 11.

Williamson, B. (2015). Access. In R. Adams, B. Reiss and D. Serlin (Eds.), *Keywords for Disability Studies* (pp. 14–17) New York: New York University Press.

35

BREAKING DOWN BARRIERS

Female Jazz Musicians in Spain

Rebeca Muñoz-García

Gendered Terms Statement: To provide context to this chapter, I would like to explain the gendered terms that have been used throughout the text. First, I will refer to 'women jazz careers' and 'female jazz musicians' as female identifying people. Second, I refer to 'male jazz musicians' and 'male counterparts or coworkers' as male identifying people. This does not mean that there are no other personal identities in the Spanish jazz scene, but the main goal of this chapter is to show how heteropatriarchal society shapes traditional gender identities in the jazz scene while intersecting with other social categories. In fact, the intersectionality approach presented here allows for finding and analyzing any different identity that the interviewees might express.

Introduction

Gender inequalities and discrimination have followed certain historical and cultural patterns. This does not mean that there is not a common framework for analyzing social inequalities, but these inequalities are expressed and materialized in different sociocultural contexts. Specifically, the study of artistic and cultural professions has been timidly approached in Spain. The particular case of jazz in Spain may well be related to, if not caused by, the fact that jazz is not viewed as a Spanish cultural creation. Although it seems that Spain has paid scant attention to analyzing jazz professional spaces, this has not prevented an increased popularity in jazz careers in recent years, especially since an undergraduate degree in jazz studies is now offered in several public and private Spanish universities. In my opinion, this lack of attention actually offers an opportunity to provide an initial analysis of jazz professional spaces in Spain from a gender perspective.

The aim of this chapter is to explore universal and specific barriers that limit the career options of Spanish female jazz musicians and the range of their professional activity. I will bring to light key issues that female jazz musicians face and some of their strategies for overcoming these obstacles and creating more inclusive and safer jazz career spaces. Initially, the first section addresses professional and personal career paths of women jazz musicians, bringing place and sociocultural context to the forefront. The second section investigates general work conditions in Spain as they relate to jazz careers. The third and fourth sections present the methodology and results of very recent fieldwork studying 21 women who are currently pursuing jazz careers in Spain. Finally, the Conclusion summarizes the main findings and reflections of this chapter.

DOI: 10.4324/9781003081876-39

Spanish Jazz Career Paths from a Gender Perspective:
A Theoretical Framework

Over the last decades, gender and feminist studies have analyzed professional jazz spaces, traditionally male-dominated, from a cross-disciplinary field of inquiry. The 1980s brought forth the first work on *compensatory history* focused on exploring the presence or absence of women from a historical perspective (Handy, 1981; Placksin, 1982; Dahl, 1989). In the 1990s some authors focused on studying how gender, race and class are shaped through jazz performances and interactions (Monson, 1995), while in the 2000s others authors have chosen a qualitative research approach to analyze the experiences of women jazz musicians (Tucker, 2000; Enstice and Stockhouse, 2004; Buscatto, 2007b; Suzuki, 2013) as well as considering new questions to explore (Tucker, 2002, 2004; Rustin and Tucker, 2008; Rustin, 2017).

Jazz studies in the United States have addressed jazz culture from an interdisciplinarity point of view, but usually some of these works have reserved only a small space to explore the jazz culture beyond the United States. However, recent research has emphasized the need to analyze jazz narratives and practices beyond American culture, which implies taking into account the fact that jazz has been shaped by different contexts (Cerchiar, Cugny and Kerschbaumer. 2012; Bohlman and Plastino, 2016; Martinelli, 2018; Johnson, 2019). Among these, we find the first Spanish jazz studies carried out in Spain (Martínez, 1996; García, 2012; Alonso, 2013; Ruesga, 2015; Ferrer, 2017; Iglesias, 2017). These works encourage thinking beyond the sociocultural context influence on jazz to understand the reflexive relationship between jazz and sociocultural context to the point where the line between them becomes blurred.

This chapter proposes the first critical approach that studies female jazz careers in Spain. It aims to address these and future questions by first considering that Spain is in the process of developing its own narrative and discourse about jazz. As shown above, a few authors have addressed jazz development and practices in Spain from different viewpoints during the last two decades. However, the gender perspective and the context outside of Spain have not yet been extensively incorporated into the field. I propose to analyze female jazz careers and musical practices in Spain within the 'New Jazz Studies' and 'Diaspora Studies' frameworks, considering intersectionality and everyday life theory as key analytical tools.

Studying Spanish jazz careers in the framework of the 'New Jazz Studies' will allow a broader view for feminist theorists and gender analysis, offering a novel framework "when 'gender and jazz' scholars are no longer solely perceived as representing the 'special interests' subcategory of jazz studies" (Rustin and Tucker, 2008, p. 8). This allows jazz issues to be expanded and developed through an interdisciplinary perspective that leads us to think in a different way and to observe jazz cultures from the 'outside.'

In this vein, 'Diaspora Studies' presents new perspectives towards rethinking jazz historiography axioms beyond the US context. We must start from the idea that "jazz was not invented and then exported; it was invented in the process of being disseminated" (Johnson, 2002, p. 39). Jazz studies in Spain can also follow this approach within their own history and practices, but also incorporating a gender perspective. As Johnson (2019) states, "jazz was globalized with a rapidity unprecedented for any other music, largely via musicians' migrations and new mass media. …. Given the global demographic, it seems likely that today most jazz is played outside the US" (p. 17). Within this scenario, analyzing female jazz careers in Spain involves delving into jazz narratives that may have not been revealed yet.

Intersectionality provides the opportunity to understand social meanings and domains of power that take place in the professional jazz spaces. This analytical tool allows us to understand the different identities that are being shaped and socially reproduced in jazz spaces within a specific sociocultural context. Accordingly, "intersectionality encourages understandings of social inequality based on interactions among various categories" (Hill Collins and Bilge, 2016, p. 26). Categories such as gender, race, ethnicity, class, and age need to be studied in the context of the Spanish professional jazz spaces and practices in order to observe how those categories intersect with one another.

Finally, the everyday life paradigm allows the inclusion of microsocial tools in order to understand how musical identities are shaped by close interactions in jazz spaces. This paradigm focuses on understanding how people give meaning to their daily practices and the discourse analysis helps us understand the significance. Furthermore, "gender, while treated in everyday encounters as a seemingly known label for dimensions of personal identity, is produced, structured and shaped within social communities" (Leonard, 2015, p. 181). Thus, gender stereotypes and gender roles associated with them are reinforced as well as questioned through social interactions. These interactions are part of the socialization and enculturation processes that affect musical and jazz practices throughout the formation of gender identity. This determines, for instance, musical taste, self-esteem, the gendering of musical education, the gender stereotyping of musical instruments, and the establishment of professional networks.

Considering this background for the analysis, I present the qualitative results of 21 in-depth interviews carried out from 2019 to 2020 in Spain.

Artistic Labor Conditions for Female Jazz Musicians in Spain

Artistic trajectories have been studied through individual experiences in relation to artistic labor market structures and cultural industries. European and American scholars have an extensive tradition in analyzing this field of inquiry, and they have revealed considerable difficulties and common socio-economic problems for all of the artistic disciplines (Becker, 1982; Menger, 1999; Cohen, 2012; Alper and Wassall, 2006, Mathieu, 2012), in music (Goldin and Rouse, 2000; Ravet, 2003; Coulangeon, 2004; Perrenoud, 2007), and specifically in jazz (Coulangeon, 1999; Buscatto, 2007b). However, except for a few cases, neither Spanish scholars nor private or third sectors have extensively explored the shape of artistic careers in Spain (Rodríguez, 1996; López and Pérez, 2017; Casals, 2018; Fundación SGAE, 2019). This makes it difficult to study cultural and artistic career paths in Spain, but at the same time it offers an ideal opportunity to integrate gender and feminist perspectives throughout, as well as use intersectionality as an analytical framework. This scarce attention may be due to the fact that jazz music is not part of the mainstream musical genres with broad social recognition in the country and has only recently been integrated into Spanish musical education programs with various degrees and levels of offerings.

In this context, two main aspects should be considered when approaching female jazz musicians' trajectories in Spain. First, analysis of the Spanish artistic labor market and cultural industries needs to be aligned with characteristics of other cultural markets and industries that have already been studied. Second, based on previous research findings showing that cultural employment is marked by temporality, uncertain trajectories, multi-activity, and low wages, we should bear in mind that in Spain cultural workers were not protected by a legislative framework for labor until 2018. That year the Artists Statute was approved in the Spanish parliament and is currently in the early stages of development and implementation. This legislation represents a major milestone for the artistic professional sector, but it also reveals the precariousness and the extreme vulnerability that artistic workers have long faced in Spain.[1]

Undoubtedly the category 'artistic work' and its heterogeneous practice is a challenge for any legal framework for social and labor protection. The artistic and cultural sector remains undervalued in Spain simply because artistic work is considered a vocational and alternative lifestyle instead of a profession from which people make a living.[2] Consequently, artistic workers are limited when exercising their social and labor rights in comparison to other fields, putting them at a great social, economic, and political disadvantage. Despite the fact that this statute represents a significant step forward, it is too early to determine its impact. Unfortunately, the implementation process is slow, and the COVID-19 crisis, which has especially impacted musicians and the performing arts sector, has slowed down the process even further. Likewise, this situation has impacted cultural researchers in Spain, making it difficult to continue developing and finding alternatives for the improvement of cultural workers' living and working conditions.

Women jazz musicians experience discrimination due to gender and their status as cultural workers. As demonstrated in the following analysis, female artists face significant obstacles to being able to afford long and stable professional careers. In male-dominated artistic professional spaces such as the music and jazz scenes, identities are being shaped by strongly gendered discursive and musical practices. Gender and work segregation is a defining characteristic of the music sector, where women's and men's professional roles determine professional possibilities for growth in terms of distribution of job opportunities, hiring and career entry, networking, social and professional recognition, gender stereotypes and social prejudices, among others (Coulangeon, Ravet, and Roharnik, 2005; Ravet and Coulageon, 2003; Buscatto, 2003). Likewise, qualitative research allows analyzing how gender identities inhabit jazz spaces and practices that affect daily life interactions where gender inequalities are being 'invisibly' shaped (Buscatto, 2007a). This sometimes prevents women from being aware of their unequal situation, especially if they are recognized within and outside of the male-dominated jazz community. Thus, the difficulty of being aware of the heteropatriarchal system shaped through daily life interactions contributes to the reproduction of social and gender inequalities where women are individually blamed for their professional difficulties, instead of considering that those difficulties are part of social structure inequalities. Furthermore, women's roles as caregivers as well as the "lack of access to masculine subjectivities necessary to succeed in such environment make women more vulnerable" (Strong and Raine, 2018, p.3), turning jazz careers for female musicians into an obstacle race.

The field of musical creativity and composition has received much attention among gender and feminist scholars focusing on the question of why musical creativity has long been a male-dominated field. The field of composition is especially of great interest as it is socially valued as the most difficult musical specialization requiring a high degree of musical knowledge and long years of musical training and education. As Buscatto states, "whereas the men, very much in the majority, are over-represented in the sector of musical creation[,] … the women, notwithstanding a vast minority in the activity, are, moreover, under-represented there" (Buscatto, 2019, p. 13). In Spain, a recent study shows that only 15 percent of women composers were able to release their works in 2014. Likewise, 72.8 percent of women in popular music are self-employed versus 66.8 percent of men, and 30.1 percent of women in this sector do not contribute to the Social Security System (Fundación SGAE, 2019, pp. 121–126).

All these studies help us understand the general career conditions in jazz from a gender perspective. However, determining exactly how many female jazz musicians are pursuing their careers in Spain is quite complex, although we do know that 15 percent of undergraduate jazz students are women (Ministry of Education and Professional Training, 2018–2019).[3] This chapter aims to contribute to the limited knowledge on musical professions in Spain, specifically in the jazz field, spotlighting women's experiences in order to analyze female jazz musicians' narratives and experiences from a sociological viewpoint.

Methodology for Qualitative Research

This chapter presents the methodology for conducting 21 in-depth interviews with female jazz musicians who are currently pursuing their professional careers in Spain as singers, instrumentalists, bandleaders and/or composers. The interviews were conducted in person and, when not possible, remotely held in the form of a video call. They were carried out in 2019 and the beginning of 2020, before the Coronavirus pandemic began in Spain. The selection process prioritizes female jazz musicians who are currently developing a professional career and who are not in the formative stage. The selection of the sample was made to seek a socio-structural representation of female jazz musicians in Spain, considering the accessibility criteria. During the participant recruitment stage, two recruitment tools were used to find participants: (1) interpersonal contacts, personal referral, and snowballing; and (2) institutional contacts through third sector organizations and local music schools.

Due to the lack of empirical research on female jazz musicians' careers in Spain, qualitative research was selected as the best method to understand how gendered identities and power relationships are being shaped into discursive and musical practices in the Spanish jazz spaces. This approach seeks to address careers of female jazz musicians through a mixed research technique that includes semi-structured interviews and life-story narratives. This combination offers a biographical approach, learning not only about specific career milestones, but also creating a broader narrative about their life experiences. To this effect, in-depth interviews were structured into three different parts: (1) Education and musical life, starting with the first contact with the music world; (2) professional career, personal difficulties, and gender interactions in socio-musical jazz spaces; and (3) women's presence or absence, and future perspectives for the jazz scene. Moreover, it is important to explain that carrying out sociological fieldwork involves conducting anonymous interviews based on the selected segmentation variables.

As noted in the first section, I propose to include the intersectionality perspective to understand how gender identity is being enacted in Spanish jazz spaces while intersecting with *age*, *musical specialty*, *place*, *ethnicity/race*, and *social class*. Race issues as related to women in jazz is usually discussed in connection to Black American culture (Tucker, 2000; Suzuki, 2013). This narrative was applied to the "old continent" after World War I and specifically to Spain with the arrival of the first foxtrot and jazz rhythms brought by Black American artists (García, 2012, pp. 21–22). However, at present, race and ethnicity must be considered beyond the US historical and cultural context, along with observing how racial and ethnic identities intersect with gender. Thus, racial, and ethnic identities in the United States may not necessarily correspond to those found in the Spanish jazz scene or another global diasporic context. In this sense, I find it more appropriate to use the term 'racialized women' when I refer to those women who receive or may receive discriminatory treatment based on the racial or ethnical category that society attributes to them.

For that matter, it is worth mentioning that these results may present certain limitations associated with finding heterogeneous profiles of racialized women willing to be interviewed in Spain. However, this only represents a part of the whole study. During the participant recruitment stage, it was difficult to find racialized women who were self-identified within the jazz genre rather than other popular music genres. At the same time, identifying racialized women who were not singers was likewise challenging. After a long search, seven racialized women were finally contacted, but only one instrumentalist responded with interest to the interviews. These difficulties, beyond limiting the research study, have demonstrated the need to study the impact of ethnicity, race, and gender on the Spanish jazz scene.

Finally, the results come from 21 women who represent the typological and socio-structural breadth of female jazz careers in Spain. This typology is composed of women who are now actively engaging in jazz careers in Spain, divided into two population groups of nine women less than 35 years old and twelve women aged 35 or older. They are non-racialized and racialized women who are categorized as instrumentalists (1), singers (2), or singers and instrumentalists (3) and, additionally, composers and/or bandleaders. Even though all of them work or have worked in different cities in Spain, most are pursuing their careers in Madrid and Barcelona.

The Results of an Intersectional Approach

The following three subsections display the universal and specific barriers that keep women from pursuing jazz careers similar to men in Spain. The barriers usually occur at two different career stages:

First, when getting into the jazz scene and, second, being part of the scene and finding challenges as professional participants. To address these issues, I present the main findings organized in three categories: Age, musical specialty, and place. Social class is later considered in the discourse analysis since it is essential to assess cultural and social capital, but mainly to determine musical education access and professional opportunities. Finally, in the third subsection, I reflect on how to approach race, ethnicity, and gender in the Spanish jazz context.

Getting into the Spanish Jazz Scene

Regarding access barriers, key factors to be analyzed are jazz education opportunities, national professional opportunities, and inclusion or exclusion mechanisms apparent in gendered daily interactions.

Foremost, women jazz musicians in Spain acknowledge the existence of a relatively small national jazz scene, where men traditionally stand out. Moreover, women's perceptions and experiences reveal a lack of female national role models, which makes them seek out models internationally, mostly in the United States and especially in New York City. The result is that gender identity is shaped through 'otherness' in Spanish jazz spaces and especially for the instrumentalists. Indeed, 'otherness' is materialized through daily interactions that can be more powerful in jazz cultures outside the United States. The identity socially attributed to jazz musicians is usually associated with being male, Black, self-assured, and creative, with an air of authority or a leader. This identity is less accessible for current and future female musicians, whose identity as jazz musicians is self-constructed from 'otherness.'

On the other hand, *jazz education access* in Spain is restricted by regional educational policies and personal financial resources, as well as by women's social and cultural capital in the sense in which Bourdieu defines these two concepts (Bourdieu, 1986). The public musical educational system taught at the conservatory and institutionally considered as 'non-university education' has recently included jazz education programs in Spain, sporadically distributed across regions. For example, undergraduate studies in jazz were first incorporated into public education as 'Jazz and Modern Music' in Barcelona in 2001. Slowly, other regions joined this initiative, although Madrid is not included among them. Hence, access to education is still limited geographically and, as a result, proximity, students' mobility opportunities and economic resources determine the access. Most of the instrumentalists interviewed have a classical educational background, except for a few women under the age of 30, who have studied in Barcelona or the Netherlands, but whose previous educational training mainly focused on classical music. Moreover, most of the interviewees who were born in Spain entered the professional scene early on. This enabled them to participate in popular music scenes as professionals rather than as students at the conservatory and official music schools.

In general, Spanish vocalists over the age of 35 have a lower level of formal training. However, the younger vocalists based in Barcelona reported higher levels of jazz education as well as music in general. This is important as musical education and musical knowledge facilitate inclusion and recognition within the jazz community. Especially vocalists are affected by this lack of educational access due to social prejudices and the belief that singing has largely been considered a natural gift that does not require musical knowledge or education.

Regarding jazz education, we note that the teacher–student relationship can determine whether female jazz musicians continue or drop out of musical education in a male-dominated field. As one of the 2020 participants, an instrumentalist and singer, explains:

> I have had teachers all my life and nobody ever treated me like he did. [...] I knew what it was about a little, but I didn't think he would make me so afraid, for example, to get into

the jams. In Holland I got in the jams a lot, but I didn't ever do it in my town because of him. […] Here I always felt like I was never going to be good enough.

Furthermore, the educational spaces, especially private studios in one-on-one situations, can be unsafe spaces for women, affecting their self-esteem and self-confidence. This also demonstrates the lack of anti-harassment protocol and measures in Spanish jazz conservatories and the normalization of chauvinistic and sexist behavior in this professional environment. As 2019 and 2020 instrumentalists and singers expressed it:

He tried to touch me a lot, like, let's see your tummy, and your back, and look how I am doing it and you … in that way. I don't know, I didn't like it at all. I was very uncomfortable, […] and some days I would even leave the class crying because we weren't getting on well. I went to ask to change teachers and they wouldn't do it. They told me if I wanted to change teachers, I would have to ask to go on a study abroad program.

And many teachers tried to hit on you! This is really awful, it's awful.

Regarding age interactions, qualitative data shows that women aged 35 and over had often entered the jazz profession later, especially as composers and band leaders. The most common reason is that families encourage them to pursue other academic careers, with jazz as a hobby. By contrast, women under 35 show early vocations, high levels of musical education and training, and an early focus on the jazz field, particularly in Barcelona.

Concerning geography, as noted before, Spanish jazz scenes are scattered and located in urban settlements, mostly determined by regional policies and private initiatives that have promoted jazz culture. Such uneven growth has reinforced regional inequalities as jazz education entered the institutions. In this context, Barcelona stands out as a key enclave for jazz development.[4] Barcelona is also the Spanish city where more women of all generations are pursuing jazz career paths. The narratives of women from Barcelona reveal a substantial change in the younger generations, not only in terms of musical educational access and level, but in self-assured, gender and feminist awareness, acquiring compositional and leadership practices from the beginning, as well as having early contact with other female musicians.

All these factors represent significant challenges for women jazz musicians, specifically the lack of cultural roots as well as education programs. As a result, the narratives of female jazz musicians show how jazz education often depends on the existence of local initiatives, family relationships, and supportive teachers.

Being Part of the Scene

The second great challenge comes when women establish themselves on a national level. At this point, precariousness, temporality, and multi-activity characterize their careers in Spain, which prevents a focus on both creative and compositional works, engagement in solo projects, and development as leaders. Women confirm the relatively small jazz employment market in Spain and a weak jazz industry, which forces them to turn to teaching and to engage in other income streams beyond the scope of the jazz field. A 2019 instrumentalist said this:

Teaching is what always evens things out because gigs come and go. You don't always get gigs and you don't know how much they are going to pay you.

As explained, until 2018 a legal framework did not exist for artistic labor protection. This has contributed to gender-based inequalities and women's social and economic vulnerability, as they are especially unprotected during maternity, retirement, unemployment, and illness. Undoubtedly, this is a sign of the uncertainty that runs through the personal experience of women-in-jazz, and which leads them to develop a life and professional experience grounded in the here and now. Heteropatriarchal structures and power imbalances produce a higher vulnerability and sense of uncertainty in female jazz musicians. This may cause women to abandon, temporarily interrupt or reduce their professional activity. Additionally, most of the interviewed women claim that many national festivals usually do not book local musicians, tending to look 'outside' when hiring artists. The preferences of festival promoters and audiences conform with what is understood as 'jazz authenticity'—as described before: male, Black, self-assured, and creative, with an air of authority or a leader. This may reduce women's employment opportunities and sense of belonging in a male-dominated field. Accordingly, some women also mention difficulties in being considered for the main national jazz venues and festival programs. Furthermore, sexism is part of the gender interactions in the scene and women note how their male workmates usually tend to undervalue women's professional success. Male counterparts argue that female jazz musicians have more opportunities due to feminism being a trend, their good looks, or their sexual or privileged relationships with colleagues. These comments correspond to post-feminist trends of cultivating the alpha-girl and competitiveness (Whelehan, 2000; Gill, 2007), especially noticeable in Spain's small jazz scene. A 2019 instrumentalist said,

> [i]n the end, it is always because of someone else's efforts. You are there because of your manager or because you have been lucky or because the festival is looking to have 50 percent women in it.

According to a 2019 instrumentalist,

> A classmate said to me: "She really doesn't play that well. Do you think if she wasn't so pretty, she would be so successful? [...] Because if you don't look at her, you will see that she doesn't play that well.

A 2020 instrumentalist said this:
> She was the only one that really stood out in the scene, right? And then I hear one of my mates say that to get where she is now for sure she has slept with all the musicians in the city.

The professional stability of female jazz musicians seems to be delayed into their thirties. At that time, women have a solid network that provides them with some confidence and solidifies their professional development in jazz. However, at this time, they also face major personal, family and professional challenges due to the caregiver role traditionally attributed to women as well as the working hours in which jazz performances take place, generally at night with fluctuating schedules. This can be observed in the interviewee comments when they explain their experiences about maternity or their desire to become mothers, to the extent that only four of the 21 participants are mothers. Some of those who are not mothers showed clear concerns about the professional repercussions that making this step would have on their career, and those who are mothers spoke explicitly of the difficulties they experience. A 2020 instrumentalist said this:

> I have seen musician couples, a girl and a guy, and he hasn't quit, and she has quit. That really makes me angry. I mean I don't want that to happen to me. So, it's like ... I have balked at that kind of thing a bit ... truthfully.

A 2020 instrumentalist said,

> When people see you with a baby bump, they won't give you tours, they won't give you gigs. And if they see you with a baby bump and a baby, they will give you even fewer ones, and if they see you with two babies, you won't get any.

As for musical specialty, major differences are apparent between women who engage in professional careers as singers versus instrumentalists. Usually, singing presents more job opportunities for female jazz musicians. Consequently, many women combine instrumental and singing practices. Singing has traditionally been equally accepted in the music field and attracts the audience's attention. Of course, the use of words usually facilitates the engagement, especially with casual audiences. The increase of women being active as instrumentalists and vocalists demonstrates a strategy to break down access barriers. However, this does not imply that women's role as instrumentalists ceases to be undervalued as critics, audiences, and male musicians recognize these women then for their vocal skills rather their instrumental work. Furthermore, while female jazz instrumentalists seem to have more opportunities to work as sidewomen, both female singers and instrumentalists usually depend on leading their own projects in order to perform. Driving forces usually include creating opportunities but also creating safer spaces. As shown below, some of them express the importance of selecting fellow group members based on the existence of professional mutual recognition and feminist commitment. A 2020 instrumentalist said this:

> Look for people with a good attitude, complicity and an interest in what you are doing. And then, commitment, a feminist vision. [...] It's important that they are committed to women's experience and have a vision of equality.

In general, a feeling of isolation and lack of belonging has been observed among women in the jazz scene, as well as difficulty in finding women with whom to share musical practices. In recent years, this situation is different in the Barcelona scene, where women observe a greater presence of female students and teaching staff in the recently created jazz music schools. However, this does not apply to jam sessions and some jazz clubs. As described in the previous section, Barcelona stands out as a key location for jazz development in Spain mainly due to having the largest national offering in jazz education programs. I also observe a lack of connection between regional scenes, which limits women's career opportunities, as well as reinforces feelings of isolation.

Race, Ethnicity, and Gender in the Spanish Jazz Scene

This section focuses on the initial findings, questions, and considerations for approaching race, ethnicity, and gender in the Spanish jazz scene. Spanish jazz representations and discourses need to be more broadly addressed, paying attention to current and further issues related to race, ethnicity, and gender in professional jazz careers. To do so, first, we need to explore Spanish migration history since the end of the nineteenth century, and its connection with jazz music development in the country from a gender perspective. Moreover, we must take into account that, since the second half of the twentieth century, Spanish migration history was determined by the Spanish Civil War (1936–1939) and the Spanish dictatorship (1939–1975). Due to the sociopolitical situation and the lack of employment opportunities, Spain primarily was a country of emigration until the late 1970s. In the 1980s and particularly during the 1990s, international migration arrived in Spain, "first there were European immigrants, followed by Latin Americans, Asians and, most recently, and in greater numbers, Africans, particularly Moroccans" (López, 1995, p.227). This migratory flow intensified between 2000 and 2007, but the 2008 crisis had two main consequences: (1) Employment opportunities for the migrant population decreased in Spain, and they then experienced higher unemployment rates (Arcarons and Muñoz, 2018), and (2) the young and skilled population migrated to other European countries and the United States in search of better job opportunities.

The Spanish jazz scene should be seriously addressed in its relation to Black culture, and three issues need more discussion: First, the meaning of Black and Blackness in Spain and its relation to Spanish jazz representations and practices; second, understanding the profile and motivation attracting the migrant population to jazz, with special attention to the cultural meanings that Blacks and the population with African roots confer to this genre—and also observe their musical and professional practices from a gender perspective; and, third, analyze the identities of non-Black, but racialized women in Spain's jazz scene.

Initial questions arose when analyzing racialized women's narrative during the fieldwork: First, while trying to contact racialized female jazz musicians, I found only singers and Cuban and American instrumentalists, some of whom do not fit into the jazz music genre; and, second, while analyzing the discourse of the non-Black, but racialized woman interviewed. Specifically, the non-Black, but racialized woman explained how complicated it was to be scheduled into the main jazz venues in her region. She stated that she was only able to get her first chance when a well-known musician in the scene who lives in Spain—male and Latin American—got a call from one of the venues asking if she was good enough to play there. As she explained:

> That American "*racialized [non-Black] girl*", is she good or not?", so then he said: "Yes, of course", then after that phone call, he called us to play not because he read my dossier, not because he listened to my music, just because that person said yes. The same thing happened in another important jazz venue. Now, we play there every year so like once you get in and when you can demonstrate what you can do, you're fine, but it's getting through the door. It's like they don't even give you the chance unless somebody says so.

Here it can be observed how both female and non-Black, though American, jazz musicians are not linked to 'jazz authenticity.' Place and race-based 'authenticity' in jazz might connect to each other when represented by American Black women, but this does not work for other racialized jazz musicians. This causes racialized women to be questioned in national jazz circles, where women can explicitly experience double discrimination and access barriers to the scene. This also reveals internal mechanisms of inclusion or marginalization represented through professional endogamy and peer group recognition when being part of the 'the boys club' (Leonard, 2016).

Finally, it is necessary to explore the reasons that make it difficult to find racialized women instrumentalists in the professional jazz scene or in the conservatories and music schools in Spain. This could lead us to think that jazz has been a genre mainly developed by white males in Spain, which goes against the historical narrative attributed to race and 'authenticity' in jazz. Hence, jazz becomes a diasporic genre which implies different analysis of the forming of identities, sense of belonging and marginalization in the jazz scenes beyond the United States.

Conclusion

Throughout this chapter, I have shown how jazz professional spaces can be addressed from gender and intersectionality perspectives to determine the universal and specific barriers that exist when pursuing jazz careers in Spain. Specifically, I have demonstrated that careers of female jazz musicians in Spain are significantly shaped by *age, musical specialty, place* and, in some cases, by *race*.

It is particularly notable that regional inequalities affect women-in-jazz educational and professional opportunities showing that Barcelona stands out for providing better support for jazz development and female presence—especially in jazz educational programs. Regarding age, women under 35 show vocations at a young age, high levels of educational training and an early focus on the jazz field. In general, the women's narratives show how gender identity is being shaped mainly through 'otherness' in the Spanish jazz spaces that are vigorously described as male-dominated. The professional endogamy, sexism and daily gender interactions reported by most of the interviewed women lead to female jazz musicians facing greater difficulties. Clearly, most of them are aware of it, especially the younger generations.

Many interviewees have expressed that the development of artistic careers involves hard-working conditions. Besides, they have revealed that culture is undervalued in Spain, as expressed by the following 2019 instrumentalists:

> I don't know how the end of my life is going to be, but the path is not being exactly easy for me. In general, people that have dedicated their lives to music, dance or theater do not have an easy life.

> We have a basic problem in Spain, there is no respect for culture.

Further research is needed to compare other artistic and cultural professions in Spain in order to find commonalities and differences in terms of barriers and opportunities. This may support the overall development of the Spanish jazz scene and boost social and employment conditions for musicians. By analyzing early barriers, similar research may foster a more inclusive and integrated jazz and musical community. This analytical perspective needs to be implemented in all career phases, paying special attention to emerging jazz education programs and evaluating the existing ones. The overall goal is to create more inclusive and safer jazz professional and educational spaces for everyone.

Finally, this chapter confirmed that further research needs to approach jazz spaces and practices beyond the United States to identify mechanisms of inclusion and/or exclusion of diasporic jazz practices and spaces. Likewise, such studies can contribute to explaining how gender identities are shaped in relation to other characteristics such as ethnicity, race, place, social class, or age, in different sociocultural contexts similar to the Spanish jazz scene.

Acknowledgments

This work was supported by the Ministry of Universities of Spain (State program for promoting talent and employability. Subprograma de Formación de Profesorado Universitario [FPU]) under Grant FPU16/03366.

Notes

1 The Statute recognizes the difficulties of typifying a heterogeneous artistic sector marked by uncertainty and intermittent work and includes a number of fiscal and labor initiatives "whose purpose is adjusting the applicable regulatory scheme to the specialties of artistic work.... All of this in the context of the rapidly changing world of employment, and especially cultural labor, and in which the cultural vocation seems at times to be misunderstood, as the opposite of professionalization" (RDL 26/2018, December 28th, p. 129855).
2 To delve into this matter, see Menger's analysis and reflections on creative work, especially in the arts field (Menger, 2014).
3 Note that only the autonomous communities of Balearic Islands, Galicia, Navarre, and Basque Country are included in these national jazz statistics.
4 Note that in the city of Barcelona there are three music conservatories that offer 'Jazz and Modern Music' bachelor's degrees. (Royal Decree-Law 26/2018, December 28, p. 129855).

References

Alonso, C. (2013). Aphrodite's Necklace Was Not Only a Joke: Jazz, Parody and Feminism in Spanish Musical Theatre (1900–1939). In S. Martinez, and H. Fouce (Eds.), *Made in Spain* (pp. 94–105). Routledge.

Alper, N. O., and Wassall, G. H. (2006). Artists' careers and their labor markets. In V.G. Ginsburggh and D. Throsby (Eds.), *Handbook of the Economics of Art and Culture* (pp. 813–864). North Holland.

Arcarons, A. F., and Muñoz, J. (2018). La generación 1.5 de inmigrantes en España ¿La crisis de empleo les ha afectado igual que a la primera generación? *REIS: Revista Española de Investigaciones Sociológicas, 164,* 21–40.

Becker, H. (1982). *Art Worlds.* University of California Press.

Bohlman, Philip V., and Plastino, G. (Eds.) (2016). *Jazz Worlds/World Jazz.* Chicago Studies in Ethnomusicology.

Bourdieu, P. (1986). The forms of Capital. In J. G. Richardson (Ed.) *Handbook of Theory and Research for the Sociology of Education* (pp. 240–268). Greenwood.

Buscatto, M. (2003). Chanteuse de jazz n'est point métier d'homme. *Revue française de sociologie, 44*(1), 35–62.

Buscatto, M. (2007a). Contributions of ethnography to gendered sociology: the French jazz world. *Qualitative Sociology Review, 3*(3), 46–58.

Buscatto, M. (2007b). *Femmes du jazz. Musicalités, féminités, marginalités.* CNRS.

Buscatto, M. (2019). Presentation. "Modest" artists standing the test of time. The artistic "vocation", yes... but not that alone. *Recherches sociologiques et anthropologiques, 50-2,* 9–26. https://doi.org/10.4000/rsa.3416.

Casals, M. (2018). *Los músicos y su profesión. Trabajo artístico y profesionalización en el jazz y la música moderna. Un análisis sociológico* (Doctoral dissertation, Universitat de Barcelona). Retrieved from: www.tdx.cat/handle/10803/586251?locale-attribute=en#page=1.

Cerchiari; L., Cugny, L., and Kerschbaumer, F. (Eds.). (2012). *Eurojazzland: Jazz and European Sources, Dynamics, and Contexts.* Northeastern University Press.

Cohen, N. (2012). Cultural Work as a Site of Struggle: Freelancers and Exploitation. *Triple C 10*(2), 141–155.

Coulangeon, P. (1999). *Les musiciens de jazz en France à l'heure de la réhabilitation culturelle: Sociologie des carrières et du travail musical.* L'Harmattan.

Coulangeon, P. (2004). L'expérience de la précarité dans les professions artistiques. Le cas des musiciens interprètes. *Sociologie de l'Art, 3,* 77–110.

Coulangeon, P., Ravet, H., and Roharik, I. (2005). Gender differentiated effect of time in performing arts professions: Musicians, actors, and dancers in contemporary France. *Poetics, 33*(5-6), 369–387.

Dahl, L. (1989). *Stormy Weather: The Music and Lives of a Century of Jazzwomen.* Limelight Editions.

Enstice, W., and Stockhouse, J. (2004). *Jazzwomen: Conversations with Twenty-one Musicians.* Indiana University Press.

Ferrer, I. (2017). Escenificando el género: estrategias corporales en los lugares de ocio de las décadas de 1940 y 1950. In B. Martínez del Fresno, and A. M. Díaz (coord.), *Danza, género y sociedad* (pp. 227–258). Universidad de Málaga (UMA).

Fundación SGAE (Ed.). (2019). *Autoras en el audiovisual, la música y las artes escénicas. Un estudio sobre el desarrollo profesional desde una perspectiva de género.* SGAE.

García, J. (2012). *El ruido alegre, el jazz en la BNE.* Ministerio de Cultura.

Gill, R. (2007). Postfeminist media culture: Elements of a sensibility. *European Journal of Cultural Studies, 10*(2), 147–166.

Goldin, C., and Rouse, C. (2000). Orchestrating impartiality: The impact of "blind" auditions on female musicians. *American Economic Review, 90*(4), 715–741.

Handy, A. (1981). *Black Women in American Bands and Orchestras.* Scarecrow Press.

Hill Collins, P., and Bilge, S. (2016). *Intersectionality.* Polity Press.

Iglesias, I. (2017). *La modernidad elusiva: jazz, baile y política en la Guerra Civil española y el franquismo (1936-1968).* CSIC.

Johnson, B. (2002). The Jazz Diaspora. In M. Cooke., and D. Horn (Eds.), *The Cambridge Companion to Jazz* (pp. 33–54). Cambridge University Press.

Johnson, B. (2019). Diasporic Jazz. In N. Gebhardt., N. Rustin., and T. Whyton (Eds.), *The Routledge Companion to Jazz Studies* (pp.17–25). Routledge.

Leonard, M. (2015). Gender and Sexuality. In J. Shepherd., and K. Devine (Eds.), *The Routledge Reader on the Sociology of Music* (pp. 197–206). Routledge. doi:10.4324/9780203736319-20.

Leonard, M. (2016). Girls at work: gendered identities, sex segregation and employment experiences in the music industries. In J. Warwick., and A. Adrian (Eds.), *Voicing Girlhood in Popular Music: Performance, Authority, Authenticity* (pp. 37–55). Routledge.

López, I., and Pérez, M. (2017). *La actividad económica de los/las artistas en España: estudio y análisis.* Fundación Antonio Nebrija.

López, D. (1995). La inmigración en España a fines del siglo XX. Los que vienen a trabajar y los que vienen a descansar. *REIS: Revista Española de Investigaciones Sociológicas, 71–72,* 225–248.

Martinelli, F. (Ed.). (2018). *The History of European Jazz. The Music, Musicians, and Audience in Context.* Equinox Publishing Limited.

Martínez, J. M. (1996). *Del fox-trot al jazz-flamenco: El jazz en España, 1919–1996.* Alianza Editorial.

Mathieu, C. (Ed.). (2012). *Careers in Creative Industries.* Routledge.

Menger, P. M. (1999). Artistic labor markets and careers. *Annual Review of Sociology, 25*(1), 541–574.

Menger, P. M. (2014). "Difference, competition, and disproportion. The sociology of creative work." Inaugural lecture delivered on Thursday 9 January 2014. Collège de France.

Ministry of Education and Professional Training (2018-2019). *Enrolled Students in Higher Music Education by Instrument, Type of Institution, and Gender.* Retrieved from http://estadisticas.mecd.gob.es/EducaJaxiPx/Tabla.htm?path=/no-universitaria/alumnado/matriculado/2018-2019-rd/re-musica//l0/&file=musica_07.px&type=pcaxis&L=0.

Monson, I. (1995). The Problem with white hipness: Race, gender, and cultural conceptions in jazz historical discourse. *Journal of the American Musicological Society, 48*(3), 396–422. https://doi.org/10.2307/3519833.

Perrenoud, M. (2007). *Les musicos: enquête sur des musiciens ordinaires.* La Découverte.

Placksin, S. (1982). *American Women in Jazz, 1900 to the Present: Their Words, Lives, and Music.* Seaview Books.

Ravet, H. (2003). Professionnalisation féminine et féminisation d'une profession: les artistes interprètes de musique. *Travail, genre et sociétés, 1,* 173–195.

Ravet, H., and Coulangeon, P. (2003). La division sexuelle du travail chez les musiciens français. *Sociologie du travail, 45*(3), 361–384.

Rodríguez, A. (1996). *Los compositores españoles: Un análisis sociológico.* Centro de Investigaciones Sociológicas.

Ruesga-Bono, J. (Ed.) (2015). *Jazz en español. Derivas hispanoamericanas.* (2nd ed.). CulturArts-Música.

Rustin, N., and Tucker, S. (Eds.). (2008). *Big Ears: Listening for Gender in Jazz Studies.* Duke University Press.

Rustin, N. (2017). *The Kind of Man I am: Jazzmasculinity and the World of Charles Mingus Jr.* Wesleyan University Press.

Spain. Royal Decree-Law 26/2018, by which emergency measures on artistic creation and cinematography are approved. Dec. 28th, BOE 314, pp. 129855 a 129862. Retrieved from: www.boe.es/buscar/doc.php?id=BOE-A-2018-17990.

Strong, C., and Raine, S. (2018). Gender politics in the music industry. *IASPM Journal, 8*(1), 2–8.

Suzuki, Y. (2013). Two strikes and the double negative: The intersections of gender and race in the cases of female jazz saxophonists. *Black Music Research Journal, 33*(2), 207–226.

Tucker, S. (2000). *Swing Shift: "All-girl" Bands of the 1940s.* Duke University Press.

Tucker, S. (2002). When subjects don't come out. In S. Fuller., and L. Whitesell (Eds.), *Queer Episodes in Music and Modern Identity* (pp. 293–310). University of Illinois Press.

Tucker, S. (2004). Bordering on community: Improvising women-in-jazz. In A. Heble and D. Fischlin., and I. Monson (Eds.), *The Other Side of Nowhere: Jazz, Improvisation, and Communities in Dialogue* (pp. 244–267). Wesleyan University Press.

Whelehan, I. (2000). *Overloaded Popular Culture and the Future of Feminism.* Women's Press.

36

THE PALE IMAGE OF THE JAZZ FEMALE INSTRUMENTALISTS IN SOUTHEASTERN EUROPE

Jasna Jovićević

Introduction

Since I was raised in a patriarchal society, the subtle discrimination I encountered during my early jazz career in Hungary and Serbia seemed normal to me. Many of my male colleagues were actually convinced that being female would be an advantage and provide me with more performance opportunities. . Needless to say, their predictions did not come true: As a girl, I was the last to be invited to the music group (of men), big band, or a professional gig. If there was no other sax player left to call it was my turn. Nevertheless, I sought out every possible opportunity to perform. Frequently I encountered comments such as, "How come that a girl is able to play the saxophone?"; "I have never seen a girl playing the saxophone before!"; "Isn't the saxophone a male instrument?"; "Are your lungs strong enough to blow?"; "Men play jazz, so are you the only one?"; "Why would a girl play jazz?"; "Why don't you do what other girls do?"; By the time I was a regular participant on the bandstand, frequent comments were: "Oh, you must be a singer!" or "Are you with the musicians?"; "Are you the trumpeter's girlfriend?"; "You play so well, I could not even hear it is not all men in the band!" (when I finally got into a professional big band, as sub); "Wow, you have balls", (a quality that describes virtuosity, strong sound, and a sense of masculinity); "You play so well (play so fast), just like a man!" or "Your solo was so lyrical, so girly"; although these comments emphasized the uniqueness of my gender[1] identity, the truth is that I did feel lonely, different, and rejected. As a result, I became a bandleader and hired musicians I feel comfortable with.

Jazz is traditionally a male-dominated genre with a high expression of masculinity and competition. Moreover, male ideas of representation dominate the aesthetics and social environment of the genre (Knauer, 2016). The focus of this chapter is specifically the geographic region of Southeastern Europe, also referred to as the Balkan cultural space. The presence of women in jazz is still very low in this geographic region due to the male-dominated culture mentioned earlier (Adkins Chitti, 2007). Patriarchal hegemony and double standards are barriers that female jazz instrumentalists have to cope with, since they are part of a system that denies access. Based on my personal experience and a cultural analysis, I propose that female underrepresentation is a direct result of the gendered cultural roles of participation in the private-public sphere and the representation of women as a novelty in the male-dominated jazz genre.

In this chapter, I analyze the portrayal of female jazz instrumentalists in the public jazz scene, together with the representation of female jazz instrumentalists in regional publications, concluding

DOI: 10.4324/9781003081876-40

an urgent need for research on gender discrepancies in jazz. Finally, I share an auto-ethnographic testimony with a subjective view of a female jazz musician's identity on the Balkan scene in support of my thesis of denial of access to a jazz career as a result of the lingering dominance of patriarchy in Balkan society.

On the Southeast Side of the Iron Curtain

Jazz has been an expression of social and political movements throughout its history. After World War I, swing bands started appearing in the salons of Eastern and Southeastern Europe representing the cosmopolitan trends of the United States. The concept of multiculturalism was appealing to this embattled region and of course, jazz was a new art form for Eastern Europe. While fascism was gaining strength in Germany in the 1920s, jazz became a symbol of resistance for Jewish musicians in Eastern Europe (Blam, 2011, p. 21). Jazz was an expression of freedom contrary to communism after World War II (Dimitrijević, 2009). Throughout the following decades, jazz was viewed as infiltration by the imperialists, and it was dangerous to create and perform in the jazz genre, even illegal, (Ibid.). After Stalin's death, jazz became popular and loudly advertised by Voice of America Radio shows behind the Iron Curtain (*Jazz Hour* radio show) (Krstić, 2010, p. 184). Broadcasting jazz programs provided opportunities for cultural contact between the West and East at that time. Jazz as an imported cultural good took on deeper social and political meaning in the framework of the Cold War situation (Kajanova, Y., Pickhan, G., and Ritter, R., 2016 p. 14). While in the United States and Western Europe jazz musicians were dealing with racial segregation and social status, Eastern and Southeastern European musicians faced problems caused by communism and later socialism (Kajanova, Y., Pickhan, G., and Ritter, R. 2016, p. 9).

Starting in the late 1950s, American musicians began touring in Eastern and Southeastern Europe, and jazz festivals flourished all over the region. The type of jazz that blossomed in this part of Europe was different in style—it was determined by the current politics, but also mentality, cultural heritage, tradition and eventually social environment. By the end of the 1970s, jazz was highly appreciated in the region a protagonist art form.

According to Serbian jazz historian and musician, Krstić (2010), the integration of jazz music was strongly intertwined with Balkan traditional music, which resulted in jazz not becoming popular in its original form. At that time, jazz could only be heard in several clubs, at taverns, or at school parties, although the music played there was not jazz in its true form. Namely, the repertoire that was played was a compilation of the popular hits, dancing, and traditional songs, but included drums (Blam, 2011, p. 125). Jazz at that time was not considered an art form or improved music genre, but the "hot" entertainment for "the rich guests" (Blam, 2011, p. 71). Starting in the 1950s due to Yugoslavia being less controlled by communist forces than Eastern Europe, musicians were free to travel outside the country and invite performances by prominent jazz musicians. American musicians started touring Yugoslavia and the first regional collaborations occurred in Bled (Slovenia) at the beginning of the 1960s (Krstić, 2010, pp. 184–187). Shortly after that, the first jazz festivals, tours, and concerts promoted jazz as "elite" music.[2] At the same time, this privileged freedom of Balkan musicians, legal permission to copy and sound like the "West", made jazz less original, daring, and innovative. The mainstream styles like swing, be-bop, and hard-bop, were considered the "original" jazz in Yugoslavia and cherished by "the gatekeepers" of the genre. Southeastern Europe (*semiperiphery*—a term coined by Blagojević (2009) for Eastern, Southeastern and Central Europe, *periphery* for the rest of the world, concerning the relation with the West as a *center*) "showed some effort to catch up with the core (the United States, West), on one hand, and to resist the integration into the core, so not to lose its cultural characteristics, on the other hand" (Blagojević, 2009, pp. 33–34). Moreover, "globalization" in Serbia had a very negative connotation in the 1990s, perceived as something that endangers "Serbian interests" rather than being a logical continuation of multiculturalism and technological progress (Hughson 2015, p. 53). One aspect of an authentic identity of the semiperipheral nations with the "desire for the West" is the preservations of the "original" traditional jazz style among players in Yugoslavia ("American jazz wanna be"). Nevertheless, I pinpoint an inability for new inventions in jazz expression, except fusion with our own folklore that reflects the tension between "modernization", "Westernization" and the opposite: "pragmatic interpretation of tradition in isolation" (Blagojević, 2009, p. 34).

Since the 1960s, regional big bands were the only "institutional" jazz in the Southeastern European region, mostly preserving said values of traditional jazz. At the same time, jazz musicians in Poland, Czechoslovakia, and Hungary went underground during the communist regime.[3] Jazz could only be heard in hidden garages and basements, and was considered politically illegal as an art form, an expression of rebellion, authenticity, and provocation by the artist community. In comparison to Southeastern Europe, East European jazz was more creative, original and freer in its form. The narrative from fifty years ago is still present today, such as cherishing the classical mainstream jazz in the Southeast, or fostering new forms with avant-garde approaches further East. Moreover, some contemporary approaches, for example experimental and novel aesthetics, are very rare in Yugoslavia, while Polish jazz became a symbol of progressive European jazz identity.

What strengthens patriarchal values of jazz tradition in Southeastern Europe is a clearly defined stylistic perception of jazz. The various interpretations of common repertoire, generally referred to as *jazz standards,* are characteristic for mainstream jazz (McBride, 2018). *Performing a* jazz standard is commonly approached by using the harmonic structure of a song as a vehicle for improvisation and harmonic interpretation. Performance practice includes well-defined roles for soloists, rhythm sections, and accompanists. Similarly to verbal communication, jazz performance is guided by a certain etiquette, such as visual cues, interaction, musical syntax, or gestures. This etiquette is similar to the rules of a game or certain sports and traditionally these rules have been created and executed by men. Musicians implemented the patriarchal ideology present in their own musical traditions and social environment also in traditional jazz. What they reproduced was the social ideological pattern of tradition as well as the canonized models of representation within the micro context of the musicians' community (Nenić, 2019, p. 9). In a society that was so rigid and restricted, advancement, innovations, and changes were not able to flourish. Therefore, I argue that the Balkan mainstream etiquette perpetuates the values of the patriarchal ideology.

The Pale Image of a Balkan Jazzwoman

In the past, the expected role of a woman in Balkan society was primarily as caretaker of children and household. In the Middle Ages, music was an activity performed solely by men (Nikolić, 2016). The same was true of troubadour music. Women were idolized but not perceived as equal performers (Ibid.). While men were performing on instruments and able to make a living at the time, women could only contribute as singers, due to the fact that singing did not involve buying the instruments which were, of course, expensive (Đurić Klajn, 2000 p. 171). Women's creative engagement was mostly through folklore and passing on the folk traditions (Blagojević Hjuson, 2015, p. 137; Dević, 1990, p. 23) of handcraft, cuisine, folk artifacts, and folksong conservation. According to Blagojević, some poetic genres, such as lyrical poems, are associated solely with women. However, female performers were rarely seen in public spaces. Not until the beginning of the twenty-first century was value attributed to creativity that prospered inside the home and only in the context of tradition and strengthening national self-awareness (Blagojević, 2015, p. 137). The traditional instrumental music of Serbia rarely features female instrumentalists and is regarded as an "outlier", as "an exception that confirms the rule that a musician is always a man by nature and the strength of his sex" (Nenić, 2019, p. 9). These attitudes have been transferred into the jazz genre, hence female instrumentalists function only at the intersection of the public and private spheres.

The end of the twentieth century brought many social changes in gender roles and attitudes in post–Yugoslavia. I am an example of a woman raised in the time of transition, where the communist and socialist ideology was coded into a new post-socialist narrative. The generation of our parents, a middle class of that time, was symbolic for a successful and happy environment, where everyone had just enough to cover what was needed. Growing up in socialism and post–socialism, I was taught that we are all equal, with equal opportunities and the right to choose. Among other things, women were portrayed as successful decision-makers, heroic nationalists, or strong workers. Images only included strong workers in the common workforce, though, not in the creative or intellectual communities. When I think back now, I cannot recall any images of female cultural workers or academics. As a teenager, I chose learning the saxophone in an environment that seemed to encourage free choice and following my dreams. However, the absence of women from public life in post–communist systems extended the effects of the communist patriarchal legacy, which gave women legal rights (to work, to equal pay, to education, divorce and abortion), but prevented them from participating in public decision-making or even making their own professional choices (Papić, 2015 p. 122).

Exclusion of women in the public sphere and engaging in cultural life during the first half of the twentieth century was justified by a sense of cultural elitism and the fact that women had limited access to education as well as the exploitation of female labor. In the 1970s and 1980s, women were referred to as a "marginal group" which, like other marginal groups, is excluded from higher professions and creative work in general. Initially, the socialist movement during the 1980s seemed to break down the elitist attitudes towards wider inclusion of marginalized groups, including women. During 1982, with new developments and technology, Yugoslavia seemed to move towards the center of Europe, away from the historical *semiperiphery* (Blagojević, 2015, p. 142).

However, during the 1990s, a focus on consumerism replaced the support of high culture, specifically in the former Yugoslavia, but also in other semiperipheral societies. One prominent example is the turbo-folk music in Serbia (Blagojević, 2015, p. 142). As a result, the real creative public work of women remained *subversive*. Some women were engaged in public life, but too often just as a side-product of said consumerism denying any options for status change. Basically, 1990s were a contextualized variant of the socialist patriarchy (Blagojević, 2015, p. 12). As a young woman at that time, I experienced this social phenomenon as a sign to be *bold and courageous*, copying the image of a nationalistic woman form the primary school textbooks; to resist, to provoke, to rebel, and to show the feminist spirit in every action and choice I made, as the only choice I could make. It became *normal* to fight for participation and equal rights. Hence, experiencing tokenism, a rare woman among men in the jazz community, confirmed the ideology that was imposed on our young women.

Historically, in jazz, as well as most cultural activities, gender roles are clearly assigned—men play the instruments, whereas women sing and/or dance (Annfelt, 2003, p. 2). In the *law of culture,* female music players were considered "others" (Nenić, 2019) in relation to the male ones, according to the dominating patriarchal values in which more power and visibility was given to instrumental music-making and from which women were, unfortunately, excluded.

There are numerous jazz history books, chapters, research papers, and articles concerning Eastern and Southeastern Europe, but none of them include female instrumentalists, as I document below. There were almost none, and there are currently only a few female active jazz instrumentalists on the scene in Southeastern Europe (Maja Avlanović, Milena Jančurić, Nevena Pejčić, Lana Janjanin, Bruna Matić, Marina Milošević, Sanja Marković, Fani Posa, Milica Božović, Jasna Jovićević).[4] This environment, with only a few role models is not a supportive environment for the next generations of female musicians to come.

As mentioned, vocalists were traditionally acknowledged as active participants, even though the numbers were still small. After analyzing the literature, I was not able to find recognition in public media for female instrumentalists active over the last two decades. Recently, women have received more space in new historical narratives in the West in an attempt to overcome gender barriers; however, no such attempts can be found in the Balkan region. Outstanding Yugoslav musicians Miša

Krstić (2010) and Miša Blam (2011) shared that women were only mentioned if they were engaged in "oriental and traditional dance and jazz ballet" aiming to "relax the guests" (Blam, 2011, p. 71). In other words, their role was to entertain the audience with jazz. Similarly, in *Vek Džeza* (*The Century of Jazz*) written by Krstić, only few female singers are mentioned, whereas female instrumentalists were not included in his review. Such exclusion erases the contribution of female instrumentalists to the art form jazz, as not even the female instrumentalists who actually performed and recorded with the bands mentioned in the same book are discussed or featured in any way.

In the most recent book on jazz history globally and regionally, Serbian writer Erčić (2015) elaborates on the genre aesthetics and styles but also provides insights into a brief world history of jazz. The jazz and aesthetics chapter of this book explains the roots and early development of jazz. In the section on influential international groups and performers, the author mentions no female players, although there are legendary all-female bands that travelled extensively in the 1940s, especially on USA tours during World War II. However, the author marginalizes the participation of female musicians in a separate section "Women in Jazz, and the Singers", a common narrative in recent historical revisions portraying their roles as outliers: "There have *also* been female ..." (Erčić, 2015). In the same book, a short biography of Lil Hardin, a remarkable piano player, is introduced with the following sentence: "Perhaps her greatest merit is that Lil Hardin was married to the legendary trumpeter Louis Armstrong, and she taught him how to read music" (Erčić, 2015, p. 237). Mary Lou Williams, a famous jazz piano player, also called the "Mother of Bebop", according to Erčić, "was praised by her colleagues, despite her gender" (Ibid.). The author explains that she developed her own style of piano playing, although her attitude was "not defensive at all, what would be expected from a lady, but it is strong and aggressive, what rather befits to a man" (Ibid.). Unfortunately, such passive-aggressive rhetoric often attributing any achievement of females to the support of men and comparing their work to male standards are quite prominent jazz history literature and analysis. The rest of the US jazzwomen biographies in this book are mostly stories about their private lives, love affairs, their famous father figures and husbands, the emotional status and behavior, with no mention of their professional achievements, music, discographies, performances, or important collaborations and contributions to the genre. Unfortunately female musicians are presented as outlier phenomena who happen to be on the jazz scene, playing an instrument "unusual for a girl" (Erčić, 2015, p. 239). This book does not include any regional female players, although it is widely used in the region as a textbook of jazz.

The cultural contributions of women in the private sphere (as wife, sister, lover of a musician, woman musician), and the representation of her identity as "novelty and exception" seem more relevant and socially more accepted in the regional literature than achievements inside the jazz practice (as musician). *Primenjena Muzika* (*Applied Music*) by Simjanović (1996), a well-known and recognized film and TV composer, is the textbook that students of Management in Culture at the Faculty of Dramatic Arts in Belgrade use during their bachelor's studies. In the entire chapter on the general and Yugoslav history of music, which includes the history of twentieth-century contemporary jazz, pop, and rock music, the only female musicians mentioned are Yugoslavian composer Ljubica Marić[5] and Ella Fitzgerald (American vocalist). The *Illustrated Jazz Encyclopedia* translated into Serbo-Croatian (Kutanjac, 1980), mentions only a handful of female jazz musicians (Carla Bley, Alice Coltrane, Blossom Dearie, Ella Fitzgerald, Billy Holliday, Ma Rainey, Annie Ross, Bessie Smith, Sarah Vaughn, and few more) elaborating mostly on their private lives and the significance of their fathers and husbands, rather than their musical contributions. For example, it presents Alice Coltrane as the second wife of a distinguished tenor saxophone player (Kutanjac, 1980). This edition portrays Mary Lou Williams's style as "too strong performance, just like a man" (ibid., p. 220), reinforcing stereotypical presentations in other Yugoslavian jazz publications. This jazz encyclopedia includes a section on regional jazz musicians, with the mention of only one female singer, Nada Knežević, and no instrumentalists at all. I suggest further studying and researching local and regional jazz histories that can offer a powerful means of addressing gender issues. It is possible that hidden histories, herstories, critical theories such as tokenism, stereotyping, gender performativity, interpellation, gender and self-efficacy, and others could provide new insights into the complexity of the process of dominant narratives' creation from the past.

What is very important for the promotion of feminist ideology is the fact that female ethnomusicologists, cultural workers, and musicologists are the ones who take an active part in this process. Some of the active female researchers in music of Southeastern Europe are Tatjana Nikolić, Iva Nenić, Jelena Novak, Adriana Sabo, Ivana Neimarević, and Olivera Vojna Nešić. By mentioning some of the remarkable female players and bands in Southeastern Europe, as well as in the rest of the World, these authors elevate female creativity, advocacy, and action by highlighting the gender inequality present on the regional music scene. Their role in the discussion on gender issues in regional music scene is pivotal since their texts provoke and enhance the changes that are truly needed.

I conclude that the Southeastern European female players have been excluded from the prominent jazz scene for two reasons; the traditional dominance of masculinity in jazz reinforced by Balkan traditions and the political struggles between communism, socialism, and democracy in a patriarchic society.

A New Spark is Born

During my professional development, I have always struggled with stereotypes. Regardless of the place I found myself—Serbia, where I live, Hungary, Austria, Brazil, the United States, or Canada, where I have worked or studied—I always felt the barriers of stereotype and limited access. In this marginalized position, I have observed the current situation critically and from a feminist point of view.

Traditionally, the goal of feminist movements was to unite and, through solidarity, fight for equality, proving that there is a place at the table in the regional scene. Similarly, at the beginning of the 2000's, I was a member of an all-female jazz saxophone quartet[6] as well as a guest in an all-female big band in Budapest.[7] At that time, female musicians started to receive more recognition in the United States and Western Europe due to an increasing awareness of lingering issues, whereas in Hungary such formations were not considered "normal" but rather "extraordinary", sometimes sexy, "girly" or sometimes "bold and courageous". All-female bands were considered entertainment and feminist movements, while the question of class, race or political statements dominated the perception of male ensembles. After spending 20 years in the Hungary, United States and Canada working with internationally acclaimed musicians of all genres as leader and sidewoman, I decided to form an all-female regional ensemble in serbia. A pilot project entitled the New Spark Orchestra—the Balkan Women in Jazz[8] (NSJO) included women from Serbia, Montenegro, and Macedonia. The goal of the project was to increase the participation of female instrumentalists and composers in the music scene of the region. Additional goals were to improve musicianship and offer professional education. The mission of the project was to directly influence the cultural development of the region, promoting the visibility of female artists and music professionals.

As discussed earlier, the Balkan countries feature mainly patriarchal societies. Therefore, major investment from both participants and consumers was needed to create and position a female jazz orchestra in a hostile market. The role of the orchestra was to highlight and uncover sociological problems by playing a prominent role in the regional music scene. Since female jazz musicians do not match the typical image of a successful woman in this social context, they often remain isolated and overlooked. Eventually, these women simply become hidden figures.

Participants of the NSJO project represented some of the pioneers in the region and forerunners of an integrated status in the industry. However, the deeply rooted perception that a woman does not play jazz in the Balkans affects not only consumers but also the musicians themselves. After two residencies, we organized two regional tours. While male jazz musicians were featured on the main stages of popular jazz festivals supported by prominent managers and agents, we were self-organized and often delegated to the smaller side stages of festivals. Not surprisingly, the tour of this orchestra was portrayed in the media as a curiosity or even completely ignored by the media and jazz audiences.

Similarly, during the presentation of workshops and educational sessions, I observed the hesitancy of some group members to contribute their own music and knowledge, lacking the needed confidence in their abilities. They were convinced that they were not "good enough" or that they "could not play as well as men do". The lack of self-efficacy caused by the social environment, was obvious and destructive. Fortunately, this program also helped jumpstart the careers of many instrumentalists who have become regional musical leaders. Some others were able to study abroad, others have become active local participants.

Unfortunately, a major cause of the small number of professional female jazz musicians is also the large dropout rate of jazz students in secondary school programs. There is a significant number of girls in high school jazz programs studying the style, learning to improvise, and becoming fluent jazz players. However, when it comes to deciding for a possible professional career as a jazz musician facing the demands of finding performances and the needed education, most women quit due to a number of obstacles. One main reason is the lack of role models in the profession and the lack of professional support for artists during their education. Also, the lifestyle required for a jazz career which includes constant organization of performances, tours, rehearsals, nightlife, long absences from home and family, and little socialization with non-musicians—all major deterrents. Especially difficult is combining responsibilities of motherhood with a jazz musician's lifestyle. Being a jazz musician in Serbia is already difficult, but being a mother and a jazz musician is close to impossible. Accordingly, the callout for participation in the NSJO encouraged especially mothers to apply. Wherever we traveled together during the program, they were allowed to bring along their babies and one more adult family member to look after the children.

There are not many female role models in current jazz scenes and history books, neither as bandleaders, composers, side women nor touring musicians. For example, there is not even one female player in all the regional big bands[9] (Serbia, Croatia, Slovenia), and those orchestras are the main representation of the regional music scene. Recently, the regional big orchestras formed a collaborative regional project called Jumbo Big Band, which united 3 big bands, consisting of 51 men on stage, playing jazz music together. There are now a few jazz departments at the university level[10] that are educating new generations of jazz musicians. Nonetheless, the percentage of female students is extremely low. In all three academic jazz education programs there is no female instrumental instructor, which raises questions of professional support, pedagogy, and safety. I analyzed the major jazz festivals' programs of the last 15 to 20 years in Serbia and lineups of the Belgrade Jazz Festival, Novi Sad Jazz Festival, and Niš Jazz Festival. The estimation shows that only 4 percent of the festival performers are female players. But, more precisely, only slightly more than 1 percent are regional female instrumentalists, while the rest are female musicians from the United States, Canada or Western Europe.

The perception of female instrumentalists as novelty lingers on. Even though I have often played as a sidewoman, every time I am a bandleader, I am recognized as different—as a "woman in jazz"— and therefore take part in the festivals that are designed for female performers exclusively. Women have been a fundamental component of new jazz styles such as free improvised music, experimental jazz, cross-over, and multidisciplinary projects (ecology, biological, experimental, free improvised, conceptual, etc.). The number of female music performers in Europe and the rest of the world is expanding[11] in all of these genres, as well as the number of supportive networks aimed at fostering their professional development.[12] The ultimate goal is to modify, intercede and reformat the narrative of traditional jazz formats and etiquette. For female creativity, the abovementioned music genres represent an important form of expression with an openness for diversity, new artistic expression, and different cultural contexts. These genres are not popular nor financially rewarding but are fertile ground for open social collaboration, transformative practices and new development of identities.

Conclusion

From its beginnings, jazz as a genre has been dominated by masculinity and competition, allowing for little female participation. Efforts are being made in supporting the creative output of the female community as well as rebranding the image of female instrumentalists and fostering initiatives in cultural policy and the music industry towards a slow-moving but noticeable shift towards representation of female identity in jazz. On the Southeast side of Europe we have the New Spark Jazz Orchestra for Jazz affirming new female actors on the jazz scene and the Female Leadership in Music (FLIM) project promoting women in music.[13] Furthermore, major music, social, educational and policy initiatives have emerged aiming to affirm, promote, and propagate gender balanced jazz music scenes in the United States and Canada: the We Have Voice Collective,[14] Terri Lyne Carrington and the Berklee Institute for Jazz and Gender Justice,[15] the Women in Jazz Organization (WIJO),[16] Local 802[17] with Roxy Coss, SHEroes[18] with Monika Herzig, Washington Women in Jazz Festival,[19] Jazz Girls Days, the Sisters in Jazz Program[20] run by the Jazz Educational Network (JEN), Women in Jazz Collective Boston.[21] Similarly to the United States and Canada but not since the early 2000s, Western European cultural and media policies focus on gender imbalanced jazz music scene. The European Jazz Network (EJN) with its Manifesto on Gender Balanced Jazz scenes[22] for European festivals, Women in Jazz Sweden,[23] Women in Jazz UK,[24] Swiss SOFIA,[25] Women in Music Italy,[26] Pafrum de Jazz Festival,[27] France, and others are taking actions towards equal female participation. In Sweden, alternative women-only and girls-only spaces offer opportunities to network, to perform, and to develop technical and artistic skills in a supportive environment.[28] Two national reports commissioned by the Swedish government (Sweden 2006; Statens kulturråd 2009) prove that jazz music is the least gender-equal performing arts sector in terms of resources distributed. These reports also uncovered a continued sex-stereotyped representation of jazz female instrumentalists.[29] There are also a few national or EU strategies, such as the equality strategy in 2010 by the Swedish Arts Council and the new Swedish agency, Musikverket, which is tasked by the government to support initiatives aiming for greater gender equality in music; the European Expert Network on Cultural and Audiovisual (EENCA); the European Music Council; and the Keychange initiative.[30] Consequently, a cultural shift towards a non-gendered creative space is noticeable.

I have been walking through my career mostly among men, but over the last few years, after I let go of my need for validation of my creativity, I realize the importance of support, the feeling of belonging, trust, and acceptance in the environment in which I am creating. Being surrounded by other women in jazz is one way to promote our work together—support the initiatives of our colleagues and deconstruct the stereotypes that are imposed on us. Fortunately, the number of women in jazz has been on the rise for the past several years, and more and more instrumentalists and composers are present in this genre building a community of support and new creative opportunities.

Notes

1 Here, I am using the term *gender* as a social construct indicating that gender identity is not innate (it is not sex as a biological category which refers to the physical differences between a man and a woman), but acquired by learning and socialization, and gender roles are culturally determined. That means that what makes a person a woman or a man (femininity and masculinity) is considered a construct of a particular time and space of society and culture (Bašaragin 2019: 2).

2 "Elite" is a concept dividing the audience between those who enjoy jazz music, because they learned how to listen and understand, and are belonging to "higher middle class", opposite to the traditional lower-class, non-bourgeoisie from the cities.

3 Vojislav Pantic, informal interview, March 13, 2020.

4 These are the names I researched, but there might be more few names to add to this list, out of my knowledge.

5 As a good example of gender analyses in music of Ljubica Marić: Nataša Kostadinović, *Rodna analiza u pisanim tekstovima o kompozitorkama Srbije krajem 20. i početkom 21. veka* (Novi Sad: Univerzitet u Novom Sadu, 2014) Doktorska disertacija.

6 Classy Four Saxophone Quartet https://novisadjazzfestival.rs/Jazz-Festival-Novi-Sad/classyfoureng.htm.
7 Swing Ladies Hungary https://youtu.be/6hGNuCgw7tk.
8 Through an open call, 15 Balkan emerging women musicians and composers participated in 15 months long program as members of the New Spark Jazz Orchestra. The program includes 2 one-week-long music residencies with ensemble, and big band workshops, an on-line educational web portal, and the promotion of new jazz learning methods via symposiums led by the Educational Team. With the new professional skills acquired, and the rehearsals with original music materials, the orchestra will have four regional concerts in three countries, and publish a promotional CD/DVD of music composed by the participants. Project was supported by the European Cultural Foundation and Serbian Ministry of Culture. Visit www.nsjo.org.
9 http://mp.rts.rs/en/ensembles/rts-big-band/, http://bigband.rtvslo.si/orkester/, https://glazba.hrt.hr/273113/o-orkestru-2,
10 Jazz Departments at Faculty of Music at the University of Belgrade (Serbia), Faculty of Music at the Goce Delčev University of Štip (Macedonia), and "Franc List" Music Academy of Budapest (Hungary).
11 https://womencreativemusic.tumblr.com/.
12 http://femalepressure.net/.
13 https://fdu.bg.ac.rs/sr/fakultet/projekti-fdu/flim-female-leadership-in-music.
14 https://calendar.pitt.edu/event/we_have_voice_collective#.XvEePZozbIU.
15 www.berklee.edu/jazz-gender-justice.
16 http://wearewijo.org/.
17 www.local802afm.org/.
18 http://music.monikaherzig.com/.
19 http://washingtonwomeninjazz.com/.
20 http://jazzednet.org/sisters-in-jazz/.
21 www.facebook.com/womeninjazzcollective/.
22 www.europejazz.net/sites/default/files/EJN_Manifesto_on_gender_balance.pdf.
23 www.womeninjazzsweden.se/in-english/.
24 www.womeninjazz.co.uk/new-page.
25 www.sofia-musicnetwork.com/en/sofia-2018-en/about/.
26 www.donneinmusica.org/womenandmedia-europe/donneinmusica.htm.
27 www.parfumdejazz.com/.
28 Cecilia Bjorck and Asa Bergman, "Making Women in Jazz Visible: Negotiating Discourses of Unity and Diversity in Sweden and the US", *Journal of the International Association for the Study of Popular Music*, Vol 8. No. 1, 42–58.
    2018, DOI: 10.5429/2079-3871(2018)v8i1.5en, 43.
29 Cecilia Bjorck and Asa Bergman, "Making Women in Jazz Visible: Negotiating Discourses of Unity and Diversity in Sweden and the US", *Journal of the International Association for the Study of Popular Music*, Vol. 8, No. 1, 42–58.
    2018, DOI: 10.5429/2079-3871(2018)v8i1.5en, 44.
30 https://keychange.eu/.

References

Adkins Chiti, P. (2007). *Women in Jazz, Donne in Jazz*. Italy: Foundazione Adkins Chiti: Donne in Musica.

Annfelt, T. (2003, July 17). Jazz as masculine space. *Kilden*. Retrieved from http://kjonnsforskning.no/en/2003/07/jazz-masculine-space.

Bašaragin, M. (2019). *Rod, kultura i diskurs razgovora u razredu* [*Gender, Culture, and the Discourse of the Language in the Classroom*]. Novi Sad, Serbia: Fondacija akademika Bogumila Hrabaka za publikovanje doktorskih disertacija.

Blagojević Hjuson, M. (2015). *Sutra je bilo juče* [*Tomorrow was Yesterday*]. Novi Sad, Serbia: Zavod za ravnopravnost polova.

Blagojević, M. (2009). *Knowledge Production at the Semiperiphery: Gender Perspective*. Belgrade: Institut za kriminološka i sociološka istraživanja.

Blam, M. (2011). *Jazz u Srbiji 1927-1944* [*Jazz in Serbia 1927–1944*]. Belgrade: Stubovi kulture.

Dević, D. (1990). *Narodna muzika Crnorečja u svetlu etnogenetskih procesa* [Traditional *Music of Crnorečje in the Light of Ethnogenetic Processes*]. Belgrade: JP Štampa, radio i film Bor, Kulturno-obrazovni centar Bojevac, FMU Beograd.

Dimitrijević, Z. (2009, November 14). Polski Jazz: Začeci. *Jazzin*. Retrieved from www.jazzin.rs/polski-jazz-1-zaceci/.

Đurić Klajn, S. (2000). Uloga žene u muzici [Woman`s Role in Music]. *Časopis za žensku književnost i kulturu ProFemina,* 21(22), 170–171.

Erčić, J. (2015). *Knjiga o džezu* [*The Book of Jazz*]. Belgrade: RTS Izdavaštvo.

Hughson, M. (2015). *Poluperiferija i rod: pobuna konteksta* [Semiperiphery and the Gender: Rebellion of the Context]. Belgade: Institut za kriminološka i sociološka istraživanja.

Kajanova, Y., Pickhan, G., and Ritter, R. (2016). *Jazz from Socialist Realism to Postmodernism.* Frankfurt: Peter Lang Edition.

Knauer, W. (2016). Gender and Identity in Jazz. *Darmstadt Studies in Jazz Research Vol. 14.* Darmstadt, Germany: Jazzinstitut Darmstadt.

Krstić, M. (2010). *Vek Džeza- Od Sent Luisa do Beograda.* Belgrade: Zavod za udžbenike.

Kutanjac, M. (ed.) (1980). *Jazz-ilustrovana Enciklopedija* [Jazz Illustrated Encyclopedia] translated by Dražen Vodoljak. Zagreb: Mladost.

McBride, C. (2018, May 8). What Makes A Jazz Standard? *NPR.* Retrieved from www.npr.org/2018/05/21/613091545/what-makes-a-jazz-standard. accessed 23.06.2020.

Nenić, I. (2019). *Guslarke i sviračice* [Female Gusla Players and instrumentalists]. Belgrade: Clio.

Nikolić, T. (2016). *Rodni odnosi na alternativnoj muzičkoj sceni Srbije i regiona* [Gender Relations on Alternative Music Scene in Serbia and Region]. Novi Sad, Serbia: Pokrajinski zavod za ravnopravnost polova.

Papić, Z. (2015). Women in Serbia: Post-Communism, and Nationalist Mutations. In J. Blagojević, K. Kolozova and S. Slapšak (Eds.), *Gender and Identity* (pp.122–140). Belgrade: ATHENA and Regional Network for Gender/Women Studies.

Simjanović, Z. (1996). *Primenjena muzika* [Applied Music]. Belgrade: Bikić Studio.

Statens kulturråd. 2009. På Väg mot jämställd Scenkonst [On the Road to Gender-Equal Performing Arts], Kulturrådets skriftserie 2009:1. Stockholm: Statens kulturråd [Swedish Arts Council]. www.kulturradet.se/Documents/publikationer/2009/pa_vag_mot_jamstalld.pdf. Accessed: 1 December 2017.

Sweden. Kommittén för jämställdhet inom scenkonstområdet [Committee for Gender Equality in the Performing Arts]. 2006. Plats på scen. Betänkande [On stage. Report]. Stockholm: Fritze. www.regeringen.se/rattsdokument/statens-offentliga-utredningar/2006/04/sou-200642/ Accessed: 27 December 2017.

37

ADDRESSING GENDER IMBALANCE THROUGH MENTORSHIP AND ADVOCACY

Ellen Rowe

Clarification of Intent: For purposes of streamlining the prose, whenever the terms "female" "woman" or "women" are used, they should be construed to mean "female-identifying" and inclusive of all who identify as female. I personally identify as a cisgender female.

Introduction

I have been blessed to have had a 35-year career in jazz education, composition, and performance. I have been privileged to have led NAfME All-Eastern and All-Northwest Honor Jazz Ensembles, in addition to many All-State and All-District high school honor groups. I get to travel around the world giving clinics, adjudicating festivals and contests, performing with my various professional groups and running or teaching at summer camps. I also chaired the Department of Jazz and Contemporary Improvisation at the University of Michigan for 10 years before stepping down to make more time for my own performing and composing. In several of these categories I was the first woman to ever serve in those capacities, and it has given me a great perspective from which to consider the issues I am addressing. Much of what is included in this chapter are my "on the ground" analyses of what I see taking place and ideas that I have been developing throughout my time as a jazz educator. I have chosen to rely less on citations and speak more from personal experience in some instances, as I believe that my status as a pioneer in certain aspects of the field has positioned me well to write in more of a narrative format.

Anyone who has attended a collegiate jazz band festival has had the experience of staring at the stage as band after band performs, and seeing the remarkable disparity between numbers of male and female instrumentalists in the groups. I often see no female members whatsoever. There are almost no women directors and generally no compositions or arrangements by female composers. The decline in numbers of female instrumental jazz from high school to college may be a contributing factor to disproportionate gender representation in collegiate jazz bands. A survey of 628 students from 15 college music programs found that women were far less likely to have played jazz in college unless they played a traditional jazz instrument in high school (McKeage, 2004). Additionally, only 26 percent of females who played jazz in high school tried

DOI: 10.4324/9781003081876-41

doing so at the collegiate level, yet 62 percent of males played jazz in both high school and college (McKeage, 2004).

In the professional world it is often not much better, as one can look at a major festival program book and find a few vocalists as headliners but often only one or two instrumentalists leading their own bands. It has only been in the last five to ten years that serious attention has been given to these imbalances and, even more recently, that organizations around the country have initiated programs to try and support young women in their pursuit of jazz performance and composition or to address the lack of representation at festivals and concert series. While more female jazz students are graduating from college and university programs than in the past, and more are finding professional success, the numbers still skew decisively in favor of men. This chapter intends to look at why this disparity exists, and what can be done to help rectify it, both in secondary school and college programs as well as during women's professional careers.

Early Development through Secondary School

As I travel around the country giving workshops or adjudicating big band festivals, I often see that there are many young women performing in elementary jazz bands and middle school bands. These numbers decline in high school, however, and even more so once these students go to college. The question then becomes, why are young women dropping out of their jazz bands as they get older and not pursuing the study of jazz seriously in high school or college?

There are many issues that contribute to this problem. While numbers of visible, successful female jazz instrumentalists are on the rise, the great majority of performers are still men, making it more difficult for young women to readily see role models. In addition, at festivals where I adjudicate, it is apparent that male high school jazz band directors far outnumber female directors while the percentages favor men even more so at the collegiate level. Shaker (2020) noted that the College Music Society *Directory of Music Faculties in Colleges and Universities, U.S. and Canada 2017-2018* listed women as representing only 11.3 percent of college band director positions in the United States and, from my experience, I would say that that percentage drops even lower when considering female jazz band directors. Even more striking is that only around 10 percent of jazz academics are female (Van Vleet, 2021). More young women might be encouraged to continue if they could see themselves in their director and received a level of mentorship and support that might more readily come from a woman. Female band and jazz band directors have often experienced gender bias themselves and are thus attuned to the needs of their female students. I remember full well the experience of being instructed by a male band director as to how I should set up my jazz band when I was selected to conduct my first All-District high school honors jazz group and the many experiences I have had at All-State festivals where sound engineers have initially disrespected me and my specific requests until they finally figured out that I knew what I was talking about. These are just a few of the many experiences that I have had where I have been forced to prove myself rather than be treated with the assumption that I was competent. In a Q&A published on the McGill University website, Dr. Tammy Kernodle, an internationally recognized scholar and teacher in the areas of African American music and gender studies, was asked what prejudices young musicians might need to unlearn. She stated:

> Train your mind and ear to know that when you see a woman in a performance space, she's not there because she's cute or slept with someone to get there. She had to navigate expectations and professional obstacles that 9 times out of 10 made her a better musician than many of her male peers. Men don't have to prove themselves. They just need to show up. A man can be mediocre and still get opportunities. A mediocre woman is non-existent in the performance space.
>
> *(McGill, 2020)*

In my experience working with middle school and high school jazz groups, I have found that young women of secondary school age often struggle with self-image and confidence and are also often more reticent to call attention to themselves than young men. As an important component of playing jazz involves improvising, or taking a solo, the idea of physically standing up to improvise (for saxophonists or trombonists, who generally play section parts while seated) or just having listeners' or peers' attention focused on you while making yourself vulnerable in that manner, can be highly intimidating or even traumatizing depending on attitudes within the group and its director. Many young women are deeply concerned with others' opinions at that age and often feel that they aren't "good enough" or lack the confidence to even try and solo (Wehr-Flowers, 2006). I've talked with many high school band directors, both male and female, and know that very often their young women will refuse to try and solo. They will state that they don't know enough or that they aren't as good as the guys, so are afraid to put themselves in that vulnerable situation. Ironically, many of the young men may also not really know very much about soloing, but that doesn't seem to inhibit them from going ahead. One director shared with me that the boys in her jazz band would frequently get together and have jam sessions but would never invite the girls.

Added to all of this is the fact that the expression of swing feel or the blues has historically been equated with expressions of masculinity; often, young women who are expected to convey those attributes in a similar fashion can feel awkward or "unfeminine" (Van Vleet, 2021). As a young educator I found that it took some time to even feel comfortable counting off a swinging jazz ensemble piece in a meaningful way. It required a physicality and confidence that I wasn't fully ready to convey to a group at that point in time. And, of course, I hadn't ever seen another woman count off a jazz ensemble before, so had no role models. For many professional women jazz artists, the phrase "she plays like a man" has often been intended as a compliment, though it completely robs her of her own identity and overlooks that she is expressing her own voice, not trying to emulate a man's. These stereotypical expectations of what a man or woman is "supposed" to sound like can be particularly difficult for younger women to navigate. And societal expectations as to how a women performer should look also still abound. When asked, in the same McGill University Q&A, how the controversy over a "women's place in jazz" has changed over time, Dr. Kernodle said:

> I don't think they have changed at all. Each generation of women musicians (vocalist and instrumentalist) have had to deal with the issue of dealing with preconceived notions about their abilities and also record companies and market strategies that often position their physical appearance over their musical talents.

> *(McGill, 2020)*

In order to start addressing these issues it is important to look at all the contributing factors from elementary school on up. For students who get to start playing music in a band or string program in grades 4–6, the first choice they get to make may have long-lasting ramifications. That choice is the selection of an instrument to start on. In too many instances, girls are encouraged to play flute, clarinet, violin or all the softer, treble-sounding instruments, while boys are encouraged to play the trumpet, trombone, string bass; the larger, often louder and lower instruments. Studies have shown a correlation between gender and instrument preference, often centered on existing gender stereotypes within performing ensembles and perceptions of musicians in relation to their gender and instrument (Johnson and Stewart, 2004; MacLeod, 2009). Van Vleet (2021) noted that gender stereotyping of instruments starts the gender divide at a young age. This then sets the stage for exclusion from traditional jazz bands where the instrumentation is often trumpets, trombones, saxophones, and rhythm section instruments.

While many wonderful educators make a point of creating flute, clarinet or other non-traditionally utilized instrumental parts for their students so that they can participate in the jazz band, that practice may not continue into high school. Directors may play demo audio versions of these pieces where the saxophonist or trumpeter is taking a solo, but not the clarinet or flute, as that part has been added to the arrangement after the fact. Publishers could help out here by including improvised solos by these non-traditional instruments in the recordings they usually include with the score and parts. The best solution for the gender stereotyping of instruments, however, is for elementary school teachers to encourage young women to try a variety of different instruments and to allow them to see and hear women playing the brass instruments, drum set or bass so that they can have role models.

Another factor that can explain why female students often don't continue with jazz after middle school is the overall underrepresentation of women jazz artists, as they don't see themselves in the profession (Van Vleet, 2021). Exposing young women to recordings and videos of professional jazz artists such as trumpeters Tanya Darby or Ingrid Jensen, trombonists Melba Liston Smith or Melissa Gardiner, bassists Linda Oh or Esperanza Spalding, or drummers Terri Lyne Carrington or Allison Miller (just to name a few artists on traditionally "male" instruments), could be a big help in inspiring them to consider those instruments as possibilities for themselves.

Regardless of what instrument a young woman may choose, directors of all secondary jazz bands, male and female, should work to create a supportive sense of community within their ensembles, where everyone gets a chance to solo and students aren't judged by how fast or loud they play. To encourage shy students of both genders, directors can experiment with group soloing where everyone plays together and create soloing situations where there are controls built in that students can utilize, such as limited note or rhythmic choices, if they aren't comfortable with having complete freedom in these areas. I spoke with one director who had her beginning students just improvise on one note, experimenting only with rhythms. Students can also trade two or four bar phrases if they are uncomfortable having to play for twelve or more. The nature of pieces that directors choose can also be a factor in encouraging less experienced or confident players to engage in improvising. Chord changes that stay in one key area for extended periods of time, or chords where possibly only one note in a scale would change between the chords can help make improvising seem less scary. Perhaps the biggest positive influence for young women, however, is having female clinicians come in as guest artists. For programs where budgets may not allow this, YouTube videos, Zoom visits, and other types of media are the next best choice. Most women jazz artists I know are happy to answer questions posed by young players online; I have even had pen pal relationships established with entire jazz bands at some schools. The Jazz Education Network, a group "dedicated to building the jazz arts community by advancing education, promoting performance and developing new audiences" (Jazz Education Network, n.d.), has a program where directors can apply for funds to bring in artists. The wonderful Women in Jazz Organization (Women in Jazz Organization, 2021), led by saxophonist Roxy Coss, has a mentorship program set up to pair professional female jazz artists with younger players. WIJO's aim is "to improve the experience of women and non-binary people in jazz through focusing our work on three main goals:

- To empower individuals in the organization;
- To foster inclusivity, solidarity, and strengthen the intersectional community of women and non-binary people in Jazz;
- To address inequalities in Jazz culture and on the Jazz scene through activism.

Another area where women jazz artists are not represented, to the detriment of all members of a jazz ensemble, is in large jazz ensemble composition. Dr. Peter Madsen, Coordinator of Jazz Studies at the University of Nebraska at Omaha, has been concerned with the lack of published jazz big band repertoire by women composers, and he recently expressed to me his dismay at the low numbers of pieces by women composers or arrangers in the J. W. Pepper "Basic Library" (J. W. Pepper, 2021), charts that are considered "essential" for every library. In reviewing the selections listed on the website, it would appear that only 3 out of the 300 or so listed are by women. This creates a self-perpetuating cycle. Young women don't get to play music by women composers, so it never occurs to them that they themselves could compose for jazz band. While there are many extraordinarily successful women jazz composers out there, many have opted to write only for their own bands or other professional ensembles. There are several possible solutions to this.

Directors or organizations that are in a position to commission works should make a point of seeking out women composers. Some of the women currently writing for professional groups could be invited to write for younger groups, given that they have the prerequisite knowledge of how to create accessible works for younger players. Directors could also reach out to women currently being published by companies like Sierra Music, Kendor Music, Doug Beach Music or ejazzlines, for example, for new pieces or for recommendations of other successful women writers who might not be published yet. All-women big bands such as Sherrie Maricle and DIVA (www.divajazz.com), Maiden Voyage, or the Seattle Women's Jazz Orchestra (www.facebook.com/seattlewomensjazzorchestra) could be contacted for the names of female composers as well. The Seattle Women's Jazz Orchestra already runs a composition contest specifically for women composers and organizations like the International Society for Jazz Arrangers and Composers (IASJAC.org) that are also considering initiatives like this. In order to start leveling the playing field, these kinds of contests and incentives need to continue to grow. Once more women are getting commissioned, published, and invited to guest-conduct their work, then more young women will be able to imagine themselves doing the same.

Another way young women can build overall confidence is through programs like "Girls on the Run," an organization devoted to empowering young women through running and community-building. GOTR has 185 chapters in different parts of the country, including Michigan, and I have had the wonderful experience of volunteering at races. Witnessing the pride and confidence that these young women exude after completing their first 5k group run (and there is no prize for "winning," each girl gets the same goodie bag and medal and all wear the race number "1") is incredibly inspiring. On their website they state

> Girls on the Run reaches girls at a critical stage, strengthening their confidence at a time when society begins to tell them they can't. Underscoring the important connection between physical and emotional health, our program addresses the whole girl when she needs it the most.
>
> *(Girls on the Run, 2021)*

Girls I have talked to who have participated in the program speak of feeling empowered by both the physical activity and the sense of community they develop with their teammates. This kind of confidence-building can have wonderful ramifications for many parts of their lives, including music-making and improvisation specifically.

College and University Programs

As female jazz students enter collegiate jazz studies programs, they are also often embarking on the beginnings of professional careers. While they are working to develop their skill sets alongside their male peers, I have found that they are often also in need of extra mentoring when it comes to marketing themselves, getting gigs and learning to display their skills with confidence. As mentioned earlier, without good role models, it's difficult for women to see themselves in the profession. In McKeage's (2002/2014) examination of one collegiate university music department, female jazz musicians couldn't identify any specific female role models. At the University of Michigan, the women jazz faculty, including myself, bassist Marion Hayden, and Contemplative Practice Lecturer

Martha Travers, take the young women in our program out once a semester for "Girls Night Out". This gives us a chance to hear about their concerns and to brainstorm strategies to address them. Providing them with the benefit of our experience is truly valuable to them, and these sessions provide a safe space for them to talk about harassment, demeaning comments and the like. They frequently ask how to be assertive and display themselves confidently, as too often women of all ages are labeled as "bitchy" or overly aggressive when they assert themselves in a manner that would be considered completely appropriate in a man. Younger women especially may also feel that they have to play "like a man" to be taken seriously. Ironically, I remember being told that I sounded too much like Bill Evans when I was in college, so while it was apparently fine for Bill Evans to often choose to play lyrically, it was a sign of weakness in a woman.

Added to the difficulty of asserting themselves in an arena where they are almost always in the minority is the issue of sexual harassment. Historically, sexism and discrimination have been common within jazz groups, and gendered statements such as, "You play good, for a girl," have added to the difficulties women face when participating in jazz (Van Vleet, 2021). While there is more awareness about this issue than ever before, it does not stop male musicians and teachers from exploiting power dynamics in the classroom and on the bandstand. Several brave young female jazz students, including Sasha Berliner, in an open letter to Ethan Iverson (Berliner, 2017), have come forward to report harassment and abuse in their university jazz programs. In 2017 the *Boston Globe* detailed what they described as a "blatant culture of sexual harassment" at the Berklee College of Music and wrote that several faculty members had been "quietly let go" (Lazar, 2017). The article continued, "Administrators at the renowned music school tolerated lecherous behavior, former Berklee students and employees said, and often silenced the accusers through financial settlements with gag orders attached." Even when a male teacher may be "quietly let go," sometimes they are easily able to get a new teaching job somewhere else.

In addition to full-time or part-time faculty, guest artists can also be problematic. Several years ago, we had a guest at our institution who told the drummers he was working with that they were "playing the drums like they were beating a woman." The young women in attendance (and many of the young men) were shocked, but even more so by the fact that when they later questioned the use of this language, the responses ranged from "you have to learn to deal with stuff like that," or "it's just a generational thing," to "guests can say problematic things." When the female student relaying the story to me asked how I would have responded had I been in attendance, I told her that I would have spoken up at the time and invited the young women to leave the room with me if they so chose. In this instance, with no women faculty there, nothing was said about it during the session. On other occasions, during conference meetings or clinics, I have been leading sessions and had a male colleague enter the room and start to take over the session from me. From these experiences and those of other female friends around the country, it becomes obvious that the patriarchy in jazz and academia in general, whether conscious or unconscious, is still alive and well despite claims to the contrary. I also find it very disheartening to see artists with documented incidents of sexual harassment in their past continuing to get hired for workshops at universities and/or summer workshops because they happen to be friends with the people in charge.

As mentioned earlier, I meet with my female students as a group several times a year and am always deeply saddened to hear their stories and to have them continue to need to ask for advice as to how to deal with uncomfortable situations when playing gigs or attending rehearsals. I now counsel them to be proactive, not reactive. Trying to address a harassment situation as it is unfolding in real time can be difficult at best; deflecting or rebuffing unwanted attention may be beyond the power of a young woman taken by surprise. I advise my students to think through situations that might possibly arise and to plan for how they might handle it in advance. Having language ready to turn down a proposition, being ready to give up a gig if an unsafe situation presents itself, planning how to not be alone with a fellow musician who may be seeking more than a musical relationship, and even carrying mace or a whistle may all be necessary, depending on the individual situation.

One resource that has been particularly helpful to me has been the "We Have Voice" collective and their Code of Conduct, which is designed to help promote safer workplaces in the art (We Have Voice, n.d.). They also list resources and articles on their website that deal with assault, consent, how to respond as a bystander, grooming and how to spot the warning signs of potential sexual misconduct, mental health for musicians, overall support, and gender and racial bias. I share the Code of Conduct and website with all my students. While I am happy and proud that the University of Michigan can provide a supportive environment for its female jazz musicians (our incoming 2021 freshman class will be 33% female), this isn't always the case, as many other institutions have no full-time female faculty.

Another aspect that may affect both high school and college age students is the omission of women jazz artists in many jazz history books. While mention is usually made of the more well-known jazz vocalists such as Bessie Smith, Billie Holiday, Ella Fitzgerald or Sarah Vaughan, there is often scant reference to instrumentalists or composer/arrangers. Out of curiosity, I recently grabbed several well-regarded texts off my shelf and found one (Gridley, 1998) that only mentioned four female non-vocalists in the index and another more recent one (Lawn, 2007), whose index included approximately 350 artists and groups, only 18 of which were female non-vocalists. To be fair, there has been a second edition of this book released in 2013 that features expanded coverage of women in jazz, but these omissions and oversights have only started to be addressed in the last seven or eight years. Fortunately, there have been some recent documentaries, such as the excellent *The Girls in the Band* (Chaikin, 2011), and the ground-breaking *Lady Be Good* (2007) and *In Her Hands: Key Changes in Jazz* (Ray, 2019) by Kay D. Ray that have highlighted the many important and overlooked women jazz instrumentalists and their contributions to the music. On *The Girls in the Band* website, Aaron Hills of the *Village Voice* is quoted as saying "It's a cultural travesty that the women of early jazz … have become a neglected footnote in music history, but Judy Chaikin's well-researched, buoyantly entertaining documentary portrait could be the corrective" (*The Girls in the Band*, 2021). Many have expressed the hope that these films will lead to a corrective view of jazz history, one that needs to be documented in revisions of previous texts or articulated in new ones.

Advocacy

Advocacy for change that will lead to greater numbers of women jazz artists and composers needs to happen on many different fronts. Young girls need to be encouraged to play whatever instrument appeals to them, and in order for that to happen it may be helpful to introduce them to videos or live performances by female jazz trumpeters, trombonists or other non-traditionally "female" instruments as mentioned earlier. For this to happen, however, there needs to be elementary or secondary school band directors attuned to these issues, which means that college music education and jazz education students need to be made aware of this kind of historical gender bias and offered suggestions to combat it. For that to happen, I feel that university music education professors need to have had gender-awareness training and must then include pertinent course materials that address these issues in their classes. This also speaks to the need for curricular reform that would include jazz education pedagogy as a requirement for all music education students and that would also address the gender imbalance issues at play and the reasons for them. At the University of Michigan, I have created a jazz pedagogy course for Music Education majors and our Jazz/Music Education double majors that is unfortunately not a required course yet but is at least a step forward. I try to hire a diverse group of lecturers for the class and make sure to address gender and social justice issues. The hiring of professors in music education and jazz departments who are attuned to issues of conscious and unconscious gender and racial bias then becomes key in the implementation of these changes. Continuing up the chain, these types of faculty members need to be hired by search committees that are actively seeking out applicants who will lead the way with regard to gender and racial discrimination.

In other areas, similar "food chains" exist. Young women who do get selected for honor jazz bands need to see women leading those groups. In order for women to lead those groups, state-wide NAfME chapters or band director association selection committees need to make a conscious effort to search out competent women directors (of which there are many!) and make those kinds of choices. This in turn means that those committees need to be populated with educators who are sensitive to gender bias issues, and are willing to be proactive with their hiring choices. As many female band and jazz band directors have expressed to me that they feel they have been the victim of an "old boy" network that has passed them over and instead rewarded male friends or colleagues for these positions, changes in selection committee processes may need to be mandated by the leadership of these various organizations. Similar situations arise with commissioning projects. Whenever I do high school or college clinics of any sort I try and promote the idea of commissions for women composers or composers of color to try to start leveling the playing field a bit. Consortiums can be a great way to realize commissioning projects—several schools or colleges can combine resources to hire a composer to create a work that they will all in turn get to perform. While I see an increase in concerts devoted to works by women composers, the actual goal should be to have women composers and composers of color represented in every concert, not just in special events. When composers representing minority constituencies are commissioned, it is also important to have them come to the schools to talk about their works, possibly conduct rehearsals, and speak at classes as well as at the concert.

The last piece of this puzzle is for these works to be published. Publishing companies need to take an active role in reaching out to underrepresented composers and arrangers to start increasing the number of published works available to jazz band directors.

Other areas where women jazz artists, educators, businesswomen, or advocates need to be represented are grant panels, award selection committees (Jazz Hall of Fame awards, magazine and radio "best of the year" type polls, Grammy awards, etc.), high school and college jazz festival adjudication, jazz education organization leadership and committees, presenting organizations' leadership, the record industry (or what's left of it), college jazz faculties, and jazz summer camp faculty. I am still amazed to see summer camp or jazz workshop faculties that either have no women at all or possibly just one female vocal instructor. There is absolutely no reason for this to continue to be the case with so many gifted women jazz artists/educators available.

A notable example of a summer jazz camp empowering young women is the New Jersey Performing Arts Council's Geri Allen All-Female Jazz Camp. Started in 2014 by the brilliant pianist, composer and educator Geri Allen, the camp has attracted young women from all over the world, representing 17 states and 6 countries, including Canada, the United Kingdom, Spain, Poland, Israel, and Australia. According to current director Regina Carter, the week-long residency for young women between the ages of 14–26, is "designed to inspire and instruct those who aspire to a professional career in performing and/or teaching jazz." Carter continues that it is the program's goal "to ensure that more young women have the opportunity to be immersed in a secure, nurturing and fun environment focusing on their instrumental and vocal skills and building confidence" (New Jersey Performing Arts Center, 2021). The camp's faculty is primarily female and includes vocalist Carla Cook, bassist Marion Hayden, drummer Allison Miller, trumpeter Bria Skonberg, myself, saxophonist Bruce Williams, and tap dancer Brinae Ali, in addition to Regina Carter. The daily schedule features music theory, the history of women in jazz, instrumental and vocal masterclasses, ensembles and tap-dancing. In my opinion, however, it is the value of the extra offerings that the camp provides the young women that really sets it apart from other kinds of camp experiences. Regina Carter states that

> The young women are involved in masterclasses, panel discussions, and listening sessions led by guest artists and faculty. There are unique challenges that female musicians can face (i.e., balancing family, performing/traveling/teaching, working in a male-dominated field,

etc.). We engage in sister-to-sister talks, where we discuss a wide range of issues and offer strategies and solutions to arm the young women for success.

(New Jersey Performing Arts Center, 2021)

Carla Cook, the marvelous jazz vocal instructor at the camp, concurred. In a recent email to me she stated,

The GAJC, I believe, provides a low pressure, 'safe' environment for young women to explore some musical ideas that are inspired by the Jazz tradition for those new to this music as well as those that have been more deeply immersed in it. I think that they also appreciate the time that is set aside to address any gender-specific issues they may encounter on the Jazz scene today.

As I am privileged to get to be a part of this camp, I can say that it is a joy to watch these young artists blossom under the tutelage of a brilliant faculty that is specifically attuned to their needs and is dedicated to helping them experience a sense of belonging and community, often for the first time.

I believe that more initiatives like this (others are listed below) can make a real difference in achieving gender parity for future generations of jazz artists and educators. While it may take some time to try to come close to gaining equal representation for women in all aspects of jazz performance, composition and education, the Geri Allen All-Female Jazz Camp and programs like it are having a significant impact. I am in awe of the women leading the programs listed below (and I apologize for any I have inadvertently left out), which includes institutes, organizations, camps, after school programs, mentoring opportunities, contests and website resources, and I hope that eventually young women from all over the country will have the resources available to them to experience this amazing art form in an environment where they are supported and encouraged by both male and female educators and artists.

Resources

Berklee School of Music's Institute of Jazz and Gender Justice: https://college.berklee.edu/jazz-gender-justice.

Seattle JazzEd's Jazz Girls USA (providing help in establishing Girls Jazz Day events around the country as well as other resources for young women): www.jazzgirlusa.org/.

Seattle JazzEd's Women's Resource Reading list: www.jazzgirlusa.org/articles.

Jazz at Lincoln Center's High School Jazz Academy Young Women's Jazz Workshop https://academy.jazz.org/high-school-jazz-academy-young-womens-jazz-workshop/.

Jazz Education Network Sisters In Jazz Collegiate Combo Competition: https://jazzednet.org/sisters-in-jazz/.

Women In Jazz Organization (WIJO) Mentors Program: http://wearewijo.org/mentors/.

New Jersey Performing Arts Center Geri Allen Jazz Camp: www.njpac.org/education-program/geri-allen-jazz-camp/.

Monterey Jazz Festival's Next Generation Women In Jazz Combo: https://montereyjazzfestival.org/education/ensembles/next-generation-women-in-jazz-combo/.

Seattle Women's Jazz Orchestra Girls Jazz Band: https://swojo.org/girls-jazz-band/.

Seattle Women's Jazz Orchestra Composition Contest: https://swojo.org/composition-contest/.

California Jazz Conservatory's Women's Jazz and Blues Camp: https://cjc.edu/jazzschool/intensives/adult-camps/womens-jazz-blues-camp/.

El Paso Jazz Girls: https://www.epjazzgirls.com/.

(New Jersey) Jazz House Kids Chica Power program: https://jazzhousekids.org/chica-power/.

References

Berliner, S. (2017, September 21). *An open letter to Ethan Iverson (and the rest of the jazz patriarchy).* www.sashaberlinermusic.com/sociopoliticalcommentary-1/2017/9/21/an-open-letter-to-ethan-iverson-and-the-rest-of-jazz-patriarchy.

Chaikin, J. (Director). (2011). *The Girls in the Band* [Film]. Artist Tribe and One Step Productions.

Girls on the Run. (2021). *Our Impact.* www.girlsontherun.org/what-we-do/our-impact/.

Gridley, M. C. (1998). *Concise Guide to Jazz* (2nd ed.). Pearson.

Jazz Education Network. (n.d.). *Title Page.* www.jazzednet.org.

Johnson, C. M., and Stewart, E. E. (2004). Effect of sex identification on instrument assignment by band directors. *Journal of Research in Music Education*, *52*(2), 130–140. https://doi.org/10.2307/3345435.

Lawn, R. J. (2007). *Experiencing Jazz*. McGraw-Hill.

Lazar, K. (2017, November 8). *Berklee let teachers quietly leave after alleged sex abuse, and pushed students for silence. Boston Globe.* www.bostonglobe.com/metro/2017/11/08/berklee-college-lets-teachers-quietly-leave-after-alleged-sexual-abuse-students-least-one-found-another-teaching-job/yfCkCCmdJzxkiEgrQK4cWM/story.html.

McGill. (2020, October 16). *Q&A with Visiting Guest Dr. Tammy Kernodle.* www.mcgill.ca/music/channels/news/qa-visiting-guest-dr-tammy-kernodle-325495.

McKeage, K. M. (2004). Gender and participation in high school and college instrumental jazz ensembles. *Journal of Research in Music Education*, *52*(4), 343–356. www.doi.org/10.1177/002242940405200406.

McKeage, K. M. (2014). "Where are the girls?" Women in collegiate instrumental jazz. *Gender, Education, Music, & Society*, *7*(3). www.doi.org/10.5561/gems.v7i3.5201. (Reprinted from "Where are the girls?" Women in collegiate instrumental jazz, 2002, *Gender, Education, Music, & Society*, *1*(1), www.queensu.ca/music/links/gems/past/No.%201?KMarticle.htm).

MacLeod, R. B. (2009). A comparison of aural and visual instrument preferences of third and fifth-grade students. *Bulletin of the Council for Research in Music Education*, *179*, 33–43. www.jstor.org/stable/40319328.

New Jersey Performing Arts Center (2021). *A letter from the artistic director.* www.njpac.org/education-program/geri-allen-jazz-camp/.

Pepper, J. W. (2021). *Basic Library Jazz Ensemble.* www.jwpepper.com/sheet-music/basic-library-jazz-ensemble.list.

Ray, K. D. (Director). (2007). *Lady be Good* [Film]. K. D. Ray Productions.

Ray, K. D. (Director). (2019). *In Her Hands: Key Changes in Jazz* [Film]. K. D. Ray Productions.

Shaker, S. (2020). "Paucity of Female College Band Directors as Faculty and Conductors at National Conferences in the United States, 2017–2018." (Publication No. 27959120) (Doctoral Dissertation, Arizona State University). ProQuest Theses and Dissertations.

The Girls in the Band. (2021). *Title Page.* https://thegirlsintheband.com/.

Van Vleet, K. (2021). Women in jazz music: A hundred years of gender disparity in jazz study and performance (1920–2020). *Jazz Education in Research and Practice*, *2*(1), 211–227. https://doi.org/10.2979/jazzeducrese.2.1.16.

We Have Voice. (n.d.). *Code of Conduct.* https://too-many.org/code-of-conduct/.

Wehr-Flowers, E. (2006). Differences between male and female students' confidence, anxiety, and attitude toward learning jazz improvisation. *Journal of Research in Music Education*, *54*(4), 337–349. www.doi.org/10.1177/002242940605400406.

Wehr, E. L. (2016). Understanding the experiences of women in jazz: A suggested model. *International Journal of Music Education*, *34*(4), 472–587. www.doi.org/10.1177/0255761415619392.

Women in Jazz Organization. (2021). *About WIJO.* http://wearewijo.org/about/.

38

SHEROES

The Role of All-Women Groups

Monika Herzig

Statement on Gender Terminology: This chapter is written from the perspective of a white European/American female jazz instrumentalist. The term all-women group is used frequently with the implication to include all female-identifying and non-binary individuals.

> As a female musician it is very important for us to see that other women can play well, write well, teach well, and so on. Once you get to see these women you can get a lot of strength and inspiration. I would say it is "life necessary."
>
> *(Olin and Aberg, 1995, p. 4)*

> "Only God can make a tree," the swing historian George T. Simon wrote in *The Big Bands* (1967, London: Macmillan, p. 261), "and only men can play good jazz."

Historical Background

All-women jazz groups are sometimes perceived as novelty acts or gimmicks. However, throughout history these formations have filled important needs and facilitated opportunities in a male-dominated environment. The concept initially became popular during World War II due to the scarcity of male musicians and because of unique performance opportunities. The most prominent of these groups, the International Sweethearts of Rhythm, completed numerous United Service Organization (USO) tours. Other notable groups at the time were Ada Leonard's All-American Girls, Ina Rae Hutton and Her Melodears, Helen Lewis and her All-Girls Syncopaters, the Parisian Red Heads, Ivy Benson and her All-Girl Orchestra, Clara De Vries and Her Jazz Ladies, Gloria Gaye and Her Glamour Girls Band, and Gracie Cole and Her Orchestra, to name just a few. While there was no shortage of capable musicians on any instrument, many of these groups were disbanded soon after the men returned from war duties and reclaimed their jobs in the entertainment business.

In the early jazz days, female musicians were active in similar bands, vaudeville acts, carnivals and theaters, but the war enabled a period of drastically new working conditions for women. A shortage of workers and entertainers opened the doors to employment and touring opportunities. Unfortunately, as Sherrie Tucker (1996) pointed out, it was a temporary support role while the men

DOI: 10.4324/9781003081876-42

were on war duty and the women were not "stealing the jobs". Once the war ended, many professional musicians had to enter alternate careers after they were replaced with their male counterparts.

The initial mission of USO entertainment was to provide a "home away from home". Hence, the visual aspect of all-women touring groups was perceived as a representation of the sweethearts left behind. The emphasis on the looks was a tough pill to swallow for these accomplished musicians but they were willing to do so in exchange for the opportunity to hone their skills and work professionally. "It was my only way to get out on the road and perform", commented Roz Cohn in a 1990 telephone interview with Sherrie Tucker, "there was virtually no integration into male bands." Music careers in all-women groups became the escape route from secretarial positions and servant careers. Payment structures were also less than equal, as Laverne Wollerman confirms: "When male sidemen were making $125–150 per week, we got $50" (Tucker, 1996). Musicians and observers at the time remember the public perception of these groups as freakish, confirmed by frequent comments such as "they play like men", and a general look first, listen second attitude.

Discrimination and glass ceilings are certainly not limited to jazz careers. It wasn't until 1982 that the Berlin Philharmonic hired the first woman, just after the US Supreme Court named its first female judge (Sandra O'Connor 1981) and Sally Ride became the first woman in space the following year. In 1987, Aretha Franklin became the first member of the Rock'n Roll Hall of Fame. Three decades after the war, in 1977, pianist Marian McPartland formed an all-women quintet to prove a point to Newport Jazz Festival promoter George Wein, who had claimed that it wouldn't be possible to find a night's worth of female talent. Two Kansas City women, Carol Comer and Dianne Gregg, challenged the lingering boys club in jazz with the presentation of the Kansas City Women's Jazz Festival, which ran from 1978 to 1985. Established performers such as Marian McPartland, Mary Lou Williams, Mary Osborne, Dottie Dodgion, Betty Carter, Toshiko Akiyoshi, Melba Liston, Carol Kaye, Joanne Brackeen, Carmen McRae, Jane Ira Bloom, Carla Bley, Stacy Rowles, Dianne Reeves, Sheila Jordan, among others, headlined next to emerging artists, competition winners and a new wave of all-women ensembles spearheaded by Bonnie Janovsky's and Ann Patterson's Maiden Voyage Big Band. Patterson formulated the mission of Maiden Voyage "to give women who have incredible potential some experience; to give women who are doing their thing and doing it well some exposure; and to give women musicians some work" (Liska, 1981).

In a 1993 interview for the *LA Times*, Patterson expanded on that mission:

We wanted to change people's attitudes toward women musicians. Back then it was assumed a woman couldn't play as well as the guys. We knew that one good woman musician could change that kind of attitude. But if there were 17 of us, it would make more of a statement. We also wanted a place for women who wanted to be in a big band to play and get experience and exposure.

The most notable aspect about this statement is that it comes nearly fifty years after saxophonist Roz Cohn joined the International Sweethearts of Rhythm for similar reasons—to have an opportunity to play, get experience and hone her skills. Hence, nearly one century into the history of jazz, female performers were still viewed as a novelty, an emerging field. Hopefully the recent resurgence of all-women ensembles, two decades into the twenty-first century, will finally succeed in shattering the lingering glass ceiling. The role of these groups is not to be a novelty or eye candy, but a fundamental need for overcoming a century of obstacles, misconceptions, and assumptions.

Many of these factors and the important role and advocacy of all-women ensembles will be discussed in this chapter. Despite frequent demands to be recognized for their musicianship rather than their gender, many prominent performers, including Renee Rosness, Terri Lyne Carrington, Roxy Coss, Ellen Rowe, Sharel Cassity, Jane Bunnett, Mayra Casales, Sherrie Marricle, and even Beyonce and Adele, have led all-women ensembles, initiated organizations, and founded the Berklee Institute for Jazz and Gender Justice over the past decade. What has triggered this recent surge of all-women groups? What is the role of these formations, and how can they help shape a future of equal participation in the art form jazz and beyond?

Post-Feminism and the Alpha Girl

In February 2012, drummer/composer Terri Lyne Carrington won a Grammy award for her *Mosaic Project* in the Best Jazz Vocal Album category. The most notable aspects about this achievement were of course the outstanding quality of the music, but also that the album's personnel happened to be all women with various guest vocalists on each track. In the first 60 years of Grammy awards, there were 1,930 male nominees and winners compared to 411 female nominees and winners. When Carrington won her second Grammy for Best Instrumental Jazz Album in 2014, she was the first woman in history to win in the instrumental jazz categories. NPR freelance reporter Lara Pellegrini gathered some of the prominent artists from Carrington's *Mosaic* project at a roundtable in 2010 to discuss the music and their careers. The general consensus was that they were all passionate about their craft and wanted to get their voices heard without any focus on gender issues. Ingrid Jensen reinforced this sentiment early in the discussion:

> If anyone knows me, they know that I avoid all women groups like the plague because I've had enough experiences where the weakest links overpower the integrity of the music. I just like to play with people who are open-minded and want to play good music.

At a later point in the conversation, Carrington is ready to shift the conversation away from the subject of women in jazz:

> I would just like to make a suggestion that we shift to talking about music and not about women. I know that's part of your thing, but none of us think about being a woman. We already said that, but I'll reiterate—none of us think about being a woman when we play or write songs or do all the other work that has to be done to organize even just a project like this. Nobody thinks about that part of it. If that makes other people attracted to it, that's fine with me, but I think in the end we're doing what we have to do. We have to do this. It's an unwritten thing.

Yoko Suzuki (2014) noticed similar attitudes during her dissertation research on female saxophonists. Her 30 interviewees frequently avoided being asked about gender-related questions and expressed their belief that the focus should be on the music rather on gender, thus eliminating the subject. In the NPR roundtable discussion, Dutch saxophonist Tineke Postma confirmed this attitude (Pellegrinelli, 2010):

> As long as the media keeps on emphasizing the female thing, you keep on putting a stamp on it. If we just emphasize the person, then maybe it will get less special, being a female artist. Then you're just an artist.

Clearly, these exceptional musicians want to equally participate in the art form based on their musicianship and feel that being categorized as female musicians could devalue their abilities. The common narrative during this period of time was that music is genderless and anyone with exceptional and outstanding musicianship will find a seat at the table. With limited spaces available in the professional jazz community and social barriers in place, the outstanding women who were invited to the table often found themselves in the role of alpha females, commonly defined as being aggressive, competitive, and ambitious. The concept of the 'alpha girl' was reinforced by popular culture during the post-feminist period, replacing the natural traits of collective female activism with competition, ambition, and meritocracy. (McRobbie, 2011). The result is actually a dangerous diminution of the natural female traits of collective spirit and political engagement. The woman who speaks out against injustice in the patriarchic system is viewed as an old-fashioned man-hater. Consequently, the idealized brand of the alpha female in media and popular culture diminishes the options of collaboration among women as a group. This strategic response to a period of feminism worked well in support of the patriarchic system. McRobbie (2011) demonstrates in her research how this wave of post-feminism actually turned the clock backwards on overcoming inequalities, terming it a "new sexual contract".

Tokenism and Stereotype Threat

On December 20, 2017, the newly formed We Have Voice[1] collective published an open letter against sexual harassment and gender discrimination, including the following statement. The initiative was formed in response to a wave of sexual harassment scandals becoming public knowledge during the *#MeToo* movement:

> We are resolved to be vigilant, and we are determined to engage in transformative ways of thinking and being in our creative professional world. We are compelled to act, not only out of solidarity with the survivors of abuse, but also to expose and eliminate a systemic structure that normalizes harassment and discrimination, allowing abusers and complicit bystanders to perpetuate these behaviors without being held accountable for their negative actions. Furthermore, we recognize that our present culture is the same one that minimizes and/or excludes artists of marginalized genders, ethnicities, sexual orientations, and so forth from venues, festivals, teaching jobs, newspaper and magazine reviews. When we bring awareness to sexual violence, we are also bringing awareness to this inequity and invisibility.

After a decade of advocacy for young women of color who were survivors of sexual violence, Tarana Burke's *#MeToo* campaign went viral with a hashtag promoted by actress Alyssa Milano on October 15, 2017 in response to the Harvey Weinstein sexual misconduct accusations. It initiated an avalanche of testimonials, scandals, proclamations, and new advocacy efforts, uncovering not only sexual misconduct but also systemic issues of discrimination and inequality. The narrative of post-feminism changed dramatically, from striving to be the competitive "alpha girl" to demanding an equal place at the table. The We Have Voice collective is one example of many advocacy efforts in the jazz community. Fourteen female and non-binary instrumentalists and vocalists released a *Code of Conduct*, articulating what a more equitable workplace might look like and setting expectations for change. Similarly, the Women in Jazz Organization (WIJO) under the leadership of saxophonist Roxy Coss, emerged as an advocacy organization, and Terri Lyne Carrington, a member of the We Have Voice collective, founded the Berklee Institute for Jazz and Gender Justice. Grammy-nominated saxophonist Tia Fuller, a member of the collective, expressed in a recent interview:

> I think slowly but surely we're doing the work and there is some shift happening, I especially see it with my students and the younger generation. That's something that's near and dear to my heart. I'm seeing the pain, psychological, physical, emotional pain that it's caused with women and sometimes men, too.
>
> *(January 14, 2019, Mesfin Fekadu, The Associated Press)*

One visible result of the shift is the emergence of a host of all-women jazz groups and projects led by some of the most prominent players in the field. Here are just a few examples of recently released recordings:

Takase, Aki, Eberhard, Silke. *Ornette Coleman Anthology*. Zürich: Intakt (2007)
Halverson, Mary, Pavone, Jessica. *Thin Air*. New York: Thirsty Ear (2009)
Carrington, Terri Lyne. *The Mosaic Project*. Los Angeles: Concord (2011)
Fuller, Tia. *Angelic Warrior*. Detroit: Mack Avenue (2012)

Bunnett, Jane and Maqueque, *Jane Bunnett and Maqueque*. Montreal: Justin Time (2014)

Bunnett, Jane and Maqueque, *Oddara*. Toronto: Linus Entertainment (2016)

Högberg, Anna. *Attack*. Gothenburg: Omlott (2016)

Herzig, Monika. *The Whole World in Her Hands*. Dartmouth: Whaling City Sounds (2016)

Johänntgen, Nicole. *Sisters in Jazz*. Independent Release (2016)

Czichowsky, Anne. *Lines for Ladies Feat. Sheila Jordan and Kristin Korb*. Villingen-Schwenningen: HGBS Blue (2016)

Scott, Rhoda. *We Free Queens*. London: Sunset Records (2017)

Marricle, Sherrie. *The Diva Jazz Orchestra 25th Anniversary Project*. ArtistShare (2017)

3D Jazz Trio. *Three Divas*. Diva Jazz (2017)

Herzig, Monika. *Sheroes*. Dartmouth: Whaling City Sounds (2018)

Rowe, Ellen. *Momentum: Portraits of Women in Motion*. Dewitt: Smokin' Sleddog Records (2019)

Lioness. *Pride and Joy*. New York: Positone (2019)

Mazur, Marilyn. *Shamania*. London: Rarenoise Records (2019)

Bunnett, Jane and Maqueque, *On Firm Ground*. Toronto: Linus Entertainment (2019)

Herzig, Monika. *Eternal Dance*. New York: Savant (2020)

3D Jazz Trio. *I Love to See You Smile*. Diva Jazz (2020)

Artemis. *Artemis*. New York: Blue Note (2020)

In 2018, the Union of German Jazz Musicians posted a declaration for equal participation of women in jazz.[2] According to their survey of the German jazz scene, only 12 percent of instrumentalists are female, and at all German jazz studies programs there are a total of two full-time instrumental faculty members and only two full-time musicians in all four German radio ensembles. The quotas are similar in the United States and around the world. Hence, despite the recent surge of female instrumentalists, the goal of equal participation is far away due to lingering and deep-rooted issues that prevent inclusion and need to be identified and resolved. In 2020 a follow-up study (Bloch, 2020) uncovered that the majority of male jazz musicians did not see any need for advocacy towards diversification. Comments often indicate that change is not even desired. This lingering passivity might be rooted in social arrangements as cited in Leslie Gourse's *Madame Jazz* (1996) from a 1977 *Daily News* interview by Ricki Fulman with trumpet player Howard McGhee:

> But you know a woman does represent problems if she's part of a male group. Someone could come up and start messing with her and that just puts a pressure on all the men. We are put in a position of having to protect the women who play with us. ... So if you're going to hire women it just means hassles.

Tucker analyzed the phenomenon of the continued perception and media treatment of women in jazz as an emerging field in her publication, *Big Ears: Listening for Gender in Jazz Studies* (Tucker, 2001). While contemporary gender theorists have overturned the belief that there are biological boundaries in the musical abilities of women, the notion seems to live on in the jazz world. Women who play like men and are exceptional musicians are good enough to be acknowledged as great jazz musicians and evolve frequently enough to not change the status quo. Tucker documents her findings with depictions of women as "sexy, ditzy, talentless singers, dumb dates who didn't appreciate jazz, provincial killjoys (often wives) who spoil hipster fun, and squealing, misguided Sinatra fans," quotes found throughout the 1950s in *DownBeat* Magazine. Further evidence is the continued representation of masculinity of iconic jazz figures in history books and biographies. The most prominent example is Miles Davis, who is torn between the claustrophobic world of women and the creative world of men. Lingering is also the common rhetoric among musicians of calling each other 'man' and 'good guys'. Hence, the continued narrative of the 'emerging' field of women in jazz still includes the branding of brass and percussion instruments as male, a remarkable female dropout rate in pre-college jazz programs (Boeyink, 2015), and a lingering perception of women instrumentalists as spectacles and novelty acts.

One of the early pioneers of European avant-garde jazz, pianist Irene Schweizer, recalls

> I was always the only woman around. Sometimes there was tension. Men want to show how fast they can play and how much technique they have. So I would have to struggle and also play as fast as possible. I found it too aggressive and competitive at times.
>
> *(Hale, 1997)*

This position of being the exception in a man's world is explained further through the theory of 'tokenism', a concept initiated by Rosabeth Kanter in her 1977 publication *Men and Women of the Corporation*. Kanter identified some of the consequences of being few amongst many as either over-achievement or underachievement due to the pressures of scrutiny and high visibility. Consequently, Schweizer explains her attraction to the women's improvisational collectives that she joined during the 1970s and 1980s as a nurturing and comfortable space.

> The interplay, the interaction was quite different than with men. Suddenly there was humor … humor in our midst, we had fun. It wasn't about achievement. We didn't need to show our stuff: I can play this run so fast. It wasn't the technique that was important. It was the expression in the music. What we wanted to say. I liked that.

All-Women Groups as Catalysts for Change

Wehr (2016) elaborates on the influence of tokenism and the possibility of stereotype threat and suggests an approach to jazz pedagogy that incorporates these findings towards building self-esteem and encouraging participation. The concept of self-efficacy, which is the belief in one's ability and has been proven to be one of the most consistent predictors of achievement (Graham and Weiner, 1996, Bandura, 1997, Watson, 2010, Ciorba, 2006), and the issue of increased performance anxiety (Wehr-Flowers, 2006) of female jazz improvisers need to be addressed early on in order to decrease the dropout rates of girls in secondary school jazz programs. Various research studies confirm the lingering issues of instrument choice, access, and even sexual discrimination (Boeyink, 2015, Alexander, 2011). Studies have also documented that it's not biological factors, but social and psychological factors, that influence female participation in jazz.

Recent efforts addressing these social and pedagogical issues include the presentation of increasing numbers of Jazz Girls Days, initially launched by trombonist and band director Sarah Kline at Berkley High School in 2012. These workshop days are free and open to all girls ages 10–18 who sing or play an instrument and are usually led by a group of all women mentors. After initial introductions and various group workshops, the girls get to work in combos and share the results in a final concert. Having presented a number of Jazz Girls Days inside and outside of the United States, my personal observations and feedback from the participants confirm the increased self-esteem and enthusiasm. As suggested by Wehr (2016), this new pedagogical approach supports building self-efficacy and higher levels of participation and performance.

Grammy-winning drummer/composer and founder of the Berklee Institute for Jazz and Gender Justice, Terri Lyne Carrington, also addressed the issue of dropout rates in a recent interview (Rees, 2019):

> "Antiquated, archaic … That's not everybody but it's the overall narrative, the system that we've all participated in, men and women," she explains. "There's been an unwritten narrative that men play music and women sing it. Sprinkled in you have these women who played instruments, but there were far more women that did play that were not supported

in the same way and many women that wanted to but didn't because it was too difficult. It's hard enough learning how to play the music. Having these extra obstacles often makes you not want to do it."

Based on the discussion of traditional barriers of female participation in jazz, all women ensembles serve to mitigate several of these barriers. These units can provide a safe and nurturing environment for musical development and help address lingering barriers towards achieving parity in performance and educational settings. Following is a list of these barriers and suggestions for solutions.

As documented earlier, all-women ensembles provide support and a safe space to create, experiment, and express. Wehr (2016) advocated for cultivating self-efficacy as it is a dominant predictor for achievement. The support and safety of all-women units can foster self-efficacy and diminish the competitive nature in the usually male-dominated environments. Participation allows for musical growth and strengthening of self-esteem, also a mission of the increasingly frequent Jazz Girls Days and all-women jazz camps. Finally, the effects of tokenism, of including a few exceptional achievers to cover diversity issues thus increasing competition for the few available opportunities, are diminished if not eliminated in all-women groups.

The presentation of female performers on major stages helps change deeply rooted perceptions that associate feminism with weakness and lower quality. This visual barrier is widespread in music and beyond. Sherrie Marricle, leader of the Diva Jazz Orchestra shared the following story in a 2018 interview with documentary filmmaker Kay D. Ray:

> When I was a kid, my fantasy was to play in the Woody Herman band. I loved that band so much and I still love it. I remember back in the day you would send a cassette tape. They sent the cassettes around blind. My friend who was playing bass in the band at the time said, "Oh, they really liked your tape." He told me this, I don't know, on the record, off the record. He said, "Yeah, everybody thought your tape was great. But then they found out you were a woman and then they laughed and threw it away.

Such attitudes and widespread nepotism were the reason for implementing blind auditions in the classical music world in the 1970s. An immediate result was a 30 percent increase of female musicians in orchestras (Golden and Rouse, 2000). There are very few positions in the jazz world that have an official application and selection process. One such example is the Jazz at Lincoln Center Orchestra, which still has no full-time female ensemble member. Advocacy efforts led by trumpeter Ellen Seeling's Equal Access for Jazz Women organization has resulted in a commitment to public job postings and blind auditions (PR Newswire, 2016). However, it will take continued advocacy and showcasing role models in performance and education in order to eliminate such visual stereotypes and, in this case, still prevalent tokenism.

Stereotyping is defined as a set of beliefs and generalizations about a certain group of people. Research has documented how the actual performance of the subjects who believe they are being stereotyped is influenced accordingly. Claude Steele's publication, *Whistling Vivaldi: How Stereotypes Affect Us and What We Can Do* (2011), discusses in detail the effect of stereotyped expectations on the achievements of a marginalized group. He provides the example of female students taking a math test and performing significantly lower when being told that their achievement is being tested versus taking the test independent of math achievement measures. Hence, the stereotyped perception of lower math ability for females causes performance pressures and lower achievements. Similarly, female jazz musicians report feeling under pressure to prove themselves, especially when entering new performance situations. From my personal experience as a touring jazz pianist, I can attest to the frequent assumption that I'm a vocalist and in need of expert backup when meeting new audiences, new presenters, and new colleagues alike. Thus, the perception of having to prove superior capacities and perform beyond expectations is especially strong when entering new situations and adds psychological and social pressures that can interfere with the quality of the performance. In a panel discussion at the 2019 Jazz Education Network (JEN) Conference in Reno, Nevada, Berkley High School Band Director and founder of Jazz Girls Day, Sarah Kline commented:

> There is a certain very small percentage of women who can deal with the stereotype threat and everything else. A lot of those 2 percent of women are sitting on this panel and are sitting amongst you. But jazz is about your voice in community, we need everyone's voice in community. We don't need 2 percent of women to break through, we don't need the big schools to get better at recruiting those 2 percent of women, we need education that reaches all of our women and all of our students, all of our men too.

Kline's very important point calls for freedom of expression and an invitation for everyone to participate in the art form jazz, in the process of communal and democratic music making. The 2009 *Jazz and Democracy*[3] curriculum created by Wesley Watkins IV indicates in its Vision Statement: Great jazz is high art that models American democratic ideals and engaging the jazz-as-democracy metaphor develops the interdisciplinary thinking, synthesis and analysis skills needed to confront complex 21st century challenges in creative ways." In order to model the American democratic ideals, equal access to the musical process needs to be offered to everyone regardless of gender or race. Diverse participation will shape the results to reflect truly democratic ideals. All-women ensembles can serve as incubators for this freedom of expression and creation away from stereotype pressures in safe and comfortable environments. They can serve as the pedagogical units that Sarah Kline recommended towards opening the doors of participation to everyone.

Conclusion

The recent surge in advocacy, awareness, and participation indicates readiness to move the concept of women in jazz from novelty to mainstream, shape perceptions and eliminate stereotypes, foster training grounds for diverse voices and move the art form away from its embedded masculinity. All-women groups play a crucial role during this process as documented through the various concepts, research results, and arguments presented in this chapter. Early leaders such as Roz Kohn, a member of the International Sweethearts of Rhythm and Ann Patterson, leader of Maiden Voyage expressed the mission of all-women groups as a space for developing the craft, a springboard for many careers, and an opportunity for integrating new voices. Contemporary groups continue to fulfill this mission and participants confirm the continued need. After a 2014 series of concerts with an all-women ensemble in celebration of Women's History Month, I collected the following feedback by the participants:

a. Everyone agreed that one of their favorite aspects of performing together was the non-pressured environment of not having to prove anything to their band mates. "We compliment and complement each other" (Carolyn Dutton, violin).
b. They also felt inspired by their peers' high level of musicality. "I would love to see a group like this go around to schools and play at jazz festivals; wouldn't that make a statement!" (Natalie Boeyink, bass).
c. The issue of raising awareness for female participation in jazz was also crucial for them. Everyone admitted how difficult it was to push the boundaries without any role models. "Promoting female improvisers and band leaders in jazz highlights the fact that women are equally as bold, creative, powerful, and intellectual as men" (Amanda Gardier, saxophone).
d. As we're still working on establishing equal rights in the workplace and at home, having mothers on the bandstand is important inspiration for the younger generations. "Just sharing the stage with such strong and musically expressive moms last night has really helped me debunk this lie for myself and renewed my faith that yes, we can have our cake and eat it too!" (Lexie Signor,

trumpet). Similarly, New Orleans trombonist Haruka Kikuchi recently became a viral sensation when she took her 9-month-old son along on a European tour with her all-women Shake 'Em Up jazz band from New Orleans and was filmed and photographed performing with her son on stage. Her picture carrying her son while playing trombone on stage became the icon for the do-it-all-motherhood image.

e. And the support in career development strategies and mentoring is much needed. "Moving to a new town and trying (as a female) to get people to let me sit in was really discouraging" (Natalie Boeyink, bass).

Vocalist Janiece Jaffe raised an important point during my 2014 informal interviews: "Equality does not mean 'sameness' though." The goal of the integration process is a cultural change that moves away from stereotyping instruments and abilities and cultivates the communal aspect of music making in jazz rather than ideals of masculinity and competition. This process includes fostering all-women groups, advocating for increased participation at all levels, revised teaching curricula, media representation, all the way to how we talk and write about all-women groups. It is not enough to promote the need for all-women groups with this dismissive concluding statement from the chapter "Going For It: All Women Bands" in Alexander Stewart's book on the contemporary New York big band scene (Stewart, 2007): "Nevertheless, as long as they remain marketable to the public, providing jobs and valuable experience, all-women bands continue to form an important part of the musical landscape."

We finally have to move beyond the emerging field and novelty act concept and embrace the essential need, function, and advocacy options of all-women ensembles. My suggestion for reformulating the statement above is that as long as we don't have equal parity in participation, opportunities, and pay rate for women in jazz, all-women bands continue to provide the safe, nurturing, and inspiring environment that supports self-efficacy, high levels of performance, and role models. Furthermore, the presentation on prominent stages eliminates perceptual barriers and counteracts lingering instrument stigmas. Once such parity is achieved the music will represent the democratic principles of creating jazz in true fashion.

Notes

1 We Have Voice is a collective of musicians, performers, scholars, and thinkers from different generations, races, ethnicities, cultures, abilities, gender identities, economic backgrounds, religious beliefs and affiliations. Together, they are determined to engage in transformative ways of thinking and being in their creative professional world, while being ingrained in an inclusive and intersectional analysis. More information can be found at https://too-many.org/.
2 www.deutsche-jazzunion.de/uber-uns/ziele/gleichstellung/.
3 http://jazzdemocracy.com/.

References

Alexander, A. (2011). "Where are the Girls? A Look at the Factors that Limit Female Participation in Instrumental Jazz" (DMA Thesis).
Bandura, A. (1997). *Self-efficacy: The Exercise of Control*. Macmillan.
Block, L. (2020). Gender macht Musik. Geschlechterberechtigung im Jazz. Deutsche Jazzunion.
Boeyink, N. L. (2015). *A Descriptive Study of Collegiate Female Jazz Instrumentalists*. Indiana University.
Brewer, C. G. (2017). *Changing the Tune: The Kansas City Women's Jazz Festival, 1978–1985*. University of North Texas Press.
Ciorba, C. R. (2006). The creation of a model to predict jazz improvisation achievement. (Doctoral dissertation, University of Miami).
Goldin, C., and Rouse, C. (2000). Orchestrating impartiality: The impact of "blind" auditions on female musicians. *American Economic Review, 90*(4), 715–741.
Gourse, L. (1996). *Madame Jazz: Contemporary Women Instrumentalists*. Oxford University Press on Demand.

Graham, S., and Weiner, B. (1996). Theories and principles of motivation. *Handbook of Educational Psychology*, *4*, 63–84.

Hale, J. (1997, November). Irene Schweizer: Many and One Direction. *Coda: The Journal of Jazz & Improvised Music*, (276), 14–15.

Jazz at Lincoln Center Adopts Blind Auditions and New Selection Procedures for Jazz Orchestra. (2016). *PR Newswire*.

Kanter, R. M. (1977). Men and Women of the Organization. *New York: Basic Books*.

Liska, A. J. (1981). Maiden Voyage. *DownBeat*, 53.

McKeage, K. (2014). "Where Are All the Girls?" Women In Collegiate Instrumental Jazz. *GEMS (Gender, Education, Music, and Society), the On-line Journal of GRIME (Gender Research in Music Education)*, 7(3).

McRobbie, A. (2011). Beyond post-feminism. *Public Policy Research*, (3), 179.

Olin, M., and Aberg, L. (1995, Autumn). The purpose of Gals'in'Jazz. *Jazz Changes*, 2(3), 4.

Pellegrinelli, L. (2010). Nine Women in the Room: A Jazz Musicians' Round Table. www.npr.org/assets/music/blogs/therecord/2010/09/NPR_JazzMusiciansRoundtable.pdf.

Steele, C. M. (2011). *Whistling Vivaldi: How Stereotypes Affect Us and What We Can Do*. W. W. Norton.

Stewart, A. (2007). *Making the Scene: Contemporary New York City Big Band Jazz*. Berkeley: University of California Press.

Suzuki, Y. (2014). "None of Us Think about Being a Woman:" Performing Gender Without Norms. *GEMS (Gender, Education, Music, and Society), the On-line Journal of GRIME (Gender Research in Music Education)*, 7(2).

Tucker, S. (1996). Working the Swing Shift: Women Musicians during World War II. *Labor's Heritage*, 8(1), 46–66.

Tucker, S. (2001). Big Ears: Listening for Gender in Jazz Studies. *Current Musicology*, 71(73), 2.

Watson, K. E. (2010). The effects of aural versus notated instructional materials on achievement and self-efficacy in jazz improvisation. *Journal of Research in Music Education*, 58(3), 240–259.

Wehr-Flowers, E. (2006). Differences between male and female students' confidence, anxiety, and attitude toward learning jazz improvisation. *Journal of Research in Music Education*, 54(4), 337–349.

Wehr, E. L. (2016). Understanding the experiences of women in jazz: A suggested model. *International Journal of Music Education*, 34(4), 472–487.

NOTES ON CONTRIBUTORS

Based in Lisbon, **Leonor Arnaut** studied voice at Escola Superior de Música de Lisboa, where she finished her degree in Jazz. During this process and until today, she works with different musicians, mainly within styles where improvisation is an important element. Currently, she explores the various possibilities of using the voice in improvised and experimental music and focuses on composing and understanding the human voice as an instrument. Her presence in different projects allows her to continue her exploratory path as a singer and composer. She also focuses on teaching, having completed her Master's in Music Education. While teaching, she aims to incorporate her vision on the instrument and its possibilities. Currently she teaches at Hot Club de Portugal school.

Kara Attrep is Lecturer in the Honors College at Northern Arizona University. Her research focuses on popular music and identity, especially gender and race. She has published on women jazz and blues club owners, and music and advertising. She received her PhD in ethnomusicology from the University of California, Santa Barbara.

Benjamin Barson is an American Society of Composers, Authors and Publishers (ASCAP) award-winning composer-saxophonist. His writings have appeared in *Black Power Afterlives* (Haymarket Press, 2020) and *The Routledge Handbook on Ecosocialism* (2021). Barson conceives his interdisciplinary work in dialogue with movements that challenge white supremacy, racism, capitalism, patriarchy, and ecocide.

Natalie Boeyink teaches full-time in the University of North Carolina system. An accomplished bassist and educator, Boeyink is an active performer and clinician. Some of her performances include appearances with Lorraine Feather, Ingrid Jensen, Terri Lyne Carrington, David 'Fathead' Newman, Christine Jensen, and John Hendricks. She is a member of Batuquê Trio which fuses contemporary Brazilian, Afro-Cuban, and Caribbean rhythms with jazz. Boeyink holds a DM in Music Education from Indiana University, a MM in Jazz Performance from the University of Louisville, and a BM in Jazz Studies from IU.

Jeremy Brown is Professor of Music at the University of Calgary and performs as a jazz and free improviser. He is also a woodwind doubler and performs frequently as a saxophonist, flautist, on recorders and clarinet. He has been conductor of the wind bands at the University of Calgary School of Creative and Performing Arts and currently directs the award-winning UCalgary Jazz Orchestra. His book *The Wind Band Music of Henry Cowell* (2018) includes recordings of Cowell's band music conducted by Dr. Brown. He was series editor and lead compiler of the first-ever *Royal Conservatory of Music Saxophone Series* (2014).

Robert Burke, Associate Professor at Monash University, Australia, is an improvising musician and composer. Rob has performed and composed on over three hundred CDs collaborating with George Lewis, Raymond MacDonald, Hermeto Pascoal, Dave Douglas, Tony Malaby, Ben Monder, Tom Rainey, Tony Gould, and Mark Helias. Books include: *Perspectives on Artistic Research in Music* and *Experimentation in Jazz: Idea Chasing,* Routledge. Rob is currently president of AJIRN (Australasian Jazz and Improvisation Research Network). His research focuses on jazz and improvisational processes investigating "What happens when we improvise?", which includes studies into the phenomenology of musical interaction, experimentation, identity, agency, and gender studies.

Marie Buscatto is Full Professor of Sociology at Paris 1 Pantheon-Sorbonne University specialised in the sociology of work, of gender, and of arts. Based on her empirical research conducted in the French and Japanese jazz worlds, her current thinking focuses on the difficulties women have to get access, to remain and to be promoted in art worlds and prestigious professions, and the ways in which artistic creation is affected by gendered processes. She is studying contemporary artists' practices, activities, and trajectories in Europe, in North and Latin America, and in Japan. She develops an epistemological reflection on qualitative methods.

Ramsey Castaneda is a Los Angeles-based educator, performer, and researcher. He currently serves as department chair for upper school music at Crossroads School for Arts and Sciences and teaches part-time at Los Angeles College of Music. He has performed in Carnegie Hall and in LA recording studios, including for Michael Bublé's most recent records. He has presented his research on jazz representation in popular culture and philosophy of music at national conferences, including Jazz Education Network, California All-State Music Education Conferences, and Documenting Jazz. He earned his DMA in jazz studies from the University of Southern California in 2018.

Jessica Chow (she/her) graduated from the joint History of Design postgraduate program between the Royal College of Art and Victoria and Albert Museum in London. This program focused on researching history through archives, museum collections, and material culture objects. Her current research specializes in studying race, gender, and class in the context of modern British history. Although she does not play any instruments, she wishes she did not quit playing jazz piano many years ago!

Brandi Coleman is Assistant Professor of jazz dance at Southern Methodist University and was a performing member, rehearsal director, and associate artistic director of Jump Rhythm® Jazz Project, founded and directed by Billy Siegenfeld. She has led more than forty choreographic and teaching residencies at universities across the country and internationally and received an Emmy Award for her performance in the documentary, *Jump Rhythm Jazz Project: Getting There.* Her creative and scholarly research explores gender-expansive jazz dance choreography that disrupts heteronormative, culturally determined gender constructs, especially as it pertains to the female moving body.

Ann Cotterrell is an independent researcher living in London, educated at the London School of Economics and at Birkbeck, University of London. She has written articles on gender history and has edited more than twenty books on American and European jazz for Northway Publications. Her current research interests include aspects of masculinity in British colonialism.

Dr. **Melissa Forbes** is a jazz singer, music educator and researcher at the University of Southern Queensland, Australia. Her research explores experiences of singing along a continuum from elite professional singers to community singing groups for health and wellbeing. She has released two albums—*No More Mondays* (2005) and *The Intimacy of Distance* (2014).

Magdalena Fürnkranz is Senior Scientist at the Department of Popular Music at the University of Music and Performing Arts Vienna. As co-leader of the project "Performing Diversity" and leader of the project "Female Jazz Musicians in Austria", her recent research has focused on performativity, gender and intersectionality in pop and rock music, Austrian music scenes, and gender/identity in jazz. She is co-editor of *Performing Sexual Identities. Nationalities on the Eurovision Stage* (2017), author of *Elizabeth I in Film und Fernsehen. De-/Konstruktion von weiblicher Herrschaft* (2019) and co-author of *Aufführungsrituale der Musik. Zur Konstituierung kultureller Vielfalt am Beispiel Österreich* (2021).

ken tianyuan Ge (he/him) is a bassist and music scholar based in Durham, North Carolina. He holds a doctorate in jazz performance from the University of Miami and is currently pursuing a second doctorate in musicology at the University of North Carolina at Chapel Hill. His work blends auto/archaeological, ethnographic, affective, and archival methodologies, interrogating case studies in gender and postwar jazz praxis, geographies of race, sound, and representation in 1940s American radio, and the everyday affects of musical life in the global cruise industry.

Clare Hall (PhD) is Lecturer in Performing Arts, Monash University, Australia. Her research, educational, and artistic practice coalesces around music, sound, and performance to promote creative arts engagements across the lifespan. Her interdisciplinary scholarship bridges boundaries between the arts, education, and sociology, with her key contribution to date in music and masculinity. She is the cofounder/leader of the *Decolonising and Indigenising Music Education* group (ISME) and is part of an Australian Research Council project: *Diversifying Music in Australia: Gender Equity in Jazz and Improvisation*. Her publications include *Masculinity, Class and Music Education* (Palgrave, 2018), *Sociological Thinking in Music Education* (Oxford University Press, 2021).

Chicago native, former US Jazz Ambassador, Fulbright Senior Music Specialist, Dr. **Lenora Helm Hammonds** is a tenured Associate Professor in the Department of Music, Jazz Studies Program at North Carolina Central University (NCCU) as Director, Vocal Jazz Ensemble, and coordinates the vocal jazz activities for undergraduate and graduate jazz majors. She holds a DMA in Music Education from Boston University, a MM in Jazz Performance from East Carolina University, and a BM in Film Scoring from Berklee College of Music. Her research is published across the intersections of intercultural maturity, jazz pedagogy, and digital humanities. Academic award highlights include the highest faculty honor, the 2021 University of North Carolina Board of Governors Award for Excellence in Teaching. P/K/A as Lenora Zenzalai Helm with seven CDs, composer awards and film scores. CD *For the Love of Big Band* features her ensemble, The Tribe Jazz Orchestra®. www. LenoraHelm.com.

Wendy Hargreaves studied jazz and popular music singing at the Queensland University Technology, Australia, completing a Bachelor of Arts (Music), Graduate Diploma in Education and Master of Music. She has worked extensively in primary, secondary and tertiary music education, and as a research assistant. She holds a PhD from the Queensland Conservatorium in vocal jazz improvisation education. Wendy has presented at conferences, including the *International Conference for Research in Music Education,* and published in journals such as the *International Journal of Music Education—Practice*. Wendy is currently a Learning Advisor at the University of Southern Queensland.

Monika Herzig, jazz pianist, has completed her Doctorate in Music Education with minor fields in Jazz Studies at Indiana University, where she is now a faculty member in Arts Administration. She is the author of *David Baker—A Legacy in Music* (IU Press, 2011), and *Experiencing Chick Corea: A Listener's Companion* (Rowman and Littlefield, 2017). She is also the head of the research committee for the Jazz Education Network and editor of *JAZZ* (*Jazz Education in Research and Practice*, IU Press). Groups under her leadership have toured the world and opened for acts such as Tower of Power, Sting, Dixie Dregs, and more. Her awards include a 1994 *DownBeat Magazine* Award for Best Original Song, a Jazz Journalist Association Hero 2015 award, as well as grants from the NEA, the Indiana Arts Commission, MEIEA, Jazz Tours, the US Embassy, among others. Her newest project *Sheroes* features the world's leading female jazz instrumentalists and was recently featured on NPR's *Here and Now* as well as cited as one of the best releases of 2018 in *DownBeat Magazine*, placing #31 on the year-end Jazz Week Charts. Monika is a CASIO Artist.

Matthias Heyman (Belgium) is assistant professor at Vrije Universiteit Brussel and lecturer at Koninklijk Conservatorium Brussel, where he leads the research group on jazz, improvised music, and popular music. He obtained his PhD at the University of Antwerp in 2018 and his MA in jazz bass performance at the Royal Conservatoire Antwerp. His current research focuses on creative agency in historical recreations in jazz and popular music. In past projects, Matthias examined jazz bassist Jimmie Blanton, Belgian jazz history, and international jazz competitions, resulting in publications in journals such as Jazz Perspectives and Popular Music. Currently, he is preparing a monograph on Jimmie Blanton (Oxford UP) and a co-edited volume on the Beatles and humor (Bloomsbury).

Karen Li-Lun Hwang seeks to promote underrepresented histories through her practice as an information and archives professional. Her work includes an ongoing engagement with the Asian American Arts Centre in New York City and linked open data research with the Semantic Lab. Previously, Karen was the Metadata and Digital Projects Librarian at the Metropolitan New York Library Council (METRO), as well as a METRO Research Fellow focusing on semantic technologies. Her research findings have appeared in Northeastern University's "Design for Diversity Toolkit" and the journal *Digital Scholarship in the Humanities*.

Aaron J. Johnson is Assistant Professor at the University of Pittsburgh, where he studies and teaches jazz, funk, film music, and MIR. He studies social aspects of how music is produced, organized, and presented; the efforts of musicians to counter powerful institutional forces; and how musicians use media of all kinds. A professional jazz musician born and raised in Washington, DC during the apex of Chocolate City, he has electrical engineering degrees from Carnegie Mellon (BSEE) and Georgia Tech (MS) and a PhD in Music from Columbia University. He plays trombone, tuba, and conch shells.

Bruce Johnson, formerly a professor of English, holds honorary professorships in a range of disciplines, including Music, Cultural History, and Communications at Glasgow, Turku, and University of Technology, Sydney. Co-founder of Finland's International Institute for Popular Culture, his academic publications number several hundred, including over a dozen books, mainly on jazz, sound studies and film music. He has also acted as a government advisor on arts policy, and is an active jazz musician.

Jasna Jovićević earned a BA from "Franz Liszt" Music Academy in Budapest, Jazz saxophone, MA in Music Composition from York University in Toronto, and is currently enrolled in PhD program on Theory in Contemporary Arts and Media in Belgrade, focusing on jazz improvisation and gender aspects in jazz. She studied and won grants to many artist-in-residency programs in New York, San

Francisco, Banff, Graz, Brazil, Spain, and Zagreb as well as music competitions in Milan, Budapest, and Ljubljana. She won a research grant by JEN in Smithsonian Institute (Washington, DC) for the Women in Jazz study, and also was a National winner of EU AI Lab Project (Ars Electronica) for her work "I Sit and Worry About Her". Jasna performed her original work around Europe, the United States and Canada at many national and international festivals,

Michael Kahr is Senior Lecturer at the Institute for Jazz at the University of Music and Performing Arts in Graz, and Chair of the Institute for Jazz at the Gustav Mahler Private University for Music in Klagenfurt. He has served as Vice Rector for Research and Quality Management at the Jam Music Lab Private University for Jazz and Popular Music in Vienna and taught at the Universities of Sydney, Linz, Salzburg, and Vienna. Kahr is a board member of the International Society for Jazz Research and convenor of the International Network for Artistic Research in Jazz. He holds a PhD in musicology from the University of Sydney and is a recipient of a Fulbright Scholar Award. Kahr edited the volume *Artistic Research in Jazz: Positions, Theories, Methods* (Routledge 2021) and published the monograph *Jazz & the City: Jazz in Graz von 1965 bis 2015* (Leykam 2016). His scholarly work has also appeared in journals such as *Jazzforschung / Jazz Research, Jazz Research Journal, Journal for Artistic Research, European Journal of Musicology,* and *Darmstädter Beiträge zur Jazzforschung*. As a pianist and composer, he has performed at festivals and in concert venues across the globe and is featured on several CDs (www.michaelkahr.com).

Keith Karns is the Director of Jazz Studies at Western Oregon University in Monmouth Oregon. His duties include directing the Western Oregon Jazz Orchestra, teaching applied trumpet, improvisation, jazz history, and jazz methods. Karns has performed, recorded, or arranged for jazz artists such as Rich Perry, Stefon Harris, Benny Golson, and the Kansas City Jazz Orchestra. His research focuses on the intersection of hard bop and free jazz. Karns is a graduate of the University of Wisconsin, Eau Claire, Indiana University, and the University of North Texas.

Wolfram Knauer is the director of the Jazzinstitut Darmstadt since its inception in 1990. He has published several books, among them critical studies of Louis Armstrong (2010/2021), Charlie Parker (2014), and Duke Ellington (2017) as well as a comprehensive history of jazz in Germany (2019). For spring semester 2008 he was appointed the first non-American Louis Armstrong Professor of Jazz Studies at Columbia University, New York.

Dr. **Sonya R. Lawson** holds a PhD in Music History with a Supporting Area in Viola Performance from the University of Oregon, and a M.M in Viola Performance from the University of Minnesota. Her dissertation presented a history of strings in jazz, and other research interests are cognitive musicology and innovations in music history pedagogy. Dr. Lawson was Principal Violist of the Tennessee Philharmonic, Assistant Principal of the Cheyenne Symphony, and has played in many orchestras. As a member of The Knotty Ensemble avant-garde chamber group, she has released two CDs on the Third Rail label.

Jennifer Leitham is known for playing with music masters Mel Tormé, Peggy Lee, George Shearing, Doc Severinsen, Woody Herman, Benny Carter, Bill Watrous, k.d. lang, and countless others. She's a bassist, vocalist, composer, arranger, lyricist, and producer. She's played on over 145 albums, including 11 of her own, was awarded the Community Leader Angel Award by Children's Hospital of Los Angeles, was lauded as one of the top 20 transgender pioneers in *Vanity Fair*, and named one of the "50 Most Interesting Angelinos" by *L.A. Weekly*. In 2019 she spoke at Jazz at Lincoln Center's Jazz Congress, was featured twice on the NowThis news site, and performed and taught at the University of North Texas.

Alexandra Manfredo, Assistant Professor of Music at Tiffin University, began teaching at the university level by the age of 24. She currently teaches musicianship and songwriting courses, directs the Songwriting Ensemble, and oversees a studio of vocal students for private lessons. She also founded the university's first recording studio, record label and production lab, TiffinMusic Studios. She holds a Bachelor of Music from Millikin University in Commercial Music and a Master's degree in Jazz Vocal Performance from the University of Miami Frost School of Music. Alex has written, recorded, produced and distributed her own EP of original music and her newest album, "bare bones" will be released this winter.

Kristin McGee is Associate Professor in Popular Music Studies in the Arts, Culture and Media Department at the University of Groningen. She teaches popular music and topics related to gender and sexuality within music cultures. She has written on jazz, popular music, and audiovisual media within a variety of articles and books, including her monographs *Some Liked It Hot: Jazz Women in Film and Television* (Wesleyan University Press, 2009) and *Remixing European Jazz Culture* (Routledge 2019). She co-edited *Beyoncé in the World: Making Meaning with Beyoncé in Troubled Times* with Christina Baade (Wesleyan University Press, 2021).

Rebeca Muñoz-García received the B.Soc.Sc. degree in sociology from Universidad Carlos III de Madrid (UC3M) in 2013, and the M.S.Sc. in Interdisciplinary Gender Studies from the Universidad Autónoma de Madrid in 2015. She holds the Professional Music Education degree (trombone specialty). She is a last-year PhD candidate at the UC3M being a recipient of an FPU Scholarship by the Spanish government. Since 2017, she has belonged to the Social Analysis Department of UC3M. She was a visiting scholar in the University of Kansas in 2019. Her current research interests include gender studies, cultural industries, and the sociology of arts and culture.

Beatriz Nunes is a Portuguese vocalist, composer and researcher based in Lisbon. As a leader, Nunes released "Canto Primeiro" in 2018 and "A Espera do Futuro" in 2021. Beatriz Nunes is Madredeus's lead singer since 2011 with the discography "Essência" (2012) and "Capricho Sentimental" (2015). Nunes studied jazz in Escola Superior de Música, completing a Master's degree in Music Education in 2020. Since 2021, Nunes is a Phd student in Ethnomusicology in Faculdade de Ciências Sociais e Humanas da Universidade Nova de Lisboa. Nunes is also a teacher in Hot Club de Portugal school and Orquestra Geração.

Carl Oser is a vocalist, pianist, and educator based in Los Angeles. He graduated magna cum laude from the University of Southern California where he studied with Grammy award-winning pianist Russell Ferrante. He is a former visiting professor at Ecuador's premier contemporary music school, Berklee College of Music's "Colegio de Música", and has taught at the Harker School in San Jose and at Sierra Canyon School in Los Angeles. In the spring of 2019 Carl earned an advanced degree in Choral Conducting from San Jose State University where he also taught undergraduate courses in music performance and appreciation.

Joshua Palkki, PhD (he/him) is Assistant Professor of Music Education at California State University, Long Beach, and co-author of *Honoring Trans and Gender-Expansive Youth in Music Education* (Oxford University Press, 2021). A sought-after guest conductor and a scholar on social justice issues, Dr. Palkki holds degrees from Michigan State University (PhD music education), Northern Arizona University (M.M. choral conducting), and Ball State University (B.S. music education). Dr. Palkki has guest conducted in several states and presented at state, national, and international research, choral, and music education conferences. His writing appears in journals including *Journal of Research in Music Education, Journal of Music Teacher Education, Music Education Research, Research Studies in*

Music Education, and *Journal of Music Theory Pedagogy*. He serves as artist-in-residence with South Bay Children's Choir in Torrance, California.

M. Cristina Pattuelli is a professor at the School of Information at Pratt Institute in New York, where she teaches courses on knowledge organization, linked open data, and art documentation. Her research focuses on the application of semantic technologies to jazz, contemporary art, and other areas of culture and media. Pattuelli is founder of the Linked Jazz Project and co-director of the Semantic Lab at Pratt. She has published extensively and received the Jesse H. Shera Award for Distinguished Published Research. She holds a Master's degree in Philosophy and in Cultural Heritage Studies from the University of Bologna, Italy, and a PhD in Information Science from the University of North Carolina at Chapel Hill.

Sarah Caissie Provost is Associate Professor of musicology at the University of North Florida. Her scholarship is primarily in the areas of early jazz and its intersections with gender, historiography, and creativity. Her work appears in the journals *Jazz and Culture*, *Jazz Perspectives*, and *Music and the Moving Image*, among others

Amanda Quinlan is a Los Angeles-based artist and graduate student at California State University, Long Beach, where she is a Master's candidate in fine arts. Amanda's work critically examines the role of contemporary photographic practices and the processes by which they help construct our understanding of the world. Her research interests include the social construction of images, artificial intelligence, and the use of machine learning in photographic editing software. She has presented research at JEN in New Orleans, and at Documenting Jazz in Birmingham, UK.

Dana Reason is a Canadian-born pianist, composer, improviser, and musicologist working at the intersections of twenty-first century musical genres and interdisciplinary practices. Reason was part of *The Space Between* trio with the electronic music pioneer Pauline Oliveros; she is documented on approximately twenty recordings and has been long-listed for Grammys in jazz, arranging, and classical music. As a film composer, arranger, and performer, she contributed music to: "Pioneers of African-American Cinema; Birth of a Movement" (PBS); "Alice Guy Blachet, Vol. 2" (Kino Lorber); "Reconstruction: America After the Civil War" (PBS). She is currently Assistant Professor of Contemporary Music at Oregon State University.

James Reddan (he/him/his) is Associate Professor and Director of Choral Activities and Music Education at Western Oregon University (Monmouth, Oregon) where he directs the Concert Choir, and Chamber Singers. Reddan is an active conductor, adjudicator, and clinician in demand regionally, domestically, and internationally. Reddan is an active scholar examining Jazz and Gender in Higher Education, specifically perception, pedagogy, and applications within the vocal jazz ensemble. He has presented at numerous conferences including *Documenting Jazz*, *Jazz Education Network*, and the *World Conference of the International Council for Traditional Music*.

Ensembles under Reddan's direction have achieved worldwide recognition throughout the United States, Europe, and Asia, including the 2008 and 2012 Olympic Games. Under Reddan's direction, ensembles competed in the Eighth World Choir Games in Riga, Latvia, winning a World Championship. Reddan received the citation for Excellence in Music Education from the American Prize in Choral Performance. Reddan received the Doctor of Musical Arts degree in Music Education from Boston University, the Master of Music degree in Choral Conducting and Music Education from the University of Oregon in Eugene and the Bachelor of Arts in Music Education from McDaniel College in Westminster, Maryland.

Chloe Resler is a vocalist, historian, and educator from Denver, Colorado. She started singing at 16, and received her Bachelor's degree from the University of Northern Colorado in Jazz Performance in 2020. She has sung lead soprano for both the Downbeat Award-winning ensembles of Vocal Lab and Northern Colorado Voices. She is currently pursuing both a Master's in Music History and Literature and a K-12 Licensure at UNC.

Ellen Rowe, jazz pianist and composer, is currently the Arthur F. Thurnau Professor of Jazz and Contemporary Improvisation at the University of Michigan. Rowe has released five CDs released as a leader, including "Sylvan Way", "Denali Pass", "Wishing Well", "Courage Music" and her newest album "Momentum—Portraits of Women In Motion". Rowe's compositions and arrangements are published by Kendor Music, Doug Beach Music, and Sierra Music Publishing, and have been performed by ensembles including the Village Vanguard Orchestra, DIVA, BBC Jazz Orchestra, Berlin, and NDR Radio Jazz Orchestras.

Kiernan Steiner (she/they/siya) is a recent graduate from Arizona State University with her DMA in Choral Conducting. Born, raised, and nourished on Ho-Chunk Nation lands in Southwestern Wisconsin, Siya's dissertation research was a Critical Discourse Analysis (CDA) of text found on current collegiate choral program websites through a decolonized framework of autoethnography. In addition to their research, she is developing vocal coaching sessions that focus on releasing stories of shame about the voice, as well as offering coaching and consulting services to educators and creatives who are interested in learning about decolonization.

Yoko Suzuki earned a PhD in ethnomusicology and a PhD certificate in gender, sexuality, and women's studies at the University of Pittsburgh. Her research, which explores the intersection of race, gender, and sexuality in jazz performance, has been published in academic journals including *Black Music Research Journal*, *American Music Review*, and *Gender, Education, Music, and Society*. She currently teaches at the University of Pittsburgh and performs as a jazz saxophonist.

Erin L. Wehr is a music educator with thirty years invested in teaching college, community, and K-12 music programs including instrumental and general music, music technology, and music psychology. Her research centers around managing social anxieties including helping girls to navigate jazz culture. As a certified professional coach, Erin utilizes her degrees in performance, education, and coaching psychology to guide creative individuals, ensembles, and organizations in employing concepts of positive psychology to enhance experiences among artists, organizations, and audiences. Erin continues to be active as a researcher and professor, specializing in applications of self-efficacy theory and positive psychology to music teaching, learning, and performing.

Tom Williams is a jazz guitarist, lecturer and musicologist specializing in improvisation, cognition, jazz and pedagogy. His PhD "Strategy in Contemporary Jazz Improvisation" (University of Surrey, 2017) created a detailed cognitive and contextual model of how expert level improvisers develop and use their craft. Tom holds lecturing posts at the Academy of Contemporary Music (Guildford) and University of Surrey.

Rebecca Zola is a musicologist and jazz musician originally from Lexington, Massachusetts, and who currently resides in Israel. She holds an MA in musicology from the Hebrew University of Jerusalem, and BA and BFA degrees in writing and jazz performance from the New School in New York City. Rebecca has presented her research at international conferences in Israel, the UK, and the United States, and plans to continue to pursue her research in gender and jazz in a PhD program.

INDEX